Saami

Bihor

Sarakatsani

Morocco

Marsh Arabs

Baluchi

Pahari

Tibet

Nepal
Kachin
Karen

Kalinga

Guam

Bilibili Island

Kababish
Arabs

Nuer
Dinka

Azande

Tallensi

Yakö

Hausa BaMbuti

Nyakyusa

Igbo

Lele

Toda Chandallas

Hanunóo

Gurumba

New
Ireland

Ponape

Semai

Samal

South Fore

Trobriand
Islands

Nauru

Batak

Bena Bena

Bougainville

Java

Dani

Solomon Islands

Plateau Tonga

Tanala

Bali Alor

Tsembaga

Mae Enga

Vanuatu

Fiji

Bushmen

Tawana

Kgatla

Wellesley Island

Maring

Torres
Strait

New Caledonia

ABORIGINES

Swazi

Mardudjara

Walbiri

Zulu Bomvana Xhosa

Pintubi

Ballardong

Tasmanians

Maori

Anthropology
Understanding Human Adaptation

Michael C. Howard
Simon Fraser University

Janet Dunaif-Hattis
Northwestern University

HarperCollins*Publishers*

Sponsoring Editor: Alan McClare
Development Editor: Philip Herbst
Project Coordination, Text and Cover Design: Carnes-Lachina Publication Services, Inc.
Cover Photo: *Front:* Stephen Ferry/JB Pictures Ltd. *Back:* Loren McIntyre
Photo Researcher: Rosemary Hunter
Production Manager: Michael Weinstein
Compositor: University Graphics, Inc.
Printer and Binder: R. R. Donnelley & Sons Company
Cover Printer: The Lehigh Press, Inc.

For permission to use copyrighted material, grateful acknowledgment is made to the copyright holders on pp. 653–654, which are hereby made part of this copyright page.

Front Cover: A Kayapo Indian uses a camcorder to record the proceedings of a meeting with government officials in Altamira, Brazil. The Indians have learned the value of recording such meetings to enable them to verify the commitments that were made. The Indians and their supporters from around the world protested the building of the Kararao Dam in the Brazilian rain forest.

Back Cover: This young Yanomami woman is being flown from her home in the Amazonian rain forest to Caracas, Venezuela, where she will be employed as a maid. Although many of her people consider this sort of paid employment a good economic opportunity, the encroachment of Western values has speeded the demise of traditional rain forest ways of life.

Anthropology: Understanding Human Adaptation
Copyright © 1992 by HarperCollins Publishers Inc.

Library of Congress Cataloging-in-Publication Data

Howard, Michael C.
    Anthropology : understanding human adaptation / Michael C. Howard,
Janet Dunaif-Hattis.
      p.   cm.
    Includes bibliographical references and indexes.
    ISBN 0-673-39811-0
    1. Anthropology.   I. Dunaif-Hattis, Janet.   II. Title.
GN25.H68 1997
301—dc20
                                                 91-24253
                                                  CIP

93 94 95 9 8 7 6 5 4 3

Contents

20
Law, Politics, and Conflict   517

Law   518
Norms ▪ *Laws* ▪ *Law Enforcement and Dispute Mediation*

Politics   523
Political Ideas ▪ *The People in Politics* ▪ *The Transfer of Power* ▪ *The Political Organization of Societies*

Conflict   530
Political Violence within a Society ▪ *Warfare between Societies*

Summary   537

Suggested Readings   538

▪ *Focus on Anthropologists*
The Clans on Capitol Hill   540

21
Religious Belief, Behavior, and Symbolism   545

Understanding Religious Belief   546
Belief Systems in Context ▪ *Choices Available* ▪ *Religious Beliefs and Adaptational Strategy*

Symbolic Expression   549
Culture-Specific Symbols ▪ *Food Symbolism* ▪ *Totems* ▪ *Myth* ▪ *Art*

Supernatural Forces and Beings   555
Unseen Power ▪ *Spirits* ▪ *Gods* ▪ *Minor Beings*

Religious Behavior and Consciousness   557
Separation ▪ *Ritual* ▪ *Altered Consciousness*

Religious Specialists   559
Shamans ▪ *Keepers of the Law* ▪ *Prophets*

Religion and Social Change   561
Change through Contact or Conquest ▪ *Millenarian Movements* ▪ *Religion and Revolution*

Summary   565

Suggested Readings   566

▪ *Focus on Anthropologists*
Religious Pluralism in a Papua New Guinea Village   567

22
Illness and Curing   571

Epidemiology   572
Endemic Diseases ▪ *Epidemic Diseases* ▪ *Diseases of Development*

Malnutrition   576
Malnutrition and Subsistence Patterns ▪ *Cultural Perceptions of Food*

Mental Illness   578
Patterns of Stress Disorders ▪ *Social Change and Stress*

Concepts of Illness Causality   581
Mind–Body Dualism ▪ *Personalistic versus Naturalistic Explanations*

Curing   582
The Effectiveness of Cures ▪ *Health-Care Delivery Systems* ▪ *The Costs of Health Care*

Summary   589

Suggested Readings   590

▪ *Focus on Anthropologists*
A View of Health and Sickness from Aboriginal Australia   591

23
Anthropology and Human Problems   595

Contemporary Adaptation Problems   596
Development and Underdevelopment ▪ *The Plight of Indigenous Peoples* ▪ *Environmental Destruction*

Toward Solving the Problems   603
The Role of Sociocultural Anthropology ▪ *Applied Medical Anthropology* ▪ *Applications of Biological Anthropology and Archaeology*

Preface

Anthropology: Understanding Human Adaptation is a comprehensive, well balanced, and up-to-date overview of contemporary anthropology. It introduces students to the diverse subdisciplines of anthropology by using a framework of unifying concepts, particularly those of evolution, ecology, adaptation, holism, relativism, and integration. Cultures are examined from an ecological perspective, in which humans are viewed as creative beings seeking to overcome problems in a multifaceted environment through particular adaptational strategies. The intent is to give students a sense of the vitality of anthropology, and then to make them aware of its social relevance in solving the major problems of immediate concern to all humankind.

Through a systems approach, with an emphasis on human adaptation, the interrelatedness of the seemingly disconnected subfields of anthropology is made clear to students. In the Amazonian Rain Forest Color Portfolio, for example, they see how one specific region is connected— ecologically, culturally, politically, and economically—to the world system. Students also gain a sense of the excitement of anthropological discovery, such as comes from finding a long-lost Mayan city in the rain forest of Belize or uncovering thousands of years of American prehistory in an Illinois cornfield. In addition, the text brings together the best of the science of anthropology by focusing on the biological and cultural aspects of human adaptation.

The theme of social consciousness runs throughout the text. Students come to appreciate the important role anthropologists play in helping a wide variety of people, serving as advocates and assisting in developmental planning. Medical anthropology, biological anthropology and archaeology, and forensic anthropology serve contemporary human needs directly. These subfields are covered in considerable detail, both in the text and in the Focus on Anthropologists sections following many of the chapters.

Anthropology: Understanding Human Adaptation is divided into three major sections. Part One, "Biological Anthropology," concerns the biological aspects of human adaptation. We examine the factors that have shaped human evolution and human biocultural adaptation. Along the way, we explore questions regarding the uniqueness of human adaptation, while stressing continuity within the natural world. We also review contemporary human biological diversity, an issue of both scientific and sociopolitical interest. A grounding in the biological foundations of human diversity shows students that our variety is an essential aspect of what makes us *all* human.

Enabled by biological evolution, cultural evolution is the ultimate expression of human adaptation. Part Two, "Archaeology and Cultural Evolution," continues to emphasize scientific thinking through the study of the cultural past. Anthropological archaeologists investigate complex questions regarding the processes of cultural evolution: Why do cultures change? Why do we see a pattern of increasing cultural complexity? Does cultural complexity create as many problems as it solves? The last question, in particular, is perhaps the most disturbing and leads us into the final section.

Part Three, "Sociocultural Anthropology," introduces students to the complexity of human life in a comprehensive and concrete manner, focusing on what anthropologists consider essential aspects of culture. We stress contemporary cultures, including the ways in which societies are interrelated, thus providing students with a framework for understanding a constantly evolving world system. The themes of change and acculturation are integrated throughout Part Three, rather than being isolated in a separate chapter.

Contemporary adaptations are placed in a historical framework, underscoring the fact that no aspects of culture can be taken for granted. Rather, we must question why activities or beliefs come into existence, why they change or disappear, and why they persist. While we may not be able to reach a consensus on why people believe and act as they do, we *can* gain insight into the complexity of the forces that influence belief and behavior.

Understanding the culture of any people today requires studying how they fit into the modern world system. We discuss the various ways in which different types of societies are incorporated into the evolving world order, with an emphasis on how the nature of this integration influences people's lives. Small-scale societies are at a disadvantage in adjusting to the world order; they have met with little success in promoting change that works to their benefit.

Special Features

- Fifteen anthropologists have contributed original essays under the general title "Focus on Anthropologists." Each essay offers a vivid account of what it is like to be a practicing anthropologist in a specific subfield. These accounts not only make for lively reading, they also put students in touch with the wide variety of options available to those who choose to pursue anthropology as a career.

- *Color Portfolio—Primates,* one of two full-color inserts, presents an overview of the contemporary nonhuman primates. The photographs graphically emphasize primate diversity, while the text summarizes the major traits associated with the different groups.

- *Color Portfolio—Amazonian Rain Forest* discusses the threats to the complex and fragile ecosystem of the Amazonian rain forest, including its indigenous peoples. It addresses the question of whether this and the other rain forests of the world can survive in a modern world subject to predominantly Western influences.

- Each chapter begins with a brief outline of the major topics to be covered in the chapter, providing students with a convenient overview.

- Concise *end-of-chapter summaries* help students review chapter material.

- A carefully selected listing of *suggested readings* follows each chapter.

- *Key terms*—boldfaced in the text—are defined within each chapter and in a comprehensive *glossary* at the end of the text.

- Following the glossary, a *bibliography* of works cited provides students with additional resources.

- The *ethnographic maps* on the inside front cover pinpoint specific peoples and places discussed in the text.

- An *Instructor's Manual and Testbank* accompanies the text. It includes learning objectives, suggestions for using the text, annotated film suggestions, and individual and class projects for each of the text chapters.

Acknowledgments

The making of this textbook was a long and complex task, involving the contributions of many individuals to whom we are indebted. In particular, we thank our friend Robert Rubinstein, who brought us together, and editor Brad Gray, who got our collaboration off to a strong start. During the book's initial development, Bruce Borland and Becky Strehlow gave us insightful and inspiring support. At HarperCollins, editor Alan McClare and our patient and talented picture researcher, Rosemary Hunter, were most helpful. Very special thanks go to our developmental editor, Philip Herbst, an anthropologist whose enthusiasm, dedication, and hard work made the timely completion of the project possible.

We are grateful for the many contributions of the numerous reviewers who commented on various stages of the manuscript. They include:

David J. Banks, State University of New York at Buffalo
Bradley A. Blake, New Mexico State University
Claude A. Bramblett, University of Texas at Austin
Robin L. Burgess, United States Air Force (formerly of Southern Illinois University at Edwardsville)
Marc Feldesman, Portland State University

William F. Fisher, Columbia University
Robert A. Halberstein, University of Miami
Laura F. Klein, Pacific Lutheran University
Joseph A. Mannino, University of Wisconsin
James J. McKenna, Pomona College
James Mielke, University of Kansas
Lloyd Miller, Des Moines Area Community College
Donald S. Sade, Northwestern University
James M. Sebring, University of New Mexico
Brian Siegel, Furman University
Richard Wilke, New Mexico State University
Ina Jane Wundram, Oxford College

I would like to thank Linda Searcy Howard for her patience and encouragement. MCH

I would like to thank William Irons, who got me started, and Donald Stone Sade, Professor of Anthropology at Northwestern University, who shaped how I think about anthropology and science. My thanks also to my family and friends, particularly Paul and Harriet Dunaif; Jon, who was patient for many years; and Daniel and Joel, who grew as the book grew. JDH

Michael C. Howard

Janet Dunaif-Hattis

Anthropology

1 Introduction: Anthropology— All Things Human

A Huli tribesman of Papua New Guinea adapts to a rapidly changing world. He hiked to nine thousand feet to help clear space for a helicopter to land. The helicopter brought supplies to oil wells where no roads exist.

Humans are an incredibly diverse group of animals. We come in so many colors, shapes, and sizes; speak so many languages; exhibit so many different mannerisms; and hold so many different ideas that it is sometimes hard to believe that we all belong to the same species. Yet, we are, in fact, unified by a common biological heritage; moreover, we do have a great deal in common with one another.

Anthropology, the scientific study of humanity, seeks to explain how and why people are both similar and different through examination of our biological and cultural past and comparative study of existing human societies. Anthropology's ultimate goal is to develop an integrated picture of humankind—a goal that encompasses an almost infinite number of questions about all aspects of our existence. We ask, for example, What makes us human? Why do some groups of people tend to be tall and lanky, while others tend to be short and stocky? Why do some people practice agriculture, while others hunt for a living? Anthropologists are interested in all things human.

ANTHROPOLOGICAL THEMES

Because of its broad scope, anthropology is divided into subdisciplines, each with its own set of specialists. However, all of anthropology is unified by certain overarching themes, including universalism, holism, integration, adaptation, and cultural relativism.

Universalism

A fundamental principle of modern anthropology is that of **human universalism**: all peoples are fully and equally human. Whether Bushman, Navajo, or Celt, we are all one species. No group of people is "closer to the ape," and none is more highly evolved than any other. Since we are all equally human, anthropologists are as interested in the Ba Mbuti (Pygmies) and Australian Aborigines as they are in people living in the industrial societies of North America and Western Europe. No human group is too small, too large, too remote, too ancient, or too unusual to merit an anthropologist's attention. *All* human beings—the living and the dead, the familiar and the exotic—are the subject of anthropological studies. All people tell us something important about the human condition, about the potentialities and limitations of the human species.

Holism

Economists study systems of production, exchange, and consumption. Political scientists study the bases of social order and conflict, as well as the distribution and dynamics of power and authority. Other scholars select other facets of human life for intensive study. Anthropologists, on the other hand, seek to comprehend all aspects of the human condition. In addition to gaining insight into a society's economy and political organization, anthropologists want to know about its religion, its rules of marriage and etiquette, its language, its technology, its art, its child-rearing practices, and its physical environ-

ment. They are also interested in a society's past as well as its present. This concept of **holism**, in which human existence is viewed as a multifaceted whole, also recognizes the biological as well as the cultural aspects of human existence. Thus, anthropologists are interested in the physical characteristics of peoples past and present. This multifaceted concern is based on the desire to understand the *whole* of the human condition.

Integration

Integration emphasizes how the various aspects of cultural life function together. It is not enough to study the politics, art, religion, kinship, or economics of, say, the Navajo. The anthropologist views these aspects of life as interwoven threads that form a social whole. They are also recognized to be integral parts of the larger biological and social environment within which the Navajo live—the arid lands of the American Southwest and United States society. To fully comprehend any belief or practice, we must view it within the context of the society of which it is a part and within the context of the broad environmental factors shaping that society.

In recent years, we have also become more aware of the extent to which all societies are an integrated part of a larger **world system**. Individual societies are not independent, and their internal characteristics must be understood in relation to a broader global social system encompassing these societies (see Wallerstein 1979, 5; Shannon 1989, 20–21). Thus, in seeking to understand such small Pacific island societies as those of Fiji or Tonga, it is not enough to study the local history and observe the local environment. These societies are also influenced by the global tourist industry, the global commodities market, international companies, and the strategic concerns of foreign powers—all of which are themselves parts of an integrated world system. The extent to which we are all part of an integrated world system is perhaps most apparent in current debates over major environmental problems: global warming, for example, or the worldwide impact of hydrocarbons and other polluting chemicals.

Adaptation

Humans, like other animals, are influenced by their surroundings, or **environment**. This includes the *physical environment*—the climate, rainfall patterns, terrain, and so forth; the *biotic environment*—all the plant and animal life in a given area; and the *social environment*—interaction with other members of our species. Thus, a coastal Californian's environment would include the beaches, the almost desertlike terrain and climate, the animals that have survived or thrived with human occupation, and the mixture of humanity that has been drawn to the region.

The study of the relationship between organisms and their physical, biotic, and social environments is called **ecology**. A major concern of anthropology, and one that strongly applies ecology, is the study of how humans and their environment are interrelated—the study of human adaptation. As a process, **adaptation** can be broadly defined as the means by which individuals or populations react to environmental conditions in order to maintain themselves and survive. The term is also used to refer to the end product of adaptation as a process—a particular behavior, social system, or physical structure. This is what is meant by *an* adaptation.

How an organism, species, or society is adapted to its environment reflects its **adaptive strategy**: the set of solutions consciously or unconsciously applied by members of a population to contend with basic environmental or biological problems (Dobzansky 1974). These problems include securing food, protecting themselves from the elements, and finding mates. The adaptive strategy of the native peoples of the Arctic, for example, includes the technologies and techniques they have devised for hunting caribou, seals, and other animals in their environment; the types of clothing and shelter they manufacture or acquire through trade to survive in the harsh climatic conditions; and the ways in which they space themselves across the landscape, distribute food, control sexual relations, and manage interpersonal tensions.

The Inuit are closely bound to the natural environment. Their short, stocky build is a biological adaptation for retaining body heat within a cold, harsh climate. Inuit cultural adaptations include clothing and equipment designed to contend with the special needs of the arctic environment.

Human adaptation has its biological side as well. In fact, the biological and cultural aspects of our adaptation evolved together, so that humans truly have a *biocultural* adaptation, one that depends on closely tied biological and cultural means of contending with environmental pressures. Our unique biological history and physical makeup—especially the human brain—make the cultural aspects of our adaptive strategy possible. In turn, aspects of our contemporary cultural adaptations, such as medical care and agriculture, have influenced human biological evolution by relieving environmental stresses. Then, too, environmental pollution and overcrowding have served to create biological stresses for the human species.

Cultural Relativism

In addition to its scientific goals, anthropology also seeks to promote understanding of people who are culturally different. The most important factor inhibiting understanding of other people is **ethnocentrism**—judging the behavior of others in terms of one's own cultural values and traditions. Why don't they eat what we eat, dress as we dress, and act as we do? At its most extreme, ethnocentrism is cultural chauvinism—the attitude that one's own customs and beliefs are inherently superior to those of others.

To a degree, ethnocentrism is a characteristic of all human societies. Every person learns from earliest childhood how to think and act. A thorough indoctrination in the values of one's own culture is a lifelong process. The basic values and standards of our culture are continuously reinforced in religious ceremonies, in school, on television, at sporting events, and at parties. Wherever we go, we are tutored in what is considered to be true, real, just, desirable, and important from the perspective of the particular social group of which we are a part. Such built-in ethnocentrism can serve as a positive force by giving people a sense of pride, well-being, and security. This is the aim of many of the consciousness-raising movements of ethnic minorities, such as the

Ethnocentrism not only entails judging others for their cultural differences but also may involve viewing others as belonging to different species. These drawings show a fifteenth-century French artist's conception of inhabitants of distant, unknown lands.

native peoples of the United States and Canada. But ethnocentrism has its negative side as well. Extreme ethnocentrism is at the heart of all bigotry and discrimination. The denial of human rights is commonly based on the notion that those being oppressed are "backward," "primitive," or in some other way inferior.

Ethnocentrism does not promote understanding. To truly understand others, one must apply the concept of **cultural relativism**; that is, judging and interpreting the behavior and beliefs of others in terms of *their* traditions and experience. What is "right" for one group of people is not necessarily "right" for another. Such contrasting views can be seen, for example, in beliefs about killing and eating animals. Many Westerners view the Hindu custom of not eating cattle as silly and wasteful; at the same time they abhor the Chinese practice of eating dogs. On the other hand, many Hindus view Westerners' slaughter

of cows as barbaric, and Chinese react to the Westerner's refusal to eat dog meat with bewilderment and humor.

Cultural relativism does not mean we should approve or accept without criticism anything a particular people does or thinks. Rather, it means evaluating cultural patterns within the context of the history, environment, and social circumstances of the people.

ANTHROPOLOGY AS A SCIENCE

Anthropology is a **science**; thus, it is a branch of study concerned with systematically observing and classifying facts and establishing verifiable laws. Anthropology is guided by the same general principles that influence all sciences. These principles include use of the scientific method, acknowledgment of differing viewpoints within a given science, and changes in the paradigms that dominate scientific thought.

The Scientific Method

The **scientific method** is a precise way of designing and conducting research. It consists of the following basic steps: (1) *establishing a hypothesis*, a general statement based upon observed facts; (2) *determining ways to test the hypothesis*, incorporating them in a research design; and (3) *testing the hypothesis* through research and further observa-tions. To these one might add steps that entail repeating the study and revising the hypothesis in light of initial and subsequent findings.

Throughout this text are examples of how anthropologists apply the scientific method. For instance, anthropological archaeologists (anthropologists of extinct cultures) sometimes generate ideas and test hypotheses about past societies by examining modern peoples whose adaptive strategies are sufficiently similar to the ones under study to serve as models (see Chapter 8). Richard Lee (1979) applied this technique to test a hypothesis regarding the evolution of human economic behavior. First, to establish his hypothesis, Lee compared contemporary human foragers, people who hunt and gather for a living, with animal societies. He concluded that the trait that set human society apart from that of other animals was exchange—the trading of resources, goods, ideas, or services. Lee thus established the hypothesis that early human economy developed on the basis of exchange.

To test this hypothesis, Lee examined exchange in contemporary foraging societies. During the day, the people dispersed to search for food and then brought their goods back to camp to share with others. Lee thus concluded that, in many foraging societies, a "carrying device" to transport food back to camp over long distances was essential to the exchange of food. To test his hypothesis, he posed that the presence of carrying devices in a society reflected the custom of exchanging food. However, since most carrying devices are made from perishable animal hides or woven plant fibers that leave no trace in the archaeological record, another means of testing the hypothesis was necessary. On further observation, Lee noted that carrying devices were also

!Kung man with a fully loaded carrying device made of woven fibers.

used to haul heavy stones back to camp, where they were made into tools. Therefore, he posed that the presence of stones that were not found locally indicated the use of carrying devices. Lee contended that his hypothesis was supported by findings at an ancient African living site—evidence that consisted of stones that were available only at locations long distances from the prehistoric camp.

Different Viewpoints

Ideally, science strives to establish verifiable laws that govern phenomena. In a practical sense, however, scientists can usually only approach a deeper understanding of "what is real." The search for scientific understanding is a long and difficult process that consists of many small steps. Often, a number of scientists will concurrently investigate the same problem. These scientists may hold conflicting viewpoints that reflect different approaches to interpreting the same information. This may sound discouraging, but without its controversies, a science would surely stagnate. With continued research, scientists eventually separate viewpoints that are sound from those that are not, thereby advancing scientific understanding.

As do all sciences, anthropology includes many differences of opinion. Controversies abound over such issues as the exact course of human evolution, the factors explaining the origin of agriculture, and the nature and causes of social change. For example, an especially controversial question concerns why the human adaptation evolved (see Chapter 6). Theories regarding this topic are based largely on information from the preserved physical and material remains of ancient life, as well as on comparisons with contemporary nonhuman species and human societies. Such theories include that our early ancestors scavenged for meat (Szalay 1972); that they hunted in the manner of social carnivores, such as lions and wolves (G.E. King 1975, 1976); that the human adaptation evolved in response to the role of females as food gatherers and as the primary socializers of children (Tanner 1981, 1987); and that the human adaptation originated based on a reproductive and sexual strategy of monogamous males carrying food home to their mates and dependent children (Lovejoy 1981).

Evolution and Revolution in Science

Sciences continually evolve. As scientists develop new methods and collect more data, they devise new ideas and clarify or discard existing ones. Every so often a scientific revolution occurs, as a major intellectual viewpoint is developed that is "sufficiently unprecedented to attract an enduring group of adherents away from competing modes of scientific activity . . . [and is] sufficiently open-ended to leave all sorts of problems for the redefined group of practitioners to resolve" (Kuhn 1970, 10). Such major viewpoints are known as **paradigms**—broad scientific explanations that provide the framework for scientific thought and research. Paradigms include Newton's laws of physics, Copernicus's view of the heavens, and Darwin's theory of evolution. Indeed, by encouraging well-structured scientific investigation, a paradigm may set the stage for its own demise and replacement by a more satisfactory alternative.

THE FIELDS OF ANTHROPOLOGY

Although the discipline of anthropology strives to create a holistic and systematic picture of humanity, no single individual can possibly command a detailed understanding of every aspect of the lives of all peoples past and present. Consequently, specialization in anthropology is practical. Most anthropologists select one or two aspects of the human condition for intensive study, but remain interested in relating their own specialized findings to what researchers are doing in other areas. The major subdivisions of anthropology are (1) biological (or physical) anthropology, (2) archaeology, (3) anthropological linguistics, and (4) sociocultural anthropology.

Biological Anthropology

Because of anthropology's concern with all things human, many anthropologists focus on the biological aspects of humankind. The various types of **biological anthropology** fall within two major categories: evolutionary studies and studies of the biological diversity of modern human populations. Evolutionary studies seek to answer questions regarding how and why humans evolved, including the ways in which biological evolution has acted to shape the living world. Some biological anthropologists study **fossils**, the preserved remains or traces of long dead animals and plants. By looking at the fossil remains of humans and related species, biological anthropologists can tell us when our ancestors began walking upright or the stage of evolution at which the human brain reached modern proportions. To form a complete picture of our ancestors and their evolution, biological anthropologists enlist the aid of other specialists. These specialists include paleobiologists, who provide data on ancient plant and animal life; geologists, who explain local physical and climatic conditions; and archaeologists, who study prehistoric tools, dwellings, and other material remains.

Humans belong to the group, or order, of animals known as the **primates**. Thus, another way of exploring human evolution is through **primatology**, which is the study of the nonhuman primates—prosimians, monkeys, and apes. These mammals are—in a biological and evolutionary sense—humankind's closest living relatives. Primatological research helps us to understand what we share with other animals, what makes us part of the natural world, and what makes us unique.

Fieldwork conducted by some biological anthropologists focuses on human evolution. Fossil-hunter Mary Leakey starts to uncover a prehuman fossil skull. She is accompanied by her Dalmations, Sally and Victoria.

Studies of these nonhuman primates also help anthropologists interpret the fossil record. For instance, if a fossilized arm bone resembles that of a branch-swinging primate, such as a gibbon, it may be that its owner swung arm-over-arm through the trees.

While some primatologists focus on primate biology, others investigate the social behavior of such primates as chimpanzees, gorillas, and baboons. Their studies help us to reconstruct the behavior of our early ancestors. For example, Jane Goodall (1964) found that wild chimpanzees consistently make and use crude tools. Many biological anthropologists therefore concluded that tool using is much more ancient than was previously believed. Even though significant differences exist in the degree to which the skill is expressed, tool using is clearly a behavior found among both chimpanzees and humans. Might, then, it also have been a characteristic of their common ancestor?

Other biological anthropologists investigate the biological diversity of modern populations.

This field is closely tied to evolutionary studies, diversity being the result of evolutionary processes. These biological anthropologists seek to describe patterns of human diversity and to explain why the differences exist. Since researchers of contemporary human populations deal with living specimens, they can study such visible characteristics as skin color and hair texture. They can also examine traits that are all but invisible, such as blood type and genetic makeup. It is therefore possible to explore the relationship that exists between the biological configuration of a local population and its environment. For example, many scientists contend that some groups of people tend to be tall and lanky and others short and stocky because of evolved adaptive responses to climatic factors, for body form is related to the conservation or radiation of body heat (see Chapter 7). Students of human biological diversity also seek to explain how biological differences develop within individuals; thus, these scientists study the mechanisms of growth and development.

Genetics, the study of biological inheritance, plays an important role in both major categories of biological anthropology. Genetics is basic to understanding how evolution works and crucial in describing the biological diversity of humankind. It is even becoming an important means of reconstructing the exact course and pace of human evolution through techniques that take biochemical and genetic differences among species as a measure of how long it has been since the forms last shared an ancestor (see Chapter 5).

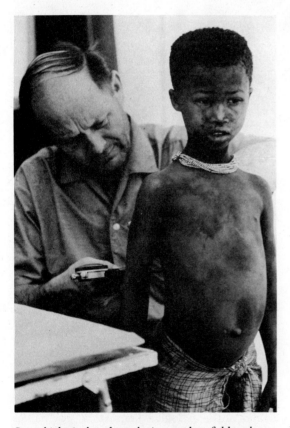

Some biological anthropologists conduct fieldwork to gather data on the biological diversity of contemporary human populations. This biological anthropologist is taking measurements of the physical stature of an African child.

Archaeology

Archaeology is the study of the cultural past through the material remains left by people. *Classical archaeologists*, who study the ancient civilizations of Europe and the Near East, are closely allied with art historians. *Anthropological archaeologists*, on the other hand, are anthropologists of earlier cultures who attempt to answer the kinds of questions that concern all anthropologists. For example, anthropological archaeologists take an integrated approach by placing cultural remains within a broad context: How did the society and its environment interact? How and why did these people and their culture evolve? Contemporary anthropological archaeologists are most concerned with explaining cultural processes rather than with describing and classifying past societies. In other words, they try to understand general principles that govern the form and development of human cultures. For example, some anthropological archaeologists are interested in the general principles that determined the origin of agriculture—a revolutionary event that occurred in different parts of the world at different times. One theory is that agriculture originated as a cultural adaptation in response to population pressure. When populations became too large to be supported by naturally occurring resources, the need for a stable food source triggered the origin of agriculture (Boserup 1981; see Chapter 10).

Many anthropological archaeologists study societies that did not leave written records. Their field is known as **prehistoric archaeology**. Besides using material remains to reconstruct prehistoric ways of life, prehistoric archaeologists also study contemporary peoples whose lifestyles are comparable to those of past societies. For most of our existence, we humans have lived by hunting and gathering wild foods; that is, by foraging. Thus, by studying present-day foragers, prehistoric archaeologists can gain insights into the ways in which our foraging ancestors lived— insights about their methods of hunting, their distribution across the land, and their religious beliefs.

Student labor is an important source of "human power" in the excavation of Native American archaeological sites. Both high school and college students provided the labor force for the excavation of the Koster site in southern Illinois.

By contrast, the field of **historical archaeology** concentrates on societies with written records, as does classical archaeology. But historical archaeologists work within the general framework of anthropology. Although many past societies left written records of their activities, these records are never a complete reflection of the people's lives. Historical archaeologists are proficient at extracting from the incomplete material remains of these societies every possible clue about what the people's daily lives were like. Archaeological excavations in California, for example, have yielded much information about the daily operation of old Spanish missions. These mission sites are helping us learn more about the early contacts between Native Americans and Europeans.

Anthropological Linguistics

The ideas and modes of behavior that constitute culture are transmitted largely by a complex system of symbols that includes language. While all organisms have ways of communicating, and some animals, such as porpoises and chimpanzees, have highly developed means of communicating, humans have evolved a unique and extremely complex system. Without it, human culture, as we know it, would be impossible. The field of **anthropological linguistics** (see Chapter 12) focuses on this aspect of human life; in turn, it is divided into a number of subfields.

Descriptive linguistics deals with how languages are constructed and how the various parts (sounds and grammar) are interrelated to form coherent systems of communication. *Historical linguistics* concerns the evolution of languages— how languages grow and change. *Sociolinguistics* studies the relationship between language and social factors, such as class, ethnicity, age, and gender. Finally, a topic of interest to many anthropological linguists is *language and culture*, which examines the ways in which language affects how we think, and, conversely, how our beliefs and values influence our linguistic patterns.

Sociocultural Anthropology

Sociocultural anthropology is the study of the social, symbolic, and material lives of contemporary and recent historical human societies. Whereas biological anthropology concentrates on the study of the biological basis of the human condition, sociocultural anthropology is concerned with the social and cultural inheritance of humankind. While sociocultural anthropology and archaeology overlap in some ways, especially in their focus on culture and their concern with the history of societies, they have many important differences. The most obvious difference is that sociocultural anthropology focuses on societies that can be studied directly, while archaeologists study extinct societies that cannot be directly observed.

The concept of culture, important to anthropology as a whole, is central to the field of sociocultural anthropology. It is also perhaps the most important defining characteristic of what it means to be human. Culture, as used by anthropologists, means much more than operas, poetry, paintings, ballet, and other such artistic endeavors. **Culture** is the customary manner in which human groups learn to organize their behavior and thought in relation to their environment. Defined in this manner, culture has three fundamental aspects: behavioral, cognitive, and material. The *behavioral* component refers to how people act, and especially interact, with one another. In child rearing, for example, parents and children tend to interact in a patterned fashion. *Cognition* involves the views people have of the

world. For example, parents have a limited range of ideas about how they should act, how their children should act, and what significance parenthood carries in the scheme of things. Finally, the *material* component of culture encompasses the physical objects that we produce and use.

Most of what goes into making up culture is a result of **learning**—modifying behavior in response to experience within an environment. Learning is practically universal among organisms. However, no other organism has a greater capacity for learning, or depends as much on learned behavior for its survival, as a human. While the survival of most other organisms is safeguarded somewhat by instincts, humans rely heavily on culture for their survival. People must learn how to live in a particular social and physical setting, with instincts playing but a minimal role. Think of the chances for survival most urban-dwelling Westerners would have if suddenly stranded in a tropical rain forest or on an arid desert. Without the help of someone who had learned how to live in that particular setting, the urbanite would probably perish.

As the term implies, sociocultural anthropology is concerned with human society, in addition to culture. Culture is not created in a vacuum or by isolated individuals; rather, it is the creation of humans interacting in groups. Through such social interactions, humans learn how to act and how to think in ways that are shared by others. We humans are social animals, with a biological makeup that predisposes us to form groups. Since the beginning of human evolution, our survival has been a cooperative enterprise. Thus, culture is a group effort and is socially shared. Those who share the same cultural perceptions and modes of behavior belong to a **society**—a group defined by the patterns of interaction of its members. It is through their common experience as members of a society that humans create shared cultural attributes. This is not a one-way process, for human society depends on culture. Neither has meaning as a separate entity.

Sociocultural anthropology is delineated by differing theoretical traditions (see Chapter 13),

*Sociocultural anthropologist Francesca Merlan
conducts ethnographic fieldwork in the highlands near
Mount Hagen, Papua New Guinea.*

and by more precise forms of specialization that
may focus on politics, economics, or kinship. By
far the largest branch of sociocultural anthropology is **ethnology**—the systematic, comparative study of patterns and processes in living and
recent cultures.

Sociocultural anthropology is built on a body
of descriptive material in which the vast array of
differing human beliefs, practices, and achievements are laid out. The process of describing individual cultures or societies—largely through
direct interaction with the people concerned, or
fieldwork—is called **ethnography**. The amount
of ethnographic information available on all
human cultures is far too vast to be studied in

depth by a single individual. Therefore, most
sociocultural anthropologists specialize in the
ethnography of one or two geographical areas,
such as sub-Saharan Africa, the Amazon Basin,
or urbanized Latin America. A sociocultural anthropologist usually does in-depth fieldwork
among one or two groups in the area, living
among them and observing and participating in
their life. For purposes of comparison and background, the anthropologist will also be informed
about other peoples in the region. This in-depth
immersion in a culture is one of the hallmarks of
sociocultural anthropology.

*Coca-Cola, one of the multinational corporations that
are a major component of the modern world system,
markets its product throughout the world. Here we
see an ad for Coke in Panama.*

ANTHROPOLOGY AND THE CONTEMPORARY WORLD

Today, humans face a world that is changing faster than ever before. It is also a world that, despite a great deal of human progress, is beset by a multitude of serious problems. Anthropology is at the forefront in the search for solutions to problems of rapid change, social upheaval, and environmental degradation; moreover, its holistic perspective is especially suited for coming to terms with the complexities of the world system. In the face of crisis and uncertainty we need, more than ever, to understand where we came from, what we are, and what we have the potential to become. By studying our evolution and comparing the ways in which we have adapted to an array of environments, anthropologists can contribute a great deal toward gaining this understanding. Furthermore, anthropology's longstanding concern with promoting the notions of universalism and cultural relativism gives it an important role in a world overrun with communal and racial intolerance, hatred, and violence.

In the chapters that follow, the reader will see how anthropology is attuned to contemporary life. We will explore, for example, the biology of human diversity, including race as an obsolete concept and the biological basis of behavior; archaeology's role in preserving and understanding cultural heritage and in instilling a sense of ethnic pride among native peoples; the problems of Third World people and how these problems are tied to the world as a whole; and the potential of worldwide ecological havoc related to the destruction of rain forests. We will see how anthropologists can further our understanding of what makes us all human, while simultaneously helping us to appreciate our differences. We will see how anthropologists can help us understand all things human.

SUMMARY

Anthropology, the scientific study of humanity, seeks to develop a whole, integrated picture of humankind. By studying all things human, anthropologists examine how and why people are both different and similar. Because of its broad scope, anthropology is separated into subdisciplines that are linked by unifying themes. Universalism is the fundamental principle that all peoples are fully and equally human. Holism dictates that all aspects of the human condition must be understood. Through the theme of integration, anthropologists recognize that the various aspects of cultural existence are interrelated. Another anthropological focus is the study of adaptation—how humans have evolved biological and cultural adaptations to contend with environmental conditions. Cultural relativism, judging and interpreting the behavior and beliefs of others in terms of their traditions and experiences, is a means of counteracting ethnocentrism, judging the behavior of others in terms of one's own cultural values and traditions.

As a science, anthropology is concerned with systematically observing and classifying facts and explaining processes. The scientific method consists of three basic steps: establishing hypotheses, determining ways to test the hypotheses, and, finally, testing them. Another aspect of anthropology as a science is the realization that the search for scientific understanding is a long and arduous process, consisting of many small steps; consequently, anthropology encompasses a wide range of viewpoints and opinions. In addition, the process of scientific inquiry represents an evolution of ideas. As scientists develop new methods and gather more data, new ideas are devised and old ones refined or rejected.

Anthropology is divided into four subdisciplines. Biological anthropology focuses on the biological aspects of humankind. The various types of biological anthropology fall into two major categories: evolutionary studies and studies of the biological diversity of modern human populations. Archaeology is the study of the cultural past through the material remains left by people. Contemporary anthropological archaeologists are largely concerned with explaining cultural processes. Anthropological linguistics focuses on how humans communicate and transmit culture, particularly through language. Its subfields include descriptive linguistics, historical linguistics, and studies of language and culture. Sociocultural anthropology is the study of the social, symbolic, and material lives of contemporary and recent historical human societies. The concept of culture is central to sociocultural anthropology, as is its focus on human society. Divided by differing theoretical traditions and by many specializations, the largest branch of sociocultural anthropology is ethnology, the systematic comparative study of patterns and processes in living and recent cultures.

SUGGESTED READINGS

Bowen, Elenore Smith. 1964. *Return to Laughter.* New York: Doubleday/Anchor. (Africa)

Cozzens, Susan E., and Thomas F. Gieryn, eds. 1990. *Theories of Science.* Bloomington: Indiana University Press.

Fernea, Elizabeth. 1969. *Guests of the Sheik.* New York: Doubleday/Anchor. (Middle East)

Liebow, Elliot. 1967. *Tally's Corner.* Boston: Little, Brown. (United States)

Read, Kenneth. 1980. *The High Valley.* New York: Columbia University Press. (Papua New Guinea)

Ruesch, Hans. 1950. *Top of the World.* New York: Harper & Row. (Arctic North America)

Siskind, Janet. 1973. *To Hunt in the Morning.* New York: Oxford. (South America)

Thomas, Elizabeth Marshall. 1959. *The Harmless People.* New York: Vintage. (Southern Africa)

Turnbull, Colin. 1962. *The Forest People.* New York: Doubleday/Anchor. (Central Africa)

Whitten, Phillip, and David E.K. Hunter. 1990. *Anthropology: Contemporary Perspectives.* Glenview, IL: Scott, Foresman/Little, Brown. (Reader on assorted topics)

Wikan, Unni. 1980. *Life Among the Poor in Cairo.* London: Tavistock. (Urban Egypt)

Wilson, Carter. 1974. *Crazy February.* Berkeley: University of California Press. (Southern Mexico)

PART ONE

Biological Anthropology

For all our cultural trappings, much of what humans are is based on biology. As did all forms of life, humans evolved over billions of years, out of the first organic molecules contained in the primeval earth's atmosphere and seas. Since then, biological evolution has fueled change and diversification in life-forms. Biological evolution still shapes the world today. We see its work each time a new strain of flu spreads across the continent, each time a new species of beetle is discovered, each time a paleontologist uncovers a unique fossil find.

In Part One, we will examine the pivotal role that biological forces have played in making us human. First we will look at the history of evolutionary theory, from its earliest roots to modern times. We will explore how biological evolution operates both to maintain continuity and to produce diversity within the living world. We will also see that science, too, evolves, as new ideas replace old ones and as scientists refine their understanding of natural phenomena.

The study of our biological heritage is essential to understanding what we are today. Thus, we will investigate the history of human evolution, which has led to contemporary human adaptations. Much of our biological heritage is still with us. When a parent responds to a child's cry, for example, or when we respond emotionally to the aggression of another nation, we reflect this heritage. Therefore, the study of other animals, especially the other primates, also sheds light on human adaptation.

Finally, we will explore how and why humans differ biologically. Ironically, this diversity is an aspect of what unites us. The human adaptation makes us an enormously flexible species, able to respond to local conditions and survive within a broad range of environments. Biology is certainly not our destiny, but it is part of what we are.

2 The Origin and Diversity of Life: Pursuit of an Explanation

An artist's view of Charles Darwin walking with a Galápagos tortoise. The Galápagos Islands, visited by Darwin during his voyage on H.M.S. Beagle, profoundly influenced his views of life and the development of his theory of evolution.

Although ways of explaining the world's creation and character vary from culture to culture, all people share a need to understand the world (see Figure 2.1). In many cultures, perceptions of the natural world and the origin of life are based on creation myths; for example, in the multilayered cosmos of the Yanomami, the layer occupied by humans is said to have been created when a section of a higher spiritual plane broke off and fell to a lower level (Chagnon 1977).

In Western society, science provides a major approach to understanding the origin and diversity of life—an approach based on observable phenomena and testable ideas. Anthropology, which seeks to explain how humans fit into nature, developed as part of the Western scientific tradition.

In Chapter 2 we will explore the concept of biological evolution, which forms the basis of the scientific approach to the natural world. Our major focus will be on the development of evolutionary theory from a historical perspective. Thus, we will introduce key scientific concepts while gaining insights as to how they influenced—and were influenced by—society.

FIGURE 2.1
Examples of non-Western
explanations of the natural world.

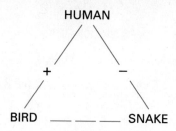

(a) Dani (New Guinea). In this small-scale farming society, the world consists of living forms and spirits who can directly intervene in the lives of people. Dani closely identify with birds, while snakes represent a hostile force.

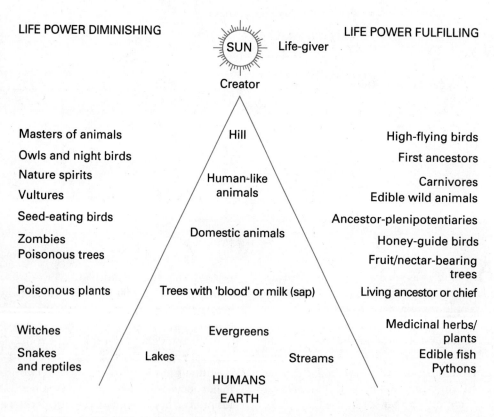

(b) Kimbu (Tanzania). In the cosmology of the Kimbu, nature consists of spiritual realities, living beings, and powers. Natural spirits control animals and plants, with the sun representing the life-giving spirit. Spiritual powers, reflecting the classification of the natural world, are divided into "life power diminishing" and "life power fulfilling."

FIGURE 2.1
(Continued)

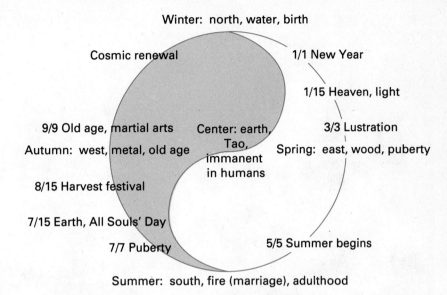

Winter: north, water, birth

Cosmic renewal

1/1 New Year

1/15 Heaven, light

9/9 Old age, martial arts

Center: earth, Tao, immanent in humans

3/3 Lustration

Autumn: west, metal, old age

Spring: east, wood, puberty

8/15 Harvest festival

7/15 Earth, All Souls' Day

7/7 Puberty

5/5 Summer begins

Summer: south, fire (marriage), adulthood

(c) Taoists (China). Taoism is based on the cyclical pattern of nature with the elements of the universe existing in a state of balance, as reflected by the dichotomy of yin/yang. The cycle of human life is equated with the cycle of nature. Festivals are associated with the cycles.

SECRETS OF LIFE: EVOLUTION SHAPES THE LIVING WORLD

How did the universe begin? Many scientists believe that 20 billion years ago, all matter and energy were concentrated in an extremely small, dense mass. In a fiery split second, an explosion projected matter and energy outward with such power that the universe is still expanding from its force. Our solar system was formed about 4.6 billion years ago, as the superheated matter cooled and condensed. Each planet was unique in its chemical composition, size, and distance from the sun. Earth, the third planet, possessed the specific conditions and materials that permitted life to develop out of inorganic elements.

As for the origin of life on earth, the first organic compounds were produced as early as 4 billion years ago. Energy from sources such as light-

ning, heat, and radiation caused very small organic molecules to be formed from chemicals contained in the primitive earth's atmosphere and seas (see Figure 2.2). Among these were the first **amino acids**, small molecules that eventually condensed, creating complex molecules. These included **proteins**, which make up living cells. Also created were molecules that could make exact copies of themselves. As we will see, these self-replicating molecules enabled both the continuity and the diversity of life.

From these few, extremely primitive organic substances sprang all the life-forms ever to exist on earth. What natural force could lead to the enormous complexity and diversity of life? What natural force could explain the existence of such

FIGURE 2.2

Re-creation of the primitive earth. Energy released by sources such as volcanic heat, lightning, and ultraviolet light fueled the breaking apart and recombination of the molecules present in the seas and atmosphere.

different forms of life as mushrooms, dogwood trees, giraffes, and humans? The answer to this ultimate biological question is evolution.

The term *evolution* means simply "change occurring through time." More specifically, **biological evolution** is the change in a population's genetic or physical makeup, or both, over time, a **population** being an interbreeding group of individuals living within a limited area. Biological evolution results from a complicated interaction of many different forces.

Scientists view biological evolution as occurring on two levels. One level, **microevolution**, consists of short-term changes that occur within a population between generations. An example of microevolution would be changes in the proportion of the ABO blood types from one gen-

eration of a human population to the next. The other level, **macroevolution**, occurs over long periods of time and results in major changes in form. For example, macroevolution was responsible for the many kinds of monkeys that now inhabit Central America and South America, all of which descended from the same ancestral population. Actually, microevolution and macroevolution represent two extremes of an evolutionary continuum, with many degrees of biological change between them.

THE DEVELOPMENT OF EVOLUTIONARY THEORY

Evolutionary theory forms the intellectual framework of the scientific approach to the natural world. Thus, a brief history of the development of evolutionary theory will help us understand the foundations of biological anthropology and, for that matter, of anthropology as a whole.

The modern-day theory of biological evolution did not spring up full-blown overnight, but is the product of an evolution of ideas. In Chapter 1, we noted that sciences evolve as knowledge is accumulated and ideas are refined. Also important to recognize is that "each age has its own 'mood' or conceptual framework which, though far from being uniform, somehow affects most thought and action" (Mayr 1982, 83). Ideas reflect the social and technological climate of their times—culture and thought evolve hand-in-hand. By viewing science from a historical perspective, we become more sensitive to the nonscientific factors that influence our search for scientific understanding.

The Earliest Roots

As is true of many aspects of Western thought, evolutionary theory has its roots in the observations and speculations of ancient civilizations. About 2,000 years ago, the society of the classical Greeks encouraged free thought and the development of scientific ideas. Even their religion was conducive to scientific thinking. The Greeks worshiped multiple gods, so that "no powerful single God {existed} with a 'revealed' book that would make it a sacrilege to think about natural causes" (Mayr 1982, 84). In addition, the Greeks traded with and colonized other lands, which made them curious about why people and places were so different. Thus, many Greeks turned to scholarly pursuits, including *Aristotle* (384–322 B.C.), who established what has come to be called the **comparative method**. Simply put, different life-forms are compared with one another to de-

cipher which traits they share and which are unique. He also focused on understanding the underlying cause of a phenomenon, rather than simply describing or categorizing nature. A devoted naturalist, Aristotle was concerned with observing animals and their behaviors; he believed in a natural order of life.

About 200 B.C., after Greece had suffered a political and intellectual decline, Rome began to dominate much of Europe and the Near East. The development of Roman culture was strongly influenced by the Greeks, and some Romans sought to continue the Greek scientific traditions. The influential Roman scholar *Lucretius* (99–55 B.C.) proposed ideas that many centuries later were reflected in evolutionary theory. His ideas included the concept of a natural hierarchy of life and the notion that some life-forms die out, leaving room for others.

After a few hundred years of prosperity, internal decay led to the decline of the Roman Empire. At the same time, Christianity became a powerful intellectual and political influence throughout Europe. The conversion to Christianity caused major changes in social attitudes toward science. During the period commonly known as "The Dark Ages," which lasted for approximately five centuries following the fall of Rome, science was held in low esteem—viewed largely as sacrilegious. Europeans repressed many of the Greek and Roman teachings because they contradicted the Biblical view of the world.

What aspects of Christian dogma conflicted most with evolutionary thinking? Christians believed that God created the world in six days and, except for the intervention of the Creator, that the world was like a "cosmic clock," ticking away in a fixed, predetermined pattern. In addition, they thought that the earth was only a few thousand years old and that life-forms were unchanged except as the result of events described in the scriptures. Clearly, such thinking left no room for ideas associated with evolution, such as extinction and change. The Christian point of view influenced the development of the natural sciences for a long time. In fact, a literal interpretation of the Bible continues to influence educational policy in the United States today (see p. 47).

While medieval Europe was repressing scientific thought, the Moslem world—the neighboring political and military power—was emphasizing scholarship and preserving the ideas of earlier civilizations, particularly those of the Greeks. These ideas included elements of evolutionary theory, including those proposed by Aristotle and Lucretius. Why was the Moslem world able to preserve European ideas that would later be used in the development of evolutionary theory? First of all, the Moslems put great emphasis on studying and preserving the scholarly ideas of *all* societies. In addition, they greatly valued education, establishing schools that accepted students from far and wide. According to Magner (1979), "one of the major contributions of the Arabs to the history of science and scholarship was their service as agents in the transmission of important discoveries and ideas between cultures" (p. 81). Most Europeans thought of the Moslems as enemies and purveyors of anti-Christian ideas. Yet, when the time was right, contact with the Moslem world helped to reintroduce Europe to enlightened scientific thinking.

By 1300, political, social, and economic changes in Europe had led to the intellectual reawakening known as the Renaissance—the "rebirth." Although Christianity was still a major influence, economic and other pressures led to a broadening of societal attitudes toward science. At the same time, a complicated mix of factors, including dominant city-states that competed for wealth and power, stimulated the expansion of trade and the search for new sea routes. In the fif-

An Australian Aborigine, as drawn in 1802 by a European naturalist. European prejudice placed the Australian Aborigines lower on the Chain of Being than Europeans.

teenth century, Europeans entered a period of world exploration that exposed them to exotic peoples and places, and Europeans became intrigued by the diversity of life they encountered.

By the late seventeenth century, science and religion coexisted peaceably—as long as science did not blatantly conflict with religious beliefs. However, religious authorities still maintained rigid control over science. In fact, during the seventeenth and eighteenth centuries, biology—the science of living things—was largely concerned with describing "God's Plan," particularly as reflected by the "Chain of Being."

The Chain of Being

The **Chain of Being** was a scheme for classifying life in which each form was placed on a graduated scale of "perfection" (theologians determined what constituted this perfection). Popular during the seventeenth and eighteenth centuries, this neat, orderly scale was viewed by scientists as having existed, unchanged, since creation. The perfectness of the scheme was thought to reflect the grandness of God's Plan. Plants were classified as the lowest, and least perfect, forms of life. Animals came next on the chain. Since theologians viewed humans as perfect among God's earthly creatures, the placement of each animal species was in accordance with its similarity to humans. For example, classifiers, going up the scale, placed insects lower than reptiles, reptiles lower than birds, birds lower than wolves, and wolves lower than monkeys. Humans were placed very high on the scale, just a step below such spiritual forms as angels, as indicated in Figure 2.3. Biologists, by characterizing and classifying life-forms, sought to clarify the order of the Chain. They added details to the scheme as new lands were explored and new organisms were discovered.

These scientists unknowingly took an important early step in the development of a scientific approach to the living world, that of classification and description. But the Chain of Being was in no way an evolutionary scheme. The classifiers viewed the natural order as forever fixed. Each type of organism was separately created and unchanging in form. However, as more life-forms were studied and added to the scheme, some scientists became dissatisfied with both the simplicity of the scale and with supernatural explanations of its character. Such scientists began to seek naturalistic ways of understanding the world, all the while emphasizing that they were attempting to better illuminate God's Plan. It was also during this period of growing dissatisfaction with simplistic explanations that Sir Isaac Newton's view of nature brought about a revolution in science.

Sir Isaac Newton: Matter in Motion

Every so often, a new paradigm is developed that revolutionizes science. The work of *Sir Isaac Newton* (1642–1727) in physics brought about one of the greatest revolutions of all time, one that affected much of science, including biology. Newton mathematically demonstrated that the universe was a single, unified, dynamic mechanical system and explained how the behavior of *all* matter was subject to the same set of physical laws. Newton's ideas were meant to illuminate the Christian point of view—"since the world exhibits order and design, it must have had a designer" (Hurlbutt 1965, xii). Newton viewed science as a way of understanding nature, and thus of better understanding God.

Newton's laws set the stage for evolutionary thinking. By clearly demonstrating that "nature . . . was a law-bound system of matter in motion" (Mayr 1982, 95), he allowed for a philosophy of change in nature that was in harmony with the Christian view of the world. In addition, Newton was a scientist par excellence who helped create an attitude toward science that emphasized careful observation and experimentation. On the negative side, the wide acceptance of Newton's approach confined biologists to strict physical laws that did not fully explain how living systems operate. Because life is a unique combination of

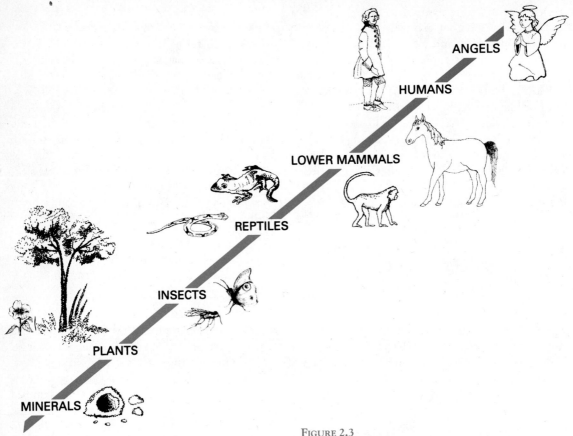

ANGELS

HUMANS

LOWER MAMMALS

REPTILES

INSECTS

PLANTS

MINERALS

FIGURE 2.3
Conceptualization of the "Chain of Being."

matter and energy, biologists had to discover their own set of natural principles. However, Newton's discovery of the laws of motion made the search for biological principles—including those of evolution—possible.

Linnaeus and Classifying the Natural World

Even with Newton's influence, most of the biologists of the eighteenth century continued to be classifiers, rather than explainers, of the natural world. Many studied **taxonomy**, the science of classifying living things. Building and improving on the work of earlier taxonomists, *Carolus Linnaeus* (1707–1778) developed the classification system we call the **Linnaean hierarchy**, a system based on traits common to different organisms. Scientists across the world currently use this system and its "binomial," or "two-name," method of labeling life forms. For example, humans are binomally labeled as *Homo sapiens*.

In the Linnaean hierarchy, life-forms—microorganisms, plants, and animals—are arranged in a graded series. Biologists group organisms on the basis of very broad similarities (such as the presence of backbones or external skeletons) at the highest levels of the hierarchy. Each level is less inclusive than the one above it and more inclusive than the one below it; thus, the highest levels contain the largest numbers of organisms. For example, as demonstrated by Figure 2.4, the highest Linnaean category is a kingdom. The kingdom *Animalia* contains all multicellular animals, from sponges to humans. The next highest category is a phylum, including *Chordata*, which contains (along with a few more primitive forms) animals with spinal cords—fish, amphibians, reptiles, birds, and mammals. The lower levels contain fewer organisms, which are grouped according to finer distinctions. In this manner, a phylum is subdivided into classes, classes into families, and so on. The Latin scientific name of each organism is derived from the two lowest levels of the hierarchy, those of genus and species. Thus derives the scientific name of humans: *Homo* (genus) *sapiens* (species).

Linnaeus viewed life-forms as unchanging and believed that similarities among organisms represented God's orderly plan. It did not occur to him that shared traits might reflect descent from a common ancestor, as we now know to be true. Still, the concept of change was preoccupying an increasing number of scientists, as was the desire to go beyond describing and categorizing life. The stage was now set for explaining the patterns of nature.

Explaining the Patterns of Nature

As knowledge of life-forms increased, some eighteenth-century scientists began to doubt that nature was as neatly ordered and fixed as people commonly believed. Newton had made it clear that change was a part of nature. In addition, the discovery of fossils led to increased speculation about changes in life-forms. Most people thought that fossil forms not represented by organisms in the present world reflected mass extinctions caused by such Biblical catastrophes as the Great Flood. But this explanation lost credibility as scientists collected more fossils. Discoveries of fossils in successive layers of earth demonstrated a progression of changes, each modification pointing to the changes seen in the next form in time. Such discoveries stimulated a search for more satisfactory ways of explaining change in nature.

James Hutton (1726–1797), the founder of modern geology, helped change some basic ideas about the age and character of the earth. After carefully studying many geological formations, Hutton concluded that the earth was much more than a few thousand years old. In addition, he realized that the earth was shaped by slow and steady natural forces that were the same in the past as they are in the present. For example, wind and rain gradually erode rocks; given enough time, such forces can tear down mountains. In the tradition of Newton, Hutton was a careful scientist who viewed the earth as a machine that continuously changed according to natural laws and processes. However, his ideas strongly contradicted the prevailing views of the time, and were difficult for others to accept.

Hutton's ideas were expanded upon by *Charles Lyell* (1797–1875). In his widely read three-volume *Principles of Geology*, Lyell clearly set forth the principle of **uniformitarianism**: the earth is tremendously old and is subject to continuous and gradual change due to everyday forces such as wind, water, heat, and pressure. This enormous time depth was the concept lacking in most earlier ideas regarding the nature of the world. Uniformitarianism directly contradicted **catastrophism**, a popular scientific doctrine of the late eighteenth and nineteenth centuries. Based on the Biblical account of creation, catastrophism proposed that supernatural forces, rather than natural and commonplace ones, were responsible for earth-bound events. For example, the Great Flood was viewed as being primarily responsible for the discontinuity between fossil and modern life-forms. Similarly, stupendous deity-driven upheavals explained the formation of mountain ranges. By contrast, uniformitarianism attributed the formation of mountain ranges to the cumulative effects of smaller-scale volcanic and tectonic activity.

Lyell was a powerful and popular figure within the European scientific community. His ideas influenced many other scientists, including naturalists who were thinking about how life, as well as the physical earth, was prone to change because of natural, rather than supernatural, forces.

The Early Evolutionists

The growing dissatisfaction with existing explanations and a slowly increasing European societal tolerance for new ideas served as an impetus for evolutionary thinking. Thus, the early evolutionists of the late eighteenth and early nineteenth centuries paved the way for Charles Darwin and the first truly comprehensive theory of evolution.

The *Comte de Buffon* (1707–1788) was an influential eighteenth-century scientist who sought to understand general laws of biology—a search fueled by his great admiration of Newton. Buffon hinted at the idea of natural selection and recognized both the diversity and the continuity of life. He also contended that species sometimes exhibited change in a slow and gradual manner. (In keeping with Newton, he viewed this change as controlled by God.) However, Buffon never presented a fully developed evolutionary theory, a failure partly based on pressures upon him to conform to Christian dogma. For example, church authorities forced Buffon to remove "offensive" passages from his works, including references to the great age of the earth.

Erasmus Darwin (1731–1802), Charles Darwin's grandfather, also contributed to the development of evolutionary theory. Inspired by Buffon and by his own observations of nature, Erasmus Darwin contended that important similarities existed among groups of organisms; that all life descended from a single, primitive entity; and that the earth was much older than commonly believed. He published his thoughts in a series of poetry books; however, the poems were difficult to understand and the form obscured his ideas. Although Erasmus Darwin died before Charles was born, he influenced his grandson in important ways. One was by establishing a particularly liberal family attitude toward science and natural history. More specifically, Charles was inspired by Erasmus's natural observations and theories.

Many of the ideas expressed by Erasmus Darwin are also to be found in the work of *Jean Baptiste de Lamarck* (1744–1829). The most famous of the early evolutionists, Lamarck was an excellent scientist who greatly contributed to the development of evolutionary theory by clearly stating key ideas. For example, he espoused the concept that biological change occurs over long periods of time and proceeds in small, uniform, and continuous steps. He also recognized that an organism's environment is a key factor in determining the nature of biological change. Unfortunately, Lamarck is best remembered for his incorrect theory of how a species changes in form. Lamarck felt that individuals unconsciously strive to fit perfectly into their environments, and thus develop beneficial "acquired characters." The acquired characters of the parents are then inherited by their offspring, thereby directing how changes occur within a species. For example, a Lamarckian explanation of the giraffe's long neck is that its ancestors stretched their necks to reach leaves high in trees. The parents then passed this trait of an elongated neck on to their offspring. Although this explanation has proven to be incorrect, Lamarck's thinking was actually quite sophisticated for his time. He *did* recognize the close relationship between changes in form and pressures of the environment, and that changes are passed on to future generations. Lamarck, however, was handicapped by not understanding how traits are passed on from parent to offspring, a problem not rectified until the discovery of the modern principles of genetics.

Many of Lamarck's contemporaries criticized his evolutionary ideas. His most damaging critic was *Baron Georges Cuvier* (1769–1832), a tremendously powerful French scientist. Cuvier is greatly respected by biologists as the father of zoology (the branch of biology that specializes in

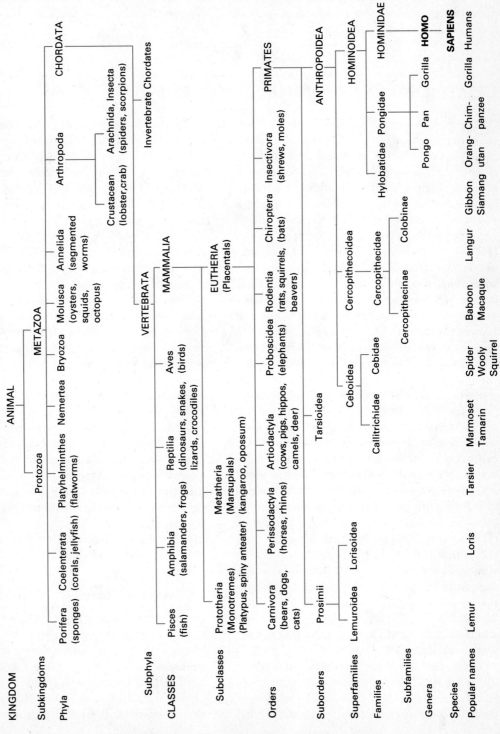

Figure 2.4

A classification chart based on the Linnaean hierarchy showing the derivation of the scientific name for humans, *Homo sapiens*. Categories connected by a horizontal line share a common ancestor. In many cases, only examples of the categories are given.

animals). He was, however, vehemently opposed to evolutionary thinking and to the concept that species could gradually change through time. A devout supporter of catastrophism, Cuvier did his best to discredit Lamarck and his theories.

CHARLES DARWIN: EVOLUTION IN FULL BLOOM

By the mid-nineteenth century, European attitudes had changed to the point where scientists could openly discuss evolutionary thinking, even though many people still objected to such ideas on religious grounds. In addition, expanding scientific knowledge could now support a new way of thinking about the natural world. It was within this context that *Charles Darwin* (1809–1882) proposed a truly unified and comprehensive theory of evolution. In doing so, Darwin created a synthesis of old and new ideas. A critical step in scientific research, a **synthesis** combines diverse ideas into a unified whole that is more than a sum of its parts because it explains how the pieces fit together. One of Darwin's contributions, the theory of natural selection, was the first explanation of how species can change that scientists could test through observation and experimentation.

The circumstances surrounding Charles Darwin's life made it possible for him to devise his evolutionary theory. He was born to an upper-middle-class family and provided with a broad education at the finest schools. Although a mediocre student, Darwin was curious about nature; even as a young man he spent much of his time carefully observing, reading, and thinking about the natural world. A story is told that young Darwin, while on one of his many long walks across the countryside, spied an interesting beetle. Having no collection jar, he popped the beetle into his mouth for safekeeping, and was promptly stung—a price he was happily willing to pay for a prize specimen.

The event that firmly committed Darwin to life as a naturalist was his world voyage aboard H.M.S. *Beagle* from 1831 to 1836. The purpose of the five-year journey was to map the coast of parts of South America, of some Pacific islands, and of other exotic locations. Darwin originally came on board as a socially acceptable companion for the ship's captain, who had to remain aloof from the lower ranking sailors. The experience directly confronted Darwin with evidence that shaped his thinking about biological evolution. For the early part of his life, Darwin had been a creationist, and had even considered becoming a minister. However, on the journey he observed geological evidence that supported the idea that the earth was very old—so old that gradual processes could be responsible for biological change. Darwin was also struck by life's seemingly endless variety—birds, ferns, beetles, flowers, tortoises, lizards, and a phenomenal array of other plants and animals inhabited the world and lived in many different environments. Darwin eventually came to appreciate the close relationship between the diversity of species and the diversity of their habitats. Furthermore, he collected fossils, which fueled his belief in extinction and convinced him that this diversity of life extended into the past. Darwin thus saw that the living world was very diverse and that change was a natural biological process. For the remainder of his life, he sought to explain the forces responsible for this diversity and change.

Devising the Theory

Once back in London, Darwin began to seriously contemplate all he had seen and read. Although he was influenced by many different scholars, two works are of special note. One major influence was Lyell's *Principles of Geology*, which provided Darwin with the idea that the living world could change slowly and gradually by way of steady

Charles Darwin in his study. Darwin spent much of his later years in solitude, contemplating ideas formed earlier in his life.

and natural processes. Lyell's theory of uniformitarianism also supplied the time depth needed for changes to occur at a slow pace. Another major component of Darwin's theory, that of the means by which evolution proceeds, was suggested to him by the work of *Thomas Robert Malthus* (1766–1834). Malthus argued that, in many cases, a human population would grow in geometric fashion (2,4,8,16,32 . . .) until it reached a critical size that could not be supported by resources, such as food, that grew only in an arithmetic progression (2,4,6,8,10 . . .). Eventually, warned Malthus, a major calamity—war, famine,

disease—would quickly and dramatically reduce the size of the population. The cycle of increases and crashes would then start over again. Applying Malthus's ideas in a more general way, Darwin contended that in times of stress and competition for resources, only animals and plants best suited to their environments would survive, thereby winning the "struggle for existence." Darwin further saw that this was an ongoing process that occurred even in noncalamitous times.

Most of Darwin's ideas had been worked out for at least 15 years before he published his complete theory. Intent on perfecting the theory and fearful about how people would react to such radical ideas, Darwin might have waited even longer. He became aware, however, that another brilliant naturalist, *Alfred Russel Wallace* (1823–1913), was about to publish a similar theory. That Wallace had come to the same conclusions indicates how right the time was for a major theory of evolution. A dedicated and competent naturalist, Wallace had read much of the same literature as Darwin, including Darwin's published journals. The two men even corresponded. In 1858, Wallace sent his own independently devised theory to Darwin. Darwin saw that he could no longer wait to make his ideas public, and their work was jointly presented before the Linnaean Society of London. However, Darwin has rightly been credited as the first to devise this comprehensive theory of biological evolution.

The Theory

In 1859, Darwin published the first version of his monumental work, titled *On the Origin of Species by Means of Natural Selection*. His theory embraces four major concepts:

1. The natural world is not fixed, but evolving. Life-forms can change through time as new species are created and others become extinct.
2. Evolution is gradual and continuous.
3. New species are not created spontaneously, but are descended from earlier forms of life; organisms with similar characteristics are likely to have descended from the same ancestor. This is known as the principle of **common descent**.
4. The principle of **natural selection** is the key to explaining how biological evolution proceeds. Darwin deduced that when differences in form are present in a population, individuals with traits best suited to the environment will live longer or be more fertile than individuals without the traits, and therefore produce the most offspring. If the traits are inheritable, then a larger proportion of the next generation will have the beneficial trait. Thus, the beneficial traits will become increasingly common within the population over time, while the less desirable ones will decrease in frequency.

Darwin's theory was clearly a synthesis, many of its elements having been derived from the work of others. For example, the nonstatic nature of life was suggested by earlier naturalists, such as Lamarck, and gradualism was emphasized by Lyell. Darwin, by combining his own insights with those of others, created a comprehensive, explanatory paradigm. For example, the theory of natural selection carries more weight scientifically in explaining the evolution of a giraffe's long neck than Lamarck's theory of acquired characters. In the ancestral population, the environment was such that neck length was not significant to survival. Purely by chance, individuals were born with inheritable differences in neck length. The environment then changed so that giraffes' major food source, leaves, were mostly found high above the ground, in trees. Individual giraffes who by chance had long necks now had an advantage over those with short necks. Over a number of generations, all giraffes had long necks because the long-necked individuals produced more offspring (which inherited the long-neck trait), while the short-necked variants produced fewer and fewer offspring (see Figure 2.5).

A close relationship exists between a beneficial trait and the environment: different traits will be most adaptive under different sets of conditions. One of the clearest illustrations of this relationship is the case of peppered moths. These moths spend most of their time lying against the bark of trees. A light-colored form of the moth lives in rural areas of England, where tree trunks are pale. In areas where tree trunks have been darkened by pollution, a dark form of the moth prevails. In both cases, protective coloration is an adaptation that evolved through natural selection, with each form at an advantage within its own environment. The adaptations evolved because it is less likely that a bird will prey upon a moth if the moth's coloration provides camouflage; that is, if it blends in with its background.

FIGURE 2.5

Comparison between (left) Lamarck's and (right) Darwin's explanations for the giraffe's long neck.

Moths that stand out quickly get eaten; hence, they produce fewer offspring.

In humans, natural selection may explain some of the differences in blood composition noted among populations. For example, the high incidence of the sickle cell trait (a variant of the gene determining the composition of red blood cells) in some tropical populations appears to be related to an increased resistance among carriers to malaria—a deadly disease common in those regions. But in regions without malaria, the sickle cell trait is much less common since the trait itself can cause another lethal disease, sickle cell anemia (see Chapter 3).

Darwin was able to test his theory of natural selection by performing experiments and observing nature. He also received support for his ideas from studies of artificial selection, an agricultural technique in which humans breed plants and animals to propagate desired traits (for example, larger fruit, meatier chickens). Darwin spent a great deal of time experimenting with plants, for "in them he could see Evolution at work, right on his study table" (Allan 1977, 17). He was intrigued by plants that captured and ate insects, such as the Venus flytrap, and saw that this unusual adaptation allowed these plants to survive in nutritionally poor soils. Such testing convinced Darwin that adaptation to different environments, through the process of natural selection, was the key to the diversity of life.

Darwin's Unanswered Question

Darwin's theory of natural selection profoundly affected the development of Western scientific and intellectual thought; in fact, his ideas exerted a strong influence on the development of cultural anthropology. Biological evolution provided the first anthropologists with a framework within which they could study the cultural differences observed among human societies (see Chapter 13). Yet, for all the greatness of his scientific contributions, Darwin had some gnawing doubts that were stimulated by the bitter debates over his theory. Although he had many support-

ers, some respected scholars objected to his ideas, especially the concept that biological changes were gradual. The most emotional attacks were triggered by Darwin's contention that the theory applied not only to the lower life-forms but to humans as well—a point that many people abhorred. The intensity of their loathing is illustrated by a famous debate between one of Darwin's staunchest supporters, Thomas Huxley, and one of Darwin's most eminent critics, the Bishop of Oxford, Samuel Wilberforce. In 1860, Huxley and Bishop Wilberforce attended a prestigious set of scientific meetings at which Darwin's theory was the major point of controversy. At one of these meetings, Bishop Wilberforce launched into an emotional harangue attacking Darwin's idea that humans descended from apes. At some point, the Bishop "turned with mock politeness to Huxley and begged to know, was it through his grandfather or his grandmother that he claimed his descent from a monkey?" (Irvine 1955, 6). In response, Huxley clearly and convincingly explained Darwin's theory and depreciated the Bishop's competency as a scientist. As a final blow, Huxley reportedly said "that he would not be ashamed to have a monkey for his ancestor; but he would be 'ashamed to be connected with a man who used great gifts to obscure the truth'" (p. 7).

Even more pressing were Darwin's own questions about the adequacy of his theory. If natural selection is to occur, there must be differences in traits among the individuals of a population, for how can selection operate without alternatives from which to select? Although Darwin could see that such variability exists within species, he could not understand its source. As did most other scientists of his day, Darwin believed in the principle of **blending inheritance**, which states that the traits of the parents are blended in the offspring. For example, he believed that a short mother and a tall father would produce children of average height, the "tall trait" and the "short trait" being forever lost. After a while, all individuals would be exactly alike, unless new traits were somehow added to the population. At a loss to explain it in any other way, Darwin incorrectly came to support the Lamarckian theory of the inheritance of acquired characters as the means of introducing new alternative forms of a trait into a population. Sadly, as Darwin and his colleagues struggled unsuccessfully with this problem, they were unaware that an Austrian monk had uncovered the mysteries of inheritance and of how variation is maintained.

GENETICS: SOLVING THE RIDDLE OF INHERITANCE

Before evolutionary theory could develop much further, scientists needed to understand how biological traits are passed on from one generation to the next. How is variability maintained within a population, and how are similarities passed on from parent to offspring? The answers to these questions can be found in the work of *Gregor Johann Mendel* (1822–1884), known as "the father of genetics."

Mendel was a member of the Augustinian Monastery at Brünn, Austria, where he was allowed to pursue his own interests. A talented mathematician, he studied in Vienna and used the monastery's gardens and extensive library to educate himself in horticulture. Mendel was fascinated by the stability of species over time and wanted to explain how this continuity was maintained from generation to generation. His interest in continuity contrasts with Darwin's interest in variability.

Mendel's thinking was stimulated by some important observations, including that, contrary to the principles of blending inheritance, the traits of the parents were *not* usually lost or muddied in later generations. Mendel designed elegant experiments, using the common garden sweet pea, to test his observations. He chose the sweet pea because different varieties had pairs of distinctly contrasting traits, making it easier to observe the patterns of inheritance. For instance, some varieties produced only tall plants or only dwarf plants, yellow seeds or green seeds, wrinkled peas or smooth peas. (We now know that most inherited traits are not so simply paired and sharply contrasted, nor do they have such uncompli-cated genetic bases. Either Mendel was extremely lucky in his choice of a subject or knew what he was doing from the start.)

Mendel crossbred two pure lines of peas, seven times for each of seven pairs of contrasting traits. In each case, one of the traits apparently disap-

Gregor Mendel tending his pea plants in the monastery garden.

peared in the offspring. For example, when Mendel crossed yellow-seeded plants with green-seeded plants, all the offspring had yellow seeds. Mendel labeled the trait that persisted as **dominant**; the trait that seemed to disappear, he labeled as **recessive**. However, when Mendel cross-fertilized these offspring plants, the recessive trait reappeared in their offspring. And not only did the recessive reappear in the next generation, but the forms were consistently distributed in a 3:1 ratio—three dominants to one recessive. For example, with the seed-color trait, there were three plants with yellow seeds for every one with green seeds.

After many such experiments, Mendel devised the *particulate theory of heredity*, now part of *Mendelian genetics*. The basis of this theory is that traits are carried as discrete units of heredity, which we now call "genes." These units do *not* blend in the offspring, but are passed on, whole and intact, to succeeding generations.

Mendel used the particulate theory to explain his observations. He noted that the initial disappearance of the recessive traits reflects the difference between genotype and phenotype. A **genotype** is the actual genetic makeup of an individual, whereas a **phenotype** is an individual's observable characteristics, such as eye color, blood type, or height. Genes usually come in pairs, one contributed by each parent. When a recessive form of a gene is paired with a dominant form, the recessive's effects are blocked, and only the dominant gene is expressed in the phenotype. However, the recessive gene has not disappeared. If two recessives are paired together in a later generation, then the recessive trait *will* be expressed in the phenotype.

Using current terminology, when two of the same form of a gene are paired, the pair is called a **homozygote**; when two different forms are paired, the pair is called a **heterozygote**. A dominant homozygote is expressed in the phenotype as the dominant trait; a recessive homozygote, as the recessive trait. In a heterozygote, with one dominant and one recessive gene, only the dominant trait is expressed. This is what happened when Mendel crossed the yellow-seeded and green-seeded plants. In the first offspring generation, each plant was a heterozygote—only the dominant yellow-seeded trait was expressed in the phenotype. But in the following generation, the genes of the heterozygotic parents were randomly recombined into new pairs. With many such breedings, the laws of probability dictate that one-fourth of the plants are recessive homozygotes and, therefore, express the green-seeded trait. The other three-fourths of this new generation are either dominant homozygotes or heterozygotes; thus, they produce yellow seeds as shown in the following diagram:

PARENTS:

genotype	=	YG	YG
phenotype	=	Y	Y

OFFSPRING:

genotypes = YY / YG / GY / GG

phenotypes = Y / Y / Y / G = 3Y:1G

Mendel also discovered that the genes for different traits were passed on separately from one another. For example, the genes determining plant height are passed on independently of those for seed color. If a plant is both tall and has yellow seeds, there is no guarantee that a future tall plant will also have yellow seeds. It *could* be tall and have yellow seeds, but it could also be tall with green seeds, short with yellow seeds, or short with green seeds.

These principles of genetics are basic to understanding how biological evolution works because they explain how both continuity and variability are maintained within a population. *Although the units are passed on intact, there is a reshuffling of genetic material in each generation.* This process of reshuffling is now called *recombination through sexual reproduction*. Because each mating involves so many genes, recombination is a potent source of genetic variability (see Chapter 3).

Mendel presented his findings in 1865 during meetings of the Natural History Society of Brünn. Copies of his report, published in 1866, were distributed throughout Europe, yet the scientific community overlooked his work. This was possibly because Mendel's complicated mathematical publications were incomprehensible to most of his contemporaries; thus, his ideas did not reach scholars who could fully appreciate his theories. In 1900, science finally caught up with his thinking, as three botanists independently rediscovered the principles Mendel had already uncovered in the monastery's garden. At that point, "Darwinism, after the rediscovery of Mendel, was to undergo a sea change" (Eiseley 1961, 206).

EVOLUTIONARY THEORY ENTERS THE TWENTIETH CENTURY

The twentieth century has been a time of extremely rapid technological and social change. While social attitudes still play a role in shaping the thinking of scientists, research has benefited from the increasingly large accumulation of scientific knowledge. In addition, advances in communication technology have increased the speed and efficiency with which scientists exchange ideas.

In regard to evolutionary theory, discoveries made during the last part of the nineteenth century, particularly in the study of living cells, enabled scientists to understand Mendel's ideas. The rediscovery of Mendelian genetics, along with twentieth-century scientific advances, has led to the refinement of Darwin's evolutionary theory. These important scientific advances include a better understanding of chromosomes, the development of population genetics, and the discovery of the molecular basis of evolution.

Chromosomes

Microscopes were improved during the late nineteenth century to the point where scientists could directly observe things that Mendel could only infer existed. Using the microscope, scientists discovered chromosomes within the nuclei of living cells. **Chromosomes** are threadlike structures that carry a cell's genetic information, including information that determines how cells are constructed and organized within an individual. Usually found in pairs, chromosomes are specific to species in their number and structure. Humans have 46 chromosomes in 23 pairs, gorillas have 48 chromosomes in 24 pairs, and dogs have 78 chromosomes in 39 pairs. The sex cells, or **gametes**, shown on the left in the following photo, contain only one from each pair of chromosomes, so that when the gametes (one from each parent) combine during fertilization, the

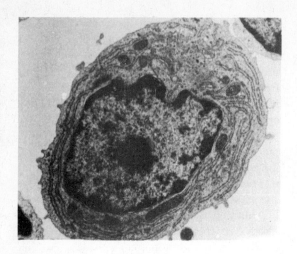

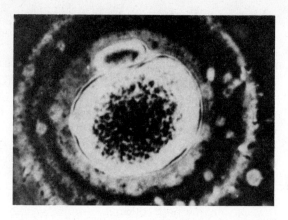

Chromosomes in living cells. (left) Electron microscopic photograph of the nucleus of a somatic (nongametic) cell. The chromosomes are visible as the threadlike structures surrounding the dark-stained central mass. (right) Human female gamete (ovum) at the moment of fertilization by a male gamete (sperm).

offspring has the same number of chromosomes as each of the parents.

A **gene** is the basic unit of heredity. It is the section of a chromosome that contains the instructions for assembling a particular protein or a section of a protein. For example, a gene, by coding for the protein responsible for pigmentation, determines the color of pea seeds. Genes also come in pairs—one on each of a pair of chromosomes. Humans have millions of these pairs of genes. One pair of genes is responsible for sickle cell anemia, another pair determines if a person will have earlobes that are attached to or separated from the head (see photos following), and so on.

The location of a gene on a chromosome—its "address"—is called its **locus**. Scientists can map the loci of genes, thus determining their distance from one another. Two loci may be close together on the same chromosome, at different ends of the same chromosome, or located on different chromosomes. For example, the locus for the human ABO-blood-group gene is close to that of a gene that causes the nail-patella syndrome, a rare disorder associated with strangely formed fingernails and kneecaps.

A gene at a particular locus may have a number of alternative forms, or **alleles**. For example, there are at least three alleles of the gene that de-

termines ABO blood type in humans: A, B, and O. Any of those three alleles may be paired together in the genotype. If both alleles are the same, they are homozygous; if they are different, they are heterozygous. Two of the alleles, A and B, are codominant: both will be expressed in the phenotype, even when the other is present. The O allele is recessive. Therefore, the relationship between the genotype and the phenotype for this trait is as follows:

Genotype	Phenotype (Blood Type)
AA AO	A
BB BO	B
AB	AB
OO	O

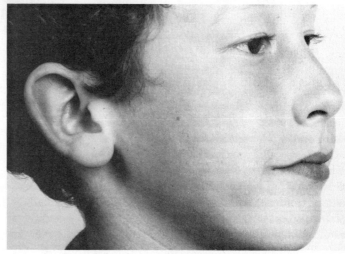

Attached and unattached earlobes. The phenotype of "human earlobe attachment" is determined by a single pair of genes located at one locus. The dominant allele is for unattached, while the attached form is recessive. The man above has two genes for attached lobes, while the boy on the right has either one or two genes for the unattached form.

The discovery of chromosomes over a century ago provided a visible structure with which scientists could understand the principles of genetics. However, a new era in genetics was born during the 1950s with the discovery of the structure of DNA—the chemical substance of which chromosomes are composed. With this discovery, scientists could truly unravel the molecular basis of evolution, and thus begin to fully understand how chromosomes carry and transmit genetic information.

DNA: The Blueprints of Life

During the early 1950s, a number of scientists competed to be the first to unveil the biochemical structure responsible for transmitting genetic information. In 1953, the race was won by the team of James Watson and Francis Crick when they described **DNA** (deoxyribonucleic acid). The discovery of the structure DNA provided the means by which scientists could thoroughly investigate the mechanisms of inheritance, thereby opening up a new scientific field, that of molecular genetics.

DNA, which is profoundly important in many life processes, makes biological evolution possible. This is because DNA molecules carry an individual's genetic code—chromosomes and genes are made of DNA. In addition, DNA is capable of making exact copies of itself. Mistakes in this self-replication, known as **mutations**, create genetic variability by introducing new, alternative genes into a population (see Chapter 3).

What vital functions are performed by DNA? The long strands that make up DNA guide the design of organisms by acting as the blueprints for the synthesis of proteins, the long, segmented strands of amino acids that are the building blocks of life. DNA molecules also contain instructions that control life processes, such as growth and reproduction. DNA's ability to du-

plicate itself allows for these instructions to be passed on to new cells, including those of an organism's offspring.

The special properties of DNA arise from its biochemical structure. DNA molecules are long and ladderlike, consisting of two chains of smaller molecules that are held together and twisted by chemical bonds. The rungs of the ladder are formed by a bonding between a pair of biochemical substances known as **bases**, as shown in Figure 2.6. The bases are the key to the genetic code—they act as the letters of a chemical alphabet. The DNA alphabet is deceptively simple, since it contains only four bases, or "letters": cytosine (C), thymine (T), adenine (A), and guanine (G). In the DNA molecule, each base can join only with one other base: A is always paired with T, and C is always paired with G. Although this complementary situation constrains what

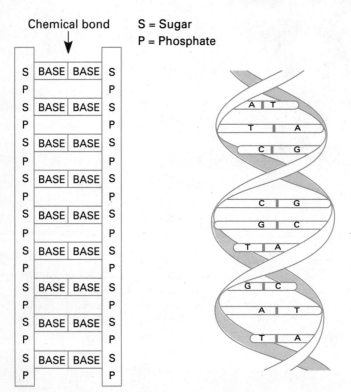

(a) Ladder-like structure of DNA   **(b)** DNA double helix

FIGURE 2.6

The structure of DNA. (a) DNA consists of two long backbones composed of alternating molecules of a sugar and a phosphate. The rungs are formed by the chemical bonding of two complementary bases. (b) The ladder is twisted by chemical bonding into a helix.

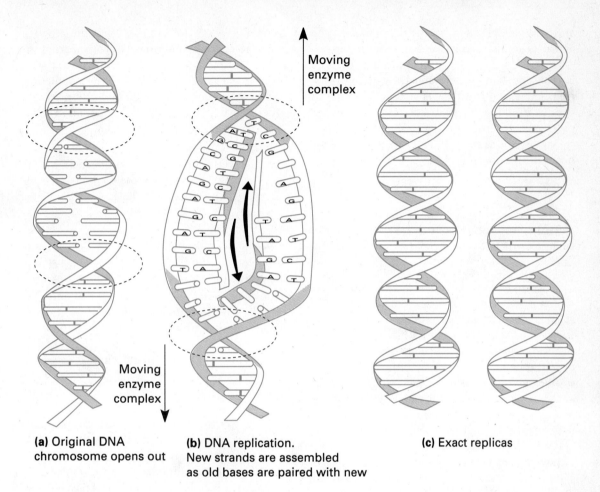

(a) Original DNA chromosome opens out

(b) DNA replication. New strands are assembled as old bases are paired with new

(c) Exact replicas

FIGURE 2.7

DNA replication. (a) Original DNA molecule is unwound and separated by the action of an enzyme complex. (b) Old bases are linked with new bases. The new backbone is built from sugars and phosphates attached to the new bases. (c) This process produces exact replicas of the original DNA.

base will be found on the opposite chain, it does not affect the order in which the bases are arranged along the length of the DNA molecules. Thus, even with only a four-letter code, a short section of DNA can contain an enormous number of possible combinations of base sequences.

DNA is able to replicate itself because of its double-stranded structure. The DNA ladder unwinds and separates, leaving the bases of both chains free to pair with unattached bases. Because of the complementary nature of the DNA bases, both strands rebuild into molecules that are usually exact duplicates of the original molecule. The new backbone is built up as each base links up with its complementary partner, since the free bases are already attached to the chemicals that form the sides of the ladder. Therefore, the new molecules are actually composed of one-half of the original DNA molecule (see Figure 2.7).

DNA builds proteins in a somewhat similar fashion. Using a closely related substance known as *RNA* (ribonucleic acid), DNA strands separate and act as templates for the stringing together of amino acids into specific protein molecules.

In DNA, we thus find the molecular basis of both Mendelian genetics and Darwinian evolution. For example, DNA is responsible for the continuity of life. It provides the mechanisms for passing genetic information from parents to offspring. At the same time, mistakes in DNA replication add new alternatives to a population's pool of genes, thereby acting as a source of a population's inheritable variability.

Population Genetics and the Genetics of Populations

So far, we have discussed how genetics applies to individuals: Mendelian genetics is concerned with how genes are passed on from parents to offspring, while molecular genetics explains how the genetic code functions within an organism. But early in the twentieth century, scientists began to emphasize the fact that *populations* evolve, not individuals. Although the individual breeds and passes on its genes, evolutionary change is the result of shifts in the genetic makeup of a population from generation to generation. This recognition led to the development of **population genetics**, a statistical study of the generational changes in a population's genetic constitution. Here, scientists apply Mendelian genetics to the study of evolutionary change in populations, closely linking the study of genetics and evolution. Population geneticists are thus concerned with microevolution—the short-term changes that occur from one generation of a population to the next. However, as we will discuss in Chapter 3, the study of microevolution helps us to understand macroevolution—the long-term evolutionary process that can result in the emergence or extinction of a species.

Population geneticists view a population in terms of its genetic makeup. They refer to all the genes in a particular population of a species as that population's **gene pool**. They further describe a gene pool as a compilation of **gene frequencies**, which indicate the proportion of an allele of a gene in relation to other alleles of the

gene. Let us say, for example, that the gene frequencies for a population's ABO blood group are 30% A, 20% B, and 50% O. This means that among all the individuals of this population, each having a pair of ABO-blood-group genes, 3 out of 10 of the genes are allele A, 2 out of 10 are allele B, and 5 out of 10 are allele O:

$$100 \text{ people} = 200 \text{ ABO genes}$$
$$60 \text{ genes} = A \text{ allele}$$
$$40 \text{ genes} = B \text{ allele}$$
$$100 \text{ genes} = O \text{ allele}$$

Population geneticists thus study evolution in terms of how and why gene frequencies change from generation to generation. When scientists study a phenomenon, they often use a control, or standard of comparison, that enables them to judge how particular variables influence an event, while other factors are held constant. Therefore, to study genetic change, scientists must understand what a stable, nonevolving population is like genetically.

In 1908, an important step was taken in furthering this understanding. At that time, scientists were active in proving the validity of Mendelian genetics and in expanding its applications. This led a number of scientists independently to derive a principle known as the **Hardy-Weinberg law**:

In the absence of forces that change gene ratios in populations, when random mating is permitted the frequencies of each allele (as found in the second generation) will tend to remain constant through the following generations. (Wallace 1987, 165)

The Hardy-Weinberg law (also known as the Castle-Hardy-Weinberg law) is a key concept in population genetics. Based on Mendelian genetics, it provides a mathematical formula for calculating what the next generation of a population should be like genetically *if* it is not evolving. A real population is compared with its mathematical ideal. If the ideal is not met, then the population is evolving, and population geneticists investigate the causes of the change.

What can cause a population's gene pool to be different from its Hardy-Weinberg prediction? It may be that mating is not random—behavioral, cultural, and geographical factors often disrupt the randomness of mating. Consider, for example, how humans choose mates. Certainly it is not in a random manner. Strong, culturally determined influences govern the choice of a mate. Is the person attractive physically or socioeconomically? Does the person meet with the family's approval? All human societies have rules regulating marriage practices. For example, according to custom, an Australian Aborigine marries a person from a different forager band, with marriages usually occurring between bands that seek to form or reinforce political alliances (see Chapter 17). On the other hand, the wealthy plantation owners of nineteenth-century Brazil encouraged marriages between first cousins to maximize the family ownership of their lands. In both cases, by prohibiting random mating, social customs affect the gene pool.

Natural selection can also cause generational changes in a population's gene frequencies, such as when one allele of a gene is favored over another. For example, natural selection seems to favor the O allele of the ABO blood group in some populations, since fetuses with type-O blood are less likely to die of haemolytic disease (caused when a mother with Rh-negative blood

Bride and groom at a traditional Korean wedding ceremony. Marriages are generally arranged in Korea, and may occur either within or between villages. However, Koreans abhor marriages between people who are even remotely related, to the extent that marriage is discouraged between those who have the same last name.

conceives an Rh-positive baby) than fetuses with type-A or type-B blood. However, people with type-O blood are apparently more susceptible to viral infections, causing natural selection to act *against* people with type-O blood under certain conditions (Mourant 1983).

As we will discuss in Chapter 3, other evolutionary processes can also shape a population's genetic makeup. Population geneticists are concerned with all the evolutionary processes and patterns of mating, since all may influence the evolution of populations.

The Modern Synthetic Theory of Biological Evolution

Besides the discoveries in cellular biology and population genetics, researchers also made progress during the early part of the twentieth century in taxonomy, paleontology, and other disciplines pertaining to evolutionary biology. By the 1930s and 1940s, a number of prominent scientists believed that, using contemporary information, it was possible to explain Darwin's evolutionary theory more thoroughly. They also believed it was important to clearly assert the validity of Darwin's theory and to reject competing evolutionary theories, such as "neo-Lamarckism" (based on the inheritance of acquired characters) and those that viewed genetic mutations as "an autonomous driving force of evolution" (Bowler 1984, 234). Thus, these scholars formulated the *Modern Synthetic Theory of Evolution* (Mayr 1978), a synthesis characterized by:

1. rejection of the Lamarckian principle of the inheritance of acquired characters;
2. clarification of the role of populations in evolution;
3. support for the idea of gradualism (evolutionary change occurring at a slow and steady pace), whereby greater variability comes about through mutation and recombination; and
4. emphasis on natural selection as the primary force giving direction to evolution.

The modern synthesis revolutionized the biological sciences by combining and clearly connecting the different areas and ideas that pertain to evolutionary biology. For example, the modern synthesis acted to connect two important groups of scholars who study evolution—the geneticists and the naturalists (as used here, those who study life-forms in their natural state). The synthesizers made one such connection by concluding that evolution proceeds gradually because of the action of natural selection (a point emphasized by the naturalists) and that it can be explained "in terms of small genetic changes and recombination" (Mayr 1982, 567). The population concept also helped bridge the gap between geneticists and naturalists because, by approaching species as reproductively isolated populations, the evolution of which is studied in relation to ecological factors, "one can explain all evolutionary phenomena in a manner that is consistent both with known genetic mechanisms and with the observational evidence of the naturalists" (ibid.).

Beyond the Modern Synthesis

For many years, this emphasis on gradualism and natural selection went almost unchallenged. However, the modern synthesis has been increasingly criticized, even from within the scientific community. We must emphasize that it is not evolution per se being questioned, but the *processes* by which it proceeds. New information, including that from fossil studies, behavioral ecology, and molecular biology, makes it necessary to rethink long-held ideas. The ideas coming into question include the overwhelming importance of natural selection as the driving force in evolution (see Chapter 3, "The Neutral Theory of Molecular Evolution") and the gradual nature of evolution's pace (see Chapter 3, "Punctuated Equilibrium").

Such debates are a natural part of scientific inquiry. However, the past few decades have also witnessed a rejuvenated religious movement that opposes *all* evolutionary ideas.

A TALE OF "APPLES AND ORANGES": "SCIENTIFIC" CREATIONISM

We have seen that social and political factors strongly influenced the development of the evolutionary sciences—for example, the religious attitudes of the classical Greeks encouraged scientific thought, while the Christian dogma of medieval Europe acted to repress evolutionary thinking. Religion has continued to shape social and political attitudes toward evolution. Ever since Darwin first published his theories, people have attacked them on religious grounds. Many of the early religious objections were based on a literal interpretation of the Bible. **Creationists**—those who believe that the story of creation as told in the Book of Genesis should be taken literally—were offended by the ideas that there are evolutionary relationships among species and that life-forms can change through time. Especially difficult to accept was the idea that humans do not hold an exalted place in the "Plan of the Creator." Within the United States, today's social climate reflects an acceptance of the need for scientific research. But this acceptance is tempered by an underlying mistrust of science, particularly in regard to the study of human evolution and behavior. Not surprisingly, the argument between evolutionists and creationists still persists, although the main battleground has shifted from the halls of higher education to the halls of state legislatures.

In 1925, the first major legal encounter between evolutionary theorists and creationists occurred, a confrontation known as the Scopes trial. In the tiny town of Dayton, Tennessee, a high school substitute teacher, John T. Scopes, broke a state law that had been recently passed forbidding the teaching of evolution in public schools. Ironically, he did so by assigning some readings on the subject in an officially approved textbook. Believing that the law infringed on academic freedom, Scopes agreed to become a legal test case. A highly publicized legal battle ensued, in which the primary issue was academic freedom,

not the validity of evolutionary theory. The judge, a devout fundamentalist Christian, favored the prosecution. After much theatrics and many stirring speeches, the jury found Scopes guilty of breaking the law, and the judge fined him $100. Because of a legal technicality, the case was not appealed to the U.S. Supreme Court, where the issue of the right to teach evolution in the classroom might have been clearly resolved.

In the years since the Scopes trial, there have been continued, though unsuccessful, attempts to prevent the teaching of evolution in public schools. Many scholars, including some prominent religious figures, believe that this animosity toward evolution is unjustified, arguing that religion and science should be viewed as two separate, yet compatible, ways of viewing the world—

GATHERING DATA FOR THE TENNESSEE TRIAL

Political cartoon lampooning the Scopes "monkey trial." Although it dealt with a serious constitutional issue, the press and the public were thoroughly entertained by the circus that surrounded the highly publicized legal battle.

a case of "apples and oranges." One view is based on faith, the other on observable facts, and they can coexist because they deal with different spheres of knowledge. Many people also believe that the Biblical version of creation is an allegory, meant as an expression of symbolic truth but not as a scientific account of the origin of life.

Since the late 1970s, there has been a vigorous resurgence of antievolutionism in which the tactic is a little different. Instead of forbidding the teaching of evolution, the movement insists that creationism be taught as an alternative *scientific* theory. "Scientific" creationism is based on supposedly scientific proof that a literal (not allegorical) interpretation of the Book of Genesis is correct (for detailed reviews of these arguments, see Eldredge 1982 and Futuyama 1983). Backed by some well-organized foundations, the supporters of this movement have been effective in distributing educational materials and in lobbying for their cause in a number of state legislatures.

Scientific creationism has been challenged by evolutionists, who believe that the movement is an affront to valid scientific practice and that it represents a powerful and potentially damaging trend. Evolutionists have organized into groups to lobby for their view that scientific creationism is based on faulty logic and on the misuse of scientific research. Emphasizing that they are not antireligion, the evolutionists' major objection is to the legislating of the teaching of religious doctrine, disguised as science, in biology classes.

The new wave of antievolutionary legislation has been successfully challenged in the courts. In 1981–82, for example, a landmark case was conducted in Arkansas, the first state to pass a law requiring the equal treatment of scientific crea-

tionism whenever evolution is taught in a science course. The goal of the plaintiffs was to prove the law unconstitutional on three grounds:

> First, it violates separation of church and state because creationism is a religion, not a science; second, it abridges the academic freedom of teachers and students; and third, it is unconstitutionally vague. (Lewin 1982, 33)

The outcome of the Arkansas case was different from that of the Scopes trial. The plaintiffs made a strong, logical, and scientifically valid case against the statute, and the state's defense lacked the strength to withstand the assault. One of the many expert witnesses noted that "science has to be testable, explanatory, and tentative and he made it plain that in his mind, creation science was none of these" (ibid., 34). The federal judge ruled that the law was indeed unconstitutional, especially since it forced teachers to present religion in the context of science (see Overton 1982 for the complete text of the judge's decision).

In 1985, a Louisiana law met a similar fate when a federal judge struck it down "on the grounds that the teaching of 'creation science' would be tantamount to the teaching of a particular religious belief" (Norman 1987, 1620). The Louisiana case went to the U.S. Supreme Court, which strongly upheld the original decision. The Supreme Court's decision may put an end to such state legislation, but not to the creationist's fight, because it will "do little to quell disputes over the selection and content of school textbooks, which is now the chief battleground over the teaching of evolution" (ibid.).

SUMMARY

Biological evolution, the change in a population's genetic or physical makeup through time, is the natural process responsible for the diversity of life. Because evolutionary theory forms the framework for the scientific approach to the natural world, a look at its historical development

provides important insights into anthropology.

The earliest roots of evolutionary theory are found in ancient civilizations, including Greece and Rome. However, during the earlier part of the Middle Ages, many scientific ideas were repressed, being viewed as sacrilegious. In the

Christian view, based on a strict interpretation of the Bible, God created the world in six days, the world was young, and life-forms were unchanged except as the result of Biblical catastrophes. By 1300, an intellectual reawakening brought many works of the ancient Greeks and Romans back into the European body of scientific knowledge. During the fifteenth century, world exploration exposed Europeans to exotic peoples and places. Although this contact further stimulated intellectual thought, religious authorities still maintained rigid control over science.

During the seventeenth century, when biology was largely concerned with classifying the living world, Carolus Linnaeus developed the Linnaean hierarchy. In the late seventeenth and early eighteenth centuries, Sir Isaac Newton stimulated a scientific revolution by mathematically demonstrating that the universe was subject to a constant set of natural laws and that change was a part of nature. Geology and the discovery of fossils also fueled the development of evolutionary theory. The late eighteenth-century geologist James Hutton concluded that the earth was very old. During the nineteenth century, Hutton's ideas were expanded by Charles Lyell, who clearly stated the principle of uniformitarianism—that the earth is tremendously old and is subject to continuous and gradual change due to everyday forces.

The early evolutionists of the late eighteenth and early nineteenth centuries, particularly the Comte de Buffon, Erasmus Darwin, and Jean Baptiste de Lamarck, and the political economist Thomas Malthus, paved the way for Charles Darwin and the first truly comprehensive theory of evolution. The major ideas of Darwin's theory are that the natural world is not fixed but evolving, that evolution is gradual and continuous, and that the principles of common descent and of natural selection are operative in biological evolution.

Darwin was at a loss to explain how the key to natural selection—the variability of traits within a population—was maintained from one generation to the next. The answer was discovered by Gregor Johann Mendel, who uncovered the basic principles of genetics—the scientific study of biological inheritance. The most basic genetic principle is that individuals carry traits as discrete units of heredity, now called genes.

During the twentieth century, researchers made great advances in the biological and evolutionary sciences. Early twentieth-century advances included the analysis of chromosomes, the basic cellular structure of inheritance, and the emergence of population genetics, the highly mathematical study of how populations evolve. During the second half of the twentieth century, scientists moved still further in deciphering the genetic code contained in DNA molecules.

During the 1940s, research from many different fields, including taxonomy, evolutionary biology, paleontology, and population genetics, led to the refinement of Darwin's theory known as the Synthetic Theory of Evolution. Since then, researchers have continued their efforts to refine evolutionary theory.

SUGGESTED READINGS

Bowler, Peter, J. 1984. *Evolution: The History of an Idea.* Berkeley: University of California Press.

———. 1990. *Charles Darwin: The Man and His Influence.* Cambridge, MA: Blackwell Science Biographics.

Darwin, Charles. 1958. *The Origin of Species.* New York: New American Library.

Eldredge, Niles. 1982. *The Monkey Business.* New York: Washington Square Press/Pocket Books. (Critique of scientific creationism)

Magner, Lois. 1979. *A History of Life Sciences.* New York: Marcel Dekker.

Mayr, Ernst. 1982. *The Growth of Biological Thought.* Cambridge, MA: The Belknap Press/Harvard University Press.

Sootin, Harry. 1959. *Gregor Mendel: Father of the Science of Genetics.* New York: Vanguard Press.

3 The Workings of Evolution

Life Nature Library/*The Primates*, Published by Time-Life Books, Inc.

A multiple photograph of a gibbon brachiating. The gibbon's body, particularly its elongated arms and fingers, is especially adapted for moving through the upper reaches of rain forests by swinging hand-over-hand through the trees.

Biological evolution is the scientific way of explaining the diversity and continuity of life. In fact, many scientists feel that biology makes sense only in the light of evolution. The study of biological evolution is an important part of anthropology, particularly because biological evolution was responsible for the origin and the present-day adaptation of humankind.

In this chapter, we will examine how evolution acts to produce the patterns of life observed in both the past and the present. We will discuss how genetic variation is produced within a population through mutation and recombination. We will also explore the processes of natural selection and random genetic drift and gene flow. And we will see how these evolutionary processes can eventually bring about the origin of new species. Finally, we will present two recent scientific challenges to the prevailing view regarding how (not *whether*) biological evolution operates.

BIOLOGICAL EVOLUTION AND ANTHROPOLOGY

Why are we devoting two chapters to biological evolution in a textbook on anthropology? Because the primary goal of anthropology is to fully understand humankind, we seek to understand *how* and *why* this particular type of biological and cultural being arose—questions that cannot be answered without an understanding of biological evolution. In addition, biological evolution continues to influence humankind, together with cultural forces, in shaping patterns of human adaptation. It follows that the study of biological evolution can help us better understand contemporary human societies, since biological evolu-

tion is basic to explaining why these adaptations came about, why cultures change, and why they continue to exist.

Chapters 2 and 3 provide us with the intellectual tools we need to understand humans in a biological light. As the text progresses, we will use these tools to examine the biological and cultural evolution of the human species and to study cultural evolution and contemporary cultural adaptations within this biological framework. In this manner, we achieve the holism that is essential to anthropology.

GENETIC VARIATION: FOUNDATION OF BIOLOGICAL EVOLUTION

The foundation of biological evolution is genetic variation. Without it, there could be no change in the diversity of life through time. Two processes, mutation and recombination via sexual reproduction, provide the solution to Darwin's "unanswered question"; they are the source of

the variability of traits that exists within species (see Figure 3.1). It is quite possible that if Darwin had known of these basic genetic processes, he would not have doubted the adequacy of his theory.

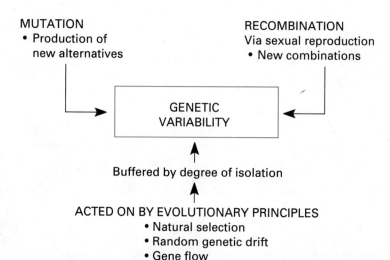

FIGURE 3.1

Genetic variability and the processes of biological evolution.

Mutations: Mistakes in DNA Replication

As defined in Chapter 2, the term *mutations* refers to mistakes in the self-replication of DNA. Mutation is the ultimate source of genetic variation because it creates new alternative genes (alleles) that can be introduced into a population's gene pool. Mutations vary in the degree to which they change the DNA molecule. Sometimes during replication, whole or large parts of chromosomes are deleted, shifted in location, or incorrectly duplicated—modifications that may give rise to differences among species in amount and organization of genetic material, as shown in Figure 3.2(b). However, such large changes can be too great for an individual to tolerate; hence, they may prove fatal even before the carrier of the mutated code can be born.

At the other extreme are *point mutations*—changes in a single base (the chemical letter of the genetic alphabet). One base may be substituted for another, or a single base may be added or deleted from a strand of DNA. Thus, point mutations can affect how the genetic code is read, much like adding or deleting a word in an instruction. Although this may sound insignificant, even small changes in the DNA sequence can cause major differences in the makeup of a protein. For example, the sickle cell trait is created by the substitution of a single base, which causes a change in one of the 146 amino acids that make up a hemoglobin protein chain (see Figure 3.2a). This change, in turn, causes red blood cells to be sickle shaped and poor transporters of oxygen.

Point mutations are also more common and more easily tolerated by an organism than larger mutations; thus, point mutations are probably more influential in evolution.

FIGURE 3.2

Point mutation and chromosomal mutation.
(a) Point mutation results from the substitution of a single base pair, such as the one that causes the formation of sickle cell hemoglobin.
(b) Chromosomal mutation (large-scale). This photograph of a person's chromosomes demonstrates that they have an extra copy of the twenty-first chromosome, causing the individual to have Down's syndrome.

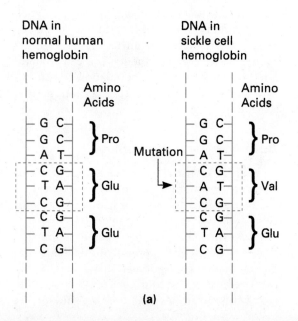

(a)

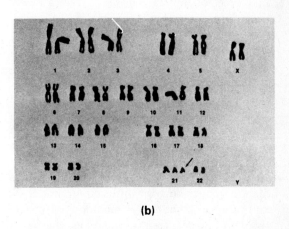

(b)

Mutations are often caused by environmental agents. These agents, called **mutagens**, are usually classified into three groups: radiation (e.g., X-rays, cosmic rays, ultraviolet light); chemicals (including substances known to induce cancer); and appreciable changes in temperature, as occur when a person is exposed to extreme heat or cold or runs a high fever. Mutations without any known cause are called *spontaneous mutations*.

Most mistakes in DNA replication are corrected by *restriction enzymes*. These enzymes compare the new strands of DNA with the original and make corrections by cutting out and replacing the faulty sections. However, because so many cells are being produced at any given time, mutations regularly occur within a population. Estimates for the average rate of mutation for a given gene range from between 1 per 100,000 and 1 per million per generation (Hartl 1983).

Mutation can take place during the production of any type of cell. However, for the mutation to be evolutionarily significant, it must be added to the next generation's gene pool. Thus, the mutation must occur in a gamete (sex cell—sperm or egg) and the gamete must be passed on during reproduction. This is a relatively common event. Taking the mutation rates into account, and considering that a single human sperm or egg contains roughly 50,000 genes, anywhere from 5% to 50% of human gametes contain a newly created mutation (ibid.).

We have noted that mutations are often caused by environmental agents. Does this mean that the form a mutation takes is also determined by the environment? The answer is no. The exact nature of the mutation, including the biochemical changes made and their effect on an organism, is *not* dictated by the character or demands of the environment. However, once a mutation occurs, whether it is maintained in a population may then depend on how it affects an organism's chances of surviving within its environment. A continuum exists as to how mutations affect survival. At one end are the deleterious (harmful) mutations that tend to disappear because their carriers do not leave many descendants. At the

other extreme are mutations that favorably affect an organism's chances of surviving and reproducing. Still other mutations are neutral: they do not bestow any advantage or disadvantage on their carriers. There are, for example, over 200 genetically based variations of the proteins that comprise human red blood cells, many of which are functionally similar to normal red–blood-cell proteins.

The evolutionary value of a mutation is strongly influenced by environmental conditions. What may be deleterious in one situation may be favorable in another. Consider the sickle cell trait. As noted previously (see p. 36), under most conditions the gene is deleterious in that it causes sickle cell anemia without providing any benefits. But in parts of western and central Africa, the sickle cell gene is maintained within each population's gene pool at high rates. This is because the pairing of a normal and a sickle cell gene increases the carrier's resistance to a dangerous form of malaria that is prevalent in these regions.

Overall, some mutations can be tolerated (in that they do not kill or sterilize the carrier), while others cannot. The mutations that can be tolerated play an important role in evolution, for they add new alternatives to a population's gene pool. When conditions are right, natural selection can select among these new alleles. Some scientists even contend that small mutations can accumulate to the extent that a population transforms into a new species without the action of natural selection.

Recombination: Reshuffling the Deck

The passing on of intact genes during sexual reproduction is responsible for maintaining continuity from one generation of a population to the next. At the same time, the recombination that occurs during sexual reproduction is the fundamental source of a population's genetic variation. Because of the continual reshuffling of the gene pool, each individual possesses a unique set

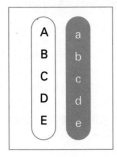 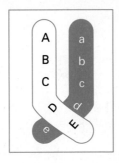 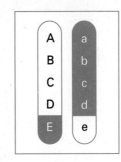

FIGURE 3.3

Crossing over occurring within a pair of chromosomes as members of the pair break and reunite (E,e). The exchange of DNA results in the recombination of genetic material.

of genes. During sexual reproduction, each parent contributes one member of each pair of chromosomes. Since each pair member has an equal chance of being passed on, an offspring may inherit one of four combinations of a pair of chromosomes:

PARENTS: Mm (mother)   Ff (father)

OFFSPRING: MF   Mf   mF   mf

This recombination is independently repeated for each set of chromosomes. Since humans have 23 sets of chromosomes, there are 2^{23} (more than 8 million) different ways that the parents' chromosomes can be recombined in a single offspring. In addition, other mixing, besides the reshuffling of whole chromosomes, occurs during sexual reproduction.

To understand the preceding concepts, we must first recognize that there are many exceptions to Mendelian genetics. One exception is that the independent passing on of traits strictly applies only when they are carried on different chromosomes, the reason being that traits carried on the same chromosome tend to be sorted out into the same gametes. But being located on the same chromosome does not *guarantee* that two traits will be passed on together. During the production of gametes, the members of a pair of chromosomes intertwine while duplicating, at which time they often exchange equivalent lengths of DNA. This process, known as **crossing over**, produces new combinations of the two original pair members, as shown in Figure 3.3.

Apparently, some crossing over takes place almost every time gametes are produced. Considering both crossing over and the reshuffling of chromosomes, we can reasonably assume that a human may produce gametes with 80^{23} (60 million trillion trillion trillion) different combinations of genes (Jolly and Plog 1987). No wonder each person is genetically unique!

Because of crossing over, traits carried on the same chromosome are viewed as "linked" to various degrees. **Linkage** is the association among genes for different traits located on the same chromosome. The closer the genes are physically, the tighter the linkage; the tighter the linkage, the greater the likelihood that two traits will be passed on together. Loosely linked traits are thus more likely to be separated during crossing over. One case of very close linkage in humans is that of the Rh blood group system and a particular type of hemoglobin protein. Scientists also note a close linkage between the human ABO blood group and the nail-patella syndrome.

Recombination and mutation are thus potent sources of genetic variability. Mutation is the force that creates new genetic alternatives, while recombination continually mixes the gene pool into new combinations. This genetic variability is molded from generation to generation by three major evolutionary principles: natural selection, random genetic drift, and gene flow. As we will see in the following sections, a population's size and degree of isolation from other groups are important factors in how these forces influence its evolution.

NATURAL SELECTION

Many scholars view natural selection as the most powerful force in evolution because it is the means by which populations adapt to their environments. Sometimes this process leads to the creation of a new species. At other times, natural selection acts to maintain a population's status quo within a stable environment. Because of these actions, natural selection explains much about both human biology and culture.

Natural selection shapes the genetic variability within a population's gene pool. It is based on inheritable differences in the ability of individuals to survive and reproduce within a given environment. Differences in survival and reproduction lead to differences in how individuals pass on their genes to the next generation. The individuals with the most advantageous traits will produce the most offspring, many of whom will inherit the favorable traits. The favorable traits will therefore occur in a greater proportion in the next generation. The individuals who have the most offspring are the most "genetically fit," genetic fitness being a relative measure of differences in reproductive success among the individuals of a population. Therefore, scientists view natural selection as the source of direction in evolution because there is a relationship between the pressures of the environment and the way that natural selection shapes a population's gene pool.

The sickle cell trait provides an excellent example of natural selection. Rain forests once covered much of western and central Africa. At that time, the people of the region were nomadic foragers (people who subsist by collecting wild plants and animals) who seldom lived near the few, well-dispersed breeding grounds of the mosquito. Their gene pools contained only a small amount of the sickle cell allele. About 2,000 years ago, people introduced slash-and-burn agriculture into these regions. This cultural practice, involving the preparation of agricultural fields by cutting down and burning off natural growth, changed the environment. As people cleared forests, they created large areas of standing water where malaria-bearing mosquitoes could breed. The agriculturalists settled close to their farmlands, thereby exposing themselves to malaria. By chance, some individuals were heterozygotic for the sickle cell trait that had randomly mutated into the population's gene pool. The heterozygotes were resistant to malaria, yet did not contract sickle cell anemia. Thus, the heterozygotes were more genetically fit and had more children than the nonresistant individuals. About one-half of these children were heterozygotic and also passed on their genes at a high rate. The gene frequency of the sickle cell allele increased over the generations until the gene pools reached a balance between the negative effects of malaria and the negative effects of sickle cell anemia.

As we saw earlier, the evolutionary value of a trait is closely tied to the pressures of the environment. When the environment is stable, the most advantageous traits remain the same; when the environment changes, the most advantageous traits often change. This is what happened with the sickle cell trait. The trait was not advantageous under the original rain-forest conditions; therefore, it was present only at a very low rate (in other words, the allele existed at a low frequency). However, when agricultural practices changed the environment, natural selection, by favoring the heterozygotic form, led to a shift in the genetic makeup of the local human population. In the contemporary United States, people of African descent are again confronted by an environment that selects against the sickle cell allele, since malaria is not a significant selective pressure.

Another human example of the relationship between trait and environment can be seen among the Black Caribs (Crawford 1983). Originating from Saint Vincent Island in the West Indies, their ancestors are a mix of American Indi-

Black Carib environments. (top) The Mosquito Coast of Central America. Slash-and-burn agriculture has increased the incidence of mosquitoes and malarial diseases. (right) Caribbean fishing village on Saint Vincent Island, where malaria is not a major problem.

ans, West Africans, and a small number of Europeans. Most of the Africans came to the island from 1517 to 1648, as runaway or shipwrecked slaves. Some groups of Black Caribs migrated from Saint Vincent to other Caribbean islands and parts of Central America. Analyses indicate genetic differences among the subpopulations of Black Caribs living in different locations. One difference is in the sickle cell allele, contributed by the West Africans to the original gene pool. Black Carib groups living on the Mosquito Coast of Honduras have a much higher frequency of the sickle cell allele than do those living on Saint Vincent. The coastal groups live within a malarial environment. Thus, natural selection, acting under different environmental conditions, may be the cause of these genetic differences. The sickle cell heterozygote confers a higher degree of genetic fitness to the coastal pop-

ulations than it does to the island Black Caribs (ibid.).

In the absence of variation, natural selection has no alternatives on which to act. Populations differ in the extent to which they vary genetically. Some have relatively little variation, while others are so genetically varied that they can adapt to devastating events. The evolution of insecticide-resistant insect populations illustrates the benefits of having a high degree of genetic variability. Although an insecticide may kill most of a population, a few of these fast-breeding organisms are likely to be unusual genetic variants that are resistant to the poison. These insects survive and produce genetically resistant offspring. The population eventually evolves a resistance to the insecticide, quickly neutralizing a substance's effectiveness as a pest control. For example, during the mid-1950s, the World Health Organization developed a global program to wipe out malaria that included widespread spraying of DDT and other insecticides (Miller 1982). By 1965, the number of malaria-bearing mosquitoes had decreased dramatically, as had cases of malaria. The frequency of the sickle cell allele also decreased in these regions, as the pressures favoring the heterozygotes subsided. However, by 1979, 61 species of malaria-bearing mosquitoes had evolved a resistance to the insecticides.

Industrial melanism in the peppered moth. (left) The original light-colored moth and a dark-colored variant lie against a lichened tree trunk. The light-colored moth is well camouflaged in this nonpolluted environment. (right) The light and dark forms against a tree trunk blackened by soot. The dark moth is the better camouflaged of the two in this polluted environment.

The number of mosquitoes rapidly increased, and malaria again became a major problem in many tropical areas of the world.

Natural Selection: Directional and Stabilizing

Natural selection can act in a number of ways, the two most frequent of which are directional selection and stabilizing selection. In **directional selection** a population adapts genetically to the different pressures resulting from shifts in the environment. This is what happened in the evolution of the DDT-resistant mosquitoes. **Stabilizing selection** maintains a population's status quo within a stable environment by weeding out disadvantageous extreme forms from the most successful forms. A human example of stabilizing selection is the relationship between birth weight and neonatal mortality. Karn and Penrose (1951) found that babies born weighing near the average birth weight (around 7.5 to 8 pounds) were the healthiest and had the highest survival rates; those who weighed a great deal more (over 10 pounds) or a great deal less (under 5 pounds) died at the highest rates. As shown in Figure 3.4, natural selection acted to select out the extreme forms.

A well-documented transformation in moth coloration provides good examples of both directional and stabilizing selection. During the nineteenth century, the Industrial Revolution caused many social and economic upheavals in England; it also drastically affected the physical environment. By the mid-1800s, the smoke from factories had created air pollution that altered the ecology of parts of the English countryside. Foliage that was once green and brown became blackened with soot. The change in the physical environment led to changes in animal life. One such change was in the peppered moth, usually light in color with small dark spots (hence, the name "peppered"). However, near industrial cities, the dark-colored, or "melanic," variants eventually became predominant. This change in color in response to a polluted environment is known as *industrial melanism*.

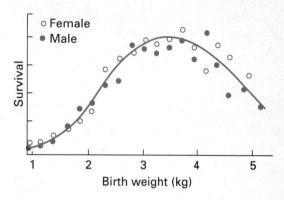

FIGURE 3.4

Graphic representation of the relationship between birth weight and survival. Optimal weight clearly lies within the range of 2.7 to 3.8 kilograms (6 to 8 pounds).

Scientists ascertained that the differences in the peppered moths' color were due to natural selection. Why is color selected for in peppered moths? We can look to their behavior for the answer. The peppered moth flies at night and spends the day lying flat against rocks or tree trunks. In nonindustrialized areas, the light-colored peppered moth blends in nicely against this background, while in polluted areas, the melanic moth seems to disappear against the blackened tree trunks (see the photo on page 58). In both cases, color camouflages the moths, so that they are less likely to be seen and eaten by birds. Natural selection favors the camouflaged forms, acting through individuals that survive and reproduce at the greatest rate under each set of conditions.

Due to mutation, the original moth population had a small proportion of dark variants. As the environment changed, directional selection shifted the composition of the population's gene pool because the dark moth became more reproductively fit than the light form. Once the population achieved the best possible level of adaptation, stabilizing selection actively maintained the status quo within both the polluted and the nonpolluted environments by weeding out the more noticeable variants. Therefore, birds acted to select out the extreme forms of the moth that occurred because of mutation or migration.

We have used the word *adaptation* in association with natural selection. Now that we have discussed the means by which biological adaptation takes place—natural selection—we can more thoroughly investigate this important evolutionary concept, which is crucial in the anthropologist's study of both biological and cultural evolution.

Biological Adaptation

It is striking how organisms seem to be so perfectly suited to the lives they lead. Natural selection is responsible for this apparent perfection because it provides the mechanism for biological adaptation. Biological adaptation can be viewed in two ways: as a process and as an object. The *process* of biological adaptation is how a population of organisms becomes better suited to its environment through time by way of natural selection. Viewed as an *object*, an adaptation is a trait or complex of traits (including behavioral) that tends to increase the chance that an organism will survive and reproduce in a particular environment. "Adaptation the object" is the result of "adaptation the process" because the objects are the features that evolve through natural selection. For example, the long, graceful arms and hands of a gibbon are an adaptation to its life high in the rain forest, where it moves by swiftly swinging hand-over-hand through the trees (see the chapter-opening photo). The process of adaptation is the means by which those arms and hands evolved.

The concept of *species* helps us better understand biological adaptation. The term can be defined in a number of ways, including as a taxonomic category that is based on shared physical and behavioral traits. A more useful approach is to address a species' evolutionary significance as a breeding population. We therefore define **species** as the largest breeding unit within which a group of organisms, under natural conditions,

are mating, or can mate, to produce healthy and fertile offspring. Members of a species make up a closed genetic system that is reproductively isolated from other groups. **Subpopulations** are small and relatively isolated breeding segments of a species. A species' subpopulations are quite capable of interbreeding. However, with complete isolation, a subpopulation may evolve to the point where it forms a new species.

Biological adaptation often plays an important role in the creation of a species, as when a subpopulation becomes geographically isolated from others of its kind and then adapts to a new set of environmental conditions. Biological adaptations reflect the character of a species' **ecological niche** (or **econiche**)—the environment within which members of a species live and *how* they live within it. A species' econiche entails both its **habitat**—the specific physical space it occupies within the larger environment—and its life-style within the habitat. A habitat can be occupied by many different species, each with its own econiche. For example, a number of species of seed-eating birds may live in the same habitat, such as in a cluster of trees. The species could coexist if their life-styles within the same habitat varied—for example, if they fed on different-sized seeds or were active at different times of the day. Thus, each would have its own econiche. As described by Miller (1982),

> {an econiche} includes all of the physical, chemical, and biological factors that a species needs to survive and reproduce in an ecosystem. To describe a species' niche we must know what it eats and what eats it, where it leaves its wastes, the ranges of temperature, wind, shade, sunlight, and various chemicals it can tolerate, the nature and range of its habitat, its effects on other species and on the nonliving parts of its environment, and what effects other species have on it. (p. 79)

For example, woodpeckers share a habitat (trees) with other birds (the larger environment

being the forest and the surrounding area). However, woodpeckers, who use their long beaks to
peck out insects from under the bark of trees, occupy a particular econiche within this habitat.
Another example is the aye-aye, a primate from
the island of Madagascar, which shares a habitat
with other tree-dwelling prosimians. Its econiche
differs, however, because the aye-aye is one of
only two Madagascan primates active at night. A
number of structural adaptations relate to this
nocturnal way of life, including very large eyes
and ears that are used for locating insect prey in
the dark. The aye-aye also has an unusual woodpecker-like dietary adaptation—a long, slender
middle finger that is used to dig for insects, as
shown in Figure 3.5(d).

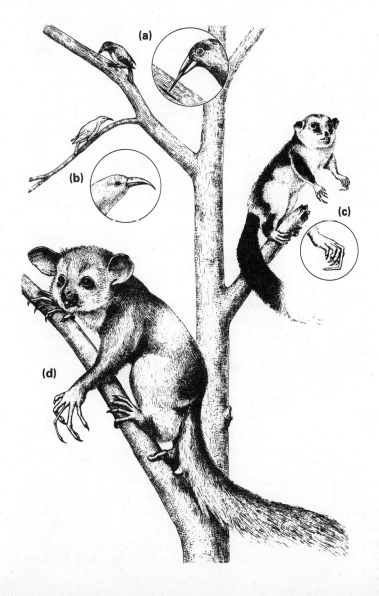

FIGURE 3.5
Surrogate woodpeckers, animals that
occupy the woodpecker's ecological
niche in places where woodpeckers
are absent, are depicted in this
idealized scene. The species shown
include (a) a Galápagos finch, which
uses a cactus spine to probe for
insects under the bark of trees; (b) a
Hawaiian bird of the honeycreeper
family, which has evolved a
woodpecker-like beak; (c) a striped
opossum from New Guinea; and
(d) the aye-aye, a primate from
Madagascar. Both mammals have
evolved long fingers that enable
them to extract larvae from trees.

One might argue that any feature could evolve as long as it improved a species' adaptation to its econiche. However, natural selection acts upon a population's genetic variation. Mutation occasionally introduces new alleles into a gene pool, but mutation occurs randomly; it does not create "needed" forms on demand, as Lamarck supposed. Therefore, most biological adaptations are selected from variations already present in the population and are thus limited by the preexisting genetic makeup of a species. For example, the nonflying ancestor of birds had feathers used for insulation. As birds began to exploit a new econiche, this preexisting adaptation was readapted to aid in flight. On the other hand, bats evolved from a featherless ancestor. Therefore, bats evolved a featherless wing, even though a feathered wing is better designed for flight. Bats were thus limited by their heritage and evolved a less-than-perfect, although still very efficient, means of flying. As for humans, we are primates—and our primate heritage imposed many constraints on our evolution. For example, human knees and spinal columns are imperfect solutions to the problem of standing and walking on two feet, but their design is the best that our heritage allows.

We have addressed only a few of the issues that concern scientists studying biological adaptation. For example, scientists know that adaptations do not act in isolation. What may be beneficial for one reason may be harmful for another. An insect's bright colors may help it attract a mate, but they also make it easier for a predator to find it. In humans, dark skin color helps protect an individual from the harmful effects of solar radiation, but it also makes that person more likely to absorb too much heat. Biological adaptation is thus a balancing act among an organism's many needs within a potentially unstable environment, where "what is adaptive" can continuously shift in small ways.

RANDOM GENETIC DRIFT

Traditional evolutionary theory views natural selection as the primary force in biological evolution. However, there is a growing scientific consensus that random events also play a significant role in evolution. (In a later section of the chapter, "The Neutral Theory of Molecular Evolution," we will consider this further.) **Random genetic drift** is a means by which chance, instead of natural selection, causes a population's gene pool to change through time.

Population geneticists study how random genetic drift causes gene frequencies, the proportion of each allele of a gene in a population's gene pool, to differ from Hardy-Weinberg predictions. Random genetic drift operates on the principle that each generation's gene pool represents a sampling of the previous generation's genes. The alleles of a particular gene may or may not be passed on in proportions that equal those of the parental generation.

Let us assume a population in which two alleles of a gene, allele A and allele B, occur in a 50:50 proportion. Further, say that the two forms are selectively equal: one allele is as "good" (adaptive) as the other. If passed on equally, the proportion of A to B in the next generation is also 50:50. But if the alleles are not passed on in the original proportions, the composition of the population's gene pool changes. For example, the alleles could be randomly passed on to the next generation, so that the proportion of A to B becomes 45:55. In later generations, the proportion of A to B may shift back to 50:50. On the other hand, the "drifting apart" might continue, eventually causing one allele to disappear (A at 0 percent), thereby leaving just one form in the gene pool (B at 100 percent) (see Figure 3.6). Random genetic drift can thus cause the population to differ from what it was in earlier generations.

Random genetic drift most greatly affects

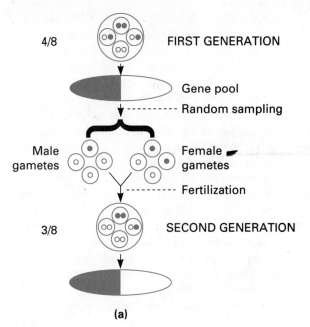

4/8 — FIRST GENERATION

Gene pool

Random sampling

Male gametes — Female gametes

Fertilization

3/8 — SECOND GENERATION

(a)

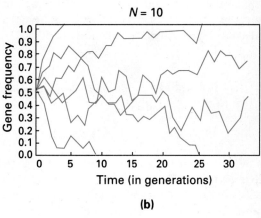

$N = 10$

Gene frequency

Time (in generations)

(b)

FIGURE 3.6

Random genetic drift. (a) Example of a random change in a population's gene frequencies from one generation to another. (b) Computer-generated examples of how gene frequencies can randomly drift. In each case, the gene frequency started at 0.5 (50%).

small, isolated populations (which may, in fact, be subpopulations of a species). The pattern of the random passing on of genes is based on statistical laws of probability, and small sample sizes magnify any fluctuations in predicted patterns. This is as true for genes in a gene pool as it is for a group of voters being polled for an election. Flipping a coin helps demonstrate this point. With each flip, a coin has an equal, or 50:50, chance of coming up either heads or tails. But it is a *probability*, not a rule, that heads and tails will come up an equal number of times. The fewer the number of trials (and, thus, the smaller the sample size), the more likely that the results will be biased and that there will not be an equal proportion of heads to tails. For example, one outcome of flipping a coin 10 times is as follows:

Try Number	Head or Tail
1	T
2	H
3	T
4	T
5	T
6	T
7	H
8	H
9	T
10	T

In this sample size of ten flips, the ratio of heads to tails is 3:7; that is, 30% heads to 70% tails.

Now suppose that, instead of coin flips, we are dealing with a very small population of humans. Originally, the population has an equal (50:50) proportion of allele A to allele B. If the preceding coin flips were to represent 10 individuals randomly passing on one allele versus the other, then the proportion of A to B in the next generation's gene pool would be 30:70—a change caused purely by chance.

Aberrations of this sort are much less significant in a large population; given a large enough sample size, such probabilistic fluctuations usually even out over time. For example, if we flip our coin 10,000 times, the proportion of heads to tails would probably be much closer to 50:50:

Heads	Tails
N = 4,823	N = 5,177
48:52 =	
48% heads	52% tails

When random genetic drift causes large changes in small groups, the gene frequencies are unlikely to adjust back randomly to the original proportions. This is because the gene pool becomes greatly biased in favor of one allele over another—so much so that an allele may drift out of the gene pool. Random genetic drift can thus decrease genetic variability within a small, isolated subpopulation, at the same time causing the group to become genetically different from the larger parent population. In fact, a subpopulation may genetically differentiate to the point where it becomes a new species.

An interesting example is that of the Galápagos finches. The Galápagos Archipelago is a string of islands approximately 600 miles west of equatorial South America, a distance that acts as a barrier isolating subpopulations of species. To a lesser degree, the islands are also isolated from one other. Charles Darwin, during his voyage on the *Beagle*, observed many different kinds of closely related species, including 14 unique species of finches (a common songbird) that were distributed among the islands. These species differ in a number of traits, particularly in beak structure, as shown in the drawings below. A reasonable hypothesis is that natural selection caused many of these differences, especially those in the finches' feeding and reproductive strategies. However, other differences appear to be of no adaptive significance and are not so readily explained by natural selection. For example, 6 species of ground finches have similar dietary adaptations, but are reproductively so different that they cannot successfully interbreed. Random genetic drift is a good way to explain such seemingly nonadaptive differences in the reproductive systems, especially since the isolation and the small size of the finch populations provide con-

Beaks of four Galápagos finches, as drawn by Charles Darwin. Darwin attributed differences in beak structure to differences in dietary adaptations. Drawings 1 and 2 are of ground finches that feed on different-sized seeds or on cactus. Drawings 3 and 4 are of tree foragers.

1. Geospiza magnirostris.
3. Geospiza parvula.

2. Geospiza fortis.
4. Certhidea olivacea.

An Amish family riding in a horse-drawn carriage.
This contemporary photograph illustrates the common
means of transportation and dress of the Amish.
Their traditional ways of life persist, despite contact
with the modern world.

ditions under which drift can become an important evolutionary force.

Other random events, besides this genetic flip of a coin, can cause evolutionary change in small, isolated populations. For example, an important random event called **founder effect** occurs under the following conditions:

1. A small group of individuals becomes isolated from its parent population, such as through migration.

2. Because of chance alone, the proportion of alleles in the founding group's gene pool is not identical to that of the original population. (Say that one founding member carries an allele that occurs 1 in 10,000 times in the original population. Because of the very small size of the founding gene pool, the rare allele now occurs at a much higher rate—that of 1 in 500 people.)

3. The small founding population then gives rise to a larger population—one that is genetically distinct from the original population, simply due to the unrepresentative genetic makeup of the founding gene pool.

Founder effect is seen among the Amish. The Amish migrated in small groups from Europe to the United States between 1720 and 1850, primarily settling in Pennsylvania, Ohio, and Indiana (Morris 1971). There are many individual Amish communities, each founded by a very small group of people. The gene pool of each founding group was too small to mirror exactly the genetic makeup of the original population.

Since only a few genotypes established each of the present-day Amish communities, the gene pools contain relatively little variation. The Amish almost always choose mates from within their own community, which further intensifies this lack of genetic variation because the subpopulations are isolated from one another reproductively. Thus, each Amish gene pool is relatively unvaried and the members of a community are genetically quite similar.

Founder effect is associated with unusually high occurrences of rare genetic disorders. One study found 82 six-fingered dwarfs among the Amish population of Lancaster, Pennsylvania (Diamond 1988). This trait is traced back to two of the few founders of the community, Mr. and Mrs. Samuel King, one of whom carried the recessive gene for this disorder. Founder effect and the small size of the population greatly increase the chances for the pairing of two recessives in an individual, thereby leading to the high frequency of the six-fingered dwarfism.

Random genetic drift reduces a subpopulation's genetic variability, while making it genetically distinct from the overall population. The mutation of new alleles only minimally counteracts the loss of variability. However, this loss can be counteracted in another, more effective, way: If a small subpopulation is not completely isolated, then the effects of random genetic drift can be reversed by the evolutionary force known as gene flow.

GENE FLOW

Gene flow occurs when a subpopulation of a species mates with individuals from another subpopulation. This is often accomplished by migration—the movement of individuals from one group into another. Gene flow thus counteracts the effects of isolation. In other words, it acts to prevent a subpopulation's genetic differentiation, which would be caused by such forces as random genetic drift, natural selection, and mutation.

Gene flow has two effects on genetic variation—effects opposite from those of random genetic drift. First, gene flow prevents the loss of variability within a subpopulation by continually reintroducing the alleles found within the overall gene pool. Secondly, gene flow decreases variability among the subpopulations by keeping the gene frequencies similar across the population as a whole. Gene flow thus prevents the subpopulations from becoming genetically varied and different from one another. In fact, only a very small amount of gene flow is needed to overcome the differentiating effects of random genetic drift (Roughgarden 1979).

In humans, marriage customs influence patterns of gene flow. Some cultures facilitate gene flow by prescribing that mates come from outside the community, as is the custom of Australian Aborigines (see Chapter 17). Other cultures, such as the Amish, inhibit gene flow by discouraging such practices, as we have just described. Geographical isolation also inhibits gene flow, as in the case of the human population of Tristan da Cunha, an island located in the middle of the Atlantic Ocean (Roberts 1968).

Yanomami Indians of South America provide an instructional example of gene flow (Smouse 1982). The Yanomami live in small, fairly isolated villages scattered through the Amazonian rain forests. Without gene flow, these villages would eventually become genetically distinct from one another. However, significant gene flow occurs among the villages through both the abduction of women during raids on enemies and the friendly acquisition of brides from allies. Gene flow thus keeps the Yanomami subpopulations from differentiating from one other by maintaining a continuous mixing of the genetic material within the overall population (see Figure 3.7).

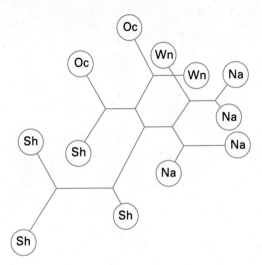

FIGURE 3.7
Gene flow between different Yanomami villages.

MACROEVOLUTION: SHAPING THE PHYLOGENETIC TREE

Having considered the short-term genetic changes that occur from one generation of a population to the next (microevolution), let us now turn our attention to macroevolution—evolution that occurs over very long periods of time, resulting in changes at the level of the organism. Macroevolutionary change can be so great as to cause the origin or the extinction of a species. Thus, macroevolution is responsible for the great diversity of life.

The processes that shape microevolution—mutation, random genetic drift, gene flow, and natural selection—also underlie macroevolution. (Although recombination is an important evolutionary process in that it creates variability in the genotypes of *individuals*, it does not cause changes in the overall genetic composition of *populations*.) But the difference in scope between microevolution and macroevolution is of considerable significance. Because of its great time

depth, macroevolution can produce enormous effects. For example, it took at least 65 million years for humans to evolve from a mammal-like reptilian ancestor, as we will discuss in Chapters 5 and 6.

Macroevolution's effects are reflected in **phylogenies**, the evolutionary histories of groups of organisms. *Phylogenetic trees*, such as that shown in Figure 3.8, illustrate the pattern of life-forms dispersed through time, with the tips of the "branches" representing present-day forms. Macroevolution shapes phylogenetic trees, causing some branches to "grow" and others to be "cropped" via extinction.

Species in the Fossil Record

Species is a crucial concept in the study of macroevolution. In defining a species, the fertility of the offspring is an important criterion. For in-

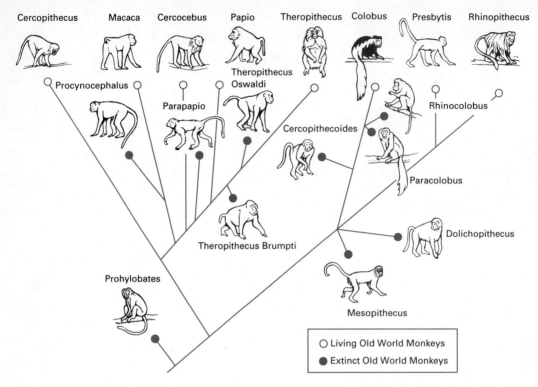

FIGURE 3.8
Phylogenetic tree for Old World monkeys.

stance, although horses and donkeys can mate and produce healthy offspring, known as mules, the mules are sterile. Therefore, horses and donkeys do not belong to the same species.

It is sometimes difficult to determine clear-cut boundaries between closely related populations. The biggest problems occur when trying to apply the species concept to the fossil record, since the "interbreedability" criterion cannot be applied in the case of extinct forms or in the case of species living at different times. This limits scientists to using differences in anatomical structure to classify fossil finds. The classification is fairly simple when large physical differences and great gaps of time exist between successive types of organisms. For example, there is a gap of at least 6 mil-

lion years between a fossil primate form known as *Ramapithecus* and an early humanlike form, *Australopithecus*. The ramapithecines and the australopithecines are easy to separate on the basis of differences in their dental remains. But seldom are divisions this clear, which often leads scientists to disagree over how to categorize fossil finds, as we will see in Chapter 5.

Dimensions of Macroevolution

There are two major ways in which species originate: phyletic evolution and speciation. Such macroevolutionary events are usually associated with ecological shifts. For example, the environment within which an entire species lives may change through time, bringing about either extinction or phyletic evolution. **Phyletic evolution** occurs when a whole species gradually changes through time until it can be called a new species (see Figure 3.9). If it persists, phyletic evolution produces a **lineage**, a succession of species through time. In a lineage, each species gradually supersedes the one before it, creating a single line of descent. Since a single population is slowly changing, phyletic evolution does not multiply the number of species coexisting at any one time.

Speciation, as diagrammed in Figure 3.10, is the process by which a lineage splits, forming new species. Life thus becomes more diversified, two or more distinct species coming to exist at the same time. An associated concept is that of an evolutionary **divergence**—the genetic separation of groups descended from a common ancestral population.

Speciation is often caused by a group moving into a new geographical area, where it becomes isolated from its parent population. This may occur if the parent population becomes so large that the local resources can no longer support it, forcing individuals to migrate into marginal areas where the resources are not as good and the selective pressures are different. Other factors can

also trigger speciation, including chance events, such as when a group is accidentally cut off from others of its kind.

Speciation accounts for much of the diversity of the primates. For example, the Old World monkey genus *Macaca* includes 16 species. The Japanese macaque (*Macaca fuscata*) lives in Japan and is isolated from other macaques by a wide water barrier. Isolation and a particular set of environmental conditions brought about an adaptation somewhat uncommon for a monkey—Japanese macaques live in a temperate climate, whereas most other nonhuman primates live in tropical and subtropical regions.

Another key element in the formation of new species is isolation, which prohibits gene flow among groups. In fact, *spatial isolation*, in which a group is physically cut off from the parent population, is usually an early step in speciation. Depending on the species, various physical or ecological features can act as effective isolating barriers, including water, mountains, glaciers, and deserts. For instance, as we saw with the Galápagos finches, water effectively isolates animals that cannot swim or fly long distances. The effects of spatial isolation are reversible up to the point where the subpopulation becomes so genetically,

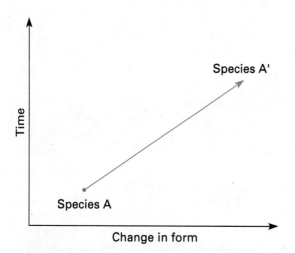

FIGURE 3.9
Phyletic evolution.

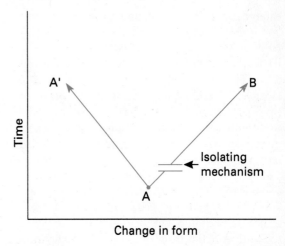

FIGURE 3.10
Speciation.

physically, or behaviorally different from the original species that *reproductive isolation* takes place. A truly distinct species is thus formed, so that even if the new and the original species come into contact, they cannot successfully interbreed.

Other Patterns of Macroevolution

Other patterns of macroevolution are variations of phyletic evolution and speciation. One of them is **adaptive radiation**, repeated speciation from a single ancestral stock (see Figure 3.11). In adaptive radiation, a generalized and very adaptable parent population confronts a wide range of empty econiches. Sections of the population move into these econiches, adapting to each particular set of conditions. This leads to the evolution of a number of new species. Because of the multiple divergences that occur, adaptive radiation is a powerful process, having played a large role in creating the striking diversity of life.

For adaptive radiation to occur, the parent population must be *generalized*, meaning that the structure of the organisms is adapted for many functions. For example, fossil evidence indicates that the dentition of some very early primates was generalized enough so that they could have eaten a range of foods, including insects, plants, and small animals (Fleagle 1988). This differs from *specialized*, meaning that the organism is narrowly adapted to a very specific set of conditions. The aye-aye referred to earlier is one of the most specialized of any of the living primates (ibid.). Its large eyes and ears, rodentlike front teeth, and extremely long middle finger reflect its dietary specialization of foraging at night for insect grubs and larvae buried in the trunk of trees.

The history of primate and human evolution consists of a series of adaptive radiations. For example, many believe that a small ancestral group of generalized monkeys accidentally rafted over to South America from Africa on a small floating island of vegetation (e.g., Ciochon and Chiarelli 1980). This apparently occurred about 50 million

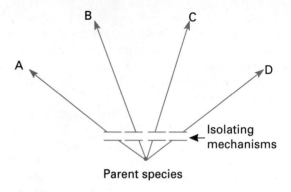

FIGURE 3.11
Adaptive radiation.

years ago, during a period when these continents were much closer than they are today. The South American continent was rich with a variety of resources and the monkeys met with little direct competition from other species. Thus, an adaptive radiation occurred, resulting in the many types of New World monkeys that now inhabit the rain forests of Central America and South America (see Chapter 4).

Another macroevolutionary pattern is **convergence**, in which different species evolve similar traits without the adaptations being derived from a common ancestor. In this manner, organisms from different lineages can evolve strikingly similar structures, physiologies, or behaviors, so that genetically diverse species appear much alike in important ways. A good example of convergence is the fishlike body shape and presence of flippers and fins in an extinct reptile, the ichthyosaur, and in sea-dwelling mammals such as dolphins (see Figure 3.12). Such convergence of form results from functional adaptations to similar environmental conditions.

Convergence causes special problems for scientists trying to decipher evolutionary relationships between species. For example, it can be difficult to establish whether similarities are the result of convergence or of inheritance from a shared ancestor. Such problems may be over-

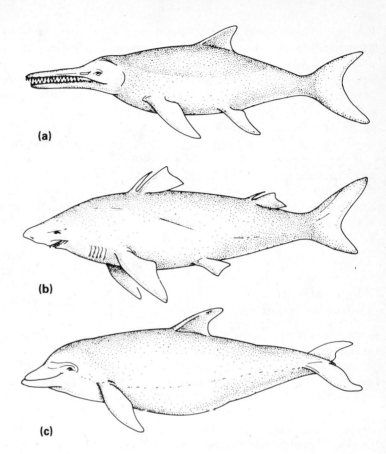

(a)

(b)

(c)

FIGURE 3.12

Evolutionary convergence. (a) A reptile (ichthyosaur) and (c) a mammal (dolphin) have evolved body forms much like those of fish, such as (b) a shark. Each evolved from different ancestors. Similarities in their forms, such as the streamlined body, flippers, and fins, evolved as the result of adapting to similar environmental conditions.

come by looking at a wide range of traits instead of only at the similar structures (see the section "Homology and Analogy" in Chapter 4).

Our discussion of macroevolution has led us to emphasize how species change through time. Not all species, however, undergo evolutionary change. Some species are stable for long periods of time, while other species become extinct. In fact, extinction is "by far the commonest fate of lineages" (Harrison et al. 1988, 13).

CHALLENGES TO THE MODERN SYNTHESIS

Biological evolution is almost universally accepted as the scientific explanation for the diversity of life. However, lively scientific debate continues over the exact ways in which it operates. For example, some scientists disagree as to the specific roles that the various forces (e.g., natural selection, random genetic drift, mutation) play in evolution. Others disagree over evolution's pace.

Thus far, we have emphasized the prevailing

view of evolution—a view largely based on the Modern Synthetic Theory (see p. 46). However, over the last 40 years, scientists have made major advances in research technology. These advances have allowed for the accumulation of massive amounts of data, which has led to the refinement of the synthesis and also to a number of significant challenges to the status quo.

In the discussion that follows, we will focus on two important scientific challenges to aspects of the synthetic theory. Keep in mind, however, that "within science, Darwin's argument that life has had a history—has *evolved*—remains intact as a profoundly solid idea" (Eldredge 1985, 13).

The Neutral Theory of Molecular Evolution

Some of the most extraordinary recent advances in science stem from the field of molecular genetics. One outcome has been a much deeper understanding of how evolution works. Previously, our knowledge of genes was limited to indirect insights gained through the study of phenotypic, or observable, traits. Evolutionary theory was therefore based largely on observations of such things as the patterns of human-blood-type distribution and the coloration of moths. As a result, most scientists currently place a strong emphasis on adaptation and natural selection in explaining biological evolution. Part of this emphasis concerns the adaptive value of mutations. The common argument is that once a mutation occurs, it usually has either a positive or negative effect on the fitness of an individual. Neutral mutations—ones with no positive or negative effects—seldom occur. Any neutral mutations that *do* exist are simply evolutionary "noise," and of no real evolutionary significance.

The advent of molecular genetics has enabled scientists to study genes more directly. For example, they can now identify the exact amino acids that make up a protein and can decode sequences of DNA. Researchers have thus learned that, scattered through the DNA molecules of higher organisms, there are many "nonsense genes" that do not code for the production of proteins. Produced through mutation, these nonsense genes represent a large, untapped supply of genetic variation within a species' gene pool.

During the late 1960s, a group of respected scientists began to use molecular genetics to challenge the well-entrenched "selectionist" approach to evolution. This group includes Motoo Kimura, who developed the "neutral theory of molecular evolution," a highly mathematical theory that focuses on evolution at the molecular level. Kimura (1979, 1983) contends that almost all the changes in a species' DNA base sequences are selectively neutral. Therefore, **neutral mutation** means that, at the time of its occurrence, the substitution of one base for another does not affect how a protein functions or the fitness of the individual. Since selection is not acting, random genetic drift, via the chance passing on of one form of a gene rather than another, determines the composition of a population's gene pool. In addition, neutral mutations for a particular protein (be it an enzyme or a chain of hemoglobin) occur at a steady rate in all species that have the protein.

The neutral theory also addresses the recently uncovered fact that populations are much more genetically varied than was earlier supposed. Why do so many types of genes have alternate forms? Selectionists contend that this is because natural selection favors the genetic variation of certain proteins, as in the case of the sickle cell trait (where an individual with a pair of two different alleles is resistant to malaria without contracting sickle cell anemia). On the other hand, neutralists argue that populations with high levels of genetic variation are at a stage at which neutral mutations have increased the number of genetic alternatives, but random genetic drift has not yet acted to decrease the variability.

As is often the case with a new scientific idea, there are many criticisms of the neutral theory.

One of the major criticisms points to the clearly observable role of adaptation in the evolution of life-forms: How can neutralists deny natural selection's overwhelming importance in shaping the character of a species? But Kimura does not believe that his theory diminishes the importance of natural selection; he argues that the two processes are both aspects of the same pattern of evolution. While neutral evolution randomly operates at the molecular level, natural selection operates on phenotypic traits in response to environmental pressures. When the environment is stable, natural selection maintains the status quo and neutral mutations create a reserve of genetic variability within a population's gene pool. With a change in the environment, adaptive evolution acts on the raw material that has already been produced by the neutral mutations.

By making use of a new body of data, Kimura and his colleagues combine the "old" with the "new" to achieve a better understanding of evolution. With continued refinement and testing, the neutral theory may eventually become part of the predominant view of biological evolution.

Punctuated Equilibrium

Punctuated equilibrium is a macroevolutionary theory developed during the 1970s by paleontologists who feel that the synthetic theory does not fully explain patterns observed in the fossil record (Eldredge and Gould 1972). The main debate is over the *tempo* of evolutionary change—the temporal pattern of the origin of species. Punctualists object to the idea that the most common pattern of macroevolution is that in which one form of an organism slowly grades into another, adapting to gradual shifts in the environment. In most fossil sequences, one form appears to abruptly replace another. Why haven't paleontologists discovered more transitional forms? Most scientists attribute this to the overall scarceness of fossil finds. However, punctualists contend that the fossil record *does* reflect reality, in that such transitional forms never existed. They argue that species seldom change. And when they do, the changes in life-forms are not gradual, but happen in rapid bursts (see Figure 3.13).

FIGURE 3.13
Gradual evolutionary change (left) versus the punctualist view of abrupt evolutionary change (right).

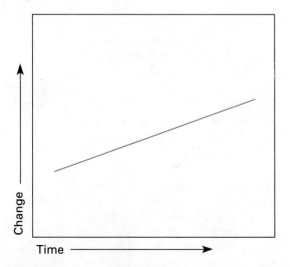 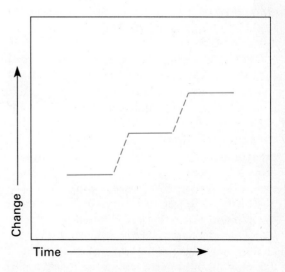

According to punctualists, a species is stable for most of its history. Natural selection maintains the species' well-adapted relationship to its environment. This is the "equilibrium" phase of the theory. The individual members of a species live in colonies that are spread across geographical space. The colonies become somewhat different from one another, primarily because of random processes such as genetic drift. Sometimes, a colony moves into a new econiche and the process of speciation then causes the colony to adapt to local conditions (Eldredge 1985). A number of closely related forms thus exist at the same time, each associated with a particular type of habitat. A local population remains stable as long as the environment is unchanged. However, with a change in the environment, the stability is punctuated as the local form is rapidly replaced by a coexisting form better adapted to the new set of conditions. This process, in which natural selection occurs among competing species (rather than among individual organisms from the same population), is called **species selection**. Punctualists contend that species selection is a "higher level" process that occurs in macroevolution but not in microevolution. In summary, then, major punctualist ideas include the following:

1. Species are stable in their adaptations for long periods of time, as natural selection maintains the status quo. This is the "equilibrium" phase.

2. Subpopulations of a species are spread across geographical space. These isolated groups become slightly varied in form, mostly as a result of random processes, and occasionally as a result of adaptation to local conditions.

3. Species selection occurs only during macroevolution. A subpopulation of a species adapts to a set of local conditions. The local environment then changes such that the original population is no longer well adapted. The original population is then replaced by a slightly different adjacent population, better adapted to the new conditions. This process explains the pattern of "jumps" in form noted within the fossil record, and represents the "punctuation."

4. Speciation, and not phyletic evolution, is largely responsible for the evolutionary history of life-forms.

Eldredge (1985) uses the example of two closely related types of trilobites (long-extinct shellfish) to illustrate punctuated equilibrium. In upstate New York, fossils of a form with 18 columns of ocular lenses were uncovered in shaley limestone, while fossils of a 17-column form were embedded in a harder type of limestone. They occupied adjacent, but not overlapping, habitats, the 18-column form living "on the limey bottoms of the midwestern epicontinental sea" and the 17-column form making a home "up and down the eastern marginal seaway, living on . . . sands, silts and muddy bottoms" (p. 82). Layers of sedimentary rock reveal that, 350 million years ago, the local inland sea dried up, leaving a marginal seaway. At that time, the 17-column form replaced the 18-column form in the fossil record. Gradualists would say that as the environment changed, it caused the 17-column form to gradually evolve directly out of the 18-column form. Eldredge contends that, because the adjacent, 17-column form was better adapted for life in a marginal seaway, it moved into the area and replaced the 18-column trilobite. Thus, selection occurred among species, and not among the individuals of a species.

Another punctualist focus is on adaptive radiation, said to have "accounted for most of the large-scale evolutionary changes in the history of life" (Stanley 1981, 86). Punctualists feel that such rapid bursts of adaptation, including that seen among mammals at the end of the Mesozoic era, provide strong support for the nongradual nature of macroevolution.

The theory of punctuated equilibrium challenges long-held beliefs regarding the pace of evolution, the role of random evolutionary processes, and the level at which natural selection acts during macroevolution. Stanley (1981) contrasted the two approaches as follows: "The *gradualistic model*, representing the traditional view, holds that most evolutionary change in the history of life has taken place within fully established species, while the *punctuational model* asserts that most change is associated with speciation that involves small populations" (p. 78).

Punctuated equilibrium is a hotly debated topic, particularly because many scientists continue to strongly support the gradual nature of evolutionary change. For example, B.J. Williams (1987) believes that the prevailing theory adequately explains macroevolution and that there is no need to invent new "higher level" processes. Others (e.g., Levinton 1986) view punctuated equilibrium as a well-publicized, trivial theory that makes invalid claims based on untestable hypotheses. Another criticism is that punctuated equilibrium contains nothing unique, for speciation, species stability, and species selection are old ideas. Further, the theory is viewed as oversimplifying reality because it reduces "all or nearly all paleontological series to two main conditions—stasis and punctuated equilibria" (Grant 1985, 345). On the other hand, many researchers believe that it is a valid theory, and they are actively applying it.

Darwinism Evolving

What role will the neutral theory and punctuated equilibrium play in the future of evolutionary theory? Stebbins and Ayala (1985) suggest that "with modifications both to the traditional views and to the competing theories most of the challenges can be accommodated within the encompassing vision of the synthetic theory" (p. 72). Such modifications would lead to a more comprehensive view of biological evolution.

More specifically, molecular biologists are producing important information that was not available to the originators of the synthetic theory—information that provides scientists with a much deeper understanding of how genes operate. The neutral theory uses these findings to expand upon traditional views of evolution. For example, the neutral theory explains the large amount of genetic variation found within gene pools without negating adaptation's importance in the evolution of phenotypic traits. However, although Stebbins and Ayala accept many of Kimura's ideas, they argue that *some* molecular changes are adaptive, such as the mutation involved in sickle cell anemia.

As for punctuated equilibrium, Stebbins and Ayala feel that while the theory contains some worthy insights, it provides few truly new ideas. For example, its apparent incompatibility with the synthetic theory may simply reflect differences in how paleontologists and geneticists perceive time scales; in other words, what is taken to be an abrupt change by a paleontologist is thought of as gradual by a geneticist. Stebbins and Ayala also believe that species may be more stable than originally thought, but not as stable as the punctualists propose. Overall, Stebbins and Ayala suggest that scientists should view punctualist ideas as valid ways of explaining *some* patterns of biological evolution, but not all.

As is all of science, Darwinian theory is evolving. Now may be the time for a *second* synthesis, as the ideas generated by recent challenges are tested, refined, and incorporated into the status quo. The natural world is a very complicated place. Not only is there room, but also a need, for a variety of ways to explain the great variety of evolutionary events.

SUMMARY

The foundation of biological evolution is genetic variation. It occurs in a population mainly as the result of two processes: mutation, by which mistakes are made in the replication of DNA molecules, and recombination via sexual reproduction. Mutation is the ultimate source of genetic variation because it creates new alternative genes. Recombination acts to continually reshuffle a population's genetic pool, so that each individual is born with a unique set of genes. A population's genetic variability is molded by three major evolutionary principles: natural selection, random genetic drift, and gene flow.

Natural selection is based on inheritable differences among individuals in their ability to survive and reproduce within a given environment. Those individuals with the most advantageous traits will produce the most offspring; therefore, the advantageous traits will occur at a higher proportion in the next generation. The evolutionary value of a trait is closely linked to the pressures of the environment, and thus can change with a change in the environment. Natural selection acts in a number of ways, including directional selection, which occurs when there is a shift in the environment and a population adapts genetically to the changed conditions, and stabilizing selection, which maintains a population's status quo within a stable environment by weeding out disadvantageous extreme forms from the most successful forms.

The process of biological adaptation is the means by which a population of organisms becomes better suited to its environment by way of natural selection. A species is the largest breeding unit within which a group of organisms, under natural conditions, are mating, or can mate, to produce healthy and fertile offspring. The biological adaptation of a species reflects the species' ecological niche, the environment within which members of a species live and how they live within it.

Random genetic drift is a means by which chance causes a population's gene pool to change. It operates on the principle that each generation's gene pool represents a sampling of the previous generation's gene pool. The alleles of a particular gene may or may not be passed on in proportions that equal those of the parental population. Random genetic drift can thus cause populations to differ from what they were in earlier generations. Founder effect is another case in which random factors influence evolution. Gene flow occurs when a subpopulation of a species mates with individuals from another subpopulation. It acts to prevent a subpopulation's genetic differentiation.

Macroevolution occurs over long periods and results in changes at the level of the organism, including the origin or extinction of a species. Macroevolution leads to the formation of a new species in two major ways: phyletic evolution, in which a whole species gradually changes through time until it can be called a new species, and speciation, the process by which a lineage splits, forming new species. Life thus becomes more diversified as two or more distinct species come to exist at the same time. Speciation is often caused by a group moving into a new geographical area, where it becomes isolated from its parent population. Other patterns of macroevolution include adaptive radiation, repeated speciation from a single ancestral stock; and convergence, in which different species evolve similar traits without the adaptations being derived from a common ancestor.

Although biological evolution is the scientific explanation for the diversity of life, details of the Modern Synthetic Theory have been challenged. The neutral theory of molecular evolution focuses on the evolutionary importance of neutral genetic mutations; it holds that not all evolutionary change is due to natural selection. Punctuated equilibrium challenges the idea that all evolutionary change occurs at a gradual and steady pace. Punctualists contend that species seldom change; moreover, when they do, the changes are not gradual, but occur in rapid bursts.

SUGGESTED READINGS

Brooks, Daniel R., and Deborah A. McLennan. 1991. *Phylogeny, Ecology, and Behavior.* Chicago: University of Chicago Press.

Eldridge, Niles. 1985. *Time Frames.* New York: Simon and Schuster. (Macroevolution and punctuated equilibrium)

Gould, Stephen Jay. 1980. *The Panda's Thumb.* New York: W.W. Norton. (Essays on evolution)

Harrison, G.A., J.M. Tanner, D.R. Pilbeam, and P.T. Baker. 1988. *Human Biology.* Oxford: Oxford University Press.

Maynard-Smith, John. 1975. *The Theory of Evolution.* Middlesex, Eng: Penguin Books.

Mayr, Ernst. 1988. *Toward a New Philosophy of Biology.* Cambridge, MA: Belknap Press/Harvard University Press.

Stanley, Steven M. 1981. *The New Evolutionary Timetable.* New York: Basic Books.

Williams, George C. 1966. *Adaptation and Natural Selection.* Princeton, NJ: Princeton University Press.

4 Humans as Part of the Animal Kingdom

Primatologist Dian Fossey sits in a rain forest close to a mountain gorilla. Fossey was dedicated to studying the behavior and ecology of the endangered mountain gorillas of Rwanda, Africa.

Humans are part of the animal kingdom. Although our species has evolved a unique biocultural adaptation, much of what we are is deeply rooted in our biological heritage. As a result, anthropologists use animal studies as a means of more fully understanding human evolution and the foundations of contemporary cultural behavior. This applies to the general study of animals, which allows anthropologists to examine fundamental principles of biology and behavior, such as the mechanics of body structure and the ways in which animals learn.

Within the animal kingdom, humans belong to a group known as the **primates**. Because the nonhuman primates are humankind's closest living relatives evolutionarily and biologically, they are of particular interest to anthropologists. Through **primatology**, the scientific study of the nonhuman primates, anthropologists gain special insights into what we share with other animals and what aspects of our adaptation are unique. Is the distinctive, finely tuned manipulator the human hand based on a general primate design? To what extent does our brain structure represent a unique adaptation? Is culture exclusive to humans? What about language? These are the types of questions that anthropologists can investigate through animal (particularly primate) studies. In this manner, animals can help anthropologists to more thoroughly understand what it is to be human.

THE HUMAN BIOLOGICAL HERITAGE

Darwin's evolutionary theory shaped the scientific view of the natural world. A major aspect of this view, which applies to humans as it does to all other forms of life, is that many of the similarities noted among species are based on descent from a common ancestor. The ancientness of the last common ancestor is reflected by the extent to which two forms share traits: the greater the number of shared characteristics, the closer their evolutionary relationship. This can be seen among the primates. For example, all of the so-called higher primates, the **anthropoids** (monkeys, apes, and humans), place more emphasis on vision and less emphasis on smell than do the more "primitive" primate forms, known as the **prosimians**. At the same time, the nostrils of monkeys native to the Americas, the New World monkeys, face sideways, while those of all Old World anthropoids (Old World monkeys, apes, and humans) point downward, as shown in the photos on the facing page. The shared emphasis on vision over smell demonstrates that the New World monkeys are more closely related to the other anthropoids than they are to the prosimians, while the differences in noses indicate that the New World monkeys are more distantly related to apes and humans than are the Old World monkeys.

Homology and Analogy

Characteristics shared among organisms as the result of common descent are called **homologies** (see Figure 4.1). Homologies are a major reason nonhuman animals are so useful in the study of human evolution. By evaluating homologous biochemical, physical, and behavioral traits, scientists can develop phylogenies (evolutionary histories) of life-forms, including humans. Researchers also use homologies in reconstructing ancestral forms. For example, since all mammals are warm-blooded, have hair, and nurse their young, it is likely that the common mammalian ancestor had these same characteristics.

Not all shared characteristics are based on common descent. Biological **analogies** are independently evolved similarities that usually arise as the result of adaptive responses to similar conditions (see Figure 4.2). Analogies are often the result of convergent evolution, in which different species evolve similar traits without the adaptations being derived from a common ancestor. In Chapter 3 we illustrated convergent evolution by the fishlike body that evolved independently in the extinct reptile ichthyosaur and sea-dwelling mammals in response to life in a watery habitat (Figure 3.12).

Analogies, too, are useful tools in evolutionary studies. Analogies nicely reflect the process of adaptation; thus, they help scientists formulate general principles of how organisms respond to environmental conditions. Scientists also use analogies in reconstructing the past. Because the form of a structure and the function it serves are closely associated, scientists hypothesize that a structure served the same adaptive function in the past as it does in the present. Thus, they use living forms as models to interpret the fossil record. R.F. Kay (1977), for example, observed that some contemporary primates have teeth designed to help them eat fruit, while leaf- and insect-eaters have other types of teeth. He concluded that many of the apelike primates of 20 million years ago ate mostly fruit because their fossilized teeth are most like those of the fruit-eating primates.

Because phylogenies reflect patterns of common descent, they need to be based on homologies. Unfortunately, it is sometimes difficult to determine whether a single shared trait is homologous or analogous. This problem can be overcome by looking at the organisms as wholes, rather than at isolated traits. If the forms share many traits, it is more likely that their similarities are due to common descent rather than to similar

Placement of the nostrils of primates. (top left) New World monkeys, such as this Bolivian red howler, have nostrils that face sideways. (bottom left) In Old World anthropoids, including this Old World monkey known as a drill, nostrils point downward. (bottom right) Humans, being Old World anthropoids, also have down-directed nostrils.

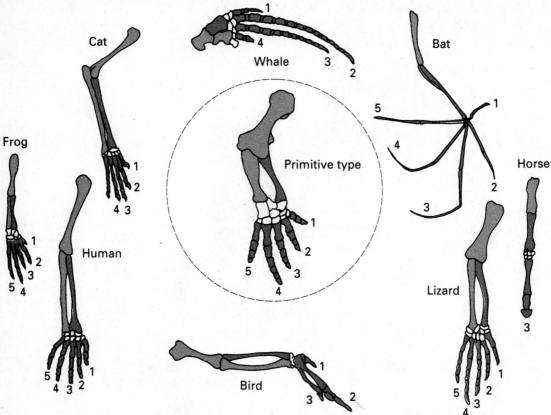

FIGURE 4.1

Homologous structures. The forelimbs of some vertebrates are compared with that of a possible common ancestor. In each case, individual bones have been modified, although they can still be traced to the ancestor. Since the shared structures are the result of common descent, they are *homologous.*

adaptive responses. In the case of birds, insects, and bats, wings evolved in each as an adaptation for flight. If one looked simply at the wings, it could not be determined whether they were homologies or analogies. But considering the whole organisms, it would be apparent that many important differences existed among them. This is clearly an analogous situation, without a basis in common descent.

Humankind's Place within the Animal Kingdom

The Linnaean hierarchy, which groups organisms into a graded series of categories, is the scheme scientists use to classify life-forms. Modern scientists know that the similarities on which the hierarchy is based are due to common descent. The evolutionary relationships between the members of each category become closer as the groupings get smaller. For example, the animal kingdom is divided into the vertebrates (animals with backbones) and the invertebrates (animals without backbones). The vertebrates are subdivided into five classes: fish, amphibians, reptiles, birds, and mammals. Although the

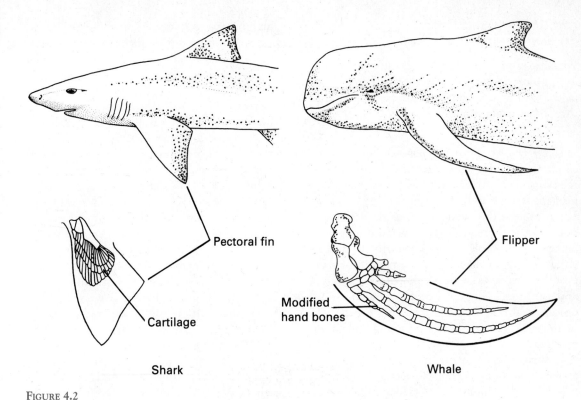

Pectoral fin

Flipper

Cartilage

Modified
hand bones

Shark

Whale

FIGURE 4.2

Analogous structures. The shark's pectoral fin and the whale's flipper are appendages that serve similar functions and are similar in appearance. However, the similarities are not based on common descent; rather, they are *analogies*—independently evolved as adaptive responses to similar conditions. Differences are seen within the structures. The appendage of the fish (the shark) is supported by cartilage, while the flipper of the mammal (the whale) is supported by modified hand bones.

members of each class are very different from members of other classes, all vertebrates have backbones and share a more recent ancestor among themselves (from about 600 million years ago) than the ancestor shared with the invertebrates. All mammals, however, are descended from a much more recent ancestor that is not shared with the other vertebrates. This ancestor dates back only about 70 million years. In addition, all mammals share a set of traits, including

internal mechanisms for maintaining a constant body temperature (warm-bloodedness), hair, and the ability to nurse their young.

Humans derive many major characteristics from their vertebrate heritage, including the presence of a backbone and a mass of nerve cells concentrated in a brain. Our mammalian heritage is also evident in that we are warm-blooded, have hair, give birth to live young (versus laying eggs), and produce milk. Within the mammals, humans belong to the order *Primates*. We thus share a greater number of traits and a more recent evolutionary history with other primates than we do with other orders of mammals (see Figure 2.4).

A large and diverse group, the primates include prosimians, monkeys, apes, and humans. Our closely shared heritage means that the other primates can provide special insights into the evolutionary and biological foundations of humanity.

Anthropology and Primate Studies

Primatology, previously defined as the study of the morphology (form and structure) and behavior of the nonhuman primates, has four major anthropological applications:

1. *Defining what is unique about the human species.* Because of the closeness of the evolutionary relationship between nonhuman primates and humans, we can look to nonhuman primates to test ideas regarding what characteristics are or are not distinctly human. For example, the ability to make and use tools was long thought to differentiate humans from all other forms of life. However, observations of wild chimpanzees making and using tools demonstrate that humans are not unique in this ability, although they *are* special in the complexity of their tool-using and tool-making skills.

2. *Reconstructing human evolutionary history by defining what traits are shared with other primates.* Scientists use homologous traits to decipher what a primate ancestor was like and to evaluate whether a fossil form is a feasible ancestor of living species. For example, contemporary apes and some humans have a particular cusp pattern (the bumps and crevices on the surface of a tooth) on the lower back molars. Anthropologists use the presence or absence of this trait to judge whether a fossil animal may have been ancestral to both apes and humans. The oldest known apelike primates, which lived about 20 million years ago, had the trait. This pattern is also present in an earlier monkeylike form, *Aegyptopithecus*. This supports the theory that *Aegyptopithecus* was ancestral to all apes and humans (see Chapter 5).

3. *Providing models for interpreting fossil finds.* Since scientists cannot directly observe ancient primates, studies of living species provide important clues about how extinct forms lived. In such studies, scientists focus on analogous characteristics that reflect similar adaptive responses. For example, Fleagle, Kay, and Simons (1980) used contemporary primates as models for reconstructing the social behavior of *Aegyptopithecus*. Fossils indicate that *Aegyptopithecus* exhibited significant sex differences in tooth and body size, the males having had larger bodies and longer canine teeth than the females. Scientists note similar differences in a number of contemporary primates, the pattern being associated with two types of social organization. One type of social organization consists of multiple adult males and multiple adult females, and the other consists of groups with a single adult male and multiple females. Sex differences of this sort do not exist in monogamous (one adult male to one adult female) nonhuman primates. Using this information, Fleagle, Kay, and Simons hypothesized that *Aegyptopithecus* lived in groups containing multiple adult females, either with a single adult male or with multiple adult males, rather than in nuclear families, which consist solely of a permanent male/female pair and their offspring.

4. *Devising general rules of evolutionary and ecological theory.* The primates afford us with an excellent opportunity to study both microevolution and macroevolution. Primate studies generate ideas about how microevolution operates in complex life-forms; for example, how mating patterns affect the genetic composition of populations. On the other hand, differences noted among primate species reflect macroevolutionary divergences. For example, the nine species of lesser apes represent a relatively recent adaptive radiation, thereby providing evolutionary biologists with a good opportunity to study speciation (Creel and Preuschoft 1984).

Besides these academic applications, the anthropological study of nonhuman primates also contributes to human welfare. For example, primate studies help medical researchers understand the degree to which various species biologically resemble humans, and thus the extent to which these species can be used as research models. Studies of sexual and social behavior contrib-

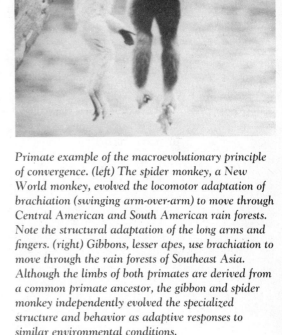

Primate example of the macroevolutionary principle of convergence. (left) The spider monkey, a New World monkey, evolved the locomotor adaptation of brachiation (swinging arm-over-arm) to move through Central American and South American rain forests. Note the structural adaptation of the long arms and fingers. (right) Gibbons, lesser apes, use brachiation to move through the rain forests of Southeast Asia. Although the limbs of both primates are derived from a common primate ancestor, the gibbon and spider monkey independently evolved the specialized structure and behavior as adaptive responses to similar environmental conditions.

ute information on how best to breed captive primates—a field becoming increasingly important as access to wild populations diminishes. Research psychologists also use primatological data. For example, field studies of rhesus monkey behavior help clarify the relationship between social status, stress, and heart attacks in humans. Other researchers use naturalistic studies of mother-infant interactions to assess the importance of proper nurturing in primate psychological development. Clearly, the anthropological applications of primate studies reach beyond the realm of abstract science into areas that have a direct bearing on our lives.

THE PRIMATE ADAPTATION

What differentiates the primates from other types of mammals? Ironically, the primates' most distinctive characteristic is that they are relatively unspecialized. Rodents, by contrast, have continually growing and very sharp front teeth that are specially designed for gnawing. The hoofed mammals, grazers that chew rough vegetation, have broad, flat molars and a hardy digestive system that includes a four-chambered stomach. Primates are not specialized in this manner; the primate order is not limited to a very specific dietary niche, but exploits a wide variety of foods. There *are* dietary and dental specializations within the order, but even the more specialized species vary their diets when conditions demand that they do so. A generalized form is more evolutionarily flexible, meaning that it can adapt to a broader range of ecological conditions than a specialized form, which is particularly well adapted to a narrow ecological niche. Therefore, this general lack of specialization has allowed the order to become highly diversified. Yet primates are still primates, whether they live in a tropical rain forest or on an arid savannah, eat leaves or insects, are active during the day or the night, or sleep in a nest in a tree or in a bed in a house.

The lack of specialization combines with a number of traits and evolutionary trends to create a pattern of primateness. The pattern is based on a generalized common ancestor that diverged from all other mammals about 70 million years ago. The earliest primate provided the foundation for the eventual evolution of all other primates—living and extinct, successful and unsuccessful, human and nonhuman.

Primate Traits and Trends

Most primate characteristics are actually evolutionary trends that are expressed to varying degrees within the order. Listing these trends may give rise to the notion that they represent a progression from an inferior to a superior state, which is not the case. Nor should it be taken that primate evolution was directed toward an ultimate primate—the human. In reality, each type of primate has adapted to its own environment with a high degree of success. As one moves from the prosimians to monkeys to apes to humans, it is more accurate to think of the increasing complexity of the traits as "embellishments" upon patterns already present in the primate stock. These embellishments evolved as the result of selection for solutions to more complex environmental demands; thus, they do *not* reflect "improvements," as such, in form and function.

Primitive primate characteristics (traits retained from the general mammalian heritage) are

1. generalized 5-digit (fingers and toes) limb structure;
2. retention of collarbone; and
3. generalized teeth, associated with the ability to eat a wide variety of foods, with some modifications among primate forms.

Primate evolutionary trends (established within the primate lineage and expressed to varying degrees among the forms) are as follows:

1. Adaptation of limbs for grasping and exploration, with flat nails replacing claws and with sensitive tactile pads at the ends of the digits. The digits become more mobile, the thumb and big toe, or both, better able to be brought together with the other digits on the same hand or foot.
2. Increasing emphasis on vision over smell, with eyes tending to be placed in front of the head rather than to the side, allowing for various degrees of binocular vision (for depth perception). The snout decreases in length. The brain becomes reorganized with proportionally smaller areas for smell and larger areas for vision.
3. Increasing emphasis on complex social organization and behavior, including changes in

On Cayo Santiago, a group of closely related female rhesus macaques sit close together. Social bonds, reflected by grooming behavior and relaxed physical contact, are crucial elements of the complex social organizations found within primate societies. The core of rhesus social groups are the bonds that exist between closely related females, such as mothers, daughters, and sisters.

patterns of growth and maturation that make this possible. The number of young from a single pregnancy decreases and gestation time and spacing between births increases. An offspring depends on its mother or other caretaker for a longer period of time, allowing for a greater degree of interaction between mother and offspring. Brain areas associated with higher mental functions, such as intelligence and learning abilities, become more extensive and elaborate. Both the increased interaction between mother and offspring and the elaborated brain allow for an increased emphasis on learned behavior. A lengthening life span permits more time for each of the various developmental stages.

The Earliest Primate

The earliest primate established the primate pattern of traits and trends that is reflected throughout the order. What was the earliest primate like?

Scientists believe that it resembled modern-day tree shrews in both form and general level of adaptation, as did many of the other early mammals. Confined to Southeast Asia, the tree shrew, a primitive mammal, inhabits the bushes and shrubs of rain forests. Small and agile, with a bushy tail, it looks like long-snouted squirrel. Tree shrews have a number of characteristics that resemble those of primitive primates, particularly in aspects of their skulls and teeth. For ex-

Modern-day tree shrew. The earliest primate is thought to have resembled the modern-day tree shrew in both form and general level of adaptation.

ample, while not as developed as those of primates, their visual systems are relatively advanced. Tree shrews also resemble primates in their grasping abilities. However, their long snouts, sideward-facing eyes, and lack of any nails clearly separates the tree shrews from the primates. In addition, the social behavior of tree shrews lacks the intense parental care associated with the primate order.

Understanding the earliest primate's adaptation is crucial to explaining why primates diverged from the other mammals. Such knowledge is also necessary in understanding the evolutionary basis of primateness. A long-standing explanation is the *arboreal theory*. It states that primate characteristics, such as limbs designed for grasping and eyes adapted for binocular vision, evolved in response to moving, feeding, and living within the complex world of the treetops. A more up-to-date theory is the *visual predation hypothesis* (Cartmill 1972), which contends that primate characteristics reflect an adaptation to a life of foraging for fruit and insects in the shrub layer of forests. The primitive primate is viewed as a hunter that depended upon good vision and limbs specialized for stalking and capturing its

prey. However, almost all living primates are arboreal, suggesting that the early primates eventually moved up into the trees. Yet another respected idea is that the origin of the primates was marked by a shift from an insect-based diet to one with a greater vegetarian component (Szalay and Delson 1979).

It has yet to be demonstrated which of these theories, if any, fully describes the adaptation of the earliest primate. Scientists must gather more evidence, including that from fossil finds and cross-species comparisons, before they can reach any firm conclusion regarding this important issue.

Primate Diversity

As we have already mentioned, the primates evolved a much broader range of adaptations than other groups of mammals. The approximately 185 species of primates, distributed within about 50 genera (plural of genus), differ in their expression of the primate trends, live in many different places, and survive in many different ways.

Although usually native to tropical and subtropical regions, the nonhuman primates exploit

Two types of primate habitats. (top) Tropical rain forests, such as this one in South America (Brazil), provide homes for many different primate species. (right) Some Old World monkeys, including species of baboons, patas, and vervets, spend most of their time on savannahs, such as this one in Africa (Kenya).

many different ecological niches. Their habitats vary greatly—some living on arid semideserts, others on grasslands, and still others in rain forests. Most primates are arboreal, making their homes in trees. However, this tendency varies in degree. Some species seldom leave the treetops, whereas others spend most of their time on the ground. Here, as in most cases, body structure reflects the animal's way of life. Highly arboreal species, such as gibbons and spider monkeys, tend to be lightly built. Terrestrial forms, such as Japanese and rhesus macaques, are heavily boned so as to withstand the stresses of walking long distances in search of food.

Primates vary not only in where they live, but also in *how* they live within their habitats. For instance, although the majority of primates are most active during the day (diurnal), a few, such as tarsiers, owl monkeys, and aye-ayes, are most active at night (nocturnal). Primates also vary in their locomotion—how they move about. Gibbons swing arm-over-arm through the rain forest; pottos are slow, cautious climbers who always have three of their limbs firmly planted on a branch; and squirrel monkeys scurry and leap their way through the trees. The terrestrial baboons and patas monkeys walk on four, equal-length limbs, while gorillas and chimpanzees knuckle-walk on the ground, with their lengthy arms stretched out in front of them.

Primates also differ in diet and feeding behavior, most preferring specific foods. Aye-ayes, galagos, and tarsiers concentrate on insect prey; mangabeys, spider monkeys, and gibbons prefer fruits; colobus and howler monkeys eat mostly leaves. However, the diets of some forms are quite diverse; for example, baboons eat many different types of plants and some meat. Other primates, such as the gum-eating loris (the angwantibo) are relatively rigid in what they will eat. In general, "selectivity and discrimination are key characteristics of the [feeding] ecology of modern primates . . ." (Richard 1985, 120). This feeding ecology is based on fine visual acuity and excellent and precise hand control.

Because of its important role in helping to explain the elusive biological and evolutionary basis of human sociality, anthropologists are especially interested in the social behavior of primates. The behaviors studied by anthropologists include grooming (the use of an animal's teeth or hands to pick small objects out of another's fur, often used as a measure of social bonding); social dominance (defined here as the ability of one group member to cause another to act submissive); mating behavior; and mother-infant interactions.

Primates demonstrate a great variety of social structures. Individuals of some species live primarily alone, such as the orangutan. By contrast, hamadryas baboons live within large and complexly organized groups (see Figure 4.3). Social organization is an important aspect of a species' adaptation. It may evolve in response to availability of resources, threats from predators, or other problems that vary with the habitat. For example, group size is an aspect of a species' adaptation affected by the distribution and availability of important resources, such as food and water; the larger the group, the more area is needed to supply the individuals. Other factors, including the need to defend against predators, may act to keep the group size from becoming notably small. Species that hide from predators, in contrast to those that put up an active defense, tend to congregate in less obvious, smaller groups (A. Jolly 1985).

The primate order is truly wondrous in the range and sophistication of its adaptations. Unfortunately, however, many primate species are in great danger of disappearing forever from the wild. As of the early 1980s, 76 species were close to extinction, threatened largely by human destruction of primate habitats. Conservationists are working with governments to try to prevent this obliteration, but economic, social, and political factors make the job difficult. The immediate needs of local human populations, many of which are poor, are often at odds with protecting nonhuman primates, as in the conversion of for-

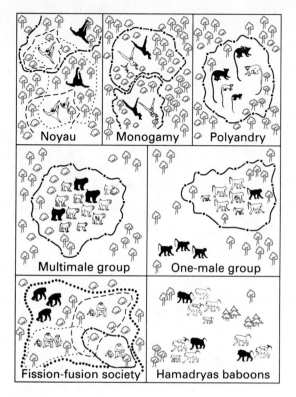

FIGURE 4.3
Common types of primate social groups.

ests to farmland or in the construction of hydro-electric projects. National and international business interests, especially those of the timber and beef industries, are also major factors contributing to rain forest destruction. There is, however, a growing awareness that natural habitats, including rain forests, are integral parts of local environments, providing watersheds and other important ecological features. Here we have a vivid case of an economic world system in conflict with the environmental world system. Even on a global scale, rain forests are crucial in that they influence worldwide climatic patterns. And the primates themselves should be saved if for no other reason than that once a species disappears, it is gone forever, leaving the earth a bit poorer. "We stand now in a special relationship to the future . . . unless we act, posterity will be unable to do so" (Passmore, in Conway 1985, 12).

Major Categories of Primates

We will now take up the question of how scientists classify the members of the primate order into taxonomic categories. In general, contemporary primates are usually divided into two major groups: the prosimians and the anthropoids, as shown in Figure 4.4. Prosimians, considered the more primitive group, are the forms most like the earliest primate. Prosimians are divided into the lemurlike and the lorislike forms. The anthropoids—the New World monkeys, the Old World monkeys, the lesser apes, the great apes, and humans—make up the more advanced, or derived (changed from the original), group, less like the earliest primate than the prosimians are. The anthropoids show a more advanced expression of the primate evolutionary trends, with the apes being the most derived of the nonhuman primates. Humans, the most derived of all the primates, have the most exaggerated expression of the evolutionary trends.

Taxonomy, the science of classifying living things, is an inexact science, in that classification of specific organisms is somewhat open to interpretation. Life-forms do not always fit nicely into humanmade categories. For example, one primate, the tarsier, is particularly difficult to classify, demonstrating characteristics of both prosimians and anthropoids. Some schemes lump the tarsier in with the prosimians, others lump it in with the anthropoids, and still others place it within its own intermediary category—the approach taken here.

The Primate Portfolio (pp. 103–114) presents an overview of the contemporary nonhuman primates. (Because there are approximately 185 species of primates, it is possible to illustrate the great diversity of the order only in general terms.) The photographs (see the end of the Portfolio) graphically demonstrate primate diversity, while the text summarizes major traits associated

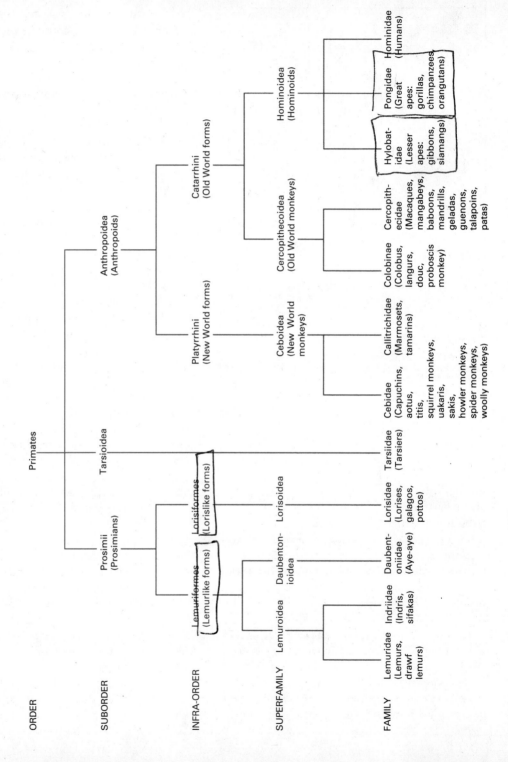

FIGURE 4.4

Classification of the living primates (to the taxomic level of family). Examples of common names are given.

with the different groups. Primate adaptations are explored through examples of how different species contend with their environments. The information is organized into four major categories of adaptation. Associated with each category are structural and functional components that evolved as a unit in response to environmental conditions:

1. *Locomotor adaptation:* How an animal moves about. Associated anatomical structures include limbs, hands, feet, the vertebral column, and the trunk.

2. *Dietary adaptation:* What an animal eats, how it obtains food, and how it eats and digests food. Associated anatomical structures include teeth and jaws, skull (including attachments for muscles), cheek pouches, hands, and the digestive tract.

3. *Information processing system:* How an animal gathers and processes information, including brain organization and the emphasis on the various special senses. Associated anatomical structures include those involved in the special senses (vision, hearing, smell, taste, touch) and processual areas of the brain.

4. *Social behavior:* How members of a species interact with one another, both within and between social groups. This category includes many topics, including group structure, mating behavior, parental behavior, dominance, grooming, emphasis on learning, communication systems, land use, and patterns of growth and maturation. Associated anatomical structures include the brain, facial muscles (for expression), hands (for grooming, etc.), the vocal apparatus, and coloration.

This approach has its limitations. For instance, while these categories cover many aspects of primate adaptation, they do not cover everything (for example, we do not address physiological responses to stress, immunological systems, or patterns of mortality). Moreover, in many cases, an aspect placed within one category will also serve a function in another. As an example, consider an animal's visual system. While we may study it as part of the animal's information processing system, it is also important to its locomotor behavior (to see where it is going); to its dietary behavior (in spotting prey, fruit, and so forth); and to its social behavior (many social signals being visually perceived, including facial expressions, gestures, body posture, and so forth). The Primate Portfolio presents a complicated wealth of information in a fairly simple manner, but one should never forget that the categories represent interactive parts of the whole of a primate's adaptive system.

ANTHROPOLOGY AND ANIMAL BEHAVIOR

R.A. Hinde, at the beginning of his 1974 book, *Biological Bases of Human Social Behaviour*, states that

> understanding human behaviour involves problems infinitely more difficult than landing a man on the moon or unraveling the structure of complex molecules. The problems are also more important and more urgent. If we are to tackle them, we must use every source of evidence available to us. Studies of animals are one such source.
> (p. xiii)

Many anthropologists are concerned with understanding the evolutionary and biological bases of human behavior. However, in the case of prehistoric behaviors, there is no such evidence as anatomical structures and their fossils to help answer questions. However, anthropologists *do* have indirect means of exploring prehistoric behavior, including the study of contemporary animal behavior.

Studying Animal Behavior

The scientific study of animal behavior, which seeks to explain how and why animals use various movements to accomplish vital tasks such as feeding and reproducing, formally began during the late nineteenth century. Charles Darwin observed that an animal's behavior is important to its survival and is therefore shaped by natural selection. Up to that point, most naturalists had simply described such behaviors without addressing their underlying functions, or they had explained them only in terms of human standards. By the early twentieth century, scientists had begun to formulate general rules of behavior that applied to all animals, including humans.

Currently there are two major scientific approaches to the study of animal behavior: experimental psychology and ethology. **Experimental psychology** studies animals under laboratory conditions, so that researchers can manipulate factors that influence behavior. Their goal is to develop general theories of behavior. A classic example of experimental psychology is the research of B.F. Skinner (e.g., 1966), who systematically varied factors in an animal's environment to investigate the relationship between stimulus and response in behavior.

There are a number of ways in which anthropologists apply experimental psychology. Some psychological anthropologists use its methods and theories in devising cross-cultural studies of human behavior. Other anthropologists directly apply psychological theories in their research; for example, in studies addressing the role of reinforcement and reward in learning.

The other scientific approach to animal behavior is **ethology**. Ethology is based on long-term, nonintervening, naturalistic fieldwork. "Naturalistic" refers to the ethologist's focus on the total organism within its environment. Well-known ethologists include Jane Goodall, who

works with chimpanzees, and Dian Fossey, who studied mountain gorillas. By focusing on the total organism within its environment, ethologists ultimately seek to answer ecological and environmental questions; for example, How does behavior function as part of a species' adaptation? This includes trying to understand an animal's motivation and internal states—an elusive goal, for while we can observe *what* an animal does, it is difficult to understand *why* it does it. What, for example, causes a monkey to grimace and cower away from another monkey? Are such actions to avoid a fight or to maintain social order?

The first step ethologists take in answering such formidable questions is the compilation of an **ethogram**—a meticulous, comprehensive catalogue of a species' behaviors, including how it moves, communicates, and breeds. Ethologists contend that once they understand the ecological and social contexts of these behaviors, they can develop theories about why the behaviors evolved as part of the animal's adaptation. A famous example is the study of rhesus macaques conducted at the Cayo Santiago facility of the Caribbean Primate Research Center. In 1938, scientists placed a group of rhesus (native to Pakistan and India) on this small Puerto Rican island. The free-ranging population has been carefully censused since the mid 1950s, permitting observers to study rhesus behavior within the context of knowing how individuals are related through maternal lines. Donald Stone Sade (e.g., Sade et al. 1985) conducted an ambitious, long-term, ethological study of the Cayo Santiago population. One social group was observed almost daily for about 10 years—an enormous length of time. Scientists working on Cayo Santiago have gathered a wealth of information, including an ethogram for rhesus monkeys (see Figure 4.5).

How is ethology used by anthropologists? One important application is in conducting cross-species comparisons, by which general theories of behavior are developed. For example, observations of how and when young deer and immature vervet monkeys play have led some researchers

FIGURE 4.5

Ethology and the rhesus monkeys of Cayo Santiago. (right) Ethologist unobtrusively observes the behavior of the monkeys, carefully noting details of social interactions. (bottom) Poses of rhesus monkeys, which is one aspect of the rhesus ethogram compiled from Cayo Santiago data. Sequence A,B shows high/low movement indicating threat. Poses C,D indicate a subordinate animal. Sequence E,F indicates an upward jerk of the head associated with appeasement. G is a neutral sitting position. H is playful wrestling. Sequence I,J,K,L shows the oblique bobbing known as a "query bob."

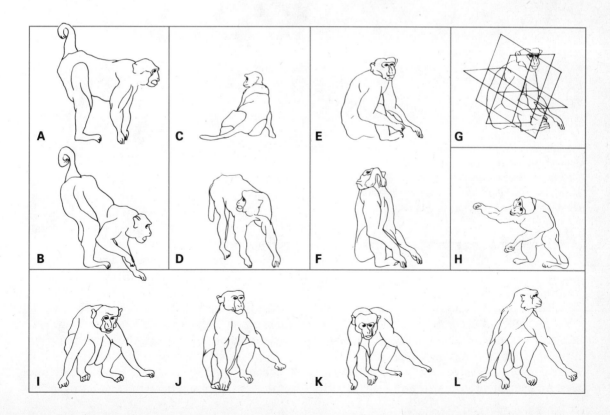

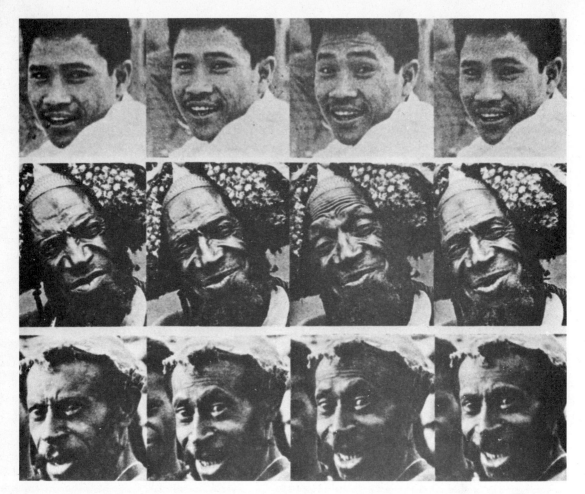

Human ethology and the universality of facial expressions illustrated by eyebrow flash during greeting in three cultures. (top) Balinese from Indonesia. (middle) Papuan, Huri tribe (New Guinea). (bottom) Papuan, Woitapmin tribe (New Guinea).

to surmise that play is a "kind of 'behavioral fat' which disappears if there are more urgent needs" (A. Jolly 1985, 401). Ethological information also helps anthropologists understand the evolution of human behavior. Observations gathered on the use of simple tools by wild chimpanzees, for example, provide anthropologists with ideas as to how our ancestors may have used tools in a limited capacity. Other anthropologists directly apply ethological techniques to the study of human behavior to collect nonjudgmental, purely descriptive, observations. These "human ethologists" concentrate on universal, inborn behavioral patterns, including the reflexive behaviors of infants (rooting for a nipple, grasping, etc.). Human ethologists also study the universality of facial expressions, such as smiles and eyebrow-raising as greetings (Eibl-Eibesfeldt 1975).

Ultimately, anthropologists seek to use the work of both experimental psychologists and ethologists to form general rules regarding the biological basis of behavior. Some of the most important of these integrated ideas pertain to learning.

The Biological Basis of Learning

The study of animal behavior has produced important insights into the biology of learning. For example, ethologists study the degree to which an animal's behavior is learned versus the degree to which it is neurologically preprogrammed, that is, genetically set within an animal's nervous system. At one extreme are *innate* behaviors, "innate" referring to genetically set behaviors, such as that of newly hatched chicks that automatically peck at shiny objects without first being taught to do so. Behaviors learned through experience are labeled *acquired*. The most extreme degree of acquired behavior is seen in humans. Much of our behavior is learned as we mature and become members of particular societies. Even so, the human capacity for learning is founded on biological structures, most notably the brain. For example, although we learn a specific language, the design of the human brain makes language acquisition of any sort possible.

Many behaviors are neither innate nor acquired, but a combination of the two. For example, *imprinted* behaviors are largely preprogrammed, but can develop properly only in the presence of specific and crucially timed experiences. A number of classic ethological studies investigated the process by which baby geese, ducks, and chickens learn to follow their mothers (Lorenz and Leyhausen 1973). These birds followed only the individual who reared them during a developmentally critical period, and continued to follow that individual—even if it was a human—until they matured. Here, the behavior is innate, but its focus depends on experience.

The degree to which behaviors are learned is selected for during a species' evolution and is an important part of an animal's adaptation. In some species, a strong genetic basis for a specific behavior can be advantageous; in others, behav-

ioral flexibility—an openness to shaping by the environment—is important to survival. The North American cowbird demonstrates the adaptiveness of an inflexible, genetically programmed behavior (Bonner 1980). The female lays her eggs in the nest of other species. Thus, she does not expend energy in nest building or in caring for her offspring, which are usually raised by the nest-owners. But once a cowbird matures, how does it know with whom to mate, since it cannot learn this from other cowbirds? Experimental studies show that females, even if raised in isolation, respond correctly to the mating song of male cowbirds but do not respond to the songs of other species. Additionally, the males sing the appropriate songs without learning them from adult cowbirds. This indicates that the cowbird's mating pattern is inborn and highly restricted—an important trait in an animal that cannot learn mating behavior from adults of its own kind.

In other cases, behavioral flexibility is an essential component of a species' adaptation. This is especially so in situations where the environment varies over a short period of time and natural selection cannot respond quickly enough to new conditions. Behavioral flexibility of this sort is possible only in animals with developmental patterns that permit learning to take place, such as the primates. Behavioral flexibility is most extremely expressed in humans, whose environment is very complex and likely to vary. Human behavioral flexibility reaches its greatest expression in our capacity to learn culture. Here again, animal studies contribute to our understanding of the evolution of an important human trait. For example, Bonner (1980) contends that the degree to which a species is cultural is selected for during evolution, and is based in behavioral flexibility and learning abilities.

Some of the first indications that nonhuman primates are capable of some degree of cultural behavior came from studies of Japanese macaques. Observers noted that a number of monkey groups, each isolated on a separate small island, behaved somewhat differently from one another. These differences in behavior, particularly in how individuals gathered and processed foods, were attributed to a simple cultural evolution of local traditions.

One famous instance of apparent cultural evolution occurred when Japanese scientists used sweet potatoes to attract the macaques from a forest to a beach, where they are easier to observe. A young female monkey, Imo, invented a method of getting sand off the potatoes by carrying them to a brook and washing them. The potato washing and other invented behaviors spread through the troop in a way that gave scientists special insights into social learning. For example, a new behavior is most readily passed among closely associated individuals, and young monkeys learn much more easily than older ones (Kawai 1965). This flexibility in learning permits macaques to rapidly respond to new environmental conditions—a pattern that makes particular sense in that the genus is known for its wide geographical and ecological distribution.

Models for the Evolution of Human Behavior

Another anthropological use of animal studies is in developing models for the origin and evolution of human behavior. Caution must be exercised, however, to limit such models to what the evidence can support. For example, Ardrey (1976) hypothesized that early humans ate meat and hunted in cooperative packs in the same way as contemporary carnivores, such as wolves and lions. He thus argued that human social behavior is based on a carnivore-like adaptation: "Humans are unique among all other primates because . . . for millions upon millions of evolving years we killed for a living" (p. 10). However, Ardrey did not take into account the many important differences that exist between carnivores and humans, especially that humans are generalized in diet. In fact, this very lack of specialization is a *crucial* aspect of the human adaptation; it makes us flexible enough to live in a wide range of environments.

Although there are problems inherent in their development, animal models provide scientists with valuable insights into the evolution of human behavior. Primates, in particular, are the source of intriguing models, including models for human mating systems based on patterns observed in monogamous primates (Kinzey 1987). We will discuss a number of such models in Chapter 6.

SUMMARY

Humans share characteristics with other species. Characteristics shared as the result of common descent are called homologies. Homologies help scientists develop evolutionary histories and reconstruct ancestral forms. Biological analogies are independently evolved similarities that arise usually as the result of adaptive responses to similar conditions. Analogies help scientists formulate general principles of adaptation and provide insights into the adaptive functions of fossilized structures.

Within the animal kingdom, humans belong to the mammalian order *Primates*, which also includes prosimians, monkeys, and apes. Humans share a greater number of traits and a more recent evolutionary history with other primates than with other orders of mammals. Primate studies have four major applications within anthropology: (1) defining what is unique about the human species, (2) reconstructing human evolutionary history by defining which traits are shared with other primates, (3) providing models for interpreting fossil finds, and (4) devising general rules of evolutionary and ecological theory.

The relatively unspecialized adaptation of primates distinguishes them from the other mammalian orders. The general pattern of primateness is based on a generalized common primate ancestor that diverged from all other mammals about 70 million years ago. Primitive primate characteristics, those traits retained from the general mammalian heritage, are a generalized 5-digit limb structure; the retention of the collarbone; and generalized teeth. Primate evolutionary trends are the adaptation of limbs for grasping and exploration; an increasing emphasis on vision over smell; and an increasing emphasis on complex social organization and behavior, including changes in patterns of growth and maturation that make this possible.

The earliest primate, resembling modern-day tree shrews in both form and general level of adaptation, was in many ways similar to other early mammals. Understanding the earliest primate's adaptation is crucial to explaining why primates diverged from the other mammals. Scientists have proposed a number of theories regarding the specifics of the earliest primate's adaptation, including the arboreal theory and the visual predation hypothesis.

Because the order is relatively unspecialized, and therefore evolutionarily flexible, the primates evolved a much broader range of adaptations than other groups of mammals. There are approximately 185 species of primates distributed within about 50 genera. These species differ in their expression of the primate trends, live in many different places, and survive in many different ways.

The contemporary primates are usually divided into two major groups: the prosimians (the more primitive) and the anthropoids (the most changed from the earliest primate). To illustrate the diversity of the living primates, it is useful to consider four major categories of adaptations: (1) locomotor adaptations, (2) dietary adaptations, (3) information processing systems, and (4) social behavior.

Anthropologists have indirect means of studying prehistoric behavior, including the study of contemporary animal behavior. Two major scientific approaches to the study of animal behavior are experimental psychology and ethology. Experimental psychology studies animals under laboratory conditions so that researchers can manipulate factors that influence behavior. Ethology is based on long-term, nonintervening, naturalistic fieldwork, the ethologist focusing on the total organism within its environment. The first step of ethology is the compilation of an ethogram—a comprehensive and complete catalogue of a species' behaviors. Anthropologists seek to integrate the work of both experimental psychologists and ethologists into general rules, including those pertaining to learning, regarding the biological basis of behavior. Another anthropological use of animal studies is in developing models for the origin and evolution of human behavior.

SUGGESTED READINGS

Bonner, John Tyler. 1980. *The Evolution of Culture in Animals.* Princeton, NJ: Princeton University Press.

Fossey, Dian. 1983. *Gorillas in the Mist.* Boston: Houghton Mifflin.

Goodall, Jane. 1986. *The Chimpanzees of Gombe.* Cambridge, MA: The Belknap Press/Harvard University Press.

Jolly, Alison. 1985. *The Evolution of Primate Behavior.* New York: Macmillan.

Kinzey, Warren G., ed. 1987. *The Evolution of Human Behavior: Primate Models.* Albany: State University of New York Press.

Napier, J.R., and P.H. Napier. 1985. *The Natural History of the Primates.* Cambridge, MA: The MIT Press.

Richard, Allison F. 1985. *Primates in Nature.* New York: W.H. Freeman.

Small, Meredith F., ed. 1984. *Female Primates: Studies by Women Primatologists.* New York: Alan R. Liss.

Aping Parents

Carol Berman

Carol Berman is a primate ethologist in the Department of Anthropology at the State University of New York at Buffalo. Before joining the faculty at Buffalo, she studied at Brandeis University, Sussex University, the University of Cambridge, and Northwestern University. In addition to her long-term studies of free-ranging rhesus monkeys on Cayo Santiago, Puerto Rico, she has studied wild rhesus in India and captive rhesus at the University of Cambridge in England.

An age-old theme in art and philosophy has been that humans tend to re-create certain themes of their childhood, or of their parents' generation, later in life — particularly in their close relationships. Many believe that parents are especially likely to carry on the styles of parenting to which they were exposed as infants and children. However, demonstrating that this is the case and understanding how parenting styles may be passed on are difficult. Although studies have shown similarities between the parenting styles of adults and the *impressions* that those adults had about their own parents' behavior (e.g., Belsky and Pensky 1988), only one study has lasted long enough to obtain direct information on both generations (Caspi and Elder 1988). This study found strong similarities between the parental styles of parents and those of their daughters, but not between parents and sons.

People who study nonhuman primate development have also wondered whether aspects of maternal style are likely to be passed on across generations through the effects of early experience. If so, studying the intergenerational transmission of parenting style in monkeys may provide some guidance for understanding how the process works in humans. Using monkeys as subjects circumvents some of the problems that arise when working with human populations. Monkeys have shorter life spans and develop more quickly than humans. Furthermore, there are fewer ethical and practical problems in observing their intimate behavior daily.

When you look at monkey mothers and infants for any length of time, you notice a great deal of variation in behavior among the pairs. For example, some mothers may be warm, others protective, and still others rejecting. We know that monkey infants are dependent on maternal care not only for their physical needs, but also for the normal development of affiliative, sexual, and maternal behavior.

I have been intrigued by variation in maternal style since 1974, when I first began observing a group of free-ranging rhesus monkeys. Since then, I have attempted to better understand the causes and consequences of that variation. I began to notice that mothers and their adult daughters seemed to exhibit similar styles of mothering, particularly with respect to rejection patterns, and I wondered whether aspects of maternal style may be transmitted across generations. But it was not until more than a decade into the study that I was able to test the idea quantitatively. Such a test required following a large number of females from infancy to motherhood.

Primatologist Carol Berman gathers data on rhesus monkeys in the field, Cayo Santiago, Puerto Rico.

My study site, Cayo Santiago, Puerto Rico, is a 45-acre island off the east coast of Puerto Rico which supports a closed free-ranging population of rhesus monkeys. The colony was established in 1938 with the introduction of about 400 rhesus from India. The population has been censused daily since 1956; hence, it is made up of known individuals with known histories and maternal kinship relationships. Early in the history of the colony, the monkeys formed species-typical social groups that grew and fissioned. My subjects came from one of these groups, Group I, formed in 1961. This group had three maternal lineages with members spanning as many as four generations. My assistants and I have collected observational data on a total of 125 mother-infant pairs. Since 1983, we have been following infants whose mothers were observed previously as younger mothers and/or infants themselves.

Over the years, my colleagues and I have found that aspects of the parenting style of a monkey's mother are associated with several factors, many of which interact in complicated ways. Among these factors are the mother's dominance rank; the infant's sex; the mother's parity (whether the infant was the mother's first or later infant); the mother's age; the number of infants she raised previously; the number, age, and sex of youngsters she still had to contend with; the size and composition of the larger social group; the terrain; the abundance and distribution of food; and the presence of predators. But what about similarities between mothers and their adult daughters? Do they really exist? If so, does this mean that daughters learned their maternal styles early in life from their mothers?

To answer these questions, my assistants and I recorded the social interactions of an infant with its mother (including all maternal rejections of the infant's attempts to gain access to the mother's nipple), as well as the infant's interactions with other group members. When analyzing the data, I focused on specific questions: Did the mothers have consistent rejection styles? Were the patterns of rejection of individual mothers similar to those of their own mothers? The answer to both questions was yes.

These results suggested that rejection styles were indeed being transmitted across generations, but the results did not establish whether the daughters had acquired the rejection styles specifically from their mothers or from other sources to which the mother was also exposed. The issue of maternally based versus lineage-based modes of transmission needed to be dealt with.

To address this issue, I reanalyzed the relationship between mothers' and adult daughters' rejection patterns in a way that controlled for differences between lineages. The results indicated that the daughters *did* carry on the rejection style of their mothers. But how, then, did the process work?

I found no evidence that adult daughters carried on the rejection patterns they experienced as infants. Instead, the rejection styles of adult daughters were more like those their mothers displayed toward their younger siblings than those they experienced directly as infants. In this sense, the results supported the suggestion that association with the mother after infancy played an important role in the transmission of rejection styles. This conclusion is tentative, however, because questions about genetic mechanisms also need to be addressed, for example, through the use of cross-fostering studies. There may, however, be alternative explanations based on the fact that mothers and daughters have similar social positions within their groups.

In summary, what I found was that monkey mothers do, indeed, have consistent rejection styles which they appear to pass on to their own daughters. Examples of learned behavior that is passed on from generation to generation are sometimes referred to as "protocultural" behavior because of their resemblance to human cultural processes. The important psychological implications of the transmission of parental style, particularly rejecting or abusive styles, are acknowledged both in humans and nonhuman primates. In monkeys, there may be additional, less widely understood implications of a biological and demographic nature. First, rejection styles influence the spacing of a mother's births; thus, particular rejection styles could significantly affect the total number of offspring a female produces in her lifetime. Second, particular rejection styles are associated with varying risks of infant illness, abnormal psychosocial development, or even death; hence, consistent rejection styles could lead to more consistent risks or advantages for the offspring of particular mothers. This could ultimately affect the mother's abilities to produce grandoffspring. Finally, the finding that adult daughters carry on their mothers' rejection styles suggests that these risks or advantages will also be carried into subsequent generations, further affecting the health and development of a female's grandoffspring.

The Prosimians
(Suborder *Prosimii*)

FORMS
Lemurlike forms, including lemurs, sifakas, indris, aye-aye; lorislike forms, including lorises, pottos, galagos.

GEOGRAPHICAL RANGE
Tropical regions of Africa and Asia.

GENERAL ADAPTATION
Mostly arboreal. Most forms are nocturnal, but a few favor the daylight. Sizes range from that of a large cat to that of a small mouse.

HABITAT RANGE
Tropical rain forests, dry forests, evergreen forests, and bamboo groves.

LOCOMOTOR ADAPTATION
Several types, varying according to food-gathering strategies. Good grasping abilities, but not as good as that of most anthropoids. Nails on most digits, but have retained a "grooming claw" on their second toe.

DIETARY ADAPTATION
Differs from one form to another; may include insects, fruits, leaves, gums, and flowers. Most forms have 36 teeth.

INFORMATION PROCESSING
Ratio of brain to body size smallest of all the primates, although large when compared with most other mammals. Greater emphasis on smell over vision than exhibited in the anthropoids; most prosimians have long snouts tipped with moist, hairless skin. Eyes are directed slightly to the sides, with binocular vision less developed than in the tarsiers and the anthropoids. Ears tend to be mobile.

SOCIAL BEHAVIOR
Territorial behavior quite common, including the use of scent marking to define territory. Prosimians have only a limited ability to use facial expression for communication. The lower front teeth are formed into a toothcomb for grooming. Many species give birth to twins and triplets, rather than to the singletons seen in most anthropoids. Life spans and periods of intense parental care are generally briefer than in the anthropoids. Most have fairly complex social organizations, although not as elaborate as those of many anthropoids. Social organization varies from solitary nocturnal species to gregarious diurnal forms.

Lemurlike Forms
(Superfamilies *Lemuroidea* and *Daubentonioidea*)

FORMS

Large group encompassing over 20 species; includes lemurs, sifakas, indris, and aye-ayes.

GEOGRAPHICAL RANGE

All are native to Madagascar, a large island off the east coast of Africa, where they are the only naturally occurring primates.

GENERAL ADAPTATION

Wide variety of adaptations; sizes range from that of the tiny lesser mouse lemur, with a body 5 inches long and a 5.5 inch tail, to that of the indri, with a 27-inch-long body. Forms include both nocturnal and diurnal. The aye-aye is the most specialized for life at night.

HABITAT RANGE

Tropical rain forests, dry forests, evergreen forests, and bamboo groves. Most are arboreal, but some forms, such as the ring-tailed lemur, spend long periods of time on the ground.

LOCOMOTOR ADAPTATION

Varies among species. Includes the four-legged scurrying through trees of the mouse lemur and the leaping and clinging between trees of the sifaka.

DIETARY ADAPTATION

Varies among species, with differing amounts of insects, fruit, leaves, gums, and flowers. Most forms concentrate on a few types of food. The aye-aye is very specialized, with a woodpecker-like feeding adaptation. It has long, slender hands and fingers, a special claw for digging insect larvae out of the bark of trees, and acute hearing to help it seek out its prey. On the other hand, ring-tailed lemurs are fairly flexible in diet and habitat, with a large fruit component in rain-forest habitats and an emphasis on foliage in evergreen forests.

INFORMATION PROCESSING

See Prosimians.

SOCIAL BEHAVIOR

Varies among species and includes some fairly complex social organizations. For example, ring-tailed lemurs live in large, multimale/multifemale groups of up to 24 individuals. They have separate social dominance hierarchies (graded orderings) for each sex, with the females dominant over the male members of the group (Budnitz and Dainis 1975). Ring-tails are somewhat flexible in behavior, populations occupying a range of habitats from lush riverside forests to dry brush plains. Indris live in monogamous family groups consisting of one adult male, one adult female, and their immature offspring (Pollock 1975). The indri families stake off exclusive forest territories. Male songs aid in defending and defining the individual territories. Aye-ayes are largely solitary animals, spending most of their time alone.

Lorislike Forms
(Family *Lorisoidae*)

FORMS
Lorises, galagos, pottos.

GEOGRAPHICAL RANGE
Continental Africa and Asia.

GENERAL ADAPTATION
Similar to that of the lemurlike forms.

HABITAT RANGE
Various levels of tropical rain forests and woodlands. For example, the angwantibo lives in shrubs, while pottos inhabit the canopies of the same forests. They are exclusively arboreal and nocturnal; thus, they do not compete for resources with the diurnal monkeys.

LOCOMOTOR ADAPTATION
Varies from the slow and cautious climbing of the slow lorises to the quick leaps and hops through the trees of the galagos. Different locomotor adaptations are associated with different food-gathering strategies.

DIETARY ADAPTATION
Most lorislike forms eat fruit, with some including leaves, gums, fungi, birds, and eggs in their diets. The insect-eating galago's rapid movements disturb hidden prey, which they then grab as the insects try to fly away. Insects are carefully located by sense of smell as lorises slowly climb through the trees.

INFORMATION PROCESSING
See Prosimians.

SOCIAL BEHAVIOR
Not well understood, since these night-dwelling forms are elusive and difficult to observe. They are believed to be primarily solitary or semisolitary animals that roam individual, but overlapping, home ranges. While solitary primates still maintain important social relationships with others of their kind, these relationships are in the form of social *networks* rather than social *groups* (Richard 1985). Although the lorislike forms spend much of their time alone collecting food in the dark, they can communicate over long distances through vocal and olfactory signals, such as by using urine for scent marking individual ranges.

The Tarsiers
(Suborder *Tarsioidea*)

FORMS
Tarsiers.

GEOGRAPHICAL RANGE
Confined to islands of Southeast Asia.

GENERAL ADAPTATION
Highly specialized nocturnal and arboreal life-style. A small primate (about the size of a rat), the tarsier's unusual flat face, enormous eyes and prominent ears are aspects of its extreme adaptation to a life of foraging in the dark for insects and small lizards. Prosimian-like traits include its nocturnal pattern, with large eyes and mobile ears, grooming claws, and aspects of the skeleton. Anthropoid-like traits include the absence of a moist nasal tip, absence of a toothcomb, and an internal ear structure similar to that of the anthropoids. Traits unique to the tarsier include the presence of 34 teeth (most prosimians have 36 teeth and most anthropoids have 32). Most distinct is the tarsier's special body design for locomotor behavior.

HABITAT RANGE
Exclusively arboreal and nocturnal.

LOCOMOTOR BEHAVIOR
Clinging to trees and leaping backwards as much as six feet at a time, its body is specially designed to accommodate such locomotion. In fact, the name *Tarsier* is derived from the extremely elongated and fused foot bones (tarsals) that provide this animal with great springing power. Hands have large pads for clinging to vertical surfaces, as does its long, thin tail.

DIETARY ADAPTATION
Mostly insects, which are trapped with a sudden and swift leap.

INFORMATION PROCESSING
Eyes are enormous and immobile, a trait compensated for by a neck that allows a tarsier to turn its head a full 180 degrees. Thus it can look behind to see where it is leaping. Large and immobile ears.

SOCIAL BEHAVIOR
Little is known about the tarsier's behavior in the wild. At least one tarsier species is monogamous (MacKinnon and MacKinnon 1980). Each family occupies a small core area that it scent marks and defends from other groups, particularly through the use of vocal displays. As is frequently the case with other monogamous primates, the mated male and female sing duets to demarcate their territory.

The Anthropoids
(Suborder *Anthropoidea*)

FORMS

All monkeys and apes. Also includes humans.

GEOGRAPHICAL RANGE

Temperate, subtropical, and tropical regions of Asia, Africa, Central America, and South America.

GENERAL ADAPTATION

The anthropoids are larger-brained than the prosimians and have more refined manual and visual systems. There is a decrease in brain areas involved in the sense of smell. The increased emphasis on vision over smell is reflected in flatter faces and eyes directed fully forward. Social organizations are more complex than those of the prosimians, with a greater stress on learned behavior. Differences among the anthropoids are extensive, as detailed in the following sections.

New World Monkeys
(Superfamily *Ceboidea*; Families *Cebidae*, *Callitrichidae*)

FORMS

Sixteen genera encompassing approximately 50 species. *Callitrichidae* includes marmosets and tamarins; *Cebidae* includes spider monkeys, squirrel monkeys, woolly monkeys, titi monkeys, howler monkeys, sakis, uakaris, capuchins, and the aotus.

GEOGRAPHICAL RANGE

The only primates native to the Americas, they are found in Central America and South America.

GENERAL ADAPTATION

New World monkeys have broad, flat noses with nostrils flaring out to the side, distinguishing them from all Old World anthropoids (which have narrow noses with nostrils directed downward). They also differ in dentition. All Old World anthropoids have 32 teeth while most New World monkeys have 36 teeth. With respect to the two major groups, the family *Callitrichidae* resembles prosimians in many ways, including being small in body and relative brain size; the family *Cebidae* is quite varied.

HABITAT RANGE

Tropical rain forests, woodlands and dry forests. All are arboreal and, except for the aotus, the only nocturnal anthropoid, all are diurnal.

Most like prosimians. Small-brained.

LOCOMOTOR ADAPTATION

Callitrichidae: Climbing and scurrying through the trees, facilitated by sharp claws on every digit except the big toe. Their manual skills are probably no better than those of lemurs.

Cebidae: Demonstrate a variety of locomotor adaptations. For example, the spider monkey brachiates (swings arm-over-arm through the trees). Many cebids, including spider monkeys, howler monkeys, woolly monkeys, and capuchins, have prehensile tails capable of grasping—an adaptation not seen in any other primate.

DIETARY ADAPTATION

Callitrichidae: Tamarins eat primarily fruit, while the common marmoset prefers insects. The smallest anthropoid, the pygmy marmoset, obtains gums and sap by gouging trees with its specialized teeth.

Cebidae: Many different dietary adaptations. For example, capuchins eat a wide variety of foods including fruits, leaves, insects, nuts, and tree frogs. Squirrel monkeys and woolly monkeys strongly favor fruit. Howler monkeys have large jaws and muscles for a diet of rough vegetation. Although the largest component of the spider monkeys' diet is fruit, they have teeth and stomachs specialized for consuming large quantities of leaves.

INFORMATION PROCESSING

Callitrichidae are relatively small-brained, while the *Cebidae* demonstrate a range of cognitive abilities. For example, the highly intelligent capuchins have manual skills and cognitive abilities rivaling those of the great apes.

SOCIAL BEHAVIOR

Callitrichidae: Limited in facial expressions. Although social behavior is not well understood, studies show that tamarins and marmosets (inclined to give birth to twins) form unusual extended family groups. Besides a monogamous mated pair and their immature offspring, the social unit often includes adult children. When not being nursed by the mother, the infants are usually carried by the father or older offspring—a rare case of shared caretaking responsibility (Cebul, in Richard 1985).

Cebidae: Exhibit many different types of social organizations. For example, squirrel monkeys live in large troops that vary in size (depending on the richness of the habitat) from as few as 20 to as many as 200 individuals. Howler monkeys live in multimale, multifemale groups that disperse through the forest as they forage for leaves. The males have a special vocal anatomy, which produces a well-amplified roar that carries for great distances. Usually before dawn or during encounters with other groups, the males of a group perform the roars in unison. These vocalizations appear to maintain proper spacing between social units (Baldwin and Baldwin 1976). In contrast to the howlers (which mostly forage alone), spider monkey groups (usually composed of about 20 adults) divide into smaller units of three or four individuals while they search for food. Moynihan (1976) notes that many New World monkeys have flexible group sizes that vary with environmental factors, such as the number of individuals living in an area and the availability of food.

Old World Monkeys

(Superfamily *Cercopithecoidea*; Subfamilies: *Colobinae*; *Cercopithecidae*)

FORMS

Colobinae includes colobus, langurs, and the proboscis monkey. *Cercopithecidae* encompasses over 50 species within 9 genera. Includes macaques, baboons, mandrills, mangabeys, patas monkeys, geladas, guenons, talapoins, and vervets.

GEOGRAPHICAL RANGE

Asia and Africa.

GENERAL ADAPTATION

All forms are diurnal. They live in a diverse range of habitats, including temperate-zone environments, semideserts, and rain forests. As do all Old World anthropoids, they have 32 teeth. Old World monkeys have sitting pads of calloused skin called ischial callosities (absent in New World monkeys). They place a greater emphasis on vision than do prosimians, evidenced in their shortened snouts. The colobines are the more specialized group, particularly in terms of diet. The cercopithecines are generalized and behaviorally flexible, with a large learned component to their behavior.

HABITAT RANGE

Colobinae: Rain forests, dry forests, mangrove swamps, and temperate forests, where they spend much of their time in trees.

Cercopithecinae: The most varied in range of any group of nonhuman primates. While most live in tropical and subtropical climates, a number of macaques live in temperate climates. Habitats include semidesert conditions (cercopithecines are the only nonhuman primates that live under such arid conditions), temperate forests, and rain forests. Some rhesus monkeys are "urbanized," inhabiting rooftops, abandoned buildings, and sacred temples.

LOCOMOTOR BEHAVIOR

Colobinae: Move about in a number of ways. The acrobatic colobus and langurs walk along branches on all fours and leap and arm-swing through the trees.

Cercopithecinae: Have a generalized locomotor anatomy, their arms and legs being about equal in length. This allows them more flexiblity in where they move about. Depending on the species, cercopithecines spend various amounts of time in the trees and on the ground. For example, baboons spend most of their daylight hours walking quadrupedally on the ground, returning to sleeping trees or cliffs at night. Geladas, which inhabit the grassy high plateau of Ethiopia, are completely terrestrial—an exception to the locomotor behavior of the nonhuman primates.

DIETARY ADAPTATION

Colobinae: Specialized for a diet that includes a large quantity of leaves. This includes a large, compartmentalized stomach. Since leaves are low in nutritional value and hard to digest, this type of stomach helps the animal to metabolize the enormous bulk of vegetation that must be consumed each day. Still, diets vary among the genera; diets may include fruit, flowers, seeds, and bark.

Cercopithecinae: Varied and generalized in diet. Cercopithecines are less specialized in their dentition and digestive tract than the colobines. Also, cercopithecines have cheek pouches in which they can temporarily store and carry food. Savannah baboons demonstrate an unusual pattern, spending large amounts of time digging for underground plants (such as roots and bulbs). Semidesert-dwelling baboons and macaques live in small groups that forage for grasses, other plants, and small animals. The forest-dwelling mangabeys eat fruits, insects, seeds, flowers, and leaves. Guenons eat leaves, bark, seeds, and insects.

INFORMATION PROCESSING

Larger-brained than the prosimians, Old World monkeys place a greater emphasis on vision over smell. Eyes are placed fully in front of the head, facilitating binocular vision. The snout is shortened (except in the case of baboons and mandrills, as previously noted).

SOCIAL BEHAVIOR

Colobinae: Variety of social organization. For example, the white colobus lives in single-male, multifemale groups that range from 3 to 15 members (including their immature offspring). There are also groups composed exclusively of adult males. Highly territorial, white colobus group members stay close together, grooming and foraging for leaves. Langurs have a variety of social organizations. One langur species, the Mentawai Island leaf monkey, is monogamous (Watanabe 1981), whereas the hanuman langurs demonstrate patterns that include multimale/multifemale groups, single-male/multifemale groups (associated with mating season), and all-male groups. This variability apparently relates to the instability of the males as group members (Richard 1985). Hanuman langur males occasionally commit infanticide shortly after acquiring a harem (a behavior also noted in other primates with similar social structures).

Cercopithecinae: Diverse in social organization, some are quite behaviorally flexible, with a large learned component to their behavior. For example, Japanese macaques demonstrate the acquisition and social transmission of food washing and other behaviors within troops. Savannah baboons tend to live in large multimale, multifemale groups that move as a unit across the grasslands. The social groups of the semidesert-dwelling hamadryas baboons vary in size according to environmental conditions and type of activity. During the day they form bands of 30 to 40 individuals that spread out in search of food. The bands are further divided into single-male, multifemale harems. At night, a number of bands come together in nearby protected cliffs, forming sleeping groups that consist of as many of 150 animals. Woodland-dwelling patas monkeys also form harems, although additional adult males may come and go, especially during the breeding season. At other times, unattached males live alone or in all-male groups. In contrast to the seemingly male-dominated hamadryas harems, an adult male patas usually lives on the edge of the group and is often chased or harassed by the females if he tries to approach the core. A male patas is most likely to associate with another group member when solicited by a sexually receptive female. The harassment by other group members continues even while the male and female consort.

Apes
(Superfamily *Hominoidea,* which also includes humans)

FORMS
Lesser apes and great apes.

GEOGRAPHICAL RANGE
Tropical and subtropical Africa and Asia.

GENERAL ADAPTATION
Apes are the nonhuman primates evolutionarily closest to humans and the least like the primal ancestor. Their relatively flat faces, with short noses and closely set eyes, reflect an increased emphasis on vision over smell. Large-brained, the apes tend to have excellent manual skills and are the most intelligent nonhuman primates. The developmental patterns that make complex social behaviors possible have the greatest nonhuman expression among the apes, with an increase in the spacing between births and a heightened emphasis on learned behavior. All apes are diurnal and live in forests, where they have adapted to a number of econiches. Some live high in the trees, while others forage on the forest floor. The greatest adaptive difference reflects the evolutionary divergence between the lesser and the great apes.

Lesser Apes
(Family *Hylobatidae*)

FORMS

Gibbons and siamangs.

GEOGRAPHICAL RANGE

Confined to Southeast Asia.

GENERAL ADAPTATION

Evolutionarily diverged from the branch that includes the great apes and humans some 15 to 20 million years ago. They are small for apes, usually weighing no more than 25 pounds. They are tailless, as are all apes, but unlike the great apes they have ischial callosities. There is very little difference in size or general appearance between the sexes.

HABITAT RANGE

Canopy of tropical rain forests.

LOCOMOTOR ADAPTATION

Specialized for brachiation. Spectacularly acrobatic, they have a lightly built body with long arms and fingers. The thumb is short, so as to not interfere with the hooking action of the long fingers; however, this decreases manual dexterity. The structure of the upper torso permits the arms to rotate completely at the shoulder. Strong muscles power this motion and support the apes as they hang, often with one arm, from tree branches. This is a common posture as they feed, rest, or copulate. When they walk (usually along branches), they do so bipedally.

DIETARY ADAPTATION

Mostly fruit and leaves, but also flowers, buds, and insects.

INFORMATION PROCESSING

Less intelligent than the great apes.

SOCIAL BEHAVIOR

Distinctive social behavior, in that not only do they form life-long, monogamous pairs (the only apes to do so), but they are the only nonhuman Old World anthropoids to have strictly defended stable territories (MacKinnon and MacKinnon 1984). Gibbons and siamangs also are exceptional for their elaborate, sex-specific songs associated with territorial behavior. Mated pairs sing in the early morning to establish territorial boundaries. The lesser ape's social adaptation is apparently associated with its dietary adaptation, which largely consists of less-abundant, high-energy foods (fruit) that must be gathered over a wide area of the forest. This encouraged the evolution of territoriality and small group size (Brockelman and Srikosamatara 1984).

Great Apes
(Family *Pongidae*)

FORMS
Chimpanzees, gorillas, and orangutans.

GEOGRAPHICAL RANGE
Chimpanzees and gorillas are found in Africa. The orangutan is the only Asian great ape.

GENERAL ADAPTATION
The largest and the most intelligent of the nonhuman primates. The African apes (chimpanzees and gorillas) share the most recent evolutionary history with humankind. Great apes are much larger than lesser apes and lack ischial callosities. Relatively long-lived, great apes may reach 50 years of age. Gorillas are the largest of all primates, males weighing about 350 pounds and females about half that. Chimpanzees are the smallest of the great apes (adult males weigh around 100 pounds and females weigh slightly less). Chimpanzees are particularly flexible in their adaptation. The orangutan has a strangely flat, almost concave, face surrounded by long, reddish hair.

HABITAT RANGE
Primarily rain forests.

LOCOMOTOR ADAPTATION
As with the lesser apes, the great apes' upper limbs are much longer than their lower limbs. However, this configuration has been adapted for walking on the ground rather than for swinging through trees. Gorillas spend almost all their time on the ground, where they use their long arms to knuckle-walk through the forest. At night, they build sleeping nests on the ground, in shrubbery, or in the low branches of trees. Chimpanzees also travel by knuckle-walking on the ground. They spend some of their time in trees, where they sleep in nests built of branches, sticks, and leaves. Orangutans spend most of their time in trees, where they are slow and cautious climbers. When on the ground, they walk using the fist side of their hands. Active during the day, orangutans build sleeping nests in the forest canopy.

DIETARY ADAPTATION
Gorillas: Their enormous jaws and skull are an adaptation to a diet of rough vegetation, including stems, vines, shoots, roots, and large quantities of leaves. Some gorillas also eat fruit and an occasional insect or snail.

Chimpanzees: Their diet is composed largely of fruits, but also includes leaves, nuts, seeds, and insects. Chimpanzees occasionally hunt and eat meat, making them the only truly omnivorous apes.

Orangutans: They favor fruit, but also eat leaves, bark, and some insects. Orangutans have heavily enameled and wrinkled back teeth that aid them in cracking nuts—a specialization not seen in the other apes.

INFORMATION PROCESSING

With their advanced cognitive skills, they are the most intelligent nonhuman primates. They place a greater emphasis on vision versus sense of smell than do monkeys.

SOCIAL BEHAVIOR

Gorillas: Social groups are relatively small, usually consisting of one mature male (called a "silverback" due to the grayish fur on its back), one or two younger black-backed males, and a few adult females and their immature offspring. Each social group occupies a large home range that extensively overlaps those of other gorilla bands. The level of aggression within a group is low, although once a male reaches full maturity (at 11 to 13 years of age), he may be forced to leave and set out on his own. The silverback male has priority in mating with the females and is responsible for challenging strangers and responding to threats to the group (A. Jolly 1985). As is true of all apes, the relationship between a gorilla mother and her young is intense and lengthy, continuing until the offspring is at least 5 years old.

Chimpanzees: Their behavioral flexibility is demonstrated by the complexity of their social behavior. The multimale, multifemale social groups consist of 30 to 80 individuals. The groups are divided into bands that are fluid in composition, individuals coming and going to a degree that is unusual for nonhuman primates. The chimpanzees have complex interpersonal relationships, including an enduring bond that exists between a mother and her offspring. Notably, male chimpanzees form life-long associations among themselves. A male chimpanzee may move from place to place, but he never changes his group affiliation. In addition, a male spends most of his time with closely related males. On the other hand, females often migrate to other groups and appear to mate in an undiscriminating fashion. Chimpanzees are clever and resourceful animals. For example, wild chimpanzees use tools including termite-reaching sticks and nutcracking rocks. Also, chimpanzees can be ingenious when confronted with a new object or situation. Jane Goodall (1971) tells of an adult male that quickly devised a way to use kerosene cans from her campsite. He would hit two cans together and make a loud noise that apparently increased the effectiveness of his "charging display"—a noisy combination of hooting and racing about that helps determine the social rank of male chimpanzees.

Orangutans: Scientists are just beginning to understand the social behavior of this elusive animal. Orangutans are semisolitary adult males living alone and females living only with their immature offspring. Males have large air sacs in their throats that amplify calls used in maintaining social spacing. These calls can be heard over one-half mile away. This pattern actually represents an extremely spread out, single-male, multifemale social network, with adult females and males coming into close contact for only a few days at a time when a female is sexually receptive. Because each individual requires its own range in which to live and forage, large areas are needed to support a relatively small number of orangutans.

A Japanese macaque mother and infant. An Old World monkey of the subfamily *Cercopithecinae*, the Japanese macaque is one of the few nonhuman primates to live in a temperate climate.

Ring-tailed lemurs. This gregarious prosimian (superfamily *Lemuroidae*) lives in large multimale/multifemale groups.

A loris from Borneo. A member of the prosimian family *Lorisidae*, this form demonstrates the large eyes and good grasping abilities of its arboreal and nocturnal adaptation.

A tarsier. The only living member of the suborder *Tarsioidea*, this highly specialized nocturnal and arboreal form has enormous eyes, prominent ears, elongated foot bones, and digit pads that enhance its grasping abilities.

A woolly monkey foraging on leaves. A New World monkey of the family *Cebidae,* this agile inhabitant of the Amazonian rain forest uses its prehensile tail as a "fifth limb."

A howler monkey howling. A New World monkey of the family *Cebidae,* the howler's large jaws and facial muscles are adapted for a diet of rough vegetation.

A golden lion tamarin. A member of the New World monkey family *Callitrichidae,* tamarins resemble prosimians in their small body and small relative brain size.

A proboscis monkey. A member of the leaf-eating subfamily of Old World monkeys (*Colobinae*), the male proboscis monkey has a highly distinctive profile.

A juvenile hanuman langur grooms another who leans on an adult. A member of the leaf-eating subfamily of Old World monkeys (*Colobinae*), hanuman langurs use their long and graceful arms to move through the forest.

A male baboon's yawn threat. The elongated muzzle and large canines of this Old World monkey of the subfamily *Cercopithecinae* are associated with its social adaptation, rather than with diet or sense of smell.

A fight between rhesus macaques and hanuman langurs at a temple in India. The hanuman langur, considered sacred in India, and the feisty rhesus macaque often inhabit towns and cities.

A gibbon family. The lesser apes of the family *Hylobatidae*
are the only apes to form lifelong, monogamous mating
pairs. The family group consists of a male, female, and their
immature offspring.

A female and male gorilla positioning for copulation. The silverback male gorilla has priority in mating over the less mature, black-backed males of a social group.

An orangutan mother and baby. This Asian great ape is semisolitary; adult females live alone, but for their immature offspring.

Mike the chimpanzee. Chimpanzees are clever and resourceful apes, known for their behavioral flexibility and intelligence.

5 Primate Evolution

The Fayum, then and now. During the Oligocene epoch, some 30 million years ago, the Fayum of Egypt teemed with plant and animal life, including early anthropoids. Located approximately 60 miles southwest of Cairo, the Fayum is now desert.

We now turn our attention to the questions of how, why, and from what form of life humans evolved. Since much of our evolutionary history is shared with that of other primates, **paleoanthropologists** (anthropologists concerned with the study of human biocultural evolution) are profoundly interested in primate evolution prior to the emergence of the hominids. The word **hominids** refers to the taxonomic group that includes all species on the human branch of the primate phylogenetic tree after it diverged from the rest of the order.

Although evolution is a scientific fact, the exact course of the history of life remains somewhat of a mystery. However, scientists have devised ingenious ways of studying our evolutionary past. Some of the methods make use of the direct remains of ancient life and environments; others use living forms as reflections of the past. Such evidence has enabled paleoanthropologists to make great progress toward reconstructing the primate evolutionary events leading to the origin of the earliest hominids.

UNCOVERING THE FOSSIL RECORD

Reconstructing the past is a difficult yet intriguing endeavor. Since we cannot directly observe extinct species within their environments, we need other means by which to study prehistoric life. The most direct evidence of ancient life comes from *fossils*, earlier defined as the preserved remains or traces of long-dead animals and plants. Fossils form the basis of **paleontology**, the scientific study of extinct life. Additional direct evidence is acquired through **paleoecology**, the scientific study of ancient environments. Scientists also make use of more indirect evidence gained through the study of modern-day species. In this section, we will consider the application of these various fields in reconstructing the past.

Fossils: The Remains of Ancient Life

Fossils provide a unique opportunity to observe the structure of extinct organisms directly, including that of our earliest ancestors. Fossils are usually formed through **mineralization**, a lengthy process by which the molecules of living tissues are chemically changed or replaced by molecules of minerals such as lime or iron oxide.

Fossilization is a rare event that depends on the composition of tissues and the conditions under which they were buried. For example, since hard tissues decay much more slowly than soft tissues, almost all animal fossils are those of bones and teeth. For burial conditions to favor fossilization, the material must be submerged in a medium that inhibits decay and promotes mineralization, such as sand, mud, lava, or tar. Climatic conditions are also important. Hot, damp climates, such as those in tropical rain forests, speed up decay; conversely, extremely dry conditions (as in a desert) or extremely cold conditions (as in arctic regions) help preserve organic materials. Since many primates lived in tropical climates, there are gaps in the primate fossil record. Furthermore, even if primates do become fossilized, their remains are not likely to be found.

The scarcity of materials and the problems of preservation create difficulties in using the fossil record to reconstruct the past. For example, paleontologists are often limited to reconstructing animals on the basis of only a few teeth or bone fragments. One monkeylike species dating from 13 million years ago is represented by a single end of an arm bone (Pickford 1982), while a number of early prosimian-like primates are known only from a few teeth or jaw fragments. Another problem is that fossils are often crushed or fragmented, making it necessary to reconstruct structures from contorted evidence. Then, too, an animal's remains may have been scattered about by a predator or scavenger, or buried materials may have been damaged or moved by disturbances of the soil or rock.

Problems in reconstructing fossils can lead to disagreement among scientists as to how to interpret finds. For example, such difficulties led to a debate over whether *Ramapithecus*, an apelike form dating from about 14 million years ago, was the first hominid (see p. 125). The previously mentioned gaps in the fossil record for specific periods of time also raise questions subject to debate. For example, almost all known fossil primates dating from about 38 to 25 million years ago come from a single African site; thus, what was occurring in primate evolution elsewhere in the world remains uncertain.

Although incomplete, the fossil record still provides us with a framework by which to understand primate evolution. For example, scientists have considerable knowledge of *Aegyptopithecus*, a monkeylike form dating from approximately 28 million years ago. The fossil material of this primate includes a well-preserved skull, some partial lower jaws, upper-jaw fragments, and a number of isolated teeth, as shown in Figure 5.1(a). In addition to this *cranial* ("of the head") material, scientists also have *postcranial* ("below the head") remains with which to work, including some arm and foot bones, as seen in Figure 5.1(b). The material is in relatively good

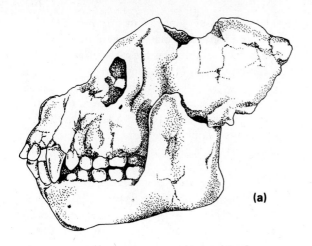

(a)

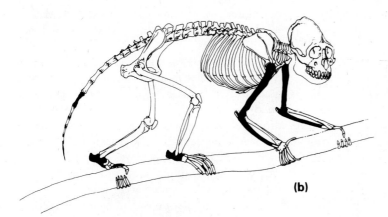

(b)

FIGURE 5.1

Fossil remains of *Aegyptopithecus*.
(a) Cranial remains include an
almost complete skull that
demonstrates primitive as well as
advanced features. Primitive features
include a long snout and small
cranium. Advanced features include
apelike teeth, including long canines.
(b) Reconstructed skeleton. Black
bones represent postcranial fossils
recovered by paleontologists.

condition, suggesting that the carcasses fell into sluggish streams and were not carried far, thereby limiting the damage done to the bones (Simons and Pilbeam 1972). Although the materials are still somewhat limited, scientists have been able to generate a number of well-founded hypotheses regarding *Aegyptopithecus*'s adaptation (p. 131).

Dating the Fossil Record

To fully grasp a fossil's significance, we need to determine its approximate age and how to place it in time, a process known in general as *dating*. Two basic types of dating techniques are used to date both fossil and cultural remains: relative dating and absolute dating (see also Chapter 8).

Relative dating does not actually establish the age of an object, but sequentially orders a set of objects in time. In other words, it labels fossil A as older than fossil B, and fossil B as older than fossil C. The most common relative-dating technique is **stratigraphy**, which is based on the geological principle that the deepest layers (strata) of rock are the oldest. Therefore, in an undeformed sequence of rocks, fossils found buried deepest at a site are the oldest, while the youngest fossils are those found closest to the surface.

Fluorine analysis, another relative-dating

technique, can be used to date only fossilized bones and teeth. Such materials are often exposed to groundwater that contains fluorine, which is slowly incorporated into the fossilizing materials. Fluorine dating is based on the premise that the longer a bone is buried, the more fluorine it will contain; thus, older fossils will contain more fluorine than younger ones. Since the fluorine content of groundwater varies from place to place, this technique can be used only to order fossils from the same location.

Interestingly, fluorine analysis helped debunk one of the most famous scientific hoaxes of all time. During the early twentieth century, fossil hunters were hotly pursuing a definitive "missing link"—a find they believed would clearly illustrate a transition from an ape to a human condition. (We now know that the concept of a missing link is an unrealistic and simplistic approach to human evolution.) Allegedly, some of the English scientists expressed high hopes that the missing link would be "homegrown" and not from far-off Africa or Asia. Their hopes were apparently realized in 1912, when the announcement came that such a find had been uncovered in a British gravel pit. Labeled the "Piltdown Man," the unearthed skull had a humanlike cranium (the part of the skull that encloses the brain) and an apelike jaw. Using animal and archaeological remains found along with it, scientists dated the find as being 500,000 years old. Although many scholars accepted Piltdown as the ancestor they were seeking, others doubted that the jaw and cranium truly were what they seemed. As the known fossil record became more extensive, it became increasingly clear that Piltdown did not fit in with the rest of the evidence. When fluorine analysis was developed during the late 1940s, it proved without doubt that the human cranium was much younger than the animal remains uncovered at the site.

Eventually, Piltdown's cranium proved to be only 500 years old; moreover, its jaw was from a modern-day orangutan whose teeth had been altered to give it a humanlike appearance. Other factors confirmed that Piltdown was a deliberate hoax—that someone had planted the animal and

archeological evidence of its antiquity. The jaw had been stained to match the cranium, and the two parts could not be properly fitted together. Piltdown fell out of our family tree with a thud. Who committed the forgery and why? Among the many suspects are the discoverer of the finds, Charles Dawson; the creator of Sherlock Holmes, Sir Arthur Conan Doyle; and Father Teilhard de Chardin, a respected philosopher. But to this day no one knows for sure.

The determination of actual age in years is performed through **absolute dating**. The two most common types of absolute-dating techniques are **radiocarbon (carbon-14) dating** and **potassium-argon dating**. Both techniques are based on the rate at which radioactive isotopes present in ancient environments naturally decay into nonradioactive chemicals. Radiocarbon dating measures isotopes in carbon-based (organic) materials, whereas potassium-argon dating uses inorganic minerals, usually rock formed by volcanic activity. For instance, potassium-argon was used to date the *Aegyptopithecus* finds that were uncovered in rock formed from sediments settling to the bottom of a river. The fossil-containing layers are capped by a volcanically formed rock called basalt, which was potassium-argon dated to be 27 million years old. The *Aegyptopithecus* fossils were dated according to how they were placed in relation to the basalt; thus, they were assigned an absolute date of approximately 28 to 29 million years old.

Fission-track dating is another absolute-dating method applied in the study of primate and human evolution. This technique uses the radioactive isotope uranium-238, contained within tiny crystals of zircon found within volcanic rock. As the uranium-238 slowly decays into lead, each atom explodes, leaving a minute "track" in the crystal. Scientists use a high-powered microscope to count the tracks contained within a crystal, thereby providing an estimate of its age.

Absolute-dating techniques are not absolutely precise. For example, materials can be contaminated by older or newer substances, thereby throwing off the accuracy of the dates. In addition, the methods can provide only approximate ages, and they are limited as to the span of time that they can measure. Radiocarbon dating is used for objects dating back no further than 50,000 to 70,000 years, while potassium-argon ac-

curately dates rocks as old as 4.5 billion years but not younger than 100,000 years. It is not surprising, then, that the ages of many fossils are still a source of controversy.

INTERPRETING THE FINDS

Besides describing the physical structure of extinct forms of life, scientists also seek to reconstruct how animals lived within their environments. By studying an animal within its environmental context, we obtain a more complete picture of the past from which to decipher the general principles of macroevolution. In the manner of many anthropologists faced with investigating such complex topics, primate evolutionists often take a *multidisciplinary approach*, in which a variety of disciplines and methods are called upon to answer a central set of questions. As indicated in Table 5.1, geology, paleoecology, and the study of living species are some of the fields that contribute in interpreting the fossil record.

The Geologic Time Scale

The general climatic and temporal framework for the study of evolutionary history is provided by the **geologic time scale**, as shown in Figure 5.2. Developed by geologists, its subdivisions reflect major changes in the earth's geology and climate, as well as the accompanying shifts in plant and animal life. The largest divisions, representing the greatest level of change, are called *eras*. For example, the Mesozoic era is known as the "Age of Reptiles," since dinosaurs were the predominant form of life. The current era, the Cenozoic, is known as the "Age of Mammals." Eras are divided into *periods*, which are further divided into *epochs*. Although they are the smallest division of the time scale, epochs can still easily encompass 10 million years—a vast amount of time when compared with the lifetime of a

human, but minute when compared with over 4 billion years of the earth's total history.

The geologic time scale provides us with the general environmental and temporal framework for our discussion of primate and human evolution. Most of the events we will cover took place during the Cenozoic era, consisting of two periods: the Tertiary, which is divided into five epochs (Paleocene, Eocene, Oligocene, Miocene, and Pliocene), and the Quaternary, which is divided into two epochs (Pleistocene and Holocene).

Geology and Our Restless Earth

The earth's surface is continuously changing. Earthquakes, glaciers, and other forces build mountains, level the land, and sculpt lakes from the soil. Continents are on the move, reflecting a phenomenon called "continental drift." This movement is explained by the geological theory of **plate tectonics**, which states that the surface of our planet is composed of six major plates and a number of smaller plates. Each plate, which contains both continental land and oceanic floor, rigidly floats on a layer of denser rock, allowing the plates to move in relation to one another. Such movement can produce great changes in the earth's surface. For example, when two plates push against one another, ridges may form on an ocean's floor; when plates move apart, the resulting volcanic activity can create new oceanic floor. The colliding of plates can cause the earth's crust to fold and form a new mountain range.

As is true of geological activity in general, tec-

TABLE 5.1
Special Skills Used to Study Fossil Sites: A Multidisciplinary Approach

IN THE FIELD

Paleoanthropologists	In charge of investigations from start to finish, paleoanthropologists must pick the site; get permission to excavate; obtain financial support; hire the labor; and organize, plan, and supervise the work in progress. Finally, they must integrate the data collected by each of the specialists and publish their conclusions.
Geologists	Often assist in selecting the site. Their knowledge of the geologic history of the region is indispensable in determining the relative ages of fossils. Geologists' study of the strata at the site determines the natural processes—erosion, volcanic action—that laid the strata down, and the conditions under which fossilization took place.
Surveyors	Map the general region of the site and the site itself, plotting it in relation to natural landmarks and making a detailed record of its contours before the contours are obliterated by digging.
Draftspeople	Record the exact position of all fossils, tools, and other artifacts as excavated, marking their relationships to each other in both the horizontal and vertical planes.
Photographers	Document fossil remains and artifacts and their associations as they are uncovered. Photographers record work in progress and the use of special equipment and provide overall views of the site as well as of personnel at work.

IN THE LABORATORY

Petrologists	Identify and classify the rocks and minerals found around the site. Petrologists can determine the nature of rocks from which tools were made and identify stones that do not occur naturally in the area, which would indicate that the stones were imported by early humans.
Palynologists	Specialize in the study and identification of fossil plant pollen, which may shed light on early humankind's environment and diet, and the climate at the time.
Pedologists	Specialize in the study of soils and their chemical composition. The findings of pedologists round out the picture of the environment as it once was.
Geochemists	With geophysicists, conduct chemical and physical tests in the laboratory to determine the absolute age of material found at the site. Geochemists may also study the chemical composition of bones and artifacts.

IN THE FIELD AND LABORATORY

Preparators	At the site, preserve and protect fossils and artifacts with various hardening agents and make plaster casts for particularly fragile bones and other organic remains. In the laboratory, preparators clean and restore the specimens, making them ready for study by various specialists.
Paleontologists	Study the fossil animal remains found at the site. From the finds, paleontologists can learn much about the ecology and eating habits of early humans.
Biological anthropologists	Specialize in the comparative anatomy of apes and humans. Biological anthropologists evaluate remains found at the site and the evolutionary status of fossil hominids who lived there.
Taphonomists	Study the condition and arrangement of the fossils in relation to the deposits which carry them to determine the origin and formation of the fossil assemblage.
Archaeologists	Study humankind's past material culture: tools of stone, bone, and wood; living sites, settlement patterns, and food remains; art and ritual.

SOURCE: Based on Bernard G. Campbell, *Humankind Emerging* (Glenview, IL: Scott, Foresman, 1988), 21.

FIGURE 5.2

Geologic time scale.

Era and Duration	Period	Epoch	Years Before Present (in millions)	Principal Events of the Era
Cenozoic 75 million years	Quaternary	Recent	Present - 10 thousand	Modern age; end of last ice age; warmer climate. First human societies; large-scale extinctions of plant and animal species; repeated glaciation.
		Pleistocene	10 thousand - 1.8 million	
	Tertiary	Pliocene	1.8 - 8	Appearance of humans; volcanic activity; decline of forests; grasslands spreading.
		Miocene	8 - 25	Appearance of anthropoid apes; rapid evolution of mammals. Formation of Sierra Mountains.
		Oligocene	25 - 38	Appearance of most modern genera of mammals and monocotyledons; warmer climate.
		Eocene	38 - 55	Appearance of hoofed mammals and carnivores; heavy erosion of mountains; angiosperms and gymnosperms dominate.
		Paleocene	55 - 65	First placental mammals; most modern angiosperm families develop.
Mesozoic 165 million years	Cretaceous		65 - 135	Appearance of monocots; oak and maple forests; first modern mammals; beginning of extinction of dinosaurs. Formation of Andes, Alps, Himalayas, and Rocky Mountains.
	Jurassic		135 - 197	Appearance of birds and mammals; rapid evolution of dinosaurs; first flowering plants; shallow seas over much of Europe and North America.
	Triassic		197 - 225	Appearance of dinosaurs; gymnosperms dominant; extinction of seed ferns; continents rising to reveal deserts.
Paleozoic 360 million years	Permian		225 - 280	Widespread extinction of animals and plants; cooler, drier climates; widespread glaciation; mountains rising; atmospheric carbon dioxide and oxygen reduced.
	Carboniferous		280 - 345	Appearance of reptiles; amphibians dominant; insects common. Gymnosperms appear; vast forests; great life abundant. Climates mild; low-lying land; extensive swamps; formation of enormous coal deposits. Many sharks and amphibians; large scale trees and seed ferns; climate warm and humid.
	Devonian		345 - 405	Appearance of seed plants; ascendance of bony fishes; first amphibians; small seas; higher, drier lands; glaciations.
	Silurian		405 - 425	Atmospheric oxygen reaches second critical level. Explosive evolution of many forms of life over the land; first land plants and animals. Great continental seas; continents increasingly dry.
	Ordovician		425 - 500	Appearance of vertebrates, but invertebrates and algae dominant. Land largely submerged. Warm climates worldwide.
	Cambrian		500 - 570	Atmospheric oxygen reaches first critical level. Explosive evolution of life in the oceans; first abundant marine fossils formed; trilobites dominant; appearance of most phyla of invertebrates. Low-lying lands; climates mild.
Precambrian 2100 million years			1,000 - 4,500	Life confined to shallow pools, fossil formation extremely rare. Volcanic activity, mountain building, erosion, and glaciation.

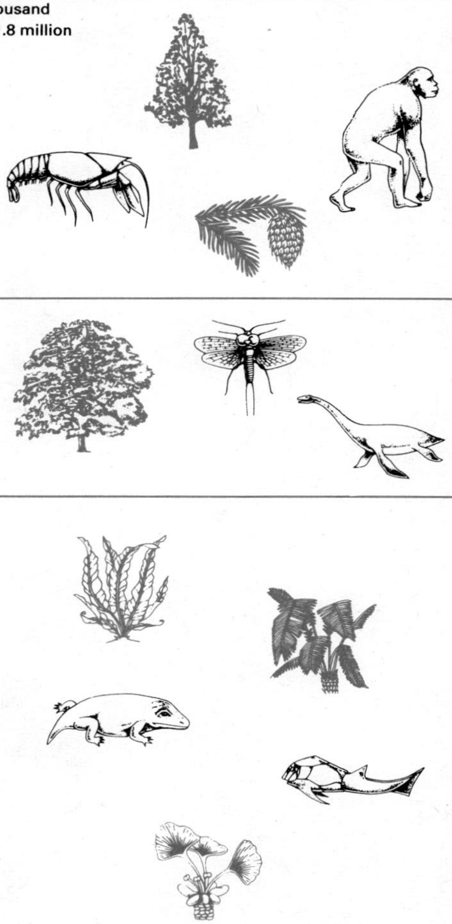

tonic movement has greatly influenced biological evolution. For example, about 12 million years ago the plate containing India pushed up against the central Asian landmass, forming the Himalayan mountains and the Mekong River drainage system. As a result, once-contiguous snail subpopulations became isolated from one another. Each isolated subpopulation adapted to its local environment, resulting in an adaptive radiation that produced at least 93 new species of snails (Stanley 1979).

How has continental drift influenced evolution? About 150 million years ago, there were two major supercontinents, Laurasia and Gondwanaland (see Figure 5.3). Over millions of years, Laurasia separated into North America, Greenland, Europe, and the northern aspects of Asia, while Gondwanaland split into South America, Africa, India, Australia, and Antarctica (Kurten 1972). Thus, areas that were once connected became separated, and subpopulations once capable of interbreeding became genetically isolated. This led to the evolution of new species. For example, continental drift apparently played a major role in the origin of the New World monkeys.

Paleoecology

We have seen that an animal's adaptation can be fully understood only when viewed within the context of its habitat. Obtaining such an understanding presents special problems when the animal lived in the distant past. Information regarding prehistoric habitats is provided by *paleoecology*, in which evidence of the past is used to reconstruct the plants, animals, climate, and physical environment of ancient times. Animals can be reconstructed using fossilized bones or droppings; for plant life, fossilized plants and pollen can be used. In addition, since specific types of plants and animals thrive only under particular conditions, reconstructing the "living" environment also helps us reconstruct the climate and physical environment. For example, remains of ferns indicate that the climate was warm and moist, while fish bones and scales in-

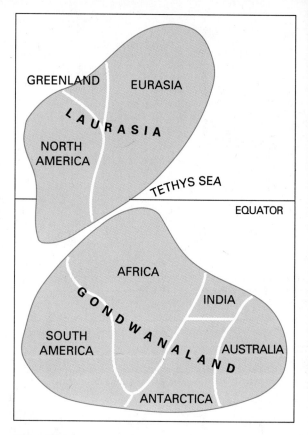

FIGURE 5.3

The supercontinents and divisions of modern-day continents.

dicate the presence of a waterway or body of water. In addition, rivers are represented in the geological strata by patterns of sediments or evidence of floodplains.

Returning to the example of *Aegyptopithecus*, paleoecologists have reconstructed what its habitat was like over 28 million years ago. Soil deposits demonstrate that many streams and a slow-moving river flowed through the area. Fossilized wood and seed pods indicate that *Aegyptopithecus* lived in a moist, warm rain forest (Simons and Pilbeam 1972). Paleontologists have also discovered fossilized birds that closely resemble modern forms living in freshwater and swamp habitats (Olson and Rasmussen 1986). Other fossils indicate that the animal life included a number of monkeylike primates, rodents, crocodiles, and some extinct forest-browsing mammals. In short, the habitat was a hospitable environment for a forest-dwelling anthropoid.

Living Primates and Understanding the Past

As we saw in Chapter 4, the study of present-day species is of great value to scientists in their attempts to understand the past. One reason is that by studying living forms, scientists can develop general rules of anatomy to use when reconstructing fragmented or incomplete fossils. Even so, there is often considerable leeway in how such material can be pieced together. For example, there was a controversy over the reconstruction of the dental arcade (tooth rows) of an ancient primate, *Ramapithecus*. This is an important issue, since paleontologists often use the shape of a form's dental arcade in evaluating its evolutionary *grade*, or stage of organization. The arcade of modern-day apes is U-shaped, with the two rows of teeth in parallel, while that of humans is "par-

abolic"—gently curving in front and diverging slightly to the rear. The apelike dryopithecines of the Miocene had a V-shaped dental arcade, a pattern that may have given rise to both the ape and the human configuration. When paleontologists first reconstructed the ramapithecine dental arcade, they could work only from jaw fragments. As a result, a number of conflicting theories were proposed regarding *Ramapithecus*'s evolutionary status. One group of scientists argued that the shape of its jaw was intermediate between the Miocene apes and hominids, demonstrating that *Ramapithecus* was a transitional form (e.g., Simons 1977). Others disputed this claim, stating that the tooth rows were actually V-shaped and similar to that of the dryopithecines (e.g., Zihlman and Lowenstein 1979) (see Figure 5.4).

Figure 5.4

Reconstructing the ramapithecine dental arcade. (a) Original ramapithecine jaw, which was reconstructed as (b) prior to the discovery of a fossil with a midline contact point. The arcade was presented as parabolic, much like that of (c) *Homo sapiens*. (d) Discovery of the complete ramapithecine lower jaw proved the arcade to be V-shaped, unlike that of humans but also unlike the parallel tooth rows of (e) great apes.

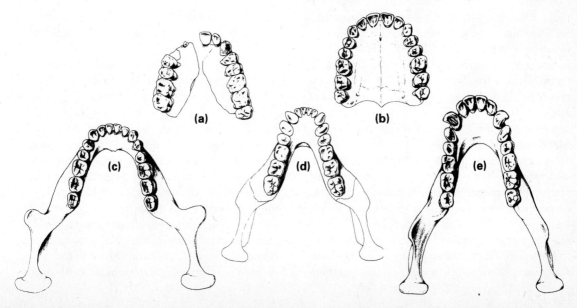

Existing species are also used as models for how structures functioned in ancient forms. For example, Every (1975) used information on tooth sharpness and its relation to diet in a variety of living mammals to reconstruct the diet of extinct primates from their fossilized teeth.

Living primates are also used to reconstruct the ways of life of extinct species. Such models are particularly useful when both structural and environmental similarities exist between the living and extinct forms. For example, *Aegyptopithecus*'s adaptation has been compared with that of modern apes and monkeys. On the basis of its size, anatomical features, and habitat, *Aegyptopithecus*, most scientists believe, had an arboreal adaptation. Its teeth and jaws indicate that it had a relatively generalized diet consisting mostly of leaves, insects, and especially fruit. Skeletal remains suggest that *Aegyptopithecus*'s locomotor adaptation closely resembled that of the howler monkey; for example, *Aegyptopithecus* moved about on all fours and had strong grasping abilities.

Earlier we noted that cross-species comparisons of living forms help scientists re-create phylogenetic histories. According to the principle of common descent, a characteristic shared by closely related species was probably derived from a common ancestor. Scientists use this concept to judge the evolutionary significance of a particular fossil find. For example, since all living Old World anthropoids have 32 teeth, it is very likely that their commonly shared ancestor had 32 teeth. Thus, a fossil-form candidate for this ancestor would be judged, in part, on its number of teeth.

Molecular Clock Studies

A relatively new and very important way in which the present is used to reconstruct the past is through **molecular clock studies**. In this field of research, biochemical and genetic differences among species are taken as a measure of the time elapsed since the forms last shared an ancestor.

Molecular clock studies are based on the neutral theory of molecular evolution, and particularly on the idea that neutral mutations occur at steady and predictable rates. Scientists determine the "molecular distance" between living species by measuring differences in the biochemical makeup of a particular substance such as a protein, in aspects of their immune systems, or in the sequencing of bases within their DNA molecules. Using a predetermined rate of molecular change, scientists then calculate the time elapsed since the species last shared a common ancestor and thus shared the same molecular makeup.

Molecular clock studies have been criticized on a number of grounds. The strongest criticism comes from paleontologists, who contend that the molecular dates for evolutionary divergences contradict those supported by substantial fossil evidence in a number of important cases. However, the molecular anthropologists counter that such contradictions will disappear with better calibration of the molecular clocks and with more accurate dating of the fossil record. In addition, they emphasize that their studies are not meant to *replace* paleontology as a means of reconstructing the past, but to provide additional means by which to evaluate the fossil record. Molecular clock studies are especially useful in setting up time frames within which fossils can be interpreted; for example, in deciding whether a find is too old or too young to have been a common ancestor of particular contemporary forms.

Another paleontological use of molecular clock studies has been in providing evidence with which to disprove questionable hypotheses. For example, Weiss (1987) called into question a hypothesis, developed on the basis of morphological features, that showed humans and orangutans descending from an ancestor not shared with the African apes. Molecular evidence clearly refutes this unusual claim by demonstrating that orangutans are genetically dissimilar to both humans and the African great apes. This evidence also supports the paleontological time frame of about 16 million years ago for the divergence of the orangutan from the evolutionary branch leading to humans and the African great apes.

Classifying the Fossil Record

Because of the complexity and incompleteness of the evidence, investigators often disagree as to how to classify the fossil record. One important issue concerns how to separate fossil finds into species. Sometimes the division of a lineage is fairly obvious, such as when large gaps in time or great physical differences exist among forms. But what happens (as is often the case) if the separation is not obvious? Since scientists cannot use the preferred criterion of interbreedability, they rely heavily on physical traits in classifying forms. This approach is complicated by the fact that modern-day forms vary in the degree to which they physically differ from one another. Sometimes this interspecies variability can be slight; at other times, the differences are great. For example, some closely related primate species are distinguishable only by coat color—a trait not preserved in the fossil record. Another consideration is the degree of intrapopulational variability—the differences among individuals of the same species. In some species, the variability among individuals is extensive, while in others it is much less. In particular, the degree of **sexual dimorphism** (differences between the sexes of a species) varies greatly among the living primates. For example, adult male and female lesser apes are similar in size, color, and structure; in gorillas, however, the males are twice as large as the females and their skulls are much more massive. Dentition may also differ, as in the case of male baboons, whose canine teeth are much larger than those of the females. Such factors can lead paleontologists to disagree over whether unlike fossils represent different genera, different species, or different sexes—an important issue in studies of early hominid evolution.

One way to contend with the difficulty of recognizing fossil species is by reducing the need to make such divisions. A growing number of paleontologists are taking what they claim to be a more practical approach to classifying the fossil record. The **cladistic approach** groups closely related organisms on a branch, or "clade," by using homologous traits to recognize their descent from a common ancestor (see Figure 5.5). Thus, by studying the fossil record in terms of clades rather than in terms of individual species, scientists circumvent the need to distinguish among closely related species. While cladists do not ignore the importance of species, they seek to avoid classification schemes based on slight physical differences in form.

For all the difficulties, steady progress is being made in our understanding of the patterns of evolution. Scientists once believed that evolution always produced a slow and gradual transition of forms; thus, they attempted to fit every find into a ladderlike progression. We now view

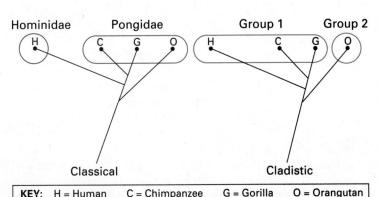

FIGURE 5.5

The classical system of classification versus the cladistic approach. Cladists group only according to branching points, whereas the classical system also considers more detailed differences in form.

From *A View of Life* by Luria, Gould, and Singer (Menlo Park, CA: Benjamin/Cummings Publishing Company, 1981), p. 681. Reprinted by permission.

KEY: H = Human   C = Chimpanzee   G = Gorilla   O = Orangutan

Contemporary
species A

SINGLE LADDER
- Every form fits
  into a ladderlike
  progression.
- Outdated,
  overly simplistic.

Contemporary
species A

BUSH
- History of life has
  many branches.
- Evolutionary
  pathway is not
  a simple
  progression.

FIGURE 5.6
Two views of the pattern of evolution.

the history of life as a "bush" with many branches. Some are capable of giving rise to new limbs; others are evolutionary dead ends (see Figure 5.6). As expressed by S.J. Gould (1977), "evolutionary 'sequences' are not rungs on a ladder, but our retrospective reconstruction of a circuitous path running like a labyrinth, branch to branch, from the base of the bush to a lineage now surviving at its top" (p. 61). This new mindset provides paleontologists with a much more realistic view of evolution and of the patterns revealed by the fossil record.

THE EVOLUTIONARY HISTORY OF THE PRIMATES

Although controversies persist, scientists have deciphered the general pattern of primate and human evolution. The following is a brief survey of primate evolution, focusing on events preceding the emergence of the hominids.

The Great Mammalian Radiation

During the *Mesozoic era* (approximately 225 to 65 million years ago), the earth was generally warm, moist, and mild, with much of the land lush with ferns and other nonflowering vegetation. A great variety of dinosaurs successfully lived under these conditions for many millions of years. However, about 70 million years ago, the earth's climate underwent a drastic and devastating change as it cooled and became prone to fluctuations in temperature. Scientists do not fully understand the cause of this change. One popular hypothesis is that an enormous asteroid or comet, some 140 miles or so in diameter, struck the earth, exploded on impact, and projected vast amounts of dust and debris into the atmosphere. The resulting clouds encircled the earth, blocking out sunlight and cooling the climate. There is good evidence in support of such an event. For example, there is a widely distributed layer of iridium, a rare chemical identified with asteroids, in geologic layers that signify the end of the Mesozoic and the beginning of the Cenozoic. Geologists have also uncovered the remains of the dust and debris, although they have not yet found the actual object (Kerr 1987). Other scientists pose alternate hypotheses for the change of climate. Hallam (1987), for example, contends that the environmental shift was more gradual than can be explained by such a catastrophic event as an asteroid impact. He strongly argues that the climatic changes were actually caused by increased volcanic activity, shifts in sea level, and other earthly geologic events.

Whatever the cause, the climatic shifts led to changes in plant and animal life, as forms evolved that were better suited to the cooler and less predictable conditions. In many areas, vegetation shifted from nonflowering plants to flowering plants, trees, and grasses. This new environment favored a different sort of animal. Some existing animal forms, including the dinosaurs, died off in mass extinctions, and the mammals came into prominence.

The early mammals did not appear overnight. Actually, a mammal-like reptile had evolved into the primal mammal long before the end of the Mesozoic. At first, it was an innocuous presence in the forest habitat. However, this small, agile animal flourished within the cooler, less predictable environment and thrived in the grassy, forested areas that covered much of the world.

Fossilized teeth indicate that this mammalian ancestor ate a wide variety of foods, most notably seeds and insects. By studying traits shared among living mammalian forms, we know that their limbs helped them to move through their forested habitats, and that their warm-bloodedness allowed them to cope with the fluxes in temperature. By nursing their young and by bearing young alive (rather than as eggs), these mammals increased the chances that their offspring would survive within an often hostile world. Also, the early mammals were generalized in structure, lacking the sorts of specializations (e.g., in diet and teeth) that interfere with the evolution of further adaptations. Because of this generalized nature, the early mammals were able to evolve in a number of directions, and were thus able to fill a broad range of econiches. This led to a great adaptive radiation of mammalian forms at the beginning of the Cenozoic era (65 million years ago to the present).

While some mammalian branches eventually died out, others diversified into the many different types of mammals now inhabiting the world. One of these branches includes the primates.

The Earliest Primates

The *Paleocene* (approximately 65 to 55 million years ago) is the first epoch of the Cenozoic era. Although the earth had cooled somewhat, the Paleocene still had a relatively mild climate. A number of primate forms lived during this epoch, including in subtropical areas of what is now North America and Europe. At that time, these areas were much closer together than they are today, and they were connected by a landbridge.

The diverse primitive primates of the Paleocene were fairly similar to other early mammals. Thus, they were similar to modern-day tree shrews, with relatively small brains and long snouts, as seen in Figure 5.7(a). Paleocene primates are primarily known from teeth and jaw fragments, although paleontologists have also uncovered some skull and postcranial materials. Among the earliest tree-shrewlike primates were the 60 plesiadapiform species, some of which persisted into the early Eocene. The plesiadapids, however, died off, apparently too specialized to have been the ancestors of modern primates.

Most of the Paleocene primates died off without leaving any descendants behind. But one branch, possibly as yet undiscovered, formed the parental stock of the primates of the next epoch, the Eocene.

The *Eocene* (approximately 55 to 38 million years ago) was warmer than the Paleocene. Thus, the earth had more of the tropical and subtropical areas that are hospitable to primates. These areas contained an abundance of the first truly prosimian-grade primates. They had larger brains, an increased emphasis on vision over smell, and better grasping abilities than the Paleocene forms (see Figure 5.7).

The Eocene saw major adaptive radiations of prosimian forms, with numerous species inhabiting regions that included North America and Europe. The Eocene primates are divided into two main groups: the adapids and the omomyids. While most of these forms were evolutionary dead ends, an adapid was probably the common ancestor of modern lemurlike and lorislike forms; an omomyid was the likely ancestor of the tarsiers. Although the anthropoids also apparently diverged during this period, scientists disagree as to their Eocene ancestor. Some contend that it was an adapid, others argue for an omo-

Plesiadapis   *Adapis*

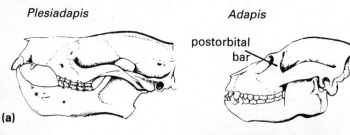

(a)

(b)

FIGURE 5.7

Examples of Paleocene and Eocene primates. (a) The partially reconstructed skulls of the Paleocene primate *Plesiadapis* and the Eocene primate *Adapis*. *Plesiadapis* appears more primitive than *Adapis*, having rodentlike teeth and lacking a postorbital bar in the back of the eye socket. *Adapis* shares many features with contemporary prosimians. (b) Skeleton of an Eocene primate and an artist's reconstruction of the animal "in the flesh." The Eocene primate has been reconstructed to resemble a contemporary prosimian.

myid, while still others claim it belonged to yet another group.

Divergence of the New World Monkeys

By the end of the Eocene, the evolutionary path of the New World monkeys had broken off from that of the other anthropoids—the Old World monkeys, apes, and humans. A controversy exists over whether the Old World and the New World monkeys, remarkable for their similarities, evolved from the same or different Eocene prosimian groups.

What was the world like at the time of the divergence of the New World monkeys? During the mid-Eocene, continental drift was distancing the Americas from Europe and Africa. However, this distance was still not very great. Also at that time

North America and South America were separated by a small expanse of water.

The most popular theory regarding the origin of the New World monkeys is that their ancestors accidentally "rafted" over on floating islands of vegetation from Africa to Central America or South America. In this view, the New World anthropoids and Old World anthropoids share a prosimian ancestor dating from the middle or late Eocene. An alternative hypothesis is that the New World monkeys and the Old World anthropoids did not share an Eocene prosimian ancestor. Supporters of this theory contend that the New World monkeys' founding ancestor evolved in North America and rafted across the short expanse of water to South America. Yet another idea is that the ancestor of all anthropoids evolved in Asia, and from there subpopulations spread into other parts of the world. The New

World monkeys' ancestor is viewed by some as having migrated across a landbridge into the Americas (e.g., Gingerich 1985).

Which of these theories is correct? Unfortunately, the evolutionary history of the New World monkeys is poorly understood, primarily because paleontologists have uncovered only a very few pertinent fossil remains. Scientists need to gather much more evidence before we can fully understand the evolutionary relationship that exists between the New World anthropoids and Old World anthropoids.

The Anthropoids of the Oligocene

The *Oligocene epoch* (approximately 38 to 25 million years ago) represents the start of a long-term cooling trend in the earth's climate. Primates disappeared from northern regions, including from North America and Europe, as areas that were once subtropical became temperate. However, many types of primates probably still existed in various parts of the world. Unfortunately, the primate fossil record of the Oligocene is extremely sparse, with almost all the known primate fossils coming from one area of Africa known as the Fayum.

The Fayum is located in Egypt, about 60 miles southwest of Cairo. At present, it is extremely hot and dry. During the Oligocene, however, the Fayum was abundant with plant and animal life; it was covered with grasslands and tropical rain forests and contained a large, sluggish river and many streams (see the chapter-opening photo). The Mediterranean Sea, which has since receded, was nearby.

Among the inhabitants of the Oligocene Fayum were small, monkeylike primates. These forms had slightly larger brains (and possibly more complex social behaviors) and better grasping abilities than prosimians. They also relied on vision rather than smell to a greater degree than the prosimians. In many habitats, monkey-grade primates outcompeted prosimians for resources; thus, prosimians were pushed into econiches where they did not directly compete with anthropoids.

The Fayum contained a number of different anthropoids, the best known of which is *Aegyptopithecus*, dating from approximately 28 million years ago. *Aegyptopithecus* was the size of a gibbon (9 to 16 pounds), making it the largest Fayum primate yet found. Because it represents an intriguing mix of primitive and advanced characteristics, it has generated much interest among anthropologists. It is a good candidate for the "connecting link" between the monkeylike forms of the early Oligocene and the apes of the Miocene (Simons 1972, 217). It is also a strong candidate for the founding ancestor of the **hominoids**, the taxonomic group that includes all ape and human species, both living and extinct. (Note that *hominoids* should not be confused with *hominids*; the latter designation refers to a subset of the hominoids and includes only the members of the human evolutionary branch.)

Some of *Aegyptopithecus*'s traits, including its fairly long snout and relatively small cranium, were primitive even for a monkey (recall Figure 5.1). In fact, its relative brain size was more like that of the larger-brained prosimians. *Aegyptopithecus*'s brain organization (as demonstrated by impressions left inside a fossilized skull) was a strange mix of features. It was monkeylike with respect to the primary senses, but primitive with respect to higher mental abilities, such as intelligence and memory. On the other hand, teeth and jaw fossils indicate that *Aegyptopithecus* could be ancestral to later apelike forms. For example, *Aegyptopithecus* had a V-shaped dental arcade, a pattern seen in the apes of the Miocene and in modern-day monkeys. In addition, its teeth have caused some to label it a "dental ape." This is because the Y-5 molar cusp pattern, a trait identified with apes and hominids, may have first appeared in *Aegyptopithecus* (see Figure 5.8). The size and shape of its teeth were also apelike, particularly its distinctively shaped, long canines.

Scientists have generated a number of hypoth-

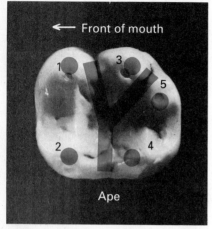

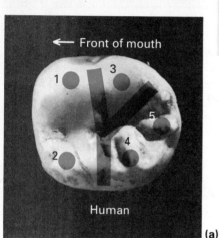

(a)

(b)

FIGURE 5.8
Aegyptopithecus **exhibited an intriguing mix of primitive and advanced traits. (a) The Y-5 molar cusp pattern. (b) Artist's reconstruction of** *Aegyptopithecus.*

eses regarding *Aegyptopithecus*'s evolutionary significance. The most popular theory is that *Aegyptopithecus* was ancestral to both the great apes and the hominids, and possibly to the lesser apes. Another idea is that *Aegyptopithecus* was ancestral to *all* Old World anthropoids, including the Old World monkeys. However, molecular clock studies indicate that *Aegyptopithecus* is not old enough to be the ancestor of both the Old World monkeys and the hominoids.

A completely different approach to hominoid origins is taken by scientists who argue that the first hominoids evolved in Southeast Asia and then spread into Europe and Africa. This claim is based on supposedly 40-million-year-old jaws and teeth uncovered in Southeast Asia. The supporters of this theory note that the materials demonstrate advanced apelike characteristics, and that the finds predate *Aegyptopithecus* by 10 million years. However, most paleontologists disagree with both the dates and the interpretation of these Asian finds. An Asian origin for the higher primates is considered to be, at best, a "very tentative" idea (Kennedy 1980, 101).

By the end of the Oligocene, the Old World monkeys and the hominoids had clearly diverged into separate branches. Both the Old World monkeys and the ape-grade primates then underwent major adaptive radiations during the next epoch, the Miocene.

The Many Apes of the Miocene

The *Miocene epoch* (approximately 25 to 8 million years ago) was a busy period in primate evolution. The earth's climate was becoming progressively cooler and drier, causing the vast forests of the Oligocene to be subdivided by belts of moist grassland. Extensive geologic activity also took place, so that by the end of the Miocene the continents were pretty much where they are today. About 17 million years ago, the drier climate and geologic activity caused the formation of a landbridge that connected Africa and Eurasia for the first time in 50 million years. During this time, the hominoids spread out across the Old World.

Why did the hominoids evolve? One theory is that they evolved to fill a dietary niche (with a greater dependency on fruit over leaves) different from that of monkeys. Another idea focuses on the increased brain size of the hominoids, which afforded them greater flexibility in behavior.

Whatever the cause, the first hominoids apparently evolved in Africa (recall that *Aegyptopithecus* is cited as a good candidate for the common ancestor). From there, the hominoids migrated across the landbridge into other forested areas of the Old World. Since these hominoids depended on forests for their livelihood, subpopulations became isolated by the encroaching grasslands that split up the forests. In addition, the isolated groups adapted to different econiches. This adaptive radiation was vast both in the number of hominoid species and in their geographical distribution.

In sharp contrast to the Oligocene, the Miocene has provided scientists with a wealth of fossil materials. Some 500 to 1,000 apelike fossils have been collected from all over the Old World, including Asia (primarily Pakistan, India, and China), Europe, and Africa. Most of the materials consist of teeth or jaw fragments, but paleontologists are discovering an increasing number of skull fragments and limb bones. The abundance of materials has given rise to some confusion over how many types of hominoids lived during the Miocene. Nonetheless, scientists have been able to form a general picture of what occurred.

Clearly, many different types of hominoids lived during the Miocene. Although most of these forms died out, among them were the ancestors of the present-day hominoids. Fossil and molecular clock evidence provide us with a general sense as to when the various lineages diverged. The lesser apes (gibbons and siamangs) had apparently diverged by early in the Miocene, while the Asian great apes (the orangutan is the only surviving form) diverged from the African hominoids (chimpanzees, gorillas, and hominids) approximately 16 million years ago. The gorilla lineage was next, diverging some 10 million years ago. Thus, chimpanzees are our "closest cousins," with the chimpanzee/hominid split occurring approximately 8 to 6 million years ago.

Unfortunately, scientists are handicapped in their search for the ancestral forms of each hominoid group. The major cause of this problem is a great lack of fossils from the period of about 14 to 4 million years ago—just the period when the divergence of the African forms most likely occurred. Even so, scientists are fairly certain that the ancestors of the great apes and humans come from the two major groups of Miocene hominoids—the dryopiths (named for the genus *Dryopithecus*) and the ramapiths (named for the genus *Ramapithecus*). The two groups are each associated with a particular geographic distribution and ecological setting.

The Dryopiths

Largely arboreal and forest dwelling, the dryopiths originated in Africa and then spread out into the warm, temperate forests of Europe. The species of dryopiths are usually classified into two genera: *Proconsul*, for the early, more generalized

East African forms, and *Dryopithecus*, for the later, more specialized forms primarily found in Europe. The East African dryopiths, which date from the early Miocene, are the earliest undisputed hominoids (see the photos that follow).

Dryopithecine materials consist largely of teeth and jaw fragments, but scientists have also uncovered some good cranial and postcranial remains. The basic dryopith dental pattern includes the Y-5 molar pattern (as found in hominids and modern-day apes) and large canines that resemble those of existing apes. Most forms had a V-shaped dental arcade that is different from, but potentially ancestral to, the dental arcades of both hominids and modern-day apes.

The great variety of fossilized structures and their wide geographical distribution indicate that the dryopiths were an especially adaptable group of primates. Although most relied on a diet of fruit and other vegetable matter, dryopiths varied in their ways of life. For example, from postcranial remains we know that some climbed through the trees on all fours, others swung hand-over-hand, while still others knuckle-walked on the ground. In addition to their different locomotor patterns, they also differed in size. Some dryopiths were no bigger than a small baboon, while others reached the size of a large chimpanzee. Eventually, they too died out, and many of their econiches today are filled by monkeys rather than by apes. Even so, some dryopithecine forms played important roles in the evolution of modern-day hominoids (see Figure 5.9).

About 15 million years ago, as the earth's climate continued to cool, increasingly larger expanses of grasslands appeared across the Old World. At this time, the fossil record indicates the presence of the other, possibly more terrestrial, group of Miocene hominoids—the ramapiths.

The Ramapiths

The ramapiths were extremely successful, in terms of both how long they survived and how broadly they spread across the Old World. Until recently, the ramapiths were known only from fossilized teeth and jaw fragments. This once-sparse fossil record now includes well-preserved cranial and postcranial remains, leading scientists to conclude that the ramapiths differed from the dryopiths in morphology, ecology, and geographic distribution.

Most researchers recognize at least two closely related genera of ramapiths: *Ramapithecus* and *Sivapithecus*. Descended from a dryopithecine population, the first ramapiths apparently evolved in East Africa at least 14 million years ago, then migrated across the landbridge into Eurasia. While most dryopiths are found in Africa and Europe, the ramapiths had a more extensive range that included large parts of Asia, where they persisted until about 8 million years ago.

What did the ramapiths look like? They were sexually dimorphic, that is, the males were larger than the females and had more exaggerated facial and dental features. Pilbeam (1978) speculates that most types of ramapiths weighed approximately 40 to 70 pounds and used a combination of quadrupedal and bipedal locomotion. Most distinctive, however, are their facial structure and teeth. The front teeth are large; the male canines are big compared with those of hominids, but smaller than those of modern-day great apes. The back teeth are particularly striking in that they are large and heavily enameled. In some cases, the molars are also quite wrinkled, much like those of orangutans. In addition, the jaws concentrated great strength on the back teeth, adding to the grinding power of the ramapith's dentition. The ramapithecine dental arcade is V-shaped and thus similar to that of most dryopiths and unlike those of hominids and modern apes. The ramapiths' concave faces and projecting front teeth were similar to those of orangutans (see the photos on the facing page).

The ramapithecine features, particularly the sturdy dentition, reflect a distinctive ecological adaptation. However, scientists disagree as to the exact nature of the ramapith's ways of life. One popular idea (e.g., Pilbeam 1978) is that the ra-

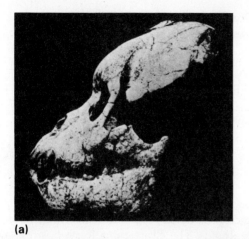

(a)

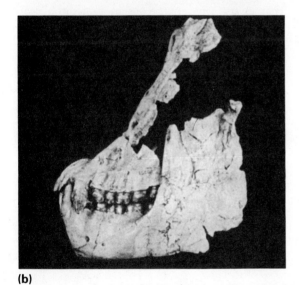

(b)

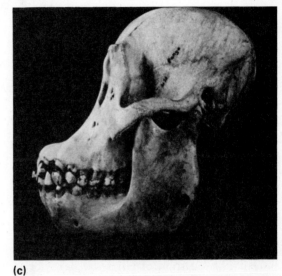

(c)

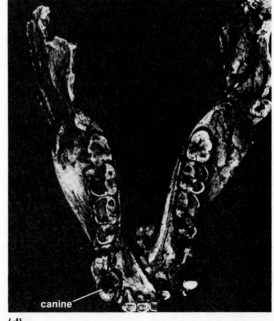

canine

(d)

Dryopithecines and ramapithecines. (a) Proconsul, the early, generalized drypothecine form. Note the similarities in general form and cranial structure to that of (b) and (c). (b) Sivapithecus, a ramapithecine form. Its concave face and projecting front teeth are similar to those of modern-day orangutans. (c) Skull of a modern-day orangutan. (d) Lower jaw of Sivapithecus. Note the relatively large size of the back teeth compared with the front teeth and the V-shaped configuration of the tooth rows.

mapiths were the first primates to exploit the expanding open woodlands and grasslands (whereas the dryopiths stayed in the forest). Ramapithecine dentition provided a powerful mechanism for chewing and grinding the tough vegetable foods, such as grasses and seeds, that are common to such habitats. This theory also contends that within this setting, the ramapiths spent much of their time on the ground. By contrast, R.F. Kay (1981) theorizes that the ramapiths lived in forests, not in the more open habitats. Comparing the ramapithecine dentition with that of modern-day forms, he argues that the ramapiths had a dietary adaptation for eating nuts, seeds, and fruits with hard, tough rinds "that require tremendous forces to open but, once opened, provide a rich source of nutrients previously available to only a few other mammals" (p. 141). Kay also notes that more postcranial evidence is needed before scientists can state definitively whether ramapiths were terrestrial. While some existing species with similar dietary adaptations are indeed terrestrial, others are arboreal. This question of terrestrial behavior is central to deciphering ramapith's role in human evolution because the hominid adaptation apparently evolved in response to a ground-dwelling niche within a grassland or savannah habitat.

The Evolutionary Significance of the Miocene Hominoids

What role *did* the dryopiths and the ramapiths play in the evolution of modern-day forms? Unfortunately, the early and mid-Miocene fossil record, although vast, is confusing, and the late Miocene record is almost nonexistent. As a result, scientists have generated a number of hypotheses with regard to this important question, including the four schemes listed in Figure 5.9.

Scientists have yet to fully comprehend the exact evolutionary significance of the Miocene hominoids. The clearest relationship is the one that exists between the Asian ramapith, *Sivapithecus*, and modern-day orangutans. The evidence for *Sivapithecus* being ancestral to orangutans includes the structure of its face and teeth, the similarities in the degree of sexual dimorphism, and the location and age of the *Sivapithecus* finds. In addition, R.F. Kay (1981) contends that the hard-fruit adaptation of the ramapiths resembles that of the orangutans. A morphological analysis of facial structure also strongly supports the status of *Sivapithecus* as the orangutan ancestor (Shea 1985).

THE FIRST HOMINID?

Clearly, *some* population of late Miocene hominoid diverged into the hominids. Who, then, *was* the first hominid? Unfortunately, the known fossil record includes only a very small fraction of the extinct primates. Also discouraging is the large gap in the record during the crucial period from about 8 to 4 million years ago. It is entirely possible, then, that paleontologists have not as yet discovered the form representing the first hominid.

Even if we cannot precisely identify the first hominid, we *can* still address other important questions concerning human evolution: How

and why did the first hominid evolve? What adaptive pattern distinguishes the hominids? The importance of such questions is emphasized by what we now know—only a few million years separate humans and the African apes. If we are so evolutionarily close to the African apes, then what accounts for our considerable differences? The key to our uniqueness is based in the origin and adaptation of the human species. Thus, we will explore these kinds of questions—questions essential to understanding what it is to be human—in the next chapter.

1. Some population or populations of dryopiths were ancestral to an evolutionary branch leading to all the great apes and to a separate branch leading to the ramapiths. The ancestor of the hominids is to be found among the ramapiths.

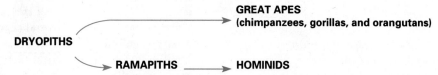

DRYOPITHS

GREAT APES
(chimpanzees, gorillas, and orangutans)

RAMAPITHS ⟶ HOMINIDS

2. The dryopiths were ancestral to an African branch leading to gorillas, chimpanzees, and hominids, and to another branch leading to the ramapiths. The ramapiths were ancestral to the Asian great ape, the orangutan.

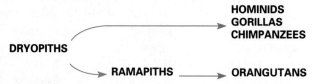

DRYOPITHS

HOMINIDS
GORILLAS
CHIMPANZEES

RAMAPITHS ⟶ ORANGUTANS

3. *Proconsul*, an early dryopithecine, was ancestral to the later dryopiths, all of which became extinct. *Proconsul* was also ancestral to early ramapiths. The early ramapiths gave rise to a late-Miocene African ramapithecine population that was ancestral to the African great apes and hominids. The same early ramapith also gave rise to an Asian ramapith (*Sivapithecus*) that was ancestral to the orangutans.

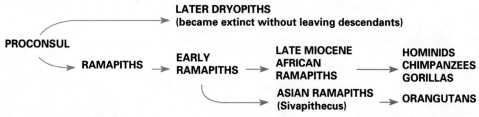

PROCONSUL

LATER DRYOPITHS
(became extinct without leaving descendants)

RAMAPITHS ⟶ EARLY RAMAPITHS ⟶ LATE MIOCENE AFRICAN RAMAPITHS ⟶ HOMINIDS CHIMPANZEES GORILLAS

ASIAN RAMAPITHS (Sivapithecus) ⟶ ORANGUTANS

4. Recently discovered remains suggest that *Proconsul* was the contemporary of an early ramapith. This indicates that the Asian and African lines already had split and that the common ancestor of all the great apes and hominids was not *Proconsul* but some even earlier form, as yet undiscovered. This fossil evidence appears to disagree with the timing predicted by molecular clock studies.

?

PROCONSUL ⟶ LATER DRYOPITHS ⟶ HOMINIDS CHIMPANZEES GORILLAS

RAMAPITHS ⟶ ORANGUTANS

FIGURE 5.9
Alternative schemes for the evolutionary roles of Miocene hominoids.

SUMMARY

Paleoanthropologists use a number of techniques to reconstruct the past. The most direct evidence of ancient life comes from fossils, the preserved remains or traces of long-dead animals and plants. Fossils form the basis of paleontology, the scientific study of extinct life. Although incomplete, the fossil record still provides a good picture of primate evolution.

An important part of interpreting a fossil find is dating, determining its approximate age and how to place it in time. Relative dating is the sequential ordering of a set of objects in time, the most common technique being stratigraphy. Absolute dating, including radiocarbon and potassium-argon dating, is the determination of an object's actual age in years.

Besides describing an extinct form's physical structure, scientists also seek to reconstruct how an animal lived within its environment. The general climatic and temporal framework for the study of evolutionary history is provided by the geologic time scale. Another geologic contribution is the theory of plate tectonics. Information regarding prehistoric habitats is provided by paleoecology, in which evidence of the past is used to reconstruct the plants, animals, climate, and physical environment of ancient times.

The study of contemporary primates helps scientists develop general rules of anatomy to use when reconstructing incomplete fossils, both as models for how structures functioned in ancient forms and as models for how extinct species lived. Molecular clock studies use biochemical and genetic differences among species as a measure of how long ago the forms last shared an ancestor.

Because of the difficulties involved with classifying and interpreting the fossil record, scientists often disagree over how to separate fossils into species. One solution is to reduce the need to make such divisions, as, for example, in the cladistic approach, which groups closely related organisms on a branch.

Although controversies persist, scientists have deciphered the general pattern of primate and human evolution. During the end of the Mesozoic era, the general climate of the earth cooled, and the resulting environmental change favored the early mammals. The early mammals were generalized in structure, thus facilitating the great mammalian adaptive radiation that occurred at the beginning of the Cenozoic era. One of the resulting branches gave rise to the primates. The earliest primates lived during the Paleocene epoch, during which the climate was relatively mild. Paleocene primates were similar to other Paleocene mammals, and thus similar to modern-day tree shrews. One branch of Paleocene primates formed the parental stock of the primates of the Eocene epoch, in which the climate was warmer than in the Paleocene; thus, more areas were hospitable to primates. There was an abundance of the first truly prosimian-grade primates in the Eocene, among which were the divergent ancestors of the anthropoids and the prosimians.

The Oligocene epoch represents the start of a long-term cooling trend, with primates disappearing from northern regions. The Oligocene primate fossil record is largely limited to finds from the Fayum in northern Africa. Of these monkeylike anthropoids, the best known is *Aegyptopithecus*. With primitive and advanced traits, *Aegyptopithecus* may represent the divergence of the hominoids, including apes and humans, from the Old World monkeys.

During the Miocene epoch, as the earth's climate became progressively cooler and drier, the first hominoids, which apparently evolved in Africa, migrated into other forested areas of the Old World. An adaptive radiation of apelike forms occurred as groups of hominoids, separated in forested areas by grasslands, adapted to different econiches. The Miocene apelike forms consisted of two major groups, the dryopiths and the ramapiths, among which were the ancestors of modern-day hominoids.

SUGGESTED READINGS

Ciochon, R.L., and A.B. Chiarelli, eds. 1983. *New Interpretations of Ape and Human Ancestry*. New York: Plenum.

Ciochon, R.L., and J.G. Fleagle, eds. 1985. *Primate Evolution and Human Origins*. Menlo Park, CA: Benjamin-Cummings.

Eldredge, N., and J. Cracraft. 1980. *Phylogenetic Patterns and the Evolutionary Process*. New York: Columbia University Press.

Fleagle, John G. 1988. *Primate Adaptation and Evolution*. San Diego, CA: Academic Press.

Kennedy, G.E. 1980. *Paleoanthropology*. New York: McGraw-Hill.

Martin, R.D. 1990. *Primate Origins and Evolution*. Princeton, NJ: Princeton University Press.

Shipman, Pat. 1981. *Life History of a Fossil*. Cambridge, MA: Harvard University Press. (Interpreting the fossil record)

6 Humankind Emerging: The Evolution of the Human Species

Artist's recreation of early hominids and their East African savannah habitat.

The history of the hominids spans millions of years and encompasses many different forms. Some forms were evolutionary side-branches; others were ancestral to modern-day humans. All hominids, however, share a common ancestor that descended from a Miocene ape.

Although biological evolution was responsible in a broad sense, paleoanthropologists seek to understand the individual factors that led to the origin of the hominids. An important part of this study is delineating the hominid adaptation—describing its components, what makes it unique, and how it can be identified within the fossil record. The next step of investigating why it evolved can then be pursued. Another major area of paleoanthropology involves studying what occurred after the origin of the hominids—reconstructing the history of human evolution, from the emergence of the earliest hominids through the appearance of anatomically modern forms.

During the course of human evolution, a genus emerged that was increasingly dependent on cultural as well as biological means of contending with the environment. Thus, human evolution is *biocultural*: physical and cultural aspects of our adaptation evolve in tandem. The cultural adaptations are based on biological structures; at the same time, cultural factors have strongly influenced the nature of humankind's biological adaptations. Because of the subject's complexity, this chapter concentrates on the biological aspects of human evolution. The cultural aspects of human evolution will be taken up in later chapters.

WHAT IS A HOMINID?

Most scientists agree that the earliest hominids adapted to life on the grasslands and savannahs of Africa. In the process, hominids began to evolve an adaptation that includes three interacting components: the behavior of *walking on two feet and habitually standing upright,* called **bipedalism**; a *distinctive, generalized dentition*; and an *enlarged and reorganized brain.* Each component has structural and functional characteristics that are expressed to varying degrees in the different forms of hominids.

Bipedalism

Bipedalism was an important component in hominid evolution. While other primates occasionally move about on two limbs, bipedalism is the primary form of hominid locomotion. The shift from quadrupedalism greatly affected the design of the hominid body. With bipedalism came a distinctive S-shaped spinal column that could withstand the stress of upright posture and feet specialized for bearing weight and walking on two limbs. Hominids also evolved straight legs, with knees that lock into place for a bipedal stride, and hips and upper bodies especially structured for bipedalism and upright posture (see Figure 6.1a).

Bipedalism is reflected in the fossil record primarily by skeletal remains (an important exception is the Laetoli footprints, described in Figure 6.5). Muscles, cartilage, and other soft materials must be reconstructed from the impressions left on bones and through analogies with living species.

Hominid Dentition

The basic pattern of hominid dentition is notable for being generalized. When compared with those of apes, the front teeth are small relative to cheek teeth. In addition, while male apes have large and protruding canines, the canines of both male and female hominids are small. Another

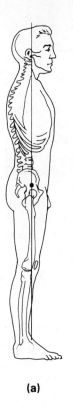
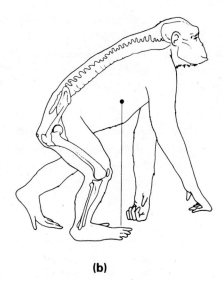

(a) **(b)**

FIGURE 6.1
Postcranial adaptations of humans versus chimpanzees. (a) Human postcranial structures are adapted for bipedal stance and locomotion. Note the placement of the head, with the spinal cord entering at the center of the base of the skull; the S-shaped curve of the spine; and the placement of the knee. (b) Chimpanzee postcranial structures are adapted for locomotion on four limbs (knuckle-walking). Compare the orientation of the head, shape of the spine, and placement of the knee with part (a).

hominid trait is that the cheek teeth have large, flat grinding surfaces. The hominid dental arcade is also distinctive, splaying at the back of the mouth to form a parabolic shape (see Figure 6.2a).

Within this generalized pattern, there are some interesting dental differences among the hominid forms. Sometimes the differences reflect the retention of primitive traits, such as large canines and more U-shaped tooth rows. Such traits help scientists evaluate the evolutionary status of a specific find. Other differences reflect dietary specializations. For example, extremely heavy jaws and oversized cheek teeth suggest a dietary specialization for chewing very rough vegetation.

Expansion of the Brain

The most dramatic aspect of human evolution has to do with the brain. During human evolu-

tion there was a progressive enlargement of the parts of the brain associated with such higher mental processes as conscious thought, intelligence, and self-awareness. The expansion of the **cerebral cortex**—the outermost layers of the brain—was particularly important in the evolution of the human capacity for cultural behavior, language, and symbolic thought.

When measured in relation to overall body size, the human brain is significantly larger than that of other primates. Brain size is also the most striking difference observed among the hominid forms. In fact, once the genus *Homo* is fully realized, brain size is the only major component of the human physical adaptation to change significantly through time.

Fossil studies of brain evolution primarily consist of two techniques: measures of cranial capacity and brain endocasts. **Cranial capacity** refers to estimates of brain size, usually expressed in

Nonprojecting canine

Projecting canine

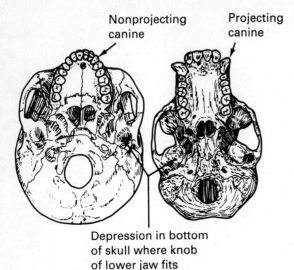

Depression in bottom of skull where knob of lower jaw fits

(a)

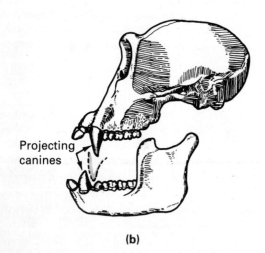

Projecting canines

(b)

FIGURE 6.2

Comparison of jaws and teeth of humans and chimpanzees. (a) The bottom of the skull of a human (left) and a chimpanzee. Note the differences in size of teeth and shape of jaw. Also note the difference in the placement of the opening for the spinal cord. (b) Side view of a chimpanzee skull. Note the projecting face, heavy lower jaw, and the placement of the projecting canines. The human pattern is much more generalized than that of apes.

cubic centimeters (cm³), made by measuring how much matter can be contained within a fossilized cranium. These measures are often inexact, however, partly because the cranium also contains materials that provide the brain with protection and nutrients. The percentage of these support materials varies among individuals, making it difficult to calculate exactly what proportion of the measurement they represent. In addition, cranial capacity is often measured from reconstructed craniums, adding to the inaccuracies of the measures. However inexact, measures of cranial capacity still provide scientists with important information regarding general stages of brain evolution.

Brain endocasts are impressions of the inside of craniums. Usually made of plastic, the molds are used to study the size, shape, and organization of the brain. Scientists attempt to distinguish the brain areas associated with particular functions, such as vision or speech. However, because of poor preservation, it is usually possible to distinguish only major subdivisions and not subtler differences in brain organization.

Fortunately, scientists have other means of investigating the complicated issue of human brain evolution. One important technique is comparing human brains with those of other living primates (see Figure 6.3). For example, such studies demonstrate that brain size relative to body size is unusually large in humans (e.g., Falk 1980). Other works (e.g., Armstrong 1979) show that primate brains differ in cellular structure.

The Complex Evolving: Which Came First?

Bipedalism, hominid dentition, and the hominid brain did not arise full-blown with the earliest form; each continued to develop over the course of human evolution. Some scientists contend that they evolved gradually at the same rate; others assert that they evolved at different rates. The latter hypothesis is supported by fossil evidence

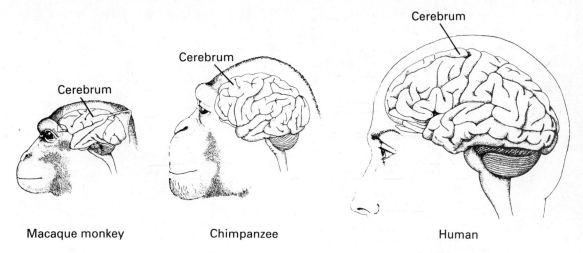

Cerebrum

Cerebrum

Cerebrum

Macaque monkey   Chimpanzee   Human

demonstrating that hominids were fully bipedal almost 2 million years before the brain began to greatly expand. Thus, walking on two feet is apparently the first trait that distinguished the hominids from the apes.

Questions of pace and the factors involved in the evolution of bipedalism, hominid dentition, and the hominid brain are basic to explaining why the hominid adaptation came about in the first place. In particular, if bipedalism preceded the other traits, does its origin help to explain why the hominid diverged from the apes? Why, then, did hominids also evolve a distinctive den-

FIGURE 6.3
Comparison of the brain of a monkey, ape, and human. Note the increase in the proportional size of the brain, particularly of the cerebrum, the region associated with higher mental functions. Also note the increase in convolutions—the folding of the outermost layer of the cerebrum. The more convoluted the cerebrum, the greater the number of nerve cells it contains.

tition and a progressively enlarged brain? How are all three of these aspects functionally and evolutionarily interrelated?

WHY DID THE HUMAN ADAPTATION EVOLVE?

The most controversial and speculative ideas regarding human evolution are those that seek to explain specifically the origin of the hominids. There are a great number of such theories, many of which use modern-day forms, especially the nonhuman primates and human foraging societies, as models for interpreting the prehistoric record. In this section, we will consider a few of the more prominent theories of human origins. While they differ as to the *whys*, all agree on the

underlying *how*: Hominids originated as the result of biological evolution, particularly through the process of natural selection.

The Scenario Approach

The earliest hominids slowly moved out of the forests and began to exploit a new habitat that consisted of grasslands and savannahs. In the process, they were confronted with new food resources. Many theories of human origins thus focus on the acquisition of a new feeding strategy that included changes in diet and in the means of acquiring food. Such changes, in turn, influenced physical, behavioral, and social adaptations.

Clifford Jolly's (1970) "seed-eating" theory, modeled on gelada baboons, contends that the earliest hominids exploited an ecological zone in which trees were few but grasslands extensive. Their feeding strategy, based on sitting on the ground and gathering seeds and grains, led to important physical and behavioral changes that foreshadowed later trends of hominid evolution, including better hand-eye coordination, upright posture, and changes in dentition. According to Jolly, another minor ecological shift then occurred as the hominids responded to a slight environmental change, "perhaps an intensification of seasonality in a marginal tropical area" (p. 21). The shift led hominids to begin eating meat. This brought about changes in social behavior, including the division of labor—the technical and social manner in which work is organized in a society—according to gender, as males became the hunters and females the gatherers of vegetable food. Cooperative behavior also became established among the members of the society, as males and females shared their gains with one another and with their offspring. The need to cooperate and refine communication skills eventually brought about the evolution of an enlarged brain capable of symbolic communication, increased intellect, and cultural advances.

An alternative dietary hypothesis was posed by Szalay (1972). His "hunting-scavenging" model argues that the primary dietary shift was to a life of scavenging for meat, and that changes in dentition reflect a functional system for tearing meat and crushing bone. Support for such a theory comes from Shipman's (1986) analysis of cut marks (microscopic patterns left on bones by the action of tools) and carnivore tooth marks, indicating that the bones of prey were handled both by carnivores (who did the killing) and by tool-using hominids, who scavenged the leftovers. Additional evidence in support of a scavenger model comes from observations of contemporary human groups and scavenging animals. Also noted by Shipman was that the locomotive needs of scavengers would have selected for bipedalism. By studying contemporary scavengers such as vultures, she determined that scavengers need to cover large areas in search of carcasses, but do not need great speed. Bipedal locomotion provides an energy-efficient means of doing so. In addition, scavengers must be able to easily locate carcasses as they move about. Thus, an upright posture "markedly improved {the hominid's} ability to spot items on the ground" (p. 33).

"Hunting and carnivore" models also focus on meat and diet and their relation to social behavior. For example, G.E. King (1975, 1976) proposed that the evolution of hunting among the early hominids had major social ramifications, including establishing the need for cooperation and for stable, highly territorial social groups. King pointed out that modern-day social carnivores, such as hyenas, lions, and wolves, demonstrate similar social patterns and can therefore serve as models for interpreting aspects of the human fossil record.

A different approach was taken by Tanner (1981, 1987). Her "gathering hypothesis" focuses on the role of food gathering by women with children. Bipedalism, according to Tanner, largely evolved to free the hands, out of women's need to carry children, food, and materials. This hypothesis emphasizes the importance of the human pattern of child rearing, including food sharing with children and their socialization, by the female caretakers, into a specific culture. A significant part of the females' role was teaching their offspring the best food-gathering techniques, including refinements in tool using. In addition, Tanner argued that chimpanzees are useful as models for early hominid behavior, noting that wild chimpanzee mothers are particularly skilled in tool using; that food is shared

!Kung San women and children returning to camp after gathering food and water. Anthropologist Nancy Tanner focused on the role of women as gatherers and the socializers of children in her theory of human origins.

among mothers, offspring, and siblings; and that chimpanzee mothers teach their young to use tools.

Owen Lovejoy's (1981) model is one of the most controversial theories of human origins. It holds that bipedalism evolved as the result of a particular reproductive and sexual strategy, based on monogamous males carrying home food to their mates and dependent offspring. Such provisioning allowed the female to space births closer together, thereby increasing the pair's reproductive fitness. This strategy provided an offspring with more intense care and nurturing, thereby increasing its chances of survival.

These are just a few of the current theories of human origins. Others focus on various social strategies, such as the origins of hominid labor division (e.g., Galdikas and Teleki 1981), and food sharing (e.g., Issac 1978). Another theory contends that bipedalism evolved to increase traveling efficiency for gathering small and scattered food resources (Rodman and McHenry 1980).

Each theory has its supporters and detractors. Some criticize many of the primate-based models as being founded on "superficial similarities between early hominids and living primates" (Potts 1987, 47). Jolly's seed-eating model has been criticized on the basis that the dental traits used to support his theory could also reflect a meat-eating diet (Szalay 1972), or that of a forest-dwelling leaf-eater (R.F. Kay 1985). Lovejoy's monogamy model is praised by some (e.g., Johanson and Edey 1981), whereas others contend that the evidence does not support his view, including that "all available evidence indicates that early hominids were polygynous and not monogamous and that male provisioning of immobile females and offspring was unlikely" (McHenry 1982, 157).

Lately there has been a growing dissatisfaction with these "just-so story" approaches to human origins. Some scholars feel that such hypotheses should be treated as literary narratives, and that most are no more than "a backward projection of current cultural beliefs and practices" (Fedigan 1986, 26). A different tack is to avoid devising exact scenarios and focus instead on general themes that reflect the uniqueness of humanness. One such theme that runs through all aspects of the human adaptation is the striking degree of plasticity in how humans contend with their environment. In this context, **plasticity** is the ability to respond and adjust to a wide range of conditions, especially during an individual's growth and development. This plasticity—in diet, habitat, behavior, and communication—may be the key to explaining what is special about the human adaptation.

Plasticity and the Human Adaptation

Humans occupy a special ecological niche. Instead of consisting of a reasonably finite and predictable set of demands, the human niche is complex, somewhat unpredictable, and prone to change through both time and space. The present-day human adaptation of great plasticity is founded on that of the first hominids, who probably evolved in response to an inhospitable niche that demanded solutions to an unpredictable set of problems. Within this context, humans became successful, as reflected by our present-day sheer numbers and by the exploitation of widely diverse habitats that span the globe from arctic tundras to equatorial deserts.

Our enormous plasticity, uniquely human, demonstrates continuity with the rest of the animal kingdom. This point becomes evident when we study the evolution of the nervous system—an animal's information-processing and motor-control mechanism, which includes the brain in more complex forms of life.

As one moves from the lower vertebrates to the primates, the organization of the nervous system becomes increasingly complex. One way to account for this increasing complexity is to focus on the concept of "perceived world"—the aspect of the physical environment an animal senses and interacts with. For example, a bumble bee and a cow both can live in the same meadow, but the environmental aspects sensed and exploited by the two are very different. The increasing structural complexity of the nervous system corresponds with an increasing complexity and unpredictability of the perceived worlds of life-forms, which dictates that a growing number of behavioral choices must be made by individual animals. This applies both to the physical environment *and* to an animal's social world. For example, social relationships are much more complicated, much less automatic, and much less predictable among the primates than among salamanders or herring gulls. Thus, complex forms need nervous systems that permit a great flexibility of response, a high degree of learning through experience, and the ability to rapidly respond to novel challenges. Humans most fully express these abilities, which are made possible by the interaction of the components of the human adaptation—bipedalism, generalized dentition, and the human brain. Of special note are human patterns of growth and development that bestow on individuals a limited ability to adjust to their own set of environmental demands, be they physical, psychological, social, or cultural. To illustrate these points, we will now examine the three components of the hominid adaptation in relation to human plasticity.

Bipedalism and Behavioral Plasticity

What is the relationship between bipedalism and hominid plasticity? One idea is that by freeing the hands from locomotor responsibilities, bipedalism allowed the hands to be adapted for carrying objects. This, in turn, liberated the mouth from such duties. Hands became specialized for manipulating and exploring the environment, thereby permitting a more detailed perception of the universe. Structurally, hands evolved extremely fine-tuned motor control based on associated changes in the brain. An important ramification of this adaptation was the refinement of tool-making and tool-using skills, which are crucial in using cultural mechanisms to exploit a broad range of habitats.

Bipedalism may also have played a key role in the evolution of language. According to Hewes (1971), for example, the first complex forms of hominid communication were gestural, and bipedalism freed the hands for this purpose. Another speculation is that the mouth, now freed from carrying, could be more easily used for "sociable chatter" (Hockett and Ascher 1964).

Generalized Dentition and Dietary Plasticity

A clear relationship exists between the generalized hominid dentition and the ability to survive under a varied set of environmental conditions. Carnivores, such as lions, have dentition specialized for killing and devouring prey, while ungulates, such as cattle and sheep, have teeth specialized for chewing rough vegetation. However, because of their lack of structural dietary specializations, humans can exploit a great range of food resources—and thus a great range of habitats. Humans are consummate **omnivores**, animals that can use both plants and animals as food resources.

Dietary plasticity is a good example of how the major components of the hominid adaptation act as a system. Besides our generalized dentition, the behavioral flexibility made possible by the human brain also factors into our great range of dietary strategies. Humans invented and learned novel ways to collect and prepare food, including innovations in hunting and the use of fire. The human ability to make and use tools, founded on bipedalism and the hominid brain, is basic to cultural means of subsistence.

Behavioral Plasticity: The Hominid Brain and Cultural Adaptation

The single most important factor contributing to the plasticity of the hominid adaptation has been the expansion and reorganization of the brain. The human brain evolved as the result of natural selection favoring increased intelligence, symbolic thought, language behavior, and a strong emphasis on learning. All of these traits allow individuals to rapidly respond to unique and complicated sets of problems. For example, reasoning, memory, and decision-making skills are crucial to surviving in an unpredictable world; fixed, reflexive responses are far too limiting.

The behavioral flexibility made possible by the human brain clearly reflects the biocultural nature of the human adaptation. Of special note is that biological evolution brought about the ability of humans to adapt via cultural means. For example, the small-scale farmers of highland Mexico use simple technology, such as tilling and weeding, to adapt to their less-than-optimal environment. At the same time, cultural patterns of exchange help distribute resources among the members of a society. Culture, in turn, provides a rapid means of solving environmental problems, by freeing humans from having to wait for natural selection to act over many generations.

Humans learn cultural behavior through **enculturation**, the process of acquiring cultural rules and values from others through social interaction. Enculturation depends on how the human brain functions and represents an extension of primate social and developmental patterns. In particular, human children have a lengthy period of dependency in which to learn specific and complex patterns of behavior.

Enculturation and human culture depend on yet another capacity of the human brain—the capacity for language. Human language evolved into a highly flexible and complex form of communication. It is a creative and open system, "open" referring to the capacity to add new signals to the system and transmit new ideas. By contrast, the call systems of most animals are considered "closed" because they are locked into a fixed set of signals. Language allows humans to communicate abstract and highly complicated concepts. Such concepts are important elements in human society, essential in the maintenance of complex social relationships. Also, technological advances (beyond the most simplistic) can be communicated only by means of language. Finally, language is basic to teaching and socializing children into the ways of their elders (see Chapter 12).

As part of enculturation, children learn language in both informal and formal settings. These American children are learning language skills in the formal setting of a primary school.

Human Plasticity in Today's World

The unique flexibility of the human adaptation is demonstrated throughout this book. For example, in Chapter 7 we will see how various physical traits develop in response to environmental factors such as altitude, disease, and nutrition. In later chapters we will explore the great range of cultural and behavioral diversity that exists in today's world. This diversity was made possible by the evolution of modern-day humans, *Homo sapiens sapiens.*

THE HISTORY OF HUMAN EVOLUTION

Sometime between 8 to 4 million years ago, the evolutionary path of humans diverged from that of all other primates. A major goal of paleoanthropology is to reconstruct the course of human evolution from the earliest hominids to fully modern forms, *Homo sapiens sapiens.* (The second "sapiens" is a subspecies designation, meaning that a form shares much with the rest of its species, but is distinctive enough to warrant its own category.) Controversies persist as to the exact role of the various fossil finds, yet most anthropologists agree on the general patterns. (See Figure 6.4 for a representative sample of important paleontological and archaeological hominid sites.) Although a number of alternative ideas are posed, the following discussion concentrates on the scheme that seems the most reasonable in the light of the current body of evidence.

WALKING ERECT: THE FIRST UNDISPUTED HOMINIDS

The earliest stages of hominid evolution occurred during the *Pliocene epoch* (8 to 1.8 million years ago). During the Pliocene, the earth continued to become cooler and drier, with savannahs and grasslands dominating increasingly larger parts of Africa and Eurasia.

As mentioned in Chapter 5, we cannot precisely identify the first hominid, especially because of the paucity of fossils from about 8 to 4 million years ago. However, since the 1970s, paleontologists working in East Africa have uncovered some very old (and very controversial) hominid finds. These finds apparently belong to the earliest group of undisputed hominids, the **australopithecines**.

The Australopithecines: Small-Brained Bipeds

In 1924, a South African quarry worker presented anatomist Raymond Dart with the skull of an ancient child. The skull was that of an individual who was not quite a human and not quite an ape. It appeared humanlike because the opening at the base of the skull through which the spinal cord enters the brain was centered, a trait found in bipeds. Moreover, its teeth and face were too small to be those of an ape. On the other hand, its brain was only a little larger than that of a chimpanzee. Asserting that this "Taung Baby" was a "man-ape," Dart labeled it *Australopithecus africanus*. His interpretation was rejected by most of his colleagues, who insisted that a large brain preceded bipedalism in human evolution. However, by the 1950s the evidence clearly supported Dart's contention that a bipedal, small-brained hominid had roamed Africa over 2 million years ago.

What distinguishes the genus *Australopithecus* from that of *Homo*? The clearest differences are in the shape and size of the head and teeth. When we take into account the smaller body size of australopithecines, their cranium is significantly smaller than that of *Homo*. The australopithecine cranial capacity averages 450 cm^3 in smaller forms and 500 cm^3 in larger types, while early forms of *Homo* average around 650 cm^3 (modern-day humans average around 1,350 cm^3). The australopithecine lower face is large relative to the vault (the top part of the skull), the reversal of what we find in *Homo*. With the notable exception of the very ancient East African form, the australopithecine's front teeth are small relative to the back teeth. This, again, is reversed in *Homo*.

Also significant is the lack of evidence that australopithecines made or used stone tools. However, they may have used less sophisticated tools made out of such materials as wood that were not preserved (Pilbeam 1984). In fact, recent findings lend support to the idea that australopithecines were capable of some form of tool use. Susman (1988) analyzed 1.8-million-year-old australopithecine hand bones uncovered in a South African cave. Scientists had assumed that primitive stone tools found at the same level of the site were made by a more modern form, *Homo erectus*, whose remains were also present. However, Susman contends that the australopithecine's hand was that of a tool-user, capable of precision grasping capabilities as reflected by the size and shape of the thumb and by the broad width of the fingertips.

If australopithecines are so different from *Homo*, why are they indisputably classified as hominids? The most important reason is that they are fully bipedal. In addition, although different from that of *Homo*, australopithecine dentition still appears more humanlike than apelike. For example, their teeth are small in comparison to those of apes, with the canines short in both

FIGURE 6.4

Important sites: Hominid evolution.

This map includes a representative sample of
important paleontological and archaeological sites.
The key below lists the sites according to country,
along with the types of finds found at the sites.

KEY TO TYPES OF FINDS*

Early hominid—very early hominid of undetermined species
Australopithecine—member of the genus *Australopithecus* of undetermined species
  A. *afarensis*—*Australopithecus afarensis*
  A. *africanus*—*Australopithecus africanus*
  A. *robustus*—*Australopithecus robustus*
  A. *boisei*—*Australopithecus boisei*

Early Homo—early member of the genus *Homo* of undetermined species
H. *habilis*—*Homo habilis*
H. *erectus*—*Homo erectus*
Trans—transitional between *Homo erectus* and *Homo sapiens*
Archaic H. sapiens—early *Homo sapiens* of undetermined type
Neandertal—early *Homo sapiens* classified as Neandertal-type
Hss—*Homo sapiens sapiens*: anatomically modern humans

*Some of the find classifications are still under debate and may vary with different sources.

AFRICA

South Africa
1. Taung—A. africanus
2. Sterkfontein—A. africanus, early Homo
3. Swartkrans—A. robustus, H. erectus
4. Kromdraii—A. robustus
5. Makapansgat—A. africanus, Trans
6. Klasies River—Hss

Zambia
7. Broken Hill—Trans

Tanzania
8. Laetoli—A. afarensis
9. Olduvai Gorge—A. boisei, H. habilis, H. erectus

Kenya
10. Chesowanja—A. boisei, H. erectus
11. Lothagam—Early hominid; Hss
12. West Lake Turkana—Robust australopithecine: WT 17000, H. erectus
13. East Lake Turkana—Australopithecine, early Homo: ER 1470, H. erectus, Hss

Ethiopia
14. Omo—A. afarensis, early Homo, H. erectus, archaic H. sapiens, Hss
15. Bodo—H. erectus, Trans
16. Hadar (Afar Triangle)—A. afarensis

Egypt
17. Fayum—Hominoids

Algeria
18. Ternifini—H. erectus

Morocco
19. Sidi Abd er-Raman—H. erectus
20. Rabat—H. erectus
21. Salé—H. erectus
22. Jebel Irhoud—archaic H. sapiens

EUROPE

23. *Gibraltar*—H. erectus, Neandertal

Spain
24. Torralba/Ambrona—H. erectus

France
25. Arago—H. erectus? Trans?
26. Terra Amata—H. erectus
27. La Chapelle-aux-Saints—Neandertal
28. La Ferrassie—Neandertal
29. La Quina—Neandertal
30. Dordogne—Hss
31. Lascaux—Hss
32. Cro-Magnon—Hss
33. Fontechevade—Trans

England
34. Swanscombe—Trans

Belgium
35. Spy—Neandertal

Germany
36. Neander Valley—Neandertal
37. Mauer—H. erectus
38. Steinheim—Trans
39. Ehringsdorf—Trans

Czechoslovakia
40. Brno—Hss

Yugoslavia
41. Krapina—Neandertal

Italy
42. Monte Circeo—Neandertal

Greece
43. Petralona—H. erectus? Trans?

ASIA

Israel
44. Tabun Cave—Neandertal
45. Skhūl—Hss
46. Jebel Qafzeh—Hss

Iraq
47. Shanidar Cave—Neandertal

Iran
48. Hota—Hss

USSR
49. Teshik-Tash—Neandertal

India
50. Hathnora—H. erectus? Trans?

China
51. Lijiang—Hss
52. Yuanmou—H. erectus
53. Maba—Trans
54. Dali—Trans
55. Lantian—H. erectus
56. Choukoutien (Zhoukoudian)—H. erectus, Hss

Borneo
57. Niah Cave—Hss

Java
58. Solo—H. erectus
59. Sangiran—H. erectus
60. Trinil—H. erectus

AUSTRALIA

61. Devil's Lair—Hss
62. Keilor—Hss

153

males and females. Also, most australopithecine dental arcades approach a parabolic, humanlike shape. The australopithecine brains also tend to be slightly larger than those of the great apes.

The australopithecines are clearly hominids. However, there is a controversy over the number of australopithecine types and their exact role in human evolution. In this text, we take a four-species approach, with two South African and two East African australopithecine forms.

The South African Australopithecines

The South African australopithecines consist of two types: *gracile* and *robust*. The smaller, more delicate graciles were about 4.5 feet tall and weighed approximately 60 pounds. The robusts stood at about 5 feet and weighed about 100 pounds. In addition, the gracile's face was smaller-boned and narrow, the robust having had larger back teeth. Both forms had grinding back teeth, suggesting that the most important component of their diet was vegetable matter rather than meat. The robust form, with its heavy skull, deep jaws, and enlarged back teeth, was more specialized for this adaptation.

The graciles and robusts have never been found at the same site (see Figure 6.4, p. 152). They apparently lived at different times and exhibited significant structural differences. This suggests that they probably represent two different species, rather than females and males of the same form. The South African graciles are called *Australopithecus africanus*; the robusts are labeled *A. robustus.*

For technical reasons, the South African australopithecines are hard to date accurately. *A. africanus* apparently lived about 2.5 to 3 million years ago, preceding *A. robustus,* who lived about 1.5 to 2 million years ago. *A. africanus* may have been ancestral to *A. robustus,* with the robust form further specializing into a "rough vegetation" dietary niche.

The East African Robust Australopithecines

The first australopithecine found outside South Africa was discovered by Mary Leakey, who was married to the famous paleontologist Louis Leakey. (Mary, in fact, was responsible for many of the Leakeys' discoveries.) The Leakeys started their search for hominid fossils in East Africa after they became intrigued by a wealth of stone tools found at a Tanzanian site, Olduvai Gorge (see Figure 6.4, p. 152). The Gorge is part of the Great Rift Valley, a 1,200-mile-long chasm along which geological activity has exposed ancient strata. It took the dedicated Leakeys from the mid-1930s until 1959 to uncover their first fossil hominid, a fragmented robust skull.

The East African robust is similar to *Australopithecus robustus,* yet different enough to merit its own species designation, *Australopithecus boisei.* *A. boisei* is best described as "super robust." It is larger and taller than the South African form, with a striking skull that has very heavy bones, exaggerated bony ridges, and a dish-shaped face. At the same time, its cranial capacity is similar to that of *A. robustus.* *A. boisei*'s back teeth are enormous and its posterior molars are heavily wrinkled. Thus, it appears to have been extremely specialized for a diet of small, hard objects (grains and nuts) and rough vegetation, embellishing the trend noted as one moves from *A. africanus* to *A. robustus.* Its dental adaptation may have included nut-cracking capabilities for the ingestion of the nutritious oil-rich nut seeds that are seasonally available on savannahs (Peters 1987).

Frequent volcanic activity along the Great Rift Valley makes potassium-argon dating both possible and desirable. *A. boisei* has been confidently dated as about 1 to 2 million years old, indicating that it lived at approximately the same time as *A. robustus.* Possibly, *A. boisei* derived from an early subpopulation of *A. robustus* that moved into eastern Africa and further adapted to a specialized diet. However, in 1985 a startling East African find was uncovered that may provide new insights regarding A. *boisei*'s place in the hominid family tree. The skull that was found, labeled WT 17000 according to the system used to label finds at the site, is estimated to be 2.5 million years old. It has strong affinities to A. *boisei*, including an advanced-looking massive facial structure. On the other hand, WT 17000's cranium is very primitive, suggesting that A. *boisei* had diverged as a separate lineage before A. *robustus* had even appeared.

Also interesting is that A. *boisei* remains have been associated with primitive stone tools. Many scientists doubt that A. *boisei* produced this technology, hypothesizing that the tools were actually made by a coexisting and larger-brained hominid, *Homo habilis*. This doubt is based on the common belief that *Homo* is the only tool-using hominid—a questionable assumption, particularly in light of chimpanzee tool use. Although evidence is lacking in support of australopithecines as tool-users, new information, particularly as advanced by Susman (1988), indicates that australopithecines were physically capable of tool-using. Such findings should lead scientists to reassess the difference between the genus *Australopithecus* and the genus *Homo*. They also may raise questions about what it means to be "human."

The Graciles of East Africa

Evidence of the most ancient hominids yet found is that of graciles unearthed in the East African Rift Valley. Two major groups of scientists discovered this evidence during the 1970s. One group, led by Richard Leakey (son of Louis and Mary), worked in Tanzania and Kenya. The finds of this group include remarkable footprints left in volcanic ash over 3.5 million years ago by two small hominids walking bipedally across an African plain (see Figure 6.5). The other group, led by paleontologist Donald Johanson and geologist Maurice Taieb, excavated in the Afar region

of Ethiopia. This desolate location is a paleontological gold mine that has produced an impressive collection of hominid finds, some of which are at least 3.5 million years old.

The most spectacular East African gracile find is "Lucy." Discovered at Hadar by Johanson and Taieb's expedition, this 3.5-million-year-old female skeleton is almost 40 percent whole, which is an extraordinary degree of completeness for any fossil hominid. Also discovered at Hadar was the amazing "First Family." This collection of fossils appears to represent an entire social group that was swiftly killed and buried under sediments, as might have occurred during a flash flood. The finds consist of bits and pieces of at least 13 individuals, including adult males, adult females, and no fewer than 4 children. While Lucy provides scientists with an excellent look at a single individual, the First Family serves to demonstrate the differences that existed between the genders and age groups of this population.

The ancient graciles of East Africa have structural traits that distinguish them from other hominids (see Figure 6.6a). Even though they are clearly bipedal, they are even more primitive than the other australopithecines, appearing to be transitional between an apelike ancestor and later hominid forms. The braincase is small—at 400 cm^3 it is more like that of an ape than that of a hominid in size. The dentition appears to be "apish with human tendencies" (Johanson and Edey 1981, 267), including tooth rows that are parallel but slightly splayed at the back, with the canines showing both human and apelike characteristics. When compared with the later forms of australopithecines, the East African gracile's dentition has a generalized aspect, devoid of specializations for digesting rough vegetation. This includes the presence of relatively small molars, as shown in Figure 6.6(b)—a condition noted in *Homo* and not in the other australopithecines. Thus, many scientists classify the gracile within its own species, *Australopithecus afarensis* (Johanson and White 1979).

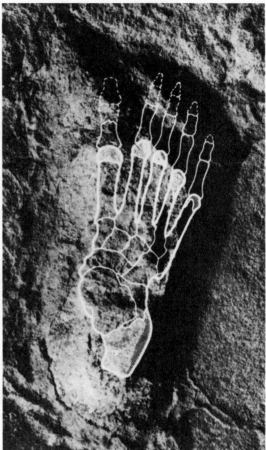

FIGURE 6.5
Early hominid footprint from Laetoli (East Africa).
The Laetoli footprints are solid evidence that
hominids were fully bipedal over 3.5 million years
ago. A superimposed outline of Lucy's foot (right)
lends proof to the theory that *Australopithecus
afarensis* was the fully bipedal creator of the
footprints.

Early *Homo*: The Brain Evolving

During the 1960s, another landmark fossil hominid was uncovered at Olduvai Gorge. Known
from only a few imperfect skulls and skull fragments, this form is about 1.75 million years old—

the same age as *Australopithecus boisei*, yet strikingly different in form. Most significantly, this
hominid had a cranial capacity of approximately
650 cm³, about 40 percent larger than that of robust australopithecines. Louis Leakey proposed
that this was a larger-brained, smaller-toothed,
tool-using hominid, deserving of the name *Homo
habilis*—"handy man."

Clearer proof of an East African early *Homo*
was made public in 1972, in the form of a remarkably well-preserved skull known as ER
1470. About 2 million years old, its skull, with a
thin face and a high cranium, is clearly different

2 SOUTH AFR. *gracile & robust*

2 EAST AFR.

AUSTRAL.

* Fully bipedal
* dentition more humanlike
  - teeth & canines smaller than apes
  - approach parabolic arcade
  - brains 2 lgr than great apes
  - date

FIGURE 6.6

Australopithecines and early *Homo*. (a) Comparison of the skeletons of *Australopithecus afarensis*, A. *Africanus*, the robust australopithecines, and *Homo habilis*. (b) The lower jaws of A. *africanus*, A. *afarensis*, and *Homo*. Note that the jaws of both A. *africanus* and *Homo* may have been derived from A. *afarensis*.

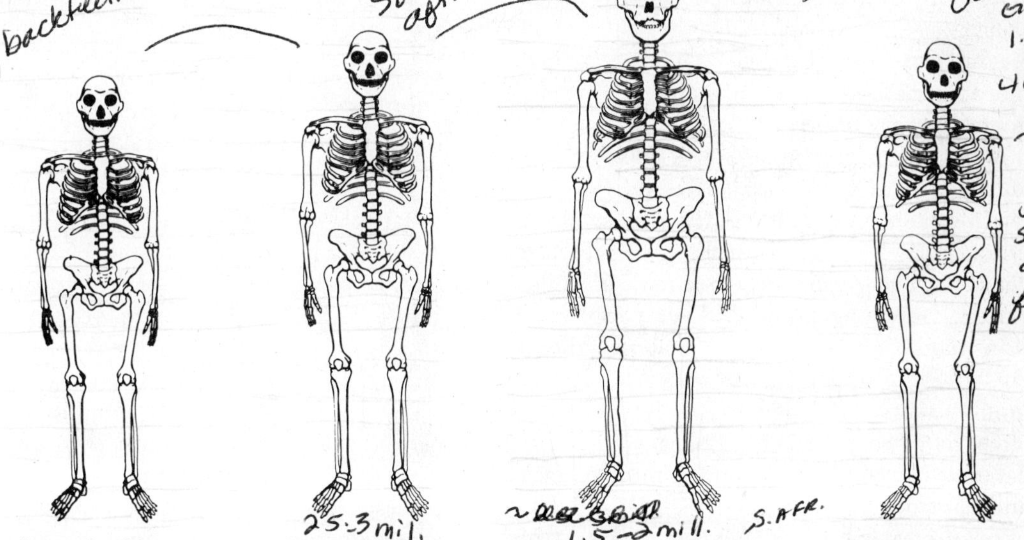

grinding backteeth - veg.

South afr.

South afr. - heavy skull - deep jaws - more spec. for veg.

OLDUVAI GORGE 1.75 mil.

40% lgr brain ~650 cm³

~ sexually dimorph.

female ~3 ft.

(a)

| *Australopithecus afarensis* | *Australopithecus africanus* | *Australopithecus robustus* and A. *boisei* | *Homo habilis* |

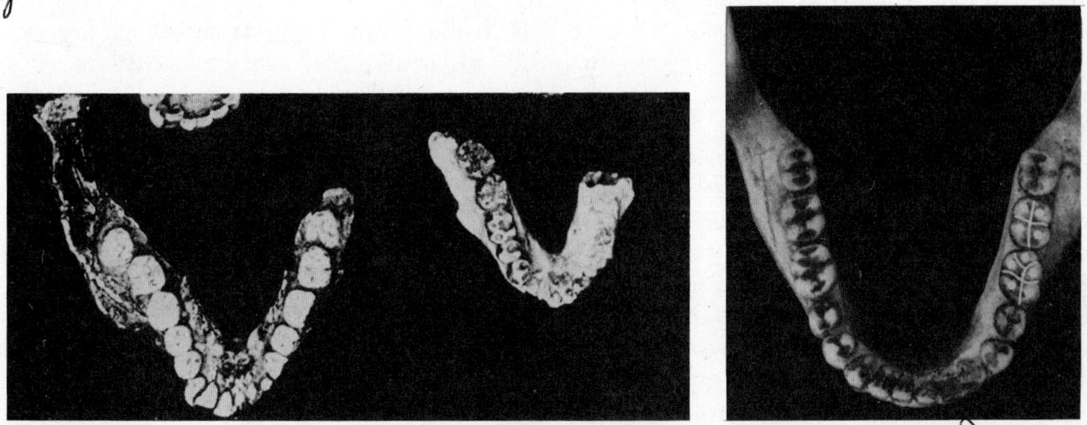

gracile

2 5.3 mil.

~ ??? 3.6 mil. 1.5 → mil.   S.AFR.

EAST (SUPER ROBUST) 1-2 mil.

"Handy man"

Gracile - ~4.5', ~60 lbs

gracile   never found @ same place   → Robust - ~5', 100 lbs

diff. times.

(b)

S. afr. gracile A. africanus

E. african gracile A. afarensis

Homo

from that of the australopithecines. ER 1470 has a cranial capacity of 775 cm³, which is much beyond the range of any australopithecine (see top left photo on p. 161).

More evidence of *Homo habilis* (or early *Homo*, as some researchers prefer) has since been uncovered in Africa. Limb materials suggest that it was taller than the australopithecines. However, a recently discovered 1.8-million-year-old partial skeleton indicates that females were only about 3 feet tall and that early *Homo* was very sexually dimorphic. Both of these traits are also noted in *Australopithecus afarensis*.

What, then, differentiates early *Homo* from the australopithecines? One important trait is that its face is small relative to its cranial capacity. In addition, early *Homo* finds clearly have been associated with very primitive stone tools of limited variety, belonging to the **Oldowan tool tradition** (named after the original materials discovered at Olduvai Gorge). First appearing about 2 million years ago, Oldowan tools are usually large, modified pebbles that have a number of flakes knocked off at one end. Simple to make and easy to transport, such tools would have been of great help in a number of tasks, from butchering meat to chopping vegetables (see Chapter 9).

In terms of temporal and spatial distribution, the *Homo habilis* finds apparently range from about 2 million to 1.5 million years old, for the most part having been found in East Africa (see Figure 6.4, p. 152). Recently discovered evidence, however, suggests that early *Homo* also coexisted with later forms of South African australopithecines.

By 2 million years ago, early *Homo* had become clearly established as a lineage separate from that of the later forms of australopithecines. *Australopithecus africanus*, *A. robustus*, and *A. boisei* had apparently diverged as a hominid lineage as they specialized for a diet of rough vegetation. On the other hand, early *Homo* continued and embellished the basic, generalized pattern of hominid plasticity first seen in *A. afarensis*. For example, as we saw in Figure 6.6(b), early *Homo*'s dentition

maintained the generalized pattern seen in *A. afarensis*, reflecting an omnivorous diet that included a wide variety of foods, including meat. In addition, *Homo*'s increased brain size indicates that it had a greater capacity for complex cultural behaviors. This dietary and behavioral plasticity may be why the genus *Homo* continued to survive in an often harsh and unpredictable world, whereas the genus *Australopithecus* disappeared around 1 million years ago.

The Role of the Australopithecines and Early *Homo* in Human Evolution

What role did the australopithecines and early *Homo* play in human evolution? Currently, the most popular scheme is that of Johanson and White (1979). These researchers contend that *A. afarensis* was ancestral both to the later australopithecines and to *Homo* (see Figure 6.7c). The age of *A. afarensis*, at least 3 to 4 million years old, permits this contention, since the oldest *A. africanus* is dated at about 2.5 million years and the earliest *Homo* is about 2 million years old. *A. afarensis*'s primitive structure is unspecialized enough to have led to the later forms of hominids. In particular, *A. afarensis*'s generalized dentition is similar to that of *Homo*. The other australopithecines also descended from *A. afarensis*, but became a sidebranch of human evolution, having diverged because of a dietary specialization for hard objects and rough vegetation. This pattern was first established in *A. africanus* and further developed in *A. robustus* and *A. boisei*.

Johanson and White's scheme is praised by many (e.g., McHenry 1982; Pilbeam 1984) but is not without its critics. In particular, Richard Leakey (1981) believes that the australopithecines and *Homo* were always separate lineages.

Human paleontology is a dynamic discipline. As new fossils come to light, the Johanson and White scheme may lose favor to another. In fact, WT 17000 already indicates that a revision is in order—one in which *A. afarensis* gives rise to

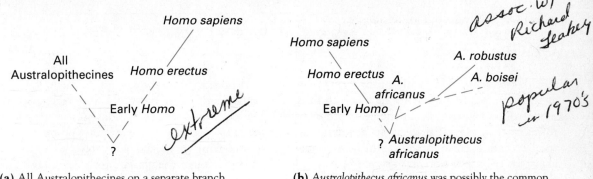

assoc. w/ Richard Leakey

popular in 1970's

(a) All Australopithecines on a separate branch from that of *Homo*. Australopithecines not considered hominids.

(b) *Australopithecus africanus* was possibly the common ancestor of the robust australopithecines and *Homo*.

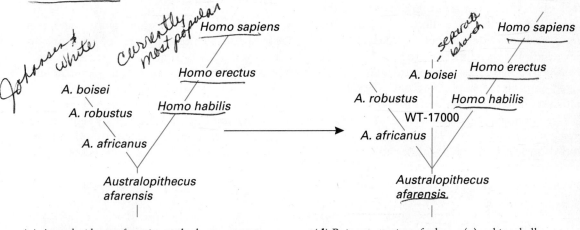

Johanson + White

currently most popular

separate branch

(c) *Australopithecus afarensis* was the last common ancestor of other australopithecines and *Homo*.

(d) Reinterpretation of scheme (c), taking skull WT-17000 into account.

FIGURE 6.7

Alternative schemes of hominid evolution. These diagrams represent only four of the many schemes that have been proposed over the years. (a) An extreme view, in which all australopithecines are regarded as nonhominids. (b) Associated with Richard Leakey, this scheme was popular during the 1970s. (c) Reflecting the approach of Donald Johanson and Tim White, this scheme is currently the most popular. However, the recent discovery of WT 17000 may lead to reinterpretations, such as the one shown in (d).

three, rather than two, branches: a South African branch, including *A. africanus* and *A. robustus*; an East African branch leading to an early then a later form of *A. boisei*; and a third branch for the genus *Homo*.

The exact pattern of early hominid evolution will be debated for some time to come. However, from about 1.5 million to 300,000 years ago, a much better known and larger-brained member of the genus, *Homo erectus*, roamed over much of the Old World. Notably, once we reach the level of *Homo*, the most significant physical change to occur within the genus is in brain size and organization.

THE PLEISTOCENE EPOCH: THE AGE OF GLACIERS

The *Pleistocene epoch* (1.8 million to 10,000 years ago) was an eventful span of time in which fully modern humans arose from the most primitive forms of *Homo*. Great strides were made in cultural evolution, running the gamut from simple chopping tools to the origin of agriculture. It was also a time of dramatic shifts in climate marked by the comings and goings of enormous continental glaciers. Because of the many events that took place, this epoch is further divided into the Lower Pleistocene (1.8 million to 700,000 years ago), the Middle Pleistocene (700,000 to 125,000 years ago), and the Upper Pleistocene (125,000 to 10,000 years ago). The Pleistocene is also subdivided into glacial and interglacial periods, of which there were eight or more in Europe.

The continental glaciers were caused by extreme fluxes in the earth's climate, as it warmed and cooled in a succession quite rapid for geologic time. The face of the earth changed as the glaciers formed, uncovering coastlines as sea levels dropped. When the glaciers melted, water levels rose, and these coastlines were reclaimed by the sea. Inland seas and landmasses were created and destroyed by the enormous power of the slow-moving ice sheets.

Even though the glaciations occurred only in northern regions, they influenced the history of humankind. This was especially so as groups of prehistoric humans began to migrate north. For example, the changes in sea level caused the creation, then the destruction, of landbridges, and ice sheets blocked access to large expanses of land for long periods of time. The changing climate and geology drastically affected plant and animal life, which in turn affected human subsistence strategies. This was a time that selected for a great flexibility and ingenuity of human behavior—a point attested to by the physical and cultural changes reflected in the fossil and archaeological record.

HOMO ERECTUS: POPULATING THE OLD WORLD

From about 1.5 million to 300,000 years ago, the Old World was inhabited by a widely distributed and physically diverse hominid, *Homo erectus*. Taller, larger-brained, and more culturally complex, *Homo erectus* apparently evolved out of an African population of early *Homo* and then migrated across the Old World. A wealth of *erectus* fossil and archaeological remains have been found in Southeast Asia, China, Germany, Hungary, Spain, and Africa (see Figure 6.4, p. 152).

Homo erectus appears to be both physically and culturally intermediate between earlier and later forms of humans. As mentioned, this form was larger-brained and taller than early *Homo*; at the same time, it was smaller-brained and shorter than *Homo sapiens*. *Homo erectus*'s cranial capacity averages around 1,000 cm³, making it significantly larger than the average of 650 cm³ of early *Homo*, yet smaller than the modern human average of 1,350 cm³.

Homo erectus is a diverse form that demonstrates regional variations. Even so, *Homo erectus*'s skull has a distinctive shape. From behind, it appears pentagonal: the widest point is low in the skull, and the top comes to a slight peak. From the front, *Homo erectus* looks relatively primitive, with a receding forehead, heavy buttressing (including pronounced brow ridges), no chin, and a slightly jutting face. Yet its expanded braincase and increased emphasis on chewing front teeth (with a reduction in molar size) cause *Homo erectus* to appear more modern than earlier

Cran cap 3 775 cm3

ER 1470 early homo

H.E. China 1000 cm³

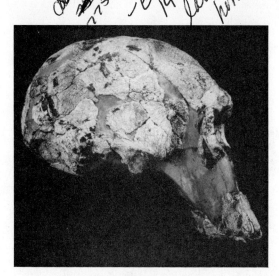

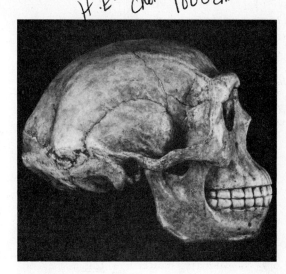

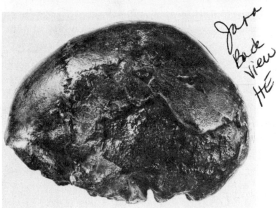

Java Back view HE

Early Homo and Homo erectus. (top left) Skull of ER 1470, an excellent example of early Homo. Dating from approximately 2 million years ago, its cranial capacity of 775 cm³ is greater than that of the australopithecines, but less than that of most Homo erectus. (top right) Homo erectus skull from China. With an average size of 1,000 cm³, Homo erectus had a larger cranial capacity than that of early Homo. Also note the heavier facial structure. (left) Back view of a Homo erectus cranium from Java. Note the distinctive pentagonal shape that is identified with Homo erectus, with the widest part low in the skull and the top coming to a slight peak.

forms. Overall, the skull is that of a heavy chewer, although much less specialized than the australopithecines (see right and bottom photos above).

One remarkable African find, dating from about 1.5 million years ago, has provided special insight into *Homo erectus*. Uncovered at the same site as was WT 17000, it is an almost complete skeleton of a 12-year-old boy, modern-looking structurally and, at 5′6″, quite a bit taller than would be expected for such an ancient human. At the same time, the cranium appears quite primitive, consisting of a braincase about half the size of that of modern humans and a heavily

boned skull. This combination of traits indicates that a modern body structure preceded a modern cranium.

Homo erectus and Increasing Cultural Complexity

Archaeological finds associated with *Homo erectus* reflect a trend toward cultural complexity (see Chapter 9). Their increasing skill as tool-users is evidenced by the frequent appearance of the **Acheulean tool tradition**. This tradition was more technically complex, more standardized, and more refined in form than the Oldowan tradition. Although marked by an increase in the number of tool types, the Acheulean is closely identified with an all-purpose, pear-shaped hand ax. In Asia, the Far East, and parts of northern Europe, *Homo erectus* still was using Oldowan tools. Thus, a number of traditions existed concurrently.

Another cultural advance was the more diversified life-style of *Homo erectus*. Sites reflect differential usage, such as kill sites and habituation (living) sites. In addition, *Homo erectus* ate a variety of foods, including large game animals, and built temporary living structures, such as oval-shaped huts. Yet another example of this increasing cultural complexity is that, by 600,000 years ago, *Homo erectus* had demonstrated the controlled use of fire. In fact, evidence from Africa suggests that fire may have been occasionally used as far back as 1.5 million years ago.

Habitat Expansion

A particularly striking feature of *Homo erectus* was its great expansion through both time and geographical space. *Homo erectus* existed as a relatively stable form for more than 1 million years—a long time for any hominid species. Prior to *Homo erectus*, hominids were apparently confined to Africa; however, by at least 1 million years ago, *Homo erectus* had migrated out of Africa into many tropical and subtropical areas of Europe and Asia. There, the populations evolved locally, leading to regional variations in form.

Physical and cultural evidence of *Homo erectus* has been found across the Old World. For example, the first discovery of *Homo erectus* was in 1891 on the Indonesian island of Java. Fossil and cultural evidence of *Homo erectus* has also been uncovered in China. Some sites, including Torralba and Ambrona in Spain, contain only cultural remains, such as the bones of butchered elephants and cutting tools. At Terra Amata in France, archaeologists have even discovered evidence of the oval-shaped huts (see Chapter 9).

What accounts for the evolution and rapid expansion of *Homo erectus*? One popular theory is that this species arose from a population of early *Homo* as natural selection acted to increase brain size and adjust the population's dietary and locomotor structure. The impetus was the need to exploit new food resources, particularly through big-game hunting. As an accomplished hunter and gatherer, *Homo erectus* had a diet that was quite varied. Why were new food resources needed? Perhaps because of a shortage of local resources or migration into less bountiful areas. Then, once the adaptations had evolved, *Homo erectus* became physically and culturally capable of exploiting a vast range of habitats.

About 300,000 years ago, *Homo erectus* began to disappear from the fossil record. Over the past 400,000 to 200,000 years, another species, *Homo sapiens*, started to evolve out of some population or populations of *Homo erectus*.

THE TRANSITION TO *HOMO SAPIENS*

The fossil record demonstrates that the transition to fully modern *Homo sapiens* occurred gradually, with a number of types sometimes coexisting in different parts of the world. Considering how stable *Homo erectus* was for so many years, why, where, and when did this transition take place? These questions remain a major anthropological mystery. However, we do know that by 200,000 years ago *Homo erectus* had disappeared and early *Homo sapiens* had become firmly established in the Old World.

Homo sapiens differs from *Homo erectus* in a number of ways. *Homo sapiens* has a larger brain, a more rounded and vaulted skull, and a more

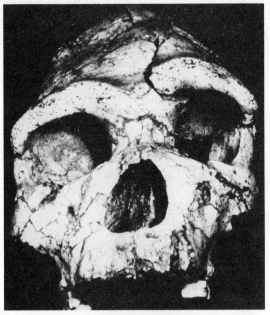
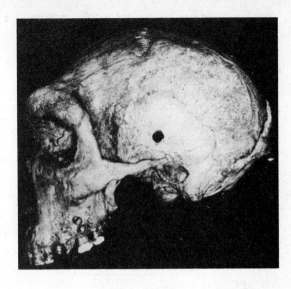
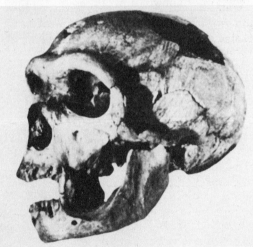
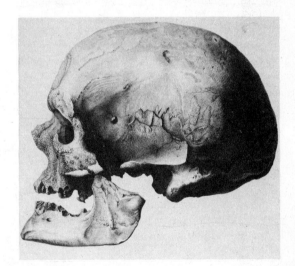

Transitional, early, Neandertal, and fully modern Homo sapiens sapiens *skulls.* (top left) *Face of transitional* Homo sapiens *skull from Arago, France. The face is heavier in structure than that of fully modern* Homo sapiens sapiens, *but more delicately structured than those of most forms of* Homo erectus. (top right) *Early* Homo sapiens *skull from Zambia, Africa. The cranium, while approaching a modern size and shape, is not as highly vaulted or as rounded as that of* Homo sapiens sapiens. (bottom left) *Classical Neandertal skull from La Chapelle-aux-Saints, France. Note the heavy brow ridges and lack of a chin.* (bottom right) Homo sapiens sapiens *skull: Cro-Magnon from Mole Grotte des Enfants, France. When compared with transitional forms, the face of* Homo sapiens sapiens *is flat and delicately structured, with a distinctive chin, a vertical forehead, and a cranium that is highly vaulted and rounded.*

delicate facial structure than *Homo erectus*. Most *Homo sapiens* have chins, while *Homo erectus* did not. In addition, sapient jaws and teeth are relatively small, and overall body build is generally more slender than that of the earlier form. Fully sapient forms have an average cranial capacity of 1,350 cm³, as do contemporary humans. This makes sense, since modern humans are a subspecies of *Homo sapiens* known as *Homo sapiens sapiens*. Thus, we have much in common with earlier forms of *Homo sapiens*.

Transitional forms—those intermediate between *Homo erectus* and *Homo sapiens*—have been found at a number of Old World sites (see Figure 6.4, p. 152). The oldest appear to be approximately 400,000 years old, although fossils 250,000 years old and younger are more common. At 1,150 cm³, the cranial capacity of these transitional forms is clearly larger than that of *Homo erectus*, yet smaller than that of most *Homo sapiens*. The skulls are less heavy than *Homo erectus* skulls, but heavier than those of later forms, as shown in the photos on page 163.

Archaeological evidence indicates that the transitional forms were fairly sophisticated tool-users and were capable of symbolic and ritualistic behaviors. The Swanscombe skull, for example, is associated with hundreds of beautifully crafted hand axes. The Ethiopian Bodo cranium, a very *erectus*-like skull with some distinctly sapient features, is also associated with some fascinating cultural evidence. Bodo was uncovered along with stone tools and cut-up hippopotamuses, at what appears to be a butchering site. In addition, the cut marks on some of the Bodo skulls suggest that scalping may have been practiced, possibly as part of a ritual. Unfortunately, the dating of Bodo is vague; age determinations of the evidence range from 700,000 to 125,000 years old.

We do not know if any of these fossils represent a direct ancestor of modern *Homo sapiens*. However, the material does clearly demonstrate that a transition had begun, at the latest by 400,000 years ago.

THE MYSTERY OF THE NEANDERTALS

The distinct set of sapient fossils commonly known as the *Neandertals* was discovered in Europe and the Near East (see Figure 6.4, p. 152). Estimated as having lived approximately 125,000 to 35,000 years ago, Neandertals (also spelled *Neanderthals*) evoke images of deformed and mentally deficient subhuman beings. In reality, the Neandertals looked much like you and me; moreover, they were quite clever, demonstrating great ingenuity in contending with a range of environments, including the harsh conditions of the last European ice ages. However, while not very different in any single way, there are a number of significant morphological differences between Neandertals and fully modern humans. When these differences are considered as a unit, Neandertals *do appear* to be a distinct group. Because of the differences and their sudden disap-

pearance about 35,000 years ago, the Neandertals continue to be one of the most intriguing mysteries of human paleontology. How should they be classified? What was their fate? What is their relationship to modern humans?

Neandertal Morphology

The distinctive Neandertal physical traits are expressed to different degrees among the finds. The most extreme, "classical" form was uncovered in Western Europe. Using this as the prototype, we can see that the overall appearance of the Neandertal skull is distinct, being long and low and bulging at the sides. By contrast, the cranium of modern *Homo sapiens sapiens* is rounder and more highly vaulted. The Neandertal skull also bulges at the lower back, a feature not apparent in modern forms. From the front, the Neandertal skull has a slightly sloped forehead, brow ridges (although less heavy than in *Homo erectus*), and little or no chin. The face is best described as big, long, and uniquely structured, with backward-sloping cheekbones and a large and prominent nose (see bottom left photo on p. 163). The Neandertal body was short, robust, muscular, and quite strong. Ranging from about $1,300^3$ to $1,750 \text{ cm}^3$, the Neandertal cranial capacity was slightly larger than that of modern humans. According to Shackley (1980), the larger capacity was not due to superior intellectual abilities, but to an expansion of neural areas associated with their very strong musculature.

Overall, Neandertals are similar to modern *Homo sapiens* in appearance, yet their differences are sufficiently great that they may warrant a different subspecies classification—that of *Homo sapiens neanderthalensis*. Support for a distinct subspecies comes from an almost complete Israeli Neandertal pelvis that is shaped differently from that of modern humans (Rak and Arensburg 1987). The pelvis indicates that Neandertals may have moved about somewhat differently from contemporary humans, a characteristic that underscores their uniqueness.

Neandertal Culture

Culturally, the Neandertals are closely associated with the **Mousterian tradition** (see Chapter 9). *Mousterian* refers to a group of five different technologies, continuing the trend of an increasing number of concurrent traditions. During this cultural period, technology was elaborated and refined, and within each tradition there was an increase in the variety and specialization of tools. For the most part, those who used the techniques of the Mousterian were Neandertals; however, some non-Neandertal populations also used them. Furthermore, some Neandertal populations used technologies that were more primitive; hence, to equate Neandertal with Mousterian, as is often done, is not justified.

The Neandertals were quite adaptable, with

different groups occupying a range of environments, from the icy tundras of Ice Age Europe to the more hospitable climates of the Near East. Although they were all accomplished hunters and gatherers, they exhibited some diversity of life-style. They lived in a variety of shelters, including caves and open-air encampments. In addition, their lives were rich in rituals and cultural traditions, as reflected by evidence of a cave bear cult and elaborate burials. A number of burial sites have been uncovered in Iraq, at Shanidar Cave. One body was posed with its legs tucked up to its chest, and pollen found in the soil indicates that the body may have been decorated with spring flowers.

The Neandertals were clearly an intelligent and skillful group of humans. Why, then, did they apparently disappear, and what was their fate?

The Fate of the Neandertals

While the Neandertals were living in Europe and the Near East, there were non-Neandertal humans in other parts of the world, including China, Java, Australia, and southern and eastern Africa. Some fossils found in Africa and eastern Asia exhibit a combination of Neandertal and modern traits, while a few fully modern specimens have been found in Africa. Such evidence, while sparse, suggests that the Neandertals were but one particular form of archaic *Homo sapiens* that coexisted with other, less specialized and more modern forms.

If the Neandertals were not the only form of archaic *Homo sapiens*, just how do they relate to modern humans? Two basic ideas have been proposed. Either they were a specialized sidebranch that became completely extinct or they were in some way ancestral to modern human beings. One long-established belief is that the Neandertals died out, outcompeted or killed off by better adapted contemporaries who moved in from other regions. Another speculation is that they were wiped out by a devastating epidemic. Or, perhaps, some Neandertals survived to interbreed and become assimilated into the more advanced population.

Recent theories are more strongly grounded in current science. For example, according to Trinkaus (1983), the first Neandertals descended from an early European form of *Homo sapiens*. Neandertals then migrated into other parts of Europe and western Asia at a time when other types of archaic *Homo sapiens* were living in Africa and eastern Asia. Noting a trend for a general reduction in the overall massiveness of the Neandertal skull and an increase in cranial capacity, Trinkaus suggested that this was due to interbreeding (thus, gene flow) between the Neandertal populations and with the more modern-looking African forms. Therefore, while the whole Neandertal population did not evolve into modern *Homo sapiens*, particular traits, such as the reduced massiveness of the skull, evolved within some groups and spread to other groups via gene flow.

Another recent model was presented by Jelinek (1982). According to this theory, a gradual transition from Neandertal to anatomically modern *Homo sapiens* occurred in the Near East. Jelinek's evidence primarily comes from a many-leveled site, Tabun Cave, located on Mount Carmel in Israel. This site has yielded a great wealth of fossil and archaeological evidence dating from about 130,000 to 50,000 years ago. The more than 44,000 artifacts, including those of Acheulean, Mousterian, and later tool traditions, demonstrate a continuity of change that can be viewed as "strong evidence for the presence of a single cultural tradition" (p. 1371). This suggests that different groups had not replaced one another, but that one population had inhabited Tabun through time. In addition, environmental shifts are associated with the changes in technology and morphology. For example, the warming and cooling of the earth's climate corresponds to changes in tool types, possibly reflecting responses to changes in food resources. However, the apparent continuity at Tabun does not negate the theory that the specialized western European form was an evolutionary dead end. The transition to fully modern *Homo sapiens sapiens* may have taken place only in the Near East within a less specialized population. Other scientists interpret the data differently. For example, a recently uncovered, 92,000-year-old, fully modern skull found in Israel lends support to the idea that the Neandertals migrated to the Near East from Europe *after* anatomically modern *Homo sapiens* had evolved in the region (Lewin 1988).

The mystery of the Neandertals is a matter of continuing debate. There is, however, a growing body of evidence regarding the origin of fully modern *Homo sapiens sapiens*. This evidence includes research conducted using a fascinating new molecular approach known as mitochondrial DNA, which we will come to shortly.

HOMO SAPIENS SAPIENS: THE APPEARANCE OF ANATOMICALLY MODERN HUMANS

By 40,000 years ago, anatomically modern humans, *Homo sapiens sapiens*, had become well established in the Old World. Compared with the Neandertals, the modern finds have slender bodies, vertical foreheads, and highly vaulted, rounded craniums. The face of *Homo sapiens sapiens* is flat and delicately structured; it has a chin and little or no brow ridge (see bottom right photo on p. 163). The cranial capacity of these fully modern skulls averages 1,350 cm^3—about the same or slightly smaller than that of the Neandertals.

The best known early group of anatomically modern humans, dating from about 35,000 to 40,000 years ago, is *Cro-Magnon*. While Cro-Magnon was discovered in France, slightly different forms have been uncovered elsewhere in Europe as well as in Africa, Asia, and Australia (see Figure 6.4, p. 152). The widespread sites reflect the great geographical and cultural diversity of early modern humans. In fact, humans may have begun to populate the New World (the American continents) as early as 40,000 years ago.

The cultures of early *Homo sapiens sapiens* are often labeled "Upper Paleolithic." The Upper Paleolithic encompasses a broad range of sophisticated Stone Age technologies, including at least five cultural types in Europe alone. For example, Cro-Magnon is identified with the **Aurignacian tradition**. The Aurignacian made use of a range of raw materials including bone, antler, and stone, and was characterized by a wide variety of tools. The Cro-Magnons also produced beautiful artwork, including refined cave paintings and pieces of sculpture. Such artwork may have played a role in their rituals (see Chapter 9).

The three major models for the origin of modern *Homo sapiens* are presented in Figure 6.8 (Lewin 1987; Tierney 1988). The Candelabra model (a) contends that there were gradual, multiple origins of modern humans, with regional groups of *Homo erectus* independently evolving into *Homo sapiens sapiens*. Thus, each regional modern group reflects traits of its *Homo erectus* ancestor. In this view, the last link among the regional groups was very ancient, possibly 1 million years old. Although the model was posed in the 1960s, its supporters have not yet found evidence to clearly support such a local continuity in form. In addition, important similarities among *erectus* finds from different areas would also argue against this model.

Cro-Magnon cave painting of a bison and a wild boar from Altamira, Spain.

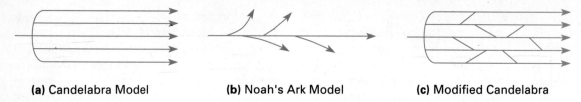

(a) Candelabra Model   **(b)** Noah's Ark Model   **(c)** Modified Candelabra

FIGURE 6.8

Models for the origin of *Homo sapiens sapiens.*

The Noah's Ark model (b) proposes a single origin of modern *Homo sapiens sapiens* in one area of the world. An extensive migration of the anatomically modern form then occurred, modern humans eventually replacing the more primitive local populations in the new regions. This model holds that contemporary regional populations are recently evolved, and that all are descended from the same ancestral group of *Homo sapiens sapiens*. Although the model nicely explains the similarities found among modern populations, it does not explain the continuities that exist between regional fossils and regional modern forms.

While the first two models represent extreme views regarding the origin of modern human populations, the Modified Candelabra model (c) is one of several less extreme approaches. This model contends that regional evolution took place, but that gene flow via migrations and interbreeding also occurred among the different populations. This explains both the regional continuities through time and those that exist among different local populations.

Which of these models best explains the origin of modern *Homo sapiens sapiens*? Much of the rapidly growing body of evidence supports an out-of-Africa, single-origin theory. For example, there are some recently uncovered and very modern-looking southern African fossils that date from about 115,000 to 80,000 years ago. Also, the Israeli remains of the 92,000-year-old modern human support the ancientness of modern *Homo sapiens* and the exclusion of the Neandertals from

our direct ancestry. Further support comes from molecular biology, including mitochondrial DNA research.

Mitochondrial DNA and the Mother of Us All

The DNA that provides an organism's genetic blueprint is contained within the nucleus of cells. However, other cellular structures, the mitochondria, contain their own unique set of DNA. Found in multicellular life-forms, including humans (not in single-celled organisms, such as bacteria), mitochondria are the "power plants" of a cell, designed for extracting energy from food and water. Biologists believe that mitochondria were originally free-living bacteria that somehow, early in the history of life, became absorbed by another kind of cell, possibly an amoeba-like form that ingested an undigestable bacteria species. As the host cell and the mitochondria established a symbiotic relationship (one in which both members benefited), the mitochondria eventually took on their present function. Having once been an independent organism, the absorbed cell had its own set of DNA. Mitochondria have maintained this independent set of genes; thus, they have a distinctive type of DNA known as **mitochondrial DNA**, or mtDNA for short.

MtDNA is passed on separately from nuclear DNA during sexual reproduction. It is structurally much less complex than nuclear DNA, having about 16,000 base pairs rather than several hundred million pairs. MtDNA is therefore easier to decode than nuclear DNA. Also, mtDNA is passed on only from mother to child, probably because only the nucleus of a sperm (and not its mitochondria) survives the fertilizing of the ovum. Therefore, any change in the composition of mtDNA from mother to offspring is due to mutation rather than to recombination. In addition, mtDNA appears to be less protected than nuclear DNA; hence, it is more susceptible to mutagens found in the environment. This apparently causes mutations to take place at the rate of 2 to 4 percent every million years—5 to 10 times faster than in nuclear DNA.

The analysis of mtDNA may prove to be an important new tool in understanding our evolutionary history. Researchers in this field contend that mtDNA provides a fast-ticking molecular clock that can reveal extremely detailed, maternally based relationships among modern populations.

One research group, based at the University of California at Berkeley, is conducting mtDNA studies that may throw considerable light on the origin of *Homo sapiens sapiens* (Cann 1987). The group obtained mtDNA from the placentas of children of African, Asian, European, Australian, and New Guinean descent. As a result, 133 distinct types of mtDNA were identified. Using a computer, the researchers mapped out lines of descent based on mtDNA similarities.

The results of these efforts are compelling. The mtDNA tree is shown to have two main branches that are joined at the base by one female—a mitochondrial "Eve"—who lived in Africa some 200,000 years ago. The name Eve is misleading, for there were many other females around, both before and during her existence. However, it was *her* mtDNA that was passed on, female to female, to all humans of today, with the only changes in composition due to the ticking of the mutational clock. One branch, probably the one established some 200,000 years ago, leads only to some Africans. The other branch apparently diverged from the first, and includes the other Africans and all other people. The divergence possibly represents the migration of groups out of a centralized African site into other parts of the world. The Berkeley researchers contend that there was little or no interbreeding among regional popu-

lations, and that racial groups do not appear as distinct mtDNA types. Thus, present-day humans represent a closely related biological family, with regional variations based on recent, and probably adaptational, events.

The value of such mtDNA studies has yet to be fully proven. Even the researchers note that the work has just begun. However, mtDNA does appear to provide a faster, simpler molecular clock with which to illuminate the fossil record. When research from mtDNA and other genetic studies is considered along with findings from the fossil record, the evidence favors a single African origin of modern *Homo sapiens*.

Combining the Fossil and Genetic Evidence

Contemporary anthropologists often seek to answer important questions by combining evidence from different research areas. For example, Stringer and Andrews (1988) used genetic and fossil data to investigate the origin of modern humans. Their focus was on two models: the Noah's Ark model, with Africa as the site of a recent, single origin, and a multiregional-origins model, with gene flow occurring among populations (earlier referred to as the "Modified Candelabra" model).

According to Stringer and Andrews, the evidence strongly supports the African-origin model (Noah's Ark). Molecular studies, for example, demonstrate that there is a very low level of protein variation among contemporary human populations, indicating that they recently descended from the same population. The mitochondrial DNA studies also suggest that the divergence was a fairly recent event. Nuclear DNA studies tend to agree with the mtDNA findings and argue against the role of gene flow in the origin of modern human populations.

Although sparse, the fossil record also supports the African-origin model. For example, paleontologists have not found evidence of the gradual transition of local populations in all regions. In fact, there are often greater similarities among populations coming from different geographic regions than there are within localized populations through time. Also, characteristics first seen in Africa arise suddenly with the appearance of *Homo sapiens sapiens* in other regions. This suggests that the modern characteristics had not spread among various populations prior to this time, and that the late forms had migrated to these areas from one parent population. In short, the earliest fossils of *Homo sapiens sapiens* apparently come from sub-Saharan Africa, with the next earliest from the Near East, as attested to by the 92,000-year-old Israelite. Europe appears to be the last place to have been colonized by *Homo sapiens sapiens*, as demonstrated by the persistence of the Neandertals and the relatively late appearance of anatomically modern humans some 40,000 years ago.

What about the Neandertals? Whereas Trin-

kaus (1983) argues for the importance of gene flow, Stringer and Andrews contend that very little, if any, gene flow took place between the more primitive local populations and modern *Homo sapiens*. Jelinek's (1982) contention of a gradual, Near Eastern transition from Neandertals to moderns is also disputed, especially in light of the genetic evidence and that of the 92,000-year-old modern fossil.

Although Stringer and Andrews provide an intriguing argument in favor of a recent and single African origin, many questions are as yet unanswered. Precisely when, where, and why did modern humans originate? It could be that the answers will be found as data continue to accumulate, and as geneticists and paleontologists improve on their exchange of ideas and information.

THE DIVERSITY OF MODERN HUMANKIND

All modern humans are physically and genetically very much the same. Even so, physical diversity is readily apparent in body types, pigmentation, hair textures, and the like. Natural selection may account for some of these differences because regional populations could have adapted to local conditions. Random evolutionary processes may account for other differences. The study of the physical diversity of humankind is, therefore, an important part of anthropology and the focus of the next chapter.

The most astounding aspect of the diversity of modern humankind is the great variety of human cultural adaptations. Cultural mechanisms have partly circumvented the slow process of human biological evolution by allowing groups to adapt rapidly to a broad range of environments. Cultural evolution and its manifestations in today's world are the focus of much of the remainder of this text.

SUMMARY

Sometime between 8 to 4 million years ago, in response to life on the savannahs of Africa, early hominids began to evolve an adaptation with three interacting components: bipedalism, a generalized dentition associated with an omnivorous diet, and an expanded brain associated with

higher mental processes and cultural behavior. These components did not arise full-blown, but continued to develop over the course of human evolution.

The most controversial ideas regarding human evolution involve specific scenarios to explain why hominids originated. An alternative approach centers on a general theme that reflects the uniqueness of the human adaptation: the striking degree of plasticity in how humans contend with their environment. Human plasticity is reflected in all three components of the human adaptation, particularly in the human brain, which allows individuals to respond rapidly to unique and complicated sets of problems.

The first hominids belonged to the genus *Australopithecus*. Australopithecines were smaller than *Homo* and had more primitive morphology and much smaller brains. Four species of australopithecines, dating from approximately 1.5 to 4 million years ago, have been discovered in Africa. Another set of early hominids, belonging to the genus *Homo*, have been uncovered in eastern Africa, and date from 1 to 2 million years ago. According to one popular scheme, the oldest australopithecine species, *Australopithecus afarensis*, was ancestral to both the later australopithecines, who represent an extinct, specialized branch, and to *Homo*.

From about 1.5 million to 300,000 years ago, the Old World was inhabited by a widely distributed and physically diverse hominid, *Homo erectus*. Taller, larger-brained, and more culturally complex than earlier hominids, *Homo erectus* appears to be both physically and culturally intermediate between earlier and later forms of humans. About 300,000 years ago, *Homo erectus* began to disappear and another species, *Homo sapiens*, began to evolve out of some population or populations of *Homo erectus*.

A distinct set of sapient fossils known as the Neandertals date from about 125,000 to 35,000 years ago. While not very different in any single way, Neandertals differ enough from fully modern humans to warrant their classification as a distinct subspecies. Some scientists contend that the Neandertals represent an extinct sidebranch; others contend that they are in some way ancestral to modern humans.

By 40,000 years ago, anatomically modern humans, *Homo sapiens sapiens*, had become well established in the Old World. Exactly when, where, and how modern humans arose is an important anthropological question. Evidence most strongly supports an out-of-Africa, single-origin theory. Besides paleontological evidence, further support comes from molecular biology, including mitochondrial DNA research.

SUGGESTED READINGS

Cann, Rebecca L. 1987. In search of Eve. *The Sciences* 27 (5):30–37. (Mitochondrial DNA)

Day, Michael H. 1986. *Guide to Fossil Man.* Chicago: University of Chicago Press.

Johanson, Donald, and Edey Maitland. 1981. *Lucy: The Beginnings of Humankind.* New York: E.P. Dutton.

Lanpo, Jia, and Huang Weiwen. 1990. *The Story of Peking Man.* New York: Oxford University Press.

Leakey, Richard E. 1981. *The Making of Mankind.* New York: E.P. Dutton.

Smith, Frank H., and Frank Spencer, eds. 1984. *The Origins of Modern Humans.* New York: Alan R. Liss.

Tanner, Nancy Makepeace. 1981. *On Becoming Human.* Cambridge: Cambridge University Press.

Trinkaus, Erik. 1983. *The Shanidar Neandertals.* New York: Academic Press.

Wolpoff, Milford. 1980. *Paleoanthropology.* New York: Alfred A. Knopf.

Identifying American War Dead from Southeast Asia

Robert B. Pickering

Robert B. Pickering served as Physical Anthropologist at the U.S. Army Central Identification Laboratory in Thailand in 1975–76. His responsibilities included identifying human remains resulting from the Vietnam War and from World War II action in the Pacific Islands. Since that time, Dr. Pickering has served as an anthropological consultant to medical examiners and coroners. He also lectures to law-enforcement agencies on forensic anthropology and recovery techniques. Dr. Pickering currently heads the Department of Anthropology at the Denver Museum of Natural History.

Forensic anthropology is the identification of human remains for medical and legal purposes (see Chapter 23). Beyond that bland description lies an incredibly interesting, complex, and socially sensitive field of study. Analyzing human remains is not like studying cultural artifacts. While the same kind of scientific rigor must be applied, these bones represent the remains of recently deceased human beings. Although no longer alive, these people have living relatives and a persona—an identity—that still exists. Scientists can describe human remains with sensitivity to the persona, but to understand the real significance of their endeavor, they must be aware of the broader social context.

A forensic anthropologist's role in an investigation is to determine as many physical characteristics as possible about the deceased; for example, the individual's age, sex, and height. Also to be determined is the nature of the changes in the body—that is, which changes occurred while the person was alive, which changes occurred around the time of death (useful in establishing the cause of death), and which changes occurred after death.

In 1975–76, I was the physical (forensic) anthropologist for the U.S. Army Central Identification Laboratory (CIL) based in Thailand. The CIL's mission was to recover and identify American personnel killed as a result of the Vietnam War. Military involvement in Southeast Asia was unpopular with many Americans. Although I was criticized by some colleagues for choosing to work for the U.S. military, I felt that identifying the war dead was a humanitarian rather than a political act. By using my scientific training to identify remains, I could alleviate some of the suffering of families who had lost their loved ones.

Today, the CIL is located in Hawaii. Since the late 1980s, the staff has been busier than at any other period of time since the Korean War. Now that hostilities have ceased, American anthropologists and military recovery teams are working with their Vietnamese, Laotian, and Cambodian counterparts to locate and recover additional remains from Southeast Asia. CIL anthropologists are also called on for special-identification assignments, such as airplane crashes or explosions on military bases. Teams have even ventured into the highlands of New Guinea to recover the remains of World War II American fliers.

Robert Pickering, forensic anthropologist, investigates the scene of a crime.

Forensic cases in a military setting have a number of distinct aspects. Most of the remains belong to young males between the ages of 19 and 30 years, few of whom died of natural causes. Evidence of the trauma that caused the death is usually obvious—trauma being the generic, polite term for what happens when a person is hit by a grenade or blown apart by a mine. While identifying massive trauma can be easy, it is not always so simple to reconstruct the details of incidents such as these.

All forensic cases have certain things in common. For example, the data associated with these cases consist of human remains, personal effects, and the context within which the remains are found. Each case is unique with respect to the completeness of the remains and the extent to which they have been modified

either by natural causes or by intentional human intervention. The remains are not always complete, clean, articulated skeletons. Sometimes a body may be represented only by a few bones; moreover, the bones may have been drastically altered by accidental or intentional burning or breaking.

During the Vietnam War, 55,000 American military personnel were listed as killed in action (KIA) or as missing in action (MIA). The bodies of most of those killed were immediately recovered and identified by standard methods of fingerprinting and visual comparison with photographs. However, only skeletons were available in the cases of some KIAs and in those of the MIAs. These are the subjects on which the forensic anthropologist focuses. The anthropologist must obtain two types of data to identify such remains: physical evidence from the remains and medical/dental records that are used to match the gathered information.

Sometimes it is possible to determine many things about a set of remains and still not be able to establish identity. For example, in one CIL case in which the skeleton was nearly complete, researchers determined the individual's sex, his age within a range of four years, and his height within three inches. The CIL also estimated the person's build and from skull characteristics, identified him as Caucasoid. From the dentition, it was clear that the person's dental hygiene had been poor, but that he had visited the dentist frequently to have cavities filled. He also had lost a tooth that had been replaced by a dental appliance, and he had stains on his teeth indicating that he had been a habitual smoker. Sometime during the person's life, he had broken his nose and it had healed irregularly. Probable cause of death was determined from metal pellets found embedded in the bone of the upper arm. The location where the body was found was accurately pinpointed, as well as the general time of death. Even though all these things were determined with a high degree of accuracy, the person remained unidentified. Why? Although the anthropological description was thorough, no medical records in the extensive Armed Services system conclusively matched the individual's characteristics. This could be explained in a number of ways. For one, the person may not have been part of the American military; he could have been a civilian or from another country. If so, his records would not have existed in the American military system. Where to go from there in seeking records in such a case is problematic.

Another case concerns a small group of American soldiers who had died while they were prisoners of war. Their skeletons, in identical small wooden boxes, were returned to American representatives around Christmas of 1975. All of the bones were in good states of preservation and had been deodorized. Each box was labeled with a person's name, indicating that the North Vietnamese had identified the remains. Yet, to ensure accurate identifications, the CIL staff conducted complete examinations. This proved to be an important step. While the Vietnamese had the correct names, they had mislabeled two of the boxes.

Working with human remains is a sensitive field in virtually all cultures. The study of mortuary behavior is the anthropological specialty that focuses on how the dead are treated and the significance of that treatment to the living. There is no better example of this important bond between the living and the dead in American society than the identification of deceased military personnel.

7 Why Do People Differ? Contemporary Human Biological Diversity

An early morning street scene in an American city illustrates the diversity of human physical types.

People are biologically different. We differ in how we look and in how our bodies respond to environmental stresses, such as severe temperatures, too much sunlight, and disease. At the same time, people from the same geographic area (or whose ancestors came from that area) tend to be somewhat similar in appearance. For example, Scandinavians are often blond and fair-skinned, while many people from southern Italy have medium complexions that tan well. Bi- ological anthropologists are concerned with explaining the patterns of contemporary human biological diversity; in this endeavor, the study of the past is a key to understanding the present.

Human biological diversity can be approached in two ways: first, as the outcome of human evolution and, second, as an ongoing process, as humans continue to adapt to environmental factors. Within these contexts, anthropologists seek to explain the diversity. Are the differences of any evolutionary significance? How should human populations be described and classified? In exploring such questions, scientists examine the biological basis of human variability, including the complex interrelationships between genes, environment, and traits, and the nature of growth and development. In their efforts to explain the genetic and evolutionary implications of the diversity, anthropologists are particularly concerned with identifying the patterns by which specific traits vary among groups.

The study of human biological diversity has long focused on grouping humans on the basis of biological traits. This focus reflects the scientific objective of classifying phenomena into orderly categories—a difficult objective when dealing with humans. In addition, attempts to pigeon-hole humankind have often impinged on crucial biological, social, and political issues. One of the most important of these issues—one that affects humans on a global scale—involves the concept of race. First posed as a biological system of classification, the term **race** has taken on meanings well beyond those originally intended, to the point where it is no longer useful in the study of human biological diversity. Thus, anthropologists are concerned with finding scientifically valid alternatives for describing and classifying human populations—alternatives that will permit us to examine our differences without losing sight of the fact that we are all basically the same.

GENES, ENVIRONMENT, AND TRAITS

The biological diversity of humankind is, in part, based on the inheritance and development of specific traits. This brings us back to the complicated relationship between genotypes, the environment, and phenotypes. In Chapter 2, we noted that a _genotype_ is an individual's genetic makeup, while a _phenotype_ is the observable expression of a particular trait, such as eye color, height, or blood type. The environment can profoundly affect both genotypes and phenotypes. For example, environmental factors (including culture) may shape genotypes by inducing mutations or by influencing natural selection. Phenotypically, environmental factors may interact with an individual's genes during the development of a trait.

Unfortunately, many people persist in viewing the relationship between genes, the environment, and traits (especially behavioral ones) in an outdated, simplistic way. According to the "nature versus nurture" school of thought, either a trait's form is dictated by genetic factors (nature) or it is purely the result of environmental influences, such as socialization (nurture). However, scientists are now aware that the issue is much more complex. A trait's expression within an individual is seldom the result of an either/or situation; instead, genotype and environment _interact_ during the development of a phenotypic trait. The degree to which genotype and environment influence a trait's development varies with the trait (see Figure 7.1).

In simple terms, one can think of an individual's genotype as parameters within which a particular trait can develop. Within these boundaries the exact course of development is influenced by environmental factors. The broadness of the boundaries, and thus the degree of environmental influence, varies from trait to trait. The more restrictive the genetic substrates, the less of a role the environment can play. For example, ABO blood type is determined by an individual's genotype with no room for environmental intervention. On the other hand, a person's height is influenced by environmental factors such as diet and disease, but height still

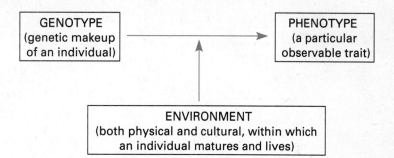

FIGURE 7.1
The relationship between genotype, environment, and phenotype.

develops within the boundaries set up by one's genetic constitution.

A related concept is that of simple versus complex traits. A **simple trait** is determined by just one gene pair (at one locus). On the other hand, a **complex trait** is controlled by a number of interacting gene pairs. Sickle cell is an example of a simple trait because one gene pair determines the presence or absence of the disorder. Skin color is an example of a complex trait, involving as many as six different gene pairs.

The more genetically complex a trait, the greater the number of genes that interact in its development. This increases the number of possible outcomes for how the trait can be expressed. Thus, the more complex the trait, the greater the environmental influence on its development. With the ABO blood type, there is no leeway to accommodate environmental action. However, with the more genetically complex trait of height, nutrition, disease, and physical environment can strongly affect how tall an adult will be (see Figure 7.2).

The concept of simple and complex traits applies to individuals. When individuals are grouped together in populations, this phenomenon is reflected by distributional patterns of traits. A simple trait is represented within a population by discrete, distinct, and *discontinuous* categories. For example, ABO blood type is determined by one pair of genes that come in three different forms (alleles): A and B (codominant) and O (recessive). The phenotypes are limited to A-, B-, AB-, or O-type blood. Therefore, a population can be described as to the specific percentages of blood types:

Population 1: 25% A 20% B 10% AB 45% O
Population 2: 35% A 25% B 15% AB 25% O

By contrast, a complex trait can be expressed in many ways, making it difficult to classify into nice, discrete categories. Complex traits thus have *continuous* distributions in large populations, expressed as statistical curves. This is the case for a trait such as height, where differences can be described using fractions of an inch (see Figure 7.3).

FIGURE 7.2
Continuum of simple and complex traits.

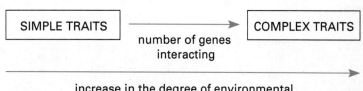

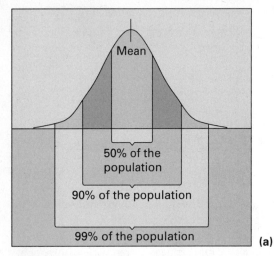

(a)

FIGURE 7.3
Continuous distribution of the complex trait of height. (a) Within a large population, the distribution of the height of individuals is expressed by a bell-shaped curve rather than by discrete categories. The majority of the population concentrates around the mean, with few individuals expressing an extreme form of the trait (very tall or very short). (b) A group of college students arranged according to height demonstrates the same bell-shaped curve.

(b)

POLYMORPHISMS AND DIFFERENCES AMONG HUMAN GROUPS

Genetic polymorphism refers to the presence in a population of two or more forms of a gene (alleles) at a particular gene site. Within individuals, a polymorphic trait may be homozygotic (both genes in a pair being the same) or heterozygotic (the two genes being different) (see Chapter 2). The ABO blood group is polymorphic because at least three alleles are found at the ABO locus.

Polymorphisms are an important source of genetic variability because they provide a population with genetic alternatives. These alternatives can be selected during natural selection. Polymorphisms are also an important tool in describing the genetic diversity of human populations inasmuch as groups can be distinguished according to allelic frequencies. For example, human populations differ in their proportion of ABO-blood-group alleles. The O allele, for instance, is present at an extremely high frequency—approximately 100 percent—in native South American populations. But in Asia, the frequency of the O allele is often as low as 40 percent.

What causes populations to differ in polymorphic traits? The answer depends on the populations and the traits in question. In some cases, such as that of the sickle cell trait, the differences may be due to natural selection acting under different environmental conditions. In other cases, the differences may be caused by random processes, such as genetic drift. This is particularly so in cases where polymorphisms exist even though one alternative appears to be as good as another; for example, in the case of the Diego blood group (a human blood factor associated with Asians and Native Americans). Whatever the cause, modern populational differences in polymorphic traits demonstrate that biological evolution continues its course in the present much as it did in the past.

MICROEVOLUTION IN MODERN POPULATIONS

In Chapter 2, we briefly discussed population genetics, the complex statistical study of how populations genetically change from generation to generation. One concern of population geneticists is to understand the microevolutionary processes that underlie human regional differences. The Hardy-Weinberg law is an important tool in this endeavor, for it enables mathematical comparisons between a real population and a nonevolving "ideal." If a population deviates from predictions, scientists then analyze such ongoing evolutionary factors as natural selection, mutation, random genetic drift, gene flow, and nonrandom mating.

Many of the biological differences that exist among human populations are apparently due to the process of adaptation occurring at a local level. These local adaptations include such traits as body shape and size, blood composition, and skin color. However, scientists have had a difficult time clearly demonstrating a relationship between adaptation and specific human traits. Sickle cell is one of the best understood (yet still somewhat controversial) cases of natural selection locally acting on a human polymorphism.

According to Meindl (1987), cystic fibrosis is another disease that reflects a regional distribution of a polymorphism. Cystic fibrosis is a debilitating and deadly genetically based disease that affects the body's mucus-producing glands, leading to the deterioration of the pancreas and the blockage of the lungs' air tubes. It occurs when an individual inherits a recessive allele from both parents, causing the individual to produce too much of a particular enzyme. This enzyme is also important in the body's defense against some microorganisms, including the one inducing the lung disease tuberculosis. Meindl examined how cystic fibrosis was distributed in present-day human populations and compared the pattern with the historical distribution of tuberculosis. He noted that cystic fibrosis was most common in populations, particularly European, in which tuberculosis had been a major problem in the past. As is seen with sickle cell, people who are heterozygotic for the cystic fibrosis allele apparently have an advantage over those with either homozygotic form. This is because they do not have cystic fibrosis, but the heterozygotic individuals *do* have an increased resistance to tuberculosis. Thus, Meindl argues that natural selection, acting in favor of the heterozygote, accounts for populational differences both in the frequency of the gene and in the occurrence of cystic fibrosis.

Microevolution in modern populations is also studied as an ongoing process within a particular population. In one in-depth study, Baker, Hanna, and Baker (1986) describe how contact with Western society is rapidly bringing about major biological and cultural changes in the Sa-

moans of the South Pacific. They contend that many of the changes, including increased body weight, a rise in fat content in the blood, and a rise in blood-pressure levels, reflect responses to environmental factors that do not drastically influence the gene pool. However, it will be interesting to see whether such changes, including a modestly reduced level of fertility, will eventually affect the population's genetic composition.

GROWTH AND DEVELOPMENT

To more fully understand how genes and environment interact to form phenotypes, we also need to understand the processes by which a human matures. The field of growth and development focuses on the degree to which heredity and environment influence an individual's adult form. Part of this concern is with *physiological plasticity*—the body's ability to adjust to environmental demands during development. Plasticity accounts for certain differences that exist among individuals and human groups. Its effects are greatest when growing individuals experience severe environmental stress, such as that from malnutrition or parasitic diseases. Physiological plasticity may repress growth as a means of conserving resources in times of deprivation (Stini 1979).

Plasticity warrants serious consideration in the study of how and why human populations are biologically different. Are the differences genetic adaptations that would develop in individuals no matter what the environment? Or do they reflect developmental plasticity acting in response to specific environmental stresses? The complexity of this issue is illustrated by a summary of Japanese studies of growth and development (K. Kimura 1984). Data on various groups (e.g., Japanese, Japanese Americans, Japanese-American hybrids, children of Okinawa) indicate that early in life Japanese grow more slowly than do Americans and Europeans. The rate of the Japanese children's growth then accelerates, so that

they reach maturity at approximately the same age as the other groups. Apparently, the prepuberty patterns of growth reflect plasticity in response to environmental factors, particularly nutritional ones; then, at adolescence, the hereditary influences become the significant factor. Thus, differences in growth may be attributable to *both* genes and environment.

Human growth and development is an extremely complex process. Not only are elements of the physical environment important, but many behavioral and cultural factors also come into play. For example, "a multitude of social, cultural, economic, and biologic factors influence the ways in which mothers and other caretakers feed and care for youngsters and the manner in which individual children respond" (Ryan and Martorell 1987, 447).

Some anthropologists use archaeological and paleontological data to study the effects of heredity and environment on development. For example, Buikstra (1976) examined regional patterns of biological variability using data from prehistoric Indian burial sites in the lower Illinois River Valley. She found an apparent association between increased stature and high social status, reflected in the tallest males being buried in the "least accessible tracts of the burial program" (p. 60). Apparently, their burials took more time and energy than those of others in the society. Analyzing the archaeological and paleontological evidence and comparing the prehistoric society with similar contemporary cultures where high-status individuals have better access to food resources, Buikstra concluded that the increased stature of the higher status males "may most reasonably be explained in terms of differential dietary access to nutrients during critical growth periods" (ibid.).

The study of growth and development has important practical applications, particularly to designers of health-related programs meant to aid the world's poor (see Chapter 23). It is essential that policy-makers in this area understand human developmental biology, and especially the role of environmental stress.

Anthropological studies of growth and development examine the processes by which people mature, reproduce, and die from an evolutionary and cross-cultural perspective. At first, the studies were descriptive, detailing maturation sequences and establishing standardized tables for the physical development of children. More recent studies focus on *how* growth takes place, ad-

An anthropological study of growth and development examined the adaptive significance of small body size in children who grew up with protein-energy deficiency in rural Mexico (above) and coastal Papua New Guinea (right).

dressing such questions as why human groups (including socioeconomic classes within the same cultures) differ in body-fat distribution, weight, skeletal growth, height, and the like. For example, cross-cultural studies have demonstrated a relationship between small stature, insufficient diet, and poor hygiene (leading to parasite infestations). As a result, "anthropologists could no longer assume that the small people of the world were simply genetically small" (Garn 1981, 525).

Another study examined the adaptive significance of small body size in children from rural Mexico and coastal Papua New Guinea who grew up with chronic protein-energy deficiency (Malina et al. 1987). The children's size, strength, and motor performance were measured against a reference population of well-nourished children from Philadelphia. Both the Mexican and the New Guinean children were smaller and weaker than the well-nourished group. However, when relative body size was accounted for, all three groups exhibited similar strength, yet varied in other measures. The researchers concluded that the situation was complex—that subtle cultural factors, as well as dietary ones, came into play during a child's development. They left the ques-

tion of the adaptive significance of small body size unresolved, noting that it varied among populations and with the type of task. For example, when adjusted for body size, the running and jumping performance (measures of explosive strength or power) was better in the New Guinean children than in those from Mexico or Philadelphia. This could be explained, in part, by selection favoring small size so as to reduce energy demands on the body. Cultural factors may also provide an explanation: children from New Guinea grow up playing sports, handling outrigger canoes, and swimming—all activities that increase explosive strength. On the other hand, grip strength was best in the well-fed group from Philadelphia—an expected outcome, since muscle mass directly correlates with the ability to apply force. Thus, small body size would not be adaptive in the case of this task.

Genes, hormones, environment, and sociocultural factors all influence the growth and development of individual humans. It follows, then, that the diversity of human populations can be attributed to the complicated interaction of such factors.

DIVERSE HUMAN TRAITS

Human biological differences vary according to the traits and populations in question. The hierarchy of phenotypic traits presented in Figure 7.4 is organized to reflect the complex relationship between genes and the environment in terms of genetic differences and developmental plasticity as causative factors. Stated in the form of a question, When differences among populations are associated with specific environmental stresses, are the differences due to natural selection acting on a localized level or to plasticity acting during an individual's growth?

Random processes may be responsible for populational differences. This is apparently the case among people living on the Aland Islands of Finland (Jorde et al. 1982; Mielke et al. 1982).

Aland, located in the Baltic Sea, is composed of approximately 6,000 islands. Because of geographical isolation caused by water barriers, the inhabitants of an island tend to marry among themselves. The more isolated the island, the higher the degree of intermarriage. The outer islands are the most isolated; to reach them entails hazardous sea travel. Researchers note that random processes are important microevolutionary forces in the Aland outer islands: "The effective population sizes of the outer island parishes are much smaller than those of the Main Island parishes. As a result, genetic drift, and hence genetic divergence, has been greater in the outer islands" (Jorde et al., 1982, 362).

Returning to the hierarchy of Figure 7.4, we see

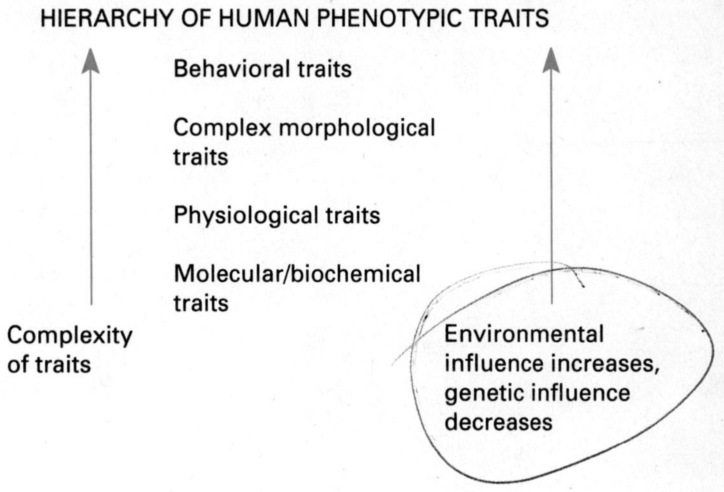

HIERARCHY OF HUMAN PHENOTYPIC TRAITS

Behavioral traits

Complex morphological
traits

Physiological traits

Molecular/biochemical
traits

Complexity
of traits

Environmental
influence increases,
genetic influence
decreases

FIGURE 7.4
Hierarchy of human phenotypic traits.

that the most genetically simple cases are at the lower levels. The simple traits are strongly dictated by genetic factors, leaving little room for the environment to act. As we move up the hierarchy, the genetic complexity of the traits increases, as does the degree of environmental influence.

At this point, it would be useful to clarify two concepts that are essential to the topics yet to be discussed in this chapter. The first concept is that of environmental stresses; the second, that of biological clines.

Environmental Stresses

Environmental stresses can be grouped into five major categories:

1. *Temperature and humidity* (for example, extremely cold climates, as in the arctic, or the hot and humid conditions in tropical rain forests).
2. *Solar radiation* (for example, ultraviolet rays that can cause skin cancer).
3. *Altitude* (for example, the low levels of oxygen found at high elevations).
4. *Nutrition* (for example, the deprivation of important nutrients or intolerance for certain nutrients).
5. *Disease* (for example, parasitic infestations, malaria, typhus, tuberculosis).

In the discussions that follow, we will consider the various relationships between specific traits and specific environmental stresses.

Biological Clines

Biological clines are graphic representations of how particular biological traits gradually vary over geographical space. Scientists use biological clines to visualize how the frequency of the alleles of a trait, or the trait itself, varies geographically. This helps them determine whether the distribution of a trait correlates with particular environmental stresses. For example, biological clines point out that the sickle cell allele is concentrated in tropical areas and correlates with the distribution of malaria (see Figure 7.5). However, clines are simply descriptive. Scientists must interpret whether the distribution of a trait has any adaptive significance. For example, a cline may represent natural selection at work, but it may also reflect patterns of gene flow via migration (Birdsell 1975). Whatever the source, clinal distributions provide insight into human biological diversity. An important case in point is that of the ABO blood group.

Molecular/Biochemical Traits

The genetically simplest traits are those at the molecular or biochemical level. Included in this

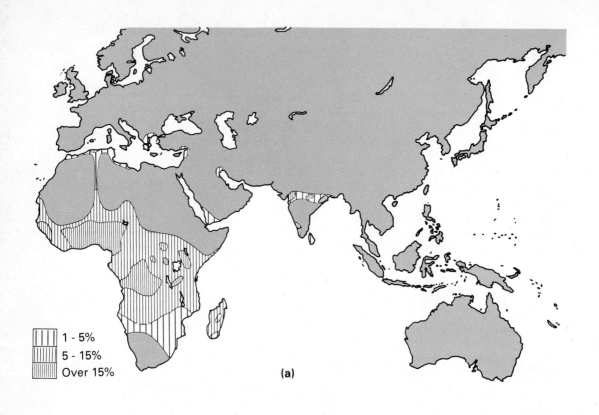

⊞	1 - 5%
⊞	5 - 15%
⊞	Over 15%

(a)

(b)

category are enzymes and components of the blood. These traits are largely determined by an individual's genetic code and are often regulated by just one gene site. However, while there is little environmental influence in how such traits develop within individuals, environmental factors are often important in the *evolution* of a molecular trait; that is, one molecular trait may be more adaptive under certain conditions than another. In this manner, environmental factors can bring about adaptive differences in a trait's expression among human populations. Environmental factors thus may lead to the evolution of polymorphisms and may influence how the variants are distributed within human groups. For example, populational differences in the ABO and HLA systems may be related to disease resistance.

ABO Blood Group and Disease

The most-studied human polymorphic trait is the ABO blood group (see Table 7.1). Many people have been tested for ABO blood type because the trait is an important consideration in blood transfusions and in other medical procedures. In addition, the test to determine ABO blood type is simple and inexpensive. Because it is a convenient trait to measure, we have a lot of data on how the ABO alleles are distributed among human populations.

Information on the distribution of ABO blood types has afforded anthropologists a special opportunity to study how a biochemical trait varies on a worldwide basis. By mapping the frequency of the alleles into biological clines, scientists have obtained a picture of how they are distributed across geographical space. While

TABLE 7.1

ABO Genotypes and Phenotypes

Genotype	Phenotype
AA	A
AO	
BB	B
BO	
AB	AB
OO	O

most groups contain all of the alleles, populations differ in the proportion of each. There are extreme cases. For example, the B allele is completely absent in the native population of Australia, as indicated in Figure 7.6.

What forces explain the distribution of the ABO alleles? Unfortunately, scientists do not have a clear answer to this question. In some cases, the differences are caused by random processes; in others, patterns of gene frequencies may have been shaped by natural selection. Selectionist explanations intuitively make sense because the ABO blood group is an antibody-antigen system, and antibodies are crucial in fighting off infection.

Do we have any evidence of natural selection acting on the ABO group? Some studies suggest that there may be a relationship between ABO blood types and resistance to disease. A number of noninfectious diseases, such as cancers, ulcers, and disorders of the circulatory system, have been tentatively associated with particular ABO blood types. In addition, there are associations between ABO blood types and infectious diseases. For example, people with A-type blood seem particularly susceptible to bacterial infections, while those with O-type blood may be more inclined to contract viral diseases (Mourant 1983).

Such evidence suggests that disease locally selected for ABO blood type, and thus influenced its interpopulational diversity. However, these

FIGURE 7.5

The clinal distribution of the sickle cell allele (a) is similar to the distribution of high levels of malaria (b). By comparing the two maps, scientists can identify a possible relationship between a high occurrence of malaria and a high frequency of the sickle cell trait.

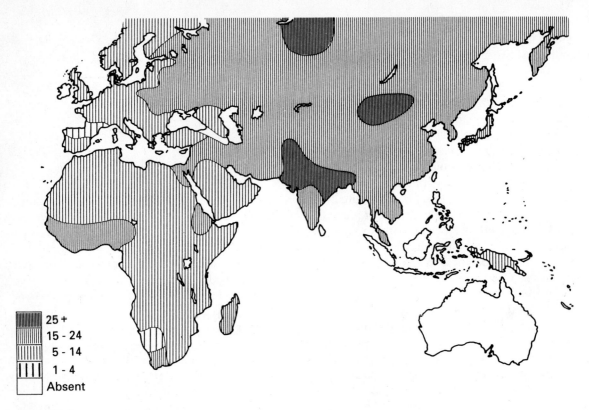

	25 +
	15 - 24
	5 - 14
	1 - 4
	Absent

FIGURE 7.6

The clinal distribution of blood group B allele in native populations of the Eastern Hemisphere. Note that the B allele is completely absent in the native population of Australia.

associations are weak at best. A much stronger case for natural selection acting on a biochemical trait comes from research on the major human histocompatibility complex, HLA.

HLA: The "Super" Polymorphism

The HLA system is composed of a group of substances (human leukocyte antigens) found in human blood and other tissues. These antigens play a pivotal role in how our bodies fight off infection and disease. The HLA system is extremely polymorphic. In some populations, no more than 1 out of 200 people share the same HLA phenotype.

Many questions arise as to why there is so much variability in such an important system. Indications that natural selection may be maintaining this high degree of variability come from studies showing that individuals with a particular HLA type are at a greater risk of contracting a specific disease. For example, one HLA type is associated with juvenile diabetes, while another is associated with rheumatoid arthritis (e.g., Bodmer 1980; Svejgaard et al. 1979). The reverse situation may also exist: specific HLA types may bestow an individual with a greater resistance to a particular disease. Possibly, individuals who are heterozygotic for the HLA gene are resistant to more diseases than people who are homozygotic for HLA. Furthermore, a population with a greater variety of HLA types may be more immune to a greater number of diseases than one with less variety. Such a population would be less likely to be wiped out by an epidemic. The hypothesis that natural selection favors variability in HLA types is supported by an interesting phenomenon. Fetuses with HLA types that are different from those of their mothers apparently have a better chance of survival than do fetuses with HLA types that are the same as those of their mothers (Bodmer 1972).

That the variability of HLA types is of selective value is also reflected by geographical patterns. For example, Northern Europeans and Japanese have different HLA allelic frequencies, with Europeans having a greater proportion of HLA types associated with diabetes. Europeans also have a greater incidence of this disease (Bodmer 1980; Thomson 1983).

Scientists have only begun to examine the evolutionary significance of the HLA system. Further research may confirm that there is a definite pattern of localized HLA-based disease resistance.

Physiological Responses to Stress

People differ in how they respond to environmental stress. For example, some people fare exceptionally well in hot and humid weather, while others are especially tolerant of the cold. Functional means of contending with environmental stress that are based on the body's capacity to adjust to its surroundings are called **physiological responses**. Physiological responses include such everyday occurrences as sweating, shivering, and panting; they also refer to permanent characteristics such as broad chests and large lung capacities.

The differences observed among human populations with respect to physiological responses pose some special questions. Are these differences due to evolved genetic adaptations, or do they reflect developmental plasticity? Are they temporary responses that are acquired by anyone exposed to particular stresses for a few days or weeks, or are they permanent traits? Such questions reflect an increased genetic complexity because more gene sites interact at the physiological level than at the molecular level. Therefore, al-

though genetic factors strongly influence physiological traits, we also see the increased influence of the environment. To add to this confused picture, the degrees of genetic and environmental influence vary in acccordance with particular physiological traits. For example, a vascular skin response to cold stress is a genetic adaptation noted in Northern Europeans. On the other hand, there appears to be an environmentally induced increase in the number of active sweat glands in children raised in hot climates.

Scientists have gathered a large and complicated body of data on physiological responses to stress. The two examples that follow are descriptive of the type of research being conducted.

Contending with Extreme Cold

Anthropologists have noted physiological differences among populations in people's physiological responses to extremely cold weather. For example, Steegmann (1975) hypothesized that physiological differences in responses to cold should be evident in hands and feet, because limbs are particularly exposed to the cold and prone to damage from frostbite. He conducted experiments on people of different ethnic backgrounds to measure their physiological response when their hands and feet were immersed in very cold water. The results were as expected. People of African descent, whose ancestors came from warm climates, fared worse than Europeans, while Inuit were superior to both groups in their physiological response to the cold. People raised in different environments reacted in a similar manner, indicating that the differences noted between the groups were based on genetic adaptations rather than on developmental responses to the cold stress.

Low Oxygen at High Altitude

Some human groups live on mountains or plateaus thousands of feet above sea level. One of the major environmental stresses found at high altitudes is the relatively low level of oxygen in the atmosphere. This can cause a condition called *hypoxia*, in which the body tissues are deprived of sufficient oxygen, especially during periods of extended activity. The sufferer may become dizzy, nauseated, and short of breath. A person newly exposed to the condition can eventually make physiological adjustments. For example, there is often an increase in the production of red blood cells, which carry oxygen through the body. However, people who habitually live at high altitudes are much more tolerant of the air's low oxygen content, demonstrating adaptive traits such as slow maturation rates, large lung capacity, and broad, barrel-shaped chests. Are these differences based on purely genetic factors, or do they reflect developmental plasticity acting during growth? Another possibility is that they are the result of **acclimatization**, reversible physiological responses that occur over relatively short spans of time in reaction to an immediate stress.

A classic study of life at high altitudes was conducted on the Quechua Indians of highland Peru (Baker et al. 1968; Baker and Little 1976). The Quechuas have been living at approximately 8,000 feet for many generations, with some settlements at 17,000 feet. In addition, some Quechuas have migrated to sea-level towns along the Peruvian coast. This combination of settlement patterns makes the Quechua an excellent population on which to conduct research concerning how humans contend with high-altitude stress. For example, the ability to use oxygen during periods of activity by Quechua raised at 13,000 feet was compared with that of Quechua raised at sea level who spent one month at the high elevations (Baker 1976; Buskirk 1976). The highland group was greatly superior to the lowland individuals in the ability to use oxygen efficiently. Since the groups were genetically from the same population, this indicates that the differences were based in developmental plasticity. However, when the lowland Quechua were compared with Europeans, the Indians did much better than the non-natives. This suggests that there is also a genetically based difference in how individuals contend with oxygen deprivation. Clearly, this is a very complex issue, involving the interactions of many factors and mechanisms.

Quechua Indians travel on a high mountain road to a market in Urcos, Peru. The town, located in the Andes Mountains, is at an elevation of 10,400 feet.

Complex Morphological Traits

The most noticeable physical characteristics of humans are referred to as the **complex morphological traits**. These characteristics are similar in many ways to the physiological traits; however, whereas physiological responses may be viewed as an active means of contending with an immediate situation, the complex morphological traits, such as height, weight, body shape, facial structure, and skin pigmentation, are more permanent features (especially in adults) that may be long-term means of contending with general environmental conditions. In fact, the complex morphological traits often influence physiological responses. For example, body weight and fat distribution affect how well an individual physiologically responds to temperature stress. Overweight people have a more difficult time cooling their bodies in hot climates, while people with a low proportion of body fat may have difficulty in metabolizing enough energy to maintain their core body temperature under conditions of extreme cold (Roberts 1978).

The relationship between the complex morphological traits and environmental stresses is an important anthropological issue. For example, rules have been developed regarding the relationship between body size and shape of warm-blooded animals and climate. *Bergmann's rule* deals with body size: Of two bodies that have similar shapes, the larger body has a relatively smaller surface area per unit of volume and will better conserve body heat (Weiss and Mann 1985). Thus, larger body size is selected for in cold climates, as evidenced in the stocky build of Inuits. *Allen's rule* focuses on body proportions in terms of surface area and the loss of body heat. In cold regions, limbs are expected to be short to limit heat radiation. In hot climates, long limbs assist in efficiently cooling bodies. We see this in the tall, long-limbed bodies of many sub-Saharan Africans.

The genetic basis of the complex morphological traits is complicated, resulting in many subtle differences in how such characteristics are expressed among the individuals of a population.

Scientific rules address the relationship between body structure and climate. (left) This Inuit's short, stocky body structure illustrates Bergmann's rule regarding the conservation of body heat. (right) The long-limbed and tall body structure of these young Africans illustrates Allen's rule regarding surface area and the loss of body heat.

Therefore, the complex morphological traits are distributed within a population in continuous, graded curves. We see this in the following two examples.

Weight and Body-Fat Distribution

Average weight, as well as the proportion and distribution of body fat, varies from one human group to another. While diet and activity influence these differences, so do genetically based factors such as metabolic rates and fat-tissue distribution. Fat is important because it stores the energy needed to maintain body functions. However, the amount of body fat and how it is spread over the body relate to problems of heat retention and radiation. In populations living under arctic conditions it is advantageous for fat to cover large parts of the body, to insulate it against the cold. In hot climates, fat is often concentrated in specific areas of the body, particularly in the buttocks. This allows the fat to be used for energy storage while lessening its insulating and heat-retention effects. Roberts (1978) found an inverse relationship between the average weight of human groups and average temperature—the hotter the climate, the lower the average weight.

Recognizing that the complex morphological traits result from the complicated interaction of genetic and environmental factors, we must be extremely careful when studying how they vary, both between and within human populations. For example, in studying weight and body-fat distribution, age and gender differences must be accounted for. Lasker and Womack (1975), for example, demonstrate trait variance both between populations and between the sexes.

Some of the research on complex morphological traits involves the influence of nutritional stress on populational patterns of fatness. Studies conducted on Polynesians and Native Americans suggest that some groups evolved the ability to rapidly increase their proportion of body fat so as to store up energy while food was plentiful. Thus, when food was in short supply, they would be safeguarded. According to Harrison et al. (1988), the ability to build up fat rapidly would

most likely evolve in populations subject to cycles of food availability, rather than in groups with stable food supplies. For example, the high degree of obesity in the tropical-living Samoans certainly has no basis in insulation against the cold. However, it may reflect Samoans' prehistoric open-sea voyaging, which subjected them to long periods of food deprivation (Baker, Hanna, and Baker 1986).

Skin Pigmentation

The complex morphological trait of skin color is easily observed and varies among human populations. Because of this, skin color has played an important role in classifying people into local groups and races. Hence, the question of why people have different-colored skins is important, not only because of its biological significance but also because of its social and political ramifications.

Regional differences in skin color logically relate to skin's adaptive functions, primarily in serving as a "first-line" environmental barrier to protect people from infection, solar radiation, too much cold, and too much heat. Skin obtains its color and tanning abilities largely from combinations of chemical substances called *pigmentations*. One such chemical is *melanin*, which is responsible for the darkness of the skin and the degree to which it tans when exposed to sunlight. *Carotene* is responsible for yellow tones, while the *hemoglobin* in red blood cells gives skin a red or pink tinge.

The complex genetic basis of skin color is not well understood. As many as four to six gene pairs are involved in producing this trait. The genes have an additive effect, resulting in a great range of genotypes and phenotypes for skin color (as many as 81 different genotypes have been estimated). Thus, skin color varies greatly even within populations, where it can be described only in terms of a continuous and graded distribution of phenotypes.

Skin color is a genetic adaptation, so individuals will have the same phenotype no matter where they are raised. It can, however, change within a population through time. Evidence suggests that much of the diversity among native populations in range of skin color is due to natural selection acting on a local level. A number of selective factors related to the skin's function as a protective agent may be at work. These factors include the following:

1. *The harmful effects of solar radiation.* Overexposure can burn skin and induce skin cancer. The damaging agent is ultraviolet light, which is most effectively blocked by melanin. In areas where sunlight is intense, selection would favor dark skin.

2. *The positive effects of solar radiation.* Sunlight stimulates the human body's production of vitamin D, which plays a crucial role in bone growth and replacement. Dark skin would be disadvantageous in areas of low sunlight, since it slows down vitamin D synthesis.

3. *Retention of heat.* Dark colors absorb more heat than light colors. However, light skin allows for a deeper penetration of heat, and thus is beneficial under cold conditions. Because of heat retention, dark skin may be a problem in very hot climates.

4. *Susceptibility to cold injury.* Dark skin may be more prone to cold injury than light-colored skin. Studies of frostbite in American soldiers indicate that dark skin is more susceptible to such damage (e.g., Post, et al. 1975).

If natural selection locally acted on skin color, then balances would have to be reached among these factors, and possibly others. For example, a cold climate without much sunlight would favor light skin. In such a climate, there would be the threat of cold injury, the need for heat retention, limited vitamin D production, and little danger of overexposure to solar radiation. In other areas, tanning would be a means of contending with conflicting needs—say, moderate protection from ultraviolet rays and yet not too much heat retention, as might occur in subtropical areas.

Although clinal distributions of skin color and climate (see Figure 7.7) support some of these claims, there is little definitive evidence regarding the evolution of skin color. In addition, we must also consider patterns of migration and interbreeding (e.g., Sunderland 1979). Even so, the complex morphological trait of skin color is an interesting case in point for those searching for examples of natural selection acting in the evolution of local human adaptations.

Behavior: What Accounts for Populational Differences?

Clearly, people from different societies behave in different ways. If this were not so, there would be no need for cultural anthropology. But the question of the degree to which behavioral differences are based on genetic factors and the degree to which they are based on environmental factors is very controversial and complex. The concept of "nature versus nurture" is of special significance in the study of human behavior. This phrase implies that behavioral differences among people and groups are determined *either* by biology (nature) *or* by social environment (nurture). The fact is, however, that most traits result from an *interaction* between genes and environment. Nowhere is this more true than for behavior. Behavior is the most genetically complex level of our hierarchy of human traits. Thus, environment exerts a very strong influence on the development of human behavior, especially through enculturation, the process of acquiring views and values from others through social interaction.

The study of the genetic basis of human behavior is best viewed within an evolutionary context. In Chapter 6, we noted that the plasticity of human behavior and our dependency on culture is a basic aspect of the hominid adaptation. This behavioral plasticity evolved along with the physical structure of an enlarged and reorganized brain. Human brain structure is based on genetic blueprints that make it developmentally plastic because much of human behavior is learned rather than genetically predetermined. Thus, the very plasticity of our behavior evolved as part of a biological system, and is based on particular genetic substrates.

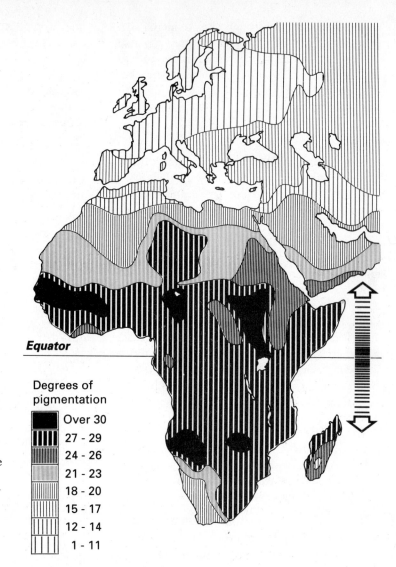

FIGURE 7.7

Clinal distribution of skin color in Africa. The arrow indicates that the degree of pigmentation in human populations decreases in a relatively even pattern with increasing distance from the equator. This is especially true in the northward direction.

Equator

Degrees of pigmentation

■	Over 30
	27 - 29
	24 - 26
	21 - 23
	18 - 20
	15 - 17
	12 - 14
	1 - 11

Intriguing yet elusive, the biological basis of human behavior (including populational differences) is studied in a number of ways. Some scientists focus on specific aspects of human behavior, as we will see shortly, in the section on race and IQ. Others focus on the relationship between brain structure and behavior, while still others study behavior across species. One currently popular and controversial approach is known as sociobiology.

Sociobiology

Since the publication of E.O. Wilson's *Sociobiology: A New Synthesis* in 1975, behavioral scientists have debated and refined this particular approach to the study of human biology and behavior. It is the best known of a number of scientific approaches that focus on the evolution of animal social behavior.

In brief, **sociobiology** draws from behavioral biology, population ecology, and evolutionary theory to understand the evolution of animal social behavior (Wittenberger 1981). As perceived by sociobiologists, social behaviors are inherently adaptive and are the result of the interaction between genetic and environmental factors. Sociobiologists view natural selection as the mechanism by which social behaviors evolve. They also view humans as part of the animal kingdom and subject to the same evolutionary forces as all other animals. Sociobiologists seek to formulate empirically testable hypotheses regarding social behavior—a difficult task indeed.

Within this general framework, many scientists include as basic to sociobiology a focus on kin selection and inclusive fitness. **Kin selection** extends the idea that natural selection acts on individuals. It is used to explain such seemingly maladaptive social behaviors as altruism, where personal well-being is sacrificed to benefit others. The idea behind kin selection is that such behaviors adaptively occur among closely related individuals, and what appears to be evolutionary suicide is actually a good way of ensuring that a greater proportion of one's genes will be passed on to the next generation. This concept is based on the principle of **inclusive fitness**, which is the *total* likelihood that an individual's set of genes will be passed on not only directly, through the individual's own children, but also indirectly, through the offspring of close relatives. This is because a proportion of one's genes is shared with one's relatives. For example, a parent and child share one-half of their genes, while a grandparent and grandchild share one-fourth of their genes. As a result, a self-sacrificing behavior will be evolutionarily beneficial when it results in the increased fitness of enough of one's relatives to ensure that the proportion of the individual's genes passed on to the next generation will be greater than if the individual had not performed the helpful act. Barash (1977) uses the example of alarm calling in prairie dogs. The prairie dog gives a loud call when it sees a coyote approaching its community. This is a self-sacrificing behavior, for while the calling warns other prairie dogs that a predator is near, it also draws atten-

tion to the calling animal and increases the chances that it will be caught. The sociobiological explanation is that such behaviors are selected for if enough relatives are saved to counterbalance the individual's personal loss of fitness.

As a new discipline, sociobiology has been subject to criticism, especially in regard to its application to humans. Some critics contend that it is dogmatic and simplistic. They point out that evolution can proceed by processes other than natural selection and that random evolutionary events also must be taken into account. Other critics object to the strong focus on kin selection; sociobiology excludes the possibility that natural selection acts on units other than the individual. An alternative idea is that *group selection*—natural selection acting on social groups rather than on individual genotypes—may also explain phenomena such as self-sacrificing behavior. Both of these criticisms represent important challenges to sociobiology. There are also those critics who pose the following question: If genes "dictate" human behavior, then what accounts for cultural diversity? However, this group misses the point that behavioral flexibility via learning and cultural mechanisms is part of the human genetic adaptation.

Particularly difficult to deal with are objections to sociobiology on social and political grounds. Controversial scientific fields, such as atomic research and genetic engineering, are likely to incur criticism of this sort. Although the basic goal of science is to enlighten humankind, some argue that scientists must consider any potential harm that could result from their work. These critics are concerned about the possible exploitation of sociobiology in developing social, political, and economic policies. They feel that sociobiology is a form of "biological determinism" that views human behavior as genetically inflexible, or incapable of change. This raises fears of racism and sexism because particular groups could be labeled as genetically inferior; thus, locked into specific behaviors.

Sociobiologists counter that such criticisms are

based on a misunderstanding of the biological basis of behavior: genes influence, but do not dictate, behavior. However, the critics' concern is not so much with scientists as with politicians and government officials who choose to manipulate sociobiological theory for their own purposes. For example, Alper, Beckwith, and Miller (1978) point to sociobiological claims that males are more naturally aggressive and cunning than females as being inherently sexist. They contend that politicians made use of such arguments in their attempts to defeat the Equal Rights Amendment.

Are the potential misuses of sociobiology enough reason to discontinue research? This is a difficult legal and moral question that touches on the rights of all scientists. It is hoped that such problems will be less of a threat as sociobiology becomes more refined and better understood.

Race and IQ

Intelligent thought is critical to the human way of life. Intelligence is an individual's capacity for problem solving through interpreting and analyzing information. It has a highly complex genetic basis and is influenced by environmental factors that may exist even prior to birth, as demonstrated by studies on prenatal care, nutrition, and maternal alcohol consumption.

Studies show that there are differences in the types and degree of intellectual skills in people of different cultures and social classes. An important controversy exists regarding the mechanisms underlying this phenomenon. Are differences in intelligence the result of environmental factors (especially socialization), are they genetically based, or both? If the differences are genetically based, then why try to enhance the academic performance of children who are inherently incapable of improvement? It is easy to see why study of the biological basis of intelligence is so emotionally charged.

The most controversial aspect of this field is that of the "race and IQ" studies, which contend that there are genetically based differences in IQ (intelligence quotient) scores in people of differ-

ent races. The best known and most hotly contested work on this topic is that of Arthur Jensen (1969, 1981). He asserts that significant differences in human intelligence are founded in racial genetic factors. His evidence comes from populational differences in IQ test scores, which supposedly measure intelligence in a culturally unbiased manner. Specifically, Jensen notes that the IQ scores of American blacks are, on the average, 15 points below those of American middle-class whites. He claims to have scientifically valid proof that such differences are based on heredity and not on environment.

Many scientists have countered Jensen's assertions. Some of the strongest criticisms center on the following aspects of his work:

1. *Problems with defining race.* The concept of race and its validity as a statistical population is, itself, doubtful. In particular, it is impossible to define "American black" as an autonomous and genetically pure population. Individuals may be of 0 percent to 90 percent Caucasian stock. Thus, American blacks are not genetically homogeneous enough to warrant definition as a biological race.

2. *Doubts as to the validity of IQ tests as a culturally unbiased measure of intelligence.* Do these tests truly measure intelligence, or is intelligence defined here as how one does on an IQ test? Block and Dworkin (1976) note that "the evidence suggests that there is no good reason to believe IQ tests *do* measure mainly intelligence and that a good number of other qualities (such as sociocultural background and personality-motivational-temperament factors) appear to have as good a claim to be measured to some degree by IQ tests as intelligence does" (p. 411). This is especially true with respect to cultural factors. Although the tests are supposedly culturally unbiased, they actually *do* reflect cultural norms and tastes (see Figure 7.8). In fact, "even the motivation of intelligence is likely to be very different in different cultures" (Harrison et al. 1988, 321).

3. *Misuse of important statistical concepts, especially that of heritability.* **Heritability** is a complex

FIGURE 7.8

IQ tests are often culturally biased, reflecting cultural norms rather than "innate" intelligence. The correct answer to this question from a Stanford-Binet intelligence test is based on Anglo-Saxon standards as to which person is "prettier."

statistical measure used by population geneticists. It focuses on the variability of a particular trait within a population and in terms of how much of the variability is caused by genetic rather than environmental factors. Heritability is *not* a measure of the genetic basis of a trait within an individual. It is a measure of the degree to which individual differences in a population are due to heritable factors. This is a subtle, but crucial, point. In addition, heritability applies only to differences *within* populations—not those *between* populations. Jensen wrongly uses heritabil-

ity to explain differences across populations, overlooking the fact that "heritability is not a concept that can be applied to a trait in general, but only to a trait in a particular population, in a particular set of environments" (Lewontin 1976, 86). In fact, even with a high degree of heritability, environment can still have an enormous effect on the development of the trait within an individual.

4. *Problems within the data base used to prove that intelligence has a strong genetic basis.* The most powerful evidence supporting a heritable basis for IQ scores is based on "twin studies." Such studies compare the performance of identical and nonidentical twins on IQ tests in relation to one another and to their parents. The most compelling studies are those of identical twins who were adopted and raised by different parents. These studies have demonstrated an 80 percent heritability of IQ scores, which has been interpreted as signifying that intelligence has a strong genetic basis. However, critics claim that a statistically invalid number of twins were used to calculate heritability. They also point out that the twins were often adopted into very similar environments, and that the researchers did not account for the influence of very early environment.

If Jensen's theories are invalid, then what are the alternatives? Other studies have demonstrated that a number of environmental factors strongly influence performance on IQ tests. These factors, such as the occupational status of the parents, socioeconomic levels, the intensity of the mother's interaction with the child, nutrition, and especially educational opportunities, are closely associated with the inequalities associated with Jensen's "racial groups." Although this question is not yet fully resolved, it is clear that the biological bases of behaviors such as intelligence are enormously complex and not easily analyzed or explained. The difficulties in quantifying such behaviors reflect the basic adaptive pattern of humankind, for "the outstanding feature of human behaviour in all its forms is its flexibility" (Harrison et al. 1988, 321).

DESCRIBING AND CLASSIFYING HUMAN GROUPS: RACE AS AN OBSOLETE CONCEPT

An important goal of biological anthropology is to describe and classify human groups according to how they physically vary. The focus in this endeavor traditionally has been on the study of human races. However, as we have noted, the validity of race as a biological concept has come into doubt, particularly because of its strong political, sociological, and emotional significance. How is race used to classify and describe human diversity? What alternatives have scientists developed?

The race concept has a long history. Upon confronting societies different from their own, humans tend to seek out ways of categorizing people. The European explorations of the sixteenth and seventeenth centuries led naturalists to categorize exotic peoples according to easily observable physical characteristics, such as skin color, hair, and skull shape and size. Once classified on this basis, these people were often viewed as not fully human, thus providing Europeans with a convenient rationale for colonizing and exploiting native populations. After colonization, European-devised racial categories were used to determine the political and economic status of the colonial population.

Early schemes were based on **racial typology**—the division of human groups into discrete categories on the basis of "ideal types" (much as was done for plants and animals). Humans were thus stereotyped into a few restrictive categories. Typological approaches have many problems. What traits, and how many, should be used to define the ideal type and the pure lines that race implies? How many races and subraces exist? And, assuming that valid criteria *can* be established, what if any purpose is served by dividing people into large categories on the basis of a few morphological traits? Modern scientists strongly criticize typological approaches to race, noting that they are often based on intuition and are of little use in the scientific study of human variability (Dobzhansky 1962).

The race concept, in regard both to typological schemes and to more modern approaches, is clearly problematic. For example, depending on the traits used, racial schemes pose that there are anywhere from 3 to 37 different races of humankind. Even so, for much of anthropology's history, the race concept has been the basic approach to the study of how human populations vary. In addition, race underlies how many people think about human diversity. Let us now consider some of the more prominent racial schemes that have influenced both popular and anthropological thought.

Racial Schemes

A long-standing problem with race as a biological concept is that scientists disagree over its definition. In 1926, Hooton grouped individuals into races on the basis of shared physical traits, contending that the similarities were derived from common descent and not from adaptation. Later, scientists began to emphasize a populational approach. For example, Dobzhansky (1972) defined races as "Mendelian populations within a species . . . which differ in the incidence of some genes in their gene pools" (p. 66).

A number of racial schemes are based on geographical divisions. One scheme, proposed by Buettner-Janusch (1973), views biological races as localized subgroups of a species. These groups are morphologically different from one another in skin color, hair, eye color, and body shape. Such differences evolved as adaptations to local conditions. At the same time, races are genetically "open" systems because mating can freely take place between the members of different groups. Although this is a popular approach to race, the problems persist: What traits should be used to classify human groups into races, and what is the rationale for doing so?

In an attempt to be precise, Garn (1965) proposed three levels of race. The largest groupings of people, *geographical races*, are separated by major geographical barriers. These groupings are what we usually think of as races and include categories such as American Indian, Polynesian, Australian, Asiatic, and European. *Local races* are breeding populations that are largely reproductively isolated from one another. At this level, adaptation occurred in response to local pressures, and then natural and social factors maintained the differences through isolation. Examples of local populations are Mediterranean, Northwest European, Northeast European, Eskimo, and Hawaiian. The smallest groups are *microraces*, which are found in densely populated areas. Microraces are somewhat ambiguous, but are the unit within which individuals will most likely find mates. In a city, a microrace may be confined to a few blocks representing a neighborhood. Although Garn's approach tries to take many populational factors into account, it is still criticized as being too simplistic and difficult to apply. For example, some critics argue that local populations are different from races and should not be defined as such. Others note that Garn's criteria cannot be used consistently to subdivide a species.

Another influential approach is Carlton Coon's (1962) "regional evolution of the races" (see Figure 7.9). Now labeled as the "Candelabra" model for the origin of *Homo sapiens sapiens* (recall Figure 6.8), it contends that five groups of *Homo erectus* evolved into modern *Homo sapiens* along separate and independent lines. Thus, there have been five geographical subspecies of humans since the mid-Pleistocene. The races were then separately molded by evolutionary processes, such as natural selection and genetic drift. The groups evolved at their own rates, so that the races became "sapient" from a "more brutal" state at different times.

At first considered "good science," Coon's scheme is now in disrepute. Many view it as racist because it implies the superiority of those races (such as Caucasoid) that supposedly crossed the sapient threshold first and the inferiority of "late crossers" such as African and Australian populations. The strongest scientific criticisms focus on Coon's misunderstanding of evolutionary biology. For example, the similarities between

FIGURE 7.9

Carlton Coon's regional evolution of the races. According to this model, five groups of *Homo erectus* evolved into modern *Homo sapiens sapiens* along separate and independent lines.

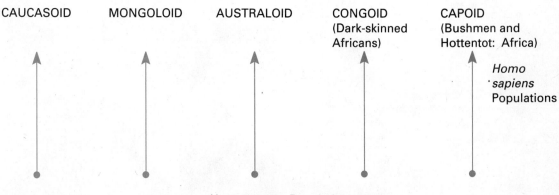

CAUCASOID   MONGOLOID   AUSTRALOID   CONGOID (Dark-skinned Africans)   CAPOID (Bushmen and Hottentot: Africa)

Homo sapiens Populations

Homo erectus Populations

human populations are much too great to allow for such lengthy independent evolutions. The hypothesis also depends on a high degree of genetic isolation of individual groups—another unrealistic assumption. The fossil record also clearly refutes the existence of five separate evolutionary pathways leading to modern humans.

A much more likely alternative is that regional populations diverged *after* evolution had reached the level of *Homo sapiens*. Migration and adaptation to local environments then led to the diversity of contemporary human populations. In Chapter 6, we noted that recent support for such a scheme comes from mitochondrial DNA studies. This evidence indicates that all modern populations are derived from a single African-based group dating from some 200,000 years ago. We also noted that fossil evidence further supports the theory that modern-day human populations are closely related and that regional variations evolved recently because of localized adaptation and genetic drift.

Alternative Approaches

Discontent with the concept of race has motivated scientists to develop more reasonable and less emotionally heated ways of approaching human biological diversity. One popular approach makes use of *clinal distributions*, which plot the occurrence of a particular trait or gene frequency over geographical space (p. 185). This technique represents a purely descriptive approach to identifying biological patterns; hence populations are not forced into a few discrete categories. Scientists then attempt to explain the clinal distributions using evolutionary principles such as natural selection, mutation, genetic drift, and migration. The clinal approach is not without its problems, however. The major shortcoming is that scientists can examine only one trait at a time, which leads to a simplistic and unrealistic picture of human variation. And, again, on what basis does one choose the trait?

Another way of analyzing human diversity is through **multivariate studies**. This technique, which applies population genetics, analyzes the distribution of several polymorphic genetic traits at the same time. Lewontin (1972) used this complicated statistical procedure (which is almost impossible without computers) to examine populational differences in the gene frequency of 17 polymorphic biochemical traits, including ABO, Rh, and other blood loci. He divided human populations in a number of ways; for example, into seven geographical groups (representing the

traditional races) and into over 150 local populations, much like Garn's "local races." The results were quite interesting. Only 6.3 percent of the genetic variation was accounted for by differences between the geographic divisions, and only 8.3 percent more of the variation was due to differences between local groups. Thus, approximately 85 percent of the genetic variation occurs *within* these populations, and not *between* them. In other words, most of the genetic differences found among people occur at the level of villages, families, and, especially, at the individual level.

Multivariate studies provide strong evidence that the genetic variation within groups is much more significant than differences between groups. Therefore, racial schemes are much too broad and much too crude to be of value in the study of human biological diversity.

What is the current status of race as a biological concept? Some scientists still view biological races as a useful way to approach human diversity when race is taken as a populational, and not as a typological, concept (e.g., Alexeev 1979). However, most scientists conclude that race has lost its value as a scientific tool. For example, J. King (1981) argues that human races are not genetically isolated enough to meet the requirements of subspecies-like divisions. The difficulties in defining the concept, its sociopolitical overtones, and the fact that our biological similarities far outweigh our differences all argue for replacing the race concept with a different approach to human biological diversity.

Racism: The Social and Political Abuse of the Biological Concept of Race

The study of race demonstrates the holism of anthropology. Biological anthropologists examine the relevance of race in understanding populational diversity, while cultural anthropologists are concerned with its use as a social and political instrument. Cultural anthropologists are particularly interested in how the concept reflects the human tendency to divide people into "we" and "they"—"we" being superior and fully human; "they" being inferior and not quite human. As we will discuss in Chapter 19, this attitude is one of **racism**—the use of perceived racial differences to determine people's position in relation to one another.

In this manner, race, originally a biological concept, has been adopted for popular use. In the process, the concept has become convoluted such that it now represents nonbiological differences. Race has become more a reflection of ethnicity than of biological variability. **Ethnicity**, selected perceived cultural or physical differences used to class people into groups or categories considered to be significantly distinct, is an important aspect of how individuals identify themselves socially. Unfortunately, ethnic differences sometimes serve as the basis for racist stereotypes. Expressions such as "the Jewish race" or "the Arab race" incorrectly raise ethnic differences to the level of biologically based divisions. With opinions already formed according to preconceived stereotypes, both race and ethnicity can be used to dismiss people as individuals.

The most damaging misuse of the race concept is when it is applied for political purposes. Race is often used to reinforce stereotypes and to emphasize the we-they distinction. Such misuse was evident during periods of colonialism. Race has also been used to justify slavery, to manipulate public attitudes toward social welfare programs, and to serve the interests of political candidates, as when a negative stereotype of a minority group member is used to raise fears among the majority.

Anthropologists should be personally concerned with the perils of racism. As members of a society, our world views are shaped by our culture. Anthropology, being a Western discipline, is influenced by the concept of race and by racism. This is why emphasizing cultural relativism is an important part of anthropology, so that we can attempt to overcome our built-in biases regarding societal norms.

HUMAN DIVERSITY IN TODAY'S WORLD

In this chapter, we saw that contemporary human diversity was brought about by biological evolution. This evolution apparently took place as the result of adaptive responses to local conditions and of random processes responding to such factors as geographical isolation and small population size. At the same time, another force also shaped the diversity of human groups: cultural evolution. Culture, made possible by the biological adaptation of humans, is enormously important to the survival of our species. How and why this is so is discussed throughout the remainder of this text.

SUMMARY

To understand human biological diversity we need to examine the complicated relationship between genotypes, the environment, and phenotypes with a view toward how this relationship determines the inheritance and development of specific traits. The degree to which genotype and environment influence a trait's development within an individual varies with the trait. The concept of simple versus complex traits reflects the number of gene pairs interacting in the development of a trait. Within populations, the forms of a trait may be distributed in a discontinuous or continuous pattern, depending on the trait's genetic complexity.

Genetic polymorphisms are an important source of genetic variability because they provide a population with genetic alternatives. Polymorphisms are also an important tool in describing the genetic diversity of human populations because groups can be distinguished according to allelic frequencies.

Many students of human biological diversity are concerned with determining how evolutionary processes cause populations to differ in polymorphic traits. Another major concern is with explaining how microevolution occurs in modern populations. The study of growth, development, and physiological plasticity also provides insights into the degree to which heredity and environment influence an individual's adult form.

Human biological traits can be organized into a hierarchy that reflects a trait's genetic complexity and the relative degree to which genetic and environmental factors influence the development of the trait within an individual. The genetically simplest traits are those at the molecular or biochemical level. Other major categories of traits include physiological responses to environmental stress, the complex morphological traits, and behavior.

An important anthropological question concerns the biological basis of human behavior and how it relates to societal differences in behavior. Behavior is a genetically complex trait. Environment exerts a strong influence on its development within an individual, especially through enculturation. Sociobiology is a controversial approach to the evolution of human social behavior. The most controversial aspect of the study of the biological basis of behavior is "race and IQ" studies, which have met with serious criticisms.

An important goal of biological anthropology is to describe and classify human groups according to how they physically vary. The traditional focus in this effort has been on the study of human races. However, the validity of race as a biological concept has been called into question.

Because of their discontent with the concept of race, scientists have developed alternative ways of approaching human biological diversity. These alternatives include the use of clinal distributions and multivariate studies, which provide strong evidence that racial schemes are much too broad and too crude to be of value. Besides its weaknesses as a biological concept, race also has serious sociopolitical implications that cannot be ignored, particularly as they relate to racism.

SUGGESTED READINGS

Baker, Paul T., Joel M. Hanna, and Thelma S. Baker. 1986. *The Changing Samoans.* New York: Oxford University Press.

Caplan, Arthur L., ed. 1978. *The Sociobiological Debate.* New York: Harper & Row.

Fancher, Raymond D. 1985. *The Intelligence Men: Makers of the IQ Controversy.* New York: W.W. Norton.

Gould, Stephen Jay. 1981. *The Mismeasure of Man.* New York: W.W. Norton. (Critique of biological determinism)

King, James C. 1981. *The Biology of Race.* Berkeley: University of California Press.

McElroy, Ann, and Patricia K. Townsend. 1979. *Medical Anthropology.* North Scituate, MA: Duxbury Press.

Molnar, Steven. 1975. *Races, Types and Ethnic Groups.* Englewood Cliffs, NJ: Prentice-Hall.

Moran, Emilio F. 1982. *Human Adaptability.* Boulder, CO: Westview Press.

Mourant, A.E. 1983. *Blood Relations.* New York: Oxford University Press. (Molecular/biochemical traits)

Tanner, J.M., and M.A. Preece, eds. 1989. *The Physiology of Human Growth* (Society for the Study of Human Biology Symposium 29). New York: Cambridge University Press.

Genetic Studies among the Hutterites

Carole Ober

Carole Ober's interest in anthropological populations and the genetics of fertility prompted her to visit the Hutterite colonies and establish ongoing investigations in this population. She visits Hutterites living in South Dakota at least twice each year. The unique features of this isolated population have allowed her to examine many aspects of fertility that have been difficult to study in outbred populations. Dr. Ober is currently an associate professor of obstetrics and gynecology and director of the Molecular Genetics Laboratory at the University of Chicago.

The Hutterites are Anabaptists whose origins trace back to 1528 in the Tyrolean Alps. They differ from other Anabaptist groups (for example, the Mennonites and the Amish) in their adherence to a communal life-style and in their literal interpretation of the New Testament, Acts 2:44,45: "And all who believed were together and had all things common; and sold their possessions and goods, and parted them to all men, as every man had need." Religious persecution and their unwillingness to serve in the military forced the Hutterites to disperse throughout Europe. Between 1874 and 1879, approximately 900 members migrated to the United States, with 423 of them settling on three communal farms, or colonies, in what is now southeastern South Dakota. Approximately half of these founders were adults, many of whom were related to each other. The remaining settlers became individual farmers in the same locale. As the population flourished, new colonies were established, and the families in the parent colony divided themselves among the parent and daughter colonies. This process of colony

"splitting" continues today. Since settling in this country, virtually no new members have joined, and relatively few Hutterites have left the community.

The current population of more than 30,000 Hutterites live in approximately 300 colonies in South Dakota, North Dakota, and Montana, as well as in western Canada. The colonies are all descendants of one of the three founding colonies. The three lines of colony descent represent the three major subdivisions of Hutterite population structure: the Schmiedenleut (S-leut), Lehrerleut (L-leut), and Dariusleut (D-leut). Marriage between members of different leut has been rare since 1910. Today, the leut differ with respect to social customs, dress, and dialect, but members of all leut speak German as their primary language and maintain a communal farming life-style.

Because many members of the founding population were related to each other, there were fewer than 100 independent genomes among the founders. As a result, the Hutterites are one of the most inbred large populations of European origins. Today the average degree of relatedness among spouses is roughly equivalent to that of first cousins once removed or 1-1/2 cousins. There are only 15 surnames in the entire Hutterite population. Hutterites usually marry between the ages of 20 and 25. Although young Hutterite men and women choose their own spouses, the union must be approved by the "elders" in the colony. Divorce is not practiced. With respect to fertility rates, Hutterites have one of the highest ever documented. About 80 percent of

Geneticist Carole Ober (left) gathers data on the Hutterites, one of the largest inbred populations of European origin in the United States.

Hutterite couples have their first child within 12 months of marriage, and the average completed family includes between 8 and 10 children. The proportion of couples who are infertile is only 2 percent, compared with 10 percent in the general population. Although all forms of contraception are proscribed by Hutterite doctrine, today birth control use for "medical indications" is not uncommon among married women. However, even among women using contraception, average families include between 5 and 8 children.

The Hutterites are educated through the eighth grade. They learn English when they start school, but continue to converse in German among themselves. English is reserved for "outsiders." Despite their limited formal education, the Hutterites are successful farmers. Many colonies practice computerized farming and use computers for record keeping. Their personal life-style, on the other hand, remains simple. Hutterite women make all their family's clothes and the men craft most of their furniture.

The Hutterites are often cited as the only successful communal group in the New World. Each colony is home to 10 to 15 families (100 to 150 people). Each family has its own house, but all food is prepared and eaten in a large central dining room. The preparation and serving of meals is the responsibility of adult women between the ages of 18 and 40, with one woman in each colony appointed as head cook who plans the menus. The men, on the other hand, are assigned a specific job at age 18 and may continue in that same job until choosing to retire at age 40. The colony is led by a "preacher" who keeps the colony's genealogical and vital statistic records.

Because of their large families, communal life-style, and detailed genealogic information, the Hutterites are uniquely well suited for genetic studies. I first visited Hutterite colonies in South Dakota to explore the possibility of conducting genetic studies of fertility. I was immediately impressed by their hospitality, openness, and willingness to participate in the studies. Over the past eight years, I have visited over 30 colonies in South Dakota, often revisiting many colonies during the twice-yearly visits of the research team. I have personally interviewed over 500 women who have participated in our studies.

The focus of these studies is a group of genes called human leukocyte antigens (or HLA). These genes play a very important role in immune response and tissue rejection; they are the antigens that must be matched between organ transplant donors and recipients. Organ transplants are likely to be rejected if donor and recipient have different HLA types. Many scientists have wondered whether these antigens also play a role in pregnancy, mediating the acceptance or rejection of the fetus. In contrast to what we observe following organ transplantation, it appears that fetuses are more likely to be rejected (i.e., miscarried) if the parents are similar with respect to their HLA types. The major aim of our studies in the Hutterites was to examine the relationship between a married couple's HLA types and their fertility.

Participation in a study involves donating one blood sample for typing of HLA and other genetic markers. An extensive interview is conducted with the wife of each couple, at which time information concerning the couples reproductive and medical histories is collected. In addition, all women who are still in their child-bearing years (about half of all married women) are asked to maintain monthly diaries

with information regarding menstrual cycles, nursing patterns, pregnancy-test results, and pregnancy outcomes (delivery or miscarriage). All female participants are given a supply of home-pregnancy-test kits and asked to test for pregnancy at the time of a missed period. Diaries are collected every six months, either through the mail or during our trips to the colonies. Currently, there are 180 women maintaining diaries and following the study protocol.

The results of these studies have demonstrated that Hutterite couples can be identical with respect to their HLA types and still have many children with few miscarriages. However, couples who are similar with respect to one particular HLA type, HLA-DR, take much longer to conceive a child after their previous conception. This increased time to conception is independent of the mother's age, of birth order, or of nursing patterns. Once pregnancy is diagnosed (30 days after previous menses), these couples are not at increased risk for miscarriage. These results could be due to factors interfering with conception or with implantation, but at this time the reason for the delayed pregnancy in couples with similar HLA-DR types is not known.

These investigations may provide insight into mechanisms that underlie successful pregnancy in outbred couples. Studies of fertility may be less complicated in the Hutterites than in outbred couples, allowing for observations that may be "hidden" in couples drawn from the general population. The Hutterite's communal life-style minimizes the effects of nongenetic factors that may affect fertility. For example, smoking is prohibited, alcohol consumption is minimal, and social attitudes toward pregnancy are uniform among Hutterites. Furthermore, their genetic homogeneity minimizes the effects of other genes that may modify fertility. Hypotheses generated from these data are currently being tested in studies of outbred couples experiencing infertility.

Archaeology and Cultural Evolution

PART TWO

During the course of human evolution, culture became an increasingly crucial aspect of the human adaptation. By reconstructing extinct societies and cultural history, anthropologists gain important insights into how cultural evolutionary processes shaped human cultural adaptations. The ultimate goal of this study is to explain the processes underlying cultural evolution and to explain how culture functions in human survival.

We begin Part Two by exploring the science of archaeology. Anthropological archaeology provides the means by which to study extinct societies within the context of anthropology as a whole. For example, our focus is not so much on the art and architecture of an ancient civilization, but on the cultural processes that led to the culture's existence and on how the culture functioned as part of the people's adaptation. Archaeology's special methods and approaches help us gain the time depth necessary to understand both the history and the processes of cultural evolution.

In the remainder of Part Two, our focus is on the history of cultural evolution, from the earliest recognized material remains to the rise of complex societies. This approach promotes understanding of how cultures change and why. A wide variety of theories and models have been proposed to explain cultural evolution, including those concerning the origin of agriculture and the rise of civilization. Cultural evolution has largely been a matter of increasing cultural complexity. However, we will see that increased complexity does not always lead to an improved way of life; indeed, cultural complexity often has created as many problems as it has solved.

8 Archaeology as a Way of Knowing the Past

Large-scale excavation of the Koster site in the lower Illinois River Valley. The massive Koster excavation was one of the first projects to be investigated using the methods developed by processual archaeologists.

The Koster Site: Illustrating the Archaeological Process _____

Archaeology as Anthropology

American Archaeology: From Description to Explanation

Archaeological Evidence

Doing Archaeology

Current Directions in Archaeology

Reconstructing Cultural History and Understanding the Processes of Cultural Evolution

Summary

Suggested Readings

***Focus on Anthropologists:* Preserving the Past: Conservation Archaeology on Guam** _____

Anthropology's concern with the cultural past is pursued through the subdiscipline of **archaeology**. Using sparse evidence, particularly the material remains of cultures, archaeologists reconstruct complex cultural worlds as a means of understanding past ways of life and of solving broad questions regarding cultural processes and evolution.

Archaeology is practiced both as a part of anthropology and as an aspect of history and art history. Our focus is on *archaeology as anthropology*—how archaeology offers anthropology a unique view into the cultural past that is essential to understanding how and why cultures evolve and how culture serves as a vital aspect of human adaptation.

In this chapter, we will explore the topic of anthropological archaeology, including how it came about. For the most part, the theories and methods of contemporary anthropological archaeology were developed in the United States, where the field was transformed from a speculative endeavor into a scientific discipline. Anthropological archaeologists make use of specific types of evidence and research techniques, with fieldwork at the core. For many, it is this fieldwork that provides the fascination archaeology holds.

THE KOSTER SITE: ILLUSTRATING THE ARCHAEOLOGICAL PROCESS

Although Americans often view archaeology as an exotic endeavor, many fascinating finds have been uncovered in the United States, often in inconspicuous farmlands and river bluffs. One such find is the Koster site. Located on the farm of Theodore Koster in the lower Illinois River Valley, the site might have been overlooked except for the interest of a neighbor, Alec Helton. Helton, a farmer, enjoyed collecting American Indian artifacts that are sometimes found lying on the ground's surface after a flood or heavy rain. Noting that Koster's cornfields contained an especially large number of such materials, Helton convinced a friend and archaeologist, Stuart Struever, to take a look.

After examining the cornfields, Struever began digging test pits—very limited excavations—which indicated that the cornfields might well contain a prehistoric Indian site. Struever then obtained Koster's permission to conduct a full-scale excavation. In the summer of 1969, a small crew of students and other volunteers dug test pits in several well-separated spots. These pits confirmed Struever's belief that this was, indeed, a very promising site, with clearly defined stratigraphy, good preservation, and at least six different cultural levels.

During the winter of 1970, Struever recruited a field crew and laboratory staff. The spring of 1970 was dedicated to setting up living quarters, classrooms, and laboratories in the small town of Kampsville, Illinois, a few miles from Koster's farm.

While taking care of such practical concerns, Struever was also busy with scientific matters, including establishing the project's research design. Struever's plan for the Koster site was one of the first to apply the tenets of a "new" archaeology, including an adherence to strict scientific methodology, that had grown out of an American intellectual revolution. Today's anthropological archaeologists seldom dig just for the sake of digging, but conduct research according to a "problem orientation"; that is, a scientifically posed question that dictates a project's research design. The problem orientation for Koster was to examine the "prehistoric subsistence and settlement patterning in the lower Illinois Valley" (Brown and Vierra 1983, 165), with the ultimate goal of explaining the relationship between culture change and the natural environment.

Another important aspect of contemporary anthropological archaeology is "teamwork"—making use of experts in a range of different fields. Struever put together an impressive group, including biologists trained to recognize the remains of plants and animals, biological anthropologists to analyze the physical remains of the Indians, and geologists. His codirector of the Koster Research Program at Northwestern University, James Brown, played the crucial role of overseeing the computer analysis of the materials. Another member of the team, John White, provided insights into the lives of Koster's prehistoric residents by re-creating their technology—how they made their pottery and tools, how they hunted, and how they built their canoes.

With a base of operations established and

funding provided from government grants and private contributions, it was time to get to work. Using the information from the test pits, the archaeologists decided where exactly to dig. Because the site was extremely large and deep, the archaeologists decided that they needed to excavate it thoroughly, rather than just a few sample squares (see p. 232). The actual excavation started in the summer of 1970. First, the site was carefully mapped so the archaeologists could accurately record where every piece of evidence had been located. A wide range of tools were used, including bulldozers, shovels, trenching equipment, brushes, whisk brooms, and small picks. As a result, a vast array of evidence—cultural, paleontological, and environmental—was uncovered. The spatial distribution of the finds was carefully recorded and the materials were ordered in time.

The Koster site's stratigraphy was wonderfully clear and well defined, which is relatively rare in a North American site (Struever and Holton 1979). The preservation was also good, including that of environmental evidence, such as animal and charred plant remains (Brown and Vierra 1983). The most impressive aspect of the Koster site, however, was its great time depth. There were a remarkable number of discrete Indian occupations (at least 13), starting as early as 9,000 years ago and continuing up into historic times.

Analysis of the Koster data has yielded interesting findings. For example, Struever and Holton (1979) used the data to re-create a picture of prehistoric life in the lower Illinois Valley. The delineation and explanation of cultural processes was also attempted. Brown and Vierra (1983), for example, sought to explain trends in sedentism (permanently settling in one location) using a model based on many concurrent factors such as the distribution of resources, the preferred types of residence of the people, and population size.

Through the efforts of Struever and his colleagues, the Koster site has proven to be a national treasure—one that was once disguised as a Midwest cornfield. Study of the Koster site also illustrates what the anthropological archaeology of today is all about: the scientific posing and testing of hypotheses and the careful analysis and interpretation of the archaeological record. Archaeology has truly become the science of humanity's past.

ARCHAEOLOGY AS ANTHROPOLOGY

Archaeology uses the material remains of extinct societies to study humankind's cultural past. For many people, archaeology evokes images of exploring ancient Greek remains or Egyptian pyramids. This represents the *classical approach* to archaeology, focusing on civilizations that left behind historical (written) records. Classical archaeology is associated with the humanistic disciplines of history and art history rather than with the field of anthropology. In our discussion, we are specifically concerned with *anthropological archaeology*, in which anthropology's general theories and methods are applied. In further contrast to the classical approach, anthropological archaeologists often concentrate on *prehistoric* *cultures*—societies that did not leave written records. Within anthropology, archaeology contributes a unique time depth to the study of culture, thus broadening our understanding of cultural processes.

Culture and Archaeology

Since archaeologists cannot observe extinct societies directly, they must think about culture in a special way. In Chapter 1, we defined the term *culture* as the customary manner in which human groups learn to organize their behavior and thought in relation to their environment. Culture has three principal components: behavioral, cognitive, and material. Archaeology concentrates on culture's material aspects through the **durable remains** of the past—those objects preserved or not completely destroyed by natural deterioration processes. There are two major categories of durable remains: **artifacts**, the products of human behavior, and **ecofacts**, objects reflecting the ancient human group's natural environment. Another crucial type of archaeological evidence is that of **context**—How are the materials placed in space and time? Under what environmental conditions were the materials found?

Because archaeologists depend greatly on the material component when reconstructing extinct societies, they approach culture as a system composed of interacting elements. If we understand the relationships of a system's parts, known components can help us to reconstruct unknown components. Thus, similar systems are used as interpretive models, making use of *analogies*. These are entities that share some traits and are assumed to share others. In particular, archaeologists use existing societies as models for ancient cultural systems.

A study by Richard Gould (1978) illustrates the application of analogies in interpreting the archaeological record. Gould sought to explain the presence of exotic raw materials at an Australian archaeological site. Local materials were much better for making tools, so why did the prehistoric foragers spend time and energy obtaining the exotic materials from hundreds of miles away? Gould investigated how contemporary foragers, living in the same area, under the same conditions, obtained and used stone. He discovered that the tools made from the special stone were of religious significance and symbolized kinship affinities. Kinship networks are extremely important among these people; for example, they ensure a friendly reception as a group moves across the inhospitable desert. This analogy provided Gould with important insights into how to interpret the archaeological find, especially since the environmental conditions and the level of

social organization were similar for the prehistoric and contemporary peoples.

Jason Smith (1976) presents a systems approach to culture that is especially useful to archaeologists. He views culture as the "learned way in which people control their environment: how they produce the necessities of day-to-day living; how they organize production—in short, the totality of their social life" (p. 37). The scheme divides culture into three interacting components: technology and technological knowledge; social organization; and ideology and ideological institutions (e.g., religions, cults, ritualistic societies). The technical component of prehistoric cultures is the major means by which archaeologists come to understand the social organization and ideology of ancient peoples. In addition, there is a larger system composed of three interacting units: culture; people (in the biological sense); and the natural and social environment (see Figure 8.1). Thus, studying the physical makeup of the people and their environment helps us understand their culture. A multidisciplinary approach, in which scientists from a broad range of fields participate in analyzing an archaeological site, increases our understanding of the larger system.

The Goals of Archaeology

Archaeology has three major goals or levels of analysis:

1. *Classifying and sequencing material culture.* The most basic goal of archaeology is to describe, classify, and temporally order material culture. This is an essential first step; it must be completed before interpretations are made.

2. *Reconstructing ancient ways of life.* The ordering and classifying of archaeological evidence takes on anthropological significance when it is used to tell us about the behavior of extinct peoples. By accumulating material cultural and contextual evidence, archaeologists reconstruct how people organized their societies, explained the

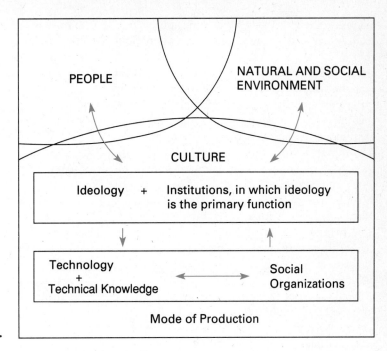

FIGURE 8.1
Smith's systems approach to culture.

world, gathered food, sheltered themselves, and so on.

3. *Explaining and delineating cultural processes.* The ultimate goal of any science is to discover scientific laws and principles. Anthropological archaeologists seek to answer questions regarding cultural processes: Why do cultures evolve? How do cultures serve as part of the human adaptation? What laws explain the patterning of all cultures?

Different goals have been emphasized as American archaeology developed as a scientific discipline. Until recently, most archaeologists did not feel that they could contend with the third goal. However, explaining cultural processes is now the primary focus of anthropological archaeology. A historical perspective demonstrates how this came about.

AMERICAN ARCHAEOLOGY: FROM DESCRIPTION TO EXPLANATION

Although archaeological concepts can be traced back to ancient civilizations, European archaeology is founded in the "humanistic antiquarianism" of the Italian Renaissance. Established in the fourteenth and fifteenth centuries, this approach to studying the past was concerned with the classical antiquity reflected by the ruins of the Greeks and Romans. Even today, the classical school continues to focus on the ancient civilizations of Europe and the Near East.

During the late 1830s, a different approach to archaeology was brought into play when Boucher de Perthes excavated some very crude, but clearly human-made, stone tools. He claimed that the tools were very old, an idea rejected by those who supported the prevailing Biblical view that the world was young (see Chapter 2). Even so, Boucher de Perthes's discoveries marked the beginning of prehistoric archaeology. This approach and its natural concern with human biology and cultural evolution was further stimulated by the publication of Darwin's theories. Although Darwin focused on biological evolution, his theory of natural selection and his support of the idea of a very old Earth presented prehistoric archaeology with a strong scientific paradigm.

While European archaeology was dividing into the classical and prehistoric schools, American archaeology was also becoming established as a scientific discipline. Although greatly influenced by Europeans, American archaeology followed its own course of development. For example, American archaeology has always been strongly focused on New World prehistory, specifically on the ancestors of the Eskimo and the North American and South American Indians. Willey and Sabloff (1980) divide the development of American archaeology into four major periods: the Speculative Period, the Classificatory-Descriptive Period, the Classificatory-Historical Period, and the Explanatory Period.

The Speculative Period (1492–1840)

This period, which started with the discovery of the Americas, is characterized by the incidental reports of explorers and travelers. Although scholars stimulated interest in the American Indians and their ancestors, they did little actual archaeological research. Most were "armchair archaeologists"—content to speculate on the past rather than actively pursue answers. One exception was Thomas Jefferson, the third president of the United States, who excavated the Indian remains on his property. However, as was generally true of scholars interested in the field during this period, archaeology was Jefferson's hobby, rather than his profession.

The Classificatory-Descriptive Period (1840–1914)

American archaeology was slowly transformed during this period from a speculative pursuit into a scientific discipline, as archaeologists became concerned with describing and classifying materials. Archaeology was greatly influenced by discoveries in other fields, including Darwin's theory and geological theories. However, archaeology still lacked a chronological perspective—the ordering of the materials through time.

Anthropological theories of cultural evolution also captured the imagination of American archaeologists. Based on simplistic interpretations of Darwinian evolution, most of these theories were *lineal*, categorizing societies along a single line of cultural development, from the "primitive" to the "advanced" (see Chapter 13, "Early Beginnings and Evolutionism"). By the end of this period, Franz Boas had guided an antievolutionary movement that shifted the focus of cultural anthropology (and, in turn, archaeology) from the devising of cultural evolutionary schemes to the factual gathering of historical and ethnographic information.

The Classificatory-Historical Period (1914–1960)

The first part of this period (1914–1940) is characterized by a concern with chronology—the time ordering of events. Goal 1, the classifying and sequencing of material culture, was now being fully pursued. Archaeologists were also becoming increasingly scientific in their methods, including how they excavated sites and analyzed data. They also began to functionally interpret cultural materials and contend with goal 2, the reconstruction of ancient ways of life.

The second part of the period (1940–1960)

continued the trend of concern with context and function. This was a time of "ferment and transition," marked by new experimental trends that began to address the third goal of examining cultural processes (Willey and Sabloff 1980, 130). Archaeologists became increasingly aware of the need to examine artifacts within their cultural and environmental contexts. In addition, cultural materials began to be viewed as reflections of human behavior rather than as abstract technological objects. In short, archaeologists began to focus on the function, context, and behavioral significance of the archaeological record, a focus that was aided by advances in other disciplines including geology, biology, and the physical sciences.

By the end of this period, American archaeology had begun to gradually shift its focus. Rather than limiting themselves to reconstructing past ways of life, archaeologists realized that they could contribute to anthropology's understanding of the processes underlying cultural evolution, which was now being viewed as a more complex, multifactorial phenomenon. The concern with explaining cultural processes became the focus of current American archaeology.

The Explanatory Period (1960 to the Present)

At the start of the 1960s, many archaeologists became concerned with explaining, rather than simply describing, the archaeological record. This concern rose to the forefront of American archaeology and remains a driving force in current research endeavors. These "new" archaeologists focused on the central issue of "how to accurately give meaning to archaeological observations" (Binford 1989, 12). Many archaeologists again embraced cultural evolutionary ideas, but ideas that were vastly different from those of the lineal evolutionists. After the turn of the century, evolutionary theory had been refined and elaborated on as scientists made discoveries in such fields such as genetics, biology, and ecology.

Particularly important to archaeology were ideas regarding the process of adaptation.

Early in the Explanatory Period, many different lines of thought were being pursued within archaeology and related disciplines. The time was ripe for a new scientific synthesis that would combine the diverse ideas into a unified whole. The person credited with achieving such an archaeological synthesis is Lewis R. Binford. In his 1962 essay, "Archaeology as Anthropology," Binford pulled together the work of many different scholars within a framework of rigorous scientific methodology. Often referred to as the "new archaeology," Binford's synthesis emphasized the following points: the need to formulate general laws of cultural processes from the archaeological record; the need to view the record within a systematic, interactive context; the need to recognize the explanatory importance of evolutionary and ecological theory; and the need to understand how the cultural present may be used to interpret the past. As discussed here, these concepts have greatly influenced the present state of American archaeology.

American Archaeology Today

American archaeology is now endowed with a scientific and anthropological validity that it lacked during earlier times. In addition, although archaeologists still reconstruct ancient ways of life and order the record into cultural histories, the overriding concern is with understanding social behavior and *why* the patterns of culture exist as they do. Because of the focus on cultural processes, this approach is often termed **processual archaeology**. What are the major tenets of this discipline?

Emphasis on Explanation

The major goal of contemporary anthropological archaeology is to explain cultural phenomena, especially by asking the broad questions that concern anthropology in general. For example, one of the first extensive applications of processual archaeology was the excavation of the Koster site in southern Illinois, described at the start of this chapter. The Koster site was excavated over a period of more than 10 years by a team of scientists particularly concerned with understanding the relationship between the environment and culture change. They investigated this issue by relating the use of natural resources to patterns of subsistence and settlement. For example, Brown and Vierra (1983) contended that "with an increased reliance on more abundant and storable resources, settlement patterns should reveal fewer short-term occupations in different environmental zones and more intense long-term occupations in the resource zone with the greatest resource productivity" (p. 186).

This desire to explain cultural processes underlies much of contemporary archaeology. In the process of fulfilling this desire, archaeologists have had to refine and further develop their scientific techniques.

Sophistication in Gathering Data
The new archaeology of the 1960s stimulated not only theorists but also "data-gatherers." The difficult theoretical goals challenged archaeologists to improve their research techniques because they had to develop more sophisticated means of identifying and analyzing relevant data. Archae-

ologists now routinely use electron microscopes for identifying wear patterns on stone tools and bones; chemical solutions for separating out tiny bits of organic material (e.g., seeds, fish scales, charcoal) from soil to gain information about ancient environments; and computers for storing, retrieving, and analyzing information.

The work of both theorists and data-gatherers is strongly influenced by a number of theoretical and methodological concepts basic to how archaeologists go about answering questions.

Scientific Rigor and the Scientific Method
In his 1962 paper, Binford noted that a major failing of archaeology was a lack of "scientific rigor." Archaeology has since become more rigorous, notably in the application of the scientific method. As introduced in Chapter 1, the scientific method is a precise way of designing and conducting research. It consists of three basic steps: establishing a hypothesis, determining ways to test the hypothesis, and testing the hypothesis.

For example, anthropologists are concerned with the relationship between the distribution of resources and social stratification (the division of members of a society into levels with unequal

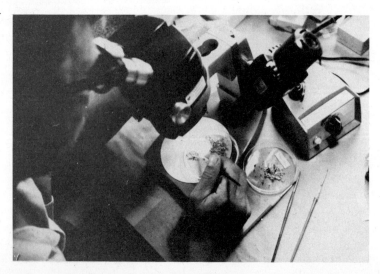

This archaeologist is using an electron microscope to analyze tiny bits of organic material gathered from a site's soil.

wealth, prestige, and power). Buikstra (1976) determined a means to examine this relationship in the archaeological record using the concept that the degree of social stratification within the society and the ranking of an individual is reflected by burial practices. She hypothesized that in highly stratified societies an individual was buried with a "symbolic representation" of wealth, while such differentiations were not made in unstratified societies. To test this hypothesis, Buikstra compared burial practices, including the distribution of artifacts, within a number of prehistoric burial mounds. After gathering and analyzing the data, she was able to determine that the hypothesis was basically valid. Moreover, she adjusted the basic premise to include an emphasis on the finding that placement within the burial mound also reflected an individual's status.

This concern with posing and testing hypotheses represents an important change in how archaeologists think about excavating sites. In the past, archaeologists would often excavate a site merely to see what it contained. Now most excavations are conducted using a *problem orientation*—archaeologists begin with a specific problem they want to solve. The problem, which is often to test a hypothesis, determines how a site is excavated. For example, Flannery (1976) wanted to investigate the factors that led to the rise of civilization; thus, he designed the excavations to reflect the distribution of settlement patterns in different areas of Mesoamerica.

Another indispensable part of the science of archaeology is the use of statistical methods and computers. Statistics play a role in determining how a site is dug (e.g., how much of a site) and is essential in analyzing patterns. Computers enable archaeologists to manage large amounts of data and perform complex analyses of information so as to test explanatory and predictive models.

Reasoning and Logic

Because archaeologists contend with indirect bodies of evidence, the significance of their data must be carefully considered. Often, they design

Excavated skeleton from the Helton burial mound in southern Illinois. Burial practices, including the positioning of the body during interment, often reflect a culture's social organization.

their research so as to apply *deductive logic*, by which laws are derived to explain specific events. Many of the explanations used by archaeologists are derived from anthropology and other social sciences (Fagan 1988). For example, Binford (1972) used the deductive method to investigate the appearance and distribution of red-ochre caches (storage vessels) in prehistoric Indian burials. Noting that the caches varied in form, both within specific sites and from one site to another, Binford examined the existence of regional patterns within the general explanatory model of "cultural drift." This theory contends that small changes can accumulate within societies that lead to big differences among cultures. Binford designed his research and analysis to test these implications.

The use of deductive reasoning was especially popular during the early days of processual archaeology. However, there is growing concern that broad laws are "so generalized . . . that it is difficult to test them with specific data" (Fagan 1988, 521). Even so, testing generalized explanations with specific cases still provides us with important insights into cultural patterns.

Another way to investigate the archaeological record is through *inference*—using evidence to make logical assumptions about a phenomenon. Inference is especially useful in archaeology, where indirect evidence is used to study behavior in extinct societies. While archaeologists cannot directly observe these peoples, they *can* make inferences about their ways of life by examining their material remains and other forms of evidence. Inferences can be quite straightforward. For example, if we find a concentration of broken pieces of clay pottery (potsherds) near the remains of a fire pit, we can infer that the people made and used pottery and that pottery was made at that particular site. We can also make more complex inferences. Further examination may reveal the techniques used to make the pottery, the firing temperature, the glazing methods, and so forth. This information, along with what we know about how pottery is used and made in other societies, helps scientists make inferences about the ancient society; for example, we can infer the types of food they ate, how they obtained and prepared the food, and the level of cultural complexity.

Scientific inferences do not involve guesswork; rather, they make use of what we have learned about a phenomenon through other means of inquiry. An important source of such information is analogies, particularly those that use information about existing cultures to make inferences about the past. (The use of ethnographic analogies will be discussed later in this chapter.)

The scientific method and deduction and inference provide the means by which we conduct archaeological research. However, these means serve us only when we use them in the context of specific theories. The theoretical framework of greatest importance to contemporary archaeologists is provided by the evolutionary/ecological perspective.

The Evolutionary/Ecological Perspective

Anthropological archaeology's current evolutionary perspective is different from that of earlier times. While the lineal evolutionists simplistically viewed human cultures as arranged in a graded series, cultural evolution is now viewed as a much more complex process consisting of many interacting factors. Essential to this is **cultural ecology**—the study of how human groups interact with and adjust to their environments, especially through the process of adaptation. For example, Julian Steward, who is credited with founding cultural ecology, hypothesized that similarities among cultures are the result of similar responses to like environments, while differences are partly the result of responses to differing ecological pressures (see also "Cultural Ecology" in Chapter 13).

The acceptance of the systems approach has permitted archaeologists to more fully understand the relationship of culture to the **ecosystem**; that is, to all living organisms and their physical environments within a specific area. As demonstrated by Jason Smith's (1976) model, the systems approach has led archaeologists to study not only how the components of culture relate to one another, but also how the culture and its environment are interrelated. For example, Struever (1968) used an evolutionary/ecological approach when he analyzed the subsistence-settlement systems of two prehistoric North American Indian cultures that lived at different times at the same location. His purpose was to investigate the theory that a change in one aspect of a culture influences the overall cultural system. To test this hypothesis in the archaeological record, he examined how material remains reflect the manner in which a social group breaks up into smaller groups so as "to exploit its biophysical environment" (p. 285).

By providing a theoretical framework for explaining cultural processes, the evolutionary/ecological perspective has greatly influenced the design of archaeological research. One of its most important methodological ramifications has been the growth of the multidisciplinary approach.

The Multidisciplinary Approach

While the multidisciplinary approach is used by anthropologists in general, it is especially important to archaeologists. Making use of the talents of a variety of scientists, archaeologists seek to extract every possible piece of information from a site.

The Koster site, the data-flow system of which is diagrammed in Figure 8.2, serves as an excellent example of the multidisciplinary approach. A range of experts participated in the project, both in the field and in the laboratory. For example, the analysis of artifacts was conducted by archaeologists, while a botanist who specialized in the study of plants used by ancient cultures was responsible for analyzing plant remains. Other specialists analyzed ancient pollen grains to help reconstruct the local climate and plants. Mussel and snail shells, fish scales, bones, and other animal remains were carefully collected and analyzed by paleozoologists. A biological anthropologist was in charge of the excavation, preservation, and analysis of the Koster site's human remains.

Ethnographic Analogy: Using the Cultural Present to Explore the Cultural Past

As we have already stated, analogies have long been used in archaeology, especially in reconstructing past ways of life and in making functional interpretations of artifacts. An important recent trend in anthropological archaeology is known as **ethnographic analogy**—the use of ex-

FIGURE 8.2

The multidisciplinary approach applied to the Koster site: The data-flow system.

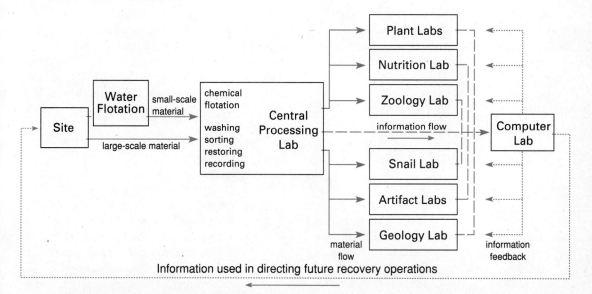

isting cultures for generating hypotheses to test in the archaeological record and for testing hypotheses derived from the record. Strongly influenced by the ecological perspective, ethnographic analogies are often based on the relationship between cultural adaptations and environmental factors. Thus, the best ethnographic analogies are made between groups that share similar environments and cultural levels, these groups being the most likely to demonstrate similar means of adaptation.

In a pioneer article on ethnographic analogy, Binford (1967) discusses the use of smudge pits—small pits dug in the ground by the prehistoric people for the purpose of smoking hides. A review of the ethnographic record of some American Indian groups to examine how variations in smudge-pit form is related to differences in function provided Binford with insight into what sort of traits to look for in the archaeological record and how to interpret the function of prehistoric smudge pits.

As ethnographic analogies grew in popularity, it became clear that many cultural anthropologists were not gathering the specific kinds of information of interest to archaeologists. As a result, some archaeologists now make their own observations of contemporary cultures in an approach known as **ethnoarchaeology**. Archaeologists most often focus on contemporary foragers because hunting and gathering was the predominant way of life during prehistoric times. For example, Richard Gould (1980) observed an Aborigine group in an Australian desert with particular attention to how their use of material goods reflected their overall way of life. He recorded how the Aborigines obtained water, hunted game, and collected vegetable matter. He also carefully studied how they made and used their stone tools, noting how many waste flakes were produced and how such debris was distributed at a site. A particular concern of archaeologists is with what campsites look like after they are abandoned, since many archaeological sites *are* abandoned campsites. Thus, Gould mapped an abandoned campsite to see how the distribu-

tion of materials reflected the activities he observed while the camp was in use.

Another "active" type of ethnographic analogy is **experimental archaeology**—controlled experiments in the use of prehistoric material culture. The idea is that "by reproducing [an ancient person's] actions, archaeologists can better understand not only his technical abilities but also his reasons for choosing one course of action rather than another" (Coles 1979, 2). Two fundamental rules must be followed in performing experiments that replicate ancient technology. First, the materials used must be the same as those available to the people being studied; second, the techniques applied must be in keeping with the people's technological level.

Many archaeological experiments are concerned with the production and use of tools, such as those conducted by François Bordes, who replicated European Stone Age technology. Some American archaeologists, such as John White (who worked at the Koster site), specialize in replicating the techniques of early Native Americans. Some studies are dramatic. For example, Thor Heyerdahl's (1950) *Kon-Tiki* expedition was an attempt to support his theory that the Polynesian islands were populated from the Americas (the predominant scientific view is that the South Pacific islands were populated from Southeast Asia). To prove his point, Heyerdahl constructed a large balsa raft, which he used to make the long and perilous voyage from the coast of Peru to the Tuamotu Islands. However, while the successful journey did demonstrate the durability of the raft, it did not positively prove Heyerdahl's theory.

Another example is that of the Overton Down earthwork, constructed by British archaeologists to study the processes by which an archaeological site comes to look the way it does (see Figure 8.3). The earthwork, which consists of a large mound and a ditch, is much like structures built during the occupation of the British Isles by the Roman Empire. Scientists buried in the mound a variety of artifacts made of materials such as wood, cloth, leather, and pottery. The experiment is long-

FIGURE 8.3
The Overton Down earthwork in
Wiltshire, England. The earthwork
is an experimental project to study
the mechanical forces that influence
the composition of archaeological
sites. The diagram illustrates changes
that occurred in the earthwork over
a period of two years.

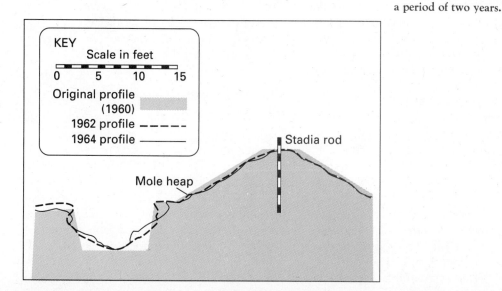

KEY
Scale in feet
0   5   10   15
Original profile
(1960)
1962 profile — — — —
1964 profile ————

Stadia rod

Mole heap

term: scientists plan to excavate sections of the earthwork at intervals from 2 to 128 years. During each excavation they will observe the preservation state of the various types of artifacts and determine how natural forces affect deterioration. Scientists plan to use this information in interpreting the archaeological remains of actual earthworks.

A relatively new approach to ethnographic analogy is that of **middle-range theory** (Binford 1977). Using ideas proposed in other social sciences (particularly sociology), middle-range theory attempts to be more sophisticated in how the present is used to make inferences regarding the past. The basic premise is that the archaeological record is a static, unchanging representation of the dynamic processes of culture and behavior. The challenge for archaeologists is to use information collected on contemporary societies to understand how these dynamic processes are reflected by the static remains of extinct cultures.

Thus, they seek refined ways of "translating" static archaeological remains into dynamic cultural processes. What distinguishes middle-range theory from other attempts is that "it is tested with living cultural systems, and provides the instruments for testing the variables identified in archaeological theory" (Fagan 1988, 411). Only a limited number of studies have actually applied middle-range theory. For example, Binford (1978) studied the Nunamiut Eskimo to see how animal remains (static evidence) reflected different ways of using sites (dynamic processes). His objective was to form an "operational definition" of a hunting camp, butchering site, and so on.

Contemporary archaeology is a complex scientific approach to understanding the remains of ancient cultures. It is essential to keep in mind that its ideas and theory are based on its special body of evidence. Now, let us consider the various types of evidence used by archaeologists to explore the cultural past.

ARCHAEOLOGICAL EVIDENCE

There are two basic aspects to archaeological evidence: (1) the physical evidence itself and (2) the context within which the evidence is found. A major category of evidence is that of *durable remains*—objects preserved and not completely destroyed by natural deterioration processes. As mentioned earlier in the chapter, durable remains include *artifacts*, the products of human behavior, and *ecofacts*, objects reflecting an ancient human group's environment.

Essential to understanding the meaning of durable remains is the *context* within which they are found. Without information regarding context, an artifact, no matter how lovely or intriguing, is virtually without scientific value. Archaeological context consists of *environmental context*, which includes both the natural and the social environments; *spatial context*, how the materials are placed in space; and *temporal (chronological) context*, the age of the materials and how they are placed in time.

The multidimensionability of both the durable remains and the context in which they are found poses many challenges to scientists. In fact, the nature of the archaeological evidence largely dictates the manner in which archaeological inquiry is conducted.

Durable Remains: Material Culture

The remains of a society's material culture, archaeological artifacts, include portable objects that can be removed from a site, such as tools, pottery fragments, and projectile points (see Figure 8.4a). Other artifacts are categorized as **features**, nonportable remnants of human activity that cannot be removed intact from a site. Features are often no more than patterned discolorations of the soil that reflect the remains of rotted wooden posts, hearths, storage pits, or burials, as exemplified in Figure 8.4(b). Once a

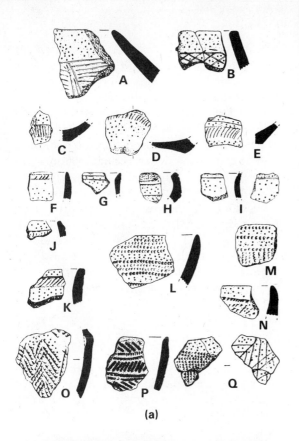

(a)

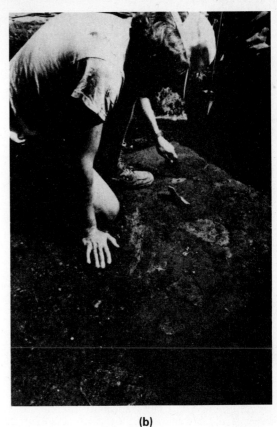

(b)

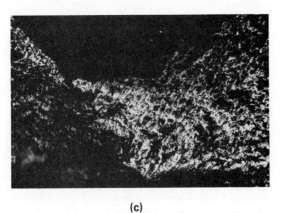

(c)

FIGURE 8.4

Artifacts: Durable remains of material culture. (a) Pottery sherds (pieces) from an archaeological site in Tanzania, Africa. Attributes of the sherds are used to classify the original vessels. The rim sherds (A, B, F, G, H, K, L, and N) vary in shape, whereas the base sherds (C–E) are all flat. Sherds A–K are decorated with incised lines and sherds L–Q are decorated with a variety of impressed and punctuate patterns. (b) An archaeological feature: Post molds uncovered at the Koster site are outlined by an archaeologist. The molds are decayed organic remains that left visible stains in the soil ground. The stains were produced by tree trunks placed upright in the ground by prehistoric inhabitants of the site, probably as the frame of a house or other structure. (c) Electron microscopic photograph of microwear (130 × actual size). This "wood polish," which appears on the edge of a flint blade used for woodworking, is a typical pattern of damage caused by the rubbing of grit particles during the use of such a tool. The implement was uncovered at a Mesolithic site in Ireland.

feature is uncovered, all the information that can be obtained from it must be gathered at the site before the feature is altered during further excavation. Artifacts may also be the discarded by-products of human activity, known as **debris**. Archaeologists learn much from this "garbage" of human behavior. For example, a large concentration of stone chips at a site suggests that tools were made there. Debris also indicates what types of materials were used for tools and the techniques involved in fashioning the tools. Garbage left from ancient meals reflects the diet of the population and how the food was prepared.

After archaeologists have systematically collected artifacts, they classify them into types, a process known as *archaeological typology*. The classification is based on the artifact's characteristics, or *attributes*. Attributes include traits such as size, shape, decoration, design, and method of fabrication. Besides being used to group artifacts into categories, attributes also may reflect an artifact's function. One attribute that can be used to determine how an artifact (especially a stone tool) was made is *microwear*, wear patterns on the edges of artifacts consisting of tiny marks and chips (see Figure 8.4c). Other attributes reflect cultural traditions. For example, decorative patterns on pottery can be used to identify the cultural traditions that influenced the thought processes of the potters, as we saw in Figure 8.4(a).

Durable Remains: Environmental Materials

Ecofacts are environmental materials such as pollen, shells, plant fibers, and bones. Sometimes, ecofacts reflect human activity; for example, in the case of food remains or charred wood from fires. Other ecofacts are the untouched residue of the environment, such as sediments from lakes and unprocessed seeds. Thus, although classified as durable remains, ecofacts are useful in reconstructing a culture's environmental context.

The scientific analysis of one type of ecofact, pollen, is known as **palynology**. By means of microscopy, palynologists classify ancient pollens found in the soil of a site. Since each type of plant has its own distinctive pollen, scientists can use this information to reconstruct the type of plant life that characterized an area during a period of time and thus gain insight into the natural resources that were available to the ancient people. Pollens also provide climatic information, since specific plants grow under specific conditions (see the photos that follow). For example, pollen analysis of the Stone Age hunting site, Starr Carr, along with information on how the material was distributed, clearly indicated that the ancient people lived in a temperate climate and that the settlement was located in a forest consisting of birch, pine, and willow trees, with a reed swamp and water lily marsh nearby (J.G.D. Clark 1954).

Environmental Context

A key aspect of deciphering the archaeological record is understanding the natural and social context within which a prehistoric society lived. Social context includes a group's contact with other societies, which can greatly influence its cultural adaptation through the exchange of ideas and technology. For example, trade and warfare can influence a society's way of life, as can the exchange of mates and other forms of migration. Archaeologists gain clues to social context through the analysis of durable remains. For instance, uncovering a decorative artifact of a design and material not associated with the group under investigation suggests that the group may have exchanged gifts with another society and perhaps were allied with another society politically.

The natural environment includes climate, physical features of the land, water resources, and the local plant and animal life. As introduced in Chapter 5, paleoecology is the scientific study that seeks to reconstruct ancient environments. Ecofacts provide important clues to what these environments were like, as do other types of evidence, including the nature of the soil and geological structures.

As noted previously, archaeologists use the

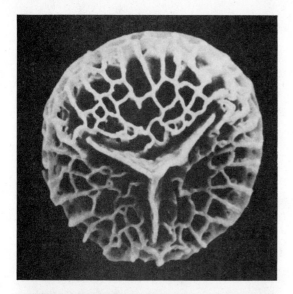

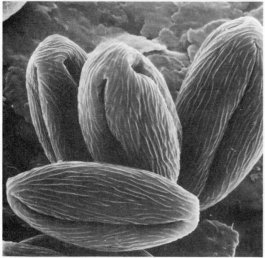

Magnified pollen grains. Palynologists use ancient pollens found in the soil of archaeological sites in the study of ancient environments. (top) Pollen grain from a fern, associated with a forested environment. (bottom) Pollen grains from cornflowers, a weed commonly found in cultivated fields.

technologies of a range of scientific disciplines when reconstructing prehistoric environments. For example, geology and soil analysis are used to obtain information from the earth. *Faunal anal-*

ysis, the specialized study of animal remains, answers questions concerning the type and number of animals that lived in the environment: Were they wild or domesticated? Do their remains reflect butchering or some other manipulation by humans? Ancient plant life is studied through *paleobotany*, which investigates questions regarding the type and distribution of plant life and how a prehistoric society used plants: Were the plants processed or stored? Were they undergoing domestication?

Spatial Context

Contemporary American archaeology is concerned with spatial context, which encompasses both how artifacts and ecofacts are distributed within a site and how sites are distributed across geological space. Spatial context tells us much about how a site was used and how the people interacted with the natural and social environments.

The study of spatial context is founded on a number of basic concepts. The usual unit of excavation is called a **site**, which is represented by a spatial concentration of durable remains. The composition of a site reflects the human activity that occurred within its boundaries. Sites are divided into components, a **component** representing a distinctive occupation of the site by one specific group of people. An excavation may reveal that only one group of people occupied the site; thus, it is termed a *single-component site*. If excavation reveals different cultural zones, indicating that the site was inhabited by a number of discrete groups through time, then this is a *multicomponent site*. Koster is a multicomponent site, with evidence of at least 13 major cultural zones.

This spatial framework is used to organize cultural remains into assemblages. An **assemblage** refers to all the artifacts contained within one component of a site. The distribution and composition of assemblages provide information about how a site was used and, therefore, how the people lived. Within assemblages, artifacts are grouped into functional categories known as *subassemblages*. For example, one subassemblage may consist of all the artifacts associated with hunting, such as arrowheads, spearpoints, and spear throwers; another, all of those associated with food processing, such as cooking vessels, pottery, and mortars and pestles. From the combined evidence of the various subassemblages, archaeologists obtain an overall picture of the society's way of life.

How an assemblage is distributed within a site provides scientists with important information regarding *site usage* (see Figure 8.5). Interpretations are made using the archaeological *law of association*; that is, objects found together in time and space are usually associated and not grouped together by chance. For example, the presence of

charred animal remains near a fire pit indicates that the area was used for food preparation and that meat was part of the people's diet.

Since studies of site usage depend to a large extent on the statistical analysis of how assemblages are distributed, archaeologists usually classify sites according to their primary functions. For example, *habitation sites* are where people lived and carried on a range of activities, as might be reflected by evidence of clusters of shelters, hearths, storage pits, and "garbage dumps" on the periphery. *Burial sites* are often characterized by the presence of human remains placed in ritualistic body positions; also, by the presence of grave goods. *Kill sites* are those areas in which

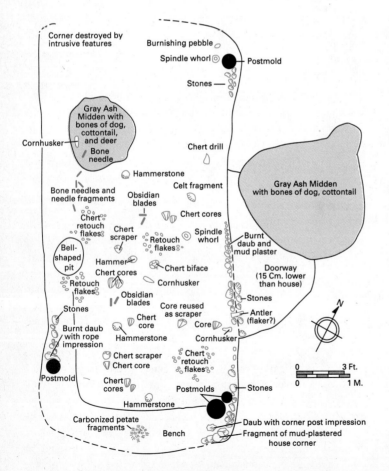

FIGURE 8.5

Spatial distribution of artifacts at the site of a house at Tierras Largas, Oaxaca, ca. 900 B.C.

large numbers of animals were slaughtered and butchered, as evidenced by a concentration of dismembered animal bones and discarded tools.

Sites themselves may be distributed in distinct patterns across geographical space. The regional patterning of sites reflects the overall cultural and ecological systems that existed within a specific area during a specific period of time. As we will discuss more fully in the section "Ordering Sites in Time and Space," understanding these patterns helps scientists to develop hypotheses about how cultures evolve and about the role that social environment plays in this evolution.

Temporal Context

Archaeology has long emphasized the importance of accurately ordering objects in time. As introduced in Chapter 5, there are two categories of dating techniques: relative and absolute dating. The specific techniques used in dating vary according to the composition of the materials; for example, different methods are used for organic and inorganic remains. The age of the object is also a factor because some techniques are valid only for very ancient materials; others are used to date objects from the less distant past.

Relative-Dating Techniques

Relative dating is not dating in the strict sense of the word; rather, it is the serial ordering of a set of objects in time. The two relative-dating techniques most often used by archaeologists are stratigraphy and seriation.

As noted in Chapter 5, stratigraphy is the most commonly applied relative-dating technique. It is based on the geological *law of superposition*, which states that, in an undisturbed sequence of layered rocks, the oldest layers are the deepest and the most shallow layers are the youngest. It follows that objects found in a geologic stratum (layer) would be of corresponding age and sequence; that is, if A is deeper than B and B is deeper than C, then A is the oldest object and C is the youngest. Stratigraphy, then, is especially useful in multicomponent sites characterized by a number of different occupations (see Figure 8.6).

Although popular, stratigraphy has its problems. For one, it can be difficult to distinguish where one stratum ends and another begins, such as in very sandy soil without sedimentary deposits. In such cases, archaeologists must make somewhat arbitrary decisions about how to divide a site into zones and hope that their decisions will

FIGURE 8.6

Stratigraphy and archaeology. In this hypothetical example, the stone ax found in stratum D is the oldest artifact. The youngest artifacts are the arrowheads found in stratum A.

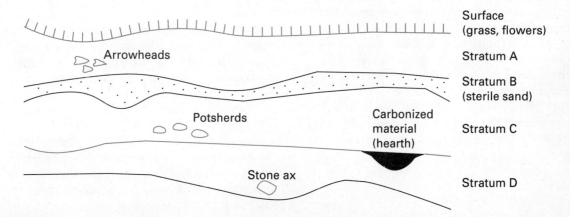

Surface (grass, flowers)

Arrowheads

Stratum A

Stratum B (sterile sand)

Potsherds

Carbonized material (hearth)

Stratum C

Stone ax

Stratum D

correspond with what the artifactual materials reveal about cultural stages. Another problem is disruptions in the neat patterning of the strata. Disruptions can be caused by natural forces (e.g., the movement of the earth, frost, and volcanic activity) and by human intervention (e.g., the reuse of burial mounds and the construction of buildings).

Seriation is a type of relative dating in which the attributes of artifacts are used to arrange assemblages so that they reflect temporal patterns of popularity in style and design. The major assumption underlying seriation is that when an attribute is introduced into a culture it occurs at a low frequency. Then, as time passes, the attribute's frequency increases as it gains in popularity. This is followed by a gradual decrease in frequency as the attribute loses popularity until it finally vanishes from the culture, superseded by another. Statistics plays a crucial role in measuring the frequency trends of attributes. From statistical data, archaeologists arrange assemblages "in such a way that the frequencies of various types of artifacts in them form 'battleship-shaped' curves through time" (Deetz 1967, 27).

Seriation is applied in two ways. The first focuses on the patterns resulting from two or more discrete styles that can be recognized as coming and going within a culture. A famous example of this application is a study of changes in colonial gravestone design (Dethlefsen and Deetz 1966). Three distinct designs went in and out of popularity: "death's head" was replaced by "cherub," which was then replaced by the "urn and willow" pattern (see Figure 8.7).

Seriation is also used to study changes within one particular style, reflecting the progression of the style. A famous study of this sort was conducted during the late 1800s by Sir Flinders Petrie, who investigated funeral pottery in Egyptian tombs. To order the finds chronologically, he was guided by changes that occurred in the handles of the vessels, which he noted became progressively smaller, until finally they were symbolically represented by painted lines.

Scientists must be prudent in their use of ser-iation. Not only must frequencies be calculated with great precision, but it must also be recognized that there are exceptions to the basic premise that battleship-shaped curves of popularity *always* exist.

Absolute-Dating Techniques

Absolute dating is a method by which the actual ages of objects are determined. Since World War II, major strides have been made in this field, particularly as the result of atomic research.

Archaeologists use a number of absolute-dating techniques, the best known of which is radiocarbon (carbon-14) dating (see also Chapter 5). Radiocarbon dating is of special use to American archaeologists because it can date objects from about 70,000 years ago up until recent New World prehistoric times. It is based on the ability to measure the radioactive carbon content of organic materials, such as charcoal, bone, skin, wood, and shells. There are a number of problems associated with radiocarbon dating, however. First of all, it converts materials into gases, thus destroying them. In addition, the process is expensive, which may limit how often tests are done. Still another problem is that extreme care must be taken in how the samples are collected; for example, it is easy to mix recent organic materials, such as leaves, sticks, and cigarette ash, in with the old. A small amount of these materials can seriously throw off radiocarbon dates. And even when care is taken, radiocarbon dates are still only approximate ages, since there have been fluctuations in the ratio of carbon-12 to carbon-14 in the atmosphere over the last 70,000 years.

Another atomically based technique is potassium-argon dating, in which a radioactive isotope of potassium decays into argon gas. Potassium-argon dating is performed on inorganic materials of volcanic origin, such as obsidian. It can accurately date as far back as 4.5 billion years but is not so accurate for materials younger than 100,000 years old. Potassium-argon dating has its limitations also; for example, scientists need very specific types of materials for the tests and it is of limited use for dating younger objects.

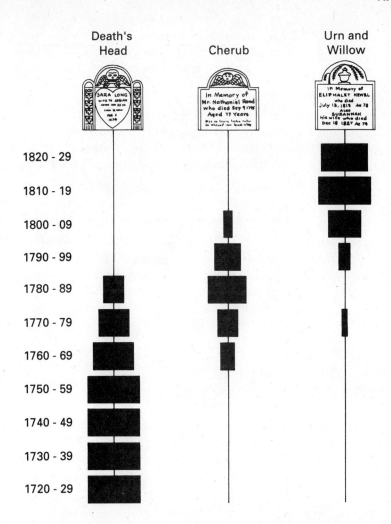

FIGURE 8.7
Seriation of stylistic sequences of gravestones in Stoneham, Massachusetts. The battleship-shaped curves illustrate the pattern of how styles come in and out of favor.

Besides nuclear techniques, there are other ways of obtaining absolute dates. In **cross-dating**, objects of known age are used to determine the age of associated materials. Cross-dating is most often applied at Old World classical sites, since it usually makes use of historical objects. For example, a Roman coin found in close association with other objects is a good indicator of their age; a specifically styled Chinese vessel of known age indicates the age of the assemblage in which it is found. Cross-dating is a very limited technique, however, and of little use in the study of New World prehistory.

A remarkably precise absolute-dating technique is **dendrochronology**, based on the fact that trees add one ring of new wood each year. The width of the annual growth ring varies with the amount of precipitation: a dry year will produce a thin ring; a wet year, a thick one—a pattern that ceases when the tree is cut down. Over each 50-year period, a unique pattern of rings is formed. Scientists have devised master charts of these patterns for specific geographical regions by working back from present-day trees and overlapping patterns with progressively older timber. Wood samples (for example, from structural posts) are obtained from archaeological sites. The pattern of growth rings for the prehistoric wood is then compared with the master sheet. When patterns match, scientists can be sure that the tree was felled in the year represented by its youngest growth ring. The tree-ring patterns also provide archaeologists with information about the ancient climate, as reflected by amounts of rainfall and the type of trees that grew in the region (see Figure 8.8).

Although an ingenious technique, dendrochronology also has drawbacks. Getting a good sample of wood can be a problem because the 25 most recent rings must be preserved to perform an analysis. Also, the wood excavated at a site does not always accurately reflect the site's age. For example, timber from a more ancient structure may have been reused. A more significant limitation is that master charts apply only to specific areas: the more homogeneous the rainfall, the broader the application. Dendrochronology is therefore most useful in semiarid regions, since in climates with a lot of precipitation there can be great fluxes in rainfall, even within a few miles.

Ordering Sites in Time and Space

To formulate broad pictures of cultural patterns, sites are ordered and grouped in terms of both time and space. The two closely related concepts of horizon and tradition are used in this analysis.

A **horizon** is a pattern characterized by cultural traits dating from the same time and distributed over a broad geographic area. These traits

FIGURE 8.8
Dendrochronology: constructing a master tree-ring chronology.

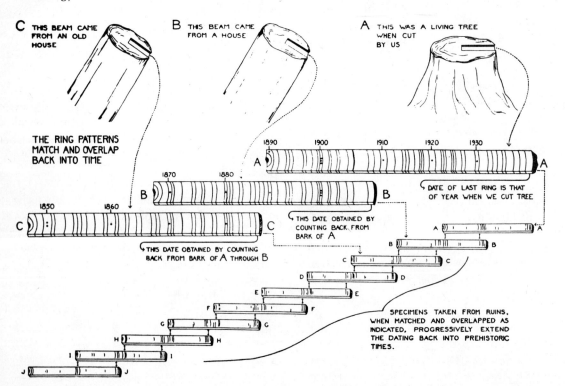

C THIS BEAM CAME FROM AN OLD HOUSE

B THIS BEAM CAME FROM A HOUSE

A THIS WAS A LIVING TREE WHEN CUT BY US

THE RING PATTERNS MATCH AND OVERLAP BACK INTO TIME

DATE OF LAST RING IS THAT OF YEAR WHEN WE CUT TREE

THIS DATE OBTAINED BY COUNTING BACK FROM BARK OF A

THIS DATE OBTAINED BY COUNTING BACK FROM BARK OF A THROUGH B

SPECIMENS TAKEN FROM RUINS, WHEN MATCHED AND OVERLAPPED AS INDICATED, PROGRESSIVELY EXTEND THE DATING BACK INTO PREHISTORIC TIMES.

serve to link the sites together culturally over large distances and over relatively short spans of time. A **tradition** is a pattern characterized by artifacts with similar attributes of widely varying ages and confined to a small geographical area. Traditions reflect ideas passed on from one generation to another, without necessarily having been spread over a large geographical area. In other words, horizons represent the spread of ideas (and possibly cultures) over large areas, whereas traditions reflect the stability of ideas or cultural behaviors within a particular society over long periods of time. These concepts are diagrammed in Figure 8.9.

Because horizons and traditions are not mutually exclusive concepts, it can be difficult to distinguish between them in the archaeological record. It is entirely possible to find a cultural horizon and a cultural tradition coexisting. For example, the Hopewell, a prehistoric Native American agricultural society, represents a tradition that was spread over a broad geographical area. The tradition dimension is reflected by magnificent art objects, such as copper bird figures and carved soapstone pipebowls that were buried with high-status individuals in mounds dating from about 200 B.C. to A.D. 600. The horizon dimension is reflected by the widespread geographical distribution of sites containing

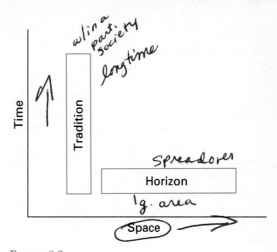

FIGURE 8.9
Tradition versus horizon.

these objects—from Illinois, to Wisconsin, to Louisiana, and east into Ohio and New York State.

Horizons and traditions are useful concepts for delineating broad patterns of how cultural traits are distributed in time and space. Such patterns help archaeologists to devise even broader units, called stages. We will discuss the stages of cultural evolution in Chapters 9, 10, and 11.

DOING ARCHAEOLOGY

Many people picture an archaeologist's life as one of adventure, filled with exciting discoveries of ancient societies. Of course, archaeology can be thrilling. Much of it, however, consists of long hours of careful and tedious excavation. Yet, such fieldwork is the basic source of information regarding the past. Archaeological research consists of three major steps: collecting information (fieldwork), describing and classifying the information, and interpreting the information. Each

of these broad steps has many different aspects, as we will now describe.

Collecting Information: Conducting Fieldwork

Archaeologists perform a number of steps before actually excavating a site. First, consistent with their problem orientation, archaeologists determine why a site should be dug. A particular problem is posed: How, for example, was the domestication of maize spread through the New World? How were living sites organized in the lower Illinois Valley? What was the relationship between settlement patterns and the use of natural resources? The problem dictates the project's *research design*—how one goes about solving the problem, including where to dig, how to dig, and how the data are to be analyzed. One factor in developing a research design is the physical condition of the site. Is the soil sandy or composed of clay? Is the site located in a desert or on the floodplain of a river? The research design is also influenced by practical matters, such as the limitations of time, money, and work force.

Next, archaeologists do *prefield research*. They review historical documents and read works concerned with the topic and geographic location. To gain information on the best place to dig, archaeologists speak with experts and residents of the area who might have noticed an interesting feature or who have found artifacts.

Archaeologists then conduct *site surveys*, the superficial scanning of a promising area. This again contributes information on exactly where they should dig. Site surveys are conducted in many ways. A well-trained person may drive around an area looking for features that suggest human activity or, perhaps, walk through a field in search of artifacts that have worked their way to the surface. Some archaeologists conduct *aerial surveys*, in which land is viewed and photographed from an airplane. Such a long-range view can reveal large features, such as burial mounds or terracing, that may not be noticeable from ground level.

Once archaeologists have a general idea of where best to dig, they perform *test excavations*. This provides them with still more information in choosing a specific site before making a major investment of time and money. Test excavations allow archaeologists to determine the nature of the possible sites, including the state of preservation of the materials and the sites' boundaries.

Using all this information, archaeologists then

choose a particular site. The problem orientation is especially important in making this decision: What site is best for answering the question at hand? Perhaps a burial site would yield the most information. Or a site with a number of ecological zones. An exception to this focus is **salvage archaeology**. Many states have laws requiring that archaeologists excavate land that is about to be drastically changed through the building of highways, dams, and other structures. Since such work permanently damages the archaeological record, salvage archaeologists attempt to glean as much information from the condemned area as possible without a specific scientific question in mind.

The next step is setting up a field camp—living quarters for the crew and a place to conduct preliminary laboratory work. Camps are often set up in nearby towns. If this is not practical, a temporary camp is set up in the field.

Before excavation takes place, archaeologists must carefully map the site. The mapping provides the framework for recording the spatial context of all the excavated materials. The most common mapping technique utilizes a *grid system*. A permanent marker, called a *datum point*, such as a cement post or steel rod, is sunk into the ground to serve as the reference point from which the grid system is laid out. The squares of the grid are labeled by a system of numbers or letters, or both. Each time material is uncovered, the code is used to record its location (see Figure 8.10).

Next comes the digging of a *control pit*. This is done close to the site, but not actually on it, so as to collect information about the site's conditions without disturbing it. Control pits provide information regarding environmental context and help archaeologists decide how to best excavate.

An important scientific decision preliminary to excavation involves *site sampling*. Because of limited time, money, and other factors, it is seldom possible to excavate an entire site. Thus, archaeologists must decide how much and what aspects of a site are to be excavated. This decision

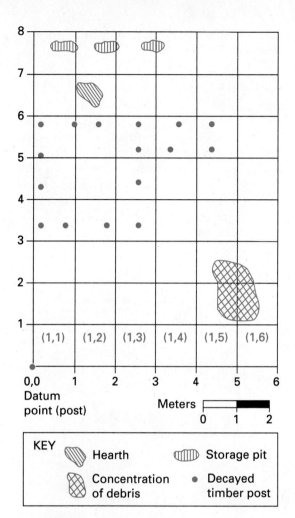

FIGURE 8.10

Hypothetical example of a grid-system map indicating the location of features.

techniques and equipment vary in accordance with the physical condition of the particular site and problem orientation. Archaeologists use a wide range of tools, including bulldozers, shovels, trowels, picks, and small brushes. Clearly, a site consisting of major architectural ruins dictates the use of different techniques than a kill site covered with thousands of small bones and tools. But no matter what the technique, archaeologists are always aware that excavation is destruction. Once an area is dug, there is no way to gather information that has been overlooked, especially data concerning spatial context and features. Thus, careful records are kept in the form of reports, journals, drawings, photographs, maps, and stratigraphic profiles (see Figure 8.11).

Analyzing the Data: Description and Classification

The second major step of archaeological research is to describe and classify the evidence so that it can be used to answer questions. The analysis of data begins in the field, with preliminary on-the-spot recording of such information as where an object was found, its spatial relationship to other items, and the excavator's impressions of how it should be classified. The objects are then cleaned, labeled, and recorded in a field catalogue. This early record keeping greatly decreases the possibility that errors will be made when the objects are closely scrutinized. The materials are then carefully packed and sent to laboratories.

During the laboratory analysis, materials are more thoroughly examined using better equipment than that available in the field. This includes more rigorously classifying materials into types, describing the attributes, and assigning objects a permanent catalogue number. Laboratory analysis may also include dating, soil analysis, and microscopic, chemical, and physical tests. The materials are then carefully stored, usually at a museum or university.

Once this analysis is completed, scientists coordinate and process the data. Most contempo-

is largely made on the basis of the problem orientation: Is a random technique best? Is it most crucial to dig around a site's parameters? Archaeologists most often take a statistical approach to site sampling, randomly selecting the grid squares to excavate. Random sampling is widely used in scientific research as a means of using parts of an entity to represent the whole.

The crew can now begin the excavation. The

rary excavations yield large amounts of extremely detailed information. Because the data must be organized in a precise and accessible manner, the computer has become one of archaeology's most essential tools.

FIGURE 8.11

Stages of the excavation of an archaeological site. A grid system is set up, using surveyor's equipment to measure and map the site. Measured squares are dug while the location of finds is carefully mapped. Tools, such as brushes and dustpans, are used for excavating small artifacts, while a sieve is used to separate materials from the soil. Archaeologists must keep accurate records of the excavation through the use of journals, catalogue books, and record cards.

Interpreting the Archaeological Record

The ultimate function of archaeology is interpreting the archaeological record. Contemporary anthropological archaeology is conducted in the manner we have just described to answer the broad questions posed earlier in the chapter: How did extinct peoples behave? What processes explain patterns of cultural evolution?

Once the archaeological record has been interpreted, the results are reported to the rest of the scientific community. Publications include reports, journal articles, monographs, and books.

CURRENT DIRECTIONS IN ARCHAEOLOGY

As is true of anthropology in general, archaeology has become diverse in its range of specific theoretical and conceptual approaches. We will now briefly describe three of American archaeology's current directions.

Historical Archaeology

While most American archaeologists focus on prehistoric sites, a growing number of researchers are studying sites dating from historic times. Unlike the classical approach, **historical archae-**

ology is a specialization of anthropological archaeology that investigates the same sorts of problems as the discipline as a whole (see also Chapter 1). However, historical archaeology is distinctive for its data base, which often makes possible the use of historical documentation.

Much of the work of historical archaeologists has been to help preserve historical sites; hence, many of their reports are purely descriptive. However, since the 1960s, historical archaeology has become more of a science, as has archaeology in general. For example, South (1977) is con-

cerned with recognizing patterns and quantifying the historical archaeological record to ultimately explain "why these lawlike regularities exist" (p. xiii). In one study, South delineated the Carolina Artifact Pattern, as defined by the types of artifacts and their frequency and distribution found at British colonial sites in North and South Carolina. The pattern was originally gleaned from five sites, each of which contained between 2,000 and 42,000 artifacts. These artifacts were counted and categorized into classes and groups, the major groups including a kitchen group (ceramics, wine bottles, glassware, tableware, kitchenware); a bone group (bone fragments); an architectural group (window glass, nails, spikes, door parts); a furniture group (hinges, knobs, locks); an arms group (gun parts, musket balls, bullets); a clothing group (glass beads, hooks and eyes, thimbles); a personal group (coins, keys, mirrors, rings); a tobacco-pipe group; and an activities group (construction tools, toys, fishing gear, military items).

World Systems Theory and Archaeology

Some archaeologists feel that the development of a given society can be understood only within a broader view of culture. These researchers seek to interpret the archaeological record using **world systems theory**, an approach of cultural anthropology that views human societies as part of an interactive social system encompassing the entire world. A key focus is the interaction of cultures at different levels of economic development.

The main point debated by those favoring a world systems approach to archaeology is the question of the appropriate unit of analysis in studying cultural evolution. They argue that

the development or cultural evolution of any society is dependent upon its relations with

other societies; that cultures are open, not closed, systems; and that studies, be they based on excavations of a site or settlement data from surveys of precisely defined, well-demarcated, but bounded areas, that fail to consider broader patterns of interaction are necessarily incomplete and partial. (Kohl 1987, 1–2)

While an admirable point of view, such a broad approach to cultural evolution is impractical because "the world" is too large a unit to analyze. What does appear to be possible, however, is the analysis of specific societies within the *context* of world events. Combining the study of specific cultural histories in a broad world view would seem to be a practical solution to an interesting dilemma.

Cognitive Archaeology

Other archaeologists also apply approaches derived from cultural anthropology. For example, *cognitive archaeology* centers on the thought processes of the people who lived in ancient societies. Ian Hodder (1982), a proponent of this approach (also known as "symbolic archaeology"), contends that human behavior follows certain rules that are reflected in the archaeological record in three major ways: (1) *signs*, consisting of durable remains such as artifacts and features, are interrelated; (2) *language* functions as the code of a culture's internal structure; and (3) cultures *transform* according to the type of logic used by the people undergoing the change.

Although an intriguing idea, this type of analysis has been applied to the archaeological record in only a few studies. Attempting to understand how ancient people thought about the world is a difficult task: It may well be that the analysis of symbols will provide the key to understanding ancient cognition.

RECONSTRUCTING CULTURAL HISTORY AND UNDERSTANDING THE PROCESSES OF CULTURAL EVOLUTION

Now that we have explored the theories and methods of anthropological archaeology, we can turn to the history of cultural evolution and cultural processes. In the next three chapters, we will review some of the major ideas that archaeologists have developed regarding cultural evolution, from the Stone Age up through the origin of civilization.

SUMMARY

Applying the general theories and methods of anthropology, anthropological archaeologists use the material remains of extinct societies to study humankind's cultural past; thus, they contribute a unique time depth to the study of culture and cultural processes.

In general, archaeology has three major research goals: (1) classifying and sequencing material culture, (2) reconstructing ancient ways of life, and (3) explaining and delineating cultural processes. As the result of a scientific synthesis that took place during the 1960s, anthropological archaeologists now focus on the third goal, explaining cultural processes, an approach often labeled "processual archaeology." The major tenets of processual archaeology include an emphasis on explanation; a new sophistication in data-gathering; a concern with scientific rigor and the scientific method; the common application of deductive logic; an incorporation of the evolutionary/ecological perspective, including a focus on cultural ecology; the extensive use of the multidisciplinary approach; and the use of ethnographic analogy.

Archaeologists make use of a special kind of evidence, which has two major dimensions: durable remains, including artifacts and ecofacts, and the context within which the durable remains are found, including the environmental context, the spatial context, and the temporal context.

Archaeological research consists of three basic steps. The first major step, collecting information, includes developing a problem orientation, developing a research design, conducting prefield research, conducting site surveys, digging test excavations, choosing a site, setting up a field camp, mapping the site, designing a method of site sampling, and excavating the site. The second step, describing and classifying information, includes field laboratory analysis, main laboratory analysis, and coordinating and processing the data. The third step is interpreting the information and publishing the results.

Anthropological archaeology includes a diverse range of specific approaches. One such approach is historical archaeology, which is distinctive for its data base. Some researchers seek to interpret the archaeological record using world systems theory; others, known as cognitive archaeologists, seek to understand the thought processes of extinct peoples. Salvage archaeologists provide a special service by gathering as much data as possible from a condemned site.

SUGGESTED READINGS

Barker, Philip. 1977. *Techniques of Archaeological Excavation.* New York: Universe Books.

Binford, Lewis R. 1972. *An Archaeological Perspective.* New York: Seminar Press.

————. 1989. *Debating Archaeology.* San Diego, CA: Academic Press.

Butzer, Karl W. 1982. *Archaeology as Human Ecology.* Cambridge: Cambridge University Press.

Cleere, Henry F., ed. 1989. *Archaeological Heritage Management in the Modern World.* London: Unwin Hyman, Ltd.

Gould, Richard A. 1980. *Living Archaeology.* Cambridge: Cambridge University Press.

Green, Ernestine L. 1984. *Ethics and Values in Archaeology.* New York: The Free Press.

Hodder, Ian. 1982. *Symbolic and Structural Archaeology.* Cambridge: Cambridge University Press.

Leone, Mark P., and Parker B. Potter, Jr. 1988. *The Recovery of Meaning.* Washington, DC: Smithsonian Institution Press.

Patterson, Thomas. 1983. *The Theory and Practice of Archaeology.* New York: The Free Press.

Struever, Stuart, and Felicia A. Holton. 1979. *Koster: Americans in Search of Their Prehistoric Past.* Garden City, NJ: Anchor Press/Doubleday.

Preserving the Past:
Conservation Archaeology on Guam

Richard D. Davis

Richard D. Davis studied anthropology at the University of Oregon. He has been actively involved with historic preservation since 1978, at first working for the Willamette National Forest in the early days of its development of a program to find and manage its historical sites. Mr. Davis relocated to Guam in 1978 and has been part of the Guam government's historic preservation program ever since. Mr. Davis has also worked at archaeological sites in eastern Virginia and central Oregon, as well as in Micronesia.

There ought to be a law . . .

When enough people can agree on an idea, it becomes a law. In recent years, national and local governments have passed laws or ordinances that require protection of archaeological or historic sites and monuments—or at least require a controlled study at sites that will be destroyed as the result of construction projects, such as highways or dams. This sort of archaeology is referred to as "conservation archaeology" or "cultural resource management," to distinguish it from research designed primarily to satisfy academic or scholarly concerns.

A conservation archaeologist typically works for a government agency or an organization that contracts to provide archaeological services to developers who have to meet legal requirements. Many universities sponsor such organizations, but many more archaeological contractors are not associated with the academic institutions that were once the dominant places of employment for archaeologists. In this practice, archaeologists, along with historians, architects, and the other historic-preservation professionals, find themselves working to balance research goals and historic values with an astounding array of valid competing interests, many of which are supported by their own laws.

I currently work for the Guam Historic Preservation Office, which implements the laws of the Territory of Guam and those of the United States regarding historic places. At this office, we have helped design intensive surveys of jungles and savannahs slated to become golf courses. One of those surveys helped establish that the prehistoric Chamorro Islanders, indigenous to Guam, had begun intensively exploiting inland hills centuries earlier than previously thought. Other development projects have redesigned facilities to avoid harming major coastal archaeological sites. Some such sites have been protected with legally enforceable easements. (Conservation archaeology is often just as actively interested in achieving such legal protections for the survival of sites as it is in the systematic studies that can be accomplished at a particular place.)

Places of interest for their historical associations are just as important to our programs as those with great potential for scientific research. For example, "pillboxes" (concrete enclosures to protect machine-gun positions) constructed by the Japanese army

Children play in the ruins of Agana, Guam, after the town was destroyed in a World War II battle between American and Japanese forces. Conservation archaeologist Richard Davis is concerned with saving sites of cultural and historic interest, including those of major battles and war crimes.

during World War II using forced labor have been legally protected through actions of our office. These fortifications are visible reminders of the 2-1/2 years during which the Chamorro Islanders suffered under occupation forces while the Japanese defended Guam against the efforts of the United States to reclaim the territory. Major battle sites and sites of war crimes, such as mass execution of Chamorro Islanders, have also been documented and saved from competing land uses.

The preservation office is also concerned with earlier sites. For example, the program has funded archival research on the early Spanish mission sites established on Guam after 1668. Many forts, bridges, and other public structures from the island's Spanish administration have also been located, documented, and formally accorded legal protection. In addition, we have helped repair historic houses and churches that were damaged when a recent typhoon passed over Guam with winds in excess of 140 miles per hour. Another example concerns our legal battle to control the research and recovery of a sunken Spanish galleon. Judges, not historians or archaeologists, were the final arbiters in this case. Archaeologists involved in the recovery must shape their practice to constraints imposed by the decisions of the courts as well as to those constraints imposed by the physical conditions of the site.

Many people are involved with the preservation of a site. They are likely to differ in the values they emphasize, which may be cultural, historic, commercial, sentimental, or aesthetic. Differing opinions can lead to strong controversies and high emotions—an occupational hazard of conservation archaeology and historic preservation. One of the rules of the Guam Historic Preservation Office has been to settle (or at least mediate) differences of opinion among landowners, neighbors, foreign and domestic investors, and even competing archaeologists. Moreover, different ethnic groups may evaluate historic factors in different ways. Even from within such groups, the range of opinion can be very wide. It is not always the archaeological or historical concern that prevails in decisions about what will happen at a site. After all, sometimes the community truly needs the sewer or highway more than it needs the perfectly preserved site. However, such projects can often be accomplished in ways that minimize damage to the most important sites.

Another important role of the preservation office is to give people the opportunity to learn about the traces of history that surround them, and thus appreciate the long history that has shaped the present. Sometimes the best reward for all the effort is to hear "That's neat! I never knew that before" from someone just noticing a site or historic building. For that person, the world became a bit richer. After all, helping people become more aware of the richness around them is a main reason why so many feel that, for historic and archaeological sites, there ought to be a law. . . .

9 Cultural Evolution before the Domestication of Food

Lascaux Cave in France contains an impressive array of Cro-Magnon cave paintings, including this portrayal of a bison and a man. Cave art may have been a form of hunting magic or other ritualistic behavior.

Essential to the human adaptation is the biologically based capacity to use culture to contend with the environment. At one time, all human cultures were similar. People had a direct relationship with their natural surroundings, their limited technologies doing little to disrupt the environment. Although a few such groups still exist, contemporary societies demonstrate a wide range of cultural adaptations. There are those groups that exploit the environment in small-scale ways, such as the Mexican farmers who use shifting cultivation. They stand in stark contrast to industrial societies, in which most individuals have little, if any, direct contact with natural resources. How and why did human groups attain different levels of cultural complexity? This fundamental anthropological question is raised in the study of **cultural evolution**—the patterns and history of culture change through time.

243

Whereas earlier we emphasized the biological ramifications of human evolution, the next three chapters examine the history of human cultural evolution as reconstructed from the archaeological record. What major processes are involved in cultural evolution? What cultural evolutionary trends help explain the patterns of cultural history? Our present focus will be on the history and trends of cultural evolution before the origin of food domestication.

THE PROCESSES OF CULTURAL EVOLUTION

To understand the human adaptation, we need to examine the processes that underlie cultural evolution. Cultural evolution is often viewed as occurring on two levels. **General cultural evolution**, the pattern of large-scale changes in culture, addresses how cultures change over long periods of time. The focus is on major shifts in sociocultural development: how and why foragers evolved into horticulturalists (small-scale, or garden, cultivators); how and why horticulturalists evolved into agriculturalists; and so on. However, localized cultural variations are often "washed out" when studying such grand patterns. Thus, **specific cultural evolution** focuses on how change occurs in particular societies over relatively short spans of time. Its theories are often concerned with explaining why cultures are so diversified: Is a society's culture the result of adaptation to the local environment? Is it the result of contact with other cultures? How do historical factors come into play?

Anthropologists have long been concerned with the study of how cultures originate and change. The late nineteenth-century anthropologists Edward Tylor and Lewis Henry Morgan proposed that cultural evolution was lineal—that there were fixed stages along a single line of development through which every culture had to pass (see Chapter 13, "Unilineal Evolution"). The differences between contemporary cultures were thought to reflect how much evolutionary "progress" had been made by a given society. At present, many anthropologists share Julian Steward's view that cultural evolution is *multilineal*—that each society evolves at its own pace in re-sponse to an interacting set of factors. These factors include elements of the natural and sociocultural environments that interact within the context of a culture's history and overall cultural system.

Specific Evolution: Sources of New Cultural Traits

Anthropologists have discovered that cultures, although dynamic, tend to resist change and conserve traditional ways of life. They have also found that cultures vary in how flexible they are in responding to the forces of change. Thus, specific cultural evolution proceeds differently, and at different paces, from culture to culture. Much of specific cultural evolution is caused by the slow accumulation of new ideas or practices. Sometimes, however, the introduction of new ideas (agriculture, for example) can swiftly bring about cultural change within a society. The acceptance or rejection of new ideas greatly depends on the needs of a society, as well as its degree of flexibility. Does a new trait serve the people's current needs? Are the people receptive to new ideas and capable of accepting them? And where do the new ideas come from? Three processes are mainly responsible for introducing culture change to specific societies: innovation, diffusion, and acculturation.

Innovation is the invention of new ideas or practices within a culture, either by accident or as the result of purposeful action. Many anthropologists contend that it is the basic source of culture change (Spindler 1977). An innovation may be a completely new idea or a practice adopted from another society and then reworked. For example, maize was apparently first domesticated in the Tehuacán Valley of Mexico, from where the innovation was introduced to other areas. Once this technology reached the southwestern United States, it was adapted for local use. _small # of traits_

In **diffusion**, a society adopts cultural traits from other societies. Diffusion can be thought of as "cultural borrowing." Since a diffused trait is often spread from culture to culture, the innovative culture may never be in direct contact with a society that adopts the trait. Diffusion does not depend on a large-scale movement of people between societies. New ideas can be introduced into a group by a very few people. For example, during the fifteenth century, European colonists learned how to use tobacco from Native Americans. This practice was then introduced into Europe by a few sailors returning from the New World. The practice of pipe smoking then quickly diffused throughout the Old World (Fagan 1986). _lg. scale influence_

In **acculturation**, a society obtains traits from another culture on an extensive basis. Although similar to diffusion, acculturation differs in a number of ways. First, acculturation always entails direct contact between the societies. Also, while diffusion usually involves a small number of traits, acculturation is the large-scale influence of one society upon another. In most cases, a more technologically advanced society exerts great influence on one that is less sophisticated. However, even though the less powerful culture is modified more than the other, cultural traits are passed both ways during periods of extensive contact.

The actual degree to which acculturation occurs depends on a number of factors, especially the "openness" of the society under transition: How willing are the people to accept change? For example, the Kaktovik Eskimos have become somewhat acculturated into the general culture of the United States (Chance 1966). The members of this north Alaskan community voluntarily adopted a range of economic and social behaviors. They were most accepting of those cultural traits they viewed as beneficial, particularly the ones that introduced new employment opportunities. Many, for example, were trained to install radar lines for the U.S. government. At the same time, many of their traditional Kaktovik cultural traits remained intact, including their kinship and religious systems.

Acculturation may occur under peaceful conditions, but it may also occur as a result of forced action; for example, when one group conquers another. Such was the case in the sixteenth-century conquest of the Mexican Aztec Empire by the Spanish conquistadors. Sometimes, forced acculturation is ethnocentrically viewed by the dominant society as "positive," as when a Catholic priest acted to halt the bartering of female infants among the Tiwi of northern Australia (Spindler 1977). Yet, even under forced circumstances, acculturation is still a two-way process: conquerors often adopt behaviors from the people they have defeated. For example, the Spanish conquistadors introduced important foods, such as maize, to Europe.

General Evolution: Increasing Complexity and Efficiency of Cultural Systems

Processes of specific evolution, including innovation, diffusion, and acculturation, influence the patterns of general cultural evolution. What are the large-scale trends noted in the history of human culture? One dominant theme is that of *increasing complexity*: of behavior, of social organization, of technology, of environmental relationships, of ideologies. This increasing complexity refers to the number of elements existing within a cultural system or subsystem. For example, whereas foraging societies often have but one basis, gender, for the division of labor, more complex agricultural societies divide their labor forces according to a number of criteria, such as gender, age, and kinship. In addition, a group of

An Alaskan Inuit sits on a snowmobile holding caribou legs. Native Alaskans have adopted aspects of American culture that they view as beneficial to their lives. For example, many Inuits use snowmobiles to facilitate a traditional subsistence practice—the hunting of caribou.

foragers is composed of a small number of people who can move to obtain resources. Thus, the foragers' social relationships are fairly straightforward. Interpersonal problems can be dealt with face-to-face and the group can split into smaller units to keep tensions under control. On the other hand, in a farming community, a large number of people are needed to work the land and support an agricultural way of life. Because they are economically and socially bound to a specific location, the social organization of these people is much more complex than that of the foragers. They must contend with many types of interpersonal relationships without the safety valve of being able to easily split into smaller groups and move to new locations.

The increased complexity of cultural systems does *not* equate with a superior way of life; rather, it represents a multifaceted response to cultural and natural environmental conditions.

However, although human behavioral flexibility makes it easier for us to adapt to environmental change, a highly complex society can become overspecialized and collapse (see Chapter 11, "The Collapse of Complex Societies").

The second dominant theme of general cultural evolution is the *increased efficiency* of the human adaptation. Behavioral flexibility, based on human cognitive skills, has allowed humans to adapt culturally to a broad range of environments, many of which are less than optimal. In an environment rich in resources where needs are limited to only a small number of individuals, there is little pressure on a society to use the resources efficiently. Groups that must survive under more stressful conditions, however, such as those imposed by low rainfall, harsh temperatures, or a large population, must become more efficient in their resource use. In response, technology becomes more complicated and the cultural system more complex. Part of the increased efficiency is the standardization of technology—finding the best tool designs and production techniques and sticking with them, until better ideas come along.

Again, increased efficiency in the use of resources is *not* equivalent to a superior adaptation. In fact, our increasing "efficiency" in how we obtain and use natural resources, along with other factors, is now endangering the world's ecological system (see Chapter 23, "Environmental Destruction"). Thus, the increased complexity and efficiency of cultural systems, while providing solutions to some problems, create new ones. For example, people must support the increased number of cultural components, leading to the differentiation of social roles (e.g., ruling class, militia, priests, craftspeople, farmers, laborers). If a society is socially stratified, then there must be enough people to fill the roles. With the increased number of people in one location, ways must be found to feed, house, and defend them all, leading to the need for technological complexity and efficiency in the use of resources. Social problems also increase when greater numbers of people who share little in common (such as bonds of kinship or the same social roles) must interact more frequently than would be the case in less complex societies.

These general themes of increased complexity and efficiency of cultural systems provide the framework for our history of cultural evolution. Although the themes do not reflect the events that occurred in every culture, they do serve to help explain why patterns of general cultural evolution occurred in different parts of the world.

Historical Patterns of Cultural Evolution

A picture of the large-scale evolution of culture has emerged from the research of archaeologists and other scientists working in both the Old World and the New World. Although many questions remain, one point is clear: Various levels of cultural complexity were reached at different times in different parts of the world. Some cultures attained the level of civilization, while others maintained less complex subsistence strategies. Why did some societies become highly complex, while others did not? Why is there often a range of cultural adaptations within a relatively small geographic area? Where have major technological innovations occurred, and why? How did important cultural traits, such as the domestication of plants, spread from the areas of innovation?

In broad terms, much can be explained by environmental demands, cultural contact, and cultural history. However, scientists disagree as to the exact processes underlying general cultural evolution. For example, cultural ecologists emphasize that a culture's subsistence strategy is greatly influenced by local environmental conditions, while world system theorists emphasize the study of a culture as part of an interactive worldwide cultural system. However, before scientists can definitively explain patterns of cultural evolution, they must first delineate the events that unfolded through time.

MAJOR STAGES IN THE OLD WORLD

Since humans did not migrate into the New World until about 30,000 years ago, the longest record of cultural evolution comes from the Old World. Old World prehistory (particularly European) is divided into stages:

Paleolithic (Old Stone Age)
Mesolithic (Middle Stone Age)
Neolithic (New Stone Age)
Bronze Age
Iron Age

The Old Stone Age was long, accounting for 99 percent of human cultural history. Because of its great time span, the Paleolithic is divided into three stages:

Lower Paleolithic: Approximately 2.5 million years ago until approximately 100,000 years ago; associated with early *Homo* and *Homo erectus*.

Middle Paleolithic: Approximately 125,000 years ago until about 35,000 years ago; associated with Neandertal and collateral forms.

Upper Paleolithic: Approximately 35,000 to 10,000 years ago; associated with anatomically modern *Homo sapiens sapiens*.

This scheme emphasizes "lithic," or stone, technology in the study of cultural evolution. Why this emphasis? First, the Stone Ages cover an extremely long period of human cultural history. In fact, the purposeful reshaping of stones into tools is taken as the earliest sign of the be-

ginnings of cultural evolution. The second reason is archaeologists' dependency on durable remains in reconstructing prehistoric cultures. Lithic tools, besides being an important part of prehistoric technology, are also extremely durable. Therefore, even though ancient peoples used other materials, such as wood, bone, and fibers, the "Stone Age" label reflects both the importance of the lithic materials and their biased representation in the archaeological record. As pointed out by Gowlett (1984), "with different conditions of preservation we might have had an 'Old String Age'; but we have no idea how far back string was in use because it always rots" (p. 38).

In the following sections we will discuss cultural evolution up through the Mesolithic. We will see that the early stages are largely distinguished according to types of **tool traditions**—artifacts grouped according to similarity of form and how they are associated in the archaeological record.

THE LOWER PALEOLITHIC: EARLIEST EVIDENCE OF CULTURE

How far back do the roots of culture extend? Cross-species studies demonstrate that some nonhuman primates make and use very simple tools, which suggests that forms just prior to the hominids may have been capable of some crude cultural behavior. This, however, is difficult to prove because such simple tools would be almost indistinguishable from rocks that had been naturally reshaped.

The earliest recognized traces of culture come from the Rift Valley of Africa, although some scientists argue that early tool-users also lived in Asia. However, there is little fossil or archaeological evidence in support of an early Asian hominid (Gowlett 1984).

The oldest known tools are simple pebble choppers and small stone flakes. The oldest of these, from the Hadar region of Ethiopia, are probably between 2.5 and 2.7 million years old (Lewin 1981). Who made these very early artifacts? The tools date from the time when early *Homo* apparently diverged from *Australopithecus afarensis*. Since many scientists believe that the australopithecine brain was not developed enough to produce this sort of technology, the most commonly accepted theory is that the tools were made by *Homo*. However, some scientists contend that australopithecines *were* intelligent enough to have made primitive tools. According to Susman (1988), australopithecines were also physically capable of making and using simple technology (see p. 151).

Little is known about the earliest use of stone tools. Much more evidence is needed, especially that which clearly associates tools and specific fossil forms, before we can truly point to a specific hominid as the first tool-user.

The Oldowan Tradition

The earliest recognized tools, including the ones uncovered in Hadar, are those of the *Oldowan tool tradition.* As noted in Chapter 6, the tradition is named for Olduvai Gorge, where the artifacts were first identified. The Oldowan tradition persisted for a very long time, from about 2.5 million years ago up to about 100,000 years ago. In addition, it is the only tool tradition associated with hominids from about 2.5 million years ago to 1.5 million years ago.

Also known as "pebble tools," the Oldowan tradition consists of a limited set of simple, yet ingenious, tool types, mostly multipurpose pebble-choppers and small flakes (see Figure 9.1). Oldowan tools were made by a technique known as the *direct percussion method*. It involved the use of a hammer stone to precisely strike a core stone, knocking off small flakes to form the desired shape. Most archaeologists believe that the tool-makers were primarily concerned with making the pebble-choppers. However, some scientists contend that the sharp flakes knocked off the core were of primary importance (Toth 1985). The latter hypothesis assumes that the flakes were used in a much broader range of activities than were the cores (e.g., butchery, hide working, and shaping wood implements).

Although Oldowan tools are simple to produce and limited in form, their production still entails a significant level of skill and technological consistency. This has led scientists to speculate about the way of life and mental abilities of the Oldowan tool-users.

Life in the Early Lower Paleolithic

Picturing how the earliest tool-users lived is particularly difficult because so much time has passed since they walked the earth. Many anthropologists picture them as early *Homo*, living in small, highly nomadic bands and subsisting as primitive foragers who used simple stone tools to kill and butcher game. Analogies with contemporary foragers suggest that the tool-users' social behavior included food sharing and a gender-based division of labor, with males as the hunters and females as the gatherers of plant food. The foragers were nomads, carrying their tools from place to place. Hence, multipurpose tools were desirable so that fewer would have to be transported. In addition, their tools had to be quick and easy to manufacture so as to be ready for immediate tasks, such as butchering hippopotamus or other large game (Gowlett 1984).

An alternative idea is that the hominids of 2 million years ago did not hunt but rather *scavenged* for meat left from carnivore kills (Shipman 1986). Evidence supporting this idea includes cut mark patterns, left by tools, on the bones of prey.

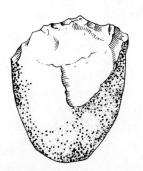 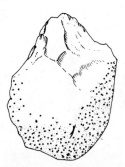 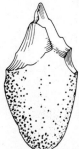

FIGURE 9.1

Oldowan pebble tools. The earliest recognized tool tradition, the Oldowan, consisted mostly of simply altered large stones. Simple choppers (left) could be further altered to produce primitive bifaces (center) or hand axes (right).

These overlay tooth marks left by carnivores. Yet another theory is that early humans were not simple nomads but that they moved among the same sites over a period of 5 to 10 years (Potts 1986).

As evidence accumulates, scientists will be able to fine-tune their ideas regarding the earliest hominid way of life. In fact, some researchers are now posing theories regarding the most enigmatic of human traits, mental abilities.

The Mental Abilities of Early Hominids

How "smart" were these early humans, whose brains were much smaller than those of *Homo sapiens*? Since anthropologists greatly depend on the use of durable remains in making such judgments, this question has been examined by focusing on the interactive evolution of the human brain, tool use, and cultural abilities. For example, Gowlett (1984) proposed a model for using archaeological remains to decipher the degree to which a hominid was aware of the future, capable of advanced planning, and able to perform complex and long sequences of actions. He noted that all three of these abilities were reflected in the Oldowan tool-users' purposeful carrying of stones over long distances to where the tools were used for particular functions. In addition, the skill and relative consistency with which the tools were made demonstrate preplanning and the need for some language skills in passing on traditions. According to Gowlett, the archaeological record reflects an increase in such complex mental abilities during the course of human evolution.

Toth's (1985) research on Oldowan stone-tool technology led him to contend, as did Gowlett, that the hominids of 2 to 1.5 million years ago were capable of advanced planning. He noted that early hominids carried suitable tool-making materials over several kilometers and carefully tested and selected the best core stones from among the raw materials available at the source site.

A number of anthropologists point to stone tools as proof that the early hominids had language abilities. For example, Kitahara-Frisch (1978) compared the tool-using abilities of nonlinguistic chimpanzees with the tool-making abilities of Oldowan users. She concluded that the level of the hominids' technical skills was such that they needed some language and symbolization abilities to pass on tool-making techniques. However, the use of stone technology in the study of language origins has been criticized by those who feel that technological skills and language abilities are two different adaptations, and that they did not necessarily evolve in tandem (Lewin 1986).

Understanding the mind of the earliest hominids is a difficult and intriguing proposition. We have much to learn through continued paleontological, archaeological, and cross-species studies.

The Lower Paleolithic Advances: The Acheulean Tradition and the Persistence of Choppers

As early as 1.5 million years ago, the archaeological record demonstrates the appearance of a more complex tool tradition, the *Acheulean*. The Acheulean tradition is characterized by a new, and more technologically advanced, type of implement, the hand ax. Thus, the Acheulean is also known as the "hand-ax tradition." While the Oldowan is usually identified with early *Homo*, the Acheulean is associated with the larger-brained hominid, *Homo erectus*.

As discussed in Chapter 6, *Homo erectus* was a physically diverse and widely distributed hominid, persisting for a long period (from about 1.5 million to 300,000 years ago). *Homo erectus* differs from earlier hominids in its expanded brain size: its cranial capacity averaged around 1,000 cm^3 versus 650 cm^3 for early *Homo*. This increased brain size is associated with more advanced cognitive and cultural skills. It thus seems likely that cultural mechanisms played a major role in allowing *Homo erectus* to expand into many different geographical and ecological zones.

Acheulean Technology

Although still a simple stone technology, the Acheulean tradition was more complex, standardized, and refined in form than the Oldowan. The Acheulean hand ax is a pear-shaped stone tool worked on two sides, as shown in the photos on page 252. Unlike the crudely shaped pebble-chopper, hand axes have sharp edges and a pointed end, and are rounded on top. They come in many sizes but are standardized in form. The hand ax, itself, went through an evolution, becoming increasingly more refined and consistent in form through time.

As was true for the Oldowan, Acheulean stone tools were produced using the direct-percussion method. The maker needed a great deal of skill to accurately strike off the desired long flakes from the cores, especially for the larger axes. As the Acheulean tradition progressed, the tools became more refined in form, with more care being taken in finishing the edges. The hand axes, which were hand-held rather than attached to a shaft, were multipurposed. Their uses ranged from cutting down trees and digging roots to butchering meat and preparing skins.

Although the hand ax is the object most indicative of the culture, the Acheulean tool kit contained other implements. At some sites, archaeologists have found lithic scrapers as well as evidence that wood and bone implements were used in a variety of ways. Here we see a pattern of increasing cultural complexity, one of the dominant themes of general cultural evolution. One major aspect of this trend is that, through time, tool traditions contained an increasing number of types of implements. We also see the beginning of another important aspect of this growing complexity: an increase in the number of coexisting tool traditions. The hand-ax technology, which must be present if a site is to be labeled "Acheulean," is associated with *Homo erectus* in Africa, the Middle East, India, and most of Europe. However, there were also contemporaneous societies that did not have hand axes, but made use of a refined chopper tradition that consisted of pebble-choppers with jagged edges, sharpened flakes, and scrapers. This chopper tradition is associated with *Homo erectus* in Asia and the Far East, including China and Southeast Asia, and in parts of northern Europe, including eastern England.

What explains the persistence of the chopper technology? One possibility is that the chopper-users never came into contact with hand-ax technology; nor did they invent it for themselves. Another idea is that tool kits are specific to environmental needs. Thus, the two traditions relate to the exploitation of habitats with different sets of technological demands. This seems reasonable, considering that Acheulean sites are usually associated with southern climates, whereas the chopper tradition is associated with colder conditions. However, the argument is weakened by evidence that both traditions are associated with similar ways of life in which the hunting of large game was central.

Whatever the specific technology, the cultural adaptations of *Homo erectus* surely facilitated its spread into a range of habitats. What do we know, then, about the life-style of *Homo erectus*?

How *Homo erectus* Lived

Several rich archaeological sites have enabled scientists to formulate some good general ideas as to how *Homo erectus* lived (see Figure 6.4, p. 152). However, we must remember that *Homo erectus* lived in many different places over a long span of time and varied regionally with respect to life-style.

Among the most remarkable *Homo erectus* archaeological finds are two Spanish Acheulean butchery sites, Torralba and Ambrona. Dating from about 200,000 to 400,000 years ago, these sites contain a wealth of butchered elephant bones along with a multitude of artifacts, including crudely made axes, choppers, and scrapers. Archaeologists have used such evidence to form a picture of *Homo erectus* as a well-organized, cooperative hunter of large game. Another important site, dating from about 300,000 years ago, is Terra Amata in France. This site contains evidence of oval huts, hearths, small animals, shell-

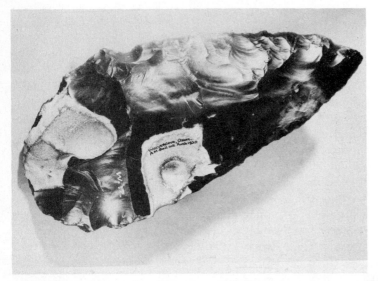

Acheulean hand axes. The Acheulean tradition is closely identified with these pear-shaped stone tools that are worked on two sides. Although they come in many sizes, Acheulean hand axes are standardized in form, with sharp edges, pointed ends, and rounded tops.

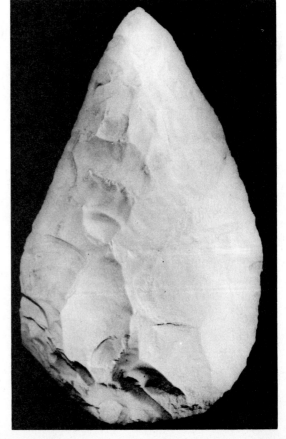

fish, and such plant foods as nuts and seeds, indicating that *Homo erectus* not only hunted, but also depended on gathered foods, returning seasonally to the same site. The hearths found at Terra Amata and elsewhere demonstrate that *Homo erectus* had mastered the use of fire. In fact, evidence from Chesowanja in East Africa indicates that *Homo erectus* was using fire as far back as 1.5 million years ago.

Another outstanding source of *Homo erectus* cultural information is the Chinese cave site, Choukoutien, which dates from about 300,000 to 500,000 years ago. Excavations at Choukoutien have unearthed more than 100,000 artifacts without any evidence of Acheulean technology. The artifacts include advanced forms of choppers, flakes, and scrapers, some of which are made of bone. The inhabitants of Choukoutien apparently were skilled hunters of big game and may have practiced ritualistic cannibalism. In addition, they had mastered the controlled use of fire. Unfortunately, the priceless Choukoutien *Homo erectus* fossils, popularly known as "Peking Man," were mysteriously lost during World War II—a loss that has hindered scientists in their study of this important site.

What of *Homo erectus*'s mental abilities? The cultural remains strongly indicate that *Homo erectus* was more cognitively advanced than early *Homo*. Gowlett (1984) has proposed that the consistency in hand-ax form, even among tools of different sizes, demonstrates that *Homo erectus* had mental "templates" for the tools, and that "the mental apparatus already existed for making basic mathematical transformations without the benefit of pen, paper or ruler" (p. 71). Furthermore, the sharing of such templates among individuals indicates that they had some form of language.

From the evidence gathered, we can draw several conclusions about *Homo erectus*'s way of life. First, humans had spread across the Old World, even into areas with harsh conditions. A major factor permitting *Homo erectus* to spread into marginal areas was its cultural adaptations, such as the controlled use of fire and the construction of huts, both of which allowed groups of these individuals to use their environments more efficiently. *Homo erectus* had at least two cultural traditions, and demonstrated an increase in the number of tool forms within traditions as well as increased skill in tool making. Subsistence was based on cooperative and well-planned big-game hunting and the gathering of plant-based foods. In addition, *Homo erectus* groups moved from one seasonal site to another. The sites, themselves, reflect differential usage: some were living sites, some were used for butchering game, and so on. Thus, *Homo erectus*'s life was apparently more varied in activity than that of earlier forms; therefore, it was more complex. Evidence also suggests that *Homo erectus* practiced ritualistic behavior, including head-hunting and cannibalism, indicating the existence of ideological systems. Mental abilities, including language, were apparently advanced over those of earlier forms. Trends reflecting *Homo erectus*'s increased cultural complexity and efficiency are summmarized in Table 9.1.

About 200,000 years ago, *Homo erectus* disappeared from the prehistoric record. Advanced forms of Acheulean technology persisted in parts

---

TABLE 9.1

Trends Reflecting the Increased Cultural Complexity and Efficiency of the Lower Paleolithic

- Refinement of tool-making techniques
- Standardization of tool-making techniques
- More technological complexity in tool making, the use of fire, and the building of dwellings
- Increased number of tools in tool kit
- Increased number of tool traditions existing simultaneously
- Exploitation of a greater number of environments
- Expansion into new geographical areas
- Diversification of ways of life
- Shift toward sedentism, with use of seasonal camps
- Appearance of ritualistic behavior, reflecting increased complexity in ideological systems
- Advanced mental abilities, including those of language and symbolization

of the Old World, suggesting that some early *Homo sapiens* used this tradition. However, by about 125,000 years ago, a new cultural level of cultural complexity had been attained—that of the Middle Paleolithic.

THE MIDDLE PALEOLITHIC

About 400,000 to 300,000 years ago, *Homo erectus* is gradually replaced in the fossil record by *Homo sapiens*. During the transition, most humans used advanced Acheulean technology. By 125,000 years ago, when all humans were fully sapient, they had entered the cultural period known as the Middle Paleolithic. The Middle Paleolithic is associated with an increase in the complexity and efficiency of stone-tool traditions, as evidenced in the increased number of traditions and tools and in the refinement of form. What factors brought about the technological shift from the Lower Paleolithic to the Middle Paleolithic? Many scientists believe that the increase in technological efficiency and complexity relates to the improved cognitive abilities of the Middle Paleolithic humans and to their expansion into a broad range of environments. This ability to exploit varied habitats was, in part, based on their capacity to preplan and on a solid knowledge of their surroundings. The great adaptability of early *Homo sapiens* is reflected in the fact that some populations lived in northern regions during the harsh Pleistocene ice ages.

The humans of the Middle Paleolithic were varied in form. Some are classified within a distinct group, the Neandertals; other populations were more generalized and similar to fully modern *Homo sapiens*. The Neandertals date from about 125,000 to 35,000 years ago, when they abruptly disappear from the fossil record. They demonstrate a range of types, from more modern-looking forms in the Near East, where they lived in temperate climates, to the extreme classic forms that lived in Western Europe during the last Ice Age. As noted in Chapter 6, Neandertals are closely associated with the Middle Paleolithic tradition known as *Mousterian*, although some populations used more primitive technologies. The less specialized and more modern-looking contemporaries of the Neandertals lived in parts of Africa and Asia. These populations also used Middle Paleolithic technology, although not necessarily the Mousterian.

Technology of the Middle Paleolithic

The most prevalent Middle Paleolithic tradition is the Mousterian. Appearing as early as 150,000 years ago, evidence of Mousterian technology has been found over much of the Old World. While the predominant artifacts are stone scrapers and points, scientists have also discovered implements made of wood, such as spear shafts.

The Middle Paleolithic continues the cultural evolutionary trend of increasing complexity. Particularly striking is the increased appearance of localized traditions within a general pattern of technological features. This variety is reflected by differences between assemblages as to specific types and number of tools. Mousterian assemblages, alone, are so varied that the Mousterian may actually be composed of a number of different industries.

Before discussing the variety of Middle Paleolithic traditions, it is useful to point out the characteristics that differentiate them from earlier traditions. An important technological advance was the *prepared-core technique* of tool making. This method involved an increased number of steps because a stone core was preshaped and then reworked to produce a specific tool. Another Middle Paleolithic trait was the introduction of implements made from several components, known as **composite tools**. An example of a composite tool is a spear made of a wooden handle, binding, and a stone point. Also during the Middle Paleolithic, we begin to see tools so elegantly and precisely made that there may have been aesthetic, rather than purely functional, considerations in their design. Yet another striking aspect of the Middle Paleolithic is the great variety of standardized tool types: assemblages may include refined axes and choppers, as well as new forms of tools, such as chisel-like burins, triangular points, drills, and double-edged knives.

Taken as a subcategory of Middle Paleolithic technology, localized Mousterian assemblages demonstrate a number of patterns. What accounts for the variety in Mousterian tool kits? According to Bordes (Bordes and Sonneville-Bordes 1970), the subtraditions reflect five autonomous cultural groups. Another idea is that the different Mousterian assemblages represent time-related cultural changes in technology (Mellars 1969), an idea not well supported by the chronological data. A third idea is that the assemblages represent different functional industries of a single cultural group and that variation in assemblages functionally relates to site usage and the ecological challenges of the particular habitats (Binford 1983). For example, an assemblage composed of points and scrapers reflects hunting and butchering activities, while a base-camp site would show evidence of maintenance tasks (such as tool manufacturing), including a large number of borers, scrapers, and burins. Generally speaking, these ideas appear to be oversimplified (Champion et al. 1984), but they *do* point to the importance of examining Mousterian variability in terms of cultural, ecological, and functional

A sample of Mousterian tools. (top) Points, which, when bound to wood shafts, formed composite tools used for hunting game. (middle) Hand ax, often used for chopping activities. (bottom) Side scrapers, often used to prepare animal hides and leather.

diversity. The technological diversity may be explained by a combination of these factors.

Middle Paleolithic cultural diversity and the relationship between technology and ecological demands are also reflected in the non-Mousterian sites. Although some Mousterian assemblages have been uncovered in North Africa, most African Middle Paleolithic sites are technologically different from the Mousterian sites. In addition, Middle Paleolithic technology may have persisted in some of these areas until 15,000 years ago. How are these sites different from those labeled "Mousterian"? Some of them strongly emphasize the use of large-blade tools, rather than the Mousterian pattern of an abundance of side scrapers. Other sites demonstrate unique, localized techniques of stone working, including the *Aterian*. Aterian technology is usually found in inland areas of North Africa that are presently desert, but which once had larger amounts of rainfall (Gowlett 1984). Here we can see the pattern of localized tool traditions: the Aterian in the inland desert regions, North African Mousterian along the coast, and an Acheulean-like hand-ax tradition in the rain forests of interior Africa (ibid.). Non-Mousterian Middle Paleolithic sites have also been found in China, Pakistan, and India.

Life in the Middle Paleolithic

During the Middle Paleolithic, we see that cultural diversity was an increasingly important element of the human adaptation. However, even though various groups used different resources, the basic subsistence level was still that of foragers. Scientists note a great deal of cultural variability among contemporary foragers and apply this knowledge in interpreting the prehistoric record.

Keeping in mind the local variability, we can still form a general picture of the Middle Paleolithic way of life. The best known Middle Paleolithic societies are those of the Neandertals, a large number of Neandertal sites having been excavated. Neandertals had a range of adaptations, from the rugged Ice Age European life to life in the temperate Near East. The specialized and diverse Mousterian tool kits reflect the richness of Neandertal life. Neandertals were accomplished big-game hunters, exploiting large territories with seasonally occupied camps. Climate and habitat permitting, they also were proficient at gathering activities, trapping small game, fishing, and collecting shellfish. Evidence indicates that the Neandertals and their contemporaries made use of fire, employed woodworking, and wore clothing.

The Neandertals are often referred to as "cavemen." This is not surprising, since the first Neandertal (which was also the first recognized human fossil) was discovered in 1857 in a small cave in the Neander Valley of Germany. In addition, many other Neandertal sites have been found in caves, which provided warmth and shelter during the northern European winters. Caves are also easy to defend against predators and possible intruders and are often high up on cliffs, making them good vantage points for surveying herds of large game and other resources. Neandertal groups also commonly used partially exposed rock shelters, the most famous being the Near Eastern site of Shanidar, Iraq. They lived in open-air sites as well, although only a few have been uncovered. However, open-air sites are not as easily preserved, which may account for the scarcity. Middle Paleolithic peoples may frequently have lived out in the open, including in tents during warm weather. A few sites, such as Molodova in Russia, contain the remains of huts and hearths.

Burials and Ritualistic Behavior

Evidence of rituals is the most striking reflection of the complexity and cultural richness of the Middle Paleolithic life. The rituals included burials and other behavior so elaborate that it bordered on the religious. The evidence, in the form of material remains, provides insights into the ideology and mental processes of early *Homo sapiens*. Although some ritualistic behavior, such as burial and cannibalism, has been associated with *Homo erectus*, it does not approach the level of complexity the Middle Paleolithic sites reveal.

More than 20 Middle Paleolithic burial sites have been excavated in parts of the Old World, including Europe and Asia. Whole-body burials have been discovered at sites dating as far back as 100,000 years ago. At these sites, individuals' bodies are deliberately arranged into configurations and are often buried with worldly goods, such as stone tools and foodstuffs. For example, at La Ferrasie in France, a whole group of burials are gathered at one spot, possibly representing an early "cemetery" (Peyrony 1934). At Shanidar, an individual was buried decorated with flowers and with red-ochre powder that may have been applied as body paint (Solecki 1972). Such finds suggest that early *Homo sapiens* had a respect for the dead (and thus for human life) and a ritual-istic sense of afterlife, since the material goods may have been intended for use in another world.

Another fascinating example of the ritualistic wealth of Neandertal life is the "Cave Bear Cult." This quasi-religious phenomenon may have been an attempt at controlling the environment through supernatural means. Evidence at a number of European cave sites indicates that the prehistoric cave bear, an enormously large and fearsome animal, was treated in a special ritual-istic manner. At one Swiss site, several neatly stacked cave bear skulls were found in a large, stone-lined pit, covered by an extremely heavy stone slab (see Figure 9.2a). All the skulls were found toward the front of the cave. A similar French find contained the skulls of at least 20 animals. Since hunting was an important part of the Neandertal way of life and the bears would prove mighty adversaries, it could be that these rituals were part of the cultists' mythology and perceptions of supernatural power.

FIGURE 9.2
Cave bear cult. (a) The discovery of bear skulls stacked in a pit helps support the theory that the cave bear was the focus of a Neandertal cult. (b) The enormous cave bear was apparently a respected adversary of the Neandertals. Hibernating bears may have been killed so that the people could move into the caves.

(a)

(b)

A number of sites reveal another form of Middle Paleolithic ritualistic behavior. Ritualistic cannibalism was apparently practiced by some groups in France, Yugoslavia, Italy, and elsewhere. For example, archaeologists have found shattered human skulls and limb bones that were split open, possibly so the Neandertals could eat the bone marrow. Some of the bones are charred, suggesting that the occupants of the site cooked human meat, or at least used the bones in some kind of ritual. We can only speculate about the significance of such behavior, although it again emphasizes the mysterious intricacies of the ideological and social aspects of Neandertal life.

Moving toward the Upper Paleolithic

The evolving complexity and increasing efficiency of the human cultural adaptation is clearly demonstrated by the Middle Paleolithic. Once the level of *Homo sapiens* had been reached, human culture became increasingly diverse, as reflected by the range of localized adaptations. Human behavior also became more sophisticated, as evidenced by the specialized tools, by

TABLE 9.2

Middle Paleolithic Cultural Evolutionary Trends

- Increased number of localized tool traditions
- More sophisticated tool-making techniques, including the use of a prepared core
- Composite tools
- Aesthetic considerations in the design of implements
- Increased number of standardized tools
- More complex ritualistic and ideological systems

the apparent aesthetic considerations that figured in their design, and by the signs of complex ritualistic behavior. Trends reflecting the increased cultural complexity and efficiency of the Middle Paleolithic are summarized in Table 9.2.

As humans became anatomically modern, cultural evolution continued to produce greater diversity and complexity in many parts of the inhabited world. By 30,000 years ago, parts of the Old World, including Europe, were in the final phase of the Old Stone Age: the Upper Paleolithic. Also at about this time, humans migrated into the New World and Australia, further extending their exploitation of the world.

THE UPPER PALEOLITHIC

The Upper Paleolithic witnessed a major change in human biocultural evolution. Physical evolution became relatively insignificant, while cultural evolution occurred at an increasingly rapid pace. Although it took at least 2.5 million years to reach this stage, cultural changes began to occur so rapidly that only an additional 35,000 years were required to go from stone-age technology to that of the atomic age.

The Upper Paleolithic continued the cultural evolutionary trends noted in the earlier stone ages. These trends involved the increasing complexity and efficiency of culture, as greater diversity and increased specialization occurred within

cultural systems. We also see technological innovations that eventually led to the origin of food domestication and the large-scale manipulation of natural resources. Another point is that the human adaptation continued to be greatly influenced by the Ice Age, a fact of special importance when discussing the populating of the Americas and Australia.

Homo sapiens sapiens: Anatomically Modern Humans

For about the last 35,000 years, all humans have belonged to the same subspecies, *Homo sapiens*

sapiens. The modern human body is more slender than that of the Neandertals, the most distinctive modern feature being the structure of the skull and cranium. *Homo sapiens sapiens*'s face is flat and relatively delicate in structure, with no or little brow ridge, a distinct chin (lacking in most Neandertals), and a vertical forehead. The modern cranium is rounded and highly vaulted, with an average capacity of 1,350 cm^3—slightly under that of Neandertals. All populations of *Homo sapiens sapiens* are similar in brain size and structure; therefore, differences in behavior and technology reflect culturally based diversity, rather than neurological distinctions.

As is the case in contemporary populations, early *Homo sapiens sapiens* is characterized by localized variations in body structure. The most famous Upper Paleolithic population is Cro-Magnon. First discovered in France and dating from about 30,000 years ago, Cro-Magnon had a large cranial capacity, a high forehead, a protruding chin, and a very slight brow ridge. Other Upper Paleolithic remains have been found throughout the Old World, as well as in the Americas and Australia. Some finds, such as the Combe Capelle fossil of France and a number of Czechoslovakian fossils, have Neandertal-like traits. Fully modern forms have been uncovered in Africa and Eastern Asia.

Having noted the physical differences between Neandertals and anatomically modern humans, let us now turn our attention to the general Upper Paleolithic changes in technology and culture.

Technology of the Upper Paleolithic

The technologies of the Middle and Upper Paleolithic periods differ both in the degree to which cultural trends are expressed and in the occurrence of innovations. In particular, the rapidity of Upper Paleolithic cultural change is quite striking, as is the increasing diversity of coexisting cultural traditions. Within each Upper Paleolithic tradition, there was a continuing in-

crease in the number of specialized tools, with greater skill needed to produce the implements. Upper Paleolithic people were very efficient hunters and gatherers, able to exploit many different resources. Thus, the variety of traditions reflects the many different types of specialized forager adaptations that existed throughout the world. For now, we will focus on the events that occurred in Europe.

According to Champion et al. (1984), the European shift from the Middle to the Upper Paleolithic can be described as a threefold technological change. First, less refined tools, such as hand axes and choppers, disappeared. Second, humans began to use new tool-making techniques, including *pressure flaking*, in which small flakes of stone were carefully pushed off a tool, and *punchstriking*, in which a pointed implement was used to apply intense pressure to make parallel-sided blades. These techniques produced long, thin blades, which could be retouched in fashioning specific tools. Compared with the Mousterian, this technology was more efficient and less wasteful. The third change involved an increase in the types of materials used to make tools. Bone, antler, and ivory, for example, had not been previously used for tool making in Europe. The addition of such materials was made possible by the tool-makers' extensive use of the burin, a flint tool with a beveled point.

Another Upper Paleolithic trend was the increasing prominence of composite tools. Small projectile points that were hafted (grooved) to nicely fit onto wooden spears or arrow shafts became commonplace. Some of the points were barbed, which increased their efficiency in hunting.

The various Upper Paleolithic traditions uncovered in Europe are distinguished by differences in the frequency and forms of tool types. An early, long-utilized tradition, the *lower Perigordian* (or *Chatelperronian*), apparently evolved out of the Mousterian. On the other hand, the *Aurignacian* represents a total departure from earlier European traditions. A bit later, about 25,000 years ago, the *Gravettian* culture (also known as the *upper Perigordian*) appeared in France. By 20,000 years ago, the Gravettian and Aurignacian were apparently replaced by a short-lived tradition, the *Solutrean*. Then, about 15,000 years ago, we see the appearance of the last European Upper Paleolithic culture, the *Magdalenian*. Quite different from the Solutrean, this tradition spread all over Europe. The Magdalenians were great hunters who made beautifully designed objects of bone and antler, as shown in the photo below.

Variety in Habitat and Ways of Life

Compared with earlier times, the Upper Paleolithic was a complex cultural period. Humans had spread across the Old World and into the Americas and Australia and had evolved specialized foraging strategies that were well adapted to local habitats. Even within a single geographical region, such as southwestern France, cultural traditions changed with habitat, particularly with the comings and goings of the last Pleistocene ice sheets. To illustrate this variation, we will now consider two Upper Paleolithic adaptations: that of southwestern France and that of the Mammoth Hunters of Europe and Russia.

The Foragers of Southwestern France

The classic European Upper Paleolithic sequence comes from southwestern France and dates from approximately 35,000 to 10,000 years

Engraved and sculpted examples of European Upper Paleolithic technologies. The objects are primarily carved from mammoth ivory or reindeer antler, except for the stone female figurine (bottom right). Most of the objects are Magdalenian, except for the ivory horse head, ivory female head, and stone female figure, all of which may be Aurignacian. The stone figurine is a famous object, known as the Venus of Willendorf (Austria).

ago. The Dordogne region, with its many caves and rock shelters, has been an especially good source of Neandertal and Cro-Magnon fossil and cultural finds. During the late Pleistocene, southwestern France provided a hospitable environment for the local groups of foragers. This was so even during the glaciation periods, the region being rich in game and marine life. Moreover, its valley and rock structures provided protection from the elements.

Technological changes in southwestern France have been associated with climatic shifts, from the arcticlike conditions that prevailed after the ice sheet had advanced, to the temperate periods that occurred when the sheet retreated north. The foragers of this region inhabited caves and rock shelters and developed elaborate and refined cultures, in which they produced impressive works of art. During the summer, they followed migrating herds of reindeer into open country, where they lived in tents and conducted game drives. Other large game included wild horses, wild oxen, mammoth elephants, and the woolly rhinoceros. Small game, such as birds and foxes, were also important sources of meat. Fish were caught from the river that runs through the Dordogne, and plant foods were gathered when available.

Upper Paleolithic art reflects an aesthetic sensibility. Beautiful paintings and engravings were created on the walls of caves and rock shelters, especially during the Magdalenian. The Magdalenians also carved figures from bone and antler as decorations for their harpoons, spear-throwers, and other implements. Most of the artwork depicted large game animals, although there are also representations of humans (see the photos that follow). Some scientists view the artwork as a part of the Magdalenians' symbolic and ritualistic attempts to control natural resources and make sense of the world (e.g., Ucko and Rosenfeld 1967; Conkey 1981). Another theory is that the artwork represented an early writing system, functioning as a calendar-like sequencing of events. Such a system would reflect a well-developed capacity for symbolization (Marshack 1972,

1976). Although we may never know its exact significance, the artwork of the Magdalenians strongly attests to the ingenuity and intelligence of these people and their desire to order the natural world.

The Mammoth Hunters

At sites in Europe and in the U.S.S.R., scientists have uncovered evidence of a specialized, mammoth-hunting society. These people concentrated on hunting the enormous woolly mammoth elephants that roamed the arctic plains of the late Ice Age. Dangerous to hunt, mammoths provided large quantities of meat in environments where smaller game and vegetable foods were scarce. The Mammoth Hunters apparently lived in the open, in huts constructed mainly of mammoth bones and skins. Skins were also turned into warm clothing. It is also very likely that fire played a crucial role in their adaptation.

An Upper Paleolithic sculpted female head from Brassenpouy, France. This delicate piece of ivory sculpture reflects the fine aesthetic character of Upper Paleolithic art.

Magdalenian harpoons carved from bone or antler.

Not surprisingly, the Hunters' art and rituals largely centered on the mammoths. Archaeologists have discovered decorated bones, carvings, clay mammoth figures, and a painted mammoth skull, which was possibly used as a ritualistic drum. They also have excavated a mass grave in which the humans were purposefully covered with mammoth shoulder blades.

About 10,000 years ago, the mammoths became extinct, taking with them the Mammoth Hunters' way of life. We do not know exactly why the mammoths, along with other large game, vanished at the end of the Ice Age. Possibly, there was a major climatic shift to which the "woollies" could not adapt. It is also possible that hunting played a part in the demise of this slow-to-reproduce species. Whatever the reason, the woolly mammoths, and the culture specialized to exploit them, forever disappeared from the earth.

As we have noted, the Upper Paleolithic is associated with a shift in emphasis from physical to cultural evolution. Table 9.3 summarizes some of the significant Upper Paleolithic cultural evolutionary trends.

Spreading Out across the World

Archaeological and paleontological evidence strongly points to the Upper Paleolithic as the period in which humans migrated into the virgin territories of the Americas and Australia. During the Pleistocene epoch, when the massive glaciers were formed from the oceans' waters, sea levels

TABLE 9.3
Upper Paleolithic Cultural Evolutionary Trends

- Increased efficiency of foraging techniques
- Increased specialization of foraging strategies
- Increased range of geographical area exploited
- Increased variety of habitats exploited
- Increased variety of resources exploited
- Increased use of seasonal base camps
- Increased number of tool traditions
- Increased number of tools in a kit, with greater specialization
- Increased efficiency in tool making
- Increased variety of materials used for tools
- Increased number of composite tools
- Innovations in tool making, including punchstriking and pressure flaking
- More sophisticated art and ritualistic behavior
- More rapid pace of cultural evolution in general, with physical evolution becoming less significant

dropped; hence, large areas of land were uncovered. These landmasses included land bridges that linked continents, which were again covered by water as the glaciers melted.

Habitation of Australia

Australia is an island continent approximately the size of the United States. Located south of Southeast Asia, it has been isolated from other continents in recent geologic times (as well as prior to the Ice Age) by wide expanses of the Pacific Ocean. However, during the Ice Age, the lowered water levels joined Australia and the nearby islands of New Guinea and Tasmania into one large landmass, known as Sahul. This area was separated from Southeast Asia by only about 60 miles of sea, a distance that humans could cross using small seaworthy boats. Such crossings apparently took place during at least two different periods about 60,000 to 40,000 years ago. These trips most likely were made by accident, without the people intending to migrate into this new land.

Australia, New Guinea, and Tasmania are dotted with a number of prehistoric sites. The oldest known sites, dating from about 35,000 years ago, are located in southeastern Australia, which indicates that the first humans—the ancestors of the aboriginal foragers—reached the northern part of the landmass about 60,000 to 50,000 years ago. Remains of these people include human skulls, clay ovens, choppers, and flake tools. By about 20,000 years ago, humans had spread across the region's southern part. Evidence of sophisticated rituals, such as the burial practice of cremation, indicate that the early inhabitants of "down under" had elaborate ways of life, which have persisted into modern times.

Into the New World

Sometime during the Pleistocene, humans migrated into the New World and spread across North and South America. These groups came from Northeast Asia, crossing a land bridge known as *Beringia*. For long periods during the Ice Age, Beringia was a dry, grassy plain that linked what is now Siberia and Alaska. Herds of large animals, such as mammoths and wild horses, apparently moved across Beringia as they grazed. The human groups that migrated into the New World may have been following these herds of game across the land bridge (see Figure 9.3).

The founding human populations came in at least two, and possibly three, separate waves. The first population to migrate into the New World was a generalized Caucasian-like group. They were the ancestors of many of the Indian populations currently spread throughout North America and South America. Another migration of a Mongoloid-type people followed. These people were the ancestors of the Eskimo and the Aleutians. The controversial third wave may represent the ancestors of the cultures contained within the Na-Dene language group. Speakers of Na-Dene include some Northwest Coast Indian societies and some groups found in the southwestern United States (Folsom and Folsom 1982).

Scientists disagree as to exactly when the human occupation of the New World, and the spread southward, actually occurred. This controversy is largely caused by problems in dating and by the scarceness of early archaeological sites. A few scientists contend that the first wave took place as far back as 100,000 years ago; others argue that migrations south of Canada did not take place before 12,000 years ago. Many scientists support a date of around 40,000 to 30,000 years ago for the earliest occupation of the New World, an estimate based on an important Alaskan site, Old Crow Flats. Evidence from this site, which includes primitive artifacts made from mammal bones, indicates that it may be up to 38,000 years old (but this is a tenuous date). Further passage was apparently blocked by massive ice sheets until the climate became milder and an ice-free corridor, located east of the Rockies, opened up, allowing groups to migrate south. When did this occur? The Meadowcroft rock shelter in Pennsylvania indicates the eastward spread of humans across North America by about 17,000 years ago (Adovasio et al. 1978). A

Eskimo

Paleo-Indians
(20,000 – 40,000 yrs ago)

BERINGIA

Aleut
(9,000 years
ago)

Na-Dene Hunters
(12,000 - 14,000
years ago)

Marmes

Gordon Creek
Los Angeles

Midland

Natchez
Vero Beach

Tepexpan

Punin

Pikimachay

Lagoa Santa
Confins

Land masses—18,000 B.P.

Ice sheets —18,000 B.P.

▲ Sites of human fossils

• Sites of Upper Paleolithic tools

Figure 9.3

Possible routes for the human occupation of the
Americas. Routes include the controversial "third
wave" of the Na-Dene language group.

264

Peruvian site suggests that humans were that far south by 19,000 years ago (MacNeish 1971). Still other remains indicate that human populations were located at the very tip of South America by 11,000 years ago.

It thus appears that, by 11,000 years ago at the latest, the humans of the New World were diversified into a range of cultural adaptations that had spread from the northern to the southern extremes of the American continents. Some of the groups developed a high degree of cultural complexity. Concentrating on North America, let us now take a look at some of these preagricultural cultures.

Paleo-Indian Adaptations

The early inhabitants of the Americas were all foragers, but regional groups rapidly adapted to local conditions. The early people of North America, who lived from about 12,000 to 6,000 years ago, are known as the *Paleo-Indians*. We know little about their ways of life, largely because these nomadic people left behind a meager archaeological record. A few Paleo-Indian sites are scattered across the Americas, as far south as Chile; however, most have been found on the Great Plains and in the southwestern United States.

Evidence uncovered at Paleo-Indian sites consists largely of animal remains, flakes, scrapers, knives, and different types of projectile points. The early inhabitants of North America apparently lived in small bands that followed grazing herds of large game animals, such as prehistoric bison and mammoths. Armed with spears, the men cooperated in well-organized big-game drives in which the animals were trapped so that they could be easily slaughtered. During the harsh winters, some groups lived off dried meat and vegetables collected during the warmer months. These groups continually moved from campsite to campsite, taking with them all their worldly goods.

The Paleo-Indians are best known from kill and butchering sites. Thus, groups are usually labeled according to their type of projectile point, which reflects the age of the site, the primary type of game hunted, and the hunting techniques. The *Clovis hunters*, who date from about 12,000 to 11,000 years ago, are also known as the Llano culture. The Clovis projectile point was made by the skilled flaking off of material on both sides of the head. As shown in Figure 9.4, the base is shallowly fluted—grooved so as to aid in attaching the point to a spear shaft. Clovis points have been found across North America, but most often at kill sites in the Great Plains and southwestern United States. Some Clovis sites contain the remains of several large game animals, particularly mammoths, indicating that the hunters were skilled mass-slaughterers of this great beast. The hunters cooperated in trapping the animals, who were apparently surprised on their way to drink water from nearby bogs.

About 11,000 to 10,000 years ago, sites of the *Folsom hunters* began to replace (and possibly overlap with) Clovis sites in the western and southwestern United States. The delicate and thin Folsom projectile points, also shown in Figure 9.4, are more deeply fluted, smaller, and of a slightly different shape than the Clovis heads. While plentiful on the Great Plains, the Folsom points are mostly scattered about and associated with only a few definite kill sites. The Folsom technology and other evidence point to a shift in the hunting adaptation of these Paleo-Indians. Apparently, they concentrated on a very large species of bison rather than on the mammoth. In addition, in contrast to the earlier emphasis on cooperative hunting, the bison were hunted either by a group of hunters *or* singly, by a lone hunter. The Folsom hunters may also have been the first Paleo-Indians to use an effective technique known as the "surround kill," a method in which the hunters cooperate in surrounding a few large animals, cutting off the animals' escape routes (Jennings 1974).

The *Plano hunters*, dating from about 10,000 to 6,000 years ago, appear to have quickly replaced the Folsom tradition on the Great Plains. The oldest known Paleo-Indian dwelling, a small,

FIGURE 9.4

Paleo-Indian projectile points from Plains cultures. Arrows indicate fluted bases.

Clovis   Folsom   Scottsbluff   Eden

round house uncovered in Wyoming, dates from the Plano tradition. Plano sites have been found over most of the continental United States east of the Rockies and are identified by an unfluted, long, slender, and parallel-flaked projectile point that differs considerably from the fluted Clovis and Folsom heads. The shift to Plano technology occurred at the time when the Pleistocene bison was superseded by the smaller, although still quite awesome, modern-day species. Not surprisingly, Plano points are often associated with these bison and other contemporary animal forms, including antelopes. An impressive example of the Plano hunters' skill comes from the Olsen-Chubbock site in Colorado (see the photo that follows). Dating from about 8200 B.C., evidence from this site indicates that approximately 200 bison were driven into a deep ravine, where they were slaughtered and butchered (Frison 1978). Such big-game drives depended on the cooperation of many hunters and may also have in-

volved the efforts of the group's women and children.

Archaeologists have found poorly preserved evidence of other Paleo-Indian cultures. Although the archaeological record is biased in favor of hunting societies (reflecting the good preservation of the projectile points), some groups apparently exploited a wide variety of animal and plant life. A number of Paleo-Indian sites that contain both fluted and unfluted projectile points along with other artifacts are distributed across the Midwest and the northeastern United States. The consistency of the tools' forms suggests that they all belong to "one technological complex" (Griffin 1978, 225), with local adaptations to a broad range of environments. However, because of poor preservation, these assemblages are almost totally lacking in animal bones or plant-food remains, which limits our ability to learn the specifics of the localized subsistence strategies. Even less is known about

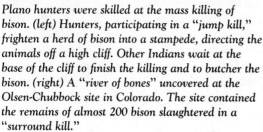

Plano hunters were skilled at the mass killing of bison. (left) Hunters, participating in a "jump kill," frighten a herd of bison into a stampede, directing the animals off a high cliff. Other Indians wait at the base of the cliff to finish the killing and to butcher the bison. (right) A "river of bones" uncovered at the Olsen-Chubbock site in Colorado. The site contained the remains of almost 200 bison slaughtered in a "surround kill."

Cultures in Transition

About 10,000 years ago, in parts of both the Old World and the New, behavioral shifts occurred that marked a period of cultural evolutionary transition. Known as the *Mesolithic*, or Middle Stone Age, in Europe and as the *Archaic* in the New World, this period represents an increased diversification of subsistence strategies. Why did new subsistence strategies appear at this particular time? At the end of the Pleistocene, many of the large game animals became extinct, possibly as the result of climatic changes, human overhunting, or a combination of both. Thus, the foragers who had concentrated on the hunting of large game had to learn to make use of a wider variety of food resources. Very significantly, this period's cultural trends eventually led to the origin of the domestication of food.

the West Coast Paleo-Indians. Limited remains suggest that they emphasized a gathering economy, as reflected by the relative abundance of shellfish remains and milling stones (used for grinding grains) and the rarity of projectile points and animal and fish bones.

THE MESOLITHIC AND ARCHAIC PERIODS

About 15,000 to 10,000 years ago, the end of the last Ice Age marked the beginning of the *Holocene*, or "recent," epoch. The earth's climate changed significantly as it stabilized, becoming much as it is today. As a result, there were changes in animal and plant life, including the extinction of many large Ice Age mammals. Important geographical changes also took place. Many of the great glaciers melted, which raised the sea level and covered land bridges and coastal regions, until the earth's surface reached its present-day form.

By the beginning of the Holocene, humans were spread over much of the inhabitable world. As the ice sheets melted, people migrated into newly uncovered regions, such as northern parts of the British Isles and Scandinavia (Champion et al. 1984). Some societies maintained their still successful foraging ways of life. Other groups were seriously affected by the environmental changes, which stimulated cultural change and innovation. In some regions, population densities increased, which also led to changes in subsistence strategies. From this point on, technological change was extremely rapid, the Mesolithic quickly leading into the Neolithic period.

The Mesolithic and Archaic periods took place at different times in different places, and, in some places, they did not occur at all. The Mesolithic is best known from northwestern Europe, from about 12,000 to 10,000 years ago, and usually refers to events that took place just prior to the origin of agriculture. The Archaic is best known from North America, where it may have first arisen approximately 10,000 to 8,000 years ago. However, while the Archaic cultures of North America most commonly date from about 7000 to 2000 B.C., the period persisted in some places until the 1850s. Furthermore, this stage chronologically overlaps with that of the Paleo-Indians.

Both the Mesolithic and the Archaic periods represent a transitional stage between early foragers and food producers. During this transition,

foraging techniques became increasingly specialized, with an intensification of food collection. These events reflect a trend toward the increased control of the natural environment—the hallmark of the domestication of food resources.

Broad-Spectrum Strategies

Because the transition to agriculture occurred in different places and under different sets of circumstances, it is difficult to sum up with generalized statements. However, according to Flannery (1973), during these transitions there was a general shift from a dependency on a specialized food base, such as large mammals, to a "broad-spectrum resource utilization" (p. 283). In other words, groups diversified their subsistence strategy to make use of a wider variety of foods. This entailed gathering many different plants, hunting small animals, and fishing. The kinds of foods varied both regionally and seasonally, according to environmental demands and the resources available.

In exploring the reasons for the shift to a broad-spectrum strategy, Flannery noted that a major factor was the change in environment, especially the decreased availability of traditional foods. He also noted that, because humans had already spread out across the world, people were less able to alleviate the pressure caused by increased population size by migrating into new regions. Consequently, there was a strain on local food resources in some locations. Societies had to use "less desirable" foods to feed all the people, thereby increasing the number of exploited types of resources. Thus, a broad-spectrum strategy was a transitional step toward the stabilizing of food resources through plant and animal domestication.

An example of a broad-spectrum strategy comes from the Near East, which is "one of those parts of the world where sedentary life . . . seems to have begun before agriculture" (Flannery 1973, 274). At the end of the Pleistocene, the climate of this region was colder and drier than it is today. The people exploited a wide range of foods, including wild plants, such as cereal grasses, nuts, and legumes. They also hunted grazing animals, such as sheep, goats and deer, and collected shellfish, turtles, and fish. Apparently, this broad-spectrum strategy led the way for the origin of agriculture, which occurred in this region about 10,000 years ago.

Technological Trends

The cultures of the Mesolithic and Archaic periods were technologically varied. Within this context, the technological trends reflect an in-creasing cultural complexity and efficiency and foreshadow the origin of agriculture. Earlier trends continued; for example, the number of tool traditions increased. Within assemblages, we see a notable increase in the number of tool types, which reflects the exploitation of a broader range of resources (see Figure 9.5). Implements were also more sophisticated and made out of a wide variety of materials, including stone, wood, bone, antler, and leather. Archaeologists also note an increase in the number of composite tools, such as bows, arrows, and harpoons.

Western European Mesolithic sites reflect this change in technology. A distinctive aspect of many of these assemblages is the great number of

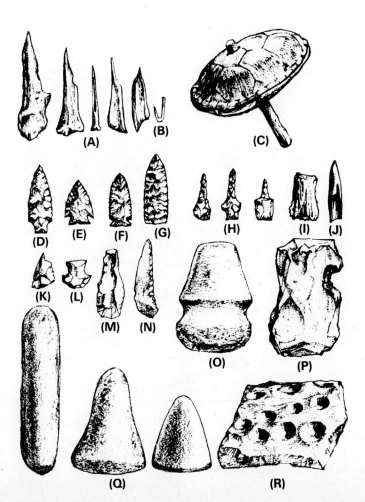

FIGURE 9.5
Archaic artifacts from Indian Knoll, Kentucky. This rich site contained over 55,000 artifacts and almost 900 human skeletons. Drawn at approximately one-fourth size, sample implements include (A) bone awls; (B) a bone fishhook; (C) a rattle; (D,E,F) projectile points; (G) a blade; (H) drills; (I) the handle of an antler spear-thrower; (J) an antler projectile point; (K) a graver; (L,M,N) scrapers; (O) a grooved ax; (P) a notched limestone hoe; (Q) pestles; and (R) a nut stone.

microliths—very small, geometrically shaped flint blades. Although they are also noted at some Upper Paleolithic sites, microliths were particularly abundant during the Mesolithic. Also common to Mesolithic sites are woodworking implements such as axes and adzes (heavy, curved cutting tools) and gear for using water resources, including fishhooks, paddles, and canoes. This technology was well designed for early Holocene life in western Europe, since the land was heavily forested and crisscrossed by rivers and streams. For example, the microliths' sharp cutting edges were well suited for cutting the abundant wood that was used for making dugout canoes, huts, tools, and weapons and as fuel for fire.

Another important technological feature of some Mesolithic and Archaic sites were *ground-stone tools*, especially axes. These implements, ground against stone and buffed to produce smooth and round edges, were used to process wood and plant materials. Ground-stone technology became an important tool-making technique in some Neolithic agricultural societies, where it was used to make mortars and other seed- and grain-grinding implements.

Social and Behavioral Trends

The Mesolithic and Archaic social and behavioral trends also represent a transitional stage between foragers and agriculturalists. Although there was much regional variation, we can make some general statements. There was an important change in settlement patterns, with a trend toward increased sedentism—a criterion for the origin of agriculture. Studies of contemporary foragers demonstrate that they can be somewhat sedentary if resources are readily available, particularly seasonally. We noted earlier that some preagricultural Near Eastern societies were completely sedentary, living in villages. A few European Mesolithic sites show evidence of seasonal occupation, including some very limited remains of huts. In the New World, a Koster Middle Archaic horizon, dating from 5,500 years ago, contains evidence of permanent houses, as well as evidence that the people continuously occupied

the same site for as long as 100 years (Struever and Holton 1979).

Another important trend associated with some societies is an increase in long-distance trade. The desire to trade over long distances is associated with sedentism, since it provides people with a means of obtaining materials they can no longer collect for themselves. For example, the Early Archaic people of the lower Illinois Valley apparently traded with groups from northern Michigan to obtain iron ore for ornamental beads (Struever and Holton 1979). Such trade established important networks of cultural contact and political alliances that may have been a factor in the origin of some state-level societies.

Examples of Mesolithic Societies

We cannot touch on all that was going on among the many and varied Mesolithic and Archaic cultures. We can, however, present a few examples of what life was like.

An early Mesolithic culture found in northwestern Europe is known as the Maglemose, named for a well-preserved Danish peat-bog site. One of the best known Maglemosian sites is Star Carr in England, which dates from about 7600 B.C. This site reflects one of the Maglemosian subsistence strategies. In the vast forests of Mesolithic northern Europe, most of the game animals, such as elk and wild pigs, were solitary. However, during the winter, red deer congregated in groups. Star Carr was apparently the winter camp site for the hunters of these red-deer herds. Clark (1972) speculated that the camp was inhabited by a small band of about 20 individuals, consisting of three or four families. This group was a small hunting party that made use of early domesticated dogs.

Maglemosian sites demonstrate that the people of the early Mesolithic exploited many different food resources. Although their diets varied with ecological zone and season, they collected a wide variety of plants; fished for such species as pike, eel, and bream; hunted storks, herons, swans, geese, ducks, grouse, gulls, and other birds; and captured mammals, such as hares, squirrels, beaver, fox, badgers, seals, and wild horses. In all, Maglemosian sites reveal the remains of at least 58 different animal species (Milisauskas 1978).

Archaeologists have uncovered clues to the Maglemosian ways of life. For example, excavations in Denmark have revealed the remains of huts with indoor fireplaces. We know that Maglemosian people used axes and adzes to cut down trees and hunted with bows and arrows that had projectile points made of microliths. Unfortunately, archaeologists have found little evidence of European Mesolithic art and symbolism. Gone are the cave paintings seen during the late stages of the Paleolithic, leaving archaeologists with only a small number of carved animal figures and decorated implements. However, collective burial sites, as well as those containing single individuals, reflect the continued importance of ritualistic activities. For example, one Polish site contains a single person buried with a wealth of goods (Champion et al. 1984).

A few early Holocene cultures spread from southern Europe into southwestern Asia, one of the best known being the *Natufian*. Dating from about 10,000 to 8000 B.C., Natufian sites are found across southwestern Asia, including Israel, Iran, Iraq, and Lebanon (Mellaart 1975). Although some cave sites have been found, the Natufians primarily lived in small open-air settlements. Their stone pit houses and nearby cemeteries indicate that they led a fairly sedentary life. Microliths, sickles, ground-stone tools, harpoons, fishhooks, and many other implements helped them take advantage of many different resources, including plants, herds of gazelle, and marine life. The sickles and grinding stones demonstrate that a major part of the Natufian diet was based on wild grains. This strategy apparently led to the early domestication of plants and animals about 10,000 years ago.

Examples of Archaic Societies

The Archaic period is characterized by localized hunting and gathering adaptations that made use of a broad range of resources. Associated with this pattern are rich and varied assemblages, such as that shown in Figure 9.5. The many types of environments exploited by Archaic people included forests, plateaus, river floodplains, and coastal regions. Archaic sites are found across the United States and Mexico.

An example of a midwestern Archaic society was uncovered at the Koster site (see pp. 210–211). Horizon 11, which dates from 6400 B.C., presents a picture of Early Archaic life (Struever and Holton 1979). At that time, it was a semipermanent seasonal camp, located near the Illinois River and surrounded by woodlands. The people's technology was fairly sophisticated. They built fire hearths and made use of some of the earliest food-grinding technology yet unearthed in North America. Using ground-stone adzes, they practiced woodworking, which included making dugout canoes. Bone awls and needles were used to make clothes out of leather; other artifacts were used in basket making. The assemblages also contain projectile points, stone knives, and scrapers. The diet of this population was varied and nutritious, consisting largely of deer, small mammals, fish, shellfish, nuts, seeds, and other plant foods.

Koster's Early Archaic people also had fairly sophisticated social practices, including elaborate rituals for the dead. Horizon 11 contains a very early cemetery in which were found the carefully arranged remains of adults and children. Even pets were interred in a ritualistic manner. Decorative beads, made out of iron, indicate that the people were involved in a trade network, since northern Michigan was the closest source of this material. Thus, Koster's Early Archaic people clearly led a rich and varied life. A more recent Koster horizon demonstrates that, by the Middle Archaic, they had come to live in preagricultural permanent villages.

Early Archaic sites, dating from at least 10,000 years ago, have been found west of the Rockies. Sometimes labeled as the "Desert Culture," these sites actually represent several traditions. This arid, sparsely vegetated environment was different from that of the midwestern forests. For example, wildlife was much less plentiful in the arid region. Within this general setting was a range of ecosystems. Some areas were covered with sagebrush, while others contained small rivers. The Colorado Plateau included a variety of resources. How did the Archaic people survive in this arid land? In contrast to the Paleo-Indians, who relied on large game, the western Archaic societies ex-

ploited a broad range of resources. Milling stones and baskets helped them to gather and prepare small seeds and other plant foods. Darts, spears, and spear-throwers served them in hunting small game. Thus, although both the midwestern and desert groups had broad-spectrum strategies, they made use of different types of resources.

THE MOVE TOWARD AGRICULTURE

Foraging was the predominant subsistence strategy for 99 percent of human history. People lived in a close and relatively well-balanced relationship with nature, in which large-scale exploitation of natural resources played no part. However, about 10,000 years ago, a major shift took place as people began to domesticate plant and animal life. This shift ushered in significant changes in technology, in social organization, and even in the environment. In addition, the pace of cultural evolution became still more rapid.

By the end of the Mesolithic, humans had expanded into many geographical regions and into a vast number of habitats. Culture now rose to

the fore as an extremely important means of contending with a varied array of environments, as people devised new and complex technologies to more efficiently contend with the conditions that faced them. Innovations led some human groups to devise a revolutionary way of life—the domestication of food resources and the large-scale manipulation of the natural environment. Since humans tend to be culturally "conservative," it is of great interest to understand the factors that might have played a part in bringing about such a radical change in the way people lived. Theories dealing with the origin and diffusion of agriculture are explored in the next chapter.

SUMMARY

Cultural evolution is viewed as occurring on two levels. General cultural evolution, the pattern of large-scale changes in culture, addresses how cultures change over time and focuses on major shifts in sociocultural development. Specific cultural evolution focuses on how change occurs in particular societies over relatively short spans of time, with an emphasis on explaining why cultures are so diversified. Specific cultural evolution proceeds differently from culture to culture, in part depending on the flexibility of the culture and the motivation to change. Three processes are mainly responsible for introducing culture

change to specific societies: innovation, diffusion, and acculturation. General cultural evolution, influenced by the processes of specific cultural evolution, has produced large-scale cultural trends. The dominant themes are the increasing complexity of cultural systems and the increasing efficiency of the human adaptation.

The history of general cultural evolution is divided into stages. The oldest stage, the Lower Paleolithic, includes the earliest recognized traces of culture. These simple pebble tools, labeled as the Oldowan tradition, were used by culturally simple foragers. Later, a more complex Lower Paleolithic tool tradition, the Acheulean, appeared in parts of the Old World. The later aspect of the Lower Paleolithic is associated with *Homo erectus.* This hominid was more complex than earlier forms, with a greater diversity of tools and types of sites.

The Middle Paleolithic represents a continuation of trends observed during the Lower Paleolithic, including a refinement and standardization of tool-making techniques, an increase in the number of tool traditions, the exploitation of a greater number of environments, a move toward sedentism, a trend toward ritualism, and advances in mental abilities. Middle Paleolithic technology included the Mousterian, often associated with Neandertal finds.

During the Upper Paleolithic, there was a major change in biocultural evolution, as physical evolution became relatively insignificant and cultural evolution occurred at an increasingly rapid pace. The Upper Paleolithic saw a continuation of earlier trends, and is associated with anatomically modern humans, *Homo sapiens sapiens.*

The Upper Paleolithic was probably the period during which humans migrated into the Americas and Australia, where human populations adapted to local conditions. The early people of North America, known as the Paleo-Indians, are associated with a number of tool traditions, including Clovis, Folsom, and Plano.

About 10,000 years ago, behavioral shifts marked a period of cultural evolutionary transition. Known as the Mesolithic in Europe and the Archaic in the New World, this period represents an increased diversification of subsistence strategies. The Mesolithic and the Archaic represent a transitional stage between early foragers and food producers, characterized by a general trend toward the increased control of the natural environment. During these transitions there was a general shift from a dependency on a specialized food base to a broad-spectrum resource utilization. Trends included greater technological sophistication, increasing sedentism, and more reliance on long-distance trade.

SUGGESTED READINGS

Browman, David L., ed. 1980. *Early Native Americans.* The Hague: Mouton Publishers.

Champion, Timothy, Clive Gamble, Steven Shennan, and Alasdair Whittle. 1984. *Prehistoric Europe.* London: Academic Press.

Fagan, Brian M. 1986. *People of the Earth.* Boston: Little, Brown. (Text on cultural evolution)

_____. 1987. *the Great Journey.* New York: Thames and Hudson.

Fiedel, Stuart J. 1987. *Prehistory of the Americas.* Cambridge: Cambridge University Press.

Gowlett, John. 1984. *Ascent to Civilization.* New York: Alfred A. Knopf.

Spindler, Louise S. 1977. *Culture Change and Modernization.* Prospect Heights, IL: Waveland Press.

Trinkaus, Erik, ed. 1990. *The Emergence of Modern Humans: Biocultural Adaptations in the Later Pleistocene.* New York: Cambridge University Press.

White, J. Peter, and James O'Connell. 1982. *A Prehistory of Australia, New Guinea, and Sahul.* Sydney: Academic Press.

10 The Origin of Agriculture

The "cliff-dwelling" Anasazi village of Mesa Verde, Colorado. The Anasazi tradition, dating from approximately 2,000 years ago, was an early agricultural society that ingeniously exploited the arid conditions of what is now the southwestern United States.

By 10,000 years ago, humans had spread across the world, various groups adapting to local conditions. While most still lived as foragers, some societies reached a new level of cultural complexity. These groups were no longer bound to the natural rhythms of the earth, but began to control food resources through the domestication of plants and animals.

We can see how humans have harnessed and reshaped the environment. Much of our food today is processed in many steps and is highly domesticated, having undergone many generations of artificial selection. These modern means of feeding people are founded in the earliest manipulations of natural resources. Thus, the origin of **agriculture**, the cultivation of plants based on the continuous and intensive use of labor and land resources, is of great interest to anthropologists.

The origin of agriculture, marking the beginning of the large-scale manipulation of natural resources, is associated with major technological and social changes. This chapter is concerned with the changes that occurred during the Neolithic, the period associated with the origin of agriculture. We will explore the questions of how, where, and why agriculture originated.

THE NEOLITHIC AND THE DOMESTICATION OF FOOD RESOURCES

During the Mesolithic, groups of foragers became more sedentary and devised broad-spectrum resource strategies. Such behavioral, technological, and social changes eventually led to the *Neolithic*—the "New Stone Age." Although technology was still largely based on stone, the Neolithic is characterized by radical changes in how people lived. Groups, for example, began to fully settle in villages and to control food resources through domestication. The rapid Neolithic transition from foraging to agricultural societies occurred from about 10,000 to 5,000 years ago, in areas of both the New World and the Old World. By 2,000 years ago, agriculture was established across much of the world. The Stone Age quickly came to a close, as societies began to prominently use metal implements.

Agriculture independently originated in at least three regions: the Near East, the Far East, and the New World. Within each region, there were centers where domestication was invented and from where it spread. Because this crucial event took place at least three times, anthropologists seek to identify unifying explanatory principles. In doing so, they hope to shed light on a range of questions: Why did societies develop food domestication, especially since people are reluctant to radically change the ways of life to which they are accustomed? Are there general processes underlying these independent, but almost concurrent, origins of agriculture? How did it spread? Why was it readily adopted by some groups and ignored by others?

Before addressing these issues, we need to clarify the concept of domestication. **Domestication** is the taming of wild plants or animals for human use. Its origin involved extreme departures from nonagricultural patterns, the most significant being

1. purposeful, large-scale land management;
2. genetic changes in plants and animals; and
3. changes in human behavior.

These components interacted during the origin of agriculture. For example, land management was necessary for cultivating crops and in caring for domesticated animals. To manage the land, people made many life-style changes; for example, they became fully sedentary, shifted residence patterns, embellished trade networks, and cooperated on large-scale agricultural projects. The genetic changes resulted from humans selecting preferred forms of plants and animals, which, in turn, made it necessary for people to change their behavior to care for the altered species.

We can view the Neolithic as an interacting set of subsystems (J. Smith 1976). The major components of the overall system are culture, people (in the biological sense), and the natural and social environment. Culture is subdivided into technology and technical knowledge, social organization, and ideology and ideological institutions (see Figure 10.1). The "people" subsystem changed in many ways. For example, as societies became more sedentary, population density increased greatly. There were also many changes in the environmental subsystem. For example, social environmental changes included an increase in intergroup trade, while natural environmental changes included the reshaping of the land through such farming techniques as irrigation and tillage. There were many changes in the technological subsystem as well; for example, the invention of pottery and of tools for cultivation. Major changes associated with social organization were the rise of tribal societies and village settlements.

FIGURE 10.1

Smith's systems approach to culture: Neolithic examples.

THEORIES OF THE ORIGIN OF AGRICULTURE

The literature concerning the origin of agriculture is vast. While much of it focuses on where and when, the more intriguing work attempts to explain *why* agriculture originated. Some researchers term it a revolution and seek to find the thresholds of its invention; others view it as an evolution, to be explained in terms of ecological theory, with reference to a natural extension of the human adaptive pattern.

Many ideas regarding the origin of agriculture are "prime-mover" or "single-cause" theories. Such approaches focus on one major stimulus, such as demography or environment. A more complex approach is provided by "multicausal," or "systemic," models, which emphasize a number of factors. Now let us take a look at some of these theories.

Early Theories

Anthropologists have been proposing scenarios for the origin of agriculture for over a century. Early ideas often focused on the site of its invention. During the early twentieth century, many anthropologists believed that agriculture was invented in a single core area of the Old World,

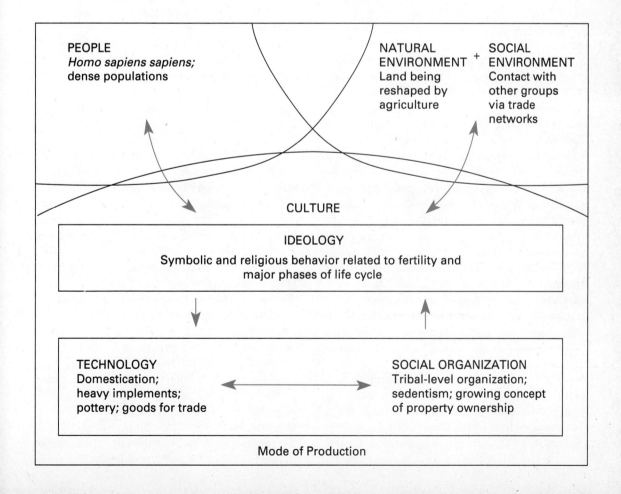

from where it diffused to the rest of the world. Most scholars now agree that domestication was independently invented in a number of regions.

Another idea, popular during the late nineteenth century, was that agriculture started "by chance." This scenario has an especially smart forager accidentally happening upon a sprouting seed and realizing that this was a means of controlling a food source. The underlying assumption here is that everyone else was insensitive to the environment and had never noticed this before. There is also the implication that, as soon as someone discovered the basics of domestication, the rest of humanity immediately seized the opportunity and started to grow food. This was certainly not the case, for nonagricultural people often coexist with farmers without ever adopting their way of life.

Ecological Theories

Modern approaches to the origin of agriculture often focus on ecological factors. One of the first ecologically based theories was devised by V. Gordon Childe (1936, 1952). His *oases theory* contends that food production arose out of a climatic crisis in an arid, subtropical region of the Near East. The invention was stimulated by a drying trend initiated by the melting of the European ice sheets that had shifted rain-bearing weather patterns to the north. As a result, the deserts' people and wildlife gravitated to oases formed around scattered springs and streams. This eventually led to a mutually beneficial relationship between humans and animals, as the people began to lead a pastoral way of life. People also began to cultivate crops, in part, to provide animals with feed. The domestication of the plants and animals provided humans with stable food sources, as well as with a surplus of food that had to be stored and managed.

Childe's theory did not hold up as more data came to light. For instance, some modern-day foragers subsist in an arid environment without domesticated food. Also, Childe's theory fails to explain why the oases-dwelling humans did not simply remain foragers. Even so, Childe stimulated the emphasis on ecological factors in theories of domestication.

Childe's ideas directly influenced another important theorist, Robert Braidwood (1958, 1971, 1975). During the late 1940s, Braidwood sought to test Childe's hypothesis in a carefully designed, multidisciplinary archaeological expedition to Iran. The evidence from that expedition refuted many of Childe's premises. For example, it was ascertained that there had been no severe climatic shifts in the region at the end of the Pleistocene, thereby eliminating the ecological basis for the oases model. As an alternative, Braidwood devised a *nuclear-zone hypothesis*, with "human nature" (people's need to understand the environment) providing the stimulus for the origin of agriculture. Nuclear zones were rich central areas, from which domestication spread to other parts of the world. According to Braidwood, as cultures became increasingly specialized, people were eager to explore the domestication of animals and the cultivation of plants, since this would allow them to settle more comfortably into their environments. Braidwood proposed that Near Eastern agriculture started in the fertile hilly flanks of the Zagros Mountains, where local people were intrigued by the cultivation possibilities of the wild grasses. This rich ecological zone was quite different from the flat, arid lowlands pointed to by Childe. Thus, Braidwood's theory has an ecological slant: a critical factor was the need for abundant plant and animal life for experimentation.

Braidwood's model was criticized by Binford (1968), who argued that major life-style changes do not occur simply as the result of human nature, but are stimulated by external factors. Another important criticism was that foragers could have lived quite well in such an abundant environment and would have had little reason to change their traditional ways of life. Also, earlier foragers probably had much of the basic knowledge, but did not apply it for purposes of domestication. To this Braidwood responded that earlier foragers were not yet culturally "ready" to be

The hilly flanks of the Zagros Mountains in western Iran. Robert Braidwood proposed that Near Eastern agriculture originated with the cultivation of wild grasses found in this ecological zone. Shown are the tents and sheep of contemporary Bakhtiari herdspeople.

farmers—not a convincing supposition from a scientific standpoint. Braidwood also overlooked the evolutionary reasoning that the plants were well adapted to the nuclear zones and would not have undergone genetic changes easily. His theory fails to explain the mechanisms underlying the alterations in genotypes. On a positive note, Braidwood championed the interdisciplinary approach and an ecological focus on local habitats.

Another important early ecological model was developed by Carl Sauer (1952). According to Sauer's model, agriculture was first invented in Southeast Asia, from where it diffused to other parts of the Old World. Sauer theorized that agriculture originated because of a gradual change in the interaction between cultures and environment, as semisedentary fishing societies began to grow root crops, such as yams, in response to ecological shifts. Most researchers disagree with Sauer's idea that the Near East was not an agricultural center. However, it is likely that agriculture occurred early in Southeast Asia. Scientists have uncovered evidence of the early domestication of ricelike grains and beans at Spirit Cave in Thailand (Gorman 1977). Additionally,

Sauer's emphasis on the relationship between cultural and environmental change has been a major influence on more fully realized ecological models of food production.

Population Pressure

Another popular focus in the study of the origin of agriculture is demographic factors, such as increased population size and density. Many demographic theories are based on the ecological concept of **carrying capacity**, the maximum population size that can be maintained by an environment under a specific set of conditions. If populations are to grow beyond their carrying capacity, then their resources must grow with them to avoid a "population crash" in which animals die from starvation or other causes. According to this reasoning, population size is an important stimulus for the domestication of food.

Ester Boserup (1965, 1981) devised a well-known prime-mover demographic model. Her model contends that population growth acted as a "trigger" that set off the rapid development of technological and environmental innovations.

In her words, "many inventions . . . have been demand-induced." Also, "radical changes in the relation between humans and natural resources occur in areas in which population multiplies" (1981, 5). Boserup's model has been criticized for not explaining why the population increase occurred at the end of the Pleistocene. Another question she left unresolved is why population size was not controlled through mechanisms such as delayed marriage or infanticide. In other words, the idea of population growth as a prime mover is too simplistic.

Another famous population model was proposed by Lewis Binford (1968), who emphasized the systemic interaction between populational factors and environmental conditions. He sought to explain why, at the end of the Pleistocene, people underwent such a radical change in culture and subsistence strategy. Binford linked the major environmental changes that occurred at the end of the Ice Age with populational pressures, contending that, as the glaciers retreated and sea levels rose, coastal populations of foragers were forced inland. This led to a rapid "disequilibrium" between population density and local resources as groups moved into territories occupied by other people. The sudden increase in population density brought about "selective advantage for increased productivity" (p. 328). Thus, in Binford's view, environmental factors were responsible for the sudden pressure on local environments where sedentary populations lived within favored habitats. Population size also increased because sedentary life was less stressful on mothers and infants than nomadic life. However, agriculture did not originate in nuclear areas, but in marginal areas into which people were pushed because of populational pressures. In addition, Binford noted that genetic changes, necessary for the domestication of plants and animals, were more likely to occur under "less-than-ideal" circumstances. People have the greatest desire and the most success in domesticating plants and animals where the species' adaptations are not fully in tune with the environmental conditions.

Binford's *demographic stress model* is an intriguing combination of ecological and populational factors, emphasizing the importance of the relationship between genetic changes and marginal zones. This hypothesis has a number of weaknesses, however, including its failure to account for why these events did not take place during earlier climatic fluxes. Nonetheless, it clearly demonstrates that simple models are inadequate in explaining the complex events that led to the origin of agriculture.

Flannery's Multicausal Approach

One of the first truly multicausal systemic models for the origin of agriculture was developed by Kent Flannery (1973). His classic work focuses on the processes underlying the transition from foraging to agricultural ways of life. Flannery argued that a single event did not cause the change, but that it occurred gradually, as food resources slowly changed along with human behavior.

Flannery also argued that no single model can fully explain the origin of agriculture because each area had its own set of conditions. He proposed at least two types of primitive agricultural, or horticultural, systems: seed-crop cultivation and vegeculture. **Seed-crop cultivation**, which occurred in the Near East, Mesoamerica, and Peru, is a relatively simple ecosystem, consisting of only a few domesticated plant species and, thus, somewhat unstable. It involves the reproduction of plants through annual introduction of seeds derived from the fruit of the plant. Although it demands a good deal of work, seed-crop cultivation *does* produce a good yield of food. **Vegeculture**, which includes the yam cultivation of Southeast Asia, is a more complex ecosystem that uses a greater variety of cultivated plants. The plants are propagated by direct cloning, such as cutting stems and dividing roots. This technique demands less attention and is less productive than seed-crop cultivation. However, because a greater variety of plants are grown, vegeculture is more stable than the simpler system.

Even though Flannery concentrated on seed-crop cultivation, he still found it difficult to come up with a general explanatory model. For the Near East, he agreed with Binford's emphasis on populational pressure and the argument that genetic changes occurred in marginal areas. He went on to expand on Binford's model, noting the multiple factors that interacted in the origin of Near Eastern agriculture, especially environmental, demographic, settlement, and social elements. In Flannery's view, agriculture originated at the end of a long, cool, dry period, in which the people had used a broad-spectrum resource strategy. They were a semisedentary people, with a higher population density than in earlier times. Thus, agriculture began "in a region of relatively great environmental diversity over a relatively small area" (Flannery 1973, 283). The genetic modifications were accompanied by technological innovations, sedentism, and changes in social organization that were necessary for the intense management of the crops.

For the evolution of Mesoamerican seed-crop agriculture, Flannery described a different set of circumstances. At first, population pressure was not a major factor, and nomadic patterns continued for quite some time after the beginning of domestication. However, there *was* a significant environmental stress: climatic fluxes that altered the productivity of gathered foods between dry and wet years. He noted that the plants domesticated by the Mesoamericans were "third-choice foods"—those which were originally eaten only under stressful conditions. The ancestral plants also shared some characteristics. They were annuals, had a high yield, stored easily, were genetically plastic, and were very tolerant of a wide range of habitats. Apparently, by domesticating these plants, the Mesoamericans were consciously seeking to stabilize their food supplies.

While acknowledging local differences, Flannery did note some unifying themes. In particular, he offered a reason why foragers would so radically change their way of life: "Since early farming represents a decision to work harder and eat more 'third-choice' foods, I suspect that peo-

ple did it because they felt they had to, not because they wanted to" (Flannery 1973, 307–8). The most likely motivation was stabilizing food resources in response to population pressures, fluxes in the environment, or other factors. Flannery also noted that a society must change as a whole system, as technological, social, and economic conditions respond to shifts in subsistence strategies.

Other Models

Most post-Flannery models are also multicausal, although they often emphasize one factor. For example, Mark Cohen (1977) pointed to population pressure as the major impetus for the origin of agriculture, with the goal of increased food supplies. Noting that agriculture started at about the same time in different areas of the world, he approached population growth in terms of a global system. According to Cohen's model, the population of the world slowly but steadily increased throughout the Pleistocene, until people could no longer contend with the growth by moving into unoccupied lands. On every continent but Australia, the increased population put stress on food resources, which first led to broad-spectrum strategies and then to agriculture. Societies accomplished these changes by further developing the subsistence techniques already practiced by foragers. People then intensified their food-production capabilities to gain a greater yield of food per acre. Cohen's model is supported by archaeological evidence that prehistoric populations underwent dietary and social stresses. Yet, if such a global system existed, what accounts for the fact that various groups adopted agriculture at different times? Critics have also criticized Cohen's model on the grounds that it does not adequately account for various social, technological, and economic factors.

Other models focus on a range of factors. Harris (1977) proposed that the local differences in timing were due to interacting variables, including population pressure, plant distribution, en-

Primitive agricultural systems. (left) Seed-crop cultivation. Here, farmers harvest corn in Amecameca, Mexico. (below) Vegeculture. The Dani of New Guinea plant sweet potato gardens; here a man sits in a watchtower looking for signs of an enemy raiding party.

vironmental flux, and technological factors that combined to make agriculture an attractive alternative to traditional foraging ways of life. Vincent (1979) emphasized the need for political centralization in response to population growth and changes in social organization. Redman (1977) focused on technological developments, such as means of storing surplus food. For Wright (1977), the role of climatic change was particularly important, allowing for the spread of wild cereal grasses across the Near East and establishing the proper conditions for its domestication.

Of special note is Fekri Hassan's (1981) complex systemic model that focuses on the Near East (see Figure 10.2). He nicely balances a range of factors by emphasizing the feedback aspect of the system's components. While noting the global increase in population size, Hassan argued that this was not the single stimulus for food domestication. Rather, he proposed a number of factors, including the climatically triggered spread of cereal grasses; the advanced technological, cultural, and cognitive level of late Pleistocene humans; and demographic factors, such as increased population density and the stresses it put on food resources. Under these conditions, very small fluxes in climate and their effects on plant and animal life acted as a "kicker." A variety of responses were initiated, "conditioned by the pre-existing state of the cultural system and the specific habitats under exploitation" (p. 225). These responses followed simple ecological principles and led to the use of less desirable and

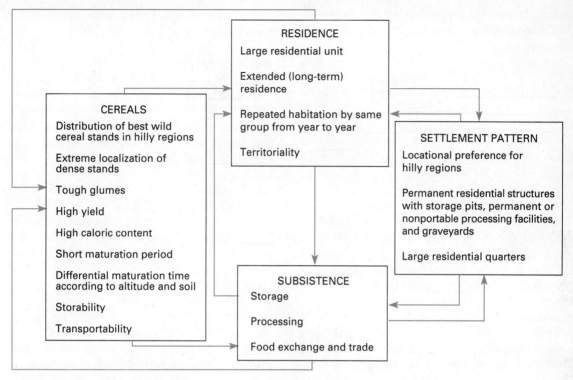

FIGURE 10.2
Hassan's feedback model for the origin of agriculture.

more labor-demanding foods as a means of stabilizing the food base. The use of one of these foods, cereal grasses, led to an "ecological trap." People began to concentrate on cereal domestication because its high yield produced food surpluses that increasingly stabilized food supplies. As they became more domesticated, the cereals demanded increasingly intensive care. Thus, the people shifted from a broad-spectrum approach to a specialized subsistence strategy. Sedentism, made possible by the stability of the food supplies, also became necessary, since the people needed to settle near the fields to care for the crops. The sedentism led to increased population density and residence size. This feedback between populational factors, sedentism, and the large size of residence is the key element of Hassan's model. Although impressive, the model needs to be thoroughly tested using data from other regions and other types of food bases.

What Model?

Clearly, it is difficult to pose a universal model for the origin of agriculture. Most successful are multicausal systemic models based on evolutionary and ecological principles. What components should be considered in such a model? A likely element is that the transition to agriculture was a gradual process that began as "just one subsystem of a larger mixed subsistence strategy" (Milisauskas 1978, 60). A feedback situation resulted from the mutual dependency of the crops and the people. This interdependency became stronger through time, with people concentrating less on wild foods and more on the demanding domesticants.

A strong model would also take into account that a strong incentive was needed to make a major shift from tried-and-true subsistence strategies. For the origin of agriculture, the most likely motivation was the stabilization and control of food resources; for example, in order to stockpile food for lean times or to provide enough food for increased populations. In addition, the model should address the people's ability to make such a change. They needed to be intellectually, socially, and technologically capable of responding to the pressures for domestication.

What about climatic and ecological factors? The model should consider both local and global conditions, particularly major or frequent fluxes in temperature or precipitation. An ecological factor was the availability of genetically plastic species responsive to domestication. The plants would have also needed attractive properties, such as storability and high productivity, especially since they may have been less desirable foods. Another ecological factor concerns the type of area that was likely to support food domestication; for instance, marginal versus primary zones. Closely related to this are demographic factors, particularly a habitat's carrying capacity. Other important demographic considerations would include increases in population size and density and shifts in settlement patterns, including sedentism.

Do any of the models put all of these components together in a solid, systemic fashion? Of those discussed, Hassan's feedback hypothesis comes the closest. As yet, however, no single model has been shown to apply to the world as a whole.

The Spread of Agriculture

A major aspect of the origin of agriculture is its spread into noncore regions. We stated that theories on the origin of agriculture need more substantiating evidence. Such evidence is also needed for theories regarding agriculture's spread. One problem is that researchers do not agree on what constitutes the core areas. Some schemes list as many as five independent seats of origin: the Near East, Southeast Asia, China, Mesoamerica, and South America. Others focus on three centers: the Near East (in contact with African influences), East Asia (particularly China and Southeast Asia), and Mesoamerica (in contact with Peru). Agriculture eventually diffused from these centers; for example, into Europe from the Near East and into North America from Mesoamerica.

Those centers listed as core areas are somewhat tentative. For example, as a result of archaeological research conducted during the 1980s, Bruce D. Smith (1989) pointed to another independent center as having been firmly identified: eastern North America. The shift from forager to agriculturalist apparently took place in this region between 2000 and 1000 B.C., when crops based on fruits and seeds, such as gourds, pumpkins, squashes, and sunflowers, were domesticated.

Anthropologists are concerned not only with where agriculture spread, but how and why it spread. Why, for example, was it adopted in some places and not in others? We know that the absence of agriculture was not due to a lack of contact, since nonagricultural people were often exposed to the necessary knowledge through Neolithic trade networks. It is likely that similar principles acted in both the invention and the adoption of agricultural ways of life. For instance, did the people have a strong incentive for making such radical changes? Adoption probably depended on the same motivations that applied in its origin, including the need to overcome demographic pressures, to contend with ecological fluxes, and to increase or stabilize food resources. Did the people possess the technological and social level and cultural flexibility that would have enabled them to adopt agricultural ways of life? Was agriculture a valid alternative within the physical and climatic setting? Were the domesticated species practical for the noncore regions? We have evidence of agricultural experimentation in noncore areas, which may reflect attempts to adapt the innovations to particular ecosystems. For example, early prehistoric desert cultures of the southwestern United States continued foraging while adopting a limited number of Mesoamerican agricultural strategies. Around 1800 B.C., the foragers (who had been living in the region since at least 11,000 years ago) made some use of maize agriculture, an event associated with a rise in population density and the occupation of winter camps by a number of bands. Although they apparently were experimenting with plant germination and irrigation techniques, these early desert societies appeared to be "helping nature along," rather than more fully manipulating their environments.

NEOLITHIC CULTURE

We have pointed out that the advent of agriculture brought with it the large-scale management and manipulation of the land, labor-intensive practices, and a mutual dependency between domesticants and humans. The technology of the Neolithic still depended largely on stone implements, but they were more sophisticated than those of earlier times. The shift to an agriculturally based economy also brought about important changes in social organization and cultural behavior.

Beyond such general characteristics, many important differences existed among Neolithic cultures. This becomes especially clear in comparing the Old World with the New World, seed-crop cultivation with vegeculture, and societies that emphasized domesticated plants with those that emphasized animal domestication.

Thus, aspects of the Neolithic applied across cultures; at the same time, diversity was apparent. To illustrate unifying trends, we will first discuss general technological and social characteristics. We will then illustrate the diversity by examining specific cultures.

Technological Characteristics

The technological changes that occurred during the Neolithic were closely tied to its social and environmental aspects. For example, a sedentary life-style allowed people to have more durable, heavy-duty implements, important in the large-scale altering of the natural environment. In addition, the diverse and specialized technology made possible the reshaping of the land, the tending of the fields, the storage and preparation of agricultural foods, and life in permanent settlements. It also reflected a trend toward increasing **social stratification**, meaning that people were becoming more specialized in terms of professions and social roles.

Neolithic people used a wide variety of raw materials, including wood, plant fibers, wool, ceramics, and leather. Late in the Neolithic, people began to experiment with copper and other metals. Yet stone was still a very important material. Toolmakers made beautifully crafted lithic implements, using highly refined techniques, such as *pecking and chipping* and *ground polished stone.*

Another Neolithic technological feature was the widespread use of pottery. It provided a sturdy but heavy means of carrying and storing large amounts of harvested materials. Pottery has special significance in archaeology because styles and production techniques are used to date sites and to decipher patterns of culture.

The Neolithic was marked by great sophistication in technology closely tied to the demands of the agrarian ways of life. What sorts of functions did the technology serve?

Agriculture and Reshaping the Land

The Neolithic represented a significant change in how people related to the natural environment. Never before had the land been reshaped through cultivation and the herding of livestock.

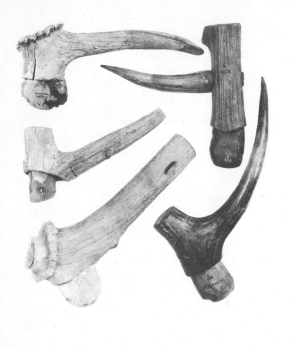

Neolithic technology. Top left: Neolithic tools from France, including flint axes with staghorn handles (bottom), a hatchet (right), and a double-edged flint chisel (top center). Top right: A European flint dagger. Left: A ceramic jar from China.

One popular agricultural strategy was "shifting cultivation." This included **slash-and-burn agriculture**, a technique by which trees are cut down and brush set on fire to prepare land for the planting of crops. As new sections are cleared, the older, less rich fields are ignored and left to return to a more natural state. Farmers eventually return to the rejuvenated sections to again prepare them for cultivation. Other labor-intensive farming methods used by Neolithic peoples included the plowing and terracing of the land and irrigation in areas of little or unpredictable rainfall.

The tools of Neolithic agriculture included ground stone axes and adzes for clearing trees; hoes and other implements for tillage (which eventually included plows); and baskets, gourds, and other containers for transporting the crops from the fields. Besides providing a stable source of food, domesticated animals were also used as "beasts of burden" for tilling fields and transporting crops and equipment.

Food Processing and Storage

Agrarian economics necessitates the preparation and storage of food. Neolithic farmers processed grains into edible forms, such as flour, by using grindstones and mortars. They cooked their food over hearths using clay pots. Specialized structures, such as grain storage bins, were used to store food and drink. Pottery—sturdy and easily designed for specific jobs—was especially useful for processing and storing food.

Clothing

Domesticated plants and animals provided a ready source of materials for the clothing, blankets, and other goods of the Neolithic peoples. Many Neolithic cultures used looms to produce fabrics from wool. Clothes were also made from skins. For example, a leather-working tool kit buried with a man in Mesoamerica demonstrates that this craft was a specialized skill in that culture (Flannery and Winter 1976).

Shelters

Shelters varied according to the environment and the available resources. The design and materials of the shelters used by a particular group reflected their degree of nomadism and their social organization. Overall, the shelters were sophisticated and sturdy. They served not only as homes, but also as storage facilities and ceremonial sites. In Europe, Neolithic farmers, using wood from nearby forests, built shelters that could withstand the damp, temperate climate of the region. Çatal Hüyük, Turkey, a town of complex design, consisted of many flat-roofed structures of sun-dried brick backed up one against the other. Apparently, some of these were shrines, as reflected by their artistically painted walls and carefully sculptured models of women, bulls, and other animals (Mellaart 1975).

Social and Behavioral Characteristics

Neolithic social and behavioral features represent cultural trends that become more fully expressed with the emergence of cities and states. These features include such closely related concepts as world view, sedentism, patterns of residence, property ownership, population density, social organization, social controls, and trade networks.

World View

A major change must have occurred in ideology, especially in how people perceived the natural world. For the first time, they began to control their resources in a major way. In addition, their world view may have actually "shrunk" since they no longer wandered, but were basically confined to home territories. Archaeological evidence of shifts in attitude is largely limited to material remains, including artwork and religious artifacts. Also of help in understanding this complex aspect of Neolithic life are ethnographic analogies with contemporary groups.

Neolithic symbolic and religious behavior took many different forms. In the Middle East, the Jericho excavation reveals that Neolithic people were sometimes buried under the floors of houses. Also, this society produced carefully crafted masks of the dead, an example of which is shown in Figure 10.3(a). Such evidence suggests that their religious activity included an ancestor-worshiping cult (Gowlett 1984). Many Neolithic rituals also centered on fertility (see Figure 10.3b). For example, the shrines of Çatal Hüyük

contain figures of women giving birth to bulls and sheep, images that may be linked to the concept of fertility and reproduction. Early Mesoamerican religious behavior included "annually recurring rituals" (Flannery 1976, 332). There were ceremonies with masked dancers and "ad hoc rituals," such as infant sacrifice and cannibalism, that were associated with the burial of important community members.

Sedentism and Village Life

In agrarian society, people settle in villages in order to tend fields and to live close to grazing lands. Agrarian technology also dictates a less nomadic way of life, since the sophisticated and durable implements are often quite heavy. Sedentism is also associated with the growing importance of territoriality and property rights.

Although all agricultural people eventually came to live in permanent settlements, the tim-

FIGURE 10.3

Evidence of Near Eastern Neolithic symbolic and religious behavior. (a) A death mask modeled of plaster found on a skull uncovered at Jericho. Realistically decorated death masks were apparently an aspect of an ancestor cult. (b) Ceramic female figurines from Tepe Sarab (Turkey), which may reflect symbolic beliefs regarding birth or fertility.

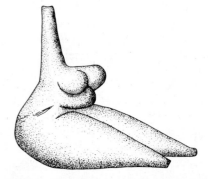

(a)

(b)

ing and degree of this pattern varied among societies. In the Near East, sedentary life actually preceded agriculture, while in Mesoamerica, nomadism was maintained for thousands of years after the beginning of plant domestication. Mesoamericans did not become fully sedentary until their major domesticated plant, maize, was productive enough to induce them to concentrate on one crop instead of exploiting a wide range of resources.

The characteristics of the settlements also differed in accordance with cultural and ecological factors, such as physical needs, demographics, cultural history, and social organization. Flannery (1976) contrasts two types of Neolithic permanent settlements: circular-hut compounds and villages composed of rectangular houses. Circular-hut compounds, common during the early Near Eastern Neolithic, consisted of small, round structures, each housing one or two people. This pattern is associated with a social organization based on a family with one husband and multiple wives, with the man and the wives each occupying his or her own dwelling. The huts are clumped together close to a surplus-grain storage bin that was shared by the man and all of his wives. Villages composed of rectangular houses varied in size and composition. These settlements were common in Mesoamerica and in the Near East late in the Neolithic.

The difference between the two forms of settlements appears to be related to differences in social organization. The rectangular houses were larger than the huts and housed whole families. They also could have been enlarged to accommodate extended family groups. Instead of one main granary, each house had its own storage facility, suggesting that the house builder's society was composed of autonomous families within a larger social grouping. These separate households maintained family-based responsibilities and privileges and came together with other families to cooperate on large-scale projects. Noting that the rectangular-house village predominated in two different parts of the world, Flannery linked the development of such villages to a

growing intensification of production. Such societies emphasized land-ownership systems, cooperation between family units, and increasing diversification of social roles.

The Concept of Property
The Neolithic emphasis on a growing concept of property ownership stemmed from the shift from nomadism to sedentary life, recognition of the importance of land properly altered for cultivation and grazing, and the role of residence and group membership in the management and organization of labor forces. In contrast to the egalitarian bands of foragers, agrarian settlements began to organize on the basis of family units, each controlling specific plots of land. This influenced the development of a system of residence, property rights, and inheritance based on family membership. Family membership bestowed people with important rights and with specific responsibilities and obligations. Thus, a structure was set up within which work parties were organized for labor-intensive projects as well as for day-to-day maintenance. The people living under such a complex system had to develop rules pertaining to group membership, property rights, and responsibilities. They also needed to establish new means of social control.

Population Density and Residence Patterns
Increased population size during the Neolithic, creating the need to feed a larger number of people, was a likely pressure contributing to the origin of agriculture. At the same time, the increased number of people in an area was necessary to the development of large-scale agriculture because it made available groups for labor-intensive projects. Population density also bears on sedentism, residential patterns, and other aspects of social systems; for example, social systems began to organize on the basis of family membership and to focus on inherited property rights. As a result, individuals tended to settle close to their original homes, creating population clusters. The denser populations meant

more complex social relationships. Moreover, disputes could not be easily resolved by simply moving away. Thus, as more people came to live in villages, major changes occurred in social organization, with mechanisms of social control playing an important role.

Tribal Level of Social Organization

One important change in social organization was the rise of tribal societies. A **tribe** is an association of bands or other groups linked by factors that cut across otherwise separate communities, uniting them at least when cooperation is needed—in times of war, for example, or when political purposes must be served. Integrating factors are kinship affiliations that transcend local groups; age grades (culturally recognized age-based categories) that can serve as political organizations; and clubs made up of people with common interests. Tribes provide a greater degree of organizational complexity than do the bands of foragers, yet they are not nearly as complex as city-states.

Tribal society fit nicely into Neolithic life. Why was this so? Bands, which tend to be mobile, depend on small group size, have a low population density, and have no social means to form larger political groups. Tribes, however, can include settlements of up to 250 people and have a more densely concentrated population; moreover, their ability to organize otherwise separate groups affords them a means of coordinating such important activities as agricultural projects.

Trade

Because people could no longer directly obtain certain raw materials and goods, sedentism created a need to trade. During the Neolithic, extensive trade networks were developed that spread for thousands of miles across both the Old World and the New. Ideas, as well as goods, were exchanged, which sometimes stimulated rapid cultural changes.

Trade networks varied from place to place. According to Flannery (1976), interregional networks linked "all the regions of Mesoamerica

into a single complex cultural area" (p. 283). Long-distance trade also linked hundreds of small and independent tribal villages in early Neolithic Europe. Goods traded included stones, shells, obsidian, flint, and ceramics (Milisauskas 1978). For example, archaeologists have occasionally found *Spondylus* shells in central Europe, usually in burial sites. These finds indicate that Central Europeans traded with southeastern Europe, since this shellfish is found only in the Black Sea and Mediterranean Sea (Shackleton and Renfrew 1970).

Examples of Neolithic Societies

During the Neolithic, in spite of general trends, cultures varied widely. To illustrate some of this variety, we describe three Neolithic societies: the Near Eastern village of Ali Kosh, Mesoamerica's Tehuacán Valley, and the central European early Neolithic Linear culture.

Ali Kosh

The Near East of Neolithic times encompassed a range of ecological zones, from the rich Fertile Crescent to sparse deserts. One important zone was a high, semiarid steppe that ran from the east bank of the Tigris River to the edge of the Zagros Mountains. Northeast of the steppe were the forested mountains that contained the wild ancestors of the Near Eastern domesticants, while to the south were the arid lands of Mesopotamia. Ecologically, the steppe represented a transition between these two zones and displayed some of the best characteristics of each. It was a fine environment for early farming. For example, the steppe had enough rain for dry farming and, like its desert neighbor, contained large rivers, making irrigation possible. The people of the Near East clearly favored life on the steppe, as reflected by the large number of prehistoric sites. These sites have permitted archaeologists to study the steppe's development of dry farming, animal herding, and irrigation. Hole, Flannery, and Neely (1969) delineated seven cultural stages, the second of which, the Ali Kosh phase, is an excellent example of an early Neolithic Near Eastern village.

The village of Ali Kosh was located in what is now western Iran, as indicated in Figure 10.4. The site contained three occupations, including an early Neolithic settlement dating from between 6500 to 6000 B.C. Evidence shows that these people were becoming increasingly dependent on cultivated crops and less on collected wild foods. In fact, about 90 percent of their plant foods came from winter-grown cereals, especially barley and wheat. Their animal foods consisted mainly of hunted large grazing animals, such as gazelle and wild cattle, although they herded some domesticated goats and sheep. The people also collected water fowl, catfish, and turtles.

During this period, a change took place in the village's architectural composition. Single-roomed huts gave way to multiroomed dwellings made of thick mud and clay brick walls, with roofs of woven reeds. Outside courtyards contained brick ovens and roasting pits. The site's size indicates that it was occupied by about 100 individuals—small, even for a Neolithic village.

The life of the Ali Kosh villagers is reflected by technological remains. Finely crafted flint blades were used to hunt wild game. Large animals were butchered using specialized tools, such as pebble-choppers for breaking up limb bones and small slabs and flint blades for cutting tendons. The site contained many scrapers, which were used for working hide and for other purposes. Drills and bone needles were also used to make clothing and other goods. Flint sickles hafted onto wooden handles helped in harvesting cereals. Grinding stones were used to pulverize grains.

Although quite advanced, the technology of this period was less sophisticated and more limited than that of later farmers. The people of this region did not use irrigation until 5000 B.C.; thus, they depended on the limited rainfall to provide enough water for dry farming. They did not, as yet, use pottery, although the villagers made other containers, such as woven wicker baskets (some of which were waterproofed with asphalt)

and carved bowls. At the same time, they did use clay for making figurines, particularly of goats, although archaeologists have also found fragmented human forms.

The burials of Ali Kosh provide insight into their social organization. Individuals were usually buried in a sitting position, tightly wrapped in a woven mat and, on occasion, painted with red ochre. The bodies were placed in shallow graves under the floor of the family's house, along with personal goods such as clothing. Sometimes a person was dug up and buried a second time, possibly because the individual had a special status and was judged to warrant a more elaborate interment. Such differences in how individuals were buried suggest that Ali Kosh society was somewhat socially stratified.

Compared with earlier stages, Ali Kosh society relied more on long-distance trade. Archaeologists have uncovered seashells from the Persian Gulf, copper from central Iran, turquoise from Afghanistan, and obsidian from Eastern Turkey (about 600 miles away). Ali Kosh was apparently part of an extensive exchange network, which included the flow of goods over inland waterways.

Tehuacán Valley

The Tehuacán Valley is located approximately 150 miles southeast of Mexico City in the arid central highlands of Mexico. It is one of the most thoroughly studied early agricultural sites in the New World, owing primarily to the interdisciplinary excavations led by Richard MacNeish (e.g., 1964, 1972, 1978). Teams of scientists excavated hundreds of sites and compiled a fascinating history of this valley, describing how the people evolved from foragers to agriculturalists to inhabitants of city-states. This research includes classic work on the evolution of domesticated maize and its role in Mesoamerican society.

One of MacNeish's interests was in comparing and contrasting the origin of agriculture in the Old World and New World. While Old World agriculturalists concentrated on only a few plant species and a relatively large number of animals, New World societies did just the opposite. In the

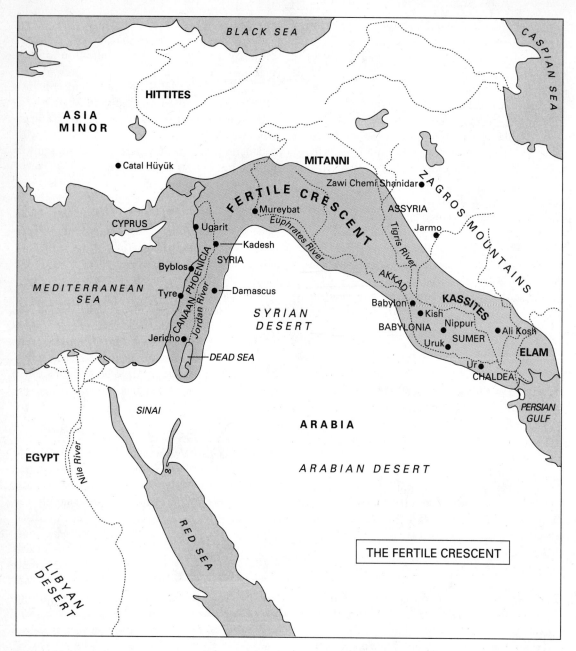

FIGURE 10.4

The Fertile Crescent and some Near Eastern sites.

Excavation of a cave in the Tehuacán Valley. Located in the arid highlands of Mexico, this excavation uncovered vital information on the domestication of maize.

New World, only a few animals were domesticated, but a wide variety of crops were exploited, including at least four kinds of beans, white and sweet potatoes, peanuts, sunflowers, chilies, pumpkins, squash, tomatoes, avocados, pineapples, and tobacco. However, the single most important crop was maize. MacNeish's interest in maize led him to investigate the Tehuacán Valley, in part because the wild ancestor of domesticated maize was a grass from the Mexican highlands and because the area's dry climate increased the chances of finding preserved remnants of maize. In fact, the Tehuacán Valley has yielded some of the earliest maize, dated to be approximately 7,000 years old.

How did the early Tehuacán agriculturalists live? About 12,000 years ago, before they domesticated food, the foragers of the valley lived in nomadic small groups of 25 to 30 individuals and exploited many different microenvironments. About 7,000 years ago, as the climate became warmer and drier, the people concentrated more

on plants and began to cultivate a few species. They were still largely nomadic, returning to their gardens as part of their cyclical pattern of movement, although some may have settled along riverbanks. The domesticants were just one aspect of their subsistence strategy, employed by the people to stabilize food resources by making use of less desirable plants in marginal regions (Flannery 1973). By about 4,000 years ago, the productivity of the maize had increased to where it became the major component of their diet. At this point, the people settled in villages and carefully tended their fields. The maize-based economy, which included other domesticants such as beans, squash, and avocados, provided a relatively stable and nutritious food base for the slowly growing population. The villages, usually located on river floodplains, consisted of long rectangular houses that could shelter large family groups. The families came together in central courtyards where they cooked, made pottery, and did other chores. The communities had facilities for storing surplus crops, which provided a stability of food resources unknown in earlier times.

Besides more casual ways of social bonding, ceremonies and other religious activities united the families into larger groups. The people of Tehuacán were linked with other Mesoamerican communities through the exchange of goods, such as pottery and marine shells, and through the sharing of ideas.

The Linear Culture

While Ali Kosh and the Tehuacán Valley were located in core areas, agriculture spread into Europe from the Near East. European societies then adopted agricultural techniques to suit their own ecological and cultural needs and made local innovations, especially in animal domestication. A good example of an early Neolithic European society is the Linear culture.

Early Linear sites are scattered throughout central Europe, including Germany, Poland, and Czechoslovakia. They are located in areas where fertile, loamy soil (loess) has been deposited on the floodplains of rivers. The Linear people cul-

tivated crops such as wheat, rye, peas, and lentils (Milisauskas 1978). Their locations were excellent for agriculture because loess is easy to farm and nearby rivers provided ready water and a means of transportation.

The Linear culture, which dates from about 6000 B.C. to about 3800 B.C., is named for the sites' pottery type. The style is distinctive for its delicately carved decorative patterns of curved and straight lines (see Figure 10.5). The culture is also identified with a polished stone ax and longhouse village settlements. The uniformity of Linear sites is striking, in terms of both the culture and the pottery style (Howell 1987).

Although part of a larger tribal society, the typical Linear village was a largely independent unit that was home to about 100 to 125 people. The village's families cooperatively farmed the surrounding fields, which they cleared using slash-and-burn techniques. During the winter, the wood longhouses may also have provided shelter for their domesticated animals, which included sheep, goats, cattle and pigs. Near the longhouses were communal pit ovens, used to dry surplus grain for storage. The grain was

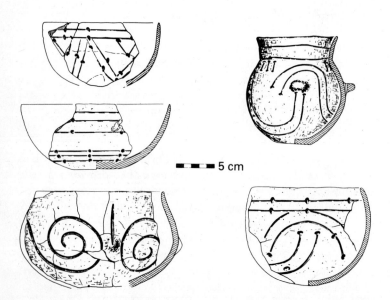

5 cm

FIGURE 10.5
Linear pottery from Neolithic Europe.

shared among the families rather than controlled by individual households. Besides the family homes, the communities apparently had even larger longhouses that were used for village meetings and ritualistic activities. The Linear people supplemented their domesticated food by collecting wild plants, such as hazelnuts, apples, and sorrel. They also hunted game, such as red deer, wild pigs, and horses.

Burials usually were along the sides of the longhouses, rather than in separate cemeteries. When cemeteries were used, they were usually located close to the Linear settlements. Evidence that some older males were buried with "status" goods, such as seashells obtained through trade networks, suggests that these early Neolithic people already had a limited degree of social stratification. In the cemeteries, the ratio of males to females is approximately equal, indicating that the Linear people did not commit female infanticide. The killing of female infants at birth was sometimes practiced by Neolithic peoples, possibly as a means of repressing birth rates. Milisauskas (1978) suggested that the absence of infanticide may reflect the fact that Linear cultures readily expanded into uninhabited areas of central Europe, thereby avoiding the stress associated with a growing population. Other evidence of Linear ideology is rare, although archaeologists have found a few human figurines.

Many researchers have surmised that the Linear culture was one in which familial membership, property rights, and residence were based on the man's maternal line. However, Milisauskas concluded that the Linear society was more flexible than traditional matrilocal systems because evidence from burials revealed that political and domestic power was firmly in the hands of men. In addition, although basically a tribal society, the individual villages may have included older males acting as headmen—a role probably based on leadership abilities rather than on inheritance of the position.

INCREASING COMPLEXITY DURING THE NEOLITHIC

The Neolithic was characterized by extremely rapid cultural evolution. With the origin of food domestication began the large-scale manipulation of natural resources, giving rise to a host of other changes. It was also an enormously complex and diverse period, in which a wide variety of agricultural and pastoral cultures coexisted with foraging societies.

As was true of the Paleolithic, a major theme of the Neolithic is that of *increasing complexity*— in technology, in behavior, in social organization, in ideology. For example, the technology of some societies became increasingly complex, as stone tools were rapidly replaced by those made of metal. There was an increase in the size of residential units, in population densities, in social stratification, and in the specialization of social roles. Such trends also reflect the *increasing efficiency* of the human adaptation. For example, as a means of supporting more individuals within limited territories, people intensified labor practices and standardized technology. Changes also occurred in relations between communities as people became more strongly identified with specific territories and as trade networks increased in size and complexity. Eventually, some groups became so complex that they reached a new level of cultural evolution: that of civilization, as expressed by cities and states.

SUMMARY

The Neolithic is associated with the origin of food domestication. The period witnessed the continuation of the cultural evolutionary trends of increasing cultural complexity and increasing efficiency of the human adaptation. The rapid Neolithic transition took place from about 10,000 to 5,000 years ago and occurred independently in at least three regions: the Near East, the Far East, and the New World. Each region contained centers in which domestication was invented and from which it spread.

Many theories have been proposed regarding the origin of agriculture. The simplistic "prime-mover" theories focus on one major stimulus, such as population pressure or environmental conditions. A more complex approach is provided by "multicausal" or "systemic" models, which emphasize a number of factors. Modern approaches often focus on ecological factors. One of the first truly systemic models for the origin of agriculture was developed by Flannery. In his view, the change was not caused by a single event; rather, it occurred gradually, as food resources slowly changed along with human behavior. People became agricultural not because they wanted to, but because they had to, with the most likely motivation being to stabilize food resources in response to various pressures. Hassan's complex systemic model emphasizes the feedback aspect of the cultural system's components and the desire to stabilize food resources.

Another important question concerns how agriculture spread into noncore regions and why it was adopted in some places and not in others. Adoption probably depended on the same motivations that applied in the origin of agriculture, including needs to overcome demographic pressures, to contend with ecological fluxes, and to increase or stabilize food resources.

The Neolithic is characterized by rapid cultural change and by traits associated with the advent of agriculture, including the large-scale management and manipulation of the land, labor-intensive practices, and the mutual dependency of domesticants and humans. The technology was still basically lithic, although the implements were more sophisticated than those of earlier times. Neolithic technology included specialized techniques for reshaping the land, tending fields, storing and preparing agricultural foods, and for life in permanent settlements. The Neolithic was also characterized by the widespread use of pottery. Sedentism and village life, a growing concept of property ownership, increased population density, and tribal-level social organization were some of the important Neolithic social and behavioral characteristics.

SUGGESTED READINGS

Boserup, Ester. 1981. *Population and Technological Change.* Chicago: University of Chicago Press.

Fagan, Brian D. 1990. *Ancient North America.* London: Thames and Hudson.

Flannery, Kent V., ed. 1976. *The Early Mesoamerican Village.* New York: Academic Press.

Hassan, Fekri. 1981. *Demographic Archaeology.* New York: Academic Press.

Milisauskas, Sarumas. 1978. *European Prehistory.* New York: Academic Press.

Phillips, Patricia. 1980. *The Prehistory of Europe.* Bloomington: Indiana University Press.

Struever, Stuart, ed. 1971. *Prehistoric Agriculture.* Garden City, NY: The Natural History Press.

Vivian, R. Gwinn. 1990. *The Chacoan Prehistory of the San Juan Basin.* San Diego, CA: Academic Press.

11 The Rise of Civilization

The Pyramid of the Sun in Teotihuacán, Mexico, the first great city-state of the New World. The pyramid, which stands 210 feet high and covers an area of 650 square feet, was the largest structure built in ancient Mesoamerica.

People often use the term *civilization* loosely, especially to distinguish highly technological societies from those we consider "primitive." While this idea is culturally biased, civilizations *do* represent the most intensive expression of the evolutionary trend toward increased cultural complexity. The earliest civilizations, which apparently began to arise some 6,000 years ago, introduced humans to a new level of cultural adaptation—one with global ramifications.

Chapter 11 explores the origin of civilization, including the traits apparently shared among the early states, and examines theories that attempt to explain it. We will also briefly address the question of why complex societies collapse. Examples of Old World and New World civilizations serve to illustrate their similarities and their enormous diversity.

CIVILIZATION, CITIES, AND STATES

What do anthropologists mean when they refer to "civilization," "city," and "state"? A thorough answer to this question would reflect an intriguing, yet frustrating, aspect of civilization: its form varies enormously, especially throughout different regions of the world. A trait of one civilization—say, the location of cities on the floodplain of a large river—may not appear in another. Similarly, a theory of why civilization arose—for example, to manage large-scale irrigation works—may apply in some regions but not in others. Thus, the extensive use of cross-cultural archaeological comparisons is crucial in responding to "what is civilization?" and "how did it arise?"

One of the first modern definitions of civilization was proposed by the famous American cultural anthropologist Alfred Kroeber (1944). Kroeber viewed cultures as composed of the same basic elements, including language, arts, religion, and ethics. He hypothesized that patterns of cultural growth led these components to become increasingly complex internally, to the point where the degree of complexity represented civilization. Unfortunately, this approach is largely descriptive; it does not address exactly *when* we can label a society as a civilization, or *why* the process takes place.

Another approach focuses on a cluster of defining traits. As the result of his study of the Near East, V. Gordon Childe (1936, 1957) defined civilization using a list of 10 characteristics, some of which are shared, to a lesser degree, by societies that are not civilizations. This list was later organized into primary and secondary characteristics by Redman (1978):

Primary
1. Settlement in cities
2. Full-time specialization of labor
3. Concentration of surpluses
4. Class structure
5. State organization

Secondary
1. Monumental public works
2. Long-distance trade
3. Standardized monumental artwork
4. Writing
5. Arithmetic, geometry, and astronomy

Childe's scheme greatly influenced the study of civilization. While the scheme has not proved to be universally applicable, aspects of it are used in more refined definitions.

In keeping with the explanatory and ecological approach, most contemporary archaeologists focus on defining civilization as a complex human *adaptive mechanism*. Rather than emphasizing lists of descriptive traits, current definitions seek to address civilization's universal functions. For example, some view civilization as a mechanism to contend with large, densely concentrated populations (e.g., Boserup 1965). Another view centers on the concept of power, such as in the control of limited resources (e.g., Hassan 1981).

In this text, we define **civilization** as an adaptive cultural mechanism for organizing very complex societies through the control and concentration of power, as expressed by the social structure of the state and the residence pattern of the city. **State** is defined as a type of social organization consisting of an autonomous integrated political unit that encompasses many communities within its territory (see also Chapter 20). States are characterized by a specialized central governing authority that has a monopoly over the powers concerned with the maintenance of internal order and the ordering of external relations. Furthermore, states are composed of highly stratified class systems. Although many nonstates are also stratified, it is the high level of stratification and organizational complexity that typifies states. Being complex, a state's social order and existing power structure are maintained through a

bureaucracy, the specialized administrative organization responsible for running the state's day-to-day activities.

City refers to a residence pattern consisting of a large and densely concentrated population. While not every civilization has a city, most have an urban or ceremonial center from which those in power operate. This dense concentration of people creates the level of social complexity associated with civilization. These people are needed to fill the many roles associated with a highly stratified society. For example, people are needed to take part in subsistence activities; to manage resources, using calculations and writing; to be architects and builders; to be traders and merchants; to serve spiritual, medical, and aesthetic needs; and to maintain internal order and defend against external forces. In most

Aerial view of the ruins of Mycenae, Greece. The densely populated city consisted of closely packed buildings contained within strong defensive walls.

cases, the lower limit of population size is 5,000 people.

We can see that civilizations depend on complex, interactive systems of people and institutions that strive to contend with an enormously detailed and complicated way of life. No wonder, then, that civilizations are also subject to collapse. For now, however, we focus on theories regarding how civilizations originate.

THEORIES OF THE ORIGIN OF CIVILIZATION

Almost from the time civilizations first came into being, proposals have been offered to explain their existence. Scientific explanations gathered strength during the mid-nineteenth century, as the social Darwinism approach to "cultural progress" and archaeological rediscoveries of ancient cities influenced Western thought. Throughout the twentieth century, scholars have sought to derive a theory broad enough to encompass the whole world, yet not so broad as to be meaningless. Although far from forming a consensus, they have proposed many explanations that embody elements crucial in the derivation of a theory so broad in scope. One of the first truly modern theories is that of V. Gordon Childe.

Childe's Urban Revolution

Childe regarded the origin of agriculture as a Neolithic revolution (see Chapter 10). He also contended that societies attained the level of civilization in a dramatic and rapid fashion, as they underwent an *urban revolution*. This event took place when the proper ecological, social, and technological conditions occurred within an agricultural society. The people then came to live in densely concentrated settlements (cities), obtained literacy (writing), and formed societies organized into bureaucratically run state political organizations. An important technological aspect of this revolution was the use of metal implements produced by a specialized class of metallurgists. Such people, who did not directly work to obtain food, had to be fed by the society's farmers, who needed to develop techniques to increase their production, such as irrigation.

The society became even more stratified as it developed bureaucracies and writing systems as a means of managing and distributing food.

While Childe's ideas greatly influenced the field, his theory lacks universality. For example, not every civilization had cities (the Minoans, for example), and some, such as the Incas of Peru, never developed a written language. In addition, Childe's theory does not clearly address the process by which the urban revolution took place, but rather simply describes its characteristics. However, despite its shortcomings, many scholars now agree that Childe's theory contains three essential components that apply to all of the world's early civilizations. Fagan (1986) described these components as follows:

1. *The creation of food surpluses* that could support nonagricultural economic classes.
2. *Diversity of food resources*, with a relatively wide subsistence base, that helped prevent famines and encouraged trade.
3. *Intensive land use* that increased agricultural productivity. This depended on advanced technology and social systems designed to provide the farmers and managers necessary to effectively use the land.

Childe's ideas laid the foundation for later theories regarding the origins of civilization. Many of these theories focus on "prime movers"—a single causal factor.

Prime-Mover Theories

Prime-mover theories propose that the origin of civilization was stimulated by a single major cause. One of the best known of these approaches is Karl Wittfogel's *hydraulic-state theory.* Wittfogel (1957) argued that societies evolved into states because of the need for large-scale irrigation. This need led to stratified societies with a state bureaucracy for controlling and managing the great irrigation works. However, although irrigation figures prominently in many early civilizations, it is not common to all of them. In addition, the causal relationship is not always as Wittfogel proposed. In some cases, such as in Mesopotamia, sophisticated irrigation systems existed well before the rise of state society (Adams 1981).

Another popular focus of prime-mover theories is ecology. The *Fertile Crescent theory* (which prevailed during the 1920s and 1930s) views civilization as originating in response to food surpluses generated by the fertile land and excellent climate found in the Nile Valley of Egypt and the Mesopotamian floodplain. Food surpluses allowed people to specialize in nonagricultural endeavors, such as crafts and religions, and established the need for resource-managing bureaucracies. Again, this theory cannot be universally applied, especially when we consider the diversity of civilizations and the complexity of ecological conditions.

Other prime-mover theories focus on pressures created by population growth. One of the best-known single-cause demographic models is that of Ester Boserup (1965, 1981). According to her model, the pressure of increased population size triggered the development of technological and social innovations needed to feed so many people. However, as we noted in Chapter 10, Boserup failed to provide a reason why populations rapidly increased.

Several other prime movers for the origin of civilization have been proposed, including the following:

Religion, particularly the establishment of ceremonial centers that were nuclei of the first cities, resulting in stratified societies with priests as figures of authority;

Technological innovations, such as metal working and the invention of the wheel, that triggered social and economic changes through shifts in subsistence strategies and the creation of craft and technological specialists;

Trade and exchange systems, to supply sedentary populations with desired nonlocal goods and establish sociopolitical links between groups; and

Warfare, including the fighting between agricultural societies for the control of desired lands.

All these prime movers were important elements in the origin of specific civilizations; some were important in the creation of many complex societies. However, the basic problem with prime-mover theories is their inherent simplicity. More sophisticated theories may emphasize a particular factor, but they all recognize that civilizations arose as a result of the interaction of a number of elements. In other words, they take a multicausal systems approach.

Adams's Multiple-Cause System

One of the first multiple-cause theories for the origin of civilization is that of Robert Adams (1966). This extremely influential theory contends that a number of interacting factors gradually led to the origin of state society in some agricultural communities.

According to Adams, the two most essential characteristics of early states were agricultural surpluses that could support nonagricultural individuals and social stratification, particularly with respect to a class that had the authority to manage the surpluses. What factors were responsible for the evolution of these characteristics, and, thus, for the evolution of the state? Although many factors were involved, Adams maintained that food surpluses primarily resulted from irrigation agriculture. Yet, not all agricultural societies that used irrigation evolved into states. Some societies were at an advantage because they could use a variety of local resources and had armed forces to protect their lands and seize control of the lands of others. Through both superior economic and military means, such societies increased their territory and number of people, with power becoming centralized in the rich communities. Through the interaction of these factors, some agricultural societies gradually evolved into states, with food surpluses to support a stratified social system in which power was concentrated in the hands of a privileged class (see Figure 11.1).

Flannery: Processes, Complexity, and Social Control

Adams's model, which came at the beginning of American archaeology's shift toward explanatory thinking, stimulated others to develop multicausal models for the origin of civilization. One such model is that of Kent Flannery (1972). As a processual archaeologist, Flannery sought to explain the processes underlying the evolution of complex cultural systems. He was particularly concerned with how this evolution was influenced by ecological factors, such as environmental stress.

Flannery's scheme is complicated. Cultures are viewed as dynamic systems composed of many subsystems. A culture may gradually increase its degree of complexity, often as a result of how the subsystems contend with environmental stress. Changes within each subsystem are regulated by social controls, so that the system as a whole is not adversely affected. Thus, social controls, such as societal rules and traditions, restrain the degree to which each separate subsystem (e.g., subsistence strategies, religious institutions, political structures) can change. In some cases, responses to such environmental stresses as population increases, unreliability of food resources, and environmental shifts result in such a degree of complexity as to lead to the origin of state society.

Flannery's model is not without problems. In the first place, it does not define the exact processes by which cultures evolve. In addition, it is enormously complex, delineating 15 "rules" for the stimulation of the origin of states. As with all multicausal models, it is also difficult to test in the archaeological record. However, Flannery's model stands as a major hypothesis for the origin of civilization and has greatly influenced the study of cultural evolution.

Hassan: Vulnerability of Agricultural Systems

In Chapter 10, we noted that Fekri Hassan's (1981) complex systemic model of cultural evolution focuses on population expansion, but that

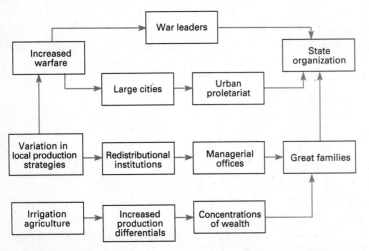

FIGURE 11.1

Adams's model for the origin of civilization.

it balances a range of factors by emphasizing the concept of feedback (see Figure 11.2).

Hassan extended his ideas on the origin of agriculture to his model for how civilizations originate. As the rapid population growth of the Neolithic continued, increased local population size and density led to the increased size of settlements, creating urban centers. The growing populations concentrated within urban centers provided larger labor forces, but they also put increasing pressure on local food resources. Thus, the need became greater to intensify agricultural techniques. These economic trends interacted with sociopolitical factors, including the "hierarchical differentiation of settlements into villages, towns, small urban centers, and large urban centers" (Hassan 1981, 250). All these fac-

tors taken together explain the emergence of large, hierarchical political systems.

Within this context, Hassan proposed an explanatory model for the origin of civilization. He stated that the emergence of civilization was a major cultural transition that was not a "revolution," but the result of a gradual sequence of processes "involving the reinforcement of certain cultural trends that had been initiated previously" (Hassan 1981, 250). These trends, interrelated through a feedback loop, include

1. *development of permanent and large sedentary residential units* that maximized economic yield;
2. *emergence of complex and formally structured social organizations* to manage the larger, sedentary groups and minimize social conflict;
3. *structured systems of food exchange and trade between communities*, especially in response to the lack of mobility created by sedentism

FIGURE 11.2

Hassan's feedback model for the origin of civilization.

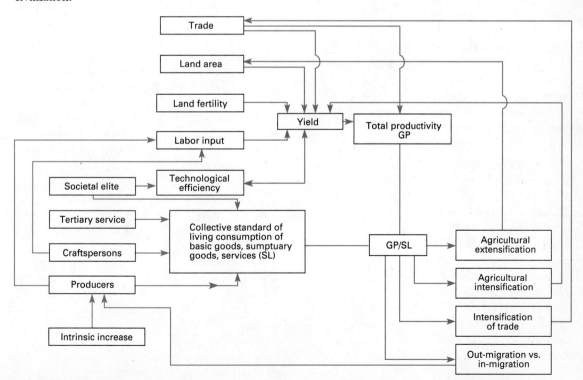

and to help cope with occasional food shortages; and

4. *social stratification*, especially as seen in a leadership for coordinating activities within and between communities.

Also important were the ecological changes associated with the origin of agriculture that led to a decrease in the number of types of food resources along with an increased emphasis on a few cultivated staple foods (see Chapter 10). However, agriculture was subject to frequent fluctuations in yield, a problem exacerbated by the increasingly large sedentary population. The response to this "vulnerability" of the agricultural system, and a means to allow for the society's economic growth, was the development of stabilizing factors, particularly "storage [of food], communal redistribution mechanisms, and interregional integration of resources" (p. 251).

In essence, Hassan's model addresses the issue of economic power:

> The primary core of civilization lies in a formal, complex hierarchical power structure. . . . [It emerged as] an outcome of the processes set in motion by the adoption of agriculture, and as a response to the vulnerability of agricultural systems to environmental and cultural perturbations. (Hassan 1981, 250)

Hassan's model has many strengths. It incorporates the important elements of earlier ideas regarding the origin of civilization, while it uses a feedback approach that nicely accounts for the interaction and the "balancing act" that occurs within such a system. Hassan goes beyond Flannery by providing specific evolutionary processes and mechanisms. His theory also emphasizes an increasingly popular theme in the study of how civilizations originate: the control of power. However, some theories take an important alternative approach. Instead of emphasizing the control of internal economic power, they emphasize the control of conflict.

Carneiro: Conflict and Warfare

An influential theory, focusing on the control of power through conflict and warfare, is that of Robert Carneiro (1970, 1981). Carneiro's theory holds that the formation of states was based on the use of force. The primary factor leading to the use of force was population pressure, specifically when populations increased within limited areas, stimulating competition for agricultural lands.

Carneiro's study is based on events that occurred in the coastal valleys of Peru. As he describes it, states originated in confined areas, where the expansion of growing populations was limited by environmental factors, such as mountains, deserts, and seas. These conditions led to a predictable series of events. At first, the population levels were low, so that the circumscribed areas contained a number of autonomous and dispersed farming villages. As the populations grew and the groups used more land, communities started to fight as they competed for the limited land resources. Within some of the villages, the leaders proved to be especially successful warlords. These communities conquered other villages, forming larger political units—tribes led by chieftains. As the populations continued to grow, so did the occurrence of warfare, until all the local communities were forcibly united within a single state, led by one powerful leader. Power was thus concentrated within the hands of a few, who lived within an urban center. Such large and complex settlements were at a great military advantage over smaller ones. The state continued to grow as the ambitious leader sent armies out of the immediate region to conquer neighboring lands. This led to the formation of more powerful states and larger civilizations.

In Carneiro's (1981) view, the most crucial changes in social organization occurred *before* the formation of the state, with the emergence of chiefdoms, social ranking, and economic inequality. These changes occurred early in the process, as the result of warfare. However, there are some critics who dismiss warfare as the *cause* of state formation, arguing rather that it was the

Aerial view of the ruins of Chan Chan, Peru. Chan Chan was the capital city and home to the powerful leader of the Chimu Empire, which once stretched for 600 miles along Peru's northern coast.

result of civilization (e.g., Fagan 1986). Others view Carneiro's model as too difficult to test in the archaeological record (e.g. Topic and Topic 1987). However, Carneiro's basic premises are gaining support. For example, Daggett's (1987) study of the Nepana Valley in Peru indicates that "developments within the valley were mainly the result of conflicts on the intravalley level" (p. 82). However, one can still question the model's application on a global scale.

Haas: The Control of Power

Jonathan Haas (1982, 1987) refined Carneiro's ideas to produce an especially strong model. Haas agreed that power is the central explanatory

framework of a model for the processes involved in the origin of states. His goal was to bring together the theories of political anthropology and archaeology in a manner that would explain the centrality of power.

Acknowledging the lack of universality of most existing theories, Haas argued that there are "patterns of similarity and diversity in the different theories that offer valuable insight into the process of state formation" (1982, 150). In reviewing the major theories, he noted a number of general patterns:

1. All the theories start with a focus on social stratification and present different explanations for how the society's members

"may gain differential access to basic resources" (p. 150).

2. In most cases, the differential access is "based on *control over the production or procurement* {of particular resources}" (p. 151).

3. Most theories contend that states develop as the internal social structure becomes more specialized and through an increasingly elaborate hierarchical bureaucracy.

Clearly, there are differences between the theories, which Haas feels reflect differences between specific states. In particular, there are major differences with respect to the resources controlled by the states' leaders. Some focus on farmland, others on irrigation systems, and still others on trade. The conditions under which various states emerge also differ. For example, states emerge in areas where agricultural expansion is limited, or in those areas where it is not.

Haas examined the essence of the theories' similarities, while allowing for their differences. He found the unifying theme to be that of *control of power in the production or procurement of resources.* This focus represents a flexible framework that is not tied to specific local conditions; that is, the exact nature of the resources is not important. It is also a systems approach, in that social stratification (particularly, the evolution of a bureaucracy and strong leader) is viewed within the overall context of a society's material and social environment. It will be interesting to see how well Haas's theory tests in archaeological records around the world.

EXAMPLES OF OLD WORLD CIVILIZATIONS

The ancient civilizations of the Old World have long been a source of fascination and scientific discovery. Excavations are found across the continents—in the Near East, Africa, Europe, Southeast Asia, and China. Although a detailed review of Old World civilizations is well beyond the scope of this book, for purposes of illustration we will now briefly describe three ancient cities: Uruk of Mesopotamia, Mycenae of Mediterranean Europe, and Zhengzhou of northern China.

Uruk

One of the best-studied civilizations is also one of the world's earliest: Mesopotamia. Located in what is now southern Iraq, Mesopotamia was spread across the semiarid floodplain of two great rivers, the Tigris and the Euphrates (see Figure 10.4, p. 292). The floodplain's soil is quite rich—with a steady water supply, it can become fertile farmland. The area is inhospitable; it contains only limited raw materials, such as ores for metallurgy and wood for building. Within this less-than-perfect environment, civilization began to emerge some 6,000 years ago.

Mesopotamia encompassed great, densely populated cities run by complex bureaucracies. The economy was based on high-yield, cultivated cereals that grew in the fertile soil, the farming of which was made possible by great irrigation works that transported water from the rivers' marshlands. Such large-scale agricultural projects depended on the cooperative efforts of many people. In turn, the farming was necessary to feed the large populations that inhabited the great Mesopotamian urban centers, some of which were home to as many as 50,000 people. In southern Mesopotamia was one of the world's oldest cities: Uruk.

The people inhabiting Uruk and other southern Mesopotamian cities were known as the Sumerians. Among their many technological accomplishments were wheeled carts, plows, and the refined use of metals. Their intellectual accomplishments included one of the first writing systems, literature, advanced mathematics, architecture that employed true arches and domes, a

The great ziggurat at Uruk, built approximately 2100 B.C.

calendar system based on some knowledge of astronomy, a complex legal system, elaborate religions, and refined arts, including sculpture and music. Sumerian trade networks provided an expansive system for managing and redistributing goods, food, and natural resources.

Uruk was one of a number of largely autonomous Sumerian city-states. During its prime, Uruk was vast, complex, and well-run. It exerted great influence on the lives of many people. Lamberg-Karlovsky and Sabloff (1979) note that the three main expressions of Sumerian society are found at Uruk: monumental temples, various stages of cuneiform (wedge-shaped) writing, and the production of elegant cylinder seals, decorated with semiprecious stones and carved with scenes of Sumerian life (see Figure 11.3).

Within the city was a central district, the core of which was a **ziggurat**, the massive, sacred temple pictured in the photo above. Around the temple were the homes of the priests and the ruling class. The higher the person's social status, the more elegant the home, and the closer its location to the central district. The temple was the focus of Uruk's religious and social life. It even functioned as the storehouse and redistribution center for food surpluses. This reflects the close relationship between the political power of the elite and the control of important resources. The temple also acted as the focal point of the network Uruk maintained with its hinterlands, through religious, economic, and military links. In these outlying areas were satellite villages, some located as much as six miles away. The villages, which had their own irrigation systems and farmlands, helped provide food to the city, formed part of Uruk's trade network, and aided in the defense against other city-states. For its part, the city administered the complex system by controlling trade, settling disputes, and running the economy.

Uruk was at its peak around 2800 B.C. Its priests and kings dominated the region for many years—exactly how long, no one is sure. Eventually, it came to lie buried in the sand, until the mid-twentieth century when archaeologists began its excavation.

Mycenae

Early in the history of mainland Greek civilization, Greece was divided into a number of city-states, each run by a single militaristic ruler who lived in a fortified city. One of the first—and the most powerful—of these city-states was Mycenae. The Mycenaean influence presided over a

(a)

	3000 B.C.			600 B.C.
Bird				
Fish				
Sun				
Orchard				

(b)

(c)

FIGURE 11.3

The Sumerian culture of southern Mesopotamia is known for its intellectual accomplishments. (a) The Sumerians developed cuneiform, one of the first systems of writing. (b) Cuneiform writing evolved from pictures to more symbolic representations of concepts. (c) Cylinder seal from Iraq, dating from about 2330–2180 B.C. Sumerians rolled the seals on clay as a means of signing their names. This seal depicts a man hunting wild goats in the mountains. Above the man is his name and profession inscribed in cuneiform writing.

great trade network. It was also extended by the aggressive endeavors of the warriors, in battles with other city-states.

The Mycenaean base of operations was the fortress city of Mycenae. The main entrance of the city's wall is pictured in the photo that follows. Dating from approximately 1650 B.C. to 1200 B.C., Mycenae was small compared with other ancient cities. Its design, as a fortified citadel, reflects that of many of its region. Within the boundaries of the defensive wall were the royal palace and religious structures and the homes of important members of the upper class. The city's

The Lion Gate, the main entrance through the great defensive wall that surrounded Mycenae, Greece.

architecture, much of it the work of highly skilled artists and craftspeople, was sophisticated for the time. Dotting the surrounding fertile countryside were the estates of major landholders, who were socially ranked below the city-dwelling rulers and administrators.

Economically, Mycenae was the focal point of an extensive sea-trade network that spread across the Mediterranean into Cyprus, Anatolia, and Egypt. Of special importance was trade in metals, such as tin and copper for making bronze. The highly valued amber, used for Mycenaean art objects, came from the far-off Baltic region. In contrast to cultures in which a written language arose largely as a means of managing food resources, the Mycenaean script was apparently invented to organize this complex system of trade. Also reflecting the importance of the trade networks are the spectacular goods buried in royal shaft graves. These burials, which emphasize the special status of the warrior kings, contain beautifully designed weapons decorated with copper and gold, as well as gold masks shaped to the faces of the graves' occupants. Famous as great warriors and horsemen, the Mycenaean kings inspired many later-day Greek stories and epics recounting their adventures.

Sometime during the twelfth century B.C., Mycenae and its influence within the Mediterranean region came to an abrupt end. Some scholars contend that it was conquered by Dorian Greek invaders. However, Tainter (1988) has suggested that the Mycenaean civilization and trade network collapsed under the weight of an unmanageable complexity, brought on by the lack of a strong internal power structure and weak economic return. More about Tainter's theories is presented in the section "The Collapse of Complex Societies."

Zhengzhou

About 5,000 years ago, great and enduring civilizations began to arise in northern China. That the evolution of Chinese civilization was an independent event is obvious from the uniqueness of its cultural characteristics. Furthermore, the region is isolated by imposing mountains and deserts. Even so, the origin of Chinese civilization was similar in some respects to that of other regions. For example, it was preceded by an increasing dependency on agriculture and increased population growth. At that time, the predominant crops were millet and rice, which were cultivated on the fertile wet lowlands of river floodplains. As the population grew, people settled in villages near the rivers, both to protect the limited, highly valued farmland and to provide enough laborers for large-scale agricultural projects. Eventually, these trends led to the origin of the first of several Chinese civilizations. These civilizations were ruled by strong, dictatorial, militaristic leaders. Their sociopolitical systems were based on kinship and firmly established alliances.

One of the greatest Chinese civilizations is known as the Shang. First formed some 3,500 years ago, the Shang civilization apparently established the roots of modern-day Chinese culture. The major cities of the Shang civilization, including Zhengzhou (Cheng-Chou), were located along the Yellow (Huang Ho) River. A Bronze Age city dating from around 1600 B.C., Zhengzhou was the capital of early Shang civilization and the fortress home of the powerful ruler. In the manner of many Chinese Bronze Age cities, Zhengzhou was well planned on a rectangular layout and enclosed by a massive wall made out of earth packed firmly between wooden structures. The wall, almost 30 feet high, formed a rectangle about 2 kilometers long and 1.7 kilometers across. Watson (1979) noted that "the estimate of labour required for its construction—put at 10,000 men working for nearly twenty years—throws impressive light on the political power" (p. 58).

The excavation of Zhengzhou has shed much light on the Shang way of life. The society's organization consisted of a tightly structured hierarchy, headed by a powerful ruler. The control of

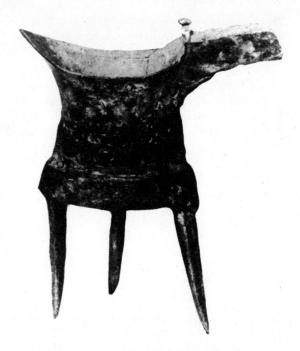

An early Chinese bronze ritual wine goblet from Zhengzhou.

power was concentrated within the city walls, which contained the ruler's residence, administrative buildings, and the dynasty's ceremonial center. Especially important was the control of the river, which was a water supply for agriculture and a means of transportation for trade.

The majority of the population lived outside the city's walls, including the peasants and most of the craftspeople. The society was rich in arts, as reflected by its beautiful architecture, artwork, and crafts—especially objects of bronze. Religion, which was based on the worship of ancestors and a supreme deity (from whom everyone was descended), played a crucial role in reinforcing the ruler's political power. We see this in the indication that leadership was inherited through ancestral lines, and that many important decisions were justified as being founded in divine

Shang oracle bones. In divination ceremonies, hot metal was applied to oracle bones, with the resulting cracks interpreted as messages from worshiped ancestors. A skilled diviner could control the cracking to manipulate the "messages" for political purposes.

guidance. For example, the Shang refined system of writing was used on sacred objects such as "oracle bones." Such writings concerned administrative and political decisions; hence, they provide archaeologists with enormous insights into early Chinese civilization. The Shang civilization also may have practiced large-scale ritual human sacrifice. In one area of the Zhengzhou site, about a hundred human skulls were unearthed, most with the top portion of the skull sawed off.

In contrast to the events at Mycenae, the end of Zhengzhou's dominance did not denote the fall of Shang civilization. Indeed, Zhengzhou apparently lost its status as the capital city when a Shang ruler moved his base of operations to another city. The Shang civilization continued to exist for hundreds of years after that, until it was overthrown by another great (and closely related) Chinese dynasty, the Chou (Chang 1983).

EXAMPLES OF NEW WORLD CIVILIZATIONS

The New World—the Americas—was home to many great civilizations. The best known of these were located in Mesoamerica, which roughly covered the modern-day countries of Mexico, Guatemala, Belize, and El Salvador. Archaeologists have identified two other major groupings of New World civilizations. One was located in the Andean region of South America; the other, in what is now the United States. By way of example, we will briefly focus on one city-state from each of the three regions: Teotihuacán from Mesoamerica, Chan Chan from Peru, and Cahokia from the midwestern United States.

Teotihuacán

The remains of the Mesoamericans fill many people with a sense of wonder. Mesoamerican civilizations left behind majestic architecture, such as the temples and pyramids in the Valley of Oaxaca and the Mayan ceremonial center complex at Tikal, Guatemala. While all of Mesoamerica shared a common history, archaeologists divide it into two regions: lowland Mesoamerica, which included cultures such as the Olmecs and Mayans, and highland Mesoamerica, which included the city-state of Tula and the Toltec and Aztec cultures. The dominance of Mesoamerican civilizations spans a period from about 3,200 years ago until the European conquest of the region during the 1500s.

Mesoamerica encompassed a broad range of environments, including swampy coastal lowlands, mountain slopes, semiarid highlands, and dense jungles. However, all Mesoamerican civilizations lacked important domesticated animals and were dependent on maize agriculture. All had complex political and religious systems founded on ceremonial centers.

The first great New World city-state, Teotihuacán, was located in highland Mesoamerica, northeast of Mexico City in the Valley of Mexico. In the beginning, it was much like the other agricultural villages that surrounded Lake Texcoco. However, about 2,100 years ago, it began to grow into the largest, and one of the most powerful, of the ancient New World cities. By A.D. 500, it covered 5 square miles and contained as many as 200,000 people. Teotihuacán's location played an important role in its growth as a city-state. The surrounding land was a rich alluvial plain, which, when irrigated, produced high yields of maize, beans, and squash. Nearby were deposits of obsidian, an important raw material used throughout the New World for tools and crafts. Obsidian was exchanged as part of a vast trade network, in which Teotihuacán had an advantageous location; it sat within a narrow valley that linked the Valley of Mexico with the Valley of Puebla, leading to the lowlands near the Gulf of Mexico. It also stood on the shores of Lake Texcoco, the waters of which were used for irrigation and for a general water supply in the semiarid environment.

Politically, Teotihuacán was headed by a domineering leader whose power was supported by "divine right." A strong bureaucracy prevailed in organizing the tremendous labor needed to build a massive system of irrigation canals and to cultivate the fields. The bureaucracy also functioned to organize the enormous labor force needed to construct majestic stone buildings.

While primarily serving as an administrative and commercial center, Teotihuacán's most breathtaking architecture emphasizes its importance as a ceremonial center. Archaeologists have uncovered fabulous temples, such as the Pyramid of the Sun, which occupied the core of the city. One of a group of temples, the Pyramid of the Sun was the largest structure built in ancient Mesoamerica—as broad at its base as the great pyramid of Cheops in Egypt. As reconstructed today, it stands 210 feet high and covers an area of 650 square feet (see the chapter opening photo). People came from all over Mesoamerica to worship at these temples. The religious rituals included human sacrifice and cannibalism, elements that grew in importance as the society became increasingly militaristic.

Other aspects of Teotihuacán also reflect the people's great skill and cultural sophistication. The city was organized into sections, with the streets carefully aligned on a grid system. The dwellings and their contents demonstrate the rigidity of the social class system and illustrate the importance of craft specialization, which included the working of stone and obsidian and making pottery. The lower classes lived in apartment-like complexes, divided according to status and occupation. Laborers, soldiers, craftspeople, and merchants each lived in their own section of the city. As was often the case, the elite ruling class and religious leaders lived in the city's central district. Food was grown by the laborers who worked the irrigated fields and was also provided by nearby satellite villages.

Teotihuacán's influence within the New World was quite extensive, in large part because of its religious significance and its key position in the Mesoamerican trade network. Pilgrims journeyed to the city to worship at its temples. From the city were exported ceramics, obsidian crafts, and other valued objects in exchange for other goods.

For reasons not fully understood, Teotihuacán eventually lost its dominance in the region and underwent internal decay. About A.D. 650, the city was dramatically destroyed as the people rampaged, burning the temples and slaughtering the ruling class. This may have been brought on by internal problems caused by disease or drought. Some scholars suggest that enemy societies plotted the city's downfall (e.g., Sanders and Price 1968). Whatever the cause, the great Teotihuacán civilization disappeared well before the arrival of Europeans in the New World.

Chan Chan

South America was home to a number of great civilizations. For the most part, these societies were located along the west side of the continent, in the Andes Mountains and the adjoining coastal lowlands. Starting around 2500 B.C., people began to settle in the narrow and arid coastal zone. These lowland people fished and used irrigation to raise Mesoamerican-type crops, such as maize, beans, and squash. They also grew cotton, which was used for textiles. As irrigation agriculture spread into the Andes, people began to live in permanent settlements in the highlands, where they adapted to a very different ecological setting. These groups emphasized starchy root crops, such as potatoes and oca, and foods derived from the tropical forests to the east, such as lima beans and chili peppers. Unlike the Mesoamericans, the highland groups domesticated animals, such as guinea pigs and muscovy ducks for food, llamas for pack animals, and alpacas for their wool.

By 1500 B.C., early sedentary villages had spread across the Andean region. From about 1000 to 200 B.C., the region began to exhibit greater cultural complexity, at a level most closely associated with the Chavín culture. Known for its unique art style, as exemplified in the photo on page 316, the Chavín society was apparently at a prestate level of organization. From approximately 200 B.C. to A.D. 600, we see the development of the first Andean city-states, Moche and Nazca. These were followed, between A.D. 600 and A.D. 1000, by the powerful regional states of Tiahuanaco and Huari. The Incan civilization, an enormously influential empire that encompassed up to 8 million people and which once covered the length of South America, was the dominant force at the start of the Spanish conquest. Preceding the Incas, from approximately A.D. 800 to A.D. 1465, the Andean region contained a number of smaller city-states, or "kingdoms." The largest of these was Chimu, which once stretched for over 600 miles along the northern coast of Peru.

As did other coastal kingdoms, the Chimu Empire built massive agricultural works, including long irrigation canals, large stone reservoirs, and hundreds of miles of terraced hillside fields. Although earlier societies also made use of irri-

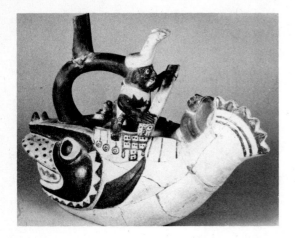

Chavín artistry from Peru. (above) Moche pottery. A fisherman paddles his fish-shaped reed boat. Note the captive tied in front of the fisherman. (right) A sculpted stone head from the inner gallery of a pyramid temple.

gation and terracing, the Chimu Empire did so on a grand scale that greatly increased agricultural yields. Such large-scale projects are based on complex administration, storage, and management capabilities—functions apparently served by the Chimu capital city of Chan Chan.

When compared with the cities of other regions, Chan Chan and most other Andean cities reveal a special character. While they were often quite spread out, they were not centers of large and densely concentrated populations. Nonetheless, Andean cities did function as the states' administrative and ceremonial centers.

Typical of most Andean cities, Chan Chan was located in a valley—the Moche Valley on the Peruvian north coast. Established during the 1200s, Chan Chan covered a large area of land: at 4 square miles, it approached the size of Teotihuacán. However, Chan Chan was different from that Mesoamerican city, being much less densely populated and much less built up. Chan Chan basically consisted of many small build-

ings, open areas, enclosed agricultural fields, and irrigation canals (see photograph on p. 307).

The center of Chan Chan reflects the differences that existed between Andean and Mesoamerican cities. While the center of Chan Chan did contain ceremonial structures, they were in sharp contrast to the grandeur of the Mesoamerican monuments. Although Chan Chan contained two somewhat modest pyramids, more striking is a series of ten extremely large rectangular compounds. Each compound was surrounded by massive adobe (mud brick) walls that enclosed courtyards, plazas, gardens, and various buildings that served as storehouses, residences, and administrative offices. The compounds also contained rectangular platforms that were, in turn, enclosed within high walls. Each platform was divided into small burial cells and functioned as a royal tomb. The tomb housed the remains of a ruler, as well as some of his riches and possibly some of his sacrificed attendants.

The rectangular compounds reflect Chan

A mummy, uncovered from a Chavín tomb.

in general) was different from that of Mesoamerica. Instead of focusing on trade and merchants, it was "shaped by and maintained for the benefit of aristocratic households and their agents" (p. 357).

Outside the city's center, Chan Chan contained two basic types of residences. The first were intermediate-sized adobe structures that apparently housed the lower-level elite. The majority of Chan Chan's people lived in residences composed of open areas, small adobe and reed structures, a hearth, and small storage areas. Some also contained small workshops for crafts and other industries.

Archaeologists consider the general function of Chan Chan to have been that of an administrative and ceremonial center. A relatively small number of the empire's people lived in the city—possibly as few as 20,000 (compared with Teotihuacán's population of 200,000). The city's inhabitants were the state's administrators, their servants, and various craftspeople. Most of Chimu's population was spread over the empire, connected by an extensive system of roads. The people were strictly ruled by the elite housed at Chan Chan, and were obligated to pay heavy taxes, work on large-scale labor projects, and serve in the military, which played an important role in Andean societies, since the kingdoms were often at war.

For all of its riches and military strength, the Chimu Empire eventually began to weaken from within, possibly because of a severe drop in agricultural production. Then, during the mid-1400s, the Chimu fell to the extremely powerful and aggressive Incan Empire.

Cahokia

Although investigators of civilization in the New World have focused largely on events to the south, the prehistory of the United States demonstrates that while many groups persisted as successful foragers, other precontact cultures evolved complex societies. In the southwestern

Chan's role as the Chimu Empire's administrative center. Chimu was ruled by a series of hereditary kings, with each rectangular compound apparently being a different king's palace. The palace, which included the king's residence and office, after death became his burial site. A new king would build his own rectangular compound and would also accumulate his own wealth. While the position was handed down intact, the late king's riches were divided among a number of heirs. The need for each king to gather his own fortune may have been the major impetus for the Chimu Empire's aggressive economic and military policy. According to Kolata (1983), the basis of Chimu's economy (and that of Andean states

United States, we see the remains of agricultural societies in which ingenious canal irrigation was used to grow maize on desert lands. Among these were the Anasazi, who built large pueblo (adobe) villages and cliff dwellings, as shown in the opening photo of Chapter 10. In the northwest United States, some societies lived in environments so rich in natural resources that they became extremely sophisticated sedentary foragers. These groups, such as the Tlingit, Kwakiutl, and Haida, lived in permanent longhouses and subsisted on salmon and other fish (which could be dried and stored), sea mammals, land mammals, shellfish, birds, and a wide variety of plants. In eastern and midwestern parts of the United States, some cultures slowly developed into complex agricultural societies. These groups, including the Adena, Hopewell, and Mississippian cultures, are known for their extensive trade networks and intricate religious practices, which involved the construction of impressive burial mounds and ceremonial platforms. Thousands of such mounds are spread across the eastern and midwestern United States, particularly along the Mississippi River and its tributaries.

Although very sophisticated, most of these North American groups did not concentrate their populations in large cities; rather, the people lived in smaller, dispersed villages. However, by A.D. 900, some Mississippian communities were expanding in both area and population. The largest of these was Cahokia.

Built on the floodplain of the Mississippi River, close to what is now St. Louis, Cahokia was once a great Mississippian capital city and ceremonial center. At its height, around A.D. 1200, it encompassed a population of approximately 30,000 people. It once contained more than 100 small mounds and many plazas, dominated by an enormous platformed earthwork, Monk's Mound. Located in the city's center, this is the largest of all North American mounds—more than 100 feet tall and covering 16 acres. It took thousands of people, carrying millions of baskets of dirt, to build the mound, the top of

which held a large thatched temple and a great plaza. Around this ceremonial mound were the homes of the elite, storage facilities, other mounds, temples, and administrative offices. Covering almost 200 acres, this central part of Cahokia was enclosed by a great log fence with gates and watchtowers. The central city was surrounded by smaller communities that had their own burial mounds, buildings, and plazas. Cahokia's urban area spread more than 5 square miles. It was very carefully planned, as reflected in the artist's reconstruction in Figure 11.4.

What was the nature of Cahokian society? Some archaeologists (e.g., O'Brien 1972) are of the opinion that it was a true state, rather than a complex chiefdom, the latter being associated with most large eastern sites. Cahokia was ruled by a strong central chief whose administrators planned the city's design, managed large labor parties, and controlled the vast trade network. The elite ruling class likely consisted of a series of powerful chiefs and their priests, who derived power from a religious system based on ancestors and multiple gods. The grand burial mounds attest to the highly stratified nature of Mississippian society: high-ranking individuals were buried with great quantities of valued items, such as robes or platforms decorated with thousands of shell beads, arrowheads, polished stones, and mica and copper ornaments. As was the case in Chan Chan, the elite were sometimes accompanied in death by sacrificed servants. The outlying settlements were apparently ruled by their own local chiefs, who were controlled by the central chief situated in Cahokia.

Around A.D. 1250, Cahokia began to decline in importance, perhaps because of exhaustion of local resources. Or possibly its trade network was disrupted by other growing Mississippi River cultures. Further investigation may provide insight into the sequence of events that resulted in the decline of this great city.

The theory that Cahokia was a true city-state is strongly supported by evidence of its great size and political complexity. Another theory—that

FIGURE 11.4
Cahokia: Now and then. (left) Monk's Mound, which was at the center of Cahokia. The largest prehistoric earthwork in the New World, Monk's Mound is more than 100 feet tall and covers 16 acres. (below) Artist's reconstruction of Cahokia as it might have appeared at its height, around A.D. 1200.

the mound-building cultures of the eastern United States originated independently of those of Mesoamerica—is also supported by evidence. Early eastern cultures did not have a Meso-american-like maize agriculture; furthermore, the practice of mound-building spread from east to west. Clearly, the eastern United States should be seriously considered as a site for the independent origin of both agriculture and civilization.

THE COLLAPSE OF COMPLEX SOCIETIES

So impressive are the remains of some ancient societies, it is hard to imagine why they ultimately collapsed. Some scholars define "collapse" loosely, in terms of any sort of societal disintegration. Some are more specific, such as Tainter (1988). In his words, "[collapse] is fundamentally a matter of the sociopolitical sphere. *A society has collapsed when it displays a rapid, significant loss of an established level of sociopolitical complexity*" (p. 4).

Theoretical parallels exist between the study of collapse and the study of how civilizations arise. For example, some researchers seek to describe specific factors, particularly a single major cause, involved in a society's collapse. Specific factors are as varied as the cultures themselves. They may include internal factors, such as epidemic disease, earthquakes or floods, overpopulation, or imbalances in the male-to-female ratio. Or external factors may be involved, such as the breakdown of trade networks or invasions. Some researchers prefer a systems approach, viewing the collapse of a society as caused by a number of interactive ecological and social factors. Still others seek to formulate broad, explanatory theories. Because space limitations do not permit a thorough review of all the approaches, we will use Tainter's model as an illustration of one way in which scholars are currently thinking about the process of collapse.

Collapse and the Declining Productivity of Complexity

Tainter's (1988) theory of collapse focuses on economic factors. Collapse is defined by him as "a sudden, pronounced loss of an established level of sociopolitical complexity" (p. 193). This indicates a reversal in the trend toward increasing complexity, including a decrease in social stratification and in the centralized control of power. Economies weaken, population levels may drop, "while arts and literature experience such a quantitative decline that a dark age often ensues" (ibid.).

Why does the trend toward increased cultural complexity so radically go into reverse? According to Tainter, four concepts are important to understanding collapse, with the first three forming the basis of the last:

1. human societies are problem-solving organizations,
2. sociopolitical systems require energy for their maintenance,
3. increased complexity carries with it increased cost per capita, and
4. investment in sociopolitical complexity as a problem-solving response often reaches a point of declining marginal returns (Tainter 1988, 194).

Societies thus create a delicate economic balance between energy expenditure and a marginal degree of return on investment. As a society becomes increasingly complex, the costs continue to rise as the society demands more food, raw materials, and information flow to support it. Tainter proposed that a society often goes into a rapid decline when the investments needed merely to maintain it reach the point where costs exceed the already marginal returns. As surpluses decrease, being used to support the status quo, the society becomes so economically weak as to fall victim to a crisis it could have earlier survived.

How can Tainter's model be applied to some of our examples of city-states? For the Mycenaean decline, he proposed the following scenario: The Greek city-state was in military and economic competition with others of the region and became caught in a competitive spiral. "The upwardly-driven costs of such a system, without any real benefits at the local level, would have induced declining marginal returns" (Tainter 1988, 204). At some point, the Mycenaean civilization was so greatly weakened from within that the society began to collapse, with repeated catastrophes taking place as the economic, political, and social structure decayed to the point that it could no longer support the society's great complexity. In the New World, Teotihuacán not only underwent a sudden collapse, but was literally destroyed by its people. In applying Tainter's model, we can point to the increasingly large allocation of resources to the military and to the increasingly large and cumbersome bureaucracy, until finally the lower classes rebelled.

Other Models

Tainter's model for the collapse of complex societies is attractive because it is broad enough to be applied globally, without concern for the specific circumstances of individual civilizations.

However, it is but one of a number of current explanatory models. For example, Rappaport (1977) described civilizations as "maladaptations," doomed to collapse because they are overspecialized and overextended social systems. Flannery (1972) approached the issue as part of his general-systems-theory model of cultural evolution. In his view, collapse is stimulated when one subsystem of a complex and delicate cultural system grows in such a manner as to negatively affect the system's other components. Renfrew (1978) proposed a "catastrophe theory," in which the collapse of a cultural system is brought on by internal stress stimulated by an abrupt and drastic change. A strongly sociological point of view is that of Eisenstadt (1969), who argued that collapse is caused by the internal instability that results from a major restructuring of social institutions, as occurs, for example, in class struggles where there is a shift in the power base. All such models are in need of further testing, especially through continued cross-cultural studies.

Besides being of scientific interest, the study of collapse also intrigues people for personal reasons. We live in a complex society. Is it also vulnerable to collapse? Noting that "civilizations are fragile, impermanent things," Tainter (1988) quoted Ortega: "The possibility that a civilization should die doubles our own mortality" (pp. 1–2).

SUMMARY

Civilization, which represented a new level of cultural complexity, is an adaptive cultural mechanism for organizing very complex societies through the control and concentration of power, as expressed by the social structure of the state and the residence pattern of the city. A state consists of an autonomous integrated political unit that encompasses many communities within its territory. States are characterized by a specialized central governing authority, a bureaucracy, and

highly stratified class systems. A city consists of a large and densely concentrated population. While not every civilization has a city, most have an urban or ceremonial center from which those in power operate.

One of the first modern theories for the origin of civilization was proposed by Childe, who contended that societies attain the level of civilization in a dramatic and rapid fashion—an event that takes place when the proper ecological, social, and technological conditions occur within an agricultural society. Childe's theory contains three essential components that apply to all of the world's early civilizations: the creation of food surpluses, diversity of food resources, and intensive land use.

Prime-mover theories for the origin of civilization include Wittfogel's hydraulic-state theory, the ecological Fertile Crescent theory, and those that focus on population growth. Adams proposed one of the first multiple-cause theories for the origin of civilization, emphasizing that a number of interacting factors gradually led to the origin of state society in some agricultural communities. In Adams's view, the two most essential characteristics of early states were agricultural surpluses and social stratification. Flannery's multicausal model focuses on the processes underlying the evolution of complex cultural systems, particularly the influence of ecological factors, such as environmental stress, on this evolution. Hassan's feedback model centers on the issue of economic power and the vulnerability of agricultural systems to environmental and cultural pressures. Carneiro also emphasized the control of power. His theory holds that the formation of states was based on conflict and warfare, with population pressure the primary factor leading to the use of force. Haas refined Carneiro's theory, contending that a unifying theme in the origin of civilization across societies is the control of power in the production or procurement of resources. Haas's model provides a flexible framework for the origin of civilization that is not tied to specific local conditions.

Ancient civilizations were found across the Old World. In the Near East, Uruk, built by the Sumerians, was a complex city-state. Mycenae was an early Greek city-state that exerted a strong influence throughout Europe and Asia by way of the aggression of its warriors and an extensive trade network. Zhengzhou, in northern China, was the capital of early Shang civilization and the fortress home of its powerful ruler.

The New World had three major locations of ancient civilizations: Mesoamerica, the Andean region of South America, and what is now the United States. Teotihuacán is an example of a great Mesoamerican city-state. It was the largest and one of the most powerful of the New World cities. Chan Chan was the capital city of the Chimu Empire, which once stretched for over 600 miles along the northern coast of Peru. Cahokia, built on the floodplain of the Mississippi River, was a great capital city and ceremonial center for the Mississippian culture.

A society is considered collapsed when it displays a rapid, significant loss of an established level of sociopolitical complexity. Theories on the collapse of civilizations include both prime-mover and multicausal models. Tainter's theory of collapse focuses on economic factors that cause a reversal in the trend toward increasing complexity. Thus, social stratification decreases and so does the centralized control of power. He proposed that a delicate economic balance exists in civilizations between energy expenditure and a marginal degree of return on investment. As a society becomes increasingly complex, the costs continue to rise. A society often goes into a rapid decline when the investments needed just to maintain it reach the point where costs exceed the already marginal returns.

SUGGESTED READINGS

Adams, Robert M. 1966. *The Evolution of Urban Society*. Chicago: Aldine.

Cohen, Mark Nathan. 1989. *Health and the Rise of Civilization*. New Haven, CT: Yale University Press.

Haas, Jonathan. 1982. *The Evolution of the Prehistoric State*. New York: Columbia University Press.

Keightley, David N. 1983. *The Origins of Chinese Civilization*. Berkeley: University of California Press.

Leventhal, Richard M., and Alan L. Kolata, eds. 1983. *Civilization in the Ancient Americas*. Cambridge, MA: University of New Mexico Press and the Peabody Museum of Archaeology and Ethnology.

Redman, Charles L. 1978. *The Rise of Civilization*. San Francisco: W.H. Freeman.

Roosevelt, Anna Curtenius. 1991. *Moundbuilders of the Amazon*. San Diego, CA: Academic Press.

Tainter, Joseph A. 1988. *The Collapse of Complex Societies*. Cambridge: Cambridge University Press.

Whitehouse, Ruth, and John Wilkins. 1986. *The Making of Civilizations*. New York: Alfred A. Knopf.

The Discovery and Preservation of a Mayan City

K. Anne Pyburn

K. Anne Pyburn, an anthropologist at Indiana University at Indianapolis, has done fieldwork in the American Southwest, Peru, West Africa, and North Yemen, but her passion is for the Maya. Working in Belize, in Central America, for about nine years, she has focused on reconstructing ancient economic patterns by looking at the houses of the prehistoric Mayan poor.

Professional archaeologists argue that ancient remains are part of the heritage of all people and should be preserved and protected for everyone. This position is a noble one, but sometimes creates serious ethical dilemmas, when the reality of life conflicts with archaeological preservation. How can we argue that people should let their families go hungry, rather than sell an old pot to an artifact dealer? What right does the archaeologist have to insist that an archaeological site is more important than a road from a rural village to a healthcare clinic?

Because of the thriving black market in ancient artifacts, people in almost all parts of the world are aware that ancient things have monetary value. All too often, new archaeological sites get documented scientifically only after they have been partly or completely destroyed by looters. Professional looters are not usually local people, but thieves who offer innocent residents some small amount of money for artifacts or for permission to dig. What they find or purchase, they sell, illegally, to unwary

museums or unscrupulous private collectors for a great deal more than they paid. In the process of looting, ancient architecture and complex archaeological sediments are destroyed, resulting not only in the loss of beautiful things, but also of scientific information.

In the spring of 1990, I was working in the north of Belize and my research was going well, so I was reluctant to take time to visit friends in a nearby village. These friends were pressing me to come see a set of Mayan mounds, and my husband, Rick Wilk, who was doing ethnographic fieldwork in the village, insisted that we should take a look. To be honest, I dreaded to see yet another looted and destroyed Mayan city—I have seen so many. Finally, I reluctantly agreed to go.

Rick and I were loaded into a small motorboat by our friend Glen Crawford, and headed down a bewildering maze of waterways. After about an hour, we came into a lagoon where the unbroken line of trees along the shore seemed to rise up several meters. I then had my first glimmer of excitement, since the tree line suggested that there was, indeed, a very large structure below. We pulled into shore and started inland along a cowpath at a breakneck pace.

Once inside the jungle, nothing was visible more than 10 feet ahead. Typical of any veteran archaeologist, I had my eyes glued to the ground searching for artifacts. Despite our rapid pace, my spirits were rising rapidly, since the ground was literally coated with stone

This photo, taken by archaeologist K. Anne Pyburn, shows the undisturbed remains of an ancient Mayan site, Chau Hiix. In 1991, the United States began imposing restrictions on the import of Mayan artifacts from Central America to discourage professional looters.

tools. When I stumbled into Rick and Glen standing dead still in front of me, I reluctantly took my eyes off the ground and looked up . . . and then up more . . . and then up more. As we later measured the height of the main building, I was looking up over 70 feet!

For the next three hours, we scrambled over one undamaged palace after another, all showing wonderful architectural preservation. Not only were the buildings unlooted, the smaller ones were undisturbed by plowing, or any later human activity whatsoever. Painted plaster walls could be seen in rodent burrows, pots left on the ground 500 years earlier were broken but still in place, bases of eroded soft limestone stelae were lined up before buildings. When we finally left, because it was growing dark, we did not feel as if we had visited an archaeological site; we felt that we had visited an abandoned but very real place, somehow still alive after hundreds of years of solitude.

We now know that the central precinct contains over 20 buildings built on a platform that stands two to five meters above the original ground surface, and covers over half a square kilometer. Several ancient elevated roads are connected to this platform by staircases, and we may have also located an ancient canal. Preliminary analysis of pottery collected from the surface of the site shows it was occupied at least from the Terminal Preclassic (A.D. 300) to the Late Postclassic (A.D. 1500). The forest covering the site is full of wonderful animals; we named the site Chau Hiix, Mayan for jaguarundi, after we saw one near the site center.

Of course, the discovery of Chau Hiix is exciting, but what accounted for such an event and what does it mean for science? First of all, the event was made possible by the very special people who live in the nearby village. They knew about the ruins for years, but protected them from destruction. As for scientific interest, my own lies in understanding ancient Mayan social and economic organization, especially evidence of the poorer classes. At other sites, a huge proportion of evidence has been eradicated by modern land use. Plowing, planting, digging, and building destroy the fragile evidence of the poorest members of a society, people with very little material culture to leave behind. Clearly, Chau Hiix offers great possibilities for finding this type of fragile evidence.

Modern archaeologists are increasingly aware that they will have to address the needs of local populations if they expect sites like Chau Hiix to be preserved. One particularly happy solution lies in the development of tourism. This means that archaeologists must reorient themselves to a responsibility that goes beyond scientific inquiry, to the consolidation and reconstruction of archaeological sites and the creation of educational settings, so that visitors can learn why archaeological materials are worth saving. For local people, the crucial factor is that tourists bring money to buy food, to buy keepsakes, to rent lodgings. This kind of archaeological industry, which is possible when sites are developed rather than destroyed, can be a source of steady income for many people over many years.

If Chau Hiix can be consolidated and reconstructed, it will be extremely attractive to visitors. The villagers hope to develop an information and educational center to teach other people about the value of Belize's heritage. If tourism brings money into the village, other people will see how it is possible to profit more from archaeology in the long run by protecting archaeological resources, and not allowing looters to steal them. Right now, the development of Chau Hiix is only a dream. But if it should come true, the villagers will be rewarded for their selflessness and vigilance.

Sociocultural Anthropology

PART THREE

Reconstructing the course of human evolution helped show us what makes the human species part of the animal kingdom and what makes humans unique. While the adaptive strategies of the first hominids still relied on the animal inheritance, these strategies became increasingly dependent on the capacity of the human brain for culture, the most important defining characteristic of being human. Culture, the customary manner in which human groups learn to organize their behavior and thought in relation to their environment, is seen in the stone tools, use of fire, and rites of the early foragers no less than in the centralized governments, class structures, and intensive agriculture of the ancient civilizations.

In Part Three, our emphasis will be on cultural adaptation. Sociocultural anthropology, which deals with the social and cultural inheritance of humankind, overlaps with archaeology in its concerns. However, sociocultural anthropology emphasizes cultures that can be studied directly. The chapters that follow survey the cultural diversity of humankind of the recent past or present. What are the various ways in which people meet their basic needs, form groups, marry, raise children, resolve conflicts, deal with the sick, and formulate views of the world? We will consider the adaptive significance of societies' activities and beliefs—what it is that holds society together and what threatens to pull it apart.

We will also examine the diverse theories anthropologists have proposed in attempting to understand human cultural existence. We will see, too, how anthropologists go about gaining information to support or refute their viewpoints.

Anthropologists have as much to say about contemporary large-scale societies as they do about small-scale societies. In the final chapter, we will show how anthropology can make an important contribution to coping with the problems faced in a world challenged by ethnic division, rapid social change, the development problems of the Third World, and environmental degradation. We will also reconsider the roles of archaeology and biological anthropology in today's world.

Our first objective, however, is to look at human communication. Through communication, individual members of a society learn about their culture and pass on its adaptive strategies to future generations. In this way cultures survive. With communication, then, we begin our sociocultural understanding of the human adaptation.

12 Communication

Mandarin, the official language of China, is the world's most commonly spoken language. Among its many dialects is Cantonese, ranked twentieth in number of native speakers. Although they share a common written script, a person who speaks only Mandarin and a person who speaks only Cantonese cannot understand each other's spoken words.

The exchange of information is one of the most universal features of life, an essential part of the adaptation of any species to its environment. Organisms are almost constantly transmitting and receiving information. Without effective means of communication, an eagle cannot locate its prey, a flower cannot attract a bee, a salmon cannot find its spawning site. Getting food, avoiding danger, and finding a mate all hinge on sending out the appropriate signals at the right time and on picking up essential information from the environment.

As we saw in Chapter 6, the hominid adaptation, made possible by the expansion and reorganization of the brain, includes increased intelligence and symbolic thought. These are the basis of much of human communication. Information exchange is a highly elaborated feature of the human adaptive strategy; without it, especially without language, culture as we know it would not exist.

How does human communication relate to culture, society, and the human adaptive strategy? This question and others are the focus of the anthropological subfield known as **linguistic anthropology**. In this chapter, we will explore aspects of communication that linguistic anthropologists study to further a holistic understanding of human life: general characteristics of communication, relationships between complexity in communication and complexity in group structure, the structure of human verbal and nonverbal communications, links between language and culture, variations within a single language, use of more than one language tradition, and the reconstruction of processes by which languages evolve.

THE COMMUNICATION PROCESS

Communication occurs whenever information is exchanged between a sender and a receiver. Information is transmitted by a sender via signals, such as a song, a sentence, a chest-thumping display, or a scent. At the other end, the information is received as a message.

Sending and Receiving Messages

As we all know from personal experience, what a signal means to the sender is not always what it means to the receiver. One person may smile at another to signal approval or friendship, for instance, but the message received may be quite different: You are making fun of me, or You think I am acting like a fool. The potential for misunderstanding exists in all communicative transactions.

Sending signals of one kind or another is inevitable. Simply by existing, any plant or animal betrays information as to its size, shape, and location. Even camouflaged organisms continue to emit signals. The flatfish, or sole, can alter its skin color to match the color and texture of the ocean floor. But it cannot camouflage its odor and electrical field, signals that mean "dinner" to a shark that swims close enough to detect them.

Since it is impossible to avoid sending signals entirely, the trick is to transmit appropriate information to appropriate receivers at appropriate times. From the point of view of the sender, the key to success lies in effective *impression management*: if signals must be transmitted, let them be to the advantage of the sender. In many instances, good impression management requires that signals be true. In other cases, it may benefit the sender to transmit purposely misleading signals.

Through impression management, the sender of signals in some way hopes to control the response of the receiver. However, there are limits to this power. Like the sole, an organism may be unable to control all the signals it emits. Another difficulty is that a sender cannot always determine who the receivers will be. A drug dealer needs to communicate his or her business to potential customers, but signals used also are likely to attract the police. A third problem is the one we mentioned earlier—the sender may intend one thing by a signal, but the receiver might get a message that means something else entirely.

Redundancy

For both senders and receivers, there is some uncertainty associated with all communication. Neither senders nor receivers have complete control over the meaning of the information they exchange. However, uncertainty can be reduced by **redundancy**—the repetition or reinforcement of a signal or message. An angry man, for example, may reinforce his verbal signal—"I'm mad as hell at you"—with other signals, such as a forceful tone of voice and aggressive gestures.

Redundancy helps in football. Coach Mike Ditka shouts and gestures, reinforcing his verbal signal.

A receiver of contradictory or misleading messages also may be helped through redundancy. If we are not certain of someone's sincerity, for instance, we will watch carefully for consistency in the signals the other person emits. If what a person says is not reinforced by how he or she says it, we are likely to suspect him or her of a lack of truthfulness. Even with overlapping cues, clear mutual understanding is rare.

COMMUNICATION AND SOCIABILITY

Effective communication is basic to the survival of all organisms, but some require more complex systems of information exchange than others. An octopus does not require a very sophisticated system of communicating. Interactions with other octopi are rare and not particularly complex. Octopi that do meet attempt to drive each other away, retreat, or mate. The signals required for these simple interactions need not be elaborate.

Communication is far more complex among social animals. Ants, bees, penguins, elephants, and primates, such as baboons, gorillas, and humans, face their environments collectively rather than as individuals. Survival depends not just on the adaptive abilities of the individual but also on the ability of the members of a group to coordinate their behavior and integrate their activities in the pursuit of common objectives. This teamwork depends on efficient communication: members of a group have to know what each is up to in order to work together effectively.

A female chimpanzee greets a male. The role relationships of social animals are complex and call for a corresponding sophistication in communication.

Communication complexity increases not only with the importance of interactions, but also with the number of roles each actor plays. The repertory of roles that loners such as octopi play in their simple, brief encounters is very limited. The role relationships of social animals are considerably more complex. In a social setting, two individuals are likely to play a multitude of roles. At various times, they may be partners in sex, parenting, grooming, defense, and food procuring; the same individuals also may compete over resources. As they work together or compete in a diversity of contexts, their behaviors must vary with the situation. This complexity in role relationships requires a corresponding sophistication in communication.

While the communication systems of any social animals are always fairly well developed,

some have more highly elaborated systems than others. Wolves, for example, have a more complex system of information exchange than ants. Most of the ant's behavior is genetically controlled, whereas wolves are much less the prisoners of their instincts. As we discussed earlier in the text, humans are virtually devoid of genetically determined instincts, depending instead primarily on culturally learned patterns of behavior.

The adaptive advantage of learned behavior is flexibility. Because of the human capacity for learning, we can alter our activities and procedures quickly to meet diverse and unstable environmental conditions. But it is not enough for individuals to be able to change their behavior.

Rather, successful adaptation requires the maintenance of maximum behavioral flexibility at the group level. To alter their activities in coordinated group fashion, social animals need to have flexible systems of communication. Among ants, much of the information exchanged is in the form of information-bearing chemicals, called *pheromones*, each of which probably has only one meaning. This one-for-one correspondence places a significant limitation on the flexibility of any communication. In contrast, humans communicate mainly through symbols. As we will see, symbols represent the ultimate in communicational flexibility, for their meaning is not fixed or automatic.

COMMUNICATION AMONG HUMANS

Humans rely more on learning, engage in a greater variety of activities, and play more diversified roles than any other animal. Of all societies, those of humans are the most complex. It is no wonder, then, that human systems of communication are so flexible and highly developed. Humans exchange information through a wide variety of channels—sight, touch, sound, and smell—but the most important mode of human communication is verbal.

If anything can be considered the most basic element of culture, it is language. Language allows us to exchange detailed information about both interior and exterior conditions. Culture is transmitted from generation to generation primarily through language, and a person's language greatly influences how he or she perceives the world. It is difficult to imagine what human life would be like without it.

Signs and Symbols

All communication is based on signs. A **sign** is anything that can convey information, including physical objects, colors, sounds, movements,

scents, and even silence. Among many animals, the meaning of a sign is *biologically determined*. A cricket does not need to learn how to chirp, nor does it need to learn what chirping by other crickets signifies: the meaning of chirping is part of its genetic makeup. In addition, the sign systems of most animals are *closed*: different signs cannot be combined to create new signs. Such animals cannot combine a sign that means "I want to mate" with one that means "danger," for example. For these animals, each sign functions independently. Such sign systems place considerable limitations on the flexibility and range of information exchanged.

Not all animals are limited to communicating through sign systems that are closed and determined; some primates have communications systems that are based on symbols. Human communication is based entirely on symbols. A **symbol** is a sign with a meaning that is *arbitrary*. Its significance is determined not by a genetic "program" but by social convention and learning. Words, whether written or spoken, are symbols, as is a crucifix, a coat of arms, or a flag.

Because the meaning of a symbol is arbitrary,

(left) In Navajo culture, the swastika, as depicted on this nineteenth-century Navajo blanket, signifies the sun. (below) In contrast, the rise of the Nazi party in Germany and its subsequent impact on the world—including, as shown here, neo-Nazi groups in the United States—has made the Nazi swastika a commonly perceived symbol of evil.

different symbols may be used to mean the same thing. What English speakers call a *dog* is called *der Hund* by German speakers and *anjing* by speakers of Indonesian. Conversely, any particular symbol may have different meanings in different cultures. The swastika, for example, has highly negative connotations today in Western cultures because of its association with Nazis, but to Hindus it signifies good fortune, and to the Navajo, it is associated with the sun. The meaning of any symbol is determined by culture, not by biology.

The flexibility of human communication is increased further by another characteristic of symbols: they may be *multivocal;* that is, often they have multiple levels of meaning. To the Christian, a crucifix, for example, is a highly multivocal symbol. It may evoke hope for the hereafter, provide relief from suffering in this life, or signify the desirability of moral behavior. It may simply function as a decoration; and, in some Eastern European societies in the past, it was used as protection against vampires. By providing a single focal point to which a diversity of experiences may be related, such a symbol may help to integrate a variety of ideas.

A symbolic system of communication is also *open*. Unlike other signs, symbols can be combined with one another to produce entirely new meanings. Rather than being restricted to a limited set of signs, humans can invent new terms and concepts freely, as when the words *smoke* and *fog* are merged to form *smog*—a new symbol with a new meaning.

Symbols also are *abstract*. The term *book* refers not only to the object you are reading but to all other like objects. This aspect of symbol use enables humans to generalize about things and events to a degree far beyond the capacity of other animals.

Because human society involves such complex relationships and because human adaptation requires responding collectively to rapidly changing conditions, it is essential that human communication systems be equally complex and flexible. Symbols are the most complex and flexible devices for communication yet formed, allowing humans to adapt them to whatever purposes necessary.

Language and Speech

The terms *language* and *speech* often are used interchangeably, but there is a distinction between them. **Speech** consists of patterned oral behavior—a concrete, observable phenomenon. **Language,** however, is an abstraction—a set of rules for generating speech. Language exists only in people's minds; therefore, it is not observable. Just as the values, beliefs, and assumptions of culture guide and condition cultural behavior, so the code of a language generates speech behavior.

The capacity for language and speech is innate in all humans. All normal human beings are, in fact, programmed for linguistic interaction. Parents do not have to force their children to learn to talk in the same way that they enforce toilet training or table manners. Linguistic skills are something human children are motivated naturally to acquire. The human brain is organized in such a way that humans are programmed for "symboling," for communicating through signs that have arbitrarily assigned meanings. In addition, all normal human beings are endowed with a special kind of vocal apparatus that allows them to make the wide range of sounds required for speaking any language.

The configuration of the anatomical complex on which speech depends—the lips, teeth, palate, tongue, and larynx—occurs only in humans. But apparently humans are not the only animals with the capacity for language. Some other primates, especially chimpanzees, have demonstrated mastery of some rudimentary language skills (see, for example, Patterson and Linden 1981; Premack and Premack 1983; Fouts and Budd 1979).

Elements of Language

Human languages have two main levels of structure: sound and grammar. The analysis of a language's sounds is called **phonology.** Grammar has two dimensions: morphology and syntax. The **morphology** of a language determines how simple sounds are organized to form units of meaning; **syntax** determines how words are strung together to form statements.

Phonology

To describe a language, linguists must first determine what sounds it uses. Humans are capable of making a wide range of vocal sounds, but no one language makes use of them all. Some languages are based on a larger number of sounds than others. In English there are 45 distinct sounds, while in most Polynesian languages there are only about 15. Nor does English have the same sounds as other languages originating in Europe. The German "ch" sound in the words *Ich* and *Buch* and the Spanish trilled "r" as in *cerro* and *burro* do not occur in English.

The smallest linguistically significant units of sound—units that alter the meanings of the words in which they occur—are called **phonemes.** In English, {p} and {b} are considered separate phonemes because one cannot be substituted for the other without changing the meaning: *pat* and *bat* have distinctly different meanings.

A phoneme may consist of a single sound or a number of closely related sounds. For example, the {pʰ} sound in *pike* and the {p} sound in *spike* are pronounced slightly differently: the {pʰ} sound in *pike* is *aspirated* (that is, it is accompanied by expelling air), while in *spike* the {p} sound is unaspirated.* But in English, the difference is not given any meaning, so speakers are largely unaware of it. Such variations of a single phoneme that do not affect meaning in a language are called **allophones.** Sounds that are allophones in one language may be distinct phonemes in other languages. In Hindi, for example, {p} and {pʰ} are not allophones, as they are in English, but separate phonemes. The difference between the two sounds is considered critical; it is as easily recognized by Hindi speakers as the dif-

ference between {p} and {b} is recognized by English speakers.

Morphology

Single sounds can be significant linguistically, but in most cases they do not have meaning in and of themselves. To create meaning, sounds are combined with one another to form morphemes. **Morphemes** are the smallest combinations of sound that convey meaning.

Leg, store, and *book,* all single morphemes in English, can each stand alone, so we call them *free morphemes.* Other morphemes, such as the suffix *-s,* which indicates plurality, cannot stand alone. Although *-s* adds new meaning and is thus considered a morpheme, it has no meaning except when attached to other morphemes; therefore, it is called a *bound morpheme.* Morphemes often are combined to form new concepts, such as *bookstores,* a word consisting of three morphemes.

We have seen that not all sound contrasts are recognized as linguistically significant in a particular language. Some contrasts are considered separate phonemes, while others are allophones of a single phoneme. Similarly, at the level of morphology, variations that have the same meaning will be considered **allomorphs** of a single morpheme. For example, the prefixes *in-, un-,* and *non-* all indicate negation of what follows; therefore, they are considered allomorphs and not distinct morphemes.

Syntax

All languages have standardized conventions for combining words to form statements that make sense to other speakers of the same language. These conventions are called the *rules of syntax.* The English sentence "If you use the light meter properly, you'll get a good picture" can be translated into German by substituting German words for English, but for a German speaker to make sense of the statement, the words would have to be rearranged as well. In German, the statement would be, "Wenn Sie den Belichtungsmesser richtig gebrauchen, dann muss es ein gutes Bild geben." Translated back into English, but keeping the German syntax, the statement

---

*Brackets around letters, as in the case of {pʰ}, are used to indicate minimal sound units. The small raised {ʰ} indicates an aspirated sound.

reads, "If you the light meter properly use, then must it a good picture give."

The rules of syntax are not learned in a fully conscious manner. All native speakers of English "know" the rules of syntax in that language, yet few could say exactly what the rules are. But the fact that a 7-year-old child can talk and be understood by others is proof that the child has, somewhat subconsciously, acquired a basic knowledge of syntax.

Syntax is a more important indicator of meaning in some languages than in others. In English, for example, there is a significant difference between "dog bites man" and "man bites dog." In Latin, however, "dog bites man" can be stated as either "canis mordet hominem" or "hominem mordet canis" without any change in meaning. In Latin, word endings (which are bound morphemes) play a special role in constructing sentences. For example, the object of a verb will often have an *-em* ending. A person with knowledge of Latin will know who bit and who was bitten by noting the noun endings; the order in which the words occur is not important. Thus, one contrast a linguist would note between Latin and English is that English is more complex syntactically, while Latin is more complex morphologically.

Other Modes of Human Communication

Language is not the only means by which humans exchange information. In conversation, for example, humans communicate not only orally but also through facial expressions, voice tones, and gestures. Style of dress and grooming also may be interpreted as messages by others, and even the ways in which people organize the space around them can have communicative significance.

Kinesics is the study of gestural communication, or "body language" (Birdwhistell 1960). Since all humans are essentially alike physically, much of our body language has universal meaning. For example, a smile probably conveys

roughly the same range of messages in any part of the world. But kinesic communication is influenced by culture, so some gestures or poses can mean one thing in one culture and something else in another (see Morris et al. 1979). In Western cultures, it makes no difference whether an individual uses the left hand or the right when he or she gives someone a piece of candy. In many Asian cultures, however, to offer anything with the left hand is considered an insult, or at least bad manners. Likewise, different gestures can convey the same meaning in different cultures. In northern Italy, as in the United States, a person shakes his or her head from side to side to mean "no," but in southern Italy and Greece the same meaning is communicated by an upward jerk of the chin.

While most of us are somewhat aware of how interaction is influenced by body language, we are probably less conscious of the ways in which information is exchanged through patterns of spacing. **Proxemics,** or the study of the cultural use of space, focuses on the "geometry of interaction" (Hall 1966). Spatial arrangements help to define interactions, such as the degree of formality or intimacy involved. In some interactions, such as a job interview, people are likely to maintain a considerable distance from one another. By contrast, the conversational distance between two good friends discussing a personal matter is more likely to be very close.

The "appropriate" use of space and the meaning of spatial arrangements are defined differently from culture to culture. For example, in a London post office, stamp buyers are expected to stand in a line without any physical contact with the others in line and patiently await their turn at the window. In Spain, however, people crowd up to the window; there may be considerable body contact, even some elbowing.

Another dimension of nonverbal communication involves bodily adornment. Everything about a person's appearance, such as clothing, hairstyle, jewelry, makeup, influences interaction with others. Conventions of dress and grooming serve as ready indicators of social status; moreover, they affect behavior, especially interactions

The use of space is defined differently in Japanese and American cultures. In the United States, bathing traditionally does not take place communally. Yet note that in the Japanese communal bath, the bathers still find ways, however subtle, to create distance between them.

between strangers. A person wearing a police uniform will elicit different behavior than someone in a clown suit. Bodily adornment thus helps to define situations within a cultural tradition.

Differences in dress and grooming often are important for cross-cultural interaction. In highland Guatemala, for instance, each Indian village traditionally had its own special customs of bodily adornment. But such styles of dress all fit within a general type identified cross-culturally as "Indian." Thus, dress also served to emphasize the cultural distinctiveness of all Indians in contrast to non-Indians. Scott Nind (1831), an early European resident of southwestern Australia, found that not knowing the language of bodily adornment in another culture can confound cross-cultural understanding. In his discussion of initial contact between Europeans and Aborigines, he noted that the Europeans' preconceived notions about native adornment and social organization led them to misinterpretation:

> We endeavored to discover whether they had any chiefs, and for a long time believed they had: indeed we had fixed upon two or three individuals to whom we supposed that rank belonged. The natives whom we selected were fine, tall active men, much painted and ornamented. . . . We subsequently discovered that they were all single men, which accounted for their constantly ornamented appearance. (pp. 40–41)

LANGUAGE AND CULTURE

Culture cannot be understood without taking into account its language, probably its single most important element. It is also impossible to completely understand a language independent of its cultural context. As expressed by anthropologist John Beattie (1964), "A people's categories of thought and the forms of their language are inextricably bound together" (p. 31). But despite the many ways in which culture and language influence each other, their integration is not absolute. Each has many unique properties that are not directly, or even indirectly, influenced by the other. People with cultures that are otherwise very similar may speak different languages, and similar languages may be spoken by people with very different cultures.

Cultural Influence on Language

There has been little research into whether culture affects the grammatical structure of a language, but it is not difficult to show that social and cultural factors influence its vocabulary. Inuit (Eskimo), Saami (Lapps), and various other native groups who live in the far north, whose livelihoods and even lives may depend on snow, can distinguish many different types of snow conditions. By contrast, native Fijians traditionally had no word for snow until one was created in the nineteenth century, following the arrival of the Europeans. However, Fijians do have "distinct words for each species of coconut, and for each stage in the growth process of the coconut" (Clammer 1976, 31).

In any language, the elaboration of a category of words is related to the importance of the category to the society, to the real-world diversity of the category, and to the uses to which the vocabulary must be put. The Samal of the southern Philippines, for example, have words for more than 250 kinds of fish. This is partly because fish are a main source of food and cash for the Samal. It is also because many different types of fish are found in the waters off the coast where the Samal live.

All languages have both highly abstract and highly specific concepts. However, languages differ in this respect. Languages such as Mandarin and English, associated with societies having an extensive division of labor and spoken by large populations, tend to have elaborate general vocabularies. Such English words as *administrator*, *mammal*, *society*, and *rights* are not found in the vocabularies of many foraging societies, but they do have their counterparts in Mandarin.

Also, research indicates that vocabulary may be influenced by cultural, environmental, *and* physiological factors. This appears to be true, for example, of color terms. While all languages have highly specific words for colors (such as *peach*), not all have the same number of general color words. Some languages have as few as two general color words, *warm-light* and *cool-dark*; others, such as English and Hungarian, have as many as

11 or 12. Berlin and Kay (1969) found that the number of color terms in a language increases with increasing economic and technological complexity. Research conducted by Kay and McDaniel (1978) has shown that the order in which general color terms are added as societies develop reflects the physiology and neurology of the eye. "Orange," for example, is never found in a language without both "red" and "yellow," reflecting the neurological characteristics of the human eye. The appearance of "orange" is not merely a reflection of neurology, however, for it also tends to be associated with societies having standard dyes, pigments, and schools. The color vocabulary, then, reflects not only the pan-human exposure to color in the environment and the generally pan-human perception of color, but also the differential need of societies to talk about color.

Linguistic Influence on Culture

On the other side of the language/culture coin, language may determine or influence certain aspects of culture. In at least one way, language clearly helps shape our cultural practices: every language serves to organize our perceptions of the world. Language establishes categories by which things considered the same or similar can be distinguished from those considered different. The categories of one language will never be precisely identical to those of another. In American culture, a person's mother is called by one kinship term (*mother*) and the mother's sister by a different term (*aunt*). Iroquois children use the same term for both mother and mother's sister. Such linguistic differences influence cultural behavior. Anglo-American children relate to aunts differently than to mothers, but Iroquois are expected to relate to both in much the same way.

Some anthropologists have gone further and claimed that we are virtual prisoners of language. The classic expression of this is known as the **Sapir-Whorf hypothesis,** named for anthropological linguists Edward Sapir (1884–1939) and Benjamin Whorf (1897–1941). According to the

Sapir-Whorf hypothesis, the structure of thought and that of language are closely related:

> Human beings do not live in the objective world alone, nor alone in the world of social activity as ordinarily understood, but are very much at the mercy of the particular language which has become the medium of expression for their society. . . . The fact of the matter is that the real world is to a large extent unconsciously built up on the language habits of the group. No two languages are ever sufficiently similar to be considered as representing the same social reality. The worlds in which different societies live are distinct worlds, not merely the same world with different labels attached. (Sapir 1929, 209–214)

The Sapir-Whorf hypothesis maintains that the tyranny of language goes beyond mere influence on the way people relate to their experiences; it forces them to perceive the world in terms that are built in to their language. If this view is correct, speakers of different languages will have correspondingly different conceptualizations of how "reality" is constructed.

Certainly language places some limitations on how a person can express his or her thoughts. For example, since verb tenses are a basic structural feature of the English language, almost any statement made by an English speaker must specify whether an event is happening now, has already happened, or will happen in the future. But a speaker of Indonesian, which has no verb tenses, is not forced to make the same kind of time specifications that are required in English. In Indonesian, one cannot say "I went to the store." Instead, one says, "I go to the store," whether that action is taking place in the present or has occurred in the past. According to the Sapir-Whorf hypothesis, the structural contrasts between the two languages give English speakers and Indonesian speakers very different views about the nature of time. The English language stresses periodicity by dividing time into distinct categories of past, present, and future; on the other hand, in Indonesia, time is seen as flowing and continuous. However, even though statements might be easier to make in one language than in the other, there are probably no thoughts or ideas that cannot be expressed in both languages. Indonesians can add a qualifier such as "yesterday", or "this morning" to their tenseless statements.

Although language and culture influence each other in many ways, both obvious and subtle, difficulties arise whenever one tries to show that culture *determines* language, or vice versa. The Sapir-Whorf hypothesis has generated interest in investigating connections between language and culture; it has also generated considerable controversy. As yet, the hypothesis remains unproved.

LINGUISTIC VARIATION

Comparisons made between languages in an effort to discover cultural influences are complicated for lack of clear-cut boundaries between languages. Further, some languages are spoken in many different dialects, and some ways of speaking are combinations of other languages. Linguistic experts find it very difficult to determine how many distinct languages are now in use.

Distinct Languages

How many languages are spoken in the world today? Estimates range from 3,000 to 5,000, but no one is really certain (see Table 12.1 for a listing of the number of speakers of the world's major languages). As many as 3,000 different languages used by South American Indians alone

TABLE 12.1

Major Languages of the World

Name	Speakers as a first language (in millions)
1. Mandarin (China)	864
2. English	443
3. Hindi (India)	352
4. Spanish	341
5. Russian	293
6. Arabic	197
7. Bengali (Bangladesh; India)	184
8. Portuguese	173
9. Malay–Indonesian	142
10. Japanese	125
11. French	121
12. German	118
13. Urdu (Pakistan; India)	92
14. Punjabi (India; Pakistan)	84
15. Korean	71
16. Telugu (India)	68
17. Tamil (India; Sri Lanka)	65
18. Marathi (India)	64
19. Italian	63
20. Cantonese (China)	63

SOURCE: Sidney S. Culbert, ed., *The World Almanac and Book of Facts* (New York: Newspaper Enterprise Association, 1990), 808–809.

have been named in the literature, but this high number is deceptive. Problems in identifying separate languages are many. In the South American studies, a single language has often been identified by more than one name. Furthermore, it is frequently difficult to tell whether the language described by one linguist is the same as that described by another. Some languages named in the literature are now extinct; other categories overlap or are inappropriate. Once such categories are eliminated, there appear to be only 300 to 400 Indian languages currently spoken in South America. Yet, as Sorensen (1973) concluded, "the linguistic map of South America remains impressionistic at best" (p. 312). Similar problems exist elsewhere.

One primary problem in compiling a list of world languages (see, for example, Voegelin and

Voegelin 1977; Ruhlen 1976) is defining what constitutes a separate language. Generally, the primary criterion for a distinct language is *mutual intelligibility*. Within any population, individual competency in a language will vary, but for the most part speakers of the same language should be able to understand one another. One common way of measuring the degree of difference or similarity between two speaking traditions is to compare their vocabularies. While vocabulary alone does not tell us all that we need to know about how languages are related, it is the major factor influencing mutual intelligibility. Vocabulary comparisons frequently are made through a carefully constructed list of *core terms* found in every language: words like *woman*, *head*, and *rain*. Words used for such core terms in each language tradition are then compared to find similarities. But even when such a systematic method is used, there is still the problem of determining where to draw the boundary. How similar must two language traditions be to constitute a single language? How different must they be to be considered two distinct languages? Morris Swadesh (1971) developed a scale for determining the boundaries of linguistic units based on percentages of shared words. Despite such techniques, however, disagreement continues over how to determine what constitutes a separate language.

Dialects

Further complicating the problem of distinguishing distinct languages, individual languages are not spoken or used in uniform fashion. Variations occur within any language tradition. A **dialect** is a patterned language variant associated with a geographically or socially distinct speech community or speech context. People who speak different dialects of the same language should be able to understand each other; the point beyond which they cannot communicate should mark the boundary between two separate languages. But these distinctions are not always clear. An English-speaking person from Alabama and an English-speaking person from Boston usually can understand each other, though they may find each other's pronunciation and grammar a bit peculiar. Their variations on a single language are known as *regional dialects* and are usually easily identifiable.

Distinctive conventions of language usage also may be associated with factors such as class, ethnicity, or situation. These are known as *social dialects.* The contrasting speech styles of English cockneys and members of the English upper class are social dialects. Classbound social dialects are found in most societies where class or caste distinctions exist. In fact, such speech differences are often cultivated for the very purpose of helping to define or maintain a separation between classes or castes. Any person coming from a lower-class background who hopes to rise in society knows from experience that "nothing stig-matizes a class more indelibly than its language" (Bolinger 1968, 138). Being able to "talk right" is almost always a critical factor in social mobility.

Other social dialects may occur in connection with such factors as religion, occupation, age, or gender. The speech style of a minister will differ from that of a dockworker. The unique speech conventions of American teenagers provide a familiar example of the age-related dialects found in most cultures. Men and women, too, can have different patterns of speech. In Japanese, for example, there are definite male and female variants; similarly, the Garifuna (Black Carib) of the Caribbean coast of Central America have very distinct male and female dialects. The original Garifuna came about from a mingling of runaway male slaves and Carib-speaking Indian women. Their different origins continue to influ-

A classic contrast in English social dialects occurs in My Fair Lady *when the cockney Eliza Doolittle is coached in speaking "proper" English by Professor Higgins. The contrasting speech styles of the cockneys and the upper class have always been significant in class-conscious English society.*

ence the speech patterns of men and women. The women speak the same dialect as the men, plus one that is used only among women. The difference between these two dialects has led investigators to conclude, erroneously, that they are separate languages. In fact, in languages that have male and female variants, the differences are often superficial.

Frequently, social dialects are linked with particular social situations. In many cultures, the same people use one distinct dialect for formal, public occasions, and another for private conversation. Presumably, the style of speech Abraham Lincoln used when he chatted with his family was not the same style he used in the Gettysburg Address. How a particular social situation is defined can have an important impact on patterns of speech.

Individual speakers of a language may use several dialects in different contexts. The number of dialects used by a person will to some extent reflect the number of groups he or she associates with that have or require different modes of speech. These dialects, combined with the individual's personal speech peculiarities, produce an **idiolect,** the speech system of each person within a language community. The range of variety in individual speech systems tends to be greater in large-scale societies, simply because there are more kinds of people—members of different ethnic groups, classes, and subcultures.

Pidgins and Creoles

In addition to dialectical variations within languages, there are variations known as pidgins and creoles that reflect contact between language traditions. Until very recently, the study of pidgins and creoles was assigned a relatively minor place in linguistic analysis. Linguists and nonlinguists alike viewed them as marginal or inferior forms of speech. Many laypeople saw them as crude attempts by mentally inferior people to mimic the speech of supposedly more advanced people. Few students of language hold such views today. Creoles are now recognized as the dominant languages of several countries, and they have been afforded official status in Haiti, Papua New Guinea, Vanuatu, and Sierra Leone. Hancock (1971) listed 80 creoles and pidgins in his world survey, and subsequent research indicates the existence of many more. Because of their social and political importance and because they can show us a good deal about the dynamics of linguistic contact and change, creoles are now being studied by language experts.

A **pidgin** is a simplified hybrid language developed to fulfill the communication needs of peoples who have no common language. The use of pidgins tends to be limited to particular situations, such as intercultural commerce and migratory labor. A pidgin is not normally used in a domestic setting, although sometimes it comes to serve as the native tongue of persons who are socially marginal. The term *pidgin* was first applied in the mid-nineteenth century to a speech form that had evolved in China as a result of interaction between Chinese and Europeans. It is now recognized as a widespread phenomenon that may occur whenever there is sustained contact among members of societies speaking different languages.

Despite considerable variation, there are features common to most pidgins. In all pidgins, the emphasis is on efficient and unambiguous communication. Pidgins usually simplify such things as gender and plurality, and they tend to reduce redundancies. For example, "the two big newspapers" becomes "tupela bikpela pepa" (two big paper) in the pidgin spoken in Papua New Guinea. Pidgins, however, also may develop distinctions not normally found in the original language. The vocabulary of most pidgins is relatively limited, reflecting the needs of the specific culture-contact situation.

When a pidgin becomes the mother tongue of a society, it is referred to as a **creole.** According to Todd (1974), pidgins become creoles for two primary reasons. In some instances, people are cut off from their mother tongue and the pidgin comes to assume linguistic primacy. Such a process occurred with African slaves who were brought to the Caribbean, where they were isolated from other speakers of their native languages. Another possibility is that pidgin becomes identified with the achievement of a higher social status, which encourages people to substitute it for their native tongue. This was essentially the case of pidgins spoken in parts of Melanesia, especially among those who moved from their villages to town.

In the process of creolization, the language is changed. The creole must be "large enough to encompass all the communication needs of its speakers" (DeCamp 1971, 16). It must become sufficiently complex and sophisticated so as to be usefully applied in a full range of social situations. This process typically involved expanding the vocabulary and evolving more elaborate syntax. Creoles themselves have changed in recent decades as they have gained legitimacy. This is especially evident in the growth of written creole for everything from newspapers and books to advertising. It has also gained greater recognition as a form of literary expression as Third World poets, novelists, and dramatists have sought to express their own experiences more accurately.

LINGUISTIC CONTACT

We have seen that linguists face many challenges in studying linguistic variation. In addition, it is difficult for them to map the regions of the world where particular languages are spoken because of overlapping. Even within very small communities, there may be speakers of more than one language or very distinct dialects living together; moreover, individuals themselves may speak more than one language.

Patterns of Contact

Patterns of social interaction result in the creation of linguistic communities. A **linguistic community** consists of any group within which communication occurs and which has a recognizable communicational boundary (Gumperz 1962). In southern Belize, for example, the linguistic community consists of members of six major ethnic groups, each with its own distinct cultural traditions and language: Spanish-speaking Hispanics from Guatemala and Honduras, Mopan-speaking Mayan Indians, Kekchi-speaking Mayan Indians, Creoles who speak Belizean creole, Garifuna who speak Garifuna, and a mixed group of mostly English-speaking expatriates. Because linguistic ability (there are, in fact, some individuals fluent in all the languages), inclination, or economic necessity is sometimes lacking, not all members of each ethnic group communicate with members of the other groups. Yet, by and large, these groups do interact and communicate regularly—a pattern that has increased as a result of greater educational opportunities, the building of roads, and increased economic integration of the region. In particular, an increasing percentage of the population speaks English in addition to one of the other languages.

Within a linguistic community, a number of subunits can be identified. In particular, there is the **speech community,** which Dell Hymes (1972) has defined as a "community sharing rules for the conduct and interpretation of speech, and rules for the interpretation of at least one linguistic variety" (pp. 54–55). Members of a single speech community share a common set of rules about language and its use. These concern forbidden topics of conversation, procedures for making requests, means of expressing humor or irony, standards for voice level and the duration of silence in conversations, and so forth. In southern Belize, the residents of a number of small mixed Mopan- and Kekchi-speaking villages may be considered a single speech community because of their shared perceptions of the so-

This sign in the town of Labasa in Fiji reflects the three languages in common use among the country's multiethnic population: English, Hindi, and Fijian.

cial use of language. This was not always the case. Not many years ago, the Kekchi and Mopan formed distinct speech communities; but over the years, through intermarriage and migration, they have come to form a single speech community.

Links between speech communities are formed on the basis of interaction and social ties among people across community boundaries. Such linkages, referred to as **speech networks**, often are formed because of economic factors. Bilibili Island of the Viataz Strait of Papua New Guinea, for instance, is inhabited by about 250 traders and potmakers. Individual islanders have trading partners on other islands who speak different languages but with whom they are able to communicate. While the speech network of each islander is limited to a few trading partners, the islanders as a community have ties with a wide range of different speech communities.

During the period of colonialism, when Western nations extended their control, European languages spread to other areas of the world. European colonialism over the past few centuries has resulted in the establishment of English and French as global languages. These were the elite languages of administration and commerce. Among colonial subjects, economic and political success became identified with an ability to speak one of these languages. For some local elites, as in India, these languages came to supplant their native languages as the primary means of communication, and thus served to distance the elite further from other members of their society.

In the postcolonial world, English and French continue to play a major role within former colonies, especially as a means of integrating these societies into the larger world community. The British Commonwealth joins together nations that share what they perceive to be a common heritage of British rule, and the clearest manifestation of that heritage is the English language. A similar body, known as "La Francophonie," was inaugurated among former French colonies in 1986. It includes more than 40 nations—as varied as Vanuatu and Vietnam—that have come together to create a forum for political, economic, educational, and cultural exchange and for cooperation on the basis of their shared colonial and linguistic heritage.

Diglossia and Multilingualism

Frequent contact with people of other language traditions may lead individuals to speak more than one variant of a single language or more than one language. Charles Ferguson (1959) coined the term **diglossia** to describe situations in which two varieties of one language ("standard" forms, dialects, pidgins, or creoles) are spoken by people in a speech community under different conditions. Use of more than one variant may have important cultural meanings. In Haiti, for instance, the vast majority of people speak what is commonly referred to as Haitian creole (derived from French), but the middle class and elite speak both Haitian creole and standard French. Standard French clearly is assigned a higher status in Haiti than is creole, and an ability to speak standard French is a requirement for upward social mobility. Even among the elite, use of the two speech forms depends on the relative social positions of those speaking and the setting of the speech situation. For diglossic Haitian elites,

creole is used exclusively in private informal situations such as among peer groups of children and adolescents and between parents at home; French is used exclusively in formal public situations, such as in administrative proceedings or in official speeches. Both Creole and French are used interchangeably in private formal situations (receptions, conversations with mere acquaintances) and public informal situations (in shops, in conversations with friends). (Valdman 1975, 66)

In situations where both French and creole are used, patterns of use signal subtle shifts of roles and attitudes among speakers.

Individuals who speak more than one language are relatively common in most societies, a fact that American students taking their first foreign-language class sometimes find amazing. Multilingualism develops for a variety of reasons: growing up in a home where more than one language is spoken, schooling, traveling to an area where another language is used, or living in border areas or mixed ethnic communities. Although the ability to speak more than one language may be little more than a convenience for the speaker, it also may have considerable social and psychological significance. When use of one's mother tongue results in stigmatization or deprivation of economic opportunities and political rights, the ability to speak another language (that of the dominant culture) may greatly enhance a person's social status and well-being.

To examine how the use of different languages influences attitudes, Wallace Lambert et al. (1960) conducted a series of tests among bilingual French and English Canadians in Montreal. Lambert asked people to evaluate the personality characteristics of the French and English speakers heard on tapes, without telling them that the speakers were bilinguals who had made matching recordings in both languages. He found that both English and French Canadians evaluated the speakers more favorably when they spoke English than when they spoke French. He interpreted this attitude on the part of French Canadians as a reflection of their minority status. They apparently assumed that the English speakers would occupy higher social positions, and seemed to have adopted many of the stereotypes held by English Canadians concerning the two ethnic groups.

Lambert was careful to choose speakers for his experiment whose use of either language exhibited little interference from the other, so that the French of a native English speaker would not betray his or her English-Canadian ethnicity, and vice versa. **Linguistic interference** occurs when familiarity with multiple languages or dialects results in a speaker's deviating from speech norms—when a person "has a funny accent" in one of the languages. Linguistic interference is often a major problem for persons learning a second language for purposes of social mobility or acceptability—for Saami (Lapp) trying to become assimilated into Norwegian society, for example. The Saami in Norway constitute a distinct ethnic group with cultural traditions and a language markedly different from those of Nor-

wegians. Because of their minority status and unfavorable treatment by Norwegians, many Saami seek to conceal their ethnic identity in public by avoiding Saami dress, modes of behavior, and speech. But the Norwegian that they speak is noticeably different from that spoken by native Norwegian speakers. This interference makes it impossible for them to disguise their ethnic identity entirely.

Social and cultural considerations usually determine when a multilingual speaker uses a given language. In a study of ethnicity in a mixed Saami-Norwegian township in northern Norway, Harald Eidheim (1971) found three spheres of social interaction: the public sphere, the closed Saami sphere, and the closed Norwegian sphere. Although Saami was the domestic language in 40 of the 50 households, Norwegian culture and language predominated in public. Even when all the persons in a public setting are Saami, the language used is generally Norwegian. In a Saami-owned store, the owner will respond in Norwegian to anyone speaking in Saami. Saami, however, is spoken in the closed Saami sphere—in interactions with kin and other Saami at home, in one's neighborhood, or occasionally in more public locales. But when Norwegians enter a closed Saami sphere, people usually switch from Saami to Norwegian. Eidheim explains: "The Norwegian not only regards Lapp {Saami} as an inferior language in a general sense, but also judges it highly improper and challenging if it is used in his presence" (p. 60). When Saami wish to speak Saami in public places, they are careful to move away from others and to speak briefly in low voices, switching immediately to Norwegian when a person of unknown or Norwegian identity approaches.

HISTORICAL LINGUISTICS

Another way of studying languages is to look at the patterns by which they change. Like the rest of human culture, language is inherently dy-

namic; no language remains fixed. Just as societies and cultural traditions can merge or diverge or become distinct, so can languages. In other words, languages evolve: they undergo systematic changes partly in response to conditions in the environment (especially the social environment) and partly as a result of forces within the languages themselves.

Evolution is not a process leading inevitably from simple to complex. Any culture that exists today has aspects of simplicity and complexity at the same time, and the same is true of language. For example, Indonesian has no verb tenses. Standard English contains a fairly large number of verb tenses, but American black English exhibits even greater complexity in its verb tenses than standard English.

Except for pidgins, all languages in the world today are fully developed, fully able to meet the communicative needs of their speakers. Evolutionary trends can be identified, however. People in small-scale societies are capable of communicating as wide a range of concepts as people in large-scale societies, but their normal communicative needs usually are met with a more restricted vocabulary. As social complexity increases and the need arises to express new ideas, existing words may take on different or additional meanings or be joined to form new words; or entirely new words may be borrowed or invented.

The study of how languages change is known as **historical linguistics**. The fate of a language and the ways in which it changes are primarily a reflection of the history of its speakers, especially their contact with speakers of other languages.

Evolutionary Processes

One of the evolutionary processes that has been identified is extinction. As a result of the subjugation of a people through conquest or other forms of forced change, languages may cease to be spoken. In the British Isles, for example, Pict and Cornish fell into disuse as their speakers either died or were absorbed into English society. Linguistic extinction does not necessarily mean that the society or people who originally spoke the language have ceased to exist, although this may well be the case. With the introduction of

writing, which allows for the preservation of languages in printed form, extinct languages can be revived if social factors favor such a development. Before a language disappears entirely, frequently there is a period of bilingualism, and it may take several generations for the language to become completely extinct.

An extinct language may be replaced by a newly created language (as in creolization) or by an already existing one. The latter is an expression of **linguistic expansion**, the spread of a language among a new population. As languages expand, they pick up traces of neighboring languages. Borrowing of words and other aspects of speech from other languages is especially noticeable in languages that have undergone considerable expansion, such as the major European colonial languages. When the Europeans subjugated indigenous peoples in North and South America, for example, they picked up some native American words and incorporated them into their language—in the case of English, producing words such as *tobacco, potato, chocolate, hammock,* and *raccoon.*

Linguistic multiplication refers to the process of differentiation within a language—the development of variant forms. Frequently it is a byproduct of expansion. As the use of Latin spread with the expansion of the Roman Empire, dialectical variants evolved, partly as a result of contact with other languages. Subsequent isolation of variant-speaking populations as the empire disintegrated led to a deepening of these differences until distinct languages evolved—the Romance languages.

Reconstructing Language History

Modern English has reached its present configuration through a long process of evolution. Because it has been a written language since the fifteenth century, reconstructing the history of English is relatively simple. But for languages that have not been written down over the years, the problems of historical reconstruction are considerably greater. Despite the lack of firm data, however, it is still sometimes possible to reconstruct the grammars and vocabularies of the ancestral forms, or *protolanguages*, and to reconstruct the process of linguistic evolution.

Hypothetical protolanguages (such as proto-German, which would be ancestral to modern languages such as German, English, and Swedish) can be reconstructed by comparing the grammars and vocabularies of the contemporary descendants of the original tongue. These reconstructions are supported by the recognition that languages are systematically structured; hence, the changes that occur must be correspondingly patterned and systematic. The comparative method of linguistic reconstruction makes considerable use of **cognates**—words that have evolved from a common ancestral word. The English word *hound* and the German *Hund* are cognates, as are *to* and *zu* and *mine* and *mein*. Regularities in the slight differences among cognates are analyzed carefully to deduce the major patterns of the protolanguage.

Just as it may be possible to reconstruct extinct languages, it may also be possible to estimate the dates when two languages diverged. For this purpose, Morris Swadesh (1971) developed a method known as **glottochronology**, or sound

dating. This approach is based on the assumption that linguistic changes are orderly, and that the rate of linguistic change is essentially uniform. If the core vocabularies of two related languages are compared and the differences between them counted, a rough estimate of when the split occurred can be determined. The ability to arrive at such dates can help in reconstructing the early histories of peoples, including their migratory patterns and contacts with other peoples. In this regard, glottochronology is sometimes used in conjunction with archaeological work to confirm patterns indicated by the material remains or to offer possible explanations for archaeological findings.

Not all scholars agree with Swadesh's methods and assumptions, however. The main critics of glottochronology challenge the idea that rates of linguistic change are as constant as Swadesh supposes. Since it is known that culture change in general is not uniform, there is little reason to assume that language changes at uniform rates. Although Swadesh's work has been of value, it is necessary to reserve judgment at this time on its ultimate reliability.

PLANNED LINGUISTIC CHANGE

Linguistic change often is not simply a result of indirect sociocultural pressures, but is brought about through the implementation of conscious policy. Because of its role in creating or denying opportunities and forging loyalties, language is closely related to economic and political life. Therefore, those concerned with building nations or empires, promoting economic development, or converting people to particular beliefs have commonly devised linguistic policies to promote their goals.

Creating a National Language

The populations of most countries exhibit considerable linguistic diversity. This is especially

true of Third-World countries, where national boundaries often are more the result of colonial conquest than cultural or linguistic affinity. Such diversity can be measured in terms of **linguistic density,** the number of languages spoken within a population. The Melanesian countries of the southwestern Pacific have the greatest linguistic density in the world. The 3.5 million inhabitants of Papua New Guinea, Solomon Islands, and Vanuatu speak more than 900 indigenous languages in addition to various local pidgins and the colonial languages French and English. In much larger, more developed countries, linguistic diversity can still be considerable. The United States and the Soviet Union possess dominant national languages (English and Russian), but other languages also are spoken by many of their inhabitants (such as Spanish in the United States) and numerous languages are spoken by smaller minority groups. In the Soviet Union, for example, there are 89 languages, including Kety and Itel'meny, spoken by around 1,000 persons each, and Jukaginy, spoken by about 400. Faced with such situations, national governments generally try to promote one or two languages as national languages to help create or strengthen a sense of national pride among the inhabitants.

Creation of a national language, however, can be extremely difficult. Moreover, it can have a profound and inequitable impact on segments of a linguistically heterogeneous country. Vanuatu provides a good example. It has the greatest linguistic diversity of any country, its 120,000 inhabitants speaking roughly 100 indigenous languages. In addition, Vanuatu was ruled jointly by two colonial powers (France and England) with different national languages for almost a century. This situation complicated the linguistic picture, as each power sought to promote its culture and language. As a result, and because the people of Vanuatu tried to make the best of a difficult situation, not only communities but also families became divided into French-speaking and English-speaking segments. Thus, some children within a family were sent to French schools and became fluent in French but lacked the ability to speak English, while their siblings attended English schools. Within the family, all might have shared the local pidgin and one of the indigenous languages, but in the wider world the French-speaking and English-speaking children would be drawn into differing social and cultural (and later political) realms.

The struggle for independence in Vanuatu in the 1970s became dominated by the English-speaking community, which gained political power upon independence in 1980. This resulted in the French-speaking population becoming disadvantaged politically and economically, although not so much that they could be ignored (they make up more than one-third of the population). While English has become the dominant language since independence, political divisions and cultural loyalties have ensured that it will not serve as the sole national language, at least for the time being. As a compromise, to bridge the gulf between speakers of French and English and to try to overcome the divisiveness resulting from so many indigenous languages, the government has promoted the use of the local pidgin, Bislama. Thus, government records and the newspaper are published in French, English, and Bislama, and Bislama is rapidly becoming the language of political discourse.

In creating a national language, political or ethical considerations sometimes compel those in power to ensure that the rights of speakers of minority languages are respected while the goal of national linguistic unity also is achieved. The compromise made in Vanuatu is only one way this problem can be addressed. In Canada, the division between French speakers and English speakers has been important economically and politically. In recent years, the national government of Canada has gone beyond simply trying to protect the rights of French speakers through antidiscrimination measures; now it actively promotes a policy of bilingualism, even though this has faced some opposition from English speakers.

Literacy

Another important aspect of language that is frequently linked to socioeconomic change and development and the subject of language planning is **literacy**, the ability to read and write in a given language. Numerous writers, planners, and politicians have argued that literacy is a crucial part of development because it allows greater participation in politics and the economy. According to Blaug (1966), on a world scale the map of illiteracy and that of poverty have striking parallels. Not only do governments, scholars, and planners perceive the political and economic implications—it is a widely recognized association. Thus, writing critically of Africa's ruling elites, Amadi (1981) argues: "Literacy . . . remains one of the few methods of gaining admission into the new ruling class. . . . {It} allows individuals to acquire the much talked about three Ms: mansion, mistress, and Mercedes" (p. 178). Once one is literate, these things do not come automatically; but without literacy, access to them is virtually ruled out.

While the preceding definition of literacy may serve in a very general way, it leaves unanswered the important question of when a person is considered literate. This issue has been addressed in an expanded definition by UNESCO (1957), which argues that a person is literate when "he {or "she"} has acquired the essential knowledge and skills which enable him to engage in all those activities in which literacy is required for effective functioning in his group and community, and whose attainments . . . make it possible for him to continue to use these skills." In this regard, it is more common to speak of *functional literacy* than simply of *literacy*. Furthermore, the UNESCO definition emphasizes that to be considered literate a person must be able to function independently; one must be able to read and write after leaving the classroom. Needless to say, measuring levels of literacy with any degree of accuracy is extremely difficult. This difficulty is related to what Amadi (1981) refers to as *cosmetic literacy*. For example, some people may possess books, degrees, and academic titles, yet show little deep-seated understanding.

As with the establishment of a national language, promotion of literacy in a particular language can have important political implications. During the nineteenth century, Christian missionaries in Fiji, who were responsible for introducing literacy to the local population, could have translated the Bible into any of 15 distinct dialects. They chose only one, however—one that was associated with the group most closely aligned with the British. This dialect subsequently became established as the written version of Fijian, to the detriment of those speaking other dialects, and helped to augment the dominant political and economic position of the group whose dialect had been chosen. Moreover, promotion of literacy in their respective languages by such colonial powers as France, England, and Spain has helped maintain ties between these countries and their former colonies long after independence. One response to this in some countries has been to promote writing and literacy in a more indigenous language.

Literacy was promoted actively by Christian missionaries in many parts of the world in the eighteenth and nineteenth centuries. Reading the Bible was seen as an essential part of spreading Christianity. It also had the effect of promoting the acceptance of values associated with the dominant colonial powers; some commentators argue that it played a crucial role in the spread of colonial rule. In the twentieth century, Christian missionaries have continued such work among tribal peoples, but more often the task of promoting literacy has fallen to national governments. Thus, in 1919, the new government in the Soviet Union passed a decree making it obligatory for everyone between the ages of 8 and 50 to learn to read and write; the government subsequently set about establishing centers around the country and organizing a mass campaign to promote literacy. In recent years, massive literacy campaigns have been launched in a number of Third-World countries, including Brazil, Cuba, Nicaragua, Tanzania, and Vietnam (see Bhola 1981; Arnove 1981; Prieto 1981). In these countries, such campaigns have been linked to the desire to promote rapid socioeconomic development.

Literacy campaigns, such as those in the countries mentioned, often have been highly successful in promoting basic literacy. In 1980, some 50,000 young people took part in Nicaragua's National Literacy Crusade. They succeeded in helping to reduce the basic rate of illiteracy from over 50 percent to around 13 percent. In many Third-World countries, however, very large proportions of the population remain illiterate in even a basic sense. In Africa, where the problem is the worst, 54 percent of the population is illiterate; in some African countries, the illiteracy rate is between 85 and 90 percent. Unfortu-

Campaigns to eradicate illiteracy are becoming more frequent in countries where the illiteracy rate is high. Here, an Ethiopian boy instructs his father in reading.

nately, according to recent UNESCO figures, in many countries the percentage of people who are literate in the population is declining, since literacy programs have not been able to keep pace with population growth.

SUMMARY

The increased intelligence and symbolic thought that are part of the hominid adaptation are the basis of much of human communication. Communication is a highly elaborated feature of our adaptive strategy.

Although all communication is essential to social life, inaccuracies arise between the sending and the receiving of messages. An organism trying to control the impression it makes may use redundant messages to get its point across.

While communication among loners can be simple, social animals require a much more complex system of communication. Humans possess the most complex and flexible system of communication, its flexibility made possible by the use of symbols. Human language and speech are unique, but other animals also may possess some capacity for language. Our language is a complex system of patterned sound and rules, or grammar, for combining sounds to convey meaning.

Humans also communicate by means of gestures (kinesics), the use of space (proxemics), and bodily adornment.

Language and culture are closely interrelated, although neither totally determines the other. Culture influences language in a number of ways; in general, those things of most cultural significance receive the most linguistic attention. Language, in turn, provides shape to a people's lives, although probably not to the extent argued by the Sapir-Whorf hypothesis, which says that language determines how we think about things.

There are thousands of languages in the world today, although the precise number is difficult to determine because of poor data and ambiguity about what constitutes a separate language. In addition to different languages, there are also regional and social dialects, pidgins, and creoles. Another problem in determining linguistic boundaries is related to linguistic contact. Individuals often are multilingual and in different situations may be called upon to use a range of distinct speech forms, as in the case of diglossia. Such contact may interfere with an individual's use of certain speech forms. It also can produce changes in the languages themselves.

Through contact and other means, languages are constantly changing. Some aspects of linguistic change are explored through the study of historical linguistics, which is concerned with the processes of linguistic extinction, expansion and borrowing, and multiplication, as well as with the reconstruction of protolanguages and patterns of linguistic change. Finally, linguistic change in the modern world is often brought about as a result of conscious planning to promote national languages and literacy.

SUGGESTED READINGS

Eastman, Carol M. 1975. *Aspects of Language and Culture.* San Francisco: Chandler and Sharp.

Hall, Edward T. 1966. *The Hidden Dimension.* New York: Doubleday. (Nonverbal communication)

Hymes, Dell, ed. 1964. *Language in Culture and Society.* New York: Harper & Row.

Jackson, Jean E. 1984. *The Fish People: Linguistic Exogamy and Tukanoan Identity in Northwest Amazonia.* Cambridge: Cambridge University Press.

Lakoff, R. 1975. *Language and Woman's Place.* New York: Harper & Row.

Sapir, E. 1921. *Language.* New York: Harcourt Brace Jovanovich.

Siegel, James T. 1987. *Solo in the New Order: Language and Hierarchy in an Indonesian City.* Princeton: Princeton University Press.

Trudgill, P. 1983. *Sociolinguistics.* New York: Penguin.

Valdman, Albert, ed. 1978. *Pidgin and Creole Linguistics.* Bloomington: Indiana University Press.

Multilingualism in Morocco

Joan Gross

Joan Gross is a linguistic anthropologist at Oregon State University. She has conducted ethnographic fieldwork in Belgium, Puerto Rico, and Morocco on multilingualism and the role of verbally artistic forms. She spent two years in Morocco with her husband, David McMurray, a social anthropologist, where she gave birth to a son. Her study concentrated on language use.

For someone raised in a monolingual environment, it is difficult to imagine living in a society where one has to speak and understand many different languages depending on the situation, the person being addressed, and the topic of conversation. Most Americans associate knowledge of foreign languages with years of training in school, but throughout the world people pick up other languages without attending school because it is a social or economic necessity. Furthermore, Americans tend to associate a language with a nation state, whereas in many places in the world, people in a single country do not share a language.

When my husband and I first arrived in Rabat, Morocco, in the winter of 1985, we immediately started intensive lessons in Moroccan Arabic. This is a variety of dialectal Arabic (called Darija), and it is the primary language of the Arab portion of Morocco, which includes all the major cities. Darija exists in a diglossic situation with Classical Arabic, or Fusha (foos-ha).* Classical Arabic is used where literacy has traditionally played a role. It is considered a sacred language, since it is believed that the Prophet Mohammed received the Holy Koran from God in this language. Prayers are said in Fusha. Political speeches by the king are in Fusha and school lectures are mostly in Fusha, although they will probably be discussed in Darija. Children do not begin to learn Fusha until they attend school, whereas Darija is learned as a mother tongue. Very seldom is Darija ever written, and Fusha is never used for informal communication.

Both varieties of Arabic arrived in North Africa with the Arab invasions of the eighth century. The population living in North Africa at the time was Imazighen, or Berber. Many of these people assimilated the language and culture of the Arab conquerors throughout the centuries. However, a large number of Imazighen still live in the rural parts of Morocco, especially in the mountain ranges. For the most part their language, Tamazight, is unwritten, although in prehistoric times a writing system was developed, and this survives in some areas for use in magic spells. On

---

*For the sake of simplicity, I am using this term to refer to both the Classical Arabic of the Koran and Modern Standard Arabic, which is more often used in formal secular contexts throughout the Arab world.

Linguistic anthropologist Joan Gross (right), who spent time in the homes of women in Morocco to learn the local languages and their social setting, here helps prepare food for her son's naming feast.

occasion, Imazighen use Arabic script to write personal letters or poems in Tamazight. No books or newspapers have been allowed to survive in this language.

After six months in Rabat, we finally received permission to proceed to our field site in northeastern Morocco. Quite proud of our ability to get by in Moroccan Arabic and the response it got us in the Arab parts of the country, we tried it out in Nador. People generally answered us, but saw no particular merit in our speaking Darija because for them it was just another foreign language. We quickly redirected our language lessons away from Moroccan Arabic and toward the local variety of Tamazight.

The language conditions that prevailed in the populous Arab portion of Morocco to the south were definitely not the same as in the north. The role of Fusha was similar, but instead of Darija, the Tarifit variety of Berber (locally called Tamazight) is learned as a mother tongue. Since the schools are run by the Arab government, Darija, not Tamazight, is used to explain formal lectures and readings in Fusha. Tamazight speakers have to learn Darija and Fusha simultaneously upon entering school.

The other language that permeates the school system of Morocco is French. The French colonized the major part of Morocco between 1912 and 1956. After independence, Moroccan schools were based on the French model, with most subjects being taught in French. Gradually they have been trying to change this through a process called "arabization," but French is still an important part of most people's education. The north, however, was colonized by the Spanish; in Nador, Tamazight speakers have been trading with the nearby Spanish city of Melilla for centuries. Furthermore, the northern region is one which many people leave in order to earn higher salaries in Europe. Typically, they leave most of their family back home and support them with their wages earned in Europe, returning home at a later date. Because of this, it is not unusual to run into people who speak French, German or Dutch, or even a Scandinavian language in addition to Spanish, Darija, and their native language, Tamazight. Yet, they may never have been to school and may not know how to read and write in any language.

Language is a complex issue in Morocco. Classical Arabic is considered to be the richest and most beautiful language, but few people know it well. While there is understandable resentment toward European colonial languages, it is hard to get ahead economically without knowing at least one of them. The native language (which varies from region to region) is considered aesthetically and expressively inferior and is seldom written. Moroccans adapt to this sociolinguistic situation by learning as many languages as possible. No one is considered educated without being at least trilingual. Besides speaking their native language, university students can read and write Classical Arabic and French and generally one other European language. English has entered the scene recently as an international language, especially of computer technology. American products and music add to its prestige.

In Nador, I spent most of my time with women in their homes. Language was often a topic of conversation, even among this segment of the population, which is considered to be the most cut off from public life, and hence the most monolingual. Frequently they mentioned that while Imazighen learned Arabic, the Arab bureaucrats sent by the government to Nador never bothered to learn Tamazight. They bragged about the various foreign languages their children were learning in school. A few of the older women had been to Spanish schools as children and therefore could speak Spanish. Younger ones in school could speak French. Others had never been to school, but even these women usually had some knowledge of Spanish, and they all said prayers in Fusha, even though some words probably were not understood.

Popular culture is sometimes more important than national borders in linguistic matters. In the afternoons, after houses had been cleaned and meals prepared, women got together with their friends to drink sweet mint tea and eat together. Sometimes they painted each others' hands and feet with henna and prepared sweets for upcoming parties. But most of the time they simply gossiped and watched television. The favorite programs were soap operas. Soap operas are about secular concerns and therefore constitute an informal situation for language use. So in the Arab world, the language used is dialectal, rather than Classical Arabic. However, Arabic soap operas all seem to come from Egypt, which means that they are broadcast in Egyptian dialectal Arabic and not Moroccan Arabic. One day, while watching soap operas, I told the women I was sitting with that I couldn't understand anything. One old woman who had recently come from the village and who didn't have a television set voiced a similar problem, but the other women were shocked. "But you speak Darija!" they exclaimed. I qualified my linguistic abilities saying that I could get by in the Moroccan variety, but this was Egyptian. "Oh, you know Moroccan!" they replied. "That's so difficult. We only understand Egyptian."

13 The Growth of Cultural Anthropology

A common Eurocentric stereotype of the Polynesian in the eighteenth century, the "noble savage," is depicted here by William Hodges in his painting Tahiti Revisited. *Classical antiquity influenced how Europeans viewed the exotic cultures "discovered" by explorers. Hodges was an artist who traveled with Captain James Cook.*

Anthropology is not a static discipline with a fixed conception of humankind. As are all other academic disciplines, it is evolving constantly.

Anthropological ideas reflect the social climate of the times. As this climate changes, so do anthropologists' views. In Chapter 2, for example, we saw how the scientific explanation of biological evolution gained acceptance as the influence of religious dogma on thought changed. In sociocultural anthropology, changes in viewpoint have taken place in similar ways. For example, until quite recently, many anthropologists ignored or minimized the place of women in society. However, during the past few decades, recognition of the male bias within Western culture has led anthropologists to reevaluate the position of women in other societies, including acknowledging that women have sometimes had more power than once believed, and to reexamine older accounts of these societies. Anthropologists now hope to present a more accurate view of women's roles and status.

But anthropology is not merely the product of the whims of a particular age; it is also the product of a gradual accumulation and testing of knowledge and ideas about people. Through the amassing of accurate information about people's behavior and beliefs, and through the constant questioning and refining of theories of human culture, anthropology has grown into a more sophisticated profession.

In this chapter we will review the growth of the subfield of sociocultural anthropology as a profession and as a body of ideas. We will look at how sociocultural anthropology changed from being a pursuit mainly of amateurs concerned with exotic (and often unimportant) "native" customs to the profession of highly trained specialists interested in all of humanity. We will also look at how the ideas of sociocultural anthropologists grew from naive assumptions about the sociocultural evolution of humankind to much more sophisticated concepts to explain how we go about living in the world around us. The story is not complete, of course; the science of humanity remains a continuously developing and ever-expanding story of discovery.

EARLY BEGINNINGS AND EVOLUTIONISM

While its roots can be traced through the history of Western culture as far back as ancient Greece, sociocultural anthropology did not begin to take shape as a distinct field until the mid-nineteenth century. At that time there were no professional anthropologists, but a growing number of amateurs were interested in tracing relationships between the "races" and in comparing the customs of exotic peoples. For these purposes, the first anthropological societies were established in Paris (1839), in London (1844), and in other major Western cities. The members shared the conviction that non-European peoples were worthy of study, but they differed as to whether all peoples should be considered "truly human" (rather than some form of nonhuman primate). They also could not agree on why people differ in appearance and behavior.

According to one popular theory of the day, humans had been created in a state of perfection, but had degenerated after the expulsion from Eden. The "degenerationists," as they were called, claimed that some peoples (i.e., nonwhites) had "fallen" further than others from the original state of perfection. Another theory held that the Christian God had created the so-called races separately. In this view, it was considered no more of a problem to explain the contrast between Africans and Europeans than it was to show why tigers and monkeys are not alike. Both theories were based on Western religious traditions, rather than on systematic observation—a major shortcoming. In addition, they considered a people's way of life to be determined largely by biological factors.

A more scientific and humanistic approach to the study of humanity developed from the school of thought that came to be known as *evolutionism*. Those who favored this approach drew inspiration from evolutionary theories that had been gaining currency in geology (e.g., those of Charles Lyell) and biology (e.g., those of La-

marck) since the early nineteenth century. They asserted that human societies, like animal species, undergo changes over vast periods of time, with primitive stages of culture succeeded by more advanced stages. Many of these first anthropologists were known as **unilineal evolutionists** because they maintained that all cultures pass through essentially the same stages along a single line of development, moving from savage to civilized. Contemporary "savages" were seen as living cultural fossils. This theory was especially important at the time as a justification for the study of non-Western peoples: by studying them, anthropologists hoped to learn something about the past of their own culture.

The concept of cultural evolution made it possible to begin studying human nature systematically, without resorting to theological dogma. In addition, the evolutionists made a clear distinction between biologically inherited characteristics and those acquired socially through learning. The distinction between biology and culture offered a solution to the fundamental paradox in the study of humanity: the question of why we are all so alike, and yet so different. The evolutionists believed in the existence of biological differences as seen in such traits as skin color, eye shape, and hair form. But they stoutly supported the principle of **psychic unity**, according to which all people have essentially the same mental capacities and potentials. They believed that the most important human differences were the result of social environment, and not biology.

Through their acceptance of the psychic unity of humanity, evolutionists were willing to acknowledge that nonwhites were the equals of whites in basic capabilities. But they were unwilling to accept that the cultures of these people were equal to those of whites. To the evolutionists, some cultures were simply more advanced than others. They saw *progress*, rather than simply change, as the most important feature of evo-

KAFFIRS RETURNING VICTORIOUS.—Drawn by Riou, from a description.

Europeans once placed the Kaffirs of southern Africa at an early stage of cultural evolution, referred to ethnocentrically as savagery.

scholar whom some came to call "the father of ethnology." Tylor's most important contribution to anthropology was his concept of culture, which he defined as "that complex whole which includes knowledge, belief, art, law, morals, customs, and any other capabilities and habits acquired by man as a member of society" (Tylor 1891, I:1). It was Tylor, more than anyone else, who established the distinction between biologically inherited characteristics and those characteristics we acquire through learning.

For Tylor, cultural evolution consisted of "the advance of reason." What distinguished the savage from the civilized was that the civilized person had progressed further in abandoning superstition in favor of customs based on more scientific or rational principles. Recognizing that Western cultures continued to exhibit customs that appeared to be irrational, Tylor labeled those customs *survivals*. Originating in earlier evolutionary stages, they had lost their original meaning and function, but persisted nevertheless. One of his examples was the custom of saying "God bless you" after a sneeze (Tylor 1891, I:98). This was a survival of the ancient belief that the soul might leave the body during a sneeze and that uttering the incantation "God bless you" would counteract the danger. The concept of survivals was important to Tylor's approach, for he believed that they provided evidence of a culture's history and could therefore be used to reconstruct cultural evolution.

lution. To them, evolution was a sequence leading from the simple to the complex, or the primitive to the advanced. This notion sometimes took the extreme form of gross ethnocentrism, in which the customs and beliefs of white people were held to be superior to those of non-whites.

Tylor: The Evolution of Reason

The most prominent of the evolutionists was Edward Tylor (1832–1917), an English armchair

Morgan: The Evolution of Technology

Another important proponent of evolution was Lewis Henry Morgan (1818–1881). A lawyer by training, Morgan began his anthropological career when he joined a young man's club in New York state called the Grand Order of the Iroquois, which Morgan patterned after the Iroquois confederacy. Besides his contributions to Iroquois and kinship studies, Morgan wrote *Ancient Society* (1877), in which he developed an elaborate developmental scheme of cultural evolution, dividing evolutionary progress into a series of stages based primarily on technological innovation. For instance, cultures passed from "middle savagery" (characterized by foragers who hunted and gathered to meet their subsistence needs, eventually learning to fish and make fire) to "upper savagery," with the introduction of the bow and arrow, and then on to "lower barbarism," with the mastery of pottery making. Morgan felt that such stages and technological innovations were associated with the evolution of cultural patterns. For example, he proposed that the family had evolved through six forms linked to his technologically based stages.

Although evolutionists such as Tylor and Morgan made great contributions to the development of anthropology, their works had shortcomings. For example, Morgan's linking of technology with other aspects of culture represented an important contribution, but his scheme suffered from ethnocentrism. Other cultures were viewed in terms of Western technology and social organization. Moreover, the categories of the evolutionists tended to be overly rigid, and their explanations of how cultures progressed from one stage to the next were not always well developed. In addition, they were hampered by poor data. Their information was obtained from travelers, traders, soldiers, explorers, missionaries, and others. Some of this information was accurate, but much of it was unreliable or simply wrong. The increasingly obvious need for more reliable data led to a new stage in the evolution of anthropology.

PROFESSIONALIZATION

By the late 1870s, anthropology was beginning to emerge as a profession. A major impetus for its growth was the expansion of Western colonial powers and their consequent desire to better understand the peoples living under colonial domination. In the United States, for example, especially in the Far West, the government sought information on Native American peoples who were being subdued and placed on reservations. Similarly, when the United States took control of the Philippines from Spain in the late 1890s, it was faced with tribal rebellions. As the tribes were subdued, anthropologists were employed to help devise means to administer these people. Britain and other European nations had a similar interest in the peoples of their far-flung empires. Anthropologists did not simply serve as agents of colonial administrations, however. Many were motivated by a desire to record local customs before they disappeared and were forgotten, both

for scientific purposes and out of a sense of humanitarian obligation.

Museum Anthropology

Anthropology became a profession primarily in museums. During the 1870s and 1880s many museums devoted to the study of humankind were founded in Europe, North America, and South America. In addition, ethnographic collections came to play a larger role in natural history museums.

Anthropology's link with museums influenced its development throughout the late nineteenth and early twentieth centuries. In the United States and continental Europe, this link remains important to some extent even today. Museums affected cultural anthropology in two ways. One was in the emphasis on material culture, stemming from museums' concern for collecting displayable materials. Second, the museum orientation encouraged anthropologists to classify their data according to natural history typologies (along the same lines as stones or butterflies) rather than focusing on the more dynamic aspects of culture. Human practices and ideas were treated as concrete and static, rather than being viewed as in a continual state of flux. Moreover, culture was seen as an assembly of distinct items, not as a system of interrelated ideas and activities.

Academic Anthropology

Professionalization during the latter part of the nineteenth and early twentieth centuries made great breakthroughs in the quality and quantity of ethnographic research. Beginning in the 1870s, the quality of ethnographic research began to improve. In the United States, for example, the Bureau of American Ethnology employed a professional anthropologist in 1879 to conduct research among native peoples in the Southwest. Franz Boas, who was to become a leading figure in American anthropology, conducted research among native peoples in Canada in the 1880s and 1890s. A major expedition from Cambridge University visited the Torres Straits between Australia and New Guinea in 1898 and 1899.

As ethnographic research was improving, anthropology gradually was being introduced into university curricula. At first, the instructors were self-taught anthropologists, since formal professional training did not yet exist. Joint appointments at museums and universities were relatively common and ensured a continued link between museum and academic anthropology. After 1900, the number of people employed as anthropologists in Europe and North America slowly grew. For example, as late as 1940, there were still only a few dozen professional anthropologists in the United States, and even fewer in England. As more of these anthropologists were employed by universities where they came into

contact with other disciplines, the museum influence was reduced.

Diffusionism

As more reliable information was amassed and as the profession of anthropology developed, there was growing dissatisfaction with the theories of the early evolutionists. New schools of thought began to emerge. One of these was **diffusionism,** the view that the main process by which cultures change is through cultural borrowing (see Chapter 9, "Specific Evolution: Sources of New Cultural Traits"). Morgan had argued that cultures passed through stages marked by important inventions, such as the wheel, metallurgy, and the alphabet. Diffusionists doubted that these important inventions occurred independently in each culture. They maintained that critical inventions were rare and that most peoples who had, say, the wheel, did not invent it themselves but picked it up from a neighboring society. Since diffusion was seen to depend on "historical accident," the diffusionists saw no need for the laws of progress espoused by the evolutionists.

Diffusionism was first developed in Germany (which was in the forefront of establishing ethnographic museums) during the latter part of the nineteenth century. German scholars studied specific culture "traits" (such as fishhook styles or myths) and sought to explain their distribution. The German diffusionists of the early twentieth century claimed that initially there were a limited number of cultural circles (*Kreise*), and that human culture had evolved through diffusion from these points of origin. They proposed that such "higher civilizations" as those of ancient Mesopotamia and Egypt had evolved in geographically favorable places. The basic inventions characteristic of civilization, diffusionists believed, had occurred in these regions, and changes elsewhere resulted from the diffusion of these inventions through borrowing, migration, and conquest. This view of cultural evolution became known as the *Kulturkreis,* or "culture-circle," theory. (In certain discredited schools of popular anthropology today, there lingers the belief, for example, that Mayan temples derived from Egyptian architecture, or that Polynesian stone monuments were products of borrowing from South American civilization.) Many of the diffusionists' propositions were little more than speculation, but diffusionism did serve to place greater emphasis on physical environment and context than had earlier notions of cultural evolution.

Historical Particularism

Diffusionist ideas were brought to anthropology in North America by Franz Boas (1858–1942). He believed that ethnology should emphasize the detailed study of the geographical distribution of culture traits. By analyzing these trait distributions, anthropologists could reconstruct historical and psychological processes of cultural change. This approach came to be called **historical particularism,** because instead of seeking to discover universal laws governing the process of culture change as had the evolutionists, Boas called for investigation of the unique histories of individual cultures. Closely associated with Boas's historical particularism were his efforts to promote cultural relativism and to demonstrate the independence of cultural and biological factors. His experience as a Jew in nineteenth-century Germany no doubt shaped the position he took against ranking cultures and against explaining culture in terms of race. His writings on these topics were important scientifically and also served to counter widespread racist notions in the United States that assumed the inferiority of nonwhite and non-Western peoples.

Many of Boas's followers turned to the study of *culture areas,* or regions where clusterings of shared, diffused cultural traits could be observed. The Great Plains of North America was one such culture area, for its native peoples shared a number of customs and institutions. All hunted buffalo and placed a high value on warfare. Most of their societies incorporated the Sun Dance ceremony and military groups. When anthropologists mapped out such culture areas in North America and South America, they discovered that each was closely correlated with a particular ecological zone, such as the Amazon Basin or the Great Basin.

Influenced by the museum tradition, diffusionists and historical particularists emphasized recording the distribution of cultural artifacts and traits and classifying them according to type. They were regarded as separate entities, with little attention given to how they were interrelated or to how cultures were integrated.

CULTURE AS AN INTEGRATED WHOLE

Throughout the first two decades of the twentieth century, the museum tradition in ethnology prevailed, but changes were afoot. Anthropologists continued to shy away from grand evolutionary "schemes," but there was dissatisfaction with the various diffusionist approaches. Armed with improving ethnographic accounts, anthropologists tried to move beyond the view of society and culture as mixed bags of traits toward a more *integrated* view. Morgan had sought to examine how a culture's parts were interrelated, but he was hampered by poor data, and his evolutionary scheme fell into disrepute. In light of the growing sophistication of ethnographic data, some anthropologists called for better analyses of how the parts of societies fit together.

Functionalism

The approach of those looking more carefully at how cultures were integrated wholes was termed **functionalism.** This new school of thought asked questions that were very different from those of the historical particularists. Functionalists believed that what was most important about the Sun Dance ritual of the Dakota, for instance, was not where, how, and when it was invented and diffused, or how it fit into some large pattern of traits in a region, but how this religious ceremony functioned—how it fit in with the rest of Dakota culture.

To understand the complex interrelationships of elements in a total cultural system, anthropologists had to carry out even more intensive fieldwork. A pioneer in the functionalist approach and in intensive fieldwork was Bronislaw Malinowski (1884–1942), who conducted research on the Trobriand Islands (eastern Papua New Guinea) between 1915 and 1918. His classic study of the Trobriand Islanders demonstrated that a long-term, in-depth involvement with an ongoing way of life could lead to far greater understanding of a culture than could a speculative reconstruction of a people's cultural past based on random interviews with a handful of informants.

Malinowski's theory of functionalism stressed that all people share *basic needs*—requirements such as food, shelter, and means of defense and reproduction. In addition, there are *derived needs*—such as economics and law—that are ultimately traceable to more basic needs associated with the fundamental requirements for biological survival. Malinowski's argument was that each part of a culture, which he saw as a working whole, functions in one way or another to fulfill these kinds of needs. This he used not only to explain the more obvious aspects of a culture, but also to make sense of seemingly irrational aspects. For example, he found that Trobriand Is-

Bronislaw Malinowski talks to a Trobriand sorcerer. When Malinowski first announced he was going to study the morals and manners of these people, he was told that "they don't have any morals and their manners are vile." Yet, in his study of ceremonial trade, he found a complex system that linked myth, magic, economic exchange, and highly developed social rules.

landers made extensive use of magic. Instead of explaining the magical customs by reference to the Islanders being "savages," or by viewing them as survivals or diffused traits, he reasoned that magic functioned to reduce the tensions and anxieties that resulted from the uncertainties of life. Thus, he found that magic was employed when people fished in the dangerous open sea, but not when they fished in the safer waters of lagoons.

Malinowski deserves a great deal of credit for his advances in fieldwork and his ability to portray the lives of Trobriand Islanders so that Westerners would perceive these peoples as thinking, rational beings—not mere superstitious savages. However, his theory of functionalism contained some serious flaws. For example, if all people have the same basic needs, then why do not all cultures meet those needs in the same way? Another problem was that by emphasizing how culture functions to meet the needs of individuals, Malinowski failed adequately to take into account those aspects of life that transcend the individual. It is difficult to argue that political revolutions or families are merely the function of the fulfillment of individual needs.

Structural Functionalism

The shortcomings in Malinowski's theory were in part offset by his contemporary A.R. Radcliffe-Brown (1881–1955), somewhat of a rival of Malinowski for the allegiance of students in England. Radcliffe-Brown was strongly influenced by the great French sociologist Emile Durkheim (1858–1917), one of the first scholars to develop the analysis of society as an integrated system of interrelated parts. Durkheim stressed that culture is the product of a community, not of single individuals. He argued that the ultimate reality of human life was sociological and not psychological—that it consisted of the social products of people interacting in groups over generations. This sociological reality (which Durkheim called "collective consciousness") existed beyond the individual; individual actions and beliefs were simply manifestations of this larger reality.

Radcliffe-Brown likened society to an organism—an integrated whole, dependent on the proper functioning of its constituent parts in order to exist. Moreover, society had a life of its own, obeying laws that transcended the individual. His mission was to investigate the anatomy of society and document the dynamics of its components. Unlike the functionalism of Malinowski, which stressed how culture works to sustain individuals, Radcliffe-Brown's theory of **structural functionalism** focused on how various elements of social structure (such as a society's major groups and institutions) function to maintain social order and equilibrium. (See also Chapter 16, "Analyzing Social Structure and Function.")

If Malinowski and Radcliffe-Brown had observed the same funeral ceremony, it is likely that they would have analyzed it very differently. Malinowski would have interpreted the lamentations of the bereaved as a custom functioning to alleviate the tensions created in these individuals by the death. Radcliffe-Brown would have looked at the social groups and institutions involved to see how the behavior of the bereaved served to reaffirm the values of the society and promote the solidarity of social groups. In other words, Radcliffe-Brown would have stressed how the funeral rites fulfill the needs of the social system, not of the individual. The two views are not so much mutually exclusive; rather, they differ in emphasis. Culture clearly has functions for the individual as well as for society.

The functionalists were instrumental in establishing the concept of cultural integration, and they refined fieldwork methods considerably. Their ideas were especially important in emphasizing the need to look at the social context within which customs and institutions occur, rather than simply viewing them as isolated components of a society. In addition, they sought to look at contemporary societies as they actually functioned rather than seeking to reconstruct the past.

But the context the functionalists recognized was still narrow. For the most part, the sociocul-

A funeral procession in Yugoslavia. According to Malinowski, a funeral helps the bereaved to deal with their loss. According to the structural functionalists, funeral rites are one of the elements of social structure that help maintain social order and equilibrium.

tural system they studied was the local community or group, and they treated the group as an isolated unit with no history. This focus often meant ignoring the impact of colonial conquest and rule, an aspect of a more general problem of the failure to deal adequately with sociocultural change. By looking at a social system as a set of mutually supporting elements in a state of equilibrium, the functionalists made it hard to explain how change took place. When pressed, as with the diffusionists before them, they tried to account for change by reference to the outside world, but by and large they ignored the world beyond the tribe or village. Dealing with the impact of the British Empire on African tribes or fitting the tribes into a wider world system was beyond their theoretical grasp. Most of the studies also paid little attention to the physical and biotic environment.

Culture and Personality

Functionalism developed largely in England (although it had its North American adherents). In the United States, the search for the mechanisms of cultural integration came to focus on psychological rather than sociological factors. Since it emphasized the relationship between culture and the individual, this new school of thought was labeled **culture and personality.** People were thought to assume certain personality characteristics in keeping with the dominant themes of their culture. Also important was the so-called nature-versus-nurture debate, concerning the extent to which behavior was learned and the extent to which it was a result of biology (see also Chapter 7). Franz Boas saw the individual as primarily being shaped by culture (nurture). Studies were carried out by a number of his students, one of whom was Margaret Mead, who became one of the best known anthropologists among laypeople. Mead (1901–1978) sought to link psychology with the study of culture, focusing specifically on the ways in which children were taught their cultures. In her work *Coming of Age in Samoa* (1928) she attempted to demonstrate how certain child-rearing practices produced certain personality traits among adults, and that the supposedly universal "strain and stress" of adolescence need not occur in societies such as Samoa, which, according to Mead, values peaceful conformity and promotes a tolerant attitude toward sex.

Another of Boas's students identified with the culture-and-personality approach is Ruth Benedict (1887–1948), who brought her training in the humanities to anthropology. She argued that a culture developed a range of potential themes into a cultural style, much as an individual develops a personality style. According to Benedict, whole cultures could be categorized according to which of these themes had been adopted. Over time, Benedict believed, aspects of a culture that contradicted the overriding theme were eliminated, until the entire system became consistent with it. Her best known work, *Patterns of Culture* (1934), discussed a few of these themes. As an example of the Apollonian type, she cited the culture of the Zuni of the American Southwest, which entailed a preference for compromise and avoidance of psychological and emotional excesses. Another type, the Dionysian, she assigned to the Kwakiutl of the northwest coast of North America. The Dionysian theme involved seeking out excitement, terror, and danger.

The search for *national characters* was an important part of the culture-and-personality school of thought. This involved establishing traits that characterized the psyches of different nationalities. National character studies became important around World War II, when the

Margaret Mead, the first woman to study the native peoples of the Pacific Islands on her own—an endeavor shocking to many in her day—in native costume in Samoa in the 1920s. Mead's work on Samoan adolescence stressed the role of culture in shaping personality.

United States government used them to assess the psychological characteristics of people involved in the war. Most influential was Benedict's book *The Chrysanthemum and the Sword* (1946), which played a role in justifying the American administration's restoration of the Japanese emperor.

The culture-and-personality approach did not break totally with the museum-derived natural history tradition. It represented a blend of the typological work of natural history with ideas current in psychology. The natural history tendency to look for types simply was moved to a higher plane of abstraction, well removed from its materialist roots.

The culture-and-personality approach was rife with problems, and by the 1950s was coming under increasing criticism. The categories proposed by Benedict and others were gross oversimplifications and removed culture from any sense of actual history or other context. For example, Douglas Haring (1949) argued that rather than looking to such things as toilet training to understand the compulsive traits exhibited by the Japanese, they could best be explained as part of the heritage of centuries of living in a police state. Beyond this was the very question of whether there was indeed such a thing as a "national character" or "psychological type" for an entire society.

SPECIALIZATION: WORLD WAR II TO THE PRESENT

By the end of World War II in 1945, the basic methods of anthropology had been developed. Non-Western peoples had become familiar to anthropologists, and their cultures were recognized as integrated and logical. At this time, new trends in anthropological theory and areas of specialization began to emerge. These trends were accelerated by an increase in the number of professional anthropologists. In the early part of the twentieth century, there were so few anthropologists that most knew one another. Today, there are thousands of anthropologists with diverse backgrounds, interests, and personalities creating a discipline of many and varied ideas, approaches, and specialties. The era of the ethnographic pioneer discovering unknown peoples is past. Today, some of the most stimulating discoveries are in the insights anthropologists derive from asking old questions in new ways and from delving into uncharted areas of knowledge.

Contemporary anthropology has been influenced by what goes on outside the discipline itself. After World War II, there was a very rapid acceleration in culture contact. People who previously were only marginally affected by the industrial world were rapidly drawn into the global economy and integrated into newly established nations. For many non-Western peoples, the past few decades have been ones of enormous upheaval and change. The Western world has experienced turbulence during this period as well. Inflation and now debt, the energy crisis, and environmental pollution are among the factors forcing us to reexamine our values and institutions. Not surprisingly, contemporary sociocultural anthropology emphasizes the study of change.

Neoevolutionism

Interest in cultural evolution had subsided by the early twentieth century, and few anthropologists have since written on the subject. Anthropologist Leslie White (1900–1975), however, played an important role in reviving interest in the nineteenth-century evolutionists and in questions of cultural evolution in general. His version of evolutionism has been labeled **neoevolutionism.**

As were the earlier evolutionists, White was in-

terested in the general evolution of human society rather than in the evolution of specific societies. White drew inspiration for his theory from
such nineteenth-century writers as Morgan,
Tylor, and Karl Marx. He was also influenced by
Durkheim and sought to blend functionalism
with evolutionism. To White, the primary force
in social evolution was technological advancement. What distinguished "advanced" from
"primitive" societies, he argued, was the amount
of energy at their disposal. In a technologically
primitive society, people have only human muscle power as an energy source. Societies evolve as
humans find ways to harness new sources of
power—domesticating draft animals and invent-
ing means of capturing energy from wind, water,
fossil fuels, and so forth. By increasing the
amount of energy available, each technological
advance makes possible greater social and cultural complexity and facilitates the growth of
ever-larger sociocultural systems.

White began writing on cultural evolution in
the 1930s, but not until the late 1950s did his
ideas start to gain some acceptance among anthropologists. He published his important work
The Evolution of Culture in 1959, the hundredth
anniversary of Darwin's *Origin of the Species*. In
addition to helping reintroduce the study of cultural evolution to anthropology, White also influenced how anthropologists perceived culture.
For Boas and his followers, culture was a loose accumulation of elements subsumed under the
heading of learned behavior. For White, this was
too sloppy. Instead, he defined culture as a class
of phenomena "made up of events that are dependent upon a faculty peculiar to the human
species, namely, the ability to use symbols" (L.
White 1949, 15). For White, without symbols
there could be no culture. He hoped to establish
a more scientific study of culture by defining culture as a distinct class of phenomena.

Cultural Ecology

Another important figure in the early postwar
period was Julian Steward (1902–1972). Stew-

ard's work laid the basis for the study of **cultural
ecology.** This approach investigates how culture
functions as a dynamic means of adapting to the
surrounding environment. In sharp contrast to
the cultural relativism of Franz Boas, who tended
to see all cultural phenomena as equal, Steward
argued that there are causal relationships; i.e.,
that certain phenomena cause others. He wrote
of "core" features of culture, such as work or
power, and "secondary" features, such as magic
and religion. His focus was on the "exigencies of
work and livelihood" and especially food-getting
activities as the most important core features. He
emphasized what people do instead of what they
believe. According to Robert Murphy (1981),
Steward's work "found its subject matter in the
more mundane aspects of culture, and it sought
explanation in sinew and sweat" (p. 176).

Steward studied resources, technology, and
labor. He saw technology and resources as fundamental. These were brought together through
human labor. Such labor was linked to a com-
mon-sense view of the world in which people
sought to create a living within the constraints of
their surroundings. He found internal and external constraints within all social systems. This
came out clearly in his early monograph *Basin-
Plateau Aboriginal Sociopolitical Groups* (1938). It
described Shoshone Indian local groups and
their subsistence activities—a description based
on an analysis of actual behavior rather than on
the statements of key informants (as was the
usual practice among anthropologists at the
time). Moreover, his analysis took into account
the constraints presented by the environment
and the situation of those living within it. He described Shoshone society as a social structure reduced to its bare essentials, reflecting its sparse
habitat and limited technology. The work was pi-
oneering in theoretical and methodological
terms.

For Steward, cultural ecology was a method for
studying the causal process by which societies are
formed through labor. However, Steward did not
believe that environmental constraints automatically caused cultural patterns, but that the en-

Julian Steward emphasized the adaptive relation between culture and environment. Shoshone Indians, studied by Steward, are shown here in summer, when conditions allowed families to come together. In winter, they had to disperse again, as resources became scarce.

vironment provided part of the *context* that shaped a culture. He believed that most subsistence activities had a degree of flexibility; it was important, however, to determine the extent of this flexibility. Thus, a simple technology limited flexibility in relation to one's environment.

Steward also championed the study of complex societies. In this pursuit, he took a different approach from many others of the time. Instead of looking at isolated pieces of a society, or making generalizations about national characters, Steward examined "subcultures" as parts of larger regions and nations. Thus, in the early 1950s, he organized a team study of Puerto Rico, with members of the team looking at specific aspects of Puerto Rican society, including coffee-growing and private and government sugar plantations, with a view to seeing the parts as segments of a larger whole.

Much of Steward's work focused on change. He looked for like sequences of cultural devel-

opment in different times and places, an approach known as *multilinear evolution*. For example, the development of agriculture in both the Near East and Mesoamerica led to similar social and political developments. Steward described "a methodology based on the assumption that significant regularities in culture change occur, and {one which} is concerned with the determination of cultural laws" (Steward 1955, 18). He did not seek to discover "universal stages" as had the unilineal evolutionists, but rather to determine "those limited parallels of form, function, and sequence which have empirical reality" (p. 19). Recognizing that particular cultures might have cultural features that were distinct, he sought to discover cross-cultural regularities relating to "levels of integration." These levels corresponded to cultural patterns found in distinct adaptive strategies, such as those associated with tribal societies and state-based societies. However, as did the functionalists and many others at that time, Steward continued to see cultures as essentially stable. This meant that change had to be based largely on such external factors as culture contact, technological diffusion, population growth, or changes in the physical environment.

Theories of Conflict

A fundamental shortcoming of the anthropological perspectives discussed to this point is their failure to deal with conflict. Pre-World War II anthropologists assumed an orderly world, neglecting competition and conflict. Motivations behind this omission probably included a desire to present cultures as integrated systems and to present the peoples being studied not as brutal savages but as humans who led orderly and sensible lives. Moreover, colonial conquest of the peoples studied usually had taken place before anthropologists arrived on the scene, leaving them to examine the lives of people existing under an externally imposed order. Employment by colonial administrations may have led anthropologists to ignore aspects of the lives of colonized peoples that might have reflected unfavorably on the colonial governments.

World War II and the postwar struggles for liberation among colonial peoples in Africa, Asia, and elsewhere changed this situation dramatically. Conflict was everywhere, and anthropologists could ignore it no longer. While some chose to view the competition and conflict they witnessed as arising out of unique postwar conditions, perceiving the period to be one of disequilibrium or perhaps a completely new situation, others argued that conflict was a normal part of human culture.

Neofunctionalism

One of the first anthropologists to try to reform the functionalist perspective to fit postwar conditions was Max Gluckman (1911–1975). His approach is known as **neofunctionalism**. Gluckman (1949) criticized Malinowski for his failure to treat conflict "as an inherent attribute of social organization" (p. 8). To Gluckman, feuds, estrangements within families, witchcraft accusa-

tions, challenges to authority, and the like were normal parts of social life. He argued that despite (or sometimes because of) conflict, social solidarity was maintained.

In *Custom and Conflict in Africa* (1956), Gluckman argued that the social order is maintained through the checks and balances of overlapping allegiances. People may quarrel in the context of one set of allegiances, but they find themselves restrained by other allegiances. Thus, people who become enemies in one situation may become allies in another. Cousins who feud with each other in support of two quarreling brothers may join forces in a dispute with another kin group. Through the web of these cross-cutting ties, the social fabric is maintained. Gluckman even viewed rebellions as no threat to the social order. Rebels, following customary norms and procedures with ritual-like precision, serve to reaffirm rather than undermine the traditional order. Their actions are "rituals of rebellion."

Gluckman succeeded in bringing conflict into the normal scheme of things, but he continued to emphasize the fundamentally unchanging social order. In this regard, he failed to deal adequately with the question of structural change—how social orders are transformed or break down. In addition, social order itself still was treated as a given, not as something to be explained.

Marxist Anthropology

Another group of anthropologists, drawing their inspiration from the writings of Karl Marx (1818–1883), also subscribed to the view that conflict was a normal part of human culture. Unlike Gluckman, **Marxist anthropologists** are concerned specifically with the transformation of social orders and the relationship between conflict and cultural evolution (see Bloch 1983; Leacock 1982; Wessman 1981). Marx, himself, in his early writings, and many later Marxist scholars employed a unilineal model of social evolution beginning with the "primitive community" and subsequently passing through the "classical," "feudal," and "bourgeois" stages. In his later writings, however, Marx recognized that the situation was much more complex; hence, a number of Marxists have recently allowed for variations in the evolutionary path (see Melotti 1977). For Marxist evolutionists, the key to understanding the process of evolution is through attention to changes within societies that lead to growing strains and conflicts as a new form of social and economic organization emerges and eventually becomes dominant.

In explaining the conditions that generated change, Marx emphasized the exploitative rather than the harmonious nature of social relations. While functionalists find the maintenance of social order of positive value, Marxists believe that most societies are characterized by an unequal distribution of resources and power. This imbalance creates a continual potential for conflict between those who are well off and those who are not. According to Marxists, cultural evolution is characterized by a reordering of the means of economic production and distribution. This transformation is rarely smooth (as exemplified by the French Revolution of the late eighteenth century and the Russian Revolution of the early twentieth century), as those who prospered under the old system try to defend their status against those seeking to establish a new order.

Marxist thought entered contemporary anthropology in France in the late 1960s, when such scholars as Maurice Godelier (1977) and Claude Meillassoux (1981) sought to analyze the structure of tribal and peasant societies from a Marxist perspective, with particular emphasis on the economic basis of social organization in these societies. Within a short time, anthropologists in the English-speaking world also began to employ Marxist concepts, paying greater attention to historical developments and acknowledging the relevance of the world system for understanding smaller social units.

Studies of Cognitive Structure

Whereas Marxists and neofunctionalists sought to explain the function of conflict in society, other schools of thought that began to emerge in the 1950s and early 1960s focused on the cogni-

tive, or mental, structures that provided order to culture. Two very different approaches are **structuralism** and **ethnoscience**. Despite their differences, both are heavily influenced by *structural linguistics,* the attempt to discover the structural principles underlying speech patterns.

Structuralism

The main proponent of the structural approach to the study of culture is French anthropologist Claude Lévi-Strauss (b. 1908). In his view, the origin of the universal principles that order the ways in which we behave and think about the world is to be found in the structure of human thought. While his ideas have influenced the study of kinship and mythology, their usefulness is limited because they are largely untestable. Furthermore, they view societies as static and do little to explain variations among cultures.

Other structuralists have pursued the less ambitious task of trying to discover the structural operating principles of specific cultural systems. One of the leaders has been another French anthropologist, Louis Dumont (b. 1911). Dumont (1970) explained the caste system in India by reference to three structural principles in that society: separation, hierarchy, and interaction. Although this approach is useful in pointing out some of the cognitive underpinnings of social behavior, it does not explain why such principles exist. This approach also treats cultural order as given. It largely ignores the adaptive dimension of culture because it fails to link underlying structural principles with the physical and social environment. Furthermore, it pays insufficient attention to the historical impact of political and economic competition and British colonialism in transforming India's caste system.

Ethnoscience

The search for the structural principles of specific societies has been refined by the largely American school of ethnoscience (sometimes known as *cognitive anthropology*). Ethnoscientists seek to discover the structural principles of specific cultures by analyzing ethnographic data in minute detail. Their main interest is in learning how people view the world—the manner in which members of a society perceive and structure their environment through language categories and the nature of the rules and principles that guide their decision making.

An early example of ethnoscientific analysis is Conklin's (1955) study of the Hanunoo of the Philippines. Conklin was interested in how the Hanunoo perceived the color spectrum. As we saw in Chapter 12, cross-cultural studies of color categorization have provided insights into the interrelationships between the cultural, environmental, and physiological factors that determine color perception. Ethnoscientists' color-perception studies also suggest that certain features of color-classification systems are universal.

Symbolic Anthropology

An approach similar to structuralism in its emphasis on ideological rather than material aspects of culture is known as **symbolic anthropology.** In this perspective, culture is viewed as a system of shared symbols and meanings.

A principal advocate of symbolic anthropology is American anthropologist Clifford Geertz (b. 1926). Instead of relying solely on people's statements about their culture, as ethnoscientists do, Geertz argues that the cultural meanings of rituals, myths, kinship, and the like need to be explored in terms of how they find expression in the context of social life. In his analyses, Geertz focuses on significant cultural events and the cultural themes that he believes they exemplify. He analyzes Balinese cockfighting (1973), for example, as an embodiment of many of the fundamental themes of Balinese culture. He sees the etiquette of people attending the fights and the masculine symbolism of the roosters as public enactments of Balinese cultural themes associated with poise, envy, brutality, status, pride, and chance. One striking aspect of Geertz's view is that he sees culture as "disconnected." He does not view culture as a thoroughly integrated whole, but as a collection of often very contradictory emotions, beliefs, and rules.

Anthropology itself is not an integrated whole. Throughout its history, anthropology has been marked by a diversity of opinion and perspective. Given the scope of the undertaking—the study of the human condition—such differences are understandable, perhaps even inevitable. In the chapters that follow, we take a perspective that emphasizes *cultural ecology, adaptation, integration,* and *change.* This is not the only approach possible. No one approach has a monopoly on the truth. Yet despite anthropologists' differing viewpoints, there is one driving force behind all anthropological thought—a constant striving for objectivity, for a view of the human condition that is as free from ethnocentric bias as possible.

SUMMARY

From its beginnings in the mid-nineteenth century, anthropology has grown from the musings of a few ethnocentric armchair philosophers to the painstaking attempts of thousands of fieldworkers to understand how and why specific cultures work. This increasingly scientific sophistication has been paralleled by continuing refinements and shifts in focus of anthropological theories.

The first important contribution to anthropological theory was unilineal evolution. Proponents of this theory saw human cultures as progressing along a single line, from more "primitive" to more "advanced" stages. Tylor felt that this progress was based on the advance of reason. Morgan attributed it to improvements in technology.

As museums and universities began to hire professional anthropologists, the quality of ethnographic research improved. Considering unilineal evolution inadequate to explain the variations they were discovering among cultures, in the late nineteenth and early twentieth centuries anthropologists developed new ways of explaining cultural change. One was diffusionism—the view that inventions and ideas were spread by borrowing, with changes perhaps radiating outward from a few advanced cultural centers. On the other hand, Franz Boas's school of historical particularism focused on the study of individual cultures, with an eye for possible patterns by which traits spread within limited areas.

In contrast to the earlier museum-oriented tendency to collect cultural specimens as individual entities, by 1920 anthropologists were attempting to envision cultures as integrated wholes, the parts of which should be examined in relation to each other. To the functionalists, such as Malinowski, cultural activities function to meet the needs of individuals. To the structural functionalists, such as Radcliffe-Brown, elements of a culture functioned to keep the social system itself working smoothly. The culture-and-personality school saw whole cultures developing certain personality themes that permeated all aspects of the system.

From World War II to the present, anthropology has diverged into many specialized areas of inquiry. The neoevolutionists looked again at cultural "progress," this time to explain why changes occur. In Leslie White's view, cultures evolved as they harnessed more energy. The cultural ecologists, led by Julian Steward, saw change as reflecting adaptation to a particular environment. Steward also emphasized that societies evolved in a multilinear fashion rather than following a universally applicable single line. In two other schools of thought, conflict has served as an explaining principle. To the neofunctionalists, conflict is simply a normal mechanism maintaining social order; to Marxist anthropologists, conflict between people with different interests continually places strains on the existing order and eventually leads to its alteration. Still other schools have focused on the cognitive structures underlying culture: structuralists such as Lévi-Strauss have sought universal patterns, while ethnoscientists have looked for culture-specific patterns. Finally, symbolic anthropologists have concentrated on cultural meanings, analyzing events and institutions as symbols of a people's beliefs.

SUGGESTED READINGS

Diamond, Stanley, ed. 1980. *Anthropology: Ancestors and Heirs*. The Hague: Mouton.

Freeman, Derek. 1983. *Margaret Mead and Samoa*. Cambridge: Harvard University Press.

Harris, Marvin. 1968. *The Rise of Anthropological Theory*. New York: Crowell.

Hinsley, Curtis M., Jr. 1981. *Savages and Scientists: The Smithsonian Institution and the Development of American Anthropology (1846–1910)*. Washington, DC: Smithsonian Institution Press.

Honigmann, John J. 1976. *The Development of Anthropological Ideas*. Homewood, IL: Dorsey Press.

Kuper, Adam. 1975. *Anthropologists and Anthropology: The British School (1922–1972)*. New York: Pica Press.

Mead, Margaret. 1972. *Blackberry Winter: My Early Years*. New York: Morrow.

Resek, Carl. 1960. *Lewis Henry Morgan: American Scholar*. Chicago: University of Chicago Press.

Stocking, George W., Jr., ed. 1974. *The Shaping of American Anthropology, 1883–1911: A Franz Boas Reader*. New York: Basic Books.

Voget, Fred W. 1975. *A History of Ethnology*. New York: Holt, Rinehart & Winston.

14 Ethnographic Research

Cave painting near Santa Barbara, California. Probably by the Chumash. Following the arrival of Spanish missionaries in 1769, native cultures in California were almost completely destroyed. The people who made drawings such as this died of epidemic diseases before the symbolic meaning of their work could be recorded.

How can we obtain sufficiently good information to support or refute anthropological theories? Because of the research method of **participant observation**, refined by anthropologists over the past hundred years, we now have a much clearer picture of the lives of other peoples. A participant observer lives with a group of people and observes their daily activities, learning how they view the world and witnessing firsthand how they behave. This form of immersion ensures that the people of interest are regarded not only as abstractions for analytical purposes, but also as real people living within a complex setting.

To intimately understand a group of people, an anthropologist must spend more than a few days or weeks with them. Even after a year of systematic research, communicating with them in their own language and sharing in their lives, an anthropologist is just beginning to appreciate and understand their way of life. But only through such experiences can we move away from static and stereotypic views of people and begin to understand what culture is all about.

PREPARING FOR FIELDWORK

While today's anthropologists may spend years living with the people they are studying, they may spend even more time preparing for fieldwork. Their preparation includes the surprisingly complex matter of choosing a topic and narrowing its focus.

Choosing a Topic

Anthropologists' research interests often are triggered by their own life experiences. Anthropologist David Maybury-Lewis (1968) provided the following description of what sparked his interest in the native peoples of South America, which eventually led him to live among the Shavante of Brazil:

> As an undergraduate I once took a course in the discovery, conquest and settlement of Spanish America. I marveled then at the skill of the early transatlantic navigators and at the audacity of the conquistadors; but what intrigued me the most were the first accounts of the American Indians. I conceived a romantic desire to know more about some of

An anthropologist in India, preparing ground-nut milk, observes as she participates in the local culture.

the people who had inspired such highly coloured narratives and who still, four hundred years later, seemed remote and exotic in a world jaded with travelogue. (p. 13)

Anthropologists who have been drawn to the discipline by their experiences with different cultures, perhaps through service in the armed forces or Peace Corps, often choose to study those cultures. Decisions about specific research projects usually require more impersonal consideration, however. For example, projects may be initiated as a result of gaps in the ethnographic literature. The study of relatively isolated, non-industrial societies historically has been a major concern of anthropology. These **small-scale societies** are characterized by an adaptive strategy that features localized social interaction and the exploitation of local resources. Studying these small-scale societies provides us with a better understanding of the human condition and improves our understanding of specific developments surrounding the frontiers of the expanding industrial world that may be poorly comprehended otherwise. Especially when the culture of people in small-scale societies is not well known, the first priority for anthropologists is to fill out the "ethnographic map" of the area. They do so by providing holistic descriptions of these peoples, gathering information on such topics as their physical environment, history, technology, productive activities, food and drink, daily routines, sexual practices, social and political organizations, medical beliefs, and religion. The goal is to understand the totality of their lives.

Once a basic familiarity with the societies of a region has been established, in-depth research can follow. At this point, instead of addressing all aspects of a culture, the field-workers will focus on a specific issue. Such topics as political leadership, religious beliefs, or the impact of regional economic development may be studied.

Anthropologists also conduct fieldwork among people who are more thoroughly inte-

grated into the world system. In contrast to small-scale societies, such **large-scale societies** are much less localized in orientation and much more dependent on extensive and highly specialized interchanges of goods, ideas, and people. It is safe to say that today most research by sociocultural anthropologists is conducted among such people—among rural farmers or peasants as well as urban dwellers. As with students of isolated societies, anthropologists studying those more integrated into the wider world initially focused on filling in the ethnographic map of these societies before moving on to more specialized studies. Until fairly recent times, studies of peasant villages or urban neighborhoods tended to treat these communities as if they, too, existed in isolation, with little or no reference to social and economic relations beyond the local level. Such studies were influenced by the more traditional studies of more isolated peoples. Contemporary anthropological studies, however, take into account the links between the community being studied and the wider society. Anthropologists see members of these communities as actors in a local setting and as participants in a much larger social system.

Narrowing the Focus

Once a topic has been selected, an anthropologist must struggle with two problems: How might the information sought be explained? From whom should it be gathered?

Forming a Hypothesis
A primary aim of anthropology is to explain why people act and think as they do. In pursuit of this goal, anthropologists continually pose and reformulate hypotheses.

As introduced in Chapter 1, a **hypothesis** is a statement that something observed, such as a pattern of behavior, is associated with or caused by a particular set of factors. An anthropologist may observe, for example, that people are moving from rural areas to a city. A hypothetical explanation might be that two major factors are caus-

Small-scale and large-scale societies are strikingly contrasted in these two scenes: (right) an isolated Pacific atoll near the equator in Kiribati and (below) a busy street in New York City.

To test the hypothesis, an anthropologist collects and analyzes ethnographic data. On the basis of these data a researcher accepts or rejects the validity of the hypothesis or recognizes the need to modify it. In trying to explain rural-urban migration, an anthropologist would probably find that other factors, such as improved transportation and the desire for better education, contributed to the process.

Anthropologists often pose hypotheses to test whether findings in a specific setting have wider applicability. David Aberle (1966), who conducted research among the Navajo of the American Southwest, extended his specific research findings to consider the wider consequences of people's involvement in a specific type of religious movement. In the 1930s, the Bureau of Indian Affairs discovered that many of the Navajo pasturelands were becoming eroded because of overgrazing. Consequently, the Bureau then ordered significant reduction in livestock, the mainstay of the Navajo economy. The measure was designed to protect the long-term interests of the Navajo, but in the short run the policy nearly

ing this shift: (1) declining employment in the countryside because of the mechanization of farming and (2) increasing opportunities for employment in the city because of an increasing demand for industrial and service workers.

nearly bankrupted some of the sheepherders. Aberle found that those most affected by reductions in herd size tended to join the Native American Church, which stressed the use of peyote to gain access to supernatural power. Moreover, Navajo who had become more integrated into mainstream American culture were less likely to join the Native American Church than those who had more traditional outlooks.

These findings led Aberle to hypothesize that, in general, the type of religious movements found among oppressed peoples was associated with how the people were incorporated into the wider social and economic system. He argued that "transformative" movements that preach withdrawal from the world would be found in a particular context. They would occur where people's life-styles had been severely disrupted and where the disruption of traditional life and forced incorporation into a largely alien society had not been accompanied by an acceptable new social status for the population. Testing such a hypothesis requires research in other settings and provides stimulus and direction for further fieldwork.

Determining Whom to Question

If, like David Aberle, a researcher decides to study the Navajo, he or she must ask some very fundamental questions. Who are the Navajo? Should only those living on the reservation be included, or should the study include Navajo living in nearby towns or more distant cities? Should all individuals who considered themselves Navajo be included, even if they were not considered Navajo by a majority of other Navajo? Should individuals be studied who did not consider themselves Navajo, but who by some standards, such as kinship, were considered Navajo by others? Deciding whom to study is not as simple as it may seem.

The people a researcher decides to include in a study are called its **population**. A population may be determined by several criteria. One is the problem being addressed. If an anthropologist is interested in studying urban migration, for example, he or she would probably select individuals who had migrated to cities. Those who had not migrated might also be examined to determine why some people left while others did not. The population may be determined by one or more other criteria: location or length of residence in the city, place of origin, ethnicity, social class, religious affiliation, or occupation. Selection of a population to be studied also may be influenced by social, residential, or environmental characteristics of the area being studied. A researcher may select a village as an appropriate population, or perhaps valley dwellers, or a group of kin because one or another appears to be a relevant unit of analysis in the particular context. Another basis for selection of a population might be local ways of classifying people, such as ethnic classification. In general, while it is important to exercise caution in specifying the population to be studied, it is equally important to be flexible. Part of this flexibility involves recognition that the study of a particular group of people may require talking to others who influence or interact with them.

RESEARCH TECHNIQUES

Precisely how anthropologists conduct their investigations depends on a variety of factors. One is the setting of the fieldwork. Urban research poses problems that are different from those encountered in a village in an isolated mountain valley. In the city, the researcher is faced with problems associated with the greater number and variety of people, while in the mountain village an important concern may be finding enough to eat or avoiding diseases. A second factor is the personal inclinations and theoretical biases of the researcher. Researchers with a psychological or cognitive perspective are likely to conduct their fieldwork in a different manner than those who stress social behavior and interaction: the former would emphasize people's statements and ideas; the latter, the people's actual behavior. A third factor is the problem being studied. There is no single formula for anthropological fieldwork; each problem and research setting is unique. Hence, anthropologists rely on different approaches in accordance with their various projects. Nevertheless, some general characteristics are common to most anthropological research: observing, questioning, and probability sampling.

Participant Observation

Understanding culture requires attention to both how people perceive the world and how they behave in it. But people's statements about their activities are not always accurate or sufficient explanations of their behavior. Whether consciously or subconsciously, an informant's reporting of events is likely to be selective and distorted in some way. If at all possible, the researcher also should view people's behavior directly. But even direct observation does not ensure objectivity, for anthropologists, too, are subject to human biases.

To appreciate the complexity of culture, an ethnographer initially must record events, ideas, and conditions in as much detail as possible. Deciding which data are relevant and searching for patterns can come later. Recording people's behavior thoroughly and systematically requires certain skills. Learning to take notes quickly and unobtrusively under conditions that are less than ideal is useful. Anthropologists also often use cameras and tape recorders; however, trying to keep a tape recorder working in a tropical rain forest may pose problems. Social difficulties may arise as well. Some people may not want their picture taken or their statements recorded. In each setting, the anthropologist must learn the most appropriate way to obtain accurate records of a people's actions and statements.

All people impose restrictions regarding who may observe their actions; therefore, the fieldworker must be sensitive to the privacy wishes of the people being studied. Some activities may be closed not only to outsiders, but also to particular members within a society. While some rules may not apply to the anthropologist, he or she should take care to learn the cultural rules that will affect research. Overzealous attempts to view behavior considered private can ruin or terminate a research project, besides violating the rights of the individuals being studied.

What anthropologists are allowed to observe in a society may change. Many Australian aboriginal societies, for example, have strict restrictions governing who may observe or participate in religious functions. In the past, after building up sufficient rapport with the people, anthropologists usually were allowed to attend and even photograph the most sacred of these. As long as they had little direct contact with members of any society besides their own, the Aborigines did not care what the anthropologist did with the material. In recent years, however, as Aborigines have become more integrated into Australian society, they have been upset to see pictures of secret rituals and sacred objects in various publications. Today, many Aborigines are much more cautious about allowing outsiders to view their rites. Anthropologists have been responsive to their concerns and have tried to limit public access to the collected material that Aborigines deem sensitive.

Questioning

Much of anthropological research consists of asking people questions about their actions. The level of questioning depends on the anthropologist's prior knowledge of a culture. Upon being introduced to a new and relatively unknown culture, the anthropologist is likely to ask very basic questions—how to eat food properly, for example, or how kin should behave toward one another. When he or she feels sufficiently at home in the culture to move on to more sophisticated ideas, subtler questions may be posed, such as how the population deals with deviations from expected behavior, why some behavior seems contradictory, and why people eat as they do.

An anthropological linguist in Highland New Guinea questions informants and listens to their responses.

At the outset of fieldwork, the anthropologist may not know the language or languages spoken by the people being studied; hence, it may be necessary to rely on interpreters. Fortunately, anthropologists often can begin their language training before leaving for the field. Some universities have native speakers on their staffs who help train prospective researchers. There are also language tapes and written material for many of even the rarest of languages. Learning the rudiments of a language in advance saves time and helps to avoid some of the initial difficulties associated with entering a foreign culture. When advance preparation of this kind is not possible, anthropologists spend the early period of their fieldwork striving to become fluent in a new language.

Asking questions takes more than simply learning basic grammar. The field-worker also must learn *how* to ask questions in a society. Most societies have prescribed ways of asking questions, often depending on the nature of the question and the relative status of the person being addressed. The social setting within which the question is being asked also is usually important. For example, it may be considered bad form to bring up a particular topic in the presence of women or children. Or the question, Is sorcery practiced in your village? may not be appropriate in a formal interview, especially if a sorcerer is among those present.

Formal Questioning

Although sensitive topics are usually best discussed in informal conversations, some questions can be dealt with more systematically. Anthropologists use structured questionnaires to provide them with survey data on such topics as residential and landholding patterns, the distribution of wealth and income within a population, and people's attitudes or beliefs on topics ranging from religion to kinship. The question may require a specific answer (How old are you?) or it may be open-ended (How do you feel about employees with AIDS?).

Before a questionnaire can be used in a meaningful way, the anthropologist must have some experience with or knowledge of a culture. Dutch anthropologist Hans Dagmar (1978) described the process that preceded his formal questioning of Aborigines living around the Australian community of Carnarvon as follows:

> During the first two months of fieldwork I collected material solely by means of participant observation including numerous informal talks and unstructured interviews. After about two months I was able to draw up a list of almost all Aboriginal households in the area. From this list I then made a selection of households the adult members (i.e., 18 years and older) of which I planned to interview with open-ended questions. In this I enquired about factual matters such as knowledge of Aboriginal culture, kinship relations, housing, education, employment, income and participation in voluntary associations and asked for opinions about Aboriginal traditional culture, internal relations within the Aboriginal community, the Aboriginal position in the institutions of the wider community and relationships with Whites including such associations of Whites as government departments.
>
> Since it was of great importance to conduct these interviews in a genial atmosphere I took extra care to be properly introduced to my respondents. Most of them I had become acquainted with during the first months of my stay in Carnarvon and to those I did not know well enough I asked to be introduced by a close relative or good friend. (pp. 13–14)

Informal Questioning

Even when formal techniques are used, anthropologists usually derive a great deal of information in a less formal manner. Julia Crane and Michael Angrosino (1974) point out that anthropologists' best interviews often are the result of chance encounters. While conducting research in the Caribbean, one of them noticed an old man out in front of his house gathering stones and arranging them in patterns. His daughter-in-law was in labor, he told the anthropologist, and newborn babies were especially susceptible to wandering demons who might have been sent by family enemies. The stones would keep any such demons from entering. Through this chance encounter, the anthropologist gained insight into the people's beliefs concerning the supernatural, social relationships within the family, and village factionalism.

Similarly, when one of the authors of this text (Howard 1977) began work in southern Belize with Mayan Indians, little effort was made to gain information concerning their traditional religious beliefs, as the existing literature stated that these beliefs largely had disappeared. Initially, this view was supported, as the people rarely discussed such things. One evening, however, while the author was visiting one of the older members of the village, a younger person present asked for a story. The "story" turned out to be a Mayan creation myth. This and similar events alerted the author to pay more attention to traditional religious beliefs and practices. Through informal questioning, a very different picture of the beliefs of these people slowly emerged—one in which many traditional aspects of their religion continued to play an important role.

Probability Sampling

The picture painted by formal and informal questioning is most accurate when the entire population is questioned, or at least, a sizable proportion. But when the population is large, interviewing everyone becomes impossible. To avoid collecting data from a nonrepresentative segment of a large population, the anthropologist can use **probability sampling,** selecting a segment of the population whose responses are taken as a miniature, relatively unbiased replica of the larger population.

One basic sampling technique is the **random sample.** This method involves selecting for questioning a significant number of individuals from the entire population. To ensure that the sample is as random and unbiased as possible, all members of the population should have an equal chance of being selected. For example, all names could be placed in a hat and the desired number to be questioned drawn out. A random sample is best used when dealing with a relatively homogeneous population, such as a group of army recruits from similar geographic areas and backgrounds. Ideally, a researcher will interview a wide enough spectrum of people to gain a general impression of how the population as a whole would have responded to the questions.

When a population contains a number of distinct subgroups, the researcher may wish to collect data separately from each one. This is called a **stratified sample.** In studying a small Pakistani village, John Honigmann (1970, 277) determined from an initial survey that the village was stratified into six levels: noncultivating landlords; cultivating landlords; tenant cultivators; craftspeople, tradespeople, and domestic servants; Marwari, a Hindu enclave in this otherwise Moslem community; and transient Brahui speakers living on the village outskirts. Consequently, Honigmann used a stratified sample of 40 subjects from each category.

Certain projects, such as trying to reconstruct the history of a people from oral sources, call for anthropologists to employ **judgment sampling.** Rather than talking to everyone or to some randomly selected population, they collect data from a limited number of key informants, selected on the basis of criteria deemed critical to the research; for example, age, gender, education, experience, reputation for reliability, or length of residence in a particular locale. Howard (1981) used judgment sampling in seeking to piece together the history of Australian Aborigines living in and around the city of Perth. After a review of the written material available (newspaper accounts, diaries, government reports), the local Aboriginal population was surveyed to discover as many likely informants as possible. Preliminary interviews with those who could be contacted and who were willing to be questioned yielded information on a range of basic topics. The sample was then narrowed to those who seemed most knowledgeable and reliable for further interviewing on specific topics.

CONDUCTING FIELDWORK

In addition to the scientific requirements of choosing a topic, observing, and questioning, anthropological fieldwork requires unusual personal adjustments. The research setting is not a library or a laboratory; the objects of study are not abstractions, but fellow human beings with whom the anthropologist must live and interact. The intensity of social relations brought about by this type of research leads to emotional commitments and to unique ethical dilemmas. In addition, the anthropologist often must learn new rules of behavior and new means of physical and psychological survival.

Gaining Entry

Rarely can anthropologists simply move into an area and start their research. To begin with, the governments and institutions of many countries require some form of research permit. Obtaining one may prove to be little more than a formality, or it may turn into a difficult and drawn-out procedure. On the positive side, this practice of prior clearance helps to ensure that research by outsiders reflects the perceived needs of the country or group being studied rather than just the needs of the researcher. Anthropologists also are often required to deposit copies of their edited notes and published works in national archives or in local libraries, so that the results of their research will be available to the host area.

While research permits obviously serve useful purposes, they also can be used as a form of censorship to forestall studies that could work against the interests of a segment of the society. For example, Fiji has long been dominated by a chiefly elite from the eastern part of the country (see Durutalo 1985, 1986). To shore up its paramountcy, this chiefly elite has attempted to ensure that writing and research on Fiji reflect favorably on its role in Fiji's history and Fijian society. One means of doing this has been through the selective issuing of permits to foreign research workers. Permits have been granted readily to those wishing to conduct research in eastern Fiji on topics that reflect favorably on the maintenance of a social order dominated by the eastern chiefs. However, permission to conduct research on more sensitive topics has been extremely difficult, if not impossible, to obtain. For example, researchers have been actively discouraged from conducting research among indigenous Fijians in the western part of the country (who have a history of resistance to eastern chiefly rule). This control of research has resulted in an ethnography of Fiji that reflects a bias toward the views of those most loyal to the country's ruling elite.

Even with official permission to work with a cultural group, projects may not always be successful. Since anthropological research requires delving into the most intimate parts of a people's culture, the researcher must establish good rapport with his or her subjects. Successful fieldwork is rarely possible without the people's support. The anthropologist must be candid about the research aims, at the same time convincing the people that he or she does not represent a threat to their well-being. Given an honest opportunity to decide whether they want to be studied, people will not feel later that they have been tricked. Honesty is also important for the sake of future research in the area.

Convincing people that a researcher is not a threat can be far from easy. Gerald Berreman (1972) found that the Pahari, who live in the hills of northern India, were very suspicious of outsiders. Most outsiders who contact the Pahari are government agents, despised and feared for their extortions and interference with local affairs. "As the variety of officials has proliferated," noted Berreman, "any stranger ... may be a government agent, and as such he is potentially troublesome and even dangerous" (p. xx). Many people have only a limited number of categories for outsiders—government official, missionary, bandit. Such categories often limit interaction to superficial interchanges.

To escape negative stereotyping, the fieldworker must get beyond the role of outsider and be brought more closely into the local society. Complete immersion is usually impossible, and from the standpoint of maintaining objectivity it is undesirable. But the anthropologist may be able to occupy a position somewhere between outsider and native. Berreman found that after he had stayed four months in the Pahari village and had spoken publicly about the need for Americans and Indians to know one another better, opposition to his presence began to wane. "Although I remained alien and was never made to feel that my presence in the village was actively desired by most of its members, I was thereafter tolerated with considerable indulgence" (Berreman 1972, xxvii). Many initial problems disappear as the field-worker's actions come to seem less exotic and as it becomes clear that no harm has resulted from his or her presence.

Survival

When fieldwork is carried out in poor and very isolated areas, mere physical survival can be a problem. Even when conditions are not severe, decisions about what to eat and where to live may affect the research.

Isolation from markets may make procurement of food difficult. This was attested to by David Maybury-Lewis (1968), who described dining with his wife on gathered fruit and rice provided by a Sherente villager in Brazil:

> Both of us ate ravenously, ignoring the children who gathered to watch the performance. I could feel my stomach distending as I forced more and more food into it. It was a habit we had learned since our arrival. When there was food, eat as much as you can. You never know when you will eat again. A couple of lean days had persuaded us of the truth of this unspoken aphorism. Today we had the sensation which Sherente cherish and which is much celebrated in their stories: the pleasure of feeling our bellies grow big with food. (p. 62)

It is sometimes possible to bring large quantities of food into the field, but doing so creates other problems. It hinders rapport with the local people by stressing the anthropologist's relative wealth. Also, one who has such a surplus usually is expected to share these goods with others. Not to do so is considered bad manners. Stocks meant to last for months may therefore dwindle quickly. In some circumstances, the aims of a research project can interfere with food sharing. For example, when Richard Lee (1969) studied foraging and food distribution among a group of Bushmen in the Kalahari Desert, the objectives of his study forced him into the role of miser, standing apart from the Bushmen's custom of sharing. This made other aspects of his research more difficult to carry out. An alternative is to live off the land in a similar way as the people being studied. One difficulty with this option is that the field-worker may strain an already overexploited environment. Problems like these usually arise only in extreme circumstances, however; most field-workers are able to feed themselves without experiencing serious problems.

Deciding where to live and what type of shelter to live in during fieldwork depends on a number of factors. First is the type of society being studied. Most desert-dwelling Australian Aborigines now live in relatively stable settlements; anthro-

Fieldwork among the Bushmen of the Kalahari Desert, as among people of any poor or isolated region, means doing your laundry by hand, as Nancy DeVore demonstrates. The water used was obtained from a source six miles away. Drinking water had to be boiled.

pologists who live with them frequently use trailers. With more mobile foragers, such as those in the Amazonian region of South America who erect very temporary camps, anthropologists are forced to live much as the people do, keeping their possessions to a minimum.

When an anthropologist is studying villagers or town-dwellers, he or she must decide whether to live with a family or to establish a separate household. Living with a family may allow greater insight into daily activities, but the field-worker's close ties with that family may inhibit other social relations. In the case of forest dwellers who all reside in a single longhouse or of Inuit living in a communal igloo, there may be no choice. Even in a village with a large number of individual households, no one may be willing to take in an outsider. Surplus houses also may be in short supply. Berremen (1972) described the three-room house he shared with two to four water buffalo as inferior to those of most villagers. A researcher may even have to construct a house.

Sometimes anthropologists must cope with health problems. A radical change in climate or diet frequently requires a period of adjustment, which may be accompanied by intestinal disorders. More severe diseases, such as malaria or hepatitis, abound in some research areas. While personal illness may be a way of gaining firsthand knowledge about a people's curing practices, or their compassion, there are rarely any other benefits. In fact, by becoming ill the anthropologist may be perceived as a threat. Charles Wagley (1977) discovered this while conducting research among the Tapirapé of Brazil: "The Tapirapé are not compassionate toward a visitor to their village when he is ill; they become nervous, fearing retaliation if he should die, and they fear that his disease will spread, as well it might" (p. 16). An anthropologist can minimize health problems by knowing what to expect and by carrying a supply of preventive medicines. In preparing a fieldwork schedule, a wise researcher will allow for time lost because of illness.

Field-workers often undergo mental strains as well. For many, the initial entry is difficult. Fear of failure and of not gaining rapport with the people are common. The researcher may not know the rules of behavior in the society, and may find it difficult to know how people are interpreting his or her actions and statements. In many ways, the beginning field-worker can be likened to a clumsy and not particularly knowledgeable child—a status that is hard for most university-educated adults to accept. The psychic distress caused by the strain of adjusting to a different culture is referred to as culture shock. It is brought on by sudden immersion in a culture very different from one's own, with different rules of behavior and different interpretations of actions and statements (see Nash 1963; Meintel 1973).

Although initial anxiety usually wears off as the field-worker's understanding of the people and their culture improves, psychological stress often persists. The intensity of social interaction required by participant observation in a small, closely knit community may be hard to handle for a person raised in a large-scale society where more individual autonomy and privacy is allowed. To escape the strain of being continually "on stage," researchers periodically allow time off from the fieldwork setting.

Not all anthropologists encounter these problems. Some individuals adjust better to stressful situations than others; also, some fieldwork conditions simply are easier than others. Even the most trying research, however, is not without personal and intellectual rewards. In time, anthropologists become accepted by most of the people they study, and often develop friendships that ease the stresses.

Acquiring a Broader World View

During the early part of this century, under the influence of Franz Boas and Bronislaw Malinowski, fieldwork became established as the "rite of passage" for aspiring anthropologists. It transformed the neophyte into a full-fledged practitioner. What the student of anthropology had learned from books and lectures was put to the test and given a grounding in the world beyond the university. Many of today's anthropologists feel that their work is much more than simply a job. It is, according to Claude Lévi-Strauss (1961), "with music and mathematics, one of the few true vocations" (p. 58). And it is ethnographic fieldwork that provides entry into the vocation.

In addition to promoting professionalism and producing ethnographic data, fieldwork can also play a role in consciousness raising. Ideally, participant observation forces the field-worker to examine his or her assumptions about the world carefully. Participant observation extends people's view of the world, revealing the complexity of human existence and the variety of possible interpretations of situations. People who were strangers or mere abstractions become real in a way not possible through films, books, or television.

In a poor southern Tunisian village we'll call "Shebika," a number of young Tunisian researchers found their education and beliefs put to a rude test by the realities of the villagers' struggle for existence on the edge of the desert. Plans for developing the village that had seemed logical and simple in the capital city appeared to be unworkable in Shebika. The group of researchers "lost the typically optimistic self-assurance which it had picked up from the ruling class in the capital city and realized what a gap there is between political programme and social reality" (Duvignaud 1970, 213). Their fieldwork taught them that plans for change had little chance for success if they were not based on a thorough understanding of people gained through participant observation.

The harsh reality of Shebika also made more tangible the concept of the unity of humankind. Shebika's inhabitants were flesh-and-blood people. Along with this recognition came a sense of obligation: "We can't but feel responsible for these people who are part of ourselves" (Duvignaud 1970, 218). Fieldwork, then, may not only increase the researcher's awareness of the realities of poverty and the difficulties of bringing about change, but also can bring home more imperatively the desperate need for changes. Unlike the

Gathering data on Efe Pygmy children of Zaire and how they learn to become members of their society helps reveal the complexity and variety of the human experience.

humanism of the distant intellectual, the humanism of the anthropologist who has done fieldwork is grounded in practical experience and an awareness of concrete situations.

ETHICAL ISSUES IN FIELDWORK

By and large, anthropologists hope that their data will benefit humanity. Anthropologists also generally feel obligated to help the people among whom they have lived and studied—those who have befriended and assisted them in their work. It is not always easy, however, to tell whether anthropologists' actions really are helpful, and long-term consequences are difficult to predict.

Cora DuBois (1960) conducted research in the village of Atimelang on the Indonesian island of Alor in 1938. She had done no apparent harm to the people by the time she left, and she had taught them a little about the outside world and provided them with a bit of excitement. As DuBois recalled, shortly after the Japanese occupied the island of Alor in 1942,

> word reached the Japanese command in Kalabahi that the village leaders of Atimelang were claiming that America would win the war. This could have been nothing but the most innocent fantasy to my friends in Atimelang since they had never even heard of the United States prior to my arrival. But to the Japanese, suffering from all the nervous apprehensions of any occupying power in a strange and therefore threatening environment, such talk could only mean rebellion . . . so the Japanese sent troops to arrest five of my friends in Atimelang. . . . In Kalabahi they were publicly decapitated as a warning to the populace.
>
> There is no end to the intricate chain of responsibility and guilt that the pursuit of even the most arcane social research involves. (pp. xiv–xv)

Anthropologists must be sensitive to the potentially adverse effects of their work. By acting as informants for government administrators or corporate employees who want information about isolated regions of a country and its cultural minorities, anthropologists can benefit the people with whom they are working, correcting misinformation or acting on their behalf. But unwittingly they may also supply information that can be used against native populations. Anthropologists sometimes are privy to such illegal activities as smuggling, tax evasion, and the brewing of illegal beer. This raises questions about maintaining confidentiality regarding the sources of such sensitive data and not making public any information that may harm people.

Discretion also is required in publishing the results of fieldwork. While most anthropological publications have not had harmful effects on people, there have been exceptions. In publishing an account of a society, data might be included that for the sake of the society would better have been left out. Thus, in one account of an impoverished East African society displaced from its original homeland, it was noted that a significant part of the people's economy was concerned with the smuggling of stolen cattle. The account was sufficiently detailed to allow government agents to move against the smugglers—a situation involving serious ethical questions.

A basic issue related to the previous example concerns the audience anthropologists address. While academics of industrial nations are the primary readers of anthropological writing, the people studied by anthropologists and those living in close proximity to them are becoming increasingly likely to read these accounts. Many people once labeled "illiterate primitives" now read, and most former colonies now boast institutions of higher education and even anthropology programs. Anthropologists from industrial countries should make their data available to these people. Most anthropologists today are careful to see that their work gets back to the national archives of countries in which they have worked and, if possible, to the residents of the actual communities. Some have written books in the local language to be read and distributed among the people who were studied. This, of course, means that anthropologists must be more sensitive than ever in the manner in which they write up their studies.

In most instances, anthropologists are confronted with few ethical dilemmas concerning sources of their financial support for research. But, as several anthropologists who worked in Thailand during the 1960s discovered, there are exceptions here also. These anthropologists were funded by a United States government agency to conduct fieldwork among isolated hill-dwelling peoples. The prospect was appealing because ethnographic data on these people were sparse. Eventually the anthropologists learned that the information they were collecting was being used for military purposes. This led a number of those involved to quit the project, feeling that the application of their work was not in the best interest of anthropology or the people being studied (see Jones 1971).

One of the issues raised in the Thailand situation is the propriety of secrecy in anthropological fieldwork. Is it *ever* proper for anthropologists to hide the sources of their support from the people they are studying, or not tell them the purpose of the research or the uses to which it might be put? Most anthropologists consider it imperative that those who are the subjects of anthropological research be provided with a clear understanding of these matters from the outset. Secrecy in this regard is ethically questionable and potentially harmful to the reputation of anthropology.

SUMMARY

Cultural anthropologists' principal method of conducting research is participant observation, which requires that a researcher live with the people under study. The anthropologist begins by selecting a general area of interest. Anthropologists gather information on relatively isolated small-scale societies as well as on subgroups of larger societies. Then they focus on specific topics and locales.

Preliminary research is usually very general. Once anthropologists have a fairly good idea of the culture of the area, they begin to focus on more specific problems in their research. They formulate hypotheses to explain what they expect to find and define the population to be studied.

In actually conducting participant observation research, anthropologists often face physical difficulties in recording information and social constraints regarding what they may view or record. Furthermore, they must learn the appropriate ways in which to conduct interviews in a society. Questions may be asked formally through questionnaires as well as informally through conversations. Since it is not always possible or desirable to speak to everyone in a population, anthropologists frequently resort to probability sampling techniques—random sampling, stratified sampling, or judgment sampling.

Anthropologists must get the permission of the people to be studied to conduct their fieldwork, and sometimes that of government or institutional officials as well. Since the anthropologist is to live among the people being studied, it is essential that he or she build good relations with them.

A number of problems associated with living in the field relate to food, residence, health, and mental stress. But fieldwork turns people into full-fledged anthropologists, and it can also help broaden their view of the world in a very concrete way.

It is difficult to assess the consequences of an anthropologist's work. To avoid negative repercussions for people studied, anthropologists must be very careful about what happens to the information they gather. Their responsibility also includes ensuring that the people they study have access to the results of the research.

SUGGESTED READINGS

Barnes, John A. 1980. *Who Should Know What? Social Science, Privacy and Ethics*. Cambridge: Cambridge University Press.

Cassall, Joan, and Murray L. Wax. 1980. *Ethical Problems of Fieldwork*. Special issue of *Social Problems* 27.

Cesara, Mr. 1982. *Reflections of a Woman Anthropologist*. New York: Academic Press. (Fieldwork in Africa)

Edgerton, Robert B., and L. L. Langness. 1974. *Methods and Styles in the Study of Culture*. San Francisco: Chandler and Sharp.

Malinowski, Bronislaw. 1967. *A Diary in the Strict Sense of the Term*. London: Routledge and Kegan Paul. (Early fieldwork in Melanesia)

Maybury-Lewis, David. 1968. *The Savage and the Innocent*. Boston: Beacon Press. (Fieldwork in Central Brazil)

Mead, Margaret. 1977. *Letters from the Field: 1925–1975*. New York: Harper & Row. (Fieldwork in the Pacific)

Pelto, Perti J., and H. Gretal. 1978. *Anthropological Research: The Structure of Inquiry*. Cambridge: Cambridge University Press.

Powdermaker, Hortense. 1966. *Stranger and Friend: The Ways of an Anthropologist*. New York: Norton.

Spradley, James P. 1980. *Participant Observation*. New York: Holt, Rinehart & Winston.

Fieldwork on Rabi Island:
An Experiment in Development

Hans Dagmar

Hans Dagmar is senior lecturer in the Department of Research Methodology and Statistics of the University of Nijmegen in the Netherlands. Between 1972 and 1984, he spent two separate one-year periods and several shorter ones among Aborigines in northwestern Australia. In the course of this fieldwork, he became closely involved in the Aborigines' efforts to regain control of land and to improve their living conditions. In 1985, with his wife and younger son, Dr. Dagmar lived for one year on Rabi Island in Fiji and went back for shorter visits in 1986 and 1988. During the last period, he cooperated with the Rabi Council of Leaders and local fishermen in working out the details of a small-scale commercial fishing project.

In a bustling street of Suva, the capital of Fiji, a brass sign marks the entrance to the "Rabi Council of Leaders." Here, in 1985, I began fieldwork to address problems of the development of Rabi Island, more than 200 kilometers away, in the northeast part of the country.

The Council is located on a block of shops and offices owned by the people of Rabi. On the office's teleprinter, messages from the Council's Australia-based economic adviser indicate the results of investments in overseas stocks and bonds.

The Rabi Council of Leaders are the elected representatives of the Banaban people, who now number more than 4,000. Most Banabans fish and plant for a living on Rabi Island, some 72 square kilometers in size. In 1945, the

Banabans bought Rabi from a private company exploiting coconut plantations; at that time, there was no longer a native Fijian population on the island. Settling on Rabi, the Banabans left behind their tiny and isolated home island, Banaba, or Ocean Island, more than 2,000 kilometers away from Fiji, in what is now the Pacific nation of Kiribati. In 1900, intensive phosphate mining began on Banaba, throwing the fishing and fruit-gathering Banabans headlong into the colonial economy. The ensuing history of these people is an extraordinary tale of its leaders learning to bargain for royalty payments, culminating in the 1970s in a lawsuit against the British government aimed at seeking compensation for the destruction of their homeland.

Because phosphate payments had ceased after termination of mining in 1980, the Council was looking for new ways of providing for the fast-growing number of Banabans. My research was seen as a possible contribution to this effort. Although I was well aware of the burden of such expectations, I did not want to back away from the task. Thorough anthropological fact-finding is a most useful basis for development planning.

It was the Council's explicit wish that I pay attention to the people's perception of the Council's role in the development process. As I was soon to find out, on Rabi there was growing uneasiness among the Banabans about their low standard of living and the Council's

Dr. Hans Dagmar (third from right) with the Rabi Council of Leaders.

performance in remedying the situation. As one informant explained:

> Development seems to be so late here; it should have been picked up long ago. We Banabans have looked to the past so much, everything seemed to revolve around the court case. I remember the British did a study on development on Rabi, but nothing really came of it. In those days the Council was concentrating on getting justice.

After arrival on Rabi, together with my wife and two Banaban assistants (a man and a woman), I began a survey of the economy and social organization of Banaban households. We formed two teams and visited every household on the island. Of course, we could permit ourselves this approach only because of the limited size of the Rabi population. After nearly 500 interviews, we not only had a very useful body of census material, we also had been able to show our faces and explain what we were doing in all four villages and smaller settlements of the island. Apart from gathering factual data on such things as types of crops planted, methods of organizing agriculture and fishing, and patterns of income and consumption, we also sought information on the people's attitudes and aspirations regarding future development of their community. Suppositions gained from the survey were then taken as the basis for a more informal and largely open-ended interview schedule with which we approached a sample of households and experts in various fields of Banaban life.

Between sessions of interviewing, and considerably helped by the presence of my family, I had ample opportunity to learn more about Banaban life by participating in family gatherings and other social events through a network of friends that we gradually developed. Performing various types of administrative tasks for the Council and participating in many of its meetings increased my insight into Council operations.

After one year of fieldwork, and contrary to popular belief in Fiji, I had detailed evidence that well over half of the Banabans were desperately poor, even according to Third-World standards. But to raise their standard of living, was it enough to have charted Rabi's social and natural resources, the wider regional impediments to development, and the limitations of the people and its Council in resource management?

From an anthropological point of view, it was also necessary to offer an interpretation. In fact, the chair of the Rabi Council, a man with exceptional leadership qualities, had asked for such an interpretation soon after I began my fieldwork. He put it in the following terms:

> The past will be explained by us. We will tell you how our economic enterprises went down. We will tell you about all this and then you can ask us questions. You will get answers from the councillors, from the old people and then you can use these answers for suggestions for the future.

While not presuming to know how the Banabans should live their lives, I had clearly learned from my research how heavily the past was still bearing down on these people. Ever since settling on Rabi, the Banabans had also retained ownership of the island of Banaba. It

was the Rabi Council who, with full support of the people, for more than 40 years had managed to maintain a "two-island identity"; by this means, the Council had secured a moral and actual entitlement to relatively large payments of phosphate money. But the reverse side of the Council's skillfully played political role was a one-sided focus on the world outside Rabi; hence, a strong reliance on outside "experts" (including myself) and a view of development primarily in terms of finance. Increasing the cash flow to the Banabans became a measure of development, and to secure this the Council invested in enterprises outside Rabi, all of which were failures.

Going beyond "pure research," I worked out a modest experiment aimed at shifting the development emphasis to one of cooperation between the Council and the people in small, locally controlled forms of enterprise. Together with members of Council, I found an agency that was willing to finance a commercial fishing project. In 1988 I returned to Rabi and, after months of very close consultation with the Banaban fishermen, presented a detailed working plan for the project. It was essentially based on local control with explicit strategies for continuous adaptation by the local management group as the project was unfolding and new information and special requirements of the fishermen emerged.

But, again, history seemed to overtake the Banabans. When funds for the project arrived, the Council did not use them to equip and organize local fishermen; rather, it chose to invest in a large-scale commercial fishing enterprise in the capital, Suva. The joint venture ended in financial disaster.

Yet, the experiment is not over. Shortly before writing this essay in early 1991, I received a letter from the Rabi Council's chair. He informed me of the Council's intention to attempt to secure new funds for implementing the fishing scheme as originally conceived.

15 Patterns of Subsistence and Economic Systems

The Loo family planting rice, near Vientiane, Laos. The spread of cultivation throughout East Asia and Southeast Asia supported the rise of sophisticated large-scale societies in that part of the world.

To survive we must eat. But unlike other animals, we humans are rarely satisfied with getting food by gathering or killing whatever we come upon by chance. We desire more security, more variety, and often simply more to eat. Accordingly, we spend a good deal of time learning how to acquire food and exploring ways to increase the amount available. In some instances, food procurement is done individually, but more often it involves group efforts. Closely related to procurement is the manufacture of implements to assist us in gathering, capturing, and producing food. While a few other animals have devised simple tools to help them in acquiring food, humans have developed much more intricate and sophisticated tools than those employed by any other species.

Human existence is more than a matter of food, of course. We expect to obtain a much wider range of things if we are to live as "hu-

mans" and not as "animals." To humans, the so-called necessities of life are not only those things we need to survive; often they are amenities prescribed by culture—companionship, physical adornment, means of transportation. We also produce many things that are not necessities—our videos, frozen yogurt, and Nikes do not sustain us, although we may sometimes think they do. Even people with relatively simple technologies and few material possessions produce an assortment of toys, trinkets, and other nonessentials.

In this chapter, we will look not only at the features of the major patterns of subsistence—the ways that humans have devised to procure the fundamental things they need or want—but also at the basic elements of economic systems. We will see how production, ownership, and exchange are organized in different societies.

PATTERNS OF SUBSISTENCE

As discussed in earlier chapters, since *Homo sapiens* appeared some 300,000 years ago and spread across the continents, human cultures have evolved and become more complex. The economic basis for most of this period was foraging (hunting and gathering). As populations grew and human knowledge increased, new subsistence patterns, based on agriculture and the domestication of animals, evolved. These in turn were intensified as large-scale societies appeared, and with them even more complex and efficient subsistence patterns.

Small-Scale Foraging Societies

In today's world, very few foraging societies exist. Foragers have not done well in competition with nonforagers. European expansion over the past few centuries, in particular, has led to the demise of many foraging groups. Today, these groups are found almost exclusively in the harshest and most remote areas of the world—in regions that no one else wants to occupy and where competition with nonforagers is at a minimum (for example, arctic regions and the deserts of Australia and southern Africa). Contemporary foraging societies differ in many ways from earlier ones because they have evolved for thousands of years, usually in contact with and under the influence of nonforagers. These modern-day foragers are not simply relics of the Stone Age; their life-style is influenced by the contemporary world, and they are active participants in the modern world system.

The popular view of foragers is one of people barely surviving on the edge of extinction. The contemporary societies that have contributed to this image, however—the Inuit, Bushmen, Aborigines of central Australia, and similar societies—are far from typical of foragers prior to contact with nonforaging societies. Most foragers previously lived in more hospitable environments with ready access to sufficient food sources,

making it possible to meet their subsistence needs with only a few hours of work per day. Real scarcity and hardship were rare.

According to Martin (1974), there are three basic types of foraging adaptation: pedestrian hunting and gathering, equestrian hunting and gathering, and aquatic foraging. Although all are associated with relatively small-scale societies, aspects of the people's lives differ considerably.

Pedestrian Hunters and Gatherers

Most foragers are pedestrian hunters and gatherers, hunting wild animals and gathering wild edible plants on foot. Contemporary pedestrian hunters and gatherers include most of the foragers in Australia, the BaMbuti and Bushmen of central and southern Africa, and the Cree and similar groups of northern Canada.

In most of these societies, men hunt and women forage, and there is little else in the way of labor specialization. The relative importance of hunting and gathering for these societies varies, but gathering generally provides the bulk of what is eaten. This means that women usually contribute the largest share of the food. Women also are usually responsible for food preparation, although men may prepare game.

Most pedestrian hunters and gatherers are organized into small nomadic groups known as **bands**—groups that wander from place to place to meet subsistence needs, rather than residing in a fixed locale. The optimum size of a band for efficient use of resources is between 15 and 25 individuals, depending on the environment. Kinship plays a prominent role in recruitment to band membership. In fact, kinship often is the principal medium for expressing social and economic relations. It is likely to be through kinship that a person acquires the right to use specific territories for foraging purposes.

The members of a foraging band may range over a territory from less than one hundred up to a few thousand square miles, according to environmental conditions and population density. Not all foragers, however, have been mobile. Records show that in some environmentally favorable areas foragers were able to live sedentary lives. Thus, groups living in coastal California who subsisted primarily by collecting acorns were able to live in settled villages. But most foragers have been nomadic.

Although the band is the primary group for social interaction and economic production and exchange among foragers, larger social groupings also are important. A band is usually allied with a number of other bands, by which arrangement common cultural features are shared. Similar dialects or languages are spoken and members are exchanged through marriage. The bands within this larger group may meet periodically when available resources permit. During these meetings, major religious ceremonies are performed, marriages arranged, goods exchanged, and disputes settled (or initiated).

The technology of pedestrian hunters and gatherers is not complex. Because, for most, mobility depends on their ability to carry all of their possessions themselves, they accumulate relatively few material goods. Such constraints limit differences in wealth, controlling the development of social inequality and de-emphasizing individual ownership. Foragers do recognize differences in individual skills, allowing for a limited degree of specialization in the manufacture of implements or performance of social and religious functions. But in these small-scale societies a person is rarely able to become a full-time specialist.

Equestrian Hunters and Gatherers

Hunting from horseback is nearly unknown today except for sport. But this subsistence pattern was widely used by societies in the Great Plains of the United States and Canada and the pampas of South America from the seventeenth to the nineteenth centuries, after Europeans introduced the horse to the New World.

Equestrian hunters and gatherers tend to differ from their pedestrian counterparts in terms of size of social units, degree of social and economic inequality, and, of course, mobility. Equestrian groups usually have been larger, more mobile, and more likely to develop a social and political hierarchy.

Before their adoption of the horse toward the end of the eighteenth century, the Patagonians of southern Argentina had lived in small, localized groups along the coast (G. Williams 1979). The horse allowed greater mobility; thus, there was a shift from reliance on coastal resources to an emphasis on hunting rhea (a type of ostrich) and guanaco (a type of llama). Adapting to the annual migratory patterns of these animals, the Patagonians moved from the coastal plain across the Patagonian plateau and into the foothills of the Andes each year. Their society changed as the Patagonians formed larger, highly structured groups. The size of these groups varied during the year. While moving across the plateau, they formed bands of 10 to 15 men and their dependents, each group totaling about 70 people; the size met the labor requirements of their hunting activities on the game-sparse plateau. At either extreme of their migratory route game was more concentrated, and a number of these bands would gather, forming a group of around 350 people sharing a common identity.

Aquatic Foragers

Hunting-and-gathering peoples who rely heavily on fishing tend to form even larger, less egalitarian societies, with more elaborate material cultures. Rather than following game on foot or horseback, these foragers settle near waters rich in marine life and pursue their prey in boats. This strategy is still used today by native peoples of the northwest coast of North America, such as the Kwakiutl and Haida, although these people now supplement their foraging activities with wage labor and commercial fishing.

Historical accounts of the Haida provide a picture of this adaptation and an extreme example of the scale and degree of social inequality that can accompany aquatic foraging. Traditionally the Haida subsisted by fishing (primarily for salmon and halibut), trapping game, and gath-

This engraving from G.C. Musters's 1897 book At Home with the Patagonians *shows equestrian hunters and gatherers swinging bolas in pursuit of game in the valley of Rio Chico, Patagonia.*

ering berries and roots. They possessed an elaborate fishing technology, including canoes more than 50 feet long. With these boats, they ranged over hundreds of miles—not always for subsistence, but sometimes to raid other peoples. Their society was divided into kin groups. It was also highly stratified, with chiefs, servants, and even slaves. This life-style was supported by an abundance of resources and a technology that allowed a relatively large number of people to live in villages of plank houses, some of which could accommodate more than 100 people. Thus, in 1840, some 8,000 Haida lived in a handful of permanent villages.

Small-Scale Farming Societies

Although fairly elaborate technologies and social structures could be built on a foraging life-style under certain circumstances, and although, at its simplest, foraging met subsistence needs with limited effort, most of the world's people

have turned away from foraging in favor of agricultural production. The cultivation or domestication of plants for subsistence usually could support higher population densities than was possible with foraging, and it generally enabled people to lead a more sedentary life.

Subsistence farmers in small-scale societies rely on human or animal labor and employ simple tools. This type of production is sometimes referred to as **horticulture,** a term for any kind of garden cultivation. This was the dominant form of agriculture from the earliest period of plant domestication some 9,000 to 10,000 years ago. It has been found among people not integrated into the market economies of large-scale societies, and it remains an important part of subsistence production among many people on the margins of the modern world economy today.

A common method of food production among small-scale farmers is **slash-and-burn agriculture**, a form of *shifting cultivation*. A few thousand years ago this type of agriculture was practiced by peoples all over the world. Today, other agricultural techniques predominate throughout much of the world, although shifting cultivation does continue to support millions of people, primarily in equatorial tropical regions.

The slash-and-burn technique entails cutting down the natural growth on a plot of land, burning it, and then planting crops in the burned area. Most tropical soils are very poor and rapidly lose nutrients. Burning produces a layer of ash that provides needed nutrients for crops. The soil fertility is rapidly depleted, however, and after one or two plantings the plot is left alone for a number of years until natural growth has again become lush enough to be burned. This *fallow period* may last only a few years in some areas, or several decades in others, depending on environmental conditions. After burning, a number of different crops may be sown together, a pattern

known as *intercropping*. Often, root crops, cereals, and shrubs are sown together in a manner that simulates the original forest cover and protects the soil from erosion. Once planting is completed, little is done to the field until it is time to harvest.

Not all small-scale farmers practice this method of shifting cultivation. In the higher altitudes of central Mexico, for example, a modified system is practiced that involves tilling, weeding, and shorter fallow periods. Some small-scale farmers employ more intensive methods, especially in more fertile environments, such as along the banks of rivers and lakes. They may also use animal waste for fertilizer or crop rotation to allow prolonged use of fields.

Many small-scale farmers augment their diet with wild game and plants. In addition, they often possess a wide variety of domesticated animals for consumption and transportation. Domesticated animals can become important in the subsistence base and in the overall social system. Among the Tsembaga of the New Guinea highlands, pigs are eaten only on special occasions, such as major rituals and during illness (Rappa-

Slash-and-burn agriculturalists in the Amazon cut and burn the growth on a plot of land and then plant their crops on the burned area.

port 1967). Pigs help clean garbage around Tsembaga settlements, and their rooting activities in fallow gardens hasten the reforestation process. They are also one of the primary items of exchange: feasts in which pig meat is distributed create and maintain vital social and political alliances.

People practicing shifting cultivation live in camps or villages of various sizes. Both the size and the stability of such settlements are influenced by the local ecology and population pressure. People living in areas with poor potential for agriculture and relatively long fallow cycles tend to live in small villages, moving every few years to remain close to their fields. Where more intensive use of the land is possible, shifting cultivators usually live in larger, more stable villages.

As with foragers, the societies of most small-scale farmers are organized around kinship, which plays a vital role in ordering social and economic relations. Land usually is owned by villages or kin-groups, and a person's place of residence and access to land are commonly determined by ties of kinship. In many ways, the family is the primary unit of production and consumption in these societies, but a good deal of work is also carried out communally. Important tasks such as clearing fields, harvesting crops, and building houses are often done by large groups rather than by individual families.

The technologies of small-scale farmers are rarely much more complex than those of foragers. Specialization in performing tasks is rare; age and gender tend to determine the kinds of activities people engage in. Among the Mundurucu, small-scale farmers of the Brazilian Amazon, women are responsible for the more tedious tasks, which also provide most of the subsistence base. Their work includes most agricultural labor, virtually all domestic chores, and the preparation and distribution of food. Men, on the other hand, hunt and fish, perform occasional heavy agricultural work, and conduct the village's external affairs.

Because of their more sedentary life-style, small-scale farmers are able to accumulate a few more things than foragers. However, the humid tropical environments in which many shifting cultivators live discourage accumulation, since many items are subject to rapid disintegration. In part because of this lack of durable goods, differences in wealth in these societies are minimal. A strong emphasis often is placed on sharing food and possessions. Sharing ensures that every villager has enough to eat and promotes village solidarity. Despite the lack of differences in wealth, members of these societies are not always social equals, for while accumulation of durable wealth may be limited, status differences can come about through the exchange of goods and services.

Pastoralism

In areas of low and unpredictable rainfall, not well suited for agricultural production, animal herding, or *pastoralism*, is a useful adaptation. Found in many parts of Asia, Africa, and Europe, animal herding was uncommon in the Americas until after the arrival of Europeans. In some pastoral societies, only the herders move with the herds, while other members live in settled villages growing some crops; in other pastoral societies everyone moves with the migrating herd. We will consider these two pastoral variants separately, for they shape cultures in different ways.

Transhumance
In this form of adaptation, only the herders move with the herds. **Transhumance** consists of limited crop production in the immediate vicinity of a village and migratory herding of animals. The pattern is found, for example, among certain Mediterranean societies, the Navajo of the American Southwest following European contact, various groups in the drier areas of southern Africa, and in the foothills of the Himalayas of South Asia.

Around the Mediterranean, with its pattern of

long summer droughts and wet winters, a production system evolved based on cereals, such as wheat and barley; tree and vine crops, such as olives and grapes; horticultural production of fruits and vegetables; and grazing sheep and goats. In the more impoverished Mediterranean environments, the grazing of sheep and goats has assumed special importance. The sheep and goats are grazed on coastal plains during the wet winter and spring and moved to the highlands when lowland vegetation dries up during the summer. The people live in sedentary villages. For those living in the lowlands, male shepherds spend a good deal of time away from the villages grazing their animals on distant pastures. Grazing is conducted on a family basis, and cooperation in the community beyond the family level is rare. Moreover, conflict between families is common as families compete for scarce resources and attempt to defend family honor and protect well-being.

Pastoral Nomadism

In regions even less suited to horticulture or transhumance, peoples have built their subsistence patterns around nomadic movement with grazing herds. **Pastoral nomadism** is an economic adaptation and life-style characterized by lack of permanent habitation and primary dependence on the herding of animals for subsistence. The development of pastoral nomadism followed domestication of the horse in the Asian steppes and the camel in southwestern Arabia, both around 3000 B.C. Over the next 2,000 years or so, pastoral nomads spread into the drier areas of northern and eastern Asia and Africa. They occupied the high mountains, lowland deserts, and dry steppes that were sparsely populated by more sedentary populations. The use of horses and camels for food and transportation allowed more mobility than had been possible before. Pastoral nomadism developed in other parts of the world as well, such as among the Saami of northern Europe, whose economy centers around reindeer herding.

Movement is a central feature of pastoral nomadism. Because of seasonal variation or unpredictability in the weather, pastoral nomads must move their herds to take maximal advantage of available pasturage. Many pastoral nomadic societies in the Middle East follow a traditional route, or "tribal road," over a widely diverse landscape. The pattern typically entails gradual movement from a low-lying area, where the nomads are in close proximity to sedentary peoples, to high and isolated mountain pastures.

The kinds of animals pastoralists herd and the extent to which they are involved in agricultural production varies considerably. Pastoralists also vary in self-sufficiency: those in Africa concentrate on meeting their own daily food needs, whereas in the Middle East pastoralists typically try to produce a marketable surplus that can be exchanged for other goods. But all pastoral nomads depend to some extent on nonpastoral products, such as grains and fruits.

Among pastoral nomads, animals are usually owned by individuals or family heads, and the primary unit of production and consumption is the family. Families, however, must work with larger groups for efficient use of resources and often for protection as well. Families are part of individual herding groups or camps. The size of the herding group will depend on factors influencing optimum herd size and composition and on the age and sex distribution within the human group. The composition of the herding group is constantly in flux. In addition to seasonal changes associated with herding requirements, groups change as individuals mature and as herds grow.

Above the camp level of organization, pastoral nomads commonly are grouped into larger social alliances, usually on the basis of kinship. The primary form of alliance is the _tribe_, sometimes formed through presumed descent from a common founding ancestor or perhaps through an alliance of associated kin-based groups. Tribes vary in size from a few hundred to several hundred thousand individuals. In the past, primarily

Pastoral nomad goatherders in Egypt near Cairo live a mobile way of life that depends on their animals.

because of the influence of central governments and pressure to organize into larger groupings for warfare, tribes sometimes joined to form larger *confederacies*. These confederacies tended to be highly unstable.

Within pastoral nomadic societies, the division of labor is based largely on age and gender. Almost all labor associated with herding and agriculture is done by men, although there are exceptions. Women generally are responsible for domestic activities and for producing items associated with the home, such as handwoven rugs. Specialization within a group is rare, but group members may depend on many goods and services produced by the specialized labor of people who are not pastoral nomads—itinerant traders and craftspeople, sedentary workers, and merchants.

Despite their mobility, pastoral nomads are able to accumulate possessions because they can carry them on large pack animals. Also, since most pastoral nomads are integrated into national economies, they can accumulate wealth in the mobile form of general-purpose money. The ability to accumulate wealth and the need to coordinate the movement of large numbers of people and animals and their access to scarce resources have led to greater differences in social status among pastoral nomads than among other small-scale societies. Status differences have also resulted from contact with centralized authority.

Large-Scale Societies

The subsistence patterns we have looked at so far involve relatively small-scale human groups. The establishment of more dense populations arose after the founding of village farming communities between 8000 and 6000 B.C. as agricultural production was intensified in certain parts of the world. Initially, there were only a few centers where early states had formed. These included the so-called cradles of civilization in the Near East, the Far East, and the New World (see Chapter 11). In these settings, previously autonomous villages were incorporated into larger political units, cities grew, and commerce beyond the village level assumed greater importance. Between A.D. 1 and A.D. 1000, the centers expanded north in Europe beyond the Mediterranean, south of the Yangtze River in China, and into southern Africa. In the New World, the civilizations in Mexico and South America spread into surrounding areas. Much of the growth in these centers was related to more systematic and intensive agricultural production, which was accompanied by population growth.

Beginning in the fifteenth century, European exploration, expansion, and colonization altered human society further by creating a more integrated world system. Societies and populations were mixed and altered to an unprecedented extent. Crops and farming techniques spread over wide areas, and commercial exchange and urbanization expanded greatly. The formation of larger scale societies was further encouraged by the development of industrial methods of production. During the second half of the eighteenth century, the economy of Britain, and to a lesser extent the economies of Western Europe and New England, were transformed by a series of mechanical inventions, especially the steam engine and important innovations in textile manufacturing. This Industrial Revolution, a shift from slow hand methods of production to mechanized factory and agricultural production, resulted in major social changes, the impact of which eventually was felt throughout the world.

As societies adopted machine technologies, they shifted from traditional subsistence activities to newer methods that greatly increased the quantities of food and other goods that each worker could produce. Those people not needed in food production could specialize in other activities, move from rural areas to urban areas where jobs were concentrated, and use the money they earned to trade for their subsistence needs. Contemporary large-scale societies using this strategy differ in degree from small-scale societies in a number of ways. The large-scale societies are characterized by reliance on machines rather than on human or animal labor; intense use of resources; large and more concentrated populations; specialization of work; emphasis on trade; interdependency of populations; and inequalities in wealth and social status.

Although a great deal of production in large-scale societies is done by machine and by highly specialized workers, this is not the only means of production. In fact, some adaptive strategies employed in many large-scale societies are modern versions of those of small-scale societies that have changed in accordance with their progressive integration into the new encompassing social and economic environment.

Foraging

The collection of wild foods persists in large-scale societies, although the methods of collection and distribution tend to be quite different from those used in small-scale foraging groups. This is true even of those who retain a close affinity with their small-scale foraging past. For example, Cree Indians today collect wild rice and trap beavers, selling a portion of what they forage to enable them to purchase industrially produced goods, such as chain saws and rifles.

One activity in particular continues to be of great significance in large-scale societies—fishing. While some fishing continues to be carried out through relatively simple means (such as that conducted by the Haida along the northwest coast of North America), most modern fishing, which can be called *industrial fishing,* employs industrial technology and considerable mechanization. Tuna fishing in the Pacific is carried out in boats costing millions of dollars, using sophisticated electronic equipment and even helicopters.

Other foraging adaptations are unique to large-scale societies because the "foragers" are excluded from the mainstream of social and economic life. These are the beggars, the so-called bag ladies, and others who live off what others discard or give away.

Peasant Farming

In Africa, Asia, Latin America, and even in parts of Europe, hundreds of millions of farmers in large-scale societies can be classified as peasants. The family farm is the peasant's basic unit of production and social organization. Although wage laborers are sometimes employed, the individual family provides most labor, and farming is carried out with a relatively simple technology and minimal reliance on mechanization. The farm furnishes the bulk of the family's needs, as well as a surplus of goods for redistribution to nonpeasants through sale, taxation, or some other means.

Peasants are part of an encompassing stratified society. One of the most significant features of peasants' lives is their underdog status—their domination by outsiders. They serve as primary producers for urban markets and rural elites, but they have little control over the means of distribution and little political power. The result is often poverty. Since peasants are incorporated into the wider society in such a disadvantageous manner, their relations with nonpeasants are characterized by extreme defensiveness. They see themselves as continually having to defend against external forces. Sometimes this defensiveness turns inward in the form of extreme suspicion and jealousy of one another; this, in turn, may lead to high rates of homicide and other forms of violence. But peasants are not always merely defensive, nor are their frustrations always taken out on one another. Periodically, peasants band together in revolt against the established order, as witnessed in the course of the leading revolutions of the twentieth century as well as in many less dramatic events around the world.

Plantation Agriculture

In a sense, peasants are small-scale farmers who have been incorporated into large-scale societies. However, a great deal of the world's agricultural production is not the result of peasant labor but of farming enterprises on a much larger scale. One form of large-scale agricultural enterprise that developed with early European colonial expansion is termed *plantation agriculture*. It served primarily to provide the world's major industrial centers in the northern latitudes with crops that could be produced solely, or more cheaply, in the tropics or subtropics—such crops as rubber, sugarcane, coconuts, sisal (a fiber used for rope and other forms of cordage), or coffee. Most of these crops require years of maturation from planting to first yield, and after several yields production may fall off and replanting may be required. All the products of a plantation are exported, in part to pay for the importation of machinery and food required to maintain the plantation.

Plantation production is labor intensive. Plantations require large, disciplined, but not especially skilled labor forces. In North America and South America, the labor was supplied initially by slaves imported from Africa. In other areas, and during the latter part of the nineteenth and twentieth centuries in the Americas, labor was supplied either by the existing local populations or was imported from such countries as India and China. The workers on a plantation may reside in compounds on the premises or in neighboring villages and towns. Their living quarters tend to be kept separate from those of the managerial staff, reflecting the hierarchy of social and economic relations on plantations.

Large-Scale Mechanized Grain Farming

Large-scale agriculture does not always require a large labor force. The type of agricultural production that has come to dominate the nontropical regions of the world—and that recently has been spreading into the tropics as well—is exemplified in the large-scale mechanized grain

Harvesting sugarcane at this plantation in Costa Rica requires considerable hand labor as well as machinery. Motorized tractors have replaced animal-drawn carts to transport the cane.

farm. In the manner of plantations, grain farms focus on growing only one or two crops, and the products are usually exported to distant markets. Unlike plantations, however, these large grain farms are capital rather than labor intensive, depending on a small work force and large inputs of fertilizer and mechanical equipment.

The form of ownership and social organization of these enterprises usually depends on the larger economic system. Thus, in many socialist countries the enterprises are collectively or state owned, whereas in market-oriented countries they are commonly owned by corporations or by private individuals. They may also be owned by communal groups, such as the Hutterites in North America.

Ranching

Yet another subsistence pattern of large-scale societies is ranching. The origins of ranching are found in medieval Europe, especially in the activities of Spanish sheepherders. Their activities gave rise to institutions such as the rodeo and to much of the equipment, attire, and vocabulary of ranching. Today ranching is confined largely to the drier regions of the world where Europeans have migrated over the past few centuries. As in plantation agriculture, the impetus behind the spread of ranching was the demand in the northern industrialized countries for goods that could be produced more cheaply elsewhere. Most ranches occupy land that is not suitable for agriculture and, moreover, that is able to support only a small number of animals per acre. This situation is changing, however, as innovations in agriculture have made farming in such inhospitable regions more feasible. The result in some cases has been a mixture of ranching and agriculture; in others, ranching has been superseded by agriculture.

Ranching is highly specialized. Most ranchers raise a single type of animal, usually cattle or sheep. Unlike the technologically unsophisticated ranches of the past, today's ranches commonly employ a wide array of industrial products. The low carrying capacity of ranch lands (that is, the sparse vegetation of the land that makes it unable to support large numbers of animals) results in low population densities and considerable social isolation. Ranching cultures reflect this situation with their emphasis on individualism, isolationism, and hospitality. Ranches have few permanent residents, with the majority of laborers hired on a seasonal basis for roundups and shearing. Small, less affluent, family-owned ranches usually have a limited division of labor and are run on a fairly egalitarian basis. By contrast, large, corporate-owned ranching operations generally exhibit a great deal of specialization, and social relations may be quite hierarchical.

Nonfood Production Patterns

In large-scale societies, more goods are produced than in small-scale societies, and in greater variety. Also, production and distribution processes are more specialized. There are two principal systems of manufacturing in large-scale societies: craft production and industrial production. *Craft production* can be carried out within relatively small social units, even within a single village, with only a limited amount of external trade. By contrast, *industrial production* represents a considerable leap in terms of scale of production, degree of specialization, and reliance on extensive exchange networks.

Industrial production uses energy sources other than human or animal to operate machinery for the extraction and conversion of resources. It requires a relatively large and diverse labor force and relatively large amounts of capital. Industrial production has been employed on a limited basis (such as in metallurgy) in various societies for thousands of years. Only during the past 200 to 300 years, however, since the beginning of the Industrial Revolution in eighteenth-century England, has it become a dominant feature of economic production. Industrialism has since become one of the driving forces behind the creation and expansion of the present world system.

Industrial production in any setting can be understood only in reference to the wider world system and to the history of its expansion. Industrial production beyond Western Europe and North America is a relatively recent phenomenon, and in much of the Third World dates only from the years following World War II. Wherever it has developed, industrial production has contributed to the growth of urban areas as people have migrated from the countryside in search of work. The precise nature of industry within a country is a reflection of that country's place within the international division of labor. Access to natural resources, transportation, technology, and labor will make a difference as well. In the more developed nations, industrial production is more highly mechanized and more skill intensive; in less developed countries, industry continues to rely heavily on less skilled labor.

While industrialization has increased the potential for productivity, it has been a mixed blessing, particularly for those unable to share in its products and for those employed in tedious and hazardous jobs. Many of the political and economic struggles in the world today center on problems related to industry—the distribution of the wealth created by industry, working conditions, and industrial pollution. In fact, recent increases in productive capability, through the use of computers and highly sophisticated electronic technology, have in many ways only made matters worse; the new technology has resulted in many benefits, but has also allowed for greater concentration of wealth, drastic alterations in the structure of employment, and further environmental problems.

PRODUCTION, DISTRIBUTION, AND EXCHANGE

Having discussed the more obvious features of subsistence patterns, now let us turn to the abstract principles on which these patterns are based—production, distribution, and exchange.

Systems of Production

When our early ancestors picked up a stone, chipped it, and put it on the end of a stick to turn it into an implement for hunting and fighting, they produced a weapon. **Production** involves the significant transformation of an object for cultural purposes. An act of production often entails physically changing an object, but it may simply be a matter of rearranging objects to alter their nature or function, such as piling stones to make a wall. It also commonly involves combining objects to produce something that is functionally different. But production is more than an act of transformation; it is a systematically ordered series of acts set in a particular social and environmental context. Anthropologists are not so much concerned with the productive act per se as they are with the *system of production* of which the act is but a part.

Production, as we have seen, varies considerably from one society to another. In our own society, the production of weapons usually involves several successive transformations of a number of objects to produce a much more complicated implement than a chipped stone on a stick. The difference reflects a more complex technology and division of labor than that of our spear-making ancestors.

Those engaged in the production of a missile are trained and organized in a manner very different from those involved in spear-making. They are also likely to have different views of work, the world, and their place in it. The same is true of peoples who have different methods of food production, such as foragers and small-scale farmers.

The Environmental Context

Systems of production are influenced by the local ecology, as well as by the social, political, and economic environment. Production by small-scale producers is especially attuned to the local ecology on which they must rely for most of their raw materials. Systems of production in large-scale societies are generally more flexible in adapting to ecological conditions because of the growth of commerce, which allows them to draw upon resources and markets over much wider areas.

Keeping a system of production going, whether in a small-scale or large-scale society, is not always easy. Disruptions, such as wars and environmental crises, must be dealt with; a steady supply of workers must be maintained; and labor and rewards must be distributed in satisfactory ways. Production systems usually have mechanisms for dealing with temporary or regular disruptions, such as droughts or other natural disasters. Foragers maintain alliances so that they may use the resources of other groups if their own are depleted. Small-scale producers also often have types of foods that they can turn to in emer-

An example of a relatively uncomplicated production process: this Inuit man uses a bow drill to cut holes in tough material, such as this walrus ivory.

gencies—items that would not be consumed under normal circumstances. In our own society, we adjust to disruptions by turning to alternate sources and by storing reserves. We also provide for the primary producers themselves through disaster-relief supplies and funds.

While many of the forces disrupting production may result from natural causes and can be dealt with in a manner that does not have long-term effects on the system of production, human action itself sometimes causes ecological prob-

lems. Many societies in the past have contributed to their own demise by abusing the lands they lived on. The Anasazi culture of the Chaco Canyon in New Mexico (A.D. 1000–A.D. 1200), for example, was very advanced for its time, but eventually fell because of environmental degradation. Abrupt deforestation for fuel and building materials led to erosion that destroyed the topsoil and ruined water channels used for irrigation; eventually, the agricultural system collapsed. Soil erosion and deforestation are severe

The expansion of agriculture into the dry center of the North American continent has been accompanied by serious environmental problems. Erosion from intensive use of the land created the so-called dust bowl in the 1930s, illustrated in this photo of a South Dakota farm in 1936. Today, the United States is estimated to lose more than 6 billion tons of soil a year through erosion. Fears rise once again of another dust bowl.

problems in much of the world today, threatening the well-being of societies scattered far and wide, and perhaps even global society as we know it.

Labor Recruitment

Another fundamental requirement of any productive system is the replacement of people. All systems of production have mechanisms for maintaining a steady flow of productive humans. This means ensuring that people are produced in the appropriate numbers. Then they must be made productive, usually through socialization whereby children of a society are tutored in the appropriate values and knowledge. Many small-scale societies seek to limit population growth through infanticide, abortion, and birth control. These practices, along with relatively high infant mortality rates, kept the world's population growth at a slow rate for tens of thousands of years, minimizing population-related stresses on economic adaptations. This situation began to

change dramatically several hundred years ago; particularly since the 1940s, rapid population growth has been a major problem confronting many societies in the Third World.

While many poorer countries face severe economic problems because of the speed with which their populations are growing, many developed countries are facing problems because of their low-to-negative rate of population growth. For many reasons, more affluent people tend to have fewer children, and today many countries in Europe and North America must meet their labor requirements by importing workers from other parts of the world. Importing workers occurs in the modern world system as a result of economic inequalities and labor requirements. Such movements began as Europeans developed plantations in the New World and set about meeting labor needs through the acquisition of millions of slaves from Africa. In the latter part of the nineteenth century, India and China provided millions of workers for construction, mining, and agriculture for the expanding colonial capitalist economies. The long-term effects of such migrations are evidenced by the large numbers of descendants of these migrants who are scattered across the globe, far from their ancestral homelands.

Nor is labor migration a thing of the past. The more prosperous economies of Europe have attracted migrants from southern Europe and the Middle East. In the 1970s and early 1980s, oil-rich countries in the Middle East recruited large numbers of workers from India, the Philippines, South Korea, and elsewhere. Such countries as the United States, Canada, and Australia continue to receive millions of workers from poorer countries around the world. As in the past, not all of those who come to work remain. Many do, however, adding further to the ethnic mix that characterizes most modern states.

Distribution and Exchange

It is not enough simply to produce things—there also must be a system for distributing them. Individuals have different needs, tastes, and desires, and often there is either not enough of something to go around or a surplus to be disposed of. How to distribute products and resources is one of the fundamental questions facing all societies, and it may be the most important source of human conflict.

Central to an understanding of distribution and exchange is the concept of **ownership**—acknowledged supremacy, authority, or power over a physical object, process, or idea. Ownership within any society is rarely a simple concept. In our society, we say that people own their homes. Yet through various ordinances and social constraints, the state and a person's kin and neighbors have a good deal to say about decisions regarding the house. Under many circumstances, police and other public employees can enter the premises regardless of the owner's wishes. The bank that holds a mortgage on a house also has rights over it; failure to pay taxes can result in a

loss of ownership. Oil companies may be able to drill holes on the site, mining companies can burrow under it, and city and state governments can tear it down to build a road, park, or civic building.

Among the Pintubi, a group of foragers in the Australian desert, ownership is denoted by the term *kanyininpa,* which may be translated as "having," "holding," or "looking after" (Myers 1982: 83). The term is used to refer to possession of physical objects ("I have two spears"), to the relationship of parent to child ("My father looked after me and grew me up"), and to the rights individuals or groups may hold over sacred sites, religious ceremonies, songs, and designs. Ownership among the Pintubi entails both control and responsibility. A person controls or "owns" a child or sacred site, but that person also has responsibilities associated with these possessions. The idea of ownership is tied to an encompassing moral order, known as the "Law," which dictates what these responsibilities are.

Ownership of land for the Pintubi comes about through the inheritance of sacred sites and the territory associated with them. It entails obligations to perform rituals linked to the sites. Failure to carry out such obligations does not merely affect a person's status in relation to the land and society, it threatens the entire moral and social order of the Pintubi. It is easy to see how such concepts are at variance with those of the Europeans who came to settle in Australia, and how such differing concepts of ownership have led to conflicts and misunderstanding.

Distribution of Wealth

No matter how ownership is defined, some people own more than others. Unequal distribution of **wealth** (objects or resources that are useful or that have exchange value) is a universal characteristic of human society. Minor inequalities exist within many small-scale societies, especially between men and women. As the productive capability of societies increases, greater inequalities tend to result. And with the rise of greater in-

Wealth is unequally distributed among Arabs in the Middle East. Traders on the floor in Kuwait City (above), where oil provides great wealth, contrast with Palestinian women in a food kitchen (right).

equality have evolved mechanisms of social control (police and military) that support unequal accumulation.

Beyond such general tendencies, there is considerable variation. Thus, traditionally wealth was much more equally distributed among the Mardudjara Aborigines who lived in Australia's harsh western desert than among the Tiwi who lived in the more abundant environment of Australia's north. Likewise, some modern industrial societies exhibit greater degrees of inequality than others. For example, wealth is much more equally distributed in a country like Denmark than in, say, the United States. But, overall, inequality is far greater in even the most egalitarian modern industrial society than in small-scale societies such as that of the Tiwi.

Inequality on a worldwide scale in the modern world has led to the division of countries into those that are considered "developed" and those that are considered "underdeveloped," "less developed," or "developing." Developed nations include those countries referred to as the **First World** (Western industrial capitalist nations). The middle range is occupied by the industrialized socialist nations, sometimes referred to as the **Second World,** as well as some of the wealthier oil-producing nations and such better-off states as Singapore. The underdeveloped group, usually referred to as the **Third World,** is a loose category of about 120 countries characterized by relatively low standards of living, high rates of population growth, and general economic and technological dependence on wealthier industrial nations. And within much of the Third World itself, inequality is often very marked. In many Third-World countries, a small, wealthy elite controls the bulk of the national wealth and has at its disposal millions if not billions of dollars, while the majority of rural and urban poor may possess barely enough to ensure their survival.

Patterns of Exchange

The distribution of wealth within a society is the result of **exchange,** the pattern of trade associated with resources, goods, ideas, and services. Economic exchange is a universal aspect of human society. Individuals in all social settings depend on others for satisfying some of their needs or wants, and our life cycle from birth to death requires that resources and ideas continually be transferred to meet changing circumstances. The process of exchange is based on principles of **reciprocity** (the mutual exchange of goods and services) and takes on various forms, such as systems of redistribution and market exchange.

Anthropologist Marshall Sahlins (1965) has delineated three forms of reciprocity: generalized, balanced, and negative reciprocity. *Generalized reciprocity* refers to gift giving without any immediate expectation of return, such as the exchange of food within domestic groups. *Balanced reciprocity* involves a more explicit expectation of

immediate return, as when a Bushman trades a Tswana an animal hide for a negotiated quantity of tobacco (Marshall 1961) or Mayan farmers exchange equal amounts of work in the field. *Negative reciprocity* is taking advantage of someone else by forcing that person to exchange something that he or she may prefer to keep, or by trying to ensure that what one receives is of greater value than what one gives in exchange.

Redistributive systems of exchange entail the accumulation of wealth and then its redistribution. Redistribution can take many forms, among which are taxation and gift giving. All societies large enough to support a government that includes an administration to provide infrastructural services (such as roads and port facilities) have developed methods of collecting wealth from their members to support the services provided. In our society, and in many others, one of the primary means of accomplishing this is **taxation.** Individuals, according to various criteria, surrender part of their wealth to the government which, in return, is expected to do such things as defend them from external threats and provide law and order, infrastructure (roads and other permanent works), and welfare services.

The **potlatch** is a form of redistribution among native peoples of the northwest coast of North America through which individuals and groups seek to enhance their status through elaborate and, at times, dramatic feast and gift-giving ceremonies. Similar forms of competitive feasting and gift giving are common among small-scale agricultural and fishing societies and serve as a focal point of economic exchange among members of different social groups.

Among the Kwakiutl of British Columbia, the gifts formerly presented in a potlatch included slaves, canoes, blankets, various manufactured articles, and highly valued shieldlike sheets of copper (Codere 1950). Hudson Bay Company blankets were the most common gift in the late nineteenth and early twentieth centuries (several thousand blankets might be presented at a single potlatch), and they served as the basic unit of ac-

A Kwakiutl potlatch, a feast and gift-giving ceremony, Alert Bay, British Columbia (photograph taken ca. 1910). By redistributing wealth, the sponsor of a potlatch validated his rank, enhanced his social status, and reinforced political ties. The redistribution of perishable goods ensured that they did not go to waste.

count; thus, the value of goods was expressed in blankets. The potlatch feast itself was sponsored by an individual on such occasions as a marriage, the birth of a first child, or the initiation of one's sister's son into a secret society, and it served to validate the sponsor's receiving a high-status title.

A person would prepare for a potlatch by accumulating the needed items largely through loans (on which interest was paid) from relatives. At the potlatch, goods would be distributed to members of one's own kin-group, to related kin-groups who had been invited, and often to people from other communities. This meant that goods were redistributed within one's own community and outside of it. Intercommunity distribution of food through the potlatch ensured that surplus perishables did not go to waste. There was keen competition among members of the elite to outdo each other in their largesse, and it was principally through the potlatch that a person could advance in social standing. Moreover, those invited were not simply the recipients of goods; they were placed in the potlatcher's debt.

Market exchange involves the buying and selling of goods. The dominant feature of these transactions is price setting, which is based more on impersonal economic factors such as supply and demand than on personal factors such as kinship and relative social status. Market exchange dominates where economic transactions are conducted among relative strangers. In the modern world, it has come to be the primary system of exchange.

Media of Exchange

The depersonalization of market exchanges is related to the use of money as a medium of exchange. The term **money** essentially refers not so much to the physical thing itself, but more important, to the qualities associated with it—durability, transferability, and acceptability over a wide range of functions. As Belshaw (1965) notes, all of these depend on the characteristic of *liquidity*—"the relative ease with which a commodity . . . can be exchanged" (p. 9). There are two basic types of money: special-purpose and general-purpose. The term **special-purpose money** refers to objects that serve as a medium of exchange in only limited contexts and that are interchangeable for only a particular range of goods and services. Cattle, pigs, jewelry, and cloth are common forms of special-purpose money. The Lele of Zaire use a special type of cloth not only to wear but mainly as a store of value and as a means of payment (Douglas 1958). It is used for trade with neighboring peoples for such items as hoes, pottery, and fish. Among themselves, the Lele use this cloth as a means of payment for particular kinds of transactions. It is presented to wives when they bear children or report would-be seducers, to in-laws upon marriage, to newly admitted members of cult groups, and to specialists who perform healing rites and divinations. The cloth is also used as a means of paying compensation for adultery and in assessing fines for fighting in a village, as well as for payment for products made by craftspeople who are not close relatives.

General-purpose money differs from the more limited versions of money in its comprehensiveness. In a society using general-purpose money, most material things and services can be bought or paid for with this one medium of exchange. This form of money makes it easier to conduct economic exchanges with strangers. One's wealth, work value, and even thoughts can be assessed in monetary terms that are widely shared. Introducing general-purpose money into societies where it had not been previously used has had a considerable impact. For example, the substitution of general-purpose money for cattle in marriage transactions in east Africa allowed young men greater personal freedom. In doing so, it also undermined patterns of parental authority and the political system based on clan alliances. In addition, it contributed to the breakdown of herd management by kin groups. The introduction of market exchange via general-purpose money into economies throughout the globe has been an integral part of the spread of the modern world system. General-purpose money is one of the most tangible forces integrating societies into the world economy; the flow of money produces both direct and indirect effects on almost all aspects of people's lives.

Commerce

The economies of societies are almost never completely self-sufficient. **Commerce**, or the exchange of goods between different countries or regions, is a feature of virtually all economic systems. The quest for resources and markets beyond the confines of one's own society is certainly not new. But the scope of world commerce today is unprecedented, as is the extent to which it influences people's lives. Even in small, relatively isolated villages, people today produce for distant markets and consume goods imported from the far corners of the globe.

Despite the many changes and growing complexity in commerce, even in the past, members of small-scale societies commonly engaged in often quite intricate exchange with members of other societies. The *Kula* of northeastern Melanesia, for example, is an elaborate exchange system involving expeditions of sailing canoes, trading partners, large feasts, ceremonial exchanges of prized shell ornaments, and bartering over a range of goods.

Shorter on ceremony, commerce between larger scale societies is characterized by a more

*Indians buy and sell goods at a market in Ecuador.
In market exchange, impersonal supply and demand
take priority over kinship and social status.*

constant flow of greater quantities and varieties
of goods and more extensive commercial networks than exchange between small-scale societies. The growth of early empires was accompanied by such networks. Thus, the ancient
Phoenicians became masters of trade routes
throughout the Mediterranean that were linked
to routes stretching as far as India. Likewise, the
Aztecs of central Mexico were at the center of an
extensive trade network over which traveled
goods from throughout Mesoamerica and from
northern South America.

European colonialism was concerned primarily with securing trade routes and, eventually,
the sources of goods around the world. Colum-
bus sailed to the New World not simply out of
curiosity but in search of trade. The Europeans'
search for raw materials and new markets for
their products led to the transformation of the
world and formed the basis for the modern world
system. The colonial period was one in which the
dominant powers sought to create a world suited
to their economic needs. Postcolonial societies
studied by anthropologists today are both a reflection of and a reaction to this colonial transformation.

SUMMARY

Subsistence activities are the strategies human groups employ to procure and produce the fundamental things they want or need. Subsistence patterns are influenced by physical and social factors, including the scale of the society. Small-scale societies have tended to be restricted, while large-scale societies are more extensive, ultimately forming part of the international division of labor.

There are three major small-scale subsistence patterns. The first is foraging, the collecting of wild foods, a basic strategy divided into three subtypes: pedestrian hunting and gathering, equestrian hunting and gathering, and aquatic foraging. The second pattern, small-scale farming, involves the use of human and animal labor and simple tools. Shifting cultivation is a common small-scale farming method, especially in the tropics. Pastoralism, the third pattern, practiced by peoples who subsist primarily on herding animals, has two main forms: transhumance and pastoral nomadism.

In large-scale societies, foraging, especially fishing, continues to be a significant activity for some people. Common forms of agriculture are peasant farming, plantation agriculture, large-scale grain farming, and ranching. The two principal systems of manufacturing are craft production and industrial production.

Economic systems consist of patterns of production, ownership, and exchange. Production, an ordered series of acts set in a particular social and environmental context, involves the transformation of an object for cultural purposes. Anthropologists are interested in the system of production of which the act is a part. Production systems must cope with disruptions and environmental crises, arrange for regular replacement of workers, and divide labor and distribute rewards.

Ownership tends not to be absolute; the concept of ownership can be complex. Considerable differences in how much is owned exist between societies and within. Differences in the distribution of wealth are greater in large-scale societies.

Wealth is distributed within and among societies in patterns of exchange. There are three basic patterns: reciprocity, redistribution, and market exchange. In reciprocal exchange, people trade one kind of good or service for another. Redistribution takes such forms as taxation, gift giving, and potlatches. Market exchange is characterized by the buying and selling of goods through the use of special-purpose or general-purpose money.

Today, few societies are isolated from the world economic system. Groups are often drawn into contact with others through commerce.

SUGGESTED READINGS

Applebaum, Herbert A. 1981. *Royal Blue: The Culture of Construction Workers.* New York: Holt, Rinehart & Winston.

Beall, Cynthia M., and Melvyn C. Goldstein. 1990. *Nomads of Western Tibet: The Survival of a Way of Life.* Berkeley: University of California Press.

Behnke, Ray H., Jr. 1980. *The Herders of Cyrenaica.* Urbana: University of Illinois Press. (Libya)

Clammet, John, ed. 1978. *The New Economic Anthropology.* London: Macmillan.

Lawrence, Peter. 1984. *The Garia.* Melbourne: Melbourne University Press. (Papua New Guinea)

Lee, Richard B. 1984. *The !Kung: Foragers in a Changing World.* New York: Holt, Rinehart & Winston.

Lehman, David, ed. 1982. *Ecology and Exchange in the Andes.* Cambridge: Cambridge University Press.

Moran, Emilio. 1981. *Developing the Amazon.* Bloomington: Indiana University Press.

Murphy, Yolanda, and Robert Murphy. 1974. *Women of the Forest.* New York: Columbia University Press. (Amazonian Brazil)

Nelson, Richard K. 1980. *Shadow of the Hunter: Stories of Eskimo Life.* Chicago: University of Chicago Press.

Wolf, Eric R. 1982. *Europe and the People without History.* Berkeley: University of California Press.

Nomads on the Roof of the World

Melvyn C. Goldstein and Cynthia M. Beall

Melvyn C. Goldstein is the John Reynolds Harkness Professor and Chairman of the Department of Anthropology at Case Western Reserve University. He is also the director of the university's Center for Research on Tibet. Dr. Goldstein's research has taken him to India, Nepal, and China. He is currently engaged in projects in Tibet and the Mongolian People's Republic.

Cynthia M. Beall is Professor of Physical Anthropology in the Department of Anthropology at Case Western Reserve University. She has conducted extensive research on human biology and adaptation to high altitude in the Peruvian and Bolivian Andes and the Nepalese Himalayas and is currently conducting research in this area in Tibet and the Mongolian People's Republic.

Professors Beall and Goldstein are the authors of Nomads of Western Tibet: The Survival of a Way of Life *(Berkeley: University of California Press, 1990).*

Tibetan nomadic pastoralists—*drokba*—exemplify an ancient and successful life-style in which domesticated animals are used to convert natural vegetation into food, clothing, and shelter for their owners. The owners do no farming, nor do they feed their animals fodder; rather, they move their tents and herds several times a year to ensure that their livestock obtain adequate grass and water.

Between 1986 and 1990, we spent about 20 months in Tibet (the Tibet Autonomous Region of China) living with and studying a group of nomadic pastoralists in Phala, about 300 miles west of Lhasa, the capital of Tibet. In a world characterized by farmers and hostile governments pushing pastoralists into increasingly marginal environments, Tibet's nomads are fortunate to still live in their traditional habitat—Tibet's *changdang*, or "northern plateau."

There they have lived with their herds of yak, sheep, and goats for untold centuries, not just eking out a meager existence, but actually producing substantial surpluses that were the backbone of Tibet's sophisticated religious civilizations. One of our research goals was to learn how they accomplished this without destroying their grassland environment.

The formidable changdang is truly the "roof of the world." Encampments range from 16,000 to 17,000 feet above sea level, and temperature lows reach well below zero—in winter, -30°F to -50°F. In midsummer, they still hover around freezing. Sitting in tents in winter, we were struck by the ferocity of the climate—while a roaring fire warmed our fronts, the relentless cold tugged at our backs, reminding us that the fire was only a small point of warmth in a world of bitter cold.

These harsh conditions, however, have actually served the nomads by protecting them from competition from agriculturalists seeking to expand production. Farming is simply not a viable alternative to herding. If there were no nomads on the changdang, the land would revert to the wildlife.

Life on the changdang is not easy. Because

*On a cold day: Cynthia Beall (left) and Melvyn
Goldstein (right) with Tibetan nomadic pastoralists.*

Tibetan livestock feed entirely on natural
vegetation, the animals must be taken to graze
every day, regardless of weather. Similarly,
lactating animals must be milked every day.
The sight of nomad women milking their yaks
as a storm deposits a layer of snow on their
backs, or of a herder returning in the evening
so numb with cold that even opening this tent
flap is difficult, epitomizes the hardship of
pastoralism on the changdang.

The nomads of Phala, however, view things
differently. They laughed when we referred to
the hardships and insisted that their way of life
was far easier than that of farmers, who had to
plow the soil and weed the fields. As one of
them explained to us: "Look, it is obvious that
we have a very easy life. The grass grows by
itself, the animals reproduce by themselves,
they give milk and meat without our doing
anything. So how can you say our way of life is
hard?"

The Phala nomads actually do have a great
deal of leisure time, but they are not passive
bystanders. Their success depends on their
active adaptation to changing conditions. They
cannot alter the cold or wind or snow, but
they can compensate for it by adjusting how
and where they herd.

Having no farms (and there being no outside
migration for jobs), these people depend
completely on their livestock, which they view
as a perpetual source of wealth. It is a simple
view—if they can provide the herd with proper
water and grasses, the animals will provide the
nomads the means to survive well. The

nomads' animals do this by yielding a wide variety of products.

As sources of food, the herd provides milk and meat products. Milk production, however, is highly seasonal. The sheep and goats (87 percent of the herd) give milk only from June to September, so there is an abundance in summer and an inadequate supply in winter and spring, when only yaks are lactating. To compensate, the nomads process the milk, converting the quickly perishable summer milk into storable butter and cheese.

During the peak summer milking season, women boil each day's fresh milk and set it aside overnight to become tart, smooth yogurt. The next morning, they eat some and churn the rest for about an hour to produce butter. When sewn tightly in "football-size" packets made from sheep stomachs, this butter can be stored for up to a year. The remaining milk solids are reboiled to produce a soft, tart cheese. Some of this is also eaten fresh, but most is dried in the sun. The resulting crumbly, rock-hard cheese can be stored indefinitely. The nomads, therefore, have developed an effective dairy-processing system that enables them to spread the summer abundance of milk calories throughout the year.

Meat, another important component of the nomad diet, is also harvested in a manner to maximize its caloric value. Rather than slaughter animals throughout the year, the nomads cull their herd for food at the end of fall. This is when the good grazing of summer and fall has built the largest store of fat on the animals. The nomads argue (correctly) that to slaughter livestock earlier or later would result in less meat and fat per animal. Also, in late fall there is no problem storing the 20 or so animals most families slaughter, since temperatures are already well below zero, with lows of -20°F to -30°F.

The nomads' animals also provide the raw materials essential for clothing, shelter, and fuel. Life on the changdang requires a portable dwelling that can stand up to the terrible wind and hailstorms that are common in this area. The Phala people weave the coarse black belly-hair of yaks into a material that they sew into their windproof and durable tents. As for clothing, 8 to 10 sheepskins or goatskins are used to make the nomads' heavy winter robelike dress, the fleece worn on the inside. Their pants are made from heavy woven wool or from sheepskin or goatskin, and their boots have yakskin soles and woolen leggings. Similarly, winter hats are generally made from lamb's fleece, and ropes, bags, and gear for their horses come from the wool, cashmere, and leather they harvest from their livestock.

The herds also provide fuel, critical for cooking and heating. There are no trees (or even shrubs) on the changdang, and life would not be possible without the dung of the animals. Thus, the nomads have a free and inexhaustible source of energy that requires little work to collect.

Intrinsic to nomadic pastoralism is moving camp. In Tibet, yak, sheep, and goats can be used as transport animals. Having their own source of transport also means the nomads can easily trade with other segments of the society; in fact, half of their total caloric intake comes from barley they obtain from farmers living about a month's walk to the southeast. In this traditional trade system, the nomads carry a variety of items, including wool; goat hair; skins of yak, sheep, and goats; butter; and live animals. They return laden with barley and other foods, such as tea and cooking oil. They also obtain products their animals cannot supply, such as wooden utensils, metalware, swords, and jewelry.

The transport animals serve still another function. They enable the nomads to exploit the enormous salt flats on the Tibetan plateau. From a distance, these look like vast snowfields, but up close they are recognized as salt deposits about one foot deep. This salt is literally there for the taking, but the task is not easy. The Tibetan nomads traditionally obtain salt in the spring, the round trip from Phala to the northwest salt flat taking 70 days on their trail. Then, the salt is transported for another month to the south to be sold.

Wild animals also play a part in the pastoral adaptation. Phala has substantial herds of antelopes, gazelles, and blue sheep—all of which are considered edible by the nomads. But they are not usually hunted heavily. When times are good, most nomads adhere more strictly to their Buddhist values and refrain from killing. However, when times are bad, literally everyone hunts. Thus, in a sense, the wildlife acts as a stockpile, used little until conditions warrant it.

The nomadic pastoralists of Phala serve as an excellent example of the nomadic pastoral mode of production. Through a sophisticated and highly efficient system of breeding, rearing, and harvesting livestock, they secure for themselves a stable and satisfactory existence in an environment that is often hostile.

16 | Society and Kinship

This pictograph, made by Sioux Indians in the late nineteenth century, documents their daily life—buffalo hunting, rituals, fighting—in a type of calendar for the past year (vegetable dyes on muslin, ca. 1 × 3 meters).

Wolf children, a few hermits, prisoners in solitary confinement, and those stranded on desert isles aside, most of us spend a great deal of time in the company of other humans. It is generally as a group that we adapt to our surroundings and seek to ensure that our subsistence requirements are met. How we perceive the world and how we behave in it are largely reflections of our interaction with others. **Society** is an abstraction of the ways in which interaction among individuals is patterned.

In the last chapter we looked at how people procure food and produce, distribute, and exchange things. This chapter focuses on the social dimension of adaptation: What are the varied ways in which people order their interaction with the human environment?

LOOKING AT SOCIETY

To figure out how society works, anthropologists study both the structure and the function of social events or processes. In their analyses, they look at varying levels of interaction—from whole societies linked by the world system down to the interaction of two individuals.

Analyzing Social Structure and Function

The term *structure* refers to the interrelationship of parts in a complex whole. When we look at the structures of whole societies, we see that groups that pursue similar subsistence strategies tend to have similar **social structures**. Their similarities will be modified somewhat by local conditions and historical circumstances, such as the availability of particular resources, weather, or contact with different peoples; nevertheless, they will share many fundamental features. Generally, we find that small-scale societies exhibit a high degree of internal cohesiveness. This is reflected in their limited division of labor. By contrast, as societies become larger they begin to lose their homogeneous nature, and the social structure comes to be made up of more specialized parts, as seen in our own society.

By **function** we mean the purpose and effects, the intended and actual consequences, of particular beliefs and actions. While one function may be of primary importance, most beliefs and actions serve a variety of functions, depending in part on the point of reference. Thus, marriage serves different functions for the individuals getting married, for the couple's respective families, and for society as a whole.

Social scientists commonly distinguish two categories of social function: manifest and latent. **Manifest functions** are the purposes or results that are most obvious and that are explicitly stated. The manifest function of washing clothing is to get it clean. **Latent functions** are the less apparent purposes. Clothes-washing by women

may perform the latent function of assessing their social standing in relation to their peers in terms of skill and diligence; as a form of drudgery, it may also symbolize a society's view that women are inferior to men.

The Individual and Society

In looking at the parts of a society, we can start with the individual. The individual is the build-

These aboriginal children at Wiluna, Western Australia, are washing clothes. The manifest function of doing the laundry is to clean the clothes; a latent function is to prepare the children to become adults.

ing block of society, for in one sense society is the product of the actions of its members. The members of a society do not act alone, however. Individuals are social actors whose behaviors are influenced by the social environment. It would be more accurate, then, to view society as the representation of the collective behavior of its members. Much of this collective behavior is highly patterned, conditioned by social forces that both spring from and transcend the individual.

Because society has no tangible existence, any permanence or regularity that it does exhibit will depend on the repetition of people's actions. Society is therefore subject to the need for continual re-creation by individuals. The pattern that we associate with the family in rural Japan does not exist except insofar as individual Japanese continue to group themselves and behave in ways that have come to be associated with a particular family structure.

Society is the product of decisions people make concerning when, how, and with whom they are going to interact. Such individual decisions are influenced by a number of factors, some of which may be based on existing social patterns. One of these factors is individual perception: how individuals view their environment and the situation in which they must act, and what they perceive their options to be. Another factor is historical precedent, because what a person does is almost always influenced by what was done in the past. The weight individuals give to this continuity depends on the extent to which they consider past actions to be relevant in their current circumstances and the degree to which they interact continually with the same people and the same physical surroundings. A third factor is the nature of a person's or group's goals. We interact with others to achieve some end. Should our goals or those of the group change, so will the pattern of our social behavior.

Social Relationships

We use the term *relationship* for any regularized pattern of action between individuals. By placing such patterns in a social context, we arrive at the concept of a **social relationship.** The interaction of a woman and her female child may be termed a mother-daughter relationship, and it can be expected to exhibit certain regularities within a particular society. However, rather than thinking about *the* mother-daughter relationship in a society in some idealized sense, we should recognize a range of mother-daughter relationships, depending on the life cycle and the varying circumstances of the two individuals involved. The relationship of an American mother and her preschool daughter will change as the child grows and becomes an adolescent. How much variation there will be in relationships is likely to depend on social scale, but even in small-scale societies there will be some variation.

Two primary questions need to be asked about social relationships: Whom are they between? What are they about? (Beattie 1964). Answers to these questions are often expressed in terms of status and role. **Status** concerns social position—what people are in relation to one another. Social scientists make a distinction between an ascribed status and one that is achieved. An *ascribed status* is assigned, usually on the basis of birth. A girl born to Nuer parents automatically is a Nuer as well as a female. An *achieved status* is attained through the actions or decisions of individuals on an optional basis. One becomes a teacher in our society as a result of individual decisions, successfully completing a course of training, and managing to find employment. A status can have both an ascribed and an achieved quality. To be born heir to a throne does not automatically ensure that the prince will become king.

The part a society expects one to play in a given relationship is a **role**—a set of activities that are thought to have some purpose and function in a particular context. A king is expected to govern; a subject is expected to submit to the king's authority. Such expectations cannot be understood in isolation, however. Precisely how a king or a subject is expected to behave will be defined by historical tradition and the contemporary situation. The status of kingship in the so-

Traditional Hawaiian chiefs in cloak and headdress. Although Hawaiian chiefs inherited their status genealogically, it was not entirely ascribed, since their practical success in leading their people helped contribute to their chiefly status.

ciety will also be a factor. A king may be expected not only to govern but also to intercede with the deities on behalf of his subjects, or to give his blessing to certain brands of cookie or tea. Such expectations are not static. Both the status and the role of Queen Elizabeth II are a far cry from those associated with Henry VIII; the difference reflects changes in the English economy, the emergence of new forms of social stratification, and the transformation of the English state.

Roles do not take place simply in pairs. Kings also have relationships with those who are not their subjects, and such relationships can influence the respective roles of king and subject. Furthermore, individuals usually occupy a number of different statuses and perform a range of roles, any one of which may influence the others. The king may also be a father, a member of a cricket team, a husband, and an airplane pilot.

Social scale is an important factor affecting statuses and roles. In small-scale societies with little specialization, the range of distinct statuses and roles available to an individual is much more limited than in large-scale societies. Among desert-dwelling foragers such as the Shoshone, almost the only distinctions made are those based on age, gender, and kinship. Furthermore, statuses and roles tend to overlap, forming a few clusters that are ascribed to individuals. Thus, all middle-aged Shoshone males can be expected to occupy more or less the same status and perform roughly the same roles. In sharp contrast, a middle-aged male in a large-scale industrial society can be anything from a wealthy and powerful business leader to an impoverished vagrant.

Institutions

Institutions are practices based on similar principles that display some degree of regularity. While there are many principles around which institutions may be organized, anthropologists identify four of major significance (Beattie 1964). Some institutions deal with *economic and property relations*—with the ways in which people produce and distribute things. Among these institutions are farms, banks, and markets. Other institutions are concerned with *social control*—with politics and law. Government, courts, and the police fall within this category. In the third category are institutions concerned with the *supernatural*—with magic and religion. These include the church, monasteries, and witches' covens. The fourth category consists of institutions based on principles of *kinship*—relations created by descent and marriage, such as the family. Anthropologists are especially interested in institutions based on kinship because of their central role in small-scale societies. We will discuss kinship in more detail in the next section of this chapter.

Any institution is likely to be concerned to some degree with more than one of these organizing principles. Thus, the family is also concerned with social control, with economic and property relations, and, in many societies, with the supernatural. But these are secondary concerns rather than primary organizing principles for the specific institution concerned—in this case, the family.

The process by which regularized patterns are created is referred to as **institutionalization,** or the standardization of patterns of joint activity. For example, when a religious prophet or cult leader succeeds in regularizing people's beliefs and practices according to his or her teachings, this type of religious belief and the social group that forms around it can be said to have undergone institutionalization. One common way of institutionalizing social relations is through kinship, the subject to which we now turn.

KINSHIP

Kinship—social relations based on culturally recognized ties of descent and marriage—is a feature of all human societies. The reasons for this universality are to some extent biological. Human infants are helpless and dependent on the care of others for a prolonged period, and bonds arise among people in relation to these conditions. But while biology provides the basis for kinship, the ways in which people define and use kinship are determined by sociocultural considerations, not biological ones. When anthropologists study kinship, they are concerned with social relations and cultural definitions. Rather than being universal, these vary widely. In different societies, people with the same biological or marital relationship may be defined differently, labeled differently, and classified variously as kin or nonkin.

Kinship Diagrams and Abbreviations

Faced with the need to understand and compare a wide variety of kinship systems, anthropologists have developed a standardized notational system as shown in Figure 16.1. At the heart of this system are six basic symbols:

1. a triangle to indicate a male;
2. a circle to indicate a female;

3. a square to indicate when a person's gender is unspecified;
4. a vertical line to indicate descent, as from parent to child;
5. a horizontal line with descending vertical lines to indicate codescent, as in the case of siblings; and
6. an equals sign or a horizontal line with ascending vertical lines to indicate marriage.

It is often necessary to use other symbols as well. For deceased persons, the symbol may be darkened or a line drawn through it. Divorce is represented by drawing a slash (/) across the horizontal bar. Kinship diagrams may be centered on a particular person. This person is referred to as **ego,** the individual from whose point of view the relationships are being traced.

Anthropologists also have devised shorthand notations to indicate people's relationships:

F for father	M for mother	S for son
D for daughter	B for brother	Z for sister
H for husband	W for wife	C for child

Other relationships can be indicated by combining these abbreviations. This is especially important because of the ambiguity in kinship terminology. Thus, what we call uncles would include mother's brothers (MB), father's brothers (FB),

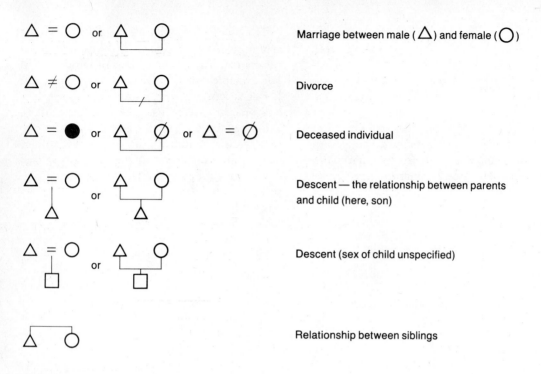

FIGURE 16.1
Standardized notations for diagramming kinship relations.

mother's sister's husbands (MZH), and father's sister's husbands (FZH). In many kinship systems, these distinctions are of considerable importance; thus, a shortened version of what are sometimes cumbersome combinations is very useful. A hypothetical family is diagrammed in Figure 16.2 with the relevant notation.

Kinship Categories

In their study of kinship, anthropologists are concerned with two separate, but interrelated, types of relationship: consanguinity and affinity. Consanguinity refers to biological relationship, that of "blood"; those so linked we call *consanguines*. Affinity concerns relationships formed through marriage; people linked in this fashion are *affines*. Not all societies view blood relatedness in the same way. In some societies, a child is con-

sidered to be related by blood to the mother only; in others, a child is related by blood only to the father.

While there are differences of opinion regarding the basic question of who should be categorized as blood relations, even more disagreement exists when we turn to more distant relatives. Take our father's brother, our uncle, for example. Some societies make no categorical distinction between him and our father; others use the same term for both of them and one of our cousins (FZS). How people categorize kin varies greatly. The variations are far from unlimited, however. There are a few general principles around which most categorical systems are built.

Defining Parents, Siblings, and Cousins

Two fundamental relationships in any system of kinship are those between parents and children and those between siblings. After all, these are our most immediate biological links. However,

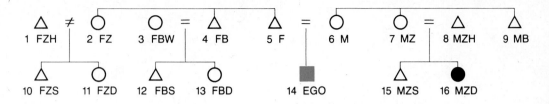

FIGURE 16.2

A hypothetical family diagram. Ego (14)—the center point of the diagram—has no brothers or sisters. Ego's father (5) has a sister (2) and a brother (4). Ego's father's sister (2) and father's sister's husband (1) are divorced. Ego's mother has a sister (7) and a brother (9), but only the sister has married. Ego's mother's sister's daughter (16) is deceased.

biology provides only the basis for these relationships. Definitions of the relationships are culturally constructed.

In our society, a distinction is made between the actual biological father, the socially and legally recognized father, and the mother's husband. The same person may occupy all three statuses, but not necessarily. When we talk about someone's father we usually mean his or her social father, who may or may not be the biological father. When divorced couples remarry, for the sake of clarity we sometimes use such terms as *stepfather* and *real father*. In other societies, things can be even more complex. The Nuer allow women and even ghosts to assume the status of social father, and in some South Asian societies a group of brothers may be viewed collectively as social fathers of a single individual.

Definitions of siblings may be equally complicated. In our society, siblings are often related by blood, but this is not always the case. We often make no distinction between siblings who are a couple's natural offspring and those who are adopted, or between children of a couple from previous marriages and those of the present one, although such distinctions are possible. The situation becomes much more complex in societies that allow individuals to have more than one spouse at the same time. And some societies dis-

tinguish siblings according to relative age. In yet other societies, siblings and cousins are categorized together. Thus, the same terms will be used for sisters and all female cousins and for brothers and all male cousins.

Cousins, the children of a parent's sibling and his or her spouse, are also basic to any kinship system. In our society, virtually the only distinction made is between those cousins considered too close for sexual or marriage purposes and those who are considered sufficiently distant. Although the reasons for making such a distinction are often couched in biological terms, the distinction in fact represents a strictly cultural pattern. In other societies, paternal cousins may be considered different from maternal cousins. And **cross-cousins**, children of a parent's sibling of the opposite sex (e.g., children of the father's sister), may be considered different from **parallel-cousins**, children of a parent's sibling of the same sex (e.g., children of the father's brother) (see Figure 16.3). These distinctions are not random. They are deeply rooted in people's cultural traditions and social structures. Thus, the distinction that many societies make between kinds of cousins is related to inheritance patterns and strategies. Many of the distinctions are also products of particular kinship systems and the manner in which descent is traced.

Principles of Descent

The organization of kinship systems involves questions of **descent**, socially recognized links between a person and his or her ancestors. It is largely through descent that our range of kin expands beyond the narrow limits of our siblings and parents and their siblings.

Many societies limit the range of people

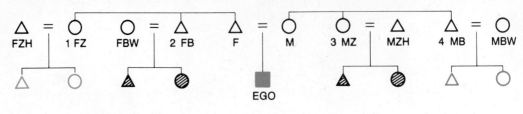

△ ○ Cross-cousins

▲ ⊘ Parallel-cousins

FIGURE 16.3

Cross-cousins and parallel cousins. Ego's cross-cousins are the offspring of ego's father's sister (1) and ego's mother's brother (4). Ego's parallel cousins are the children of ego's father's brother (2) and ego's mother's sister (3).

through whom descent can be traced. One of the most important reasons for doing this is to control access to resources. In this way, descent becomes an adaptive strategy. The most restrictive way of tracing descent is **unilineal descent**— through a single line, male or female. Unilineal rules of descent affiliate a person with a line of kin extending both back in time and into the future, but select only those kin who are related through male or female lines. We refer to the tracing of descent through female lines as **matrilineal descent.** According to this principle, children of each generation trace descent from their social mother, and only those who are related through female lines are considered part of the same kin group (see Figure 16.4). Descent traced in a similar manner through male lines is referred to as **patrilineal descent** (see Figure 16.5). Unilineal descent patterns are found among more affluent or stable foragers, certain small-scale farmers, and pastoral nomads.

A few small-scale societies define kinship on less restrictive terms, yet continue to adhere to principles of lineality. Some trace descent separately through both male and female lines. According to this principle of **bilineal descent** (sometimes known as double descent), an individual may trace descent patrilineally for some purposes and matrilineally for others. Other societies recognize both matrilineal and patrilineal descent, but it is up to the individual to choose between them. This principle is referred to as **ambilineal descent**. Lastly, in some societies women trace descent through female lines and men trace descent through male lines, a principle referred to as **parallel descent.**

Another form of descent predominates in large-scale societies, foraging societies occupying harsh environments or experiencing pressure

patrilineal

FIGURE 16.4

Matrilineal descent. The symbols outlined in color in this diagram are all related through the female line to a common ancestor.

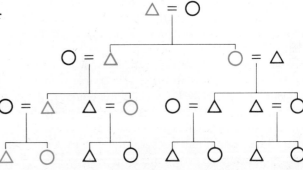

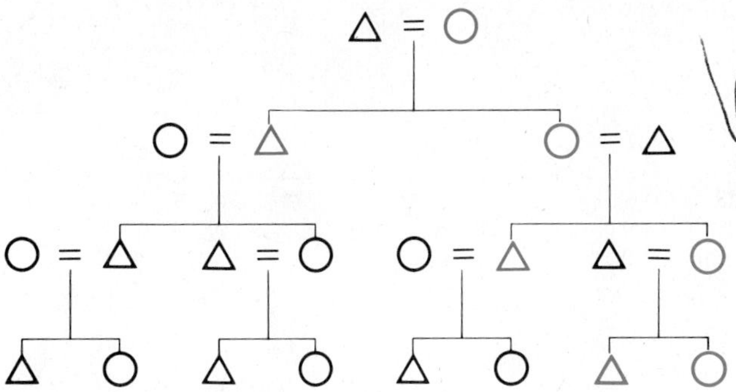

[handwritten margin notes: mother's uncle is important / matrilineal]

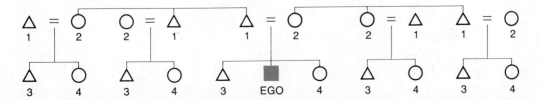

FIGURE 16.5

Patrilineal descent. The symbols outlined in color in this diagram are all related through the male line to a common ancestor.

from nonforaging peoples, and among family-oriented transhumants and farmers living in fairly poor environments. This pattern, often called **cognatic descent,** allows a person to trace descent through all ancestors, male and female. All relatives on both sides are considered kin.

Systems of Labeling Kin

Not only do societies base descent on different principles, they also use different labels for relatives. Although a vast array of kinship terminologies are in current use throughout the world, anthropologists have been able to isolate a limited number of general patterns in the ways people label kin. We will now review some of the more common of these patterns.

The system employed in our own culture and commonly associated with cognatic descent systems is known as the *Eskimo System* (Figure 16.6). In this system, cousins are distinguished from brothers and sisters, but all cousins are placed in the same category. Aunts and uncles are distin-

guished from parents and are labeled separately according to sex. Unlike most other systems, in the Eskimo System no other relatives are referred to by the same terms used for members of the nuclear family—mother, father, brother, sister. This restrictiveness of terms may be related to the lack of large kin-based groups in these societies and their emphasis on small family groups instead.

The *Hawaiian System* (Figure 16.7) is the least complex system, using the smallest number of terms. All relatives of the same sex in the same generation are referred to by the same term. Thus, all female cousins are referred to by the same term used for ego's sisters, and all male cousins by the same term used for ego's brothers. Likewise, all known male relatives of ego's parents' generation are called by the same term, as are all female relatives of this generation. This system is often associated with ambilineal descent, which allows for a person to be affiliated with the kin group of either father or mother, or with nonunilineal systems. At the other extreme is the *Sudanese System* (Figure 16.8), which makes the most distinctions possible. It uses distinct

FIGURE 16.6

Eskimo kinship system.

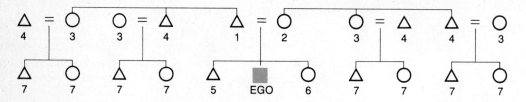

FIGURE 16.7
Hawaiian kinship system. Symbols with the same number are referred to in the same way by ego.

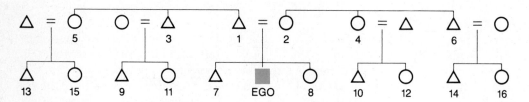

FIGURE 16.8
Sudanese kinship system.

terms for all cousins on the basis of their relationship with ego, for example. The Sudanese System is common in societies characterized by a complex division of labor, marked social stratification, and patrilineal descent groups.

The *Omaha System* (Figure 16.9) is the one usually associated with patrilineal descent. It uses the same term for a number of kin of the same generation within the patrilineal group. For instance, ego's father and father's brothers are all given the same label. Distinctions are not made with regard to most maternal relations, however. Ego's mother, mother's sister, and mother's

brother's daughter are all assigned the same title, as are the mother's brother and mother's brother's son. Within ego's generation, different labels are applied on the basis of gender. Male siblings and male parallel cousins are all given the same title, and ego's female siblings and female parallel cousins are lumped together under another label.

The *Crow System* (Figure 16.10) may be considered the matrilineal equivalent of the Omaha System. The primary difference between the two is that in the Crow System relatives in the father's matrilineage (F, FB, and FZS on the one hand, and FZ and FZD on the other hand) are labeled as one respectively, while generational distinctions are made on the mother's side. Accordingly, ego's mother and mother's sister are given the same name, ego's female siblings and female

FIGURE 16.9
Omaha kinship system.

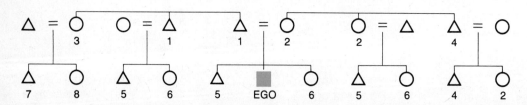

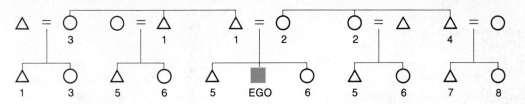

FIGURE 16.10
Crow kinship system.

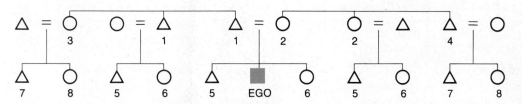

FIGURE 16.11
Iroquois kinship system.

parallel cousins are given the same name, and ego's male siblings and male parallel cousins are also called by one name.

Finally, the *Iroquois System* (Figure 16.11) is similar to the Crow and Omaha systems in the way individuals of ego's parents' generation are treated. Ego's father and father's brother are assigned the same name, and ego's mother and mother's sister are likewise merged. The primary difference between the Crow and Omaha systems and the Iroquois System is in how cross-cousins are treated. In the Crow and Omaha systems, they are given separate terms or merged with the previous generation. In the Iroquois System, male cross-cousins are categorized together (FZS, MBS), as are female cross-cousins (FZD, MBD). This pattern may be linked with societal preferences for cross-cousin marriage, since cross-cousin marriage and Iroquois terminology often occur together (Goody 1970).

SOCIAL GROUPINGS

We use the term *group* very broadly in common discourse, but anthropologists are much more careful in their use of the word. When referring to a group, anthropologists usually mean what more specifically can be labeled a corporate group. A **corporate group** is theoretically permanent; its members are recruited on the basis of recognized principles, they have common interests or property, and they have norms or rules fixing their rights and duties in relation to one another and to their property or interests. A patrilineage is a corporate group to which members are recruited on the basis of kinship, the principle being descent through the male line from a common ancestor (see p. 432). A business corporation is also a corporate group, but one that recruits people for specific purposes on the basis of their skills and particular modes of behavior. Although both the patrilineage and the business corporation are corporate groups, membership in the former is ascribed, whereas membership in the latter is on a nonascriptive basis.

This important distinction bestows groups with significantly different characteristics.

Ascribed Groups

In **ascribed groups**, membership is acquired at birth. Assembling people into multipurpose groups on the basis of ascribed categories is the chief principle of group formation in small-scale societies. With increasing social scale, groupings tend to become more voluntary and specialized. The most common types of ascriptive multipurpose groupings are based on age, gender, and kinship.

Age-based Groups

Age is a universally important factor determining social behavior. All societies include a series of recognized age-based categories, or **age grades**. Most societies at least divide their members into categories associated with youth, adulthood, and old age, and in many societies these age grades are further refined. There are behavior expectations associated with each of the age grades and sometimes they are accorded specified rights and privileges, but individuals within the same age grade do not necessarily function as a corporate group.

In a number of small-scale societies, especially in Africa, those belonging to the same age grade are formed into corporate groups. These groups, known as **age sets**, are composed of individuals of similar age and of the same sex who share a common identity, maintain close ties throughout their lives, and together pass through a series of age-related statuses. The structure of age sets varies from one society to the next. Some follow a linear progression, in which those born during a specified period belong to a single set that moves through a series of grades as the members grow older. Others adhere to a cyclic pattern, in which new members are periodically accepted. In some societies, age sets are fairly unimportant, performing a limited range of functions and exerting little influence on the overall functioning of

society; in other societies, they are of tremendous importance.

The Nyakyusa of southeastern Africa have a well-developed system of age sets (Wilson 1963). At age 12, boys who have grown up working closely together leave their parental homes and move to a village of their own. They return to their parents for meals and to their fathers' fields to work until they marry and set up their own households, at about age 25. Younger brothers of the village founders join the community until it becomes large enough for the members to decide to close admittance. After a decade or so, when there are a number of new age-set villages in the area, the fathers hold a ceremony to hand over full political authority to their sons.

Gender-based Groups

All societies categorize people by gender, as well as by age. In small-scale societies, people are automatically divided into gender-based groups that serve many purposes, such as carrying out subsistence activities delegated to one or the other sex. Large-scale industrial societies also commonly include gender-based groups (such as the League of Women Voters, the Boy Scouts, and fraternities and sororities), but membership in these is usually on a voluntary basis, and the groups serve a narrower range of purposes.

Again, within small-scale societies, the structure and significance of these sex-based groups can differ a great deal. In Amazonian Brazil, the Mundurucu household contains a gender-based group consisting of several closely related women of two generations. Usually the women are from the same village and have grown up together. They carry out most of their productive tasks as a group—gardening, preparing manioc, and cooking together. It is a secure group that is to a large extent self-sufficient. The males in a Mundurucu village have moved there from other villages upon marriage. When not engaged in subsistence activities, they spend much of their time in a central men's house, a common feature in small-scale farming societies. The men's groups

Kuikuro Indian men painting up for a tribal dance in their men's house, a common gender-based feature in small-scale societies. The use of a men's house, from which women are excluded, often functions to maintain men's control of special forms of ritual and knowledge.

are not as well integrated as are those of women, since the men come from different villages. Also, male economic tasks are performed alone or in small groups, further diminishing their unity.

Changes brought about by integration into larger societies have served to undermine gender-based groups such as those of the Mundurucu. The Mundurucu have become increasingly dependent on collecting rubber to meet their economic needs, and especially to earn money to purchase consumer goods from traders. Rubber trees are widely scattered, so that many Mundurucu now live as isolated nuclear families to be nearer rubber-collecting areas. Others have moved to a mission settlement. Such moves have resulted in the breakdown of the prior pattern of separate gender-based groups and their replacement by new forms of association.

Kin-based Groups

People use kinship for two primary social functions. First, kinship serves as a medium for transmitting status and property from one generation to the next. We refer to this process as **inheritance.** Second, kinship serves as a principle by which to establish and maintain social groups. Kin-based groups themselves can be formed for a variety of purposes. They are often property-owning bodies, with the ownership of land, animals, ceremonial objects, and other forms of property vested in the collective membership. They may also provide a basis for mutual aid, with their members helping one another in anything from agricultural labor to burying the dead. They may also serve military purposes, or ceremonial ones, or even political and administrative functions. The most basic kin-based group is the family, which will be discussed in the next chapter. For now, we will focus on kin-based groups beyond the family level.

Unilineal descent is one of the most common principles on which the formation of kin-based social groups is based. Membership in a unilineal kinship group generally is ascriptive: a person becomes a member at birth. Its ascriptive nature allows for the formation of discrete social groups, dividing everyone in a society into members and nonmembers. The four basic types of groups based on unilineal principles are indicated in Figure 16.12. These groups are lineages, clans, phratries, and moieties.

FIGURE 16.12

Unilineal descent groups. Lineages, clans, phratries, and moieties are groups that can form an organizational hierarchy. A lineage is a subdivision of a clan, a clan is a subdivision of a phratry, and a phratry is a subdivision of a moiety. Societies are not always subdivided into four groups, however; some societies may have only one or two of these groups.

A **lineage** is a group of kin who trace descent from a common ancestor or ancestress through known links. When descent is traced through the male line, the group is known as a **patrilineage.** When descent is traced through the female line, the term **matrilineage** is used. In small-scale societies, lineages can serve a primary role in the distribution of wealth and power. In such societies land, and sometimes other important forms of wealth, are held jointly. Lineage members often cooperate economically and are expected to assume some responsibility for one another's well-being. Religious life in lineage-based societies frequently emphasizes the worship of lineage ancestors.

In contrast to a lineage, a **clan** is a group of kin who believe themselves to be descended from a common ancestor, but who cannot specify the actual links back to that ancestor. In some societies, clan members form close-knit groups not unlike lineages. Often, however, clan members are widely dispersed, rarely interacting on a clan-wide basis. A point of unity for clan members commonly is a shared **totemic emblem**—an animal or plant. Clan members are expected to acknowledge certain mutual obligations, but these may be limited to assisting one another in times of need.

Clans often encompass a number of localized lineages. The Yakö of eastern Nigeria, for example, have small, landowning patrilineages (they also have matrilineages, which serve other func-

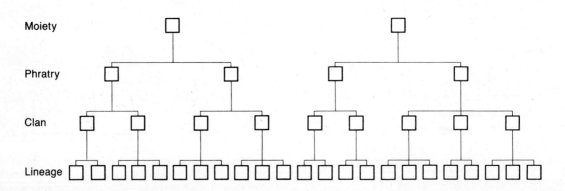

Moiety

Phratry

Clan

Lineage

*Tsimshian chiefs of the wolf crest (clan emblem),
Giltadamaxs, 1903: Andrew Nass, shirt with coppers;
John Nass in white; James Skean, chilkat blanket;
Philip Nass, chilkat blanket with neck ring; Charlie
Brown in shirt with inverted face and holding drum.*

tions). Patrilineages occupying a section of a village are usually united by common clan membership. Each clan has a ritual leader who is in charge of the clan shrine and who presides over informal meetings of lineage elders and notables. Under normal circumstances members of Yakö clans recognize their common descent. When disputes arise over household sites or agricultural land, however, lineage members tend to emphasize their distinctiveness (Forde 1964).

A **phratry** is a descent group composed of a number of supposedly related clans, the actual links usually being unrecognized. The Haida of the northwest coast of North America, for example, have phratries that are subdivided into a large number of clans. Each phratry has its own identifying totemic emblem. The two main phratries of the Haida are the Raven phratry, with the killer whale as its emblem, and the Eagle phratry, with the eagle as its emblem. Phratry members have the exclusive right to use of their emblems on material belongings—houses, boats, utensils, hats, and so forth. Haida settlements generally include members of both the Raven and the Eagle groups. Phratries rarely serve an important social function. Among the few exceptions were Aztec phratries, which were the basis for common ceremonial activities in addition to serving significant political functions.

Many small-scale societies are divided into **moieties,** two distinct unilineal descent groups that perform reciprocal functions for one another. Where moieties exist, members usually must marry members of the opposite moiety, and moiety affiliation is often an important consideration in religious or ceremonial activities. The Mardudjara Aborigines have moieties based on patrilineal descent, and at large ceremonial gatherings they group their camps into two "sides," each performing distinct roles in the ceremonies. Among the Seneca Iroquois of North America, each moiety performs mourning rituals on behalf of the other. And in some North American native societies, moieties compete against one another in games of lacrosse. Moieties are frequently associated with dualities in the universe: land and water, night and day, sky and earth, war and peace. Accordingly, moieties commonly are assigned names that identify them with these dualities.

Whereas lineal descent provides a ready basis for groups with nonoverlapping memberships, cognatic descent is much more messy. In cognatic descent systems, individuals can be members of more than one group at the same time, and any person can serve as the founder of a group. Thus, all of ego's grandparents might be the founders of separate groups, and ego could be a member of all of them. From the perspective of the individual, such a system is advantageous because of its flexibility, which offers ego a range of choices. On the negative side, the system makes it difficult to form unified groups, and property and loyalties can be widely and almost randomly dispersed.

There are two ways to approach the formation of groups on the basis of cognatic descent. In the *ancestor-focused approach*, groups are formed by tracing descent from ancestors. In the *ego-focused approach*, groups are formed around a shared relative who is not an ancestor. The network of individuals linked to ego through ego-focused cognatic principles is called a **kindred** (see Figure 16.13). One of the distinguishing features of a kindred is that no two individuals except siblings (and double first cousins) will have the same potential kindred. Furthermore, a kindred cannot persist beyond the life of the person on whom it is centered.

Kindreds are common among the tribal peoples of island Southeast Asia. These societies traditionally lacked states and had no fixed social hierarchies. Emphasis was placed on ideas of fam-

FIGURE 16.13
A kindred. Kindreds are groups that are formed using ego-focused cognatic descent principles. People are related to a living person (ego) through both male and female lines. This diagram shows ego's kindred; ego's mother's kindred, however, is confined to within the dashed border. (Arrows indicate continuation of the lines.)

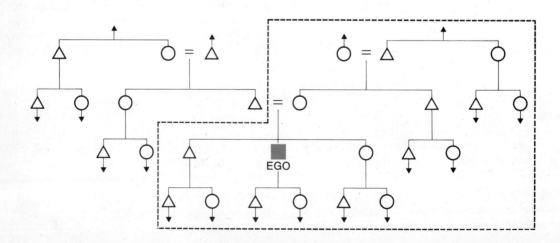

ily gift giving and obligation. Male prestige was associated with war and especially head-hunting, and kindreds often served as the basis for recruiting head-hunting parties. Among the Kalinga of the northern Philippines, kindreds served to form vengeance parties when someone was killed, as a means of sharing meat, and occasionally for other forms of assistance. In general, such kindreds do not form stable groups, the individuals coming together only for a limited purpose.

The ancestor-focused approach allows for the formation of groups that are more like groups formed on the basis of lineal descent, but to do so requires the imposition of some kind of restriction. The most common type of restriction has to do with residence. A person may have the right to membership in a number of groups, but is able to exercise that right only by living in a group's territory. Individual New Zealand Maori, for example, may have many cognatically recognized ancestors and may belong to a number of different descent groups. But a person can reside only with one of these groups, and for males it is usually the father's group.

Voluntary Associations

Special-purpose groups, the members of which are recruited on a nonascriptive basis, are a common feature of life in large-scale industrial societies. These **voluntary associations** are found less often in small-scale societies, where most groupings tend to be ascriptive. Nevertheless, several types of voluntary association may play a part in small-scale societies.

Voluntary Groupings in Small-Scale Societies

Specialized *military associations* are formed in some small-scale societies that engage in warfare regularly, although kinship groups and age sets are more likely to be the primary military units. The Cheyenne traditionally had five such societies: the Fox, the Dog, the Shield, the Elk (or Hoof Rattle), and the Bowstring (or Contrary),

each with its own leaders, costumes, songs, and dances (Hoebel 1978).

Secret societies are another form of voluntary grouping found in small-scale societies. The Poro society, found in Liberia and Sierra Leone, is an example of such a group (Little 1965/66). Members of the Poro society are said to have close contact with the supernatural and to possess magical powers. Its leadership comes from among those who hold public power, and the society serves to support their public statuses. Young men who are initiated into the society attend "bush school" in an isolated part of the forest for several years, at which time they learn secret rituals, the society's version of the history of their people, as well as a variety of useful survival skills.

There are also *religious cults,* such as those of the Tupi-Guarani of Brazil, reported by early European explorers and settlers (Lanternari 1963). Tupi-Guarani prophets would gather large numbers of followers and then set off in search of a promised land. The so-called cargo cults of the South Pacific (see Chapter 21) are another example of this type of voluntary association.

Voluntary Groupings in Large-Scale Societies

Voluntary associations have developed in large-scale societies in response to two processes: urbanization and industrialization. The dislocation, alienation, and impersonalization of modern, large-scale societies have given rise to the formation of voluntary associations directed toward the varied interests of those living in these societies. While anthropologists have studied a wide range of such associations, they have been especially interested in those formed by ethnic minorities and recent migrants to cities.

Recent urban migrants frequently form associations on the basis of their place of origin, ethnicity, religion, or line of work. These associations sometimes play an important role in securing employment and social services for their members. But their precise roles can vary a great deal. Moreover, anthropologists have questioned

A voluntary association: the Cheyenne Lance Society (photograph taken in the late 1880s). A social and military group, the Lance Society, also known as the Coyote, was part of a ruling group along with chiefs. The group also served a police function on buffalo hunts.

the actual importance of these associations to members of the community within which they exist. Abner Cohen (1969), in a study of West African ethnic associations, found that only a small percentage of the total number of migrants actually joined these associations, and that for many of those who did join, the activities of the associations were of little relevance to the members' daily lives. Cohen's study alerts us to the need for caution when placing modern voluntary associations in the context of social life in large-scale societies.

Voluntary associations, of course, need not directly affect the daily lives of their members to exert a great deal of influence on them. We can see this in the case of trade unions, a form of voluntary association that arose out of the new work conditions of large-scale industrial societies. Unions have influenced the lives of workers in many countries indirectly by having such an important effect on the evolution of acceptable conditions of work and, more specifically, through individual negotiations that set wages and work standards. Workers tend only to be reminded of the importance of unions when negotiations take place or disputes occur. A similar point can be made concerning political parties. Indirectly, political parties influence almost every aspect of the lives of people in modern states; yet, most people in these societies do not directly participate in these associations and are only directly con-

cerned with them when elections take place. In this way, we can see that voluntary groups differ a great deal from the ascriptive groups of small-scale societies where the link between daily life and association is much more direct and constant.

SUMMARY

Humans shape and are shaped by their social environment. These interactions can be analyzed by looking at their structure or functions. Within a society, beliefs and activities may serve certain obvious, or manifest, functions and less obvious, latent, functions.

The individual is the basic building block of society. Society is the result of the decisions individuals make about when, how, and with whom they are going to interact. Social relationships, regularized patterns of action between individuals, are often institutionalized according to the status and role given to those involved.

Individuals organize or are organized into various kinds of groups. They are born into nonvoluntary groups on the basis of gender, age, and kinship. Such groups tend to be rather strictly adhered to and multipurpose in small-scale societies. Voluntary associations are more common in large-scale societies, where they may serve a variety of functions.

Biology provides the basis for kinship, but the ways in which kinship is used and defined are determined by sociocultural considerations. Even consanguineal, or blood, relationships with parents, siblings, and cousins are defined differently in different societies.

One way to understand varying kinship patterns is to study how descent is perceived. Some societies trace descent unilineally—through either male or female ancestors and descendants; other societies use bilineal, ambilineal, parallel, or cognatic descent principles.

The "same" relatives are also given different labels in different societies. The many relatives we call "cousins," for example, are given more explicit labels in some other naming systems. The major kin-naming systems are Eskimo, Hawaiian, Sudanese, Omaha, Crow, and Iroquois.

Kinship has two main social functions: inheritance and group formation. In order of increasing inclusiveness, kin-based groups formed on principles of unilineal descent are lineages, clans, phratries, and moieties. Societies using cognatic descent principles may form ancestor-focused cognatic descent groups or ego-focused kindreds.

In kin-based societies, kinship is of fundamental significance to the social order and to the lives of individuals. Differences in the significance of kinship reflect societies' differing adaptational strategies.

SUGGESTED READINGS

Beattie, John. 1964. *Other Cultures: Aims, Methods and Achievements in Social Anthropology.* New York: Free Press.

Blau, Peter M. 1975. *Approaches to the Study of Social Structure.* New York: Free Press.
Boissevain, Jeremy, and J. Clyde Mitchell, eds. 1973.

Network Analysis: Studies in Human Interaction. The Hague/Paris: Mouton.

Burnham, P.C., and R.F. Ellen, eds. 1979. *Social and Ecological Systems*. London/New York: Academic Press.

Epstein, A.L. 1981. *Urbanization and Kinship*. New York: Academic Press. (Zambia)

Evans-Pritchard, E.E. 1940. *The Nuer*. Oxford: Clarendon Press.

Firth, Raymond. 1936. *We the Tikopia: Kinship in Primitive Polynesia*. London: Allen & Unwin.

Pasternak, B. 1976. *Introduction to Kinship and Social Organization*. Englewood Cliffs, NJ: Prentice-Hall.

Stack, Carol B. 1975. *All Our Kin: Strategies for Survival in a Black Community*. New York: Harper & Row.

Land and Genealogy in New Caledonia

Donna Winslow

Donna Winslow is an associate researcher in the Department of Anthropology at Université de Montréal. She did doctoral and postdoctoral research in New Caledonia on ethnic and national identity and has published a number of articles on the independence movement. She is currently working on a book on the relationship between custom and independence in the territory.

The nuclear family is the basic unit of Kanak society in New Caledonia. It is incorporated into an extended family, lineage, and clan, which represent successively larger patriarchal units sharing the same rites, symbols, and marriage customs based on clan exogamy, patrilocality, and marriage to classificatory cross-cousins.

Genealogical memory expresses itself in a series of personal and geographical names. The system of personal names functions to regulate behavior between living individuals. Each person traces his or her line to the last known living paternal relative and, collaterally, to the descendants of the father's father's brother and his descendants. Beyond that, genealogy is expressed geographically. Extended families are assembled into wider groups of lineages and clans by reference to a common place (homestead mound) of origin. These homestead sites refer to the raised mounds in ancient settlements where a large central dwelling was erected.

The clan reference point is the homestead mound founded by the clan ancestor, and each clan knows its history over multiple generations marked by a succession of occupied mounds. The history of each clan is a description of a long series of displacements. Within each clan, the lineages are positioned hierarchically according to the antiquity of their first residence in the genealogical itinerary of the clan. Land is thus the material representation of the clan.

The clan discourse, recited at festivals, is the song of the march, beginning with the homestead mound of origin and describing the journeys of each branch of the clan. This establishes the legitimacy of each lineage in the social order. The name of each lineage is that of the first mound occupied by the lineage ancestor. Social status and land are allotted according to one's name because one has access to land in all the sites occupied by one's ancestors. Names are not always hereditary. A child can receive the name of an extinct lineage or one that has no male inheritors so that its name may continue.

A person can also gain access to land through marriage. A man has access to the land of his wife's family. He can seek a mate and land from his mother's family, his mother's mother's family, or his father's mother's family. In the past, strangers were often welcomed to a region by the offering of wives and, in times of conquest, the conquering group would take wives and go on to occupy land in the conquered area. All these acts could be accompanied by a change

The recovery of ancestral lands is a prime objective of the Kanak independence movement, New Caledonia.

of name. This shifting of names and resulting manipulation of genealogies emphasize the dynamism and flexibility of precontact Kanak society.

When New Caledonia was annexed by France in 1853, the development of the colony became tied to settler colonialism, mineral exploitation, ranching, and the establishment of a penal colony—all necessitating the expropriation of large tracts of native land. The first settlers encountered violent opposition from the Kanaks. This was the result of the confusion surrounding the Kanak idea of land use versus the permanent possession of the land. Settlers would give a gift thinking they had purchased the land, but in Kanak terms the settler was making an exchange that permitted only temporary use of the land. The massacre of a few settlers led to a series of reprisals aimed at pacifying the colony. Kanak lands were confiscated and redistributed to colonists.

In addition, the French administration reasoned that the natives, with their long fallow periods, were wasting land, and that part of this unused acreage could be given over to colonization. The expropriation of vacant land completely disrupted the Kanak agricultural system. The size of the allocations was calculated at 7 hectares of mediocre soils per inhabitant, while it has been estimated that the Kanaks need an average of 30 hectares per person in order to carry out traditional subsistence activities based on yam and taro production. Moreover, the dispossession of Kanak lands was not only an uprooting, it represented a rupture with the symbolic ties that bound people and land.

The first land reserves were created in the 1860s and, from their inception, the notion of reserve was fraught with ambiguities. But whatever the interpretation, it always meant a dispossession of Kanak lands in favor of colonization. The French colonialists also created a crisis situation by sending clans to live on the lands of other clans. The uninvited guests, dispossessed of their own lands, were installed on other lands belonging to the original inhabitants of the village, who found themselves submerged under the flood of immigrants.

By the turn of the century, New Caledonia was primarily a penal colony with very few settlers. The governor at the time decided to recruit settlers from France, but ironically there was little land left to offer them. Thus, the colonial administration turned to the reserves. At this time, the Kanak population was in a steep decline due to epidemics, the aftermath of a revolt, and a low birth rate. This was used as an excuse to expropriate even more land and reduce all reserves to 3 hectares per inhabitant. Some reserves disappeared altogether, and the displaced clans were grouped together in new areas.

This was the most systematic and radical reduction of Kanak lands to date. Kanak geopolitical space no longer bore any resemblance to that of the traditional past. An arbitrary, artificial, imposed system had replaced it totally. The culturally cohesive and contiguous clan territories had been reduced to a shattered collection of isolated communities. In New Caledonia, colonial land expropriation has marked the collective Kanak memory deeply, and the fear of having land confiscated is omnipresent, even though the colonial period has ended and the process has been turned around by the Kanaks themselves.

After World War II, there was a liberalization of French colonial rule. In New Caledonia, Kanaks were given the right to vote, which changed the political relations of power as they began to use their new-found political leverage for land claims. In the early 1970s, when the Kanak-based Front Indépendantiste was being formed, sovereignty over the land and recognition of Kanak cultural identity were the core demands. By the mid-1970s, the land problem on the reserves had become critical because of an economic crisis in the territory. Unemployed youths returned to the reserves only to find that there was no space for them. Their response was to agitate for the recovery of traditional lands. Demanding the return of ancestral lands was also a way of affirming group identity.

By the 1980s, the total recovery of ancestral lands had become a prime objective of the Kanak independence movement. Land claims and the political claim to independence became fused. For the Kanaks of New Caledonia, independence means sovereignty over their land and their genealogical history. Land has become an essential political element in a liberation movement that bases its quest for political power in the establishment of a cultural identity. The ancestral way of life, in this case the relationship to land, is being invoked by Kanak independence leaders. Its symbolic power as a political force is undeniable.

17 Marriage and the Family

Henry Moore's Family Group (1948–49), a Western image of the family. Bronze (cast 1950), 59¼ × 46½ in.; at base, 45 × 29⅞ in.

Among humans, the interaction between men and women involves more than occasional sexual encounters and sharing of food.
Male-female relations are, in fact, an integral
part of most aspects of social life. Every human
society has developed institutions to regulate
these relations, two of the most universal being
marriage and the *family*. These institutions may
be found in all societies; however, as with so
many human institutions, the form they take can
vary a great deal, as can the functions they serve.
This chapter focuses on the varied forms and
functions of these two institutions.

MARRIAGE

Marriage can be defined as a socially sanctioned sexual and economic union between men and women. In some societies, this definition can be expanded to include unions between members of the same sex. The near universality of marriage in human society is related to our mastering several problems common to the human species. One of these is the prolonged period of dependency of the human infant. Especially in labor-intensive foraging and agricultural societies with little division of labor, this dependency places a severe burden on the person (usually a woman) responsible for child care, since it interferes with subsistence activities. During this period, the person tending the child becomes, in turn, dependent on others. Marriage is the most common way of ensuring that the child and its caretaker are supported.

The second problem marriage seeks to solve is sexual competition. Unlike females of other species, mature human females are more or less continuously receptive to sexual activity, which increases the likelihood of disruptive rivalry among males and females. Some scholars (mostly male) have argued that sexual competition is a reproductive and economic threat to the survival of society and that the relative stability provided by marriage is the best way of coming to terms with this threat.

A third adaptational factor encouraging marriage is the division of labor based on gender. Among foragers—the primary human economic adaptation for millions of years—men usually hunted large game and women gathered edible plants and killed smaller animals. Numerous authors argue that such a pattern best meets the needs of a foraging society. Among the Mardudjara Aborigines, women gather food in groups if possible, which allows them to share child-care responsibilities. Mardudjara men, on the other hand, usually hunt alone or in pairs without children to care for, because hunting requires far greater mobility than the slow-paced foraging activities of women. Marriage ensures that men and women gain access to the fruits of the other's labor. Marital partners share with each other the food that they find.

Some scholars also suggest that marriage was traditionally, and in some instances still is, a means for men to gain dominance over women. Thus, although female foragers could meet most of their own subsistence needs, marriage ensured that males gained access to the substantial products of female labor and thereby reduced their own workload. In our own society, there is considerable debate over the labor performed by so-called housewives and their dependency on male wage-earners. Many feminists argue that the "housewife" is an exploited laborer who performs necessary and often very tedious services for which she is compensated only as her husband sees fit.

The adaptive advantages of marriage may diminish as social scale increases, so that marriage becomes increasingly optional. Members of many small-scale societies assume that all adults will marry and that the only unmarried adults are either looking for a spouse or have lost their spouse and are too old to remarry. In large-scale societies such as our own, parents, relatives, and peers usually place pressure on individuals to marry. But it is also possible to be accepted in society without ever having been married. This liberalization, which reflects the increasing degree of specialization in these societies and the diminishing importance of kinship, might lead one to speculate that marriage will eventually disappear. Such a development is not likely to occur in the near future, however, for sufficient pressures and adaptational advantages remain to ensure that most people will choose to marry.

Marriage as Formation of Alliances

Marriage is rarely just a matter of uniting two individuals. Those joined in wedlock have kin and friends who are affected by the creation of the relationship, and the act has other broad implications as well. More often than not, marriage unites a wide network of people, providing a relatively durable bond or series of bonds of widespread social importance.

Marriage as Exchange

Viewed from a group perspective, marriage becomes an exchange of personnel and resources that creates alliances based on reciprocal rights and privileges. Not only is there an initial exchange of people and wedding gifts, but there are usually expectations of future transactions among those associated with the married couple. These expectations may be little more than the promise of help should the need arise, or they may entail a firm commitment to assist in warfare or political struggles. They may also involve a pledge to reciprocate at some future date with the exchange of yet another man or woman in marriage.

Anthropologist Claude Lévi-Strauss (1969) has argued that marriage in small-scale societies serves as a generalized exchange system centering on the exchange of women between groups. Lévi-Strauss makes a distinction between what he terms elementary and complex systems. *Elementary systems* are those in which the rules specify which category or group of persons one should or should not marry into. For example, the prescribed form of marriage among the Mardudjara is between cross-cousins. For a man, approved mates would include his mother's brother's daughters and his father's sister's daughters; for a woman, they would include the mother's brother's sons and the father's sister's sons. Marriage to any other category of person would be considered wrong and possibly even incestuous (Tonkinson 1978). In *complex systems*, the rules state whom one *cannot* marry, but they do not specify whom one *should* or *must* marry. A complex system might prohibit one from marrying certain categories of kin or individuals in certain social strata, but otherwise the possibilities are left open.

Lévi-Strauss further distinguishes between systems in which the exchange is direct and those in which the exchange is more indirect. The simplest system is that of *direct exchange,* whereby group A provides wives for group B, and group B provides wives for group A. Such exchanges can take place immediately within the same generation or be delayed over generations: Group A gives group B wives in one generation and group B reciprocates in the next. *Indirect exchange* occurs when women move in one direction only. Group A provides wives for group B, group B provides wives for group C, and group C provides wives for group A, forming a circle of marriage exchanges. The so-called marriage-alliance cultures of Southeast Asia, such as the Batak of Sumatra, are an example of societies in which indirect exchange plays an important social role. Such societies emphasize giving and receiving gifts within and between social groups. Spiritually and ritually, wife-giving lineages are viewed as superior to wife-receiving lineages. Givers and takers are bound to each other through a series of gifts and countergifts of women, food, textiles, jewelry, and livestock. These alliances serve as the focus of village social life.

Endogamy and Exogamy

Endogamy refers to a rule that one must or should marry within one's own group or category; **exogamy** refers to rules or preferences for marrying outside of a social group or category. Basically, exogamy links groups together, while endogamy isolates groups and maintains them as distinct units.

The distinction between endogamy and exogamy depends on how one's own group is defined. In our society, we tend to marry people outside our own kin group but within our own socioeconomic stratum. A doctor would not be imprisoned for marrying someone of blue-collar background, but social pressures and practices help to maintain strata endogamy. The family (nuclear or extended) is the primary exogamous unit in our society, and it is primarily between families, usually of the same social stratum, that marital exchanges take place.

Social strata in our society are not, of course, homogeneous, and marriage can serve in forming alliances between segments of a stratum. This can be illustrated by marriage patterns among the wealthy elite of the United States and European nobility during the latter part of the nineteenth century and early twentieth century, which were endogamous in terms of social strata but exogamous in terms of nationality. The newly affluent Americans of this period were seen as rather crude by the more established elites of their own country. In Europe, the newly rich found poorer aristocrats who were all too willing to trade their family name for a share of American wealth. The principal marketplace was the Riviera:

> Daughters of the American rich could here be traded for the esteem that went with older landed wealth and title, or sometimes merely the title. By this single simple step the new wealth achieved the respectability of age. And the anciently respectable got money, something they could always use. So inevitable was this bargain that they were negotiated by the scores, and brokers—often impoverished women of imagined social rank—appeared to make the deals. . . . By 1909, by one estimate, 500 American heiresses had been exported for the improvement of the family name, along with $220 million. (Galbraith 1977, 68)

Perhaps the most notable of these exchanges was between the Vanderbilts and the Churchills. Cornelius Vanderbilt arranged to have his daughter marry into the Churchill family, one of the most honored in British history, for an initial payment of $2.5 million. With this (and eventually another $7.5 million), he was able to help rid his family of its robber-baron stigma and transform it into one of high repute.

Australian Aborigines also seek marriage partners outside their immediate group for strategic reasons. The alliances created through such marriages serve to give them access to a wider hunting-and-gathering range. For desert-dwelling Aborigines, faced with the ever-present threat of scarcity and drought, such a strategy especially makes sense.

Families or social groups do not always favor a strategy of seeking alliances through marriage with others. They may instead follow a narrowly defensive endogamous strategy, usually to maintain a group's identity and wealth. One way of achieving this is to prescribe marriage to certain categories of cousin. Among patrilineal Moslem peoples in the Near East and North Africa, for example, the preferential marriage for a man is to his patrilateral parallel cousin (his father's brother's daughter). This marriage practice ensures that property is kept within relatively narrow bounds, overcoming the threat to maintenance of family wealth posed by Islamic law, which calls for inheritance by sons and daughters. It also creates a strong social group of allied brothers and their children, particularly useful in the hostile and faction-ridden social environment that has existed in this area. Such a social environment, however, is to some extent a result of the isolationist principles by which these groups are formed and separated from others in the first place. The result is a cycle in which the practice of patrilateral parallel-cousin marriage encourages factionalism, which in turn promotes this form of marriage.

Number of Spouses

Societies typically prescribe not only whom one should marry, but also how many people one may marry. In our own society, a person married to more than one spouse at the same time is known as a bigamist; if caught, he or she can be imprisoned. Many societies, however, allow men to have more than one wife, and some allow women to have more than one husband. In fact, **plural marriages**, in which a person has more than one spouse, historically have been accepted in the vast majority of societies. There are no natural reasons for either practice. Whether a society tries to restrict marriage to a single spouse or encourages plural marriages reflects the particular way in which the society has evolved. And, such practices change over time as conditions change. Some societies that formerly allowed plural marriages no longer do so, one reason being the

Anna Gould, the youngest daughter of American financier Jay Gould, became a countess when she married Count Marie Ernest Paul Boniface de Castellane in 1895. Upon marrying, the Count acquired access to Anna's yearly income of about $650,000 from her trust fund. In spite of this income, by the time this picture was taken in 1900, the couple had run up debts totaling $4.5 million. Anna left the Count shortly after this, went to France, and married the Count's cousin, the Duc de Talleyrand-Perigord.

spread of European colonialism and the Christian morality that accompanied it.

Monogamy

The form of marriage found in the United States and other Western industrial nations is **monogamy,** the state or custom of being married to one person at a time. Monogamy is not simply a norm in these societies; it is prescribed. Plural marriages are illegal. In societies where divorce is fairly common, individuals may enter into a series of marriages—marrying, divorcing, and mar-

rying again—but still they may have only one spouse at a time. We refer to this pattern as **serial monogamy.**

Polygamy

Many other societies prefer not to limit the number of spouses available to a person at one time. The practice of having more than one spouse at the same time we call **polygamy**. There are two principal types of polygamy: polygyny and polyandry.

The term **polygyny** refers to marriage between

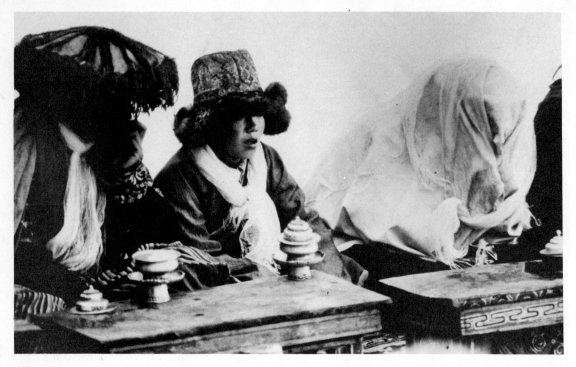

Polyandry is a rare form of marriage, found mostly in South Asia. Shown here is a polyandrous family, Nepal: two grooms at left, bride swathed in veiling, during ceremonial tea-drinking at wedding.

one man and two or more women simultaneously. Historically, polygyny has been common to many societies around the world. The possibility of polygynous marriage in a society, however, does not mean that all adult men in that society will have more than one wife. For them to do so in most cases would be a demographic impossibility. In a survey of the Aboriginal inhabitants of Jigalong in western Australia, Tonkinson (1974) found that despite the preference of married men for two wives, only 11 of the 40 married men in the sample had polygynous marriages. Among the Tiwi of northern Australia (Hart and Pilling 1979; Goodale 1971), some older men marry up to one or two dozen women, while others will have only one wife and younger

men may have to wait until their late thirties to marry. Tiwi men do not necessarily remain celibate before marriage, but their premarital sexual relations with women are considered illegitimate.

Jealousy and interpersonal rivalry among co-wives is recognized as a potential problem in most societies with polygynous marriage. Maintaining a separate household for each wife is one way of trying to avoid conflict. Among the Plateau Tonga of Zambia, husbands with more than one wife not only place their wives in separate dwellings, but also divide their property among them. Sharing of attention in such an arrangement can lead to conflict when husbands demonstrate noticeable preferences. The Tanala of Madagascar have dealt with this issue by ruling that a husband spend a day with each of his wives in succession or be accused of adultery; a slighted wife is entitled to sue for divorce and receive considerable alimony. Another common means of reducing jealousy among co-wives is to assign the wives hierarchical statuses. The senior wife among the Lacandon of southern Mexico is the only woman allowed to enter the family shrine when specially prepared ritual offerings are to be presented (Tozzer 1907). In other societies, the older wife can dictate to the younger.

The potential for tension is acute when the co-wives share no other social bonds except that with their husband. One strategy for getting around this problem is for a man to marry sisters, in the belief that they will get along well because they are accustomed to cooperating and living together in the same household—a belief that sometimes proves to be false. In the practice of **sororal polygyny**, upon marriage to a woman, the man acquires the right to claim her younger sister in marriage, sometimes without additional ceremony or payment. Sororal polygyny occurs most often in societies with patrilineal descent groups, where co-wives are bound not only as siblings but also by the duties imposed on them by lineage affiliation.

While the practice of polygyny is not as widespread as it once was, it persists nevertheless. It is estimated that as many as 25 percent of the men in Africa have more than one wife, despite attempts by Christian churches to end the practice and despite its being stigmatized among many urban-dwelling, educated Africans. According to Hazel Ayanga (1986), men report looking for second wives because the first wife is too busy with an outside job to run the household. They want a less educated, more manageable second wife. Others simply state that they have a second wife because they "think it's fun." Also, where divorce is frowned upon in Africa, it is easier to take a second wife than to divorce the first. Looking at it from a woman's perspective, Ayanga noted: "When a young woman becomes a second wife, it's usually on the understanding that the first wife is going to be sent away. . . . But most of the time this doesn't happen and you end up being a second wife" (p. 10). Some of the potential complications are avoided when the two wives are physically separated, as when one stays in town and the other is in the village. In fact, the two may not even know one another.

Polyandry, marriage of one woman to two or more men at the same time, is a rare form of marriage. The majority of societies in which polyandry is practiced are in South Asia: Tibet, India, Nepal, and Sri Lanka. The most common form of this type of marriage is **fraternal polyandry**, where a group of brothers share a wife. Nancy Levine (1988) described one such polyandrous arrangement among a group of ethnic Tibetans in Nepal. The household was composed of three generations, including three brothers and their wife and their five sons and their wife. In most such households, the eldest brother, as first-married, is accorded a higher status and exerts some authority in household affairs. In the case of the group studied by Levine, the brothers sought to determine paternity of children, placing a great value on male offspring. This is not always the case. Thus, among the Pahari of northern India studied by Gerald Berreman (1962), biological paternity was disregarded.

There are various practical reasons for the practice of polyandry beyond the simple weight of tradition. Among the Pahari, for example, there may have been a shortage of women. In other cases, it seems related to situations in which men are away to make war or trade much of the time. Polyandry ensures that at least one man will always be at home. The women Levine (1988) studied commented that polyandry provided them with the security of knowing that should one husband die, there would always be another. She also pointed to several important functions of fraternal polyandry: It serves to maintain a low rate of population growth; it prevents the dispersal of property, especially land; and it serves to maintain a united group of brothers, and often their male offspring, as the core of a highly self-sufficient household unit.

The Marriage Process

Marriage cannot be treated as a single event; it is a process that occurs over time. The process essentially has three parts: finding a potential spouse (or spouses), securing the marriage, and maintaining it. In all societies, there are certain expectations regarding what course this process is supposed to take and there are sanctions against extreme deviations. Practices vary, however, and the norms themselves undoubtedly change over time.

Choosing a Spouse

In many societies, personal choice in selecting a spouse is limited. In small-scale or village-level societies, for simple demographic reasons there are unlikely to be many potential spouses. In a village of 200 people, no more than one or two dozen choices are likely at best. If the village population is relatively stable and families have been intermarrying for generations, the number of possible marriage partners will be reduced even further by rules of exogamy. Those unable to find a spouse locally will be forced to look elsewhere.

Systems of marriage exchange, such as those discussed earlier in the chapter, are one way of overcoming local shortages of potential spouses. Another way is to seize mates from elsewhere. *Marriage by capture* typically involves the capture of women from groups perceived to be hostile. Capturing wives was once fairly common among small-scale farmers in Melanesia and Amazonian South America, where the practice was closely related to warfare, and it is still practiced by some peoples in these areas. Capturing a woman does not always automatically make a woman a man's wife, however. Among the South Fore of New Guinea, for example, for the marriage to be recognized, the man still has to provide appropriate payment to the woman's kin (Glasse 1969).

Whether spouses are drawn from the local population or from elsewhere, it is common practice in many societies for marriage to be arranged by one's family or kin. Among the Bena Bena of highland New Guinea, for example, marriage is seen as the responsibility of the subclan. A man decides after consulting with other members of his subclan that it is time for his son to be married, and a search for a bride is begun. The marriage arrangements may be made by the father,

but they are just as likely to be made by his brother or some other member of the subclan, or in some instances even by more distant relatives (Langness 1969).

Australian Aborigines have two means of arranging marriages: wife bestowal and mother-in-law bestowal (Maddock 1972). In *wife bestowal,* a man is given a wife (often a widow). In *mother-in-law bestowal,* a woman becomes a man's potential mother-in-law with the promise that he will be able to marry a future or existing daughter when she is old enough. Meanwhile, the man waits, often for years, currying favor with his "in-laws" until the time for the marriage arrives. During this long wait, things can go amiss. The "mother-in-law" may die before having a daughter, the daughter may die, or one of the parties may try to back out. In general, the bestower gains a great deal from the arrangement because of the dependent relationship it establishes; the young man must endure it because of the relative shortage of potential spouses in these small societies. The right to bestow a daughter or mother-in-law may be assigned to the father or brother of the girl or the girl's mother's brother. Bestowal, however, is never decided by a single individual, although one person may have the final say. Also, the girl herself is unlikely to remain entirely silent in the matter.

In Indian society, the majority of marriages are arranged, although so-called love matches are becoming more common. Marriage arrangements traditionally have been the responsibility of parents, although today a young man may take an active part—calling the parents of a girl whose picture he has seen or placing an advertisement in the newspaper: "Handsome Delhite, British degree, suitable government position for sophisticated virgin 22 years old. . . ." Families and unmarried individuals also sometimes resort to professional matchmakers and even matchmaking services in the search for a spouse. In any arrangements, such factors as caste, relative wealth of the family, educational background, citizenship, and employment of those being matched will be important considerations.

Meeting the Terms

Once a man has obtained the right to marry a woman, he may be expected to perform tasks, called **bride service**, for his bride-to-be's parents. This service may consist of little more than bringing his future wife and her parents corn and firewood for a few months, as is expected among the Kekchi of southern Belize. By contrast, the man may be expected to live with his future in-laws and work for them for several years, the traditional practice among Kekchi in highland Guatemala. Bride service may continue for some time after the couple is married, or in some instances it may begin only after the marriage takes place. The most common reason given for the practice of bride service is that it compensates the family of the bride for losing one of its members.

In most societies, it is customary to exchange more than just people through marriage. Money, labor, animals, and land may be exchanged by individuals or groups. This exchange may take the form of **bridewealth**, or **brideprice**, in which wealth of some sort is passed from the husband's group to the wife's. Like bride service, it is sometimes considered payment for the loss of the bride's companionship and labor. The practice is common in societies with patrilineal descent groups, where it is viewed as compensation for transferring the woman's labor and potential offspring to her husband's group. Bridewealth is rarely paid in societies with matrilineal descent groups, where the children automatically become members of their mother's group.

Among the Nuer, as with many other pastoral societies, young men use their family's cattle for bridewealth. The family itself may not have enough cows and may have to borrow cows from other relatives, widening the network of those involved in the exchange. The cows are then distributed to relatives of the bride's father and mother. The exchange of cows reinforces the alliance between patriclans formed as a result of the marriage, and also redistributes cows throughout Nuer society.

Monetization of economies has had important implications for brideprice customs in many parts of the world. The introduction of general-purpose money often breaks the hold that parents and other kin have over the exchange because money, unlike traditional forms of wealth, is more likely to be individually owned rather than owned by the family or group. Also, the in-

The Nuer of East Africa use cattle as bridewealth. It is passed from the husband's group to the wife's, promoting the alliance between clans and redistributing cows throughout the society.

troduction of money often creates inflationary cycles, whereby ever-greater amounts are paid, usually as a result of competition for prestige. Such inflation is possible when the supply is not subject to the same constraints as more traditional forms of wealth. It is commonly associated with migratory labor.

Many Asian and southern European societies have a different exchange custom called **dowry**. The dowry is usually seen as the woman's share of her inheritance from the group of her birth, which is taken with her upon marriage. For example, among the Sarakatsani of Greece, parents are expected to contribute to the establishment of new households by their children (Campbell 1974). Family wealth—animals, money, and goods—is held in common, with the idea that it will be eventually distributed among the family members as inheritance. Upon marriage, a son usually continues to reside near his parents in an extended family group, and wealth is still held in common. A daughter, however, leaves to live with her husband and his family. The dowry that she takes with her upon marriage is her portion of the family estate. As a result, both the husband's and the wife's family provide roughly equal amounts toward establishing the new household.

Dowry has been an important part of the marriage tradition in Indian society and remains so today despite its having been outlawed in 1961 and in the face of protest from many women's rights groups. Such opposition is based on social problems associated with the practice. For example, there are reports of young women committing suicide for fear their parents will be unable to provide them with dowries. Another problem is the practice of parents demanding increased dowries of their daughter-in-law's family after marriage. Such demands are sometimes accompanied with threats to kill the bride, or they may lead her to commit suicide. Linked to this are hundreds of cases each year in India of brides being burnt to death, beaten, tortured, or starved because their families failed to supply the level of dowry promised at the time of marriage. In one case, in a rural Indian community, a woman's mother-in-law and brother-in-law were sentenced to hang for burning her to death because her family had failed to provide a radio and bicycle promised as dowry. The husband was jailed for life.

The Marriage Ceremony

Marriage is formalized by different means in different societies, but in all cases there is some publicly recognized act or rite. The act may be a very simple one. After coming to an understanding with a woman, a young Brazilian Tapirapé man will deposit a load of firewood at her family's dwelling as a means of publicly announcing their intention to be married (Wagley 1977). He then moves his hammock next to her hammock and becomes part of the household.

Village-level agricultural societies often have more elaborate ceremonies. The Kgatla of Botswana, in southern Africa, begin the marriage process with an engagement that may last two to three years, during which time gifts are exchanged and the couple is referred to as "husband and wife" (Schapera 1940). The husband-to-be is allowed to sleep with the woman to whom he is betrothed. (Before Christianization this was done openly; now it must be done in secret.) Before the wedding, the bride spends time in seclusion in her hut. Only her "supporter," generally a daughter of a maternal aunt or uncle, is allowed to see her. During this time she is supposed to get fat by eating porridge, milk, and meat. The bride and groom are also doctored to protect them from witchcraft and other evils. When it is time for the wedding, the bride and her companions go to the dressmaker's house, where she puts on her wedding costume. Her parents then summon their future son-in-law and his companions to the dressmaker's house by sending him a pot of beer. If it is not a church wedding, a senior male relative tells the couple to link arms, and the procession heads to the bride's home. At Christian weddings, the party goes from the dressmaker's to the church, returning to the bride's home after the marriage ceremony.

(above) In a Pokot wedding, Africa, the young bride mourns that she is about to leave her home and father. (above right) In a contemporary Jewish wedding ceremony in the United States, the parents share their daughter's joy as they give her away.

After an elaborate and lengthy feast at the bride's home, the couple goes to the groom's residence or village, where another celebration is held. Before the couple is considered legitimately married, the brideprice transactions must also be completed.

Establishing a Residence

Once a couple is married, where will they reside? In our own society, the ideal residence is their own dwelling, which may or may not be near either set of parents. We refer to such a pattern as **neolocal residence**. This pattern fits with our economic system and pattern of kinship relationships. We sell our labor and move where jobs are available. Neolocal residence is associated not only with geographic mobility, but also with financial independence. A newly married couple who are poor or unemployed often reside with one set of parents until their financial situation improves, but in general the goal of a married couple is to set up a household of their own.

Neolocality is not a universal residential preference; in many societies newly married couples do not aspire to owning their own homes and living independently. In societies where social bonds among closely related males are important, the couple usually resides with the husband's group, and even in the same household as other male relatives of the husband. Wives in such situations may find themselves cut off from their natal group and may become permanent members of their husband's group instead. We refer to such a pattern as **patrilocal residence**. This is the predominant pattern in virtually all patrilineal societies, as well as in a small number of matrilineal societies.

Among peoples with matrilineal kin groups, it is common for a woman to live with her own group after marriage and for her husband to come to live with her. This is a **matrilocal residence** pattern. In this case, the man does not give up membership in his natal group, as does the woman in patrilocal residence. A man in this type of society exercises authority in the group of his birth over his sisters and their children because he occupies the important status of mother's brother. Because of this status, particularly powerful mother's brothers sometimes can establish residence with their natal groups, taking their wives with them. Such forms of residence may benefit women, allowing them to form strong social units for work and mutual support.

Another residence pattern found among matrilineal societies is **avunculocal residence**. In this case, the couple lives near the husband's mother's brother. In such societies, the residential unit includes a group of brothers and their sisters' sons. Dival and Harris (1976) found this pattern to be associated with warfare and male dominance; it is a practice that can shift to patrilocality should the brothers begin to allow some of their sons to remain with them after marriage.

There are other types of residence patterns as well. In **ambilocal residence**, the couple has a choice of living with or near the parents or kin of either bride or groom. **Bilocal residence** is somewhat different: the couple is expected to live for a period with or near the bride's parents and for another period with or near the groom's.

Residential patterns are not always rigidly prescribed or uniform. Among the Kekchi of southern Belize, there is a patrilocal bias in residency, but the situation is very mixed and fluid (Howard 1977). During the first few years of marriage, a couple may shift between patrilocal and matrilocal residence a few times before settling down more permanently. Where the couple settles can be determined by personal factors, such as inability to get along with in-laws. Villages are often divided into factional groupings, and choice of residence can also be related to the formation of factional alliances. In such cases, not only may the sons of a factional leader live near him, but the leader may convince his daughters' husbands to live nearby as well. There are physical considerations, too. Because of heavy rainfall during the rainy season, houses must be built on high ground, and the hilly terrain places a premium on suitable residential sites as well as sometimes limiting the number of residences that can fit on a site.

Remarrying

After the marriage is legitimatized, much of married life centers on the family, which we will take up in the next section. The final part of the marriage process concerns events after a person's first marriage ends, either through divorce or death. While in a large-scale society such as our own, there is considerable variation in what people do once they are no longer married—from starting careers to enjoying the singles life to getting remarried—in many societies patterns are more institutionalized, especially for widows and widowers.

In the remarriage custom called **wife inheritance**, when a man dies, his heir (usually his next of kin) is expected to marry the widow. Wife inheritance is found in conjunction with both patrilineal and matrilineal descent, where it is customary for a man's brother or some other member of his lineage to marry his widow after he dies. In a matrilineal system, a man inherits from his mother's brother, and one of the things he may inherit is the obligation to care for the deceased's wife or wives. The rationale for this custom is that since the marriage involved the group of the man who died, a member of that group should replace him. When found in conjunction with polygyny, with patrilineal descent groups, and usually with patrilocal residence as well, the custom is commonly referred to as **levirate**. This practice ensures that the widow's children continue to belong to the patrilineage. A complementary practice is the **sororate**, in which a man marries the sister of his deceased wife. It, too, is associated with polygyny, patrilineal descent groups, and patrilocal residence, and is sometimes a natural extension of sororal polygyny.

Ghost marriage is a related practice found in many African societies. Among the Nuer, the brother of a deceased man may marry an unmarried woman "to the name of" the deceased. The children of this marriage are considered children of the deceased, and thus his heirs (Evans-Pritchard 1940). The Zulu of South Africa have two forms of ghost marriage (Gluckman 1950). In one, when a man who is betrothed dies, his fiancée is married to one of his kinsmen and she then bears children for the dead man. In the second form, a man "wakens" a dead kinsman who has not been betrothed by marrying a wife to his name.

All these practices reflect a belief that people should remain married until they clearly are too old to function properly in society. While they limit personal freedom and may emphasize the low status of women in these societies, they also provide security for those who are widowed. In some situations today, however, the tradition of wife inheritance is subject to abuses that stem from changing values. Thus, in Zimbabwe, wife inheritance is as often as not used by relatives to seize the mobile property of a couple (television sets, furniture, etc.) when the husband dies, leaving the widow destitute (Chandler 1986).

Many societies stop short of dictating who is to marry a widow, while formulating rules to ensure that someone is responsible for taking care of her. A Kekchi widow may be taken care of by her own kin, by her husband's, or by her own children, depending on circumstances, but it is expected that someone among her relatives will care for her. If she is not too old, she is expected to remarry, but there are no more restraints on her selection of a new spouse than if she were marrying for the first time.

There are, however, societies that discourage widow remarriage. The Roman Catholic Church discourages remarriage of widows and widowers, and in former times priests were empowered to refuse to sanctify unions in which one or both partners had been married previously. Among the Sarakatsani, Greek pastoralists, it is extremely difficult for a widow to remarry, because the family into which a woman has married does not want to lose her labor, her children, or their honor (since she would be having sexual relations with someone from another family).

Even more extreme are instances where spouses are killed or kill themselves upon the death of their husband or wife. A well-known example of this was the Indian practice of *sati* (or suttee): self-immolation of a widow in the belief that a faithful wife who followed her husband into death would become a demi-goddess (see Datta 1988). Based on a religious cult, the practice gained increasing support among the Indian priesthood and aristocracy from the fourth century B.C. It was not universally supported, and the British set about to ban it in the nineteenth century. It spread among the common people in later years, and is still practiced on rare occasions in rural villages, despite its being illegal. Thousands of people turned out to honor an 18-year-old widow as she committed sati in a village in Rajastan in 1987.

Similar to sati was the Fijian practice of *loloku*, whereby the wife or wives of chiefs were strangled beside the deceased husband (T. Williams 1858; see Mariner 1827). There are also a few societies in which husbands were killed upon the death of a wife, such as the Natchez of the Mississippi region. This custom was associated with matrilineal societies, in which high-ranking female common-ers married male commoners.

The practices we have discussed are for the most part tied to kin groups with vested interests in what happens to widows of their members. These practices can be expected to be maintained only so long as the social conditions that generated them remain. In many parts of Africa, for example, the destruction of corporate kin groups has led to the end of related forms of remarrying widows.

Divorce, too, is a reflection of social and economic processes in a society. Thus, the near im-possibility of divorce among the Sarakatsani fits their overall pattern of social organization and their attitudes toward the family and toward women in general. By contrast, the ease with which Mundurucu women can divorce their husbands is related to the social and economic autonomy of Mundurucu women and to their matrilineality and matrilocal residence pattern. In our own society, a higher divorce rate can be linked to ideological and economic changes concerning the role of women and the nature of the family in recent decades.

FAMILY GROUPS

One of the functions of marriage is the creation of the family. Families may exist independently of marriage, but it is through marriage that families usually come into being as socially recognized, legitimate entities. An intimate kin-based group that consists of at least a parent–child nucleus, the **family** is the minimal social unit that cooperates economically and assumes responsibility for the rearing of children. Various people may be added to the parent–child nucleus, forming an economically cooperating, childrearing family group that may or may not share the same dwelling.

Types of Family Groups

The "typical American family" so thoroughly incorporated into our ideology consists of a husband, a wife, and two or more children, all of whom live in a single detached household. However, this image does not typify families in our society today. There are single parents with children, and there may be other relatives living with the family. And if we look at families in other societies, we find that our American ideal is, in fact, rather rare worldwide.

The **nuclear family** is composed of a man, a woman, and their children. This group is not the ideal in societies that practice polygyny or polyandry, nor is it considered normal in most societies with unilineal kin groups. The nuclear family group is fairly rare among small-scale agriculturalists and, in fact, occurs infrequently among any rural peoples. The nuclear family group is most often found in segments of American society where housing is not in short supply and where social mobility, the hunt for jobs and improved social status, and the existence of specialized support systems (such as schools and nursing homes) reduce the central caring role of the family. It is also associated with more marginal foragers, whose precarious economic adaptation favors organizing into small, very mobile units for most of the year.

Since few environments encourage the existence of small, independent social groups, more common types of family organization are those referred to as complex or compound. Polygynous marriage leads to the creation of **polygynous family groups**, consisting of a man, his wives, and their children. The members of this family group sometimes live in the same household, each wife perhaps having her own territory centering on her fire hearth. Since this living arrangement often exacerbates tensions, however, co-wives often have separate dwellings. This re-

Although many families in our society are not nuclear families, a traditional ideal in America has been a family of two parents and two or three children. (left) Here you see it represented in TV's "Growing Pains." (below) Among the Kekchi Indians of Belize, it is not unusual to find a family consisting of the mother and her children.

sults in matricentric households, where each wife lives in her own dwelling with her own children.

Polyandry leads to the creation of **polyandrous family groups.** The members of a polyandrous family group—a woman, her husbands, and children—may live under a single roof, or the husbands may jointly occupy a separate men's hut.

There are also various forms of **extended family groups**, in which two or more families of at least two generations live together. A *patrilocal extended family group* consists of a man and his sons and their wives and children. A *matrilocal extended family group* consists of a woman and her daughters and their husbands and children. An *avunculocal extended family group* consists of a man, his sister's sons, and their wives and children.

Finally, there are **joint family groups**, in which two or more relatives of the same generation and their spouses and children live together. The *fraternal joint family group* is a common example of this type; it consists of at least two brothers and their wives and children.

While one or two of these family groups may represent the normative ideal of a society, in practice many of these forms may coexist in the same social setting. In Kekchi villages in southern Belize, it is common to find nuclear families, various extended and joint family groups, and even an occasional polygynous family group (usually curers and the wives they have inherited from deceased patients). In each case, the pattern reflects the strategies of people in relation to their broader social environment—the size of the village, factionalism, the social network of the married couple, and how long they have lived in a village.

The Development Cycle

Family groups are formed and evolve in accordance with the ongoing cycle of birth, maturation, and death. There are three main phases, or stages, in this development cycle (Fortes 1958).

First is **expansion**. It begins with marriage and lasts until all children of the family are born and raised to reproductive age. The duration of this phase is limited primarily by the length of time a woman is fertile. During this period, the offspring are highly dependent on their parents.

The second phase is **dispersion and fission**. This may overlap with the first phase, for it begins with the first marriage of one of the children and continues until all of the children are married. Where it is customary for the youngest child to remain to take over what remains of the family estate, this commonly marks the beginning of the final phase. The third phase, **replacement**, includes the death of the parents and their replacement in the social structure by families of their children.

At any given time, the phase a family group is going through may influence its residential patterns. Among the Iban of north Borneo (Freeman 1958), a couple may choose to live with the wife's or husband's family group, depending on where they are in the cycle. If one of the spouses is the last child remaining in the family after the others have married and left, for instance, he or she stays on as prospective heir.

Precisely what happens in the final stage, as well as residential decisions throughout the cycle, often depends on inheritance customs. In some societies, the eldest child inherits most of or all of the property. This is referred to as **primogeniture**. Younger siblings either depend on the eldest or seek their fortunes on their own. In other societies, the youngest (usually male) child remains in the natal household and inherits the property of the parents. This is referred to as **ultimogeniture** and usually leads to that child's taking over directly from the parents when the cycle begins anew. Such a child is also usually expected to care for the aged parents.

As with other aspects of the institution of the family, the form that family groups take and the cycle of their development vary from society to society. This variation reflects the larger environment of which the family is a part.

SUMMARY

Marriage is a socially sanctioned sexual and economic union between men and women. It is an adaptive measure, related to the prolonged period of dependency of human infants, sexual competition, the sexual division of labor, and, perhaps, to male domination. It is also a means of forming useful social, economic, and political alliances. Systems of marital exchange between groups may be elementary or complex, direct or indirect, endogamous or exogamous.

Although one spouse at a time is the only form of marriage allowed in our society, monogamy is not universal. Two forms of plural marriage, or polygamy, are found in many societies: polygyny (multiple wives) and polyandry (multiple husbands). Our version of marriage is not universal either. Societies place varying restrictions on the choice of a spouse. The terms of the marriage may involve bride service, brideprice, or dowry. The actual ceremony can vary greatly in elaborateness. After the ceremony, residential possibilities include neolocal, patrilocal, matrilocal, ambilocal, bilocal, and avunculocal residence. Lastly, there is the question of what happens when a spouse dies or a divorce takes place. Many societies have institutionalized remarriage through practices such as levirate, sororate, and ghost marriage.

In our society, the traditional family includes husband, wife, and children. This nuclear family is not the only way of grouping close kin, however. In addition to the nuclear family group, there are four principal types of complex or compound family groups: polygynous, polyandrous, extended, and joint.

The family group follows a rhythmic cycle of expansion, dispersion, and replacement. Expressions of this pattern are influenced by a number of factors, including inheritance customs such as primogeniture and ultimogeniture.

SUGGESTED READINGS

Bohannon, Paul, and John Middleton, eds. 1968. *Marriage, Family and Residence*. New York: Natural History Press.

Croll, Elisabeth. 1981. *The Politics of Marriage in Contemporary China*. Cambridge: Cambridge University Press.

Goodale, Jane C. 1971. *Tiwi Wives: A Study of the Women of Melville Island, North Australia*. Seattle: University of Washington Press.

Goody, Jack R., ed. 1958. *The Developmental Cycle in Domestic Groups*. Cambridge: Cambridge University Press.

Goody, Jack R., and S.J. Tambiah, eds. 1973. *Bridewealth and Dowry*. Cambridge: Cambridge University Press.

Kennedy, Theodore R. 1979. *You Gotta Deal with It: Black Family Relations in a Southern Community*. New York: Oxford University Press.

McNetting, R., R.R. Wills, and E.J. Arnold, eds. 1984. *Households: Comparative and Historical Studies of the Domestic Group*. Berkeley: University of California Press.

Potter, Sulamith H. 1980. *Family Life in a Northern Thai Village: A Study in the Structural Significance of Women*. Berkeley: University of California Press.

18 Socialization

A classic American rite of passage, or ritualized transition between an old and a new status, is the graduation prom, seen here in a high school group in California.

To the Semai, a small group of relatively isolated forest-dwellers in Malaysia, the thought of becoming angry is absurd. "We do not get angry," they explain (Dentan 1968, 55). Of course, the Semai *do* get angry on occasion, but they deny the existence of such an emotion within their culture. And, indeed, their cultural values minimize the likelihood of their becoming angry. They see themselves as nonviolent people. Almost from birth they are taught to avoid aggression and to feel shame for aggressive behavior. Should an individual hurt someone physically or emotionally, the injured party has the right to ask compensation, and more than likely the aggressor will seek to make up for the illfeeling he or she has caused.

The Semai attitude toward aggression seems peculiar to most people in American society, where anger and hostility are everyday aspects of life. To many brought up in a Western cultural tradition the Semai may seem weak and cowardly, or perhaps carefree and naive. Either perception reflects the Westerner's own cultural views concerning violence and anger. Both Western and Semai attitudes are part of cultural traditions that have been shaped by distinct historical and environmental conditions. In this chapter, we will see how people acquire such attitudes and how acquiring them is related to the larger society. In looking at how individuals become part of their society, our orientation, as in the previous three chapters, is still toward how society is put together.

AN OVERVIEW OF SOCIALIZATION

The general process by which we learn social roles from others is known as **socialization**. While part of what is learned is a result of formal instruction, much socialization occurs simply through interacting with others. As we learn to behave as members of a particular society, we undergo a process of **enculturation** by which we learn the rules and values of the culture.

We acquire an image of the world that is highly conditioned by the practices and beliefs of those around us. We are taught how to categorize the physical and social world and what these categories mean. The Semai categorize animals according to their habitat; fish, whales, and turtles are all in the same category. Likewise, the categories into which they divide their social and physical world differ from our own in many ways and reflect attitudes that are very different from those of Westerners. Thunder squalls, for instance, are considered unnatural by the Semai (Dentan 1968). They are thought to be the result of human action, in contrast to natural phenomena over which humans have little control.

Socialization results in a degree of uniformity among the members of a society as they come to share values and attitudes. But there will always be considerable variation. Such variation is partly a reflection of the particular statuses and roles of individuals within a society. Beyond this, there is always some room for individual choice and individual peculiarities. This is especially so in large-scale societies, where pressure to conform is less than in small-scale societies.

Socialization begins at birth. Although the early years of life are particularly important in shaping an individual's views, the process continues until death. As people grow older, their place in society changes, and they must learn new modes of behavior. Expectations for children differ from those for adults, and as people achieve adult status they must learn how to behave in accordance with new expectations. What these differences are, and how great, will vary from one society to another; but there will always be differences.

Socialization is also influenced by changes

Reprinted under license from Morriseau Syndications, Burlington, VT.

within the environment. Societies and their settings are changing constantly, and people must adapt to these changes. The kinds of adjustments people make will depend partly on the nature of the changes taking place and partly on prior behavioral patterns and views of the world. For example, the introduction of television in the 1940s altered socialization patterns as it became a source of information, a mediator between members of a household or between individuals and the outside world, and a baby-sitter for millions of children. But its impact on society was not uniform. Reactions to television varied with age, gender, class, ethnicity, and a host of other factors.

CULTURAL ORIENTATIONS

What is learned within a particular society is part of the adaptational strategy of its members. This strategy is reflected in their way of looking at life and how best to go about doing things.

World View

The basic cultural orientation of the members of a society—the way in which people perceive their environment—may be referred to as their **world view**. As Robert Redfield (1952) noted, a person's world view is the organization of ideas that answer such questions as Where am I? Among what things do I move? What are my relations to things? World view concerns the fundamental assumptions of a people about the nature of the world, as expressed more or less systematically in their philosophy, ethics, rituals, and scientific beliefs (Wallace 1970). Not all members of a society adhere to the same beliefs, but a society's world view is thought to represent the dominant themes of that society's culture as a whole.

People living in similar types of societies share broadly similar views of the world. How foragers in the deserts of Australia view the world resembles the view of foragers roaming Africa's Kalahari desert. Likewise, it is possible to speak of a world view of those living in modern industrial societies in the West and to some extent globally. This situation is complicated, however, by differences associated with class. Oscar Lewis (1966) developed the concept of a "culture of poverty"—common cultural attitudes and life-styles that he found among poor people in Western industrial nations: a feeling of helplessness, a withdrawal from political activity, and an orientation toward immediate consumption. Lewis's idea of a culture of poverty has many shortcomings, but it does point out that living in impoverished circumstances with little real chance of improvement may lead to certain shared perceptions of the world.

Some writers divide world views into two very different types: "primitive" and "civilized." The so-called primitive world view is associated with small-scale or tribal societies in which face-to-face social relationships predominate. The **tribal world view**, as we will refer to it, is a personal view of the universe in which humans are seen as united with nature rather than separate from it. The physical world within which humans find themselves is seen as animate; thus, humans relate to trees and water, for example, as they do to other humans. As a part of nature, humans assume the responsibility for maintaining the natural order of things, rather than trying to dominate or change nature (Wallace 1970). Their efforts find expression through ritual.

The tribal world view reflects the close social relationships that the members of small-scale societies maintain with each other and the close relationship with nature that their technology and adaptive strategies entail. Australian Aborigines, for example, assign religious significance to the entire physical landscape and see themselves as united with animals and with particular territo-

These masks on display at the Field Museum in Chicago represent a world view that differs considerably from that of most urbanites in the United States.

ries through kinship and ritual. Their religion emphasizes the unchanging aspect of the universe. Furthermore, it not only makes them a part of nature, but it also requires that they perform rituals to maintain the natural order.

The **civilized world view**, by contrast, reflects the more impersonal aspect of social relationships in large-scale societies—as in our relationships with the government—and a technology that allows people to distance themselves more from nature. In many ways, it is the opposite of the tribal world view. Instead of emphasizing the unchanging nature of the universe and placing humanity within this natural order, the civilized world view stresses our separation from nature and our role as its conqueror. Instead of living in harmony with the desert or the forest, we seek to dominate it, to transform it to suit our perceived needs.

Values

Bound up in the world view of a culture are the values of its members. **Values** are emotionally charged beliefs about what is desirable or offensive, right or wrong, appropriate or inappropriate. Within any society there will be some diversity in the values held by individuals. Even within our own families we are unlikely to have precisely the same values as our parents or siblings. And with work associates or neighbors, value differences may be even greater.

Despite individual variation, many common values are often held by residents of a region or by members of a social class or ethnic group. In our own society we speak of national values, middle-class values, or city values, recognizing that different life-styles can be associated with different value orientations. In each of these cases, the values will be related to the particular setting, history, and adaptive strategy of the people. Peoples with long histories of warfare or military conquest will possess a range of values associated with militarism and aggression: a willingness to sacrifice and to pledge blind obedience to those in command.

In most cultures, it is possible to identify a set of central values that are systematically related. These **core values** provide the basis for social behavior and for the goals pursued by the members of the society. The Japanese emphasis on duty, respect, and filial piety provide examples of such core values.

Many core values of a culture do not apply equally to all members of the society. This is true, for example, of values associated with men and women in Hispanic society; for example, *machismo* (manliness, bravery) and *verguenza* (modesty, bashfulness, shame). Moreover, just what constitutes the core values of a society may be subject to controversy, and defining core values can have a political dimension. For example, Mouer and Sugimoto (1986) are critical of attempts to portray consensus and acceptance of hierarchy as being values universally accepted in Japanese society. To them, this portrayal reflects the view of a conservative elite and obscures the fact that Japan's history has largely been one of conflict.

Although core values are resistant to radical change, they are not static. And under certain circumstances they may change drastically in a short time. Shifts in values are generally associated with a changing social or environmental context. Japanese values placing women in a subservient position to men have come under increasing pressure to change in recent years as a result of Japan's economic prosperity, greater educational opportunities, and more exposure to cultures characterized by greater equality in male-female relations.

PERSONALITY AND PERSONALITY TYPES

In the individual, world view and values manifest themselves in the personality. The term *personality* refers to personal beliefs, expectations, desires, and values derived from the interaction of physiological and environmental influences. Anthropologists approach the study of personality by looking at its various components and trying to discern their meanings and causes in their social context. Thus, most anthropologists focus their studies of personality on social and environmental, rather than physiological, factors. One component that receives a good deal of attention is emotion. In her study of Inuit life in northern Canada, for example, Jean Briggs (1970) found that in trying to adapt to life in a harsh environment, the Inuit have promoted sociality by avoiding expression of anger.

An individual's personality has unconscious as well as conscious aspects. The unconscious aspect involves a core of values, attitudes, and orientations of which we are largely unaware. This core serves as a "blueprint" for the conscious aspect of our personality, which includes the overall view that we have of ourselves—our **self-concept**. Self-concept is based, among other things, on a person's perception of how others view him or her. In forming a self-concept, individuals usually choose to emphasize certain personality traits over others. What the individual comes to emphasize tends to coincide with more general cultural values. Thus, most Semai would include an image of themselves as nonaggressive as part of their self-concept in keeping with the more general Semai values concerning the avoidance of aggression.

We all like to think we are unique individuals, and to a degree we are distinct. Nevertheless, it is possible to generalize about personality types in a population. However, we must be careful to avoid stereotypic thinking and rely instead on careful analysis in making such generalizations. In compiling personality types, anthropologists usually focus on what they find to be dominant themes in the personalities they study, at the same time recognizing that individual personalities will be more complex and varied.

David Riesman (1953) distinguished three general personality types in the United States: tradition-oriented, inner-directed, and other-directed. The *tradition-oriented personality* is most commonly associated with small-scale societies, where the majority of activities are very routine, rather than with life in large-scale societies, such as the United States. Values and behavior in small-scale societies are oriented toward and legitimatized on the basis of tradition. Riesman maintains that because tradition alone does not suffice to give direction to life for most people in large-scale societies, the other two personality types are more common.

The *inner-directed personality* is characterized by a strong conscience and a sense of righteousness, as exemplified by the Puritans of colonial New England. A person with such a personality is compulsively driven and is the ideal type to expand a frontier, to conquer other peoples, and to exploit resources with a fervent single-mindedness. This type of personality was presumably common in the early years of American history, when the nation was in its expansive phase. In contrast, the *other-directed personality* is characterized by ambiguous feelings about what is right and wrong. Other-directed personality types are more adaptable and more responsive to the actions and expectations of others. To Riesman, this type of personality is more suited to the United States of the latter half of the twentieth century.

Riesman's personality types do not coincide with the personalities of particular individuals; they indicate tendencies or themes associated with personalities. Also, they point to the important relationship between personality and a society's environment and adaptive strategy.

SOCIALIZATION THROUGH THE LIFE CYCLE

Socialization is a continuous process. It lasts from birth to death, and according to some cultural traditions, continues even after death. Within any society, this process tends to follow a general pattern associated with the **life cycle**: birth, maturation, old age, and death. Precisely how these periods are divided and interpreted, however, varies from one society to another.

Childhood in some societies is seen as a single continuous phase, lasting until the onset of puberty. In other societies, it is divided into a series of clearly defined phases. The Mardudjara Aborigines, for example, divide early childhood into distinct stages, with a particular label for each: newborn, able to sit up; walking, but only just; walking properly; no longer breast-fed; and no longer carried. After that, a person is simply referred to as a child until he or she becomes an adult. The precise age at which childhood ends also varies among societies. In different societies, the beginning of adult life may be variously defined as the onset of puberty, the time of marriage, or an age determined almost at random, as in our own society.

Even death is not treated the same in all societies. The Judeo-Christian tradition, for example, views the period after death from a linear perspective; death is considered to lead to a permanent existence in a noncorporeal or spiritual state. To Hindus, on the other hand, death is part of a cycle in which the spirit of the deceased eventually will be reborn.

However life's phases are defined, the socialization process will not be the same at different periods of the life cycle. Our experiences and requirements change with age. In any society the experience of a 1-year-old child will be limited and his or her needs fairly basic—affection, feeding, and a bit of looking after. This situation contrasts sharply with that of middle-age, when a person possesses decades of prior experience and has much greater and more complex social and psychological needs than those of a child. From the point of view of the society, its members' statuses and roles vary throughout the life cycle, and each individual must become socialized to change in his or her social position. Thus, in our society, we say that adolescents need to learn to behave like adults, and refer to the adjustments people must make upon retirement.

Childrearing and Family Influence

Early childhood experiences are critical in forming an individual's personality and in socializing the individual to the ways of the society. These early experiences are, for the most part, unstructured and unplanned. Much of early childhood socialization is not the result of acts explicitly aimed at shaping the child's view of the world, although some acts will be. Rather, most of what goes on in the socialization process during this period is informal as people feed, care for, and play with the child.

The range of people influencing a child varies from one society to the next and among different groups within the same society. To free the mother and father from the "burden" of childrearing, elites in large-scale societies often leave early child care largely up to nurses or nannies. Childhood socialization among the urbanized middle classes of these societies tends to take place within the nuclear family. By contrast, in many small-scale societies, virtually everyone in the community assumes some responsibility for looking after children. Thus, unlike most Western children, Australian Aboriginal children are not separated from the rest of the community. The life of the camp goes on all around the child, and all adults take an active role in his or her rearing, whether they are the child's parents or not.

How those involved in childrearing interact with the child also varies. In contrast to societies such as our own, where children are subject to stricter discipline, Semai infants are indulged by members of the community. Physical punishment is rare, consisting merely of a pinch on the cheek or a pat on the hands. This does not mean that Semai do not seek to control the behavior of their children. Instead of using physical means, they instill fear in their children—fear of strangers, of evil spirits, and of violence in nature.

Whatever they are, the child's experiences are internalized and organized unconsciously, gradually shaping the personality of the emerging adult. Early childhood relationships shape our personality for the remainder of our lives, despite our growing independence from those who raised us.

Rites of Passage

Although much of our socialization takes place gradually, during certain times of transition the social shaping of our lives is accelerated. Some of these transitions may be closely associated with biological developments, such as first menstruation; other transitions, such as school graduation or marriage, are influenced by sociocultural factors. For both the individuals involved and the society as a whole, these transitions are important and often rather stressful. Marriage is thus a period when individuals and groups must adjust to a new set of relationships and roles.

Transitional periods frequently are occasions for ceremonies that focus on the importance of the person's change in status and affirm his or her new place in society. The rituals associated with these transitions are called **rites of passage**. These rites commonly are composed of three stages (Van Gennep 1960): separation, transition, and incorporation. The individual first symbolically and often physically is separated from society and his or her normal place in it. Separation is followed by a transitional stage in which the person is suspended between the old and the new. Finally, there is the ritual incorpo-

Childrearing and the influence of the family on the child differ in different societies. (right) Very young Polynesian children enjoy every comfort and attention from indulgent parents, other adults, and older children, but they soon take on the responsibilities of child care themselves. (below) An upper-class English child may not be indulged as much by parents, but as shown here, receives the attention of a nanny, who socializes the child in the ways of English culture.

ration into the new social position as the individual reenters society.

The college graduation ceremony in our own society provides a good illustration of the stages of a rite of passage. We begin by having the graduates wear distinctive costumes and separating them from the others present. During the transitional stage, ritualized speechmaking takes place, in which graduates are provided with words of wisdom intended to help them as they leave a protected environment for the wider world. The speeches are followed by the handing out of diplomas, after which the graduates and parents mingle and the graduates once again become part of the normal order. But now they occupy a new status: they hold a college degree.

In addition to affirming an individual's movement through stages in the life cycle, rites of passage may serve to reinforce, through ceremony and speech, some of the dominant values of a society. Thus a marriage ceremony can be used to emphasize values associated with social, economic, or political relationships. Likewise, the graduation ceremony instills in the graduates a sense of belonging to a community—a community from which they have been estranged during their years of study—and reminds them of their responsibilities toward the community.

Education

Another important mode of socialization is **education**, systematic instruction or training. Through education individuals are given instruction concerning beliefs, ways of behaving, and the means of producing things according to

The graduation ceremony in American society serves as a rite of passage for young people as they leave school to enter the wider society.

the cultural traditions of their society. People are not simply taught history, reading, or weaving; rather, they are given a distinct view about these things or a specific way in which to perform tasks. As Jules Henry (1963) noted: "The function of education has never been to free the mind and the spirit of man, but to bind them" (p. 32). The history taught in American schools represents a distinctly American view; it does not provide a student with a completely unbiased account of past events. This holds not only for how material is presented, but also relates to what is left out. Students learn about the westward expansion of the United States more from the perspective of the pioneers than from that of the Native Americans at whose expense the expansion took place.

Informal and Formal Education

In nonindustrial societies, most educational instruction is given by example; learning results from observation and imitation of relatives, peers, and neighbors. Children see how adults perform tasks and how they behave. At first, children's imitation is in the form of play—making toy bows and arrows, shooting at insects, or making mudpies. Play slowly disappears as children begin to take a more substantial role in community work. From an early age, children accompany their parents on their daily round of activities, watching and then assisting until eventually they can perform required adult tasks on their own. Some education in small-scale societies is more formalized. This especially applies to more esoteric subjects such as magic, curing, and playing a musical instrument. Sometimes formal education is also more universal, as when all Mardudjara Aboriginal male children are isolated for weeks and given instruction about religious and legal traditions in preparation for initiation into adulthood.

In large-scale societies, formal education is more pervasive. Individuals are instructed formally in a wider range of topics, and they spend more time in schools. This is not necessarily because there is more to learn; rather, it reflects a shift of emphasis in the way people are taught

and who is responsible for their instruction in keeping with a greater division of labor. In most large-scale societies, some governmental authority or nonfamilial institution, such as the church, assumes a primary role in education, resulting in a loss of instructional autonomy at the family or community level. Under state control, education functions not simply to provide instruction, but also to promote homogeneity and a sense of identification with the state that supersedes more local and personal loyalties.

The governments of many newly independent states that have emerged since the 1940s have emphasized formal education. Such education is used to provide technical skills in order to lessen dependence on foreigners and to promote a basis for economic development. Since many of these states include peoples from very different backgrounds, schools also are used to foster a sense of nationalism and to reduce cultural differences.

Education and Economic Advancement

For individuals in underdeveloped countries and for the poorer citizens of wealthier industrial states, education may be an avenue to desired economic rewards and higher social status. Even in many poor countries, the potential social and economic rewards available to the educated can be substantial, the alternative being extreme poverty.

In many Third-World countries, the "white-collar" jobs available to the educated allow them to live a life-style of relative affluence, in sharp contrast to that of the impoverished majority. Such desirable positions, however, are scarce, and the cost of the education that enables one to seek such a job is considerable. Tuition and board for a year at a grammar school can easily amount to more than the yearly earnings of most parents—and the cost of attending a university is even greater. Nevertheless, the potential rewards of education prompt many parents to devote all their available resources and even to go into debt to provide for their children's education. In some instances, entire communities will pool their incomes to support a student, hoping that they will be rewarded when their native son (or occasionally daughter) lands an influential position.

As the number of highly educated people in a country increases, it becomes more difficult for those with higher education to find suitable employment, especially when universities produce more graduates than can readily be absorbed in the workforce. This is in part a result of people's aspirations for individual socioeconomic advancement outpacing the productive capability of their society to support "white-collar" workers. For many poorer countries, however, this has yet to become a problem, and they continue to suffer from a shortage of trained personnel at the higher levels.

Education's Effect on Traditional Values

Western-style education frequently conflicts with the traditional values of non-Western peoples, which may cause serious social problems. At the university level, education patterned on Western models often creates an educated elite whose values are more Western than the values shared by the majority of their fellow citizens. Such education can play a positive role in the society's development, but it can also encourage the elite to view indigenous segments of their society as uncivilized barbarians rather than as people with whom they share a common bond.

Western education in societies with non-Western cultural traditions may also promote sociocultural marginality; that is, it may lead students to become disenchanted with their traditional culture but not fully integrate them into the new, leaving them marginal to both the old and the new ways of life. Until recently, it was common practice in rural Australia for missionaries or government authorities to take Aboriginal children away from their parents and place them in schools, which usually were run by Christian missionaries. At the schools, the children were encouraged to reject their cultural heritage and to adopt the views of the missionaries. Almost no attempt was made to adapt the curriculum to the

Western-style education of Aboriginal children in Australia is imparted here by an Aboriginal teacher. In the past, formal schooling among Aborigines trained them in little they could use in either their world or that of the white people.

cultural needs of the Aboriginal children. As a result, the children performed poorly and learned little that was of use to them in either the white or the Aboriginal world. As a result of their formal education, many of these children lost their attachment to traditional Aboriginal culture. Since they did not fit into white culture either, they became people "in between" (Sackett 1978).

The values promoted by Western-style education are associated with the crisis of rapid urbanization facing many Third-World countries.

Writing on the Marsh Arabs of Iraq, Wilfred Thesiger (1985) described how people go to the city believing that their "meager education" will allow them to find their fortune; they have no idea of the limitations facing them as they are forced to compete for scarce jobs with hundreds of thousands of others possessing similar qualifications. Michael Dobbs (1987) writes of how Marsh Arab schoolchildren no longer are interested in occupations such as farmers and fishermen; instead they dream of becoming airline pilots or engineers. The situation is not entirely negative, however. One Iraqi government official is quoted by Dobbs as chiding Thesiger for implying that the Marsh Arabs should continue to live as they had for centuries. Dreams and ambitions will, in fact, enable some of these children to become airline pilots and engineers.

The shortcomings of traditional Western education in non-Western settings have become apparent to educators in recent years. Educational reformers have sought to develop alternative approaches that better fill the needs of particular populations. Such reform requires an understanding of traditional local educational practices. It also requires a thorough knowledge of the people being educated, and of their needs. Anthropologists, with their understanding of culture and their focus on the integration of sociocultural factors, are providing analyses to help bring about this reform.

Socialization in Later Life

The period up to adulthood is the most important for the incorporation of values and the formation of an individual's personality. But socialization does not stop at this point. Three patterns of socialization are of particular significance in later life: the reinforcement of the values of one's society, learning how to adjust to new phases in the life cycle, and learning how to adapt to changes in the environment.

Reinforcement of Values
During our early formative years we are socialized to accept the core values and views of our so-

ciety. As we grow older and our experiences widen, we are faced with more choices, and life becomes more uncertain. People may then be inclined toward different values and world views. Such tendencies to change are countered by the lasting effects of early socialization, general social pressure to conform, and other forms of continuing socialization.

One means of reinforcing core values and views is through public gatherings in which members of a society are subjected to desired messages as a group. Group sharing of the experience makes the individual concretely aware of being part of society. Among Australian Aborigines, periodic gatherings for religious ceremonies remind individuals of the dominant values of their society. In these dramatic representations of mythical events, the members of the society as a group are made to feel part of the mythical events through which the world was created. Public gatherings in our own society serve similar purposes. In Fourth of July parades, for example, millions of people join in a celebration of American patriotism.

People's adherence to prescribed values and views is also reinforced in other ways. In our daily interaction with those around us, public values and attitudes are a constant topic of conversation. In most societies today, continual reinforcement comes from newspapers, magazines, radio, and television as well. The news reports that we receive, the fashion articles that we read, and the music that we listen to all channel our perceptions and, frequently, reinforce the prevailing values of our society. Through the media in our society, we are pressured to consume, compete, and get ahead. And we are encouraged to view such behavior as the most rational possible.

Adjusting to Life-Cycle Changes
As we mature, we must adjust to new phases in the life cycle, coming to terms with new roles and physical changes. Sometimes these changes are small, as in the case of a person receiving a minor promotion at work. In other instances the changes may be considerable, as when a person retires from a job that has been the focal point of

An important message from PAUL NEWMAN and JOANNE WOODWARD

"We share our love with seven wonderful children we have never seen.

"We'd like to tell you why."

Sponsored children pictured: Pedro, Gustavo, Carlos, Johnny, Andres, Jaime, and Laki.

Advertisers and promoters of social causes make use of celebrities as role models to gain acceptance of their products or views.

his or her life for 40 years. The greater the change, the more one will have to adjust and the more one will have to learn.

Adjusting to new statuses and learning new roles are characteristically different in small- and large-scale societies. In most small-scale societies, the range of roles and statuses available is relatively limited and fairly well known. There is room for individual choice, but the basic guidelines are pretty well established. Among the Mardudjara Aborigines, for example, everyone is expected to marry and have children. There are

fairly rigid rules for determining potential spouses, and the prospective bride and groom probably have known each other for years by the time they actually marry. Learning how to behave in their new role is relatively simple for the bride and groom, for they were able to observe in considerable detail the interaction of married couples in the camp as they grew up. Family and other kin also are likely to give them plenty of advice on how to behave. And because of the public nature of the camp, their behavior will be subject to continual scrutiny and comment by other members of the community.

In large-scale societies, the range of statuses and roles is much greater. True, there are limitations, and chances are that the life of a Bolivian tin miner's son will be very much like his father's, but for most people there is much more potential for variation than in small-scale societies. In our own society, a substantial minority do not get married, and many of those who do marry do not have children. The life-style of parents is a poor indicator of what their children's lives will be like, except in very general terms. That a person is an accountant who married his childhood sweetheart and lives in a well-appointed suburb where he plays golf or tennis on the weekend tells us little about what the lives of his children will be like once they leave home. Chances are that his children will lead lives roughly similar to his own or that of his wife, but they are likely to pursue other occupations and some of them may lead very different lives.

Although some of the socialization for new statuses and roles in large-scale societies is carried out by parents or kin, much of it is not. Teachers and professional counselors assume an active role in socialization where labor is highly specialized and generational differences exist. If one's father is a welder or chef, there is a limited amount of advice he can give his child about adjusting to life as a lawyer. People also can turn to books or the radio or television for assistance. Furthermore, role models include not only those with whom one is acquainted, but also a much wider assortment of celebrities and public figures, to say nothing of fictional characters, than is available to those in small-scale societies. For these reasons, socialization to changing roles in large-scale societies tends to be far less personal than in small-scale societies.

Adjusting to Environmental Changes

In addition to trying to adjust to the more predictable changes that accompany growing older, we must also come to terms with changes in our world. For those born in relatively isolated, small-scale societies, integration into the wider world can be traumatic. Sometimes the trauma is so great that people cannot adjust. Many of those who perished as a result of contact with Western civilization did not die from disease or murder, but from loss of the will to live in a world that was too different from the one they knew. In adjusting to environmental change, age is often an important consideration; the younger members of a society are usually better able to cope with drastic changes.

Adapting to changes in the world around us can be hard even for those brought up in a Western cultural tradition, especially for older people who have formed fairly rigid ideas about how the world should be. Most people in a society like ours do adjust, however grudgingly, partly because we are socialized to expect and, to some extent, even to desire change. Our flexibility is also made possible by our reliance on a relatively wide range of impersonal socializing devices. Socialization based on the personal experiences of parents and others of older generations has its limitations in dealing with completely new circumstances. Adjustments to such changes are made easier when people can draw on the experiences of a much greater range of people through books and the media and through the use of professional counselors.

DEVIANTS

In all societies there are standards for judging appropriate behavior. Views about what constitutes an ideal person and a normal person are fairly well established. The normal person usually is not expected to live up to the ideal. In fact, to do so sometimes can lead to criticism: "Who does she think she is, acting so prim and proper?"

Those who are judged to be normal simply are expected to behave in ways generally deemed acceptable and to hold views that are not considered too strange or threatening. Normal people are allowed a few peculiarities and occasional slips, but there are limits. Behavior that goes beyond certain limits is considered deviant, and those who think or behave in ways radically different from the norm, especially if they do so with some consistency, are considered **deviants**.

Identifying Deviants

Anthropologists are concerned primarily with how members of a society jointly reach a consensus about deviance. Definitions of deviance vary from one society to the next. A person labeled crazy in our society might be considered gifted or normal in another. In our society if you catch someone trying to cheat you and become angry, you are considered to be behaving normally, provided your anger does not lead you to act violently. Semai or Inuit would view such anger as deviant.

In all cultural traditions, there is leeway for rationalizing occasional improprieties. For example, although the Semai consider violence abnormal, many took an active part in the British campaign against Communist insurgents in the 1950s. Some Semai justified their action by attributing it to temporary insanity, to "blood drunkenness." In this way, they avoided labeling themselves as deviants and upheld the Semai view that violence is wrong.

How members of a society define deviance usually reflects their collective experience over generations and their adaptational strategy. Semai or Inuit consider violent individuals to be deviant because they are seen as threats to an adaptational strategy that stresses harmonious social relations. Early childhood socialization fosters the transmission of such perceptions over generations. These learned attitudes toward deviance are reinforced in later life by the actions and statements of others with similar views. Experiences that result in frustration and insecurity may also shape attitudes toward deviance because the deviant acts of others often are seen as linked to one's own problems. To a Mayan Indian, frustration in hunting or in courting may be blamed on the work of a sorcerer. In our own society, we are likely to blame bums, hoodlums, and drug pushers for our problems, but the list of "troublemakers" is long—for some people including rock musicians and homosexuals.

Members of small-scale societies, because of their relative homogeneity, tend to exhibit a high degree of consensus regarding deviance. Most Mardudjara Aborigines would agree as to which acts and individuals were deviant. There is usually less consensus in large-scale societies because of the greater diversity of socialization patterns, individual experiences, and goals. For instance, while some members of American society consider it deviant to drink anything alcoholic, most Americans do not.

Groups also can be singled out as deviant. Members of small-scale societies usually reserve this designation for communities or groups outside their own. Thus, the members of another kin group or community may be seen as "a gang of cutthroats and cheats" or "a den of thieves." More heterogeneous large-scale societies commonly contain groups that are designated deviant. Throughout Europe, gypsies are seen as such a group, as are motorcycle gangs such as the Hell's Angels in North America.

Definitions of deviance and attitudes toward deviants are not static. They vary according to one's place in the life cycle. While it may be acceptable for an American male to be something of a "hell-raiser" in his teens, to continue such behavior into middle age is viewed with disfavor. Moreover, attitudes can change significantly over time in the face of social change. For example, during the cold-war hysteria of the 1950s many people in the West considered anyone with Communist leanings a deviant who threatened the social order. As the cold war waned in the 1960s, fear of menacing Communists lessened and Americans turned their attention to other deviants, more relevant to current problems— rapists, welfare cheats, robbers. Such changes in defining deviance are often related to attempts by particular members of a society to promote their views about deviance and, as with the so-called witch hunts against suspected Communists in the 1950s, definitions of deviance can assume a political dimension.

The Hell's Angels accept their society's consensus regarding their status: they even take pride in being considered deviant.

The Deviant's View

To this point, we have been discussing how people identify others as deviant. But what about the deviants themselves? Do they see themselves as deviants, as normal people, or as unjustly censured members of society? While there are people who consider themselves to be witches, often those accused of witchcraft do not agree with their accusers. Likewise, while some members of a society might consider prostitutes to be deviants, the prostitutes themselves (for example, those involved in such organizations as Coyote in the United States and the Indian Prostitutes' Welfare Association in India) may not share such a view. Citing the fact that prostitution was legal by licensing in 56 countries, in the late 1980s the

Indian association called on the government to legalize prostitution and to set up a body to protect prostitutes' rights.

While people may agree with a society's general view of deviants, they may be unwilling to identify themselves as deviant. Middle-class people in our own society who engage in acts generally held to be deviant, such as stealing or smuggling, may not consider themselves deviant. They often have a stereotyped vision of what a deviant is like ("the criminal type"), which differs considerably from their own self-image. A similar situation can exist with groups considered deviant by most members of a society. Those who belong to the Ku Klux Klan certainly do not consider the group to be deviant. In fact, they feel that it functions to uphold the fundamental values of American society.

Many deviants accept the general consensus regarding their status. This is not surprising, since deviants take their cues about how to identify deviants from the same cultural tradition as do others around them; should their acts lead others to see them as deviant, they are likely to agree with the label. Billy the Kid was quite aware of his deviant status, just as the Hell's Angels are of theirs. In fact, some people may derive satisfaction from being labeled deviant.

By and large, deviants are still members of the wider society and are influenced by its cultural traditions. Indian and French prostitutes still share much of their respective cultures, just as Maori biker gangs in New Zealand have many distinctively Maori characteristics. In fact, deviants may be so labeled not because they reject cultural values, but because they exaggerate certain values, as in the case of the "patriotism" of the Ku Klux Klan.

Within the wider society, deviants often form distinct groups or subcommunities with their own adaptational strategies, values, and methods of organization. The *hinjaras* of India (eunuchs, transsexuals, hermaphrodites, and transvestites), for example, form groups of up to 200. These groups have various rituals and are organized hierarchically under the leadership of a single guru (with transvestites occupying the lowest status).

They support themselves by singing and dancing at celebrations for newborns and newlyweds, where their presence is supposed to bring good luck. Many of them also work as prostitutes. In 1986, over 6,000 eunuchs gathered in Bhopal for their first national meeting since 1906 to elect a new leader.

As individuals become members of deviant groups or subcommunities, they become socialized to a new set of values and expectations. Those sent to prison for the first time undergo a process of socialization as they adjust to prison life. The adjustment can be considerable, especially if the prisoner comes from a segment of society in which imprisonment is uncommon. Such an adjustment may be only temporary, as with "white-collar" criminals who are likely to assimilate into law-abiding middle-class society upon their release. On the other hand, it may result in a more fundamental transition. Some inmates of prisons and psychiatric hospitals become so thoroughly socialized to the ways of the institution (becoming, in a sense, normal in the institutional context) that they later cannot adapt to life on the outside. Those who undergo such thorough transformations are likely to remain deviants from the perspective of the encompassing society, unless some other drastic change of circumstance forces or encourages them to move in another direction.

SUMMARY

Members of different societies learn to view themselves and their world in different ways. The basic cultural orientation of the members of a society is called their world view. A society's world view is linked with its adaptational strategy and its environment. Similar economic circumstances produce roughly similar world views, as exemplified in Lewis's culture of poverty. Very generally, world views may be divided into the primitive and the civilized: the former views things in largely personal terms; the latter, more impersonally. Within any cultural tradition, it is possible to isolate core values, which are fundamental in providing shape and meaning to people's lives.

On the level of the individual, culturally learned attitudes are expressed in the personality. It is based on a set of core values of which we are largely unaware, with a conscious aspect that includes our self-concept. Although each personality is unique, it is possible to generalize about personalities in particular societies. Thus, some anthropologists have described personality types, such as those that are tradition-oriented, inner-directed, and other-directed.

World views, values, and personality develop throughout the life cycle by way of socialization. The life cycle is divided and defined differently in different societies. However childhood is defined, socialization during this early period is critical in forming an individual's personality. Transitional periods in the life cycle are often marked by rites of passage, which may ease a person's move into the next stage of life and may be used to reinforce cultural values.

In most societies, education plays a significant role in socialization. In small-scale, nonindustrial societies, education is largely a matter of observation and imitation, with little specialized instruction. In large-scale societies, education is conducted more formally in specialized institutional settings. Since World War II in particular, Western-style education has spread throughout the world, with important consequences—some good and some not so good—for the nations concerned.

Even after formal education ends, socialization continues in later life. The culture's values are reinforced and there are continual adjustments to the life cycle and to environmental changes.

Although these processes tend to shape individuals who conform to the world view, values, and personality of their society, there is always some deviance from these patterns. How members of a society define deviance is largely a product of their collective experience over generations and of their adaptational strategy. Those identified as deviants may or may not define themselves as deviant, but they are clearly still members and products of their society.

SUGGESTED READINGS

Barnovw, Victor. 1985. *Culture and Personality*, 4th Ed. Homewood, IL: Dorsey Press.

Berry, John W. 1976. *Human Geology and Cognitive Style*. New York: John Wiley and Sons.

Chisholm, J.S. 1983. *Navajo Infancy: An Ethnological Study of Child Development*. Chicago: Aldine.

Herdt, Gilbert H., ed. 1982. *Rituals of Manhood*. Berkeley: University of California Press. (Papua New Guinea)

Hsu, Francis L.K. 1984. *Rugged Individualism Reconsid-ered*. Knoxville: University of Tennessee Press. (United States)

Rohlen, Thomas P. 1983. *Japan's High Schools*. Berkeley: University of California Press.

Whiting, B.B., and J.W. Whiting. 1974. *Children of Six Cultures: A Psycho-cultural Analysis*. Cambridge, MA: Harvard University Press.

Williams, Thomas R., ed. 1975. *Psychological Anthropology*. The Hague/Paris: Mouton.

Central American Refugees: Learning New Skills in the U.S.A.

James Loucky

First working in highland Guatemala in 1973, before the onslaught of tourists or of massive political repression, James Loucky has continued to work with the Mayan people both in their homeland and in exile. Using a mix of observation and time-recall methods, he has documented the significance of children in their rural household economy. Since the mid-1980s, Dr. Loucky's research has focused on Mayan families now living in the United States. Currently he teaches at Western Washington University.

Enrique's public schooling in Los Angeles ended the day he was jumped on the way home. Demanding that the 15-year-old join their gang, several youths forcibly tattooed a mark on his arm before letting him go. Filled with a fear that he had not experienced since fleeing Guatemala with his family several years earlier, he never returned. At the urging of his parents, he attended night school for several months until the family left for the perceived safety of a farm community, where Enrique now labors in the fields alongside his father.

The contrast between the remote mountain villages of highland Guatemala and inner-city neighborhoods in the United States could hardly be more striking. In addition to being uprooted from traditional means of adaptation and learning, Mayan refugees living in cities such as Los Angeles confront challenges in the areas of social and economic roles, language, and values. As with the immigrants and refugees before them, how well they adjust to the new conditions and the stresses of a major

metropolitan area depends largely on the children and their achievement in school.

When I first went to Guatemala, I became fascinated with how fully the Maya utilize natural resources available to them, and I quickly realized how important children are in this way of life. From an early age, Mayan children begin running errands and caretaking, gradually assuming responsibility for an increasing variety of food-gathering, cultivation, and food-processing tasks. By adolescence, they are working nearly as intensely as do adults. Parents and older siblings offer encouragement, and the children soon come to realize that their help is essential to an interdependent family effort.

The skill acquisition and value formation inherent in this informal education provide a built-in cultural intervention for a population at risk. However, the pressure that comes from having insufficient land also prevents many Mayan children from attending or staying in school. In contrast to their socialization in the work setting, the possibility and efficacy of socialization by formal means are far less apparent.

During the 1980s, Guatemala's glaring social inequities escalated into popular unrest, which the military countered with brutal and massive repression. Tens of thousands of Maya fled scorched-earth campaigns, kidnappings, and forced recruitment into the fighting. Many joined other Central Americans in the movement north, eventually settling in communities throughout Mexico, the United

Mayan refugees enjoying the marimba during a community fiesta.

States, and Canada. Several thousand now live in urban barrios west and south of downtown Los Angeles.

Ironically for Guatemalans, the insecurity and fears related to poverty and violence in Central America have been replaced by new uncertainty and danger in the inner city of Los Angeles. People crowd into one- or two-room apartments in aging brick tenements, doubling up with extended kin or even unrelated people to pay the high rents. Most Maya over the age of 15 toil for 50 to 60 hours a week doing menial sewing work in the sweatshops of the garment district. They are underpaid and have little job security. When not in school, Mayan children stay in or near the apartment, since street crime and drug dealing can make even the front steps or hallways dangerous places to play.

Completely removed from their natal circumstances, these children quickly find out that they need to learn new skills and ways of thinking. Their economic value is clearly not as evident as in the normally occurring family structure of highland Guatemala. However, as I developed close relationships with the Mayan refugee community through my work with a cultural organization that they formed in 1986, I saw how the children continue to play an essential role in contributing to the family's well-being. They facilitate household management by helping to clean and by taking care of younger brothers and sisters. And as they get older, they take on part-time jobs and do mending at home.

The competence of children in Los Angeles, compared with that of children in Central America, increasingly revolves around schoolwork rather than physical labor, yet it is of no less benefit to the family, both immediately and in the long term. The children's school attendance is often the main sustained contact recently arrived families have with the institutions of their new society. Children daily cross the threshold between home and host society and play a valuable culture-broker role by translating and channeling English and other information from classroom to home. In this way, they help to expand their family's skills and resources and provide an anchor in the midst of change.

So while their activity lacks the survival significance it has in rural Guatemala, and while they tend to be ignored by researchers and politicians alike, immigrant children are still best viewed as integral parts of an interdependent family. They both influence and are influenced by their family's adaptation to Los Angeles, helping to enhance mutually effective social interaction. Education is thus part of a strategy for holding together and furthering the family and an actualization of the age-old immigrant dream of "something better" for their children.

Guatemalan parents laud the benefits of school, particularly as it promotes proficiency in English. However, there is considerable variation in the degree of success Central American children achieve in Los Angeles schools. For some children, the student role is new, home-study space is limited, and parental role models are few. Intergenerational conflicts emerge as the children acquire new roles and power that may be disturbing to their non-English-speaking parents. The classroom itself can create cultural conflict. Quick second-language acquisition is required. Teachers often lack knowledge of the students' cultural background, or misperceive their insecurity or cultural differences as lack of intelligence or motivation. For some children, academic underachievement may snowball into low self-esteem as they blame themselves for falling further and further behind.

By contrast, other immigrant children are incredibly creative and resilient, in some cases progressing toward higher education despite (and perhaps in reaction to) traumatic uprooting, family separation, or privation. These successes can usually be traced to families that offer a supportive environment for schooling. This may include effective management of joint space and activities, frequent encouragement, and early inculcation of faith to maintain positive vision. However, individual children differ; for example, one indigenous Guatemalan girl won a scholarship to college, while her sister dropped out of school in the seventh grade.

Their minority status and their concern about the disruptions they frequently experience have led Guatemalan refugees in Los Angeles and in other communities across North America to try to maintain their cultural identity. Social ties and cultural competency have been reaffirmed through nonformal educational means, such as music, dance, language, lore for children, and fiestas. Though less structured than schooling, community activities to restate and re-create culture are examples of the diverse ways in which education both empowers and transforms immigrants in the United States today.

19 Ethnicity and Social Stratification

A view of the city of Rio de
Janeiro, with its stark contrast
in wealth and life-style.

The Ballardong say that some remote tribes to the eastwards are cannibals, and that they mark children at their birth who are eventually to be eaten. . . . I am convinced, however, that little dependence can be placed on stories of this sort respecting cannibalism; what we positively know being that most tribes practiced it more or less, and that nearly all stoutly deny the fact, and accuse their neighbors of it.

So reported police constable David E. Hackett about the Aborigines of York, Western Australia, in the late nineteenth century (in Curr 1886–87, 1:342–43). None of the Ballardong had ever actually seen anyone eaten, but they were prepared to believe anything about their neighbors to the east that cast them in a bad light. The Ballardong had no clear evidence that their neighbors were cannibals, basing their beliefs instead on misinterpretation of the purpose of circumcision (for the Ballardong did not circumcise, a practice which, of course, has nothing to do with cannibalism). But the Ballardong's unfounded beliefs reinforced their perception of cultural differences between themselves and the York Aborigines and supported a feeling of group identity among the Ballardong by helping them to define themselves as distinct. Such beliefs in a we-they distinction are central to **ethnicity**, previously defined as selected perceived cultural or physical differences used to class people into groups or categories considered to be significantly distinct (see Chapter 7).

Hackett's statement reveals not only the Ballardong's prejudices, but also the prejudices of white Australians toward Aborigines. His remark about Aboriginal cannibalism was based no more on observation than was that of the Ballardong, but most white Australians during the nineteenth century were certain that Aborigines did eat each other. (For that matter, many primitive peoples believed that whites were cannibals.) European settlers simply assumed that the practice of cannibalism was a feature of most "savage" societies; the claims fit with their commonly held stereotypes, and proof was by and large not thought necessary. Such beliefs helped

489

white settlers to justify their maltreatment and displacement of Aborigines.

In this chapter, we will look at two closely related dimensions of sociocultural differentiation: ethnicity and social stratification. In doing so, we will turn our attention to forces that threaten to pull society apart. A wide range of factors is involved in these ways of differentiating people, for ethnicity and social stratification influence and are influenced by almost all aspects of our lives. Both are dynamic processes that continually adapt to the ever-changing conditions in the world around us.

ETHNICITY

Ethnicity, or ethnic-group affiliation, is one major basis on which to draw we-they distinctions. Ideas about ethnic groupings involve concepts of race, people's perceived ethnic identity, ethnic symbols, and relations among ethnic groups.

The Concept of Race

Categorization of humans according to physical or racial characteristics took place among very early human societies. Prehistoric cave paintings in various parts of the world and decorations on ancient Egyptian tombs depict people with markedly different physical characteristics. Anthropologists find that people often make distinctions between groups according to observed or presumed biological differences. Usually one's own type is considered normal—the Yanomami call themselves "true men," the Aboriginal inhabitants of southwestern Australia refer to themselves as "the people"—as compared to all others. The concept of **race,** or categorization according to physical traits, is virtually universal, as is the mistaken belief that the features chosen for purposes of categorization parallel differences in behavior (see also Chapter 7).

As European civilization spread across the globe, race became the subject of systematic scientific enquiry. It became an important issue as Europeans encountered people who differed so much from themselves as to raise doubts about their humanness. From the great variety of observable physical differences, Europeans developed universal classifications. Carolus Linnaeus (1758–59) divided all humanity into four races: white, yellow, Negro, and Indian. In colonized areas, where there was concern over the products of *miscegenation*, or mixing of these presumed races, racial categorization became even more complex. The Spanish carried such racial classification to an extreme in their American colonies. In eighteenth-century Mexico, for instance, the Spanish created 16 racial categories based on degrees of mixture among European, Negro, and Indian (Morner 1967).

As in the case of colonial Mexico, such classifications often were used to determine the political and legal rights and economic statuses of people. More generally, it was common to rank races. The noted philosopher David Hume (1748) stated that since Negroes were the only race not to have developed a major civilization (an idea since proven false), they were "naturally inferior" to whites. Even today, many people think that humanity is divided into a small number of distinct races and that their differences reflect social and intellectual as well as physiological differences. When such perceived differences are used to determine people's position in relation to one another, it is known as **racism**.

Racism in small-scale and large-scale societies is significantly different. In small-scale societies, it entails hatred or oppression of strangers—those outside one's own society. This is true of large-scale societies as well, but in these societies it

Much of American blacks' "racial" identity arises from their experience with economic inequality and perceived injustice. Here, demonstrators march in Minneapolis to protest the police shooting of a young black man.

commonly involves oppression of groups within one's own society. This is to be expected, since larger societies generally incorporate a greater mixture of people than do smaller ones.

As noted in Chapter 7, race as a biological concept has come under attack in recent years. No fundamental biological differences have been found among contemporary races, and race is equally insignificant as a determinant of social or cultural differences. No longer important scientifically, race is relevant only as a sociocultural phenomenon. Race stands as a symbol of non-biological differences—a reflection of cultural differences, different religious beliefs, and economic inequality and exploitation. As Brazilian anthropologist Verena Martinez-Alier (1974) noted: "Strains and tensions in society that may be the result of a variety of factors are often justified and rationalized in terms of racial distinctions" (p. 6).

Ethnic Identity

During the decades immediately following World War II, buoyed by optimism concerning the prospects for rapid global change, some social scientists believed that racism and ethnicity were rapidly disappearing throughout the world. They felt that race and ethnicity were ceasing to be significant issues in Western industrial nations, and that they would soon be irrelevant elsewhere, as countries became more urbanized and industrialized.

In both industrial and industrializing countries, predictions of the demise of racism and ethnicity have been incorrect. If anything, ethnicity has undergone a period of revitalization. Many people thought to have lost their sense of ethnic identity once again are proclaiming their pride in being members of distinct ethnic groups with their own cultural traditions. And, as conflicts in South Africa, Sri Lanka, and Eastern Europe have demonstrated, ethnicity remains a central fact of much of political life.

The persistence of ethnicity is tied to identity formation in early socialization. As young children, we learn to value certain aspects of the cultural traditions of our society. We acquire what may be called primordial, or original, attachments to a particular way of life, and in the process learn to value that way of life more than other ways. In other words, we become *ethnocentric.*

While our ethnic identity may be rooted in early childhood socialization and in the perceived cultural traditions of our society, the significance of this identity at any given time will, for the most part, reflect current situations. The resurgence of ethnicity in the Soviet Union and elsewhere in Eastern Europe, as exemplified in the formation of separatist political movements, is not simply a reflection of primordial attachments to cultural traditions. Such attachments are important, but recent ethnic militancy in these countries is primarily a reaction to current political and economic conditions, such as the collapse of Communist regimes and major economic disruptions.

Census figures in Australia in 1987 showed 225,000 people identifying themselves as Aborigines. In 1981, the figure was only 160,000. Since the population growth rate for Aborigines is 3 percent per year, how can such a rise be accounted for? Part of the answer is fairly simple. In 1987, Aboriginal census workers were hired to help count fellow Aborigines for the first time. State institutions often play a role in ethnic identification in this way, sometimes creating or encouraging such identification where it had been weak or nonexistent. But the increased self-identification among Aborigines also was

These Soviet Georgians, a militant ethnic minority in the Soviet Union, protest Soviet rule.

brought about by the work of Aboriginal political activists. The clearest example of this was in Tasmania, where most Australians believed the last Aboriginal inhabitants had died in the nineteenth century. In recent years, however, Aboriginal political activists in Tasmania have struggled for the recognition of local Aborigines, and people of Aboriginal ancestry increasingly have come forward and identified themselves as Aborigines.

Ethnic identification may result from the imposition of ethnic categories by others rather than simply from self-identification. The creation of such categories is a common feature of state formation, especially when linked to colonial expansion. For example, Australian Aborigines did not see themselves as Aborigines until they were treated as a single ethnic group by their European conquerors. Similarly, the Makah are a native American tribe that was created around 1870 by the U.S. government from an aggregation of formerly autonomous villages. In such situations, it may take time before the people categorized begin to assume their new identities; if there is no pressure to do so, they may never adopt them.

Ethnic Symbols

To lump others into ethnic groups—or to see oneself as part of an ethnic group—usually involves the selection of particular aspects of a culture as defining ethnic identity. For example, how people speak, what they eat, how they build their houses, and what they wear serve as markers identifying members of a distinct ethnic group. Often there will be clusters of symbols, only some of which will be seen as essential for defining identity. This applies especially when physical differences exist among populations. Thus, in the southern United States it is possible to list numerous traits associated with the black population, although few of these are universal. The essential characteristic is that of skin color.

The nature of ethnic symbols may vary a great deal from one group to another and even among members of a single ethnic group. Not all whites in the southern United States have the same views about black ethnic identity, and their ideas will not correspond entirely with the blacks' own views. Also, while poorer blacks may view certain foods and patterns of behavior toward kin as part of being black, upwardly mobile blacks may not. Indeed, the latter may wish to identify more with the dominant white culture and thus may assume characteristics identified with that culture. To some extent, use of ethnic symbols depends on a person's strategy in a particular situation.

The evolution of ethnic symbolism is related to efforts to define ethnic groups in relation to one another. Defining groups becomes especially important under conditions of national integration—the incorporation of groups of people, at one time relatively autonomous and distinct, into an encompassing state structure. For example, when the Kekchi- and Mopan-speaking Maya who today occupy the southern part of Belize moved into the area from Guatemala during the latter part of the nineteenth and early twentieth centuries, they had little contact with members of other ethnic groups in Belize—Garifuna, Creoles, whites, Chinese, and others. Since World War II this situation has changed, as the Kekchi and Mopan have been integrated into the multiethnic Belizean society (Howard 1980). As a result, they have had to consciously define their ethnic identity—to develop a general, idealized picture of what it means to be a Mopan or Kekchi Maya. They have also developed conscious ideas about what it means to be a member of one of the other ethnic groups. These images, known as "basic value orientations" (Barth 1969, 14), include the Maya's view of themselves as hard-working and honest in contrast with "lazy" Creoles and Garifuna and "crafty and dishonest" East Indians and Chinese. Among the values of the Maya were those emphasizing sociocultural homogeneity, playing down differences among themselves.

Out of this general picture of what it is to be a Maya, the Mopan and Kekchi selected specific symbols to characterize their identity. The symbols chosen were items, institutions, or practices that they perceived as central to their life-style and to the social fabric of their communities. These included growing maize and black beans, practicing reciprocal labor exchange, wearing certain kinds of clothes, and eating certain foods. The thatched hut emerged as a particularly important symbol of Mayan identity, in contrast with the corrugated-metal-roofed houses of board or brick common among non-Maya. Construction of a thatched house traditionally has involved reciprocal labor exchange and the use of local forest products, whereas corrugated-metal-roofed houses are built by paid laborers and require the purchase of externally produced building materials. When constructed by Maya, the latter type of houses came to be seen by other members of the community as a means of flaunting one's wealth and social superiority. As a result, those who built such houses were stigmatized by other Maya.

In the face of rapid change in southern Belize in recent years, the use of ethnic symbols by the Maya has evolved. Dress now almost never serves as an ethnic marker, for the men no longer wear distinctive clothing, and fewer and fewer women want or can afford to wear the traditional clothes.

Ethnic Relations

Ethnic identity is primarily a product of interaction among members of social groups who perceive themselves to be different. While it may be of little importance for members of small-scale societies who rarely interact with members of other societies, for those living in large-scale societies it is often very significant. Especially in urban areas, a person is likely to encounter people of different ethnic identities at work, while shopping, or in the course of other daily activities. Whether we-they distinctions arise depends on factors that promote either **boundary maintenance**—the process by which ethnic distinctiveness is maintained—or **assimilation**—the process by which cultural distinctions between ethnic groups are minimized or eliminated. These factors include marriage patterns, patterns of occupational specialization, demographic characteristics, and politics.

Marriage Patterns

Marriage within an ethnic group maintains ethnic boundaries because it enhances group homogeneity (and hence, indirectly, group distinctiveness). By contrast, marriage across ethnic boundaries *may* promote assimilation. Faced with a shortage of women in the 1960s, the Tapirapé of central Brazil began to intermarry with the neighboring Carajá, speeding up the loss of a distinctive culture by the Tapirapé (Shapiro 1968). Young Tapirapé men who marry Carajá

women form important social bonds with their Carajá in-laws by joining them as commercial fishermen and ceasing to live as Tapirapé agriculturalists. Both Tapirapé and Carajá nevertheless remain part of an encompassing ethnic category—Indian—which distinguishes them from non-Indian Brazilians.

Rather than assimilating one group into another, marriage between members of different ethnic groups may lead to the creation of new ethnic groups. In colonial Mexico, for example, there were 16 ethnic categories that were generated from only a few initial groups—Spanish, Indian, and African (categories themselves representing a synthesis of an earlier plethora of ethnic divisions)—as a result of miscegenation.

Occupational Specialization or Competition

Within multiethnic settings, occupational specialization often is a feature of ethnic groups, playing a significant role in maintaining ethnic distinctiveness. Although this specialization may promote interdependency between ethnic groups, relations between the groups are not necessarily harmonious or egalitarian. The nomadic Baluchi pastoralists of southern Iran and Pakistan historically have dominated other non-nomadic ethnic groups who share the same territory. For instance, many non-Baluchi agriculturists farm as sharecroppers on land owned by the Baluchi.

Members of different ethnic groups may compete for jobs. When people from rural areas move to the city, they often seek assistance from members of their ethnic group who live in the city. The central figure in Nigerian novelist Chinua Achebe's *No Longer at Ease* is supported while at school in England and assisted in getting a job upon his return home by members of a voluntary association of fellow tribespeople. In his study of the Liberian city of Monrovia, Fraenkel (1964) described how tribal-based voluntary associations function to exploit and maintain a monopoly over particular occupations. [*Main text continues on page 499.*]

The Amazonian Rain Forest:
Ecosystem and World System

Amazonia, the enormous basin of the Amazon River, which is 4,000 miles long and fed by more than 1,000 tributaries, contains a rain forest that covers two-fifths of the South American continent. This vast rain forest harbors an incredibly rich array of plant and animal life and has been home to numerous Indian groups for thousands of years. Yet this natural and cultural diversity, in what some regard as the last great primeval wilderness, is now vanishing at an alarming rate.

Hardly an isolated backwater, although it may seem so, the Amazonian rain forest has, in fact, been a part of the world economy since the seventeenth century. More recently, it has been the focus of major initiatives of South American industries and colonists to exploit the land and its resources. This exploitation of the rain forest has been encouraged by national government policy and international economies. (For an account of exploitation of the rain forests of the world, see Repetto 1990.) The rain forest's role within the world system—particularly in the service of extractive enterprises that deplete resources, such as timber, minerals, and plant products, without provision for replenishment—has resulted in the degradation of the forest's natural environment and the extermination of many Indian tribes.

The Amazonian rain forest is a complex ecosystem—a web of millions of interacting plant and animal species and nonliving components, such as soil and water. For millions of years, the forest environment has been stable, facilitating the evolution of the great variety of species. The diversity of life also reflects the existence of many ecological zones, distributed from the forest's top, a massive canopy, to the bottom. Between the forest's top and bottom are a large variety of miniecosystems that teem with life: airborne plants dangle from vines, filled with insects, spiders, and small reptiles. Thousands of birds and mammals also inhabit the forest, including primates, as discussed in Chapter 4. Besides being of scientific and aesthetic interest, rain forests are also "climate controllers, desert preventers and huge storehouses of as yet untapped natural resources" (Mitchell 1986, 9).

Rain forests are inherently fragile and highly susceptible to disturbances, such as those caused by the clearing and burning of land for agriculture and other purposes. Once disturbed, a rain forest is extremely difficult to reestablish. The forest ecology is based on the presence of large, ancient trees; in fact, most of the life-forms are sustained by the trees, not by the soil, which lacks nutrients. This type of ecosystem means that the soil is not suited to large-scale agriculture. In addition, the soil is rapidly washed away by torrential rains as the protection of the forest's canopy and root system is destroyed.

The rain forest's ecosystem is also linked with the global environment, which many experts fear is being altered with deforestation around the world. Environmentalists have expressed widespread concern over the "greenhouse effect"—global warming associated with increased atmospheric carbon dioxide due to burning. They are also concerned with ozone depletion and with desertification. They also fear the extinction of countless plant and animal species, which, in addition to enriching our world, hold promise for new scientific discoveries in medicine and other fields. We now use drugs from rain-forest plants to treat childhood leukemia, cancers, heart ailments, and arthritis. Yet little more than 1 percent of rain-forest species have been examined for their potential medical applications.

Humans are enmeshed in the rain-forest web of life. Indigenous societies for the most part were well adapted to the environment, although sometimes they severely altered the environment in the process of feeding themselves. Many scientific studies, however, suggest that traditional Indian social organization and technology in Brazil supported relatively large societies without upsetting the regenerative cycles of plant and animal life. Indian communities that were located along rivers coordinated their planting of crops, such as maize and manioc; their hunting, using arrow and dart poisons; and their fishing with the annual rise and fall of the water level of the river (Lathrap 1968, 1977). For example, yearly floods deposit fertile silt across a large floodplain, which enriches the soil and enhances the cultivation of crops. Riverine Indians adapted their agriculture to this seasonal cycle. Indian communities also adapted their technologies to other ecological zones, such as savannah (Nimuendaju 1967), and modified otherwise unfavorable environments by building causeways, canals, and raised fields (Denevan 1970). Political alliances and extensive trade networks between communities living in different ecological zones ensured that resources were distributed from one area to another.

Thus, while Indians utilized the forest environment, they did so largely without disturbing the ecological balance. In the absence of a market economy, as long as land was abundant and people few, there was no excessive exploitation of any narrow range of resources that would prevent natural regeneration. The Indians' vast knowledge of the natural environment has sometimes helped them conserve resources. Some Brazilian Indians, for example, would release the tropical birds they had captured after taking a few feathers for headdresses.

Europeans entered the Amazonian rain forest with a different orientation to the forest environment, creating a succession of transformations. The human and natural worlds of the Amazon were increasingly subjected to the pressures of a wider and more complex economic and political world (Bunker 1985).

Early European relations with Brazil began with exploratory expeditions and continued with the military conquest of the Amazon River. Soon after came the enslavement of Indians, who were conscripted to work on plantations; the importing of large numbers of indentured workers to tap rubber trees; and eventually the expulsion of the descendants of those workers by large companies seeking to use the land they occupied to cut lumber, raise cattle, or extract minerals. The powerful groups behind each penetration of the rain forest, whether they used slave labor, fire, bulldozers, or chain saws, all transformed it in ways that limit its further use (Bunker 1985).

This progressive limitation of the use of the rain forest as a result of exploitation is evident ecologically. For example, early European traders exploited turtles for egg and meat products in demand in international markets. This exploitation interfered with the ecosystem, with the consequent disappearance of turtles as a natural resource on which the traders relied. The indigenous people also suffered. Turtles meant food for the Indians and were also part of the food chain supporting another food source—fish. Thus, the traders' exploitation of turtles limited the availability of protein sources for Indian populations.

Since the first European penetration of the Brazilian rain forest, many Indian groups have been demoralized, displaced, or decimated. It is estimated that the Indian population has fallen from around 6 million at the time of European contact to about 100,000 today. In the twentieth century alone, about 87 Brazilian Indian groups have become extinct, or nearly so (Ramos 1984). Imported Western disease, to which the indigenous peoples had no immunity; massacres organized by colonists, cattle-ranchers, and coffee-growers seeking land; and slavery all contributed to the Indians' demise. For example, the discovery of minerals on some Indian territories provoked air bombings, food poisoning, and other acts of violence against native groups. Furthermore, with the construction of dams and highways, trees are destroyed, diseases are spread, and pressure is put on Indian groups to give up their traditional ways of life.

Why haven't governments acted to better protect the Indians? Because of their unique way of using the resources of the rain forest and their small numbers, Amazonian Indians have not been regarded as productive occupants of the forests. Their cultural differences—signs, to many non-Indians, of inferiority—often divest them of the protection accorded "legitimate" citizens of the nation, including the right to occupy land (Schmink and Wood 1984). Corruption within institutions established to protect Indians' rights and the vulnerability of these institutions to outside pressure have also worked against Indian interests (Ramos 1984). In 1967, for example, Brazil's Indian Protection Service was dissolved when administrators were implicated in the slaughter of Indians by dynamite, machine guns, and sugar laced with arsenic. Indian groups, largely because of communication difficulties between them, fragmentation into numerous small societies, and official action regarding their wardship, have been slow to organize in fighting for their rights, although such organization has been coming about.

The exploitation of the rain forest is rationalized in the name of development. It results, however, in severe and irrevocable injury to human life as well as to natural resources. The prospects for indigenous peoples are not bright, although if they are afforded some protection from disease and given sufficient land to sustain them, they may be able to survive and maintain their ethnic identities.

We have seen that human biological and cultural diversity account for the spread and adaptation of humans across the globe. However, as the world modernizes and becomes part of a system of predominantly Western influences, such diversity is threatened (Bogin 1990). As a result, we have fewer choices for change and adaptation. The influence of Western technologies and economies in the Brazilian rain forest, however beneficial to special-interest groups, is nevertheless bringing the region to the brink of ecological disaster and has already destroyed much of the ethnic diversity the forest has long provided.

Is there any hope for the survival of the Amazonian rain forest or for the other rain forests of the world? In 1990, the rate of forest loss in Amazonia dropped, but the drop may have had more to do with economic recession than with environmental policy. Brazil does have its Operation Amazonia to control deforestation, but it is limited by budget problems and by landowners' violent opposition to its campaign. However, just as the economy of the world system can lead to the destruction of the rain forests, it may also help to preserve them. People around the world are becoming increasingly aware of the importance of the rain forests. Growing social and political movements are beginning to pressure governments into developing ways to use the forests without using them up. One solution may lie with us as consumers. We can become more aware of the source of the wood products on the market, and not buy them if they come from rain forests. A more direct approach is to have developed countries make it economically feasible for financially distressed countries, such as Brazil, to stop the destruction of the rain forests. These countries are saddled with enormous foreign debts. As the result of a growing movement, "debt-for-nature" swaps are taking place, as conservation and other groups take over the debts, on the condition that the forests are turned into national parks (Nichol 1990). Finally, we can learn from the indigenous peoples, who know methods of sustaining resources. With such creative efforts at work, the rain forests may yet endure.

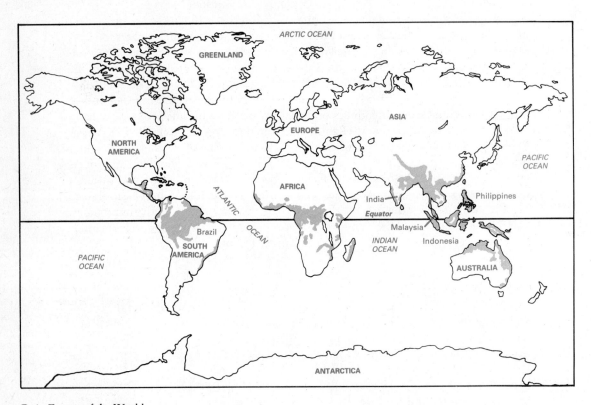

Rain Forests of the World

Ominous vision: The Amazonian rain forest afire. Once destroyed, this primeval wilderness is not likely to ever return.

A hummingbird probing the nectary of a flower. The long-stable environment of the Amazonian rain forest favored the evolution of countless species of plant and animal life.

The diverse ecological zones of the rain forest reach from the forest's floor to the canopy. Poised with a blowgun, a Yagua Indian is engulfed in the forest environment.

An Urueu-Wau-Wau boy, making a practice target of a wounded bird, learns to hunt at an early age.

Traditional Yanomami living quarters. It was from Amazonia that Europeans borrowed the idea of the hammock.

Yanomami fishing the river. Along with hunting and agriculture, fishing supported relatively large Indian societies without upsetting the fragile ecological balance of the rain forest.

Urueu-Wau-Wau villagers perform a victory dance to celebrate the killing of a rubber tapper who encroached on their land. Because their territory is off-limits to outsiders, the warriors face no reprisals from the government.

A young Urueu-Wau-Wau Indian woman totes a macaw, her tribal totem, atop a backpack and a steel blade in her hand.

Rain forest is destroyed to clear land for a farm in Brazil. Deforestation is a drain on valuable resources and a source of greenhouse gases; it represents a loss of habitat for plant and animal species.

In Brazil, unemployment and concentration of land in large holdings result in migration to the frontier. Small-scale farmers, such as this settler working a cornfield, may encroach on Indian land or square off against wealthy ranchers also occupying the area.

Logging in Amazonia supplies an international market. Logging is a major cause
of deforestation, especially where stands are not allowed to recover.

Deforestation is rapid where roads for logging and other activities
are constructed to open up a region for development.

Erosion caused by deforestation.

Wildcat mining for stream tin in the state of
Rondônia, Brazil. Indian forest is torn up,
while Indians provide labor.

What is the fate of the Amazonian Indian? Many have already died as a result of exploitation. A Venezuelan pilot is taking this Yanomami girl to Caracas to be a household maid.

Demography

Demography, or population characteristics such as birth rate and geographical distribution, also influences ethnic relations. For example, rapid population growth among members of a particular group may put pressure on them to expand their place in a society at the expense of another group. Conversely, a group's rapid loss of population may invite others to exploit a perceived advantage. Greater numbers do not always mean greater power, however. Very tense situations may be created when relatively small ethnic minorities dominate the politics and economy of an area at the expense of much larger groups. South Africa serves as a prime example, where some 4 million whites dominate around 20 million blacks and 2 million people categorized as "colored." On the other hand, when larger groups do gain economic and political ascendancy, and when their interests and those of the smaller groups are in conflict, they may feel little compunction about oppressing ethnic minorities.

Politics

Ethnic relations influence political activities and are also affected by them. To the extent that people's use of ethnicity is related to their desire to enhance their position, ethnicity may be seen as inherently political. The Saami, by choosing which language to employ in multiethnic settings, are at least indirectly acting politically. The political role of ethnicity often is even more direct; in many settings, ethnicity is central to political dialogue. This is especially true in postcolonial societies, where diverse peoples were brought together under colonial rule. Thus, in

A South African white man, claiming to be a policeman, and carrying a whip, implements the policy of apartheid by arresting a black man in Johannesburg. The political success of apartheid in past years has meant greater economic prosperity for the Afrikaaners.

Fiji, ethnic differences between the descendants of Indian immigrants and the indigenous population, each making up roughly half the population, have provided a focal point for political competition for many years (see Howard 1991). In settings such as this, ethnicity obscures other differences, such as those associated with social class.

In South Africa, during the early part of this century, the Afrikaaner minority (descendants of early Dutch settlers) found themselves progressively losing out to the English community. The Afrikaaners sought to reverse this trend by implementing racist policies aimed at curtailing the rights of nonwhites. In particular, they sought to restrict land ownership and to relegate nonwhites to the role of servile laborers. By 1948, through an alliance with some whites of English origin, the Afrikaaners assumed control of the government. Through the 1950 Suppression of Communism Act, supported by a wide spectrum of the white population during a wave of anti-communist hysteria, they suppressed any organization or individual opposed to them or their policies. At this time, the Afrikaaners also began to strictly enforce the "apartheid" policies of ethnic separation and domination that became the object of international condemnation.

SOCIAL STRATIFICATION

As the South African example illustrates, ethnicity can be closely linked to economic and political inequality. The Afrikaaners used ethnicity as a means of attaining power and of defining the relative socioeconomic statuses of groups of people, assigning nonwhites lower statuses than whites. Ethnicity is not the only basis for inequality in South Africa, however, and even among whites there is a great deal of inequality in wealth and power. Virtually all societies have developed some degree of inequality through the process of **social stratification**—the division of members of a society into *strata* (or levels) with unequal wealth, prestige, and power.

Increasing social scale, productive capacity, and specialization of labor increase the potential for stratification. In small-scale foraging and farming societies there is little specialization and a relatively small food surplus to appropriate. Accordingly, differences in wealth and power in these societies are limited. By contrast, more intensive forms of agricultural and industrial production, and attendant increases in social scale and division of labor, result in far more potential for inequality.

Beliefs Supporting Stratification

Systems of social stratification are accompanied by beliefs that obscure or legitimatize inequality. These beliefs maintain the existing system of stratification by drawing attention away from threatening areas and by emphasizing common bonds or interests. Widespread adherence to egalitarian ideals in the United States and the Soviet Union, for example, helps to obscure inequality and allows for the survival of a ruling class. Such a ruling class consists of a small group that dominates the country's wealth and holds considerable political power. In addition to sharing economic and political interests, the group has a high degree of social and cultural unity. Thus, writing of the wealthy families that in his view make up the core of the ruling class in the United States, G. William Domhoff (1974) notes that they "are part of interlocking social circles which perceive each other as equals, belong to the same clubs, interact frequently, and freely intermarry" (p. 86). In some societies, differences between social strata are promoted as part of the natural order of things. Louis XIV of France said he ruled by the will of God, and the Nazis in Germany sought to rule as representatives of a supposedly superior race. In feudal societies, those on top view the world as hierarchically ordered and consider themselves part of a "natural" aristocracy. The peasants are encouraged to accept their position, likewise as part of a natural order.

Ideologies supporting systems of stratification also are linked to notions of exchange. In all societies, those who have less wealth and power are conditioned to think that they are getting something in return that justifies existing differences. Aboriginal women give up a portion of the food they gather to men, who in turn perform rituals to ensure the survival of the world. The serf in medieval Europe gave a large part of his crop to his lord in exchange for protection.

Conflict versus Stability

The potential for conflict exists in all stratified systems. As long as there is a feeling among the members of a society that the exchange is fair, and as long as the supportive ideology is maintained, a degree of stability is possible. If a particular segment of society becomes dissatisfied with the arrangement, however, it may seek to change things. The likelihood of this happening in small-scale societies is minimal. Inequalities are not so glaring as in large-scale societies, pressure to conform is strong, and few alternative views are available. The differences between strata in large-scale societies are much greater and tensions are more pronounced. Also, increased heterogeneity in experience, socialization patterns, and the range of views available to those in large-scale societies increases the likelihood of conflict. While fundamental changes in systems of stratification in large-scale societies are rare, tensions as expressed in protests, riots, and rebellions can lead to reforms and gradual changes.

Adherence to an existing system of stratification is associated with the stability of a people's overall adaptation. Should the essential features of their adaptation begin to change, the traditional system of stratification will be threatened. The rise of the world system, the Industrial Revolution, increased population, and a number of other factors combined in the late eighteenth and early nineteenth centuries to undermine the aristocratic hierarchy that prevailed in Europe, replacing it with a system of stratification linked to capitalist production. Thus, as adaptational and economic patterns evolve, so do the ways in which the members of a society are stratified.

Systems of Stratification

While stratification exists in all societies, the forms it takes differ in both degree and kind. In egalitarian societies, stratification is minimal. In nonegalitarian societies, people differ with respect to wealth, prestige, and power according to systems of hierarchical ranking, caste, feudalism, or class.

Egalitarian Societies

The least stratified of societies are known as egalitarian because people tend to treat each other as equals. **Egalitarian societies** are characterized by few individual or group differences with respect to wealth and power. Many foraging and small-scale agricultural societies are relatively egalitarian. Norms in these societies center on sharing and ideals of interpersonal equality. This is not to say that social stratification is nonexistent in these societies. Thus, although the Copper Eskimo of northwestern Canada traditionally emphasized equality, they were not blind to the existence of differences. There were those who were held in high esteem for personal qualities; there were the *ataniq*, who organized hunts; and there were shamans (those thought to be in direct contact with the spirit world), who were sometimes feared because of their ties to the gods (Damas 1972). The Mardudjara-speaking Aborigines of Australia are stratified according to gender and age, and individuals can attain high status as curers or "law-men" (those responsible for maintenance of traditional rules and rituals).

An Inuit shaman in Point Hope, Alaska, chants a song for good luck in hunting whales. The bones in the background are whale rib bones; the drum is made from sealskin. Although part of an egalitarian society, shamans are accorded more respect than others because they are believed to be connected with the gods.

Compared with nonegalitarian societies, however, such differences are relatively insignificant.

The egalitarianism of small-scale societies frequently is undermined by contact with more hierarchical societies. As a result of contact with Indian Hindu society, for example, the Bihors (foragers of the Chota Nagpur plateau of central India) have come to adopt an array of officials—headmen, priests, curers, conveners of meetings, and so forth—all of whom occupy higher positions than other members of Bihor society (Sinha 1972). Often this transformation from egalitarian to nonegalitarian society is part of the process of colonial expansion. White settlers in southwestern Australia made changes among the Aborigines to ease the administration of these conquered people: they created "kings" and gave them brass plaques to wear around their necks to signify their status (Howard 1981).

The egalitarian ideal does not necessarily disappear in large-scale societies. A degree of economic and social equality may be maintained within segments of the larger society. The egalitarian norm is most pronounced among those occupying the lower socioeconomic strata of large-scale societies—peasants, industrial workers, and pastoral laborers. Among peasants, egalitarian beliefs find expression in what has been termed the "image of the limited good" (Foster 1965). Proponents of this view hold that a limited amount of wealth is available; by gaining more than one's share of this wealth one is depriving someone else. This is not to say that all peasants within a village will, in fact, have equal resources or be of the same social status. Those who do have more, however, are careful not to flaunt what they have; moreover, they are expected to share some of their surplus with others.

Since the eighteenth century, a number of industrial societies have adopted ideologies proclaiming social equality as their goal. These include various schools of communist, socialist, anarchist, and utopian thought. Their theories have been put into practice in communes, cities, and nations with varying degrees of success. (Socialist countries will be considered in further detail later on in this section.)

Rank Societies

In contrast to egalitarian societies, many societies divide people into hierarchically ordered groups, which differ in status and perhaps in occupation and wealth. Often this hierarchy is accepted fatalistically by those in the lower as well as in the upper strata as being part of the natural order.

Members of **rank societies** differ in prestige according to a series of graded ranks. In ancient Panama, for instance, high chiefs ruled a number of villages. The high chiefs were respected, traveled by litter, had the sole right to wear many fine ornaments, possessed large and well-provisioned households, and were given elaborate funerals that included the sacrifice of servants. Below the high chiefs were others of high rank: aristocrats born to high status who served as administrators; warriors who served under the aristocrats, controlling villages; and a lesser group consisting of commoners who had achieved social distinction in their own lifetime for prowess in battle. Under this elite were other commoners, primarily farmers, who provided services for those above them—fishing for the elite, planting their crops, fighting for them, and building their houses. The lowest stratum consisted of slaves, who were captives of war (Holms 1976).

In a rank society, those of higher rank tend to be wealthier, to live in better houses, and generally to live a more comfortable life than those of lower rank, who provide them with goods and services. In exchange for this support, the higher ranking members undertake public service, and sometimes are expected to redistribute some of their wealth through feasts and religious ceremonies.

Kinship is an important criterion in determining status in rank societies. Individuals generally are born into a particular stratum, and often there are ranked kin groups. Upward mobility is sometimes possible for individuals who show exceptional aptitude in a particular domain, such as warfare. Religion, too, plays an important role in many rank societies. Priests are afforded high status and the elite justify their special position on the basis of religion.

Historically, the formation of rank societies was associated with intensification of production by farming communities and, in some instances, foraging societies as well. This increased productive capability allowed for greater specialization, increased organizational complexity, and greater population density.

Rank societies consisted of confederations or a number of centrally administered villages; thus, they can be associated with the transition from small-scale societies to large-scale societies. Warfare and competition among rival elites often played an important role in the expansion and development of rank societies (as well as in their subsequent transition into larger sociopolitical units). Sometimes the development of rank societies was stimulated by contact and trade with larger societies.

European colonial expansion destroyed or enveloped many rank societies. In western Panama, for instance, members of rank societies who were not slaughtered by the Spanish in the sixteenth century, or killed by diseases introduced by them, fled into the mountains or were incorporated into the Spanish colonial state. Eastern Panama was out of the main thrust of Spanish conquest and colonization. Although the indigenous people, the San Blas Cuna, suffered some disruption, they were able to adjust more gradually.

The creation of the modern world system has not put an end to all systems of stratification based on rank. In some parts of the world, traditional systems of rank remain a significant part of contemporary patterns of stratification. Indigenous ranking systems were often employed by European colonial powers to establish control over populations through a pattern known as **in-**

The street preacher was a newly created occupation of Christian colonial Fiji. Although ranking considerably below the chief, who continues to enjoy substantial prestige and influence, the Fijian minister may exchange his services in spreading the word of God for some contributions to his coffers.

direct rule, whereby ranking individuals in the native population aided foreign colonial authorities in administering those in their charge. This was the case in Fiji (see Howard 1991), where the chiefs held a variety of posts under the British from the 1870s until independence in 1970. After independence, the highest ranking chiefs were able to assume dominance in the new government, holding such posts as prime minister and governor general and forming a body known as the Great Council of Chiefs, which was granted important powers under the constitution. The Fijian state today is very different from the archipelago of warring chiefdoms of the early nineteenth century, but the traditional system of ranking does continue to exert an influence in contemporary Fijian politics.

Caste Societies

Rank societies are divided primarily horizontally, with only limited differentiation within strata, especially at the lower levels. In some parts of the world, however, as social stratification (and along with it the division of labor) became more complex, some societies developed the practice of dividing individuals at birth into one of a number of occupationally specific, largely endogamous, and hierarchically ordered statuses known as **castes**. Caste systems are viewed as elaborations of rank systems. Perhaps the most comprehensive and striking example of a caste system is the one in India. Other examples are provided by preindustrial Japan and by several societies in northern Africa.

The Indian caste system probably evolved in northern India more than 2,000 years ago out of a blending of the indigenous Harappan civilization of chiefdoms unified by a priesthood and the nomadic Aryan tribes that invaded northwestern India around 1500 B.C. Hindu religion and culture and the related caste system developed out of the mixing of these two peoples and the emergence of larger, more hierarchical, and urbanized societies.

Hindu religious beliefs rationalize and stabilize the caste system. It divides society into four categories, called **varna**, on the basis of occupation. The varna are ranked according to their relative purity—the extent to which their members are considered in a sacred sense to be clean or unclean. The highest varna is occupied by Brahmins—priests and scholars, who are held to be the purest. Below the Brahmins in descending order of status and purity are the Kshatriyas, or warrior castes; the Vaisha, or merchant castes; and the Shudras, or castes of artisans and menial workers. A fifth group, occupying a position below the four varna, consist of the untouchables (commonly referred to as Harijans), who perform work held to be too polluting for others. According to Hindu belief, the varna into which a person is born reflects the quality of his or her actions in a previous life.

Hindu beliefs also provide guidelines for the behavior of caste members. Higher caste persons will not accept food or drink from the polluted hands of those belonging to a lower caste. Likewise, traditionally, they could not have sexual relations with or marry members of lower castes. And higher caste members are expected to avoid consuming polluting substances, such as meat or alcohol. While members of all castes are supposed to try to live up to the Hindu ideals of behavior, those of the higher castes are expected to come closest to ideal behavior.

Castes traditionally functioned within rather narrow localities—a village, or at most a few linked villages. Within this setting, the population would be divided into a series of exclusive castes numbering from a few to 20 or more, called *jati*, ranked according to their place within the varna hierarchy (the relative ranking often being subject to dispute among the jati). These are the most important focal points of caste identity. Each local caste or jati formed a closed, endoga-

mous descent group with an occupational specialization that it offered in exchange for the products and services of other castes. Each caste group usually lived within its own quarter; untouchables lived either on the fringes of villages or in a separate hamlet altogether. Often a dominant family or caste controlled the arable land and monopolized the use of physical force.

In northern India, relations between higher and lower castes often took the form of **jajmani relationships**—patron–client relationships between families of different castes. The jajmani system served as a means of economic exchange within village settings, both reflecting and helping to maintain the relative inequality of castes. Especially important was the giving of grain by members of the dominant castes to families in exchange for services.

The caste system is often seen as static—as an unchanging social structure in which a person's status and occupation are determined at birth. This was not entirely the case during British colonial rule. The British brought about significant changes in the caste system to suit their own administrative and economic needs. Thus, they promoted classes of people who owned land privately, in part as a means of increasing revenues from taxes. This led to widespread debt peonage and promoted migration to towns and plantations (and later overseas) in search of wage employment. India became independent in 1948, and the decades that followed have seen further changes in the caste system as a result of urbanization, industrialization, political reforms, and other factors. New employment opportunities in the industrial and service sectors and increased education also have undermined caste-imposed limits on economic advancement.

Despite many changes, caste continues to be important in India. Most Indians still marry within their own jati, which serves to reinforce many other caste practices and values. Caste also continues to play a role in competition with respect to land, wealth, business, education, and politics. As members of localized castes have come into contact with those from similar castes

This Brahmin woman, a teacher of dance in Bombay, specializes in Bharat Natyam, the temple dance of South India. Although her family's apartment is small, the musicians live there, using the balcony as sleeping quarters.

in cities and towns and in new occupations, new castes have evolved—supercastes that fuse or incorporate the more specialized local castes. Nevertheless, caste now takes its place among many other factors, such as those associated with a modern class society, in shaping the pattern of social stratification in contemporary Indian society.

Feudal Societies

Various agrarian societies, as they have increased in scale, have evolved systems of social stratification that can be termed **feudal**. Within feudal societies, there is an essential difference between those who work the land and those who support themselves by appropriating some of the produce and labor of the agriculturalists. This division is reflected in the pattern of social stratification. In medieval Europe, those who worked the land were often referred to as serfs or vassals, while the primary group appropriating their surplus were referred to as lords. The lord provided military protection and served as a patron for the serf. In return, the serf was expected to provide the lord with a substantial amount of his agricultural product and to render numerous services. There was some degree of reciprocity in the lord–serf relationship, but it was not a balanced relationship. The lord clearly got the better of the deal. Another group that appropriated agricultural surplus was the clergy.

Feudalism is associated with the rise of chiefdoms or the breakdown of larger centralized political authority. In western Europe, feudalism emerged out of the chaos that ensued after the death of the emperor Charlemagne (A.D. 768–

Feudal society in Europe. Serfs till the field to provide a large portion of their agricultural produce to the knights and their ladies.

A.D. 814). In India, China, and Japan, feudalism was linked to the rise and decline of various empires and to the struggles for power among warlords. Feudal societies are prone to warfare and instability; it was partly out of a desire to secure protection and a degree of stability that relations between lord and vassal first arose, for lords provided military protection to the farming population and assumed the rights of government.

With the rise of modern capitalist societies and the nation-state, feudalism has disappeared in many settings. Where it has survived, it has done so within the context of the modern world; thus, it is different in many ways from earlier forms. As André Gunder Frank (1972) pointed out, the more modern feudal societies provide a large part of their product to external markets rather than

being largely self-contained, as was the case in the past. Thus, what is produced by these societies and the value that is placed on products depend more on external market conditions than on local needs.

In Latin America, feudal relations took hold where the authority of Spanish colonial or postindependence governments had been weak. The **hacienda** exemplifies feudalism in Latin America. In highland Peru, where this feudal system continues, there are three classes of persons: the landlord, or *hacendado*; the tenant-workers, called *colonos*; and the administrators or foremen hired by the hacendado (Long 1975). While the hacendado has legal control of the land, the colono works most of it. The colono also works as a servant in the hacienda, and periodically clears roads and water channels and makes repairs around the hacienda. Performing these services usually leaves the colono only enough time to satisfy his subsistence requirements. Besides providing the colono with a small plot of land, the hacendado pays small sums of money for the work done on the hacienda, provides alcohol and cigarettes for those involved in collective work parties, provides pasturage for the workers' animals and access to firewood for cooking, and feeds people working for the hacienda.

Modern feudal systems are unstable in the face of an expanding modern world system. For the elite owners of land, for example, there is the option of replacing feudal labor-intensive methods with more mechanized production, or replacing such a paternalistic system of labor with a more flexible system of wage employment. For the serf, there are also options: moving to town, for example, or finding employment elsewhere. Also, most governments in recent years have sought to take a more active role in the affairs of those regions characterized by feudalism. Thus, the Peruvian government has tried to implement land reform and to exert greater control over agricultural production through administrators.

Modern Class-based Societies

The development and spread of Western industrial capitalism has given rise to a fourth system of social stratification: a hierarchical structure composed of **social classes**. These classes can be associated with life-style or income, but primarily they are defined in terms of the role they play in production.

In Chapter 11, we saw how economic classes evolved in association with the Neolithic revolution and the rise of civilizations. The creation of agricultural surpluses supported nonagricultural classes, and leadership resided in a class of people who could manage surpluses and coordinate activities within and between communities. Modern classes developed first in response to the growth of extensive trade within and beyond Europe largely between the fifteenth and seventeenth centuries, and then assumed greater importance with the rise of industrial production beginning early in the eighteenth century. The first period can be referred to as the era of mercantile capitalism and the second as industrial capitalism. In this way, the system became established and then consolidated.

Class distinctions arose in particular between those who controlled commerce and owned factories on the one hand and those who provided productive labor on the other. Modern social classes have accompanied the diffusion of industrial production from Western Europe and North America to the rest of the world over the past two centuries.

Membership in a class is determined by the means by which people acquire wealth rather than by wealth per se. In a capitalist industrial society, there are two primary classes: one is composed of those who sell their productive labor in return for a wage; the other, of those who own the means of production. Included in the first class are workers engaged in the production of agricultural and industrial goods, the **proletariat**—factory workers, farm laborers, and the like. Also included are those whose labor is connected with the movement or distribution of what is produced. This group includes such occupations as clerical worker, truck driver, and stevedore. The second primary class, the **capitalist**, is made up of those who own the means of production; they appropriate value or wealth from what is produced (i.e., profits) and control the circulation of the wealth that is appropriated.

Often closely related to the capitalist class are wage-earners in supervisory or management roles. There are also those employed in technical positions (such as engineers) and others whose class position is more ambiguous—a reflection of the complex division of labor found in modern industrial societies. Such people are sometimes labeled *middle class*.

Another important segment of modern class-based societies consists of those at the margins or beneath the other classes. These people serve as a *reserve army* of surplus workers who can be employed when the need arises. Braverman (1974) described this reserve army as follows:

> {It} takes a variety of forms in modern society, including the unemployed; the sporadically employed; the part-time employed; the mass of women who, as houseworkers, form a reserve for the "female occupation"; the armies of migrant labor, both agricultural and industrial; the black population with its extraordinarily high rates of unemployment; and the foreign reserves of labor. (p. 386)

In many societies, the role of domestic (largely female) unpaid labor within this reserve army is especially important because it subsidizes relatively low wages paid to the members of a household employed in wage labor. Another form of such subsidy is the partial support of laborers by relatives who are active in semisubsistence agriculture; the laborers themselves may resort to subsistence agriculture when wage labor is not available.

Members of the capitalist class are generally wealthier than those of the wage-earning class, but this is not always the case. Moreover, there are wealth differences within classes. The wealth of wage-earners is determined largely by how much they are paid for their labor. Their pay is influenced by a number of factors: how much their work is considered to be worth by members of the capitalist class, the relative demand for their particular skills, and the political power they exert as a result of unionization or lobbying. Highly skilled laborers usually are paid more than semiskilled and unskilled laborers. Workers in countries where labor is abundant and political rights of workers are few may be paid much less than workers in comparable jobs in countries where labor is less abundant and workers have more political power. Semiskilled textile workers in many Asian and Latin American countries, for example, may be paid as little as $20 a week, while in the United States their weekly pay may exceed $200.

Wages of even the best paid of such laborers, however, are considerably lower than those earned, for example, by managers of large corporations. Also, laborers' wages tend to be much lower than those in technical fields such as medicine. Relative wage differences between the working class and middle class vary considerably from one country to another. Thus, in many Third-World countries, members of the middle class earn a great deal more than factory workers. In developed countries, the gap between the wages of the middle class and factory workers is much smaller, largely because of the better bargaining position of factory workers in these societies.

The wealth of capitalists comes principally from their profits—the difference between what goods cost to produce and what they can be sold for. The actual wealth of individual capitalists depends on their success in finding and controlling sources of profit. Some capitalists may be completely unsuccessful in their search for profits, and others may be able to find only small sources. By contrast, the wealthiest capitalists control enormous sources of profit. Japanese businessman Yoshiaki Tsutsumi, for example, is one of the world's wealthiest people, with a personal fortune estimated in excess of $20 billion. He inherited his father's railway and real estate business and, as head of the Seibu Railway Group, controls some 70 companies (mainly in real estate and transportation).

Whereas in rank, caste, and feudal societies people are aware of their precise position in the social hierarchy, in modern class-based societies consciousness of class position often is ambiguous. Class consciousness evolves through the perception of common interests. For example, for those engaged in industrial production and, later, service work, class consciousness came about largely through the organizing and actions of labor unions. Class consciousness among capitalists is promoted by organizations such as chambers of commerce. For the middle class, things are more ambiguous, but they, too, sometimes form associations to promote their specific

Japanese businessman Yoshiaki Tsutsumi (right), named one of the world's richest men, controls enormous sources of profit.

interests, for example, as consumers or property-owners.

People do not always view themselves as members of a distinct class; rather, they may view themselves as individual actors. Or they may see themselves as belonging to a specialized segment of society with its own distinct interests—bankers, lawyers, or electricians. Such views reflect important ideological values in capitalist societies that stress individual achievement. Alliances across class boundaries based on perceived common interest also serve to undermine class consciousness. In many countries the most significant alliance is between the capitalist class and the military. In return for creating optimal conditions for corporate profit (for instance, by stifling labor unrest), the military in such countries as Chile and Guatemala has been rewarded with higher wages, better living conditions, and greater amounts of military equipment.

Relations between the two primary classes are characterized by an underlying competitiveness regarding distribution of wealth. In capitalist in-dustrial societies, this tension underlies any surface stability and occasionally breaks out into open conflict. For example, in the Russian Revolution of 1917, industrial laborers, peasants, members of the middle class, and others revolted against the Russian aristocracy and those members of the capitalist class allied with it.

Socialist Societies

The Russian Revolution of 1917 led to the founding of the first modern socialist society. In this century, socialist governments have been established in about 30 countries. These countries vary considerably in population, level of economic development, and political institutions. They range from giants, such as China (with a population in excess of 1 billion) and the Soviet Union (275 million), to the Congo and Mongolia (with fewer than 2 million people each); from the relatively developed countries of Eastern Europe to some of the poorest countries in the world, such as Ethiopia, Laos, and Cambodia.

Their political structures have included the relatively liberal governments of Yugoslavia and Hungary on the one hand and the highly authoritarian regimes of North Korea and Romania on the other. But even if they vary in the kind of socialist society they have created or aim to create, these states do share certain characteristics—at least in theory. They share a stated goal of creating a society in which inequality of wealth and hierarchies of status and power are minimized. They also have relied more heavily than most capitalist societies on state planning and other forms of intervention in the economy. And private ownership of the means of production has been replaced to a greater degree by state or collective ownership than in capitalist societies. One other common feature of most socialist societies today is that they have undergone dramatic change after years of relative stability.

In practice, existing socialist societies are not egalitarian. Yet the transition to socialism does bring about important changes in social stratification, making it different from that in capitalist societies. The former ruling classes are eliminated, whether they were landed aristocrats or wealthy capitalists. Most existing socialist societies inherited extensive peasantries. Collectivization of farms and industrialization has led many peasants in these countries to move to towns to become urban workers. For those remaining in the countryside, life changes as they are incorporated into a more centralized state structure. Among the middle sectors, socialism creates a need for expertise in planning and management as the government assumes a central place in the daily lives of people. Greater educational opportunities also produce a larger middle class of technical and professional people.

Taking Hungary as an example, during the immediate postwar era efforts were made to change the country using the Soviet Union as a model. This had a major impact on social classes as the old capitalist–feudal class structure was transformed into one more in keeping with socialist ideals and the Soviet model. The subsequent period of extensive industrialization and collectivization of agriculture in the 1950s created a much larger group of industrial workers. As peasants came to work in cooperatives, they resembled industrial workers. A new stratum of professionals and white-collar workers also arose, initially coming mostly from the working class.

Social stratification in socialist Hungary was shaped largely by how occupations were positioned in the structure of redistribution (of goods, services, and income). Kolosi and Wnuk-Lipinski (1983) identified four main socio-occupational categories in Hungary: unskilled and semiskilled workers; skilled workers; white-collar workers; and professional workers (including managers). The socio-occupational status of the parents does not necessarily influence the status of their children. In fact, social mobility is high. As in other socialist countries, education serves as the main channel of social mobility. Moreover, Kolosi and Wnuk-Lipinski found that membership in socio-occupational categories did not correlate neatly with socioeconomic strata, as indicated by material living conditions and other criteria. The position of many skilled workers was identical to that of many professionals.

Whereas social stratification may be blurred in socialist countries such as Hungary (in part because of the absence of both an impoverished underclass and a superrich ruling class), differences do exist. Of considerable importance in recent years has been the rise of a large middle class in socialist countries such as the Soviet Union and those of Eastern Europe. Real incomes rose significantly in the 1960s and 1970s (2.2 times in the case of Hungary between 1960 and 1978), resulting in a more prosperous stratum of intellectuals, managers, scientists, doctors, lawyers, technicians, and other professionals. With increased prosperity came greater consumer and political demands that proved difficult to meet in the face of the economic decline or slow growth in the 1980s. The result has been a period of reform unprecedented in the postwar period that has led to significant changes in social stratification in these societies.

SUMMARY

Ethnicity and social stratification are two major ways by which humans divide themselves into we-they groupings. Ethnicity is a complex of ideas about race, perceptions of ethnic identity, ethnic symbols, and relations between ethnic groups. The notion that observed physical differences such as skin color are biologically related to different ways of behaving is now largely discounted by scientists, yet it continues to influence people's perceptions of racial "groups." Consciousness of ethnic identity—of belonging to some group that is physically or culturally distinct—has not disappeared either; in fact, it is resurging in some areas. Often this sense of ethnic identity is expressed through selected symbols.

Ethnic awareness arises through the interaction of groups that perceive themselves to be different. Factors that determine whether boundaries will be maintained or distinctions eliminated include marriage patterns, occupational competition or ethnic-group specialization, demographic features, and politics.

Social stratification, although sometimes linked to ethnic distinctions, is a different way of classifying people. In stratified societies, people are divided into broad categories with unequal wealth, prestige, and power. Such divisions are legitimatized by a society's beliefs, but may change if the society's fundamental adaptation changes.

Stratification differs in degree and kind from one society to another. The least stratified societies are called egalitarian. In ranked societies, people are divided into strata that differ in prestige. In societies with caste systems, people are born into occupationally specific, hierarchically ordered statuses. Feudal societies divide people into two primary strata: those who work the land and those who appropriate the products of their labor in return for certain services. Industrial class societies have evolved distinctions between wage-earners and those who own the means of production. Such distinctions have been modified in the case of socialist societies, in which inequality is based largely on occupation and level of skill.

SUGGESTED READINGS

Berreman, Gerald D., and Kathleen M. Zaretsky, eds. 1981. *Social Inequality: Comparative Developmental Approaches.* New York: Academic Press.

Beteille, Andre. 1977. *Inequality among Men.* Oxford: Blackwell.

Blu, Karen I. 1980. *The Lumbee Problem: The Making of an American Indian People.* Cambridge: Cambridge University Press.

Holloman, Regina E., and Serghi A. Arutiunov, eds. 1978. *Perspectives on Ethnicity.* The Hague/Paris: Mouton.

Howard, Michael C., and Rodolfo Stavenhagen, eds. 1988. *Ethnicity and Nation-building in the South Pacific.* Tokyo: United Nations University Press.

Sanbacka, C., ed. 1977. *Cultural Imperialism and Cultural Identity.* Helsinki: Finnish Anthropological Society.

Sanday, Peggy R. 1981. *Female Power and Male Dominance: On the Origins of Sexual Inequality.* Cambridge: Cambridge University Press.

Strathern, Andrew. 1982. *Inequalities in New Guinea Highlands Societies.* Cambridge: Cambridge University Press.

Wasserstrom, Robert F. 1983. *Class and Society in Central Chiapas.* Berkeley: University of California Press.

Social Stratification in Guatemala

Beatriz Manz

Since her first visit to conduct ethnographic field research in the Indian province of El Quiché in 1973, Beatriz Manz has been actively involved in human rights issues in Guatemala. Currently teaching at the University of California, Berkeley, Dr. Manz has lectured and published extensively on political, economic, and social conditions of Guatemalan Indians.

Anthropologists have long been attracted by Guatemala's extraordinary ethnic richness and diversity. The majority of the country's people are descendants of the Mayas. They speak 22 different languages, wear distinctive, colorful hand-woven clothing, and practice varied rituals and customs, some a heritage from their pre-Columbian Mayan civilization and others intertwined with the legacy of Spanish conquest. Those Guatemalans who are not of Indian descent or who no longer practice Indian customs are called *ladinos*. Although there are ladinos in all social classes, a tiny ladino elite has ruled the country since the Spanish conquest over 450 years ago.

I first went to Guatemala in the summer of 1973 to do field research in the western highlands at the site of the pre-Columbian capital of the Quiché-Maya kingdom. This site, now the municipality of Santa Cruz del Quiché, is the capital of the populous Indian province of El Quiché. I was part of a large ethno-historical project seeking to develop a history of the Quichés since the Spanish

conquest. Whereas other anthropologists had investigated their language, history, and archaeological remains, I was to observe and record their present culture. I began by visiting small hamlets and peasant homes, which dot the eroded hillsides. I observed the peasants and asked them about their agricultural techniques, religious beliefs, and household practices. I also gathered ethno-historical data for the other members of the team.

In the process of my ethnographic research, I soon became aware that insufficient land was the overwhelming concern of these Indians. Inadequate land translated into some of the worst social statistics in the hemisphere, such as extreme poverty, high infant mortality, short life expectancy, chronic disease, and a severe economic insecurity. Moreover, not having enough land to survive in their highland communities compels many Indians to migrate to the large coffee, sugar, and cotton plantations on the Pacific coast for months at a time every year. The pay is abysmal, the climate hot and humid, and the working conditions extremely arduous. In these circumstances, disease is rampant. As an anthropologist, I realized I had to go beyond studying the people of this community solely as Indians; I also needed to understand their lives and relations as peasants.

Santa Cruz del Quiché was peaceful and appeared complacent in 1973. Beneath the surface, however, discontent was seething and was to flare into open conflict less than a decade later. Sensing these tensions, I began to

*Anthropologist Beatriz Manz (center) with
Guatemalan refugees in the Lacandon jungle, Mexico.*

focus on the dynamics of social stratification in
Guatemalan society and sought to place these
peasants within the larger economic and social
structure of the country.

Guatemala has the most unequal
distribution of land in all of Latin America. At
one end of the spectrum, 1 percent of all farms
control 34 percent of all farmland in holdings
of 450 hectares or more. At the other end, 88
percent of all farms control 16 percent of all
farmland. This striking inequality is
exacerbated by the fact that the larger farms
also control the best land. Moreover, the
situation is deteriorating. In El Quiché, the
arable land per capita declined precipitously
from 1.04 hectares in 1950 to 0.56 in 1980.
More than 309,000 peasants in Guatemala had
no land at all in 1980. Despite this need for
land, plantation owners keep hundreds of

thousands of acres idle, denying access to
landless peasants. Consequently, a desperate
peasantry is available to harvest the
commercial crops at virtually any wage and
under almost any conditions.

The only serious talk of land reform took
place in the early 1950s. President Jacobo
Arbenz proposed that the government acquire
idle land on large plantations for distribution
to landless peasants. However, before these
reforms could be fully implemented, Arbenz
was overthrown in a CIA-backed military
coup. Since then, military rule has enforced
the existing social stratification and extreme
inequality in the country.

To prevent reforms, the military has sought
to repress or eliminate independent
organizations throughout the society. In the
1970s peasants in the highlands began
organizing producer and consumer
cooperatives as well as other organizations to
protect their interests. These organizations were
viewed as a threat and were therefore

suppressed. The same was true for many trade unions, student groups, and even religious organizations.

With peaceful means for democratic change blocked, armed conflict flared in the early 1980s. Unlike a guerrilla movement of the 1960s, this time the Indian peasantry participated in and supported the insurgent movement. The province of El Quiché was the center of conflict. The army mounted a widespread counterinsurgency drive in an effort to terrorize and subjugate the civilian population.

The military's activities have caused a major disruption in community life. Following the destruction and depopulation of an area, the army often seeks to entrench its control in the countryside; in the process, the culture of the indigenous population may be forcibly transformed. In addition to setting up large bases, the military has two major programs to extend its authority: civilian patrols and "model" villages. The civilian patrols, consisting mostly of Indian males conscripted by the army, are required to monitor, control, and report on the activities of the civilian population and the patrollers themselves. This pervasive military role at the community level displaces traditional community forms of organization and maintenance of order. The system disregards community elders and elected leaders and the judicial settlement of disputes. The "model" villages are designed by the military to concentrate the scattered Indian peasant population and closely supervise and direct their activities.

In the past, many anthropologists studying rural communities have ignored the central government or the powerful wealthy elite and military. In Guatemala, even the most remote village cannot be studied in isolation. The existing social stratification pervades the entire society, and no village remains unaffected. The unequal access to resources or means to sustain a basic standard of living has resulted in the ever-increasing impoverishment and disenfranchisement of the majority of the population. This impoverishment has continued during good economic times as well as bad. In the 1960s and 1970s, for example, the Guatemalan economy grew at about 5 percent a year in real terms. Nonetheless the poorest 20 percent of the population saw their share of income distribution fall from 6.8 to 5.5 percent, while the wealthiest 20 percent saw their share rise from 46.5 to 55 percent. In the bad economic times of the 1980s, the share of the poorest 20 percent declined further to 4.8 percent, while the share of the wealthiest 20 percent continued to increase to 56.8 percent.

20 | Law, Politics, and Conflict

Conflict erupts in all societies, but varies with the specific adaptations and environment of the society. In Tiananmen Square, Beijing, 1989, prodemocracy protesters confront helmeted soldiers.

In all societies there will be competition for resources and disputes over how they are to be acquired and used. In adapting to their harsh environment, the Mardudjara Aborigines emphasize cooperation in the acquisition and distribution of goods largely through kinship and through rules that are religiously sanctioned. Despite such rules, however, disputes arise, conflicts occur, and laws are broken. The Mardudjara response is to seek recognized means for handling disputes and conflicts and for dealing with those who break the rules. As societies become larger and more complex, the potential for conflict increases, and mechanisms for dealing with disputes, conflicts, and rule-breakers likewise become more complex.

In this chapter, we will examine various beliefs as to what constitutes proper behavior and the means people have devised to regulate social life, especially when competition and disputes occur. We will also look at politics, the competition for power, which plays an important role in all human societies. Finally, we will discuss what happens when competition or disputes within and between societies erupt into conflict. In general, we will look at how these processes are related to the adaptational strategies of societies, and thus how they change as societies evolve.

LAW

Most of us have fixed notions about how people should behave. Children should obey their parents, parents should support their children, drivers should stop for red lights, doctors should care about their patients, and public officials should not take bribes. Such conceptions of appropriate or expected behavior are called **norms**. Obviously, a mixed lot of conceptions fall into this grouping. While we may think of norms as part of a system, to do so presumes an order, which actually exists only in part. Although many of our ideas about what people ought to do are closely related, not all are; people often adhere to beliefs that are contradictory. Norms vary from ambiguous guides, such as Be good to your parents, to very specific directives, such as Do not covet your neighbor's wife.

Members of a society frequently systematize norms and elevate them to the status of laws. A **law** is a binding rule, created through enactment or custom, that defines right and reasonable behavior. It is common for such matters of law to be placed in the hands of the courts or a comparable legitimate group, such as certain elders in Aboriginal society. Legal systems are constantly changing as societies themselves change, and they are part of the overall adaptational strategy of a society. An important aspect of any legal system is the overt or underlying threat by those in authority to use force to ensure obedience or to punish wrongdoers.

Norms

Norms generally fall into three categories: reality assumptions, ranking norms, and membership norms (Cancian 1975). *Reality assumptions* are general beliefs taken for granted regarding what actions are meaningful or possible in a particular context. For example, in our society, if a bank teller took our check and ate it before giving us the money we had requested, this would be a violation of a reality assumption—it would be seen as crazy. *Ranking norms* evaluate people and their actions on the basis of how closely they conform to some standard. Such norms may be used to distinguish rank or status. A student is ranked on the basis of certain criteria—SAT scores or grade-point averages, for example. *Membership norms* are standards for admission into a particular group or social stratum. To be a king, president of a bank, or member of the Ku Klux Klan, one must meet certain criteria. These may include the performance of tasks, adherence to specific behavioral guidelines, or willingness to wear a certain costume.

People use norms in social situations in accordance with particular goals. This usage is closely related to our perceptions of social identities—what a bank teller is and does, and what it means to be a good one. People's support of norms is commonly based on what they think others perceive to be normative behavior, rather than simply on their own values. Good bank tellers wear a smile and tell customers to have a nice day. Such behavior does not necessarily mean that they care about their customers or that they are happy; it shows that they are trying to live up to their image of what others expect.

Norms change continually to keep pace with new social or environmental realities. The obsequious behavior of such cinematic characters as Step-n-Fetchit in American movies of the 1920s and 1930s typifies the normative expectations held by many white Americans during this period regarding relations between blacks and whites. In the American movies of today, there is a noticeable difference in how black-white relations are portrayed, reflecting changing attitudes about how members of the respective ethnic groups should behave. The normative beliefs of many small-scale societies underwent profound changes as a result of colonialism and integration into modern nation-states. In many parts of Africa, for example, belief in allegiance to the extended kin group was at odds with new ideas favoring the social and economic autonomy of individuals and nuclear families. This situation often led to the breakdown of extended kin groups and of the normative order surrounding them.

Laws

Systems of law are not exclusive to modern large-scale societies, although such societies do have unique procedures for administering and codifying laws. Traditional Australian Aborigines adhered to a system of law that dictated personal relationships with the supernatural, with physi-

---

Although they have since changed their ways, British royalty once derived legitimacy from the concept of the divine right of kings.

cal surroundings, and with other humans. Aboriginal law included the responsibility to perform rituals associated with mythical events and established conventions of behavior toward kin. These laws were not written down, but they were as binding and as systematic as our written laws.

As previously mentioned, a law is a norm that states with relative precision what form of behavior is expected or appropriate in a specific situation. All legal systems ultimately are based on more general normative concepts, such as the god-given right of a king to rule or the right of the state to maintain order, and it is from these more general norms that laws derive their legitimacy. Ultimately, **legitimacy** refers to the traditional moral system of a society (M.G. Smith 1960). Australian Aboriginal law, for example, derives its legitimacy from Dreamtime mythol-

ogy: the laws are said to have been laid down by the creative beings of the Dreamtime. Reference to the supernatural for support of a legal system is fairly common; it is a feature of many aspects of the legal systems of modern Western nations ("one nation under God").

Support for a legal system also may be based on reference to a more secular idea of morality or well-being. For example, many legal systems embrace the concept of the "reasonable man": culturally acceptable ideas about what constitutes reasonable behavior in a given situation. According to Max Gluckman (1973), "the reasonable man is recognized as the central figure in all developed systems of law" (p. 83). Gluckman argued further that the concept was equally important in non-Western systems, such as that of the Barotse of Zambia, on whom his own study focused. He also noted the absence of a concept of the "reasonable woman" in many legal systems, reflecting the lower legal status of women.

Laws and legal systems change in small ways in response to social or environmental conditions. For example, environmental protection laws have been enacted during the past decade in response to society's growing awareness of environmental problems and a greater desire to do something about environmental destruction. But such changes take place on the basis of recognized principles within an overall legal structure that remains much the same. Changes in legal structure require much more fundamental alterations in the adaptive strategy of a society, as is associated with increasing social scale or a change in state structure, such as that from a monarchy to a republic. Even in these instances, legal systems do not always change completely, and often there is some continuity from the old system to the new.

The existence of more than one legal tradition within a single state is relatively common. In many of its colonies, Britain adopted a policy of "indirect rule" that allowed subject peoples to retain many features of their own legal systems. British law took precedence over "native" law whenever there was a conflict, and native law underwent some changes as a result of codification, but this new system allowed some continuity with the past. Such dualism (two traditions) occurs in a number of Western states where native peoples have retained features of their traditional legal systems. Australian Aboriginal communities, and to some extent Australian courts, have come to recognize both Aboriginal law, which is linked to the Dreamtime, and Australia's Western legal system, which is associated with the majority population and the power of the state.

Many states today are subject to conflicting views about the basic legal structures they should employ. In modern times, Shariah, or Islamic law, has been enforced only in Saudi Arabia, in the Gulf sheikdoms, and in revolutionary Iran. But other states with large Muslim populations have faced controversy over the extent to which their laws should conform to Islamic injunctions, as well as how such injunctions should be interpreted. While Pakistan's constitution bars legislation contrary to the spirit of Islam, the practice has been for the judiciary to use common law rather than Shariah. Fundamentalist Islamic interests in Pakistan have pressured the government to adhere more closely to Shariah; however, opposition has come from those who are Western-educated, from women's rights advocates, and even from some Islamic groups wary of how Shariah will be interpreted. Thus, there is debate over the relative power of Parliament versus the *ulama* (religious scholars).

Law Enforcement and Dispute Mediation

It is never enough simply to establish laws. In every society, there are always individuals whose actions fall beyond established legal limits. Furthermore, laws may be interpreted differently or not accepted by certain individuals. Therefore, societies have developed formal or informal mechanisms for enforcing their laws and handling disputes.

Attitudes toward Laws

While all societies have ideas about what is proper and improper behavior and means for ensuring a degree of conformity, precisely how order and its maintenance are viewed can vary. To begin with, there are considerable differences in the degree to which societies have transformed their ideas about correct behavior into a set of laws. The Comanches, for example, traditionally did not possess abstract rules about appropriate behavior (Hoebel 1940). The society did not lack norms, but they were not formulated into a roster of general laws. Societies also vary in the extent to which compliance with laws or norms is expected. At one extreme are those societies placing strong emphasis on compliance, where absolute compliance is seen as necessary for survival or to achieve goals (e.g., to withstand external threats or to create an empire). At the other extreme are societies that are more tolerant, emphasizing manipulation and bargaining. There are also differences in the kind of behavior that is tolerated. Some societies, such as the Inuit, take the theme of peace and harmony to an extreme, seeking to avoid controversy and aggressive behavior. At the other extreme, disputative and aggressive behavior may be seen as desirable, with a high value placed on individual achievement. These differences represent different adaptive strategies.

Adherence to laws is greater when laws are based on widely accepted norms. Most people in Western societies accept and comply with laws against the murder of an adult or child, while laws relating to abortion are subject to considerable debate. This is because there is no prevailing view concerning the rights of the fetus. Likewise, Prohibition did not succeed in the United States before World War II because norms regarding the consumption of alcoholic beverages were not well established in the society as a whole. As with both of these examples, laws will affect some segments of a society more than others. This is particularly an issue in states where cultural diversity is great. Laws about abortion are of more relevance to women, and attitudes on the issue are related to one's religion. Drinking laws are more important to those for whom the consumption of alcohol is an option than to those who, say on religious grounds, would never consider drinking under any circumstances.

Handling Disputes

Because laws will not automatically be adhered to by all members of a society, every society has mechanisms for dealing with those who break or disagree with the laws. The need for such mechanisms is particularly pressing in large-scale societies because of their greater heterogeneity; but even small, relatively homogeneous societies require means for handling antisocial behavior and disputes.

The two major points of tension in foraging societies are sexual relations and the distribution of food. All foraging societies have rules for sharing food, but the actual process is often marked by suspicion and stress as people worry about getting their just share. Disputes over infidelity and sexual jealousy are minimized in some societies by liberalizing sexual access, but in many others behavior such as extramarital affairs is a major source of tension and conflict. In most foraging societies, the emphasis is on reestablishing social equilibrium. Because of the small, close-knit nature of these societies, many disputes are handled at an interpersonal level through discussions or fights. Other members of the society may become involved informally through shaming, gossip, and ridicule.

Disputes are not always settled easily, however, and sometimes it is necessary to try to end tensions by more formal means. A common way of easing tensions among foragers is through dispersal: bands split up to avoid further quarrels. The ease with which this occurs depends in part on environmental conditions. Where scarce resources or hostile neighbors make dispersal difficult, the prime protagonist(s) may be ostracized. Some foraging societies use more elaborate methods of settling disputes. In many Australian Aboriginal societies, individuals accused of wrongdoing were able to get a public hearing at certain ceremonial gatherings and could be forgiven through the ritual of penis holding, in the case of a man, or giving herself to the men involved in the hearing in the case of a woman (Berndt 1965). Reciprocity was the focal point of such actions. This theme permeates much of the legal thought in foraging societies. Compensation tends to be negotiable. Groups may negotiate over the precise goods and services they are to receive; where death is demanded, they may negotiate over who, how many, or what type of people are to be killed.

The change from foraging to farming leads to new stresses and new legal requirements. In farming societies, more people are packed into a smaller space, they are residentially more stable, and they have more material possessions. In short, there is more to fight over and a greater likelihood that people will fight. The primary legal problems for small-scale farmers have to do with distribution of the surplus they produce, property inheritance, land rights, and sexual relations. Disputes usually increase as critical resources, such as land, become exceptionally scarce.

Small-scale farmers handle many of their legal problems in the same ways as foragers, with some important differences. Many problems are handled by kin; for example, when older brothers or fellow lineage members are held responsible for a person's behavior. Shaming and ridicule also play a role. The Melanesians of Goodenough Island practice a form of shaming with food (Young 1971). A man who feels that he has been wronged will give the wrongdoer the finest and largest yam or other food item that he has with the intent of shaming the person by giving him something far better than he can reciprocate. In many small-scale farming societies, even in dealing with mundane tensions and disputes, people also practice sorcery and witchcraft and accuse one another of practicing them.

Dispersal and ostracism also are practiced by small-scale farmers. Farmers, however, find dispersal much more difficult because of their commitment to their crops and greater population densities. In southern Belize, which until recently had a low population density, Mayan villages would fragment every few years because of factional disputes. Members of factions would move to other villages or establish a new village in an unoccupied region. Ostracism is a relatively common strategy among small-scale farmers. In southern Belize, the leading adult males of the village may decide to ostracize an individual when it is felt that other means of dealing with the person have failed. This person must then either seek permission to reside in another village or leave the area altogether.

The legal requirements of large-scale societies organized into states are different from those of small-scale societies. States are characterized by a greater array of tensions, and their increased scale and complexity make it more difficult to rely on informal and interpersonal means of settling disputes. While gossip, shaming, and the like remain important means of ensuring order, the state also relies on specialized institutions, such as a judiciary for defining laws and police for upholding them. While small-scale societies sometimes employ individuals in special judicial or policing roles, such specialization is much more pervasive in states. Ostracism is practiced in states in the form of deportation, but it is more common to remove the offending individual through imprisonment, an almost unheard-of act in small-scale societies.

How laws are enforced in states depends in part on the distribution of power and wealth. Where one segment of society is able to control the state apparatus, that segment will seek to use the laws and legal institutions for its own ends. This is the case in such Third-World countries as Guatemala and El Salvador, where political power is mainly in the hands of wealthy landowners and capitalists (and their allies in the military) who have had laws passed that favor their interests at the expense of the poorer majority, and who use the military, police, and courts to control threats to their power. Where political power is more widely distributed, as in many Western countries, there is more debate surrounding the passage of laws and greater recognition of the legal rights of a larger spectrum of the population.

The soldier or policeman in the state of Guatemala today helps to enforce laws, but they may be laws passed to favor the small elite of this country, who use the militia or police to prop up their rule.

POLITICS

Power may be defined as the ability to act effectively on people or things; it is instrumental in influencing people's perceptions and behavior. What we know as **politics** is the competition for power. Shaking hands or kissing a baby may signify nothing more than a wish to demonstrate friendship or affection, but when these actions are intended to influence power relations, they become political acts. Viewed from such a perspective, politics is a universal of social existence. But politics is not the same in all settings. Despite some underlying similarities, Amazonian Indians, urban-dwelling Canadians, and Javanese rice-farmers have very different politics. Different environmental conditions, forms of social organization, and cultural traditions produce a wide variety of political goals and different means of achieving them.

Political Ideas

Politics is based not simply on brute force but also on **political norms**—ideas about appropriate political goals and behavior. Through a process of political socialization, people develop goals within a specific environment and learn preferred means of achieving them. Although these norms may not be strictly adhered to in practice, they still influence political behavior.

Among the most fundamental political norms are those concerned with **authority**, the right (versus simply the ability) to make a particular decision and to command obedience (M.G. Smith 1960). Authority reflects the acceptable or tolerable bounds of power—a government's right to tax activities *up to a certain level*, to police the activities of citizens in certain spheres *according to accepted procedures*, and the like. What is acceptable or tolerable, though, is not simply a matter of voluntary consent on the part of the governed, for any government controls sufficient resources (personnel and wealth) to allow it to influence what people perceive to be the scope of its authority. Any powerful group or institution will be restrained by the need to seek authority, while also being in a position to manipulate notions of authority.

Within any society there are likely to be distinct realms of authority. Talal Asad (1970) distinguishes two major realms of authority among the Kababish Arabs, pastoral nomads of Sudan: the household and the tribal. Power within the household sphere is held largely by the male household head on the basis of his role as husband, father, and manager of the family enterprise and its animal property in particular. Power within the wider, tribal sphere is held by a *shaikh* (chief or headman) and the lineage of which he is a member. The shaikh and his lineage gained authority by cultivating ties with the colonial and later national authorities who rewarded them with administrative posts. These posts allowed them to control access to and allocation of significant resources, such as water. The majority of Kababish feel that members of the shaikh's elite lineage are entitled to their authority to speak for the Kababish, to collect taxes, and to make other political decisions because they have the power to enforce their will. The elite themselves base their authority on historical precedent (in the past, members of other kin groups pledged their allegiance to the shaikh in return for his protection) and on the legal rights associated with the offices they hold.

Ideology

When ideas consciously and systematically are organized into some form of program or plan, they constitute an **ideology**. Political ideologies are concerned with the distribution of power: the maintenance, reform, or overthrow of the existing structure. Australian Aboriginal law serves as political ideology by providing justifications for existing power relations. In recent history, various capitalist and socialist ideologies have been concerned with maintaining or changing power relations.

There are two forms of ideology: organic and rationalistic (see Hoare and Smith 1971; Rude 1980). An *organic ideology* consists of ideas held by members of a society (or segment of a society) about how the world is or should be ordered based on their historical experience. Included are popular ideas about what constitutes a just government. A *rationalistic ideology* consists of a program of action based on observation or introspection, or both, by those seeking ordered sets of laws of social behavior. Examples of the latter

Among the Kababish Arabs of the Sudan, the shaikh, or headman, here seated in his tent, holds power within the tribe. The shaikh and his lineage gained authority through favorable ties with the national authorities of the Sudan.

are the eighteenth-century revolutionary ideologies inspired by the Enlightenment philosophers and the interests of the emerging capitalist class pertaining to the nature of government in France and the United States. Each form of ideology may contain elements of the other. Ideas from rationalistic ideologies creep into popular beliefs through sermons, political speeches, the printed word, radio, and television. Rationalistic ideologies in turn contain distilled elements of organic ideologies: folk wisdom based on people's experiences, ideals, and dreams.

As small-scale societies have been incorporated into the modern world system, their members have been subjected to the rationalistic ideologies of large-scale industrial societies. Thus, the indigenous peoples of the Soviet Union and the United States have been subjected to the respective ideologies of these states through coercion, education, and the offering of political and economic incentives. Receptivity to these ideologies has varied. Societies with traditions of co-operation and an emphasis on homogeneity have been unreceptive to the individualism and competitiveness of capitalist ideologies. However, others with traditions of entrepreneurship and trade have had little trouble accepting such ideas.

Symbols

Political ideologies and activities rely heavily on symbolic imagery. Most of us are familiar with the time-honored symbols of American politics: Uncle Sam, the flag, the national anthem, and catchphrases dealing with patriotism and equality. Similarly, the communist government of the Soviet Union relied on statues and portraits of Lenin, the hammer and sickle, use of the color red and other images and words associated with revolution, and reference to Mother Russia. Symbols are useful politically because they appeal to strong basic emotions—feelings of hatred, of well-being, of happiness or despair. To be able to manipulate such powerful imagery benefits those with political ambition. This is why politicians like to be surrounded with patriotic paraphernalia and why competition among politicians over identification with symbols can be so intense.

Political symbols are based on cultural experiences and traditions, but their use reflects current political realities. Chinese politicians relied heavily on Maoist imagery as long as the revolutionary tradition associated with Mao was in favor. After the Cultural Revolution, as Maoism fell out of favor, new images came into use. The same symbol can also mean different things under different circumstances. In the United States, Uncle Sam is a symbol of goodness, but in

The president of the United States, in the political tradition, calls up strong emotions by surrounding himself with the symbols of patriotism. The flag is manipulated in the competition for power.

many parts of the world it is a symbol associated with imperialism.

The People in Politics

Whether electoral, hereditary, or seized by force, political power ultimately resides in people. Within most societies there are three categories of people involved in politics: the political community, the political elite, and political teams (Bailey 1969).

The Political Community

The political community consists of people who adhere to roughly similar political norms and goals, and for the most part follow the same political procedures. Political communities may be as small as a nuclear family or as large as the British Commonwealth. Each political community is unique in some way, for it has evolved particular modes of behavior and specific potential avenues for the acquisition of power. Some degree of generalization is possible, however. Thus, we find similar patterns of political behavior among people with similar socioeconomic adaptations, and political communities in modern states can be placed within a few categories.

Individuals often belong to several political communities at the same time. These may be interrelated, as with family, town, and national communities. Membership in a community is not always rigidly defined, nor do people always consider themselves members of the communities with which others choose to associate them. For example, during World War II, many people in the United States and Canada felt that citizens of Japanese origin necessarily had mixed loyalties because of their ancestry, and that those citizens sought to identify with the Japanese forces, with whom the United States and Canada were at war. On the other hand, Japanese living in Canada and the United States considered themselves loyal citizens of those countries.

The Political Elite

The political elite are those within a community who wield power and leadership. Sometimes the political elite consists of a homogeneous and rigidly bounded group, but often its membership is diverse and flexible. Among those included in the political elite are leaders. A **political leader** is an individual who has the power to make decisions within and for a group. Although the scope of this power and how it is maintained vary, the political power of all leaders is personal, within the broad sweep of the socioeconomic setting within which the individual leader lives. Such things as administrative office or the status of one's parents may work to a leader's advantage (or disadvantage), but the actual dimension of power a leader possesses is a matter of his or her personal manipulation of available resources—connections, wealth, charisma, speaking ability, or physical strength—within this larger context.

The status of leader is insecure in most societies. The person who has attained it is rarely able to sit back and take leadership for granted. Threats come from those who covet the leader's position and from those who are jealous or resentful of anyone exercising power over them. To achieve some security, leaders develop a network of supports. The wider and more overlapping the network, the more secure the status. One source of support for a leader is to be an *intermediary*—one who seeks to benefit from the political, economic, and sociocultural gaps between groups or significant individuals. Not all intermediaries are political leaders; but even when they are not, they often exert considerable political influence. Thus, the American military officer Oliver North, associated with the Iran-Contra scandal of the Reagan presidency, was himself not a political leader, but his actions as an intermediary in relation to American strategic interests in Central America and the Middle East had important political implications (see Bryne 1987).

Political Teams

Political teams are organized groups of people actively involved in politics. Within all societies there are loosely structured political groups that can be designated *coalitions*—temporary alliances for a limited political purpose (Boissevain 1974).

The least institutionalized of these, an *action set*, comes into being when individuals call on other people within their own personal networks to act for some specific purpose (such as to win an election). A more institutionalized form of coalition is a *faction*—a group that acts within a larger unit, in opposition to some other element of the unit. Any analysis of factions must be dynamic, viewing their evolution over time. In the case of the Kekchi-speaking village of Pueblo Viejo in southern Belize, factions evolved as the village population grew, as land pressure increased, and as social and economic differences among villagers became greater (Howard 1977). Initially, the factions were recruited by individuals primarily on the basis of kinship and *compadrazgo* (ritual godparenthood). Eventually, they became relatively permanent features of the village, and as they did the role of leaders who were responsible for their formation in the first place tended to wane.

The most institutionalized form of political grouping is a *political party*. Parties are a product of modern large-scale societies and reflect the high degree of specialization in such societies. The closest thing to a party in smaller, nonindustrial societies is a multipurpose group, such as a lineage or clan, which functions as a political organization in some contexts. Political parties, however, are formed with one purpose in mind: to direct the policies of a government. In addition, their greater degree of internal organization is different from that of other political groups. Parties usually are organized around particular political beliefs and interests and are more impersonal than other political groups.

After World War II, political parties became more important to small-scale societies as they were integrated into the new states. For example, previously, the people of Pueblo Viejo had been little affected by party politics in Belize (then known as British Honduras), of relevance largely in the capital city. From the 1960s onward, as roads and schools were built and as political reforms reached into even the most isolated villages, agents of political parties visited the village in search of votes, and villagers in turn sought the spoils of political patronage. The villagers became increasingly aware that roads, schools, and the like were political commodities, and that their own political behavior helped determine who got these resources. Political parties have come to affect indigenous and ethnic minorities in other ways as well, playing a role in the development of communalism in many ethnically plural societies, influencing land-rights struggles, and in general serving to articulate the place of these groups within the nation.

Finally, mention should be made of the political role of multipurpose organizations that exist alongside, within, and even in opposition to political parties. Religious organizations and trade unions play an active role in politics, as do a variety of clandestine organizations and secret societies such as Masonic lodges. In Sierra Leone, for example, the small Creole elite sought to retain its political influence through Masonic lodges after the country became independent in 1961 (Cohen 1974).

The Transfer of Power

A fundamental feature of political power is that it is not permanent; hence, the members of a society are faced with crucial questions about how it is to be transferred. Those in power not only must contend with those competing for their power, but also with the problem of human mortality. Just how orderly this transfer of power is varies from one political setting to another. *Political contests* are the processes through which power is sought and challenged, and through which ideologies can be tested. While political contests can become chaotic and even violent (as we will discuss later in the chapter), all societies attempt to provide some order to the processes of challenging and transferring power.

Since power is never secure from challenge, those wishing to remain in power must constantly maneuver to ward off threats to their position. The Melanesian Big-Man, for instance, who builds his reputation and amasses wealth in pigs and other valuables by strategic manipulation of gift-giving ceremonies, is continually maneuvering to maintain or enhance his position.

The Big-Man, a type of leader in parts of Melanesia, achieves his power by amassing wealth in pigs and other valuables and by holding gift-giving ceremonies that enhance his reputation and influence. This Te Enga Big-Man of New Guinea, seen on the raised platform, engages in a continual contest for power.

Should he stop holding pig-feasts, he would soon stop being a Big-Man. Likewise, politicians in our own society never seem to stop running for office, and even absolute monarchs must always be alert to palace intrigues and signs of trouble beyond the palace.

Political competition is especially keen when individuals holding power die. Communities in which politics is structured through kinship usually designate a suitable heir or heirs to bring some order to this potentially disruptive situation. An eldest son or senior brother may be the preferred successor, for instance. Whatever the preference, almost always allowance is made for an alternative to avoid the risk of the normally preferred heir being judged by others as unsuitable. Despite these provisions, disputes often erupt when the order of succession is challenged by rival heirs within the kin group, by rival kin groups, and even by those who view the situation as an opportunity to challenge the system as a whole. Sometimes there are recognized means for handling such disputes, such as avenues of appeal to a higher authority. Or, if things get too bad, rival groups may separate. But even once the succession is settled, underlying tensions often remain, waiting to resurface when the new incumbent dies or when some other opportunity presents itself.

Today, heredity is less relevant in most political contexts than it was in the past, or at least not so automatically a determinant of political succession. It is often still an important factor, however. Thus, political leaders, such as Lee Kuan Yew of Singapore and Kim Il Sung of North Korea, have sought to position their sons to enable them to assume power. Towns, provinces, and even nations may be ruled by oligarchies or elite families, such as the landed oligarchs of the Philippines. And it still helps to be a Rockefeller or a Kennedy in the United States. In large-scale societies, unlike kin-based societies, heredity rarely is viewed as the primary or only legitimate means for assuming power. It is used in combination with other resources, such as wealth or military power.

During the past few centuries, elections have emerged in many nations as the focal point of political activity surrounding the means for transferring power. Since World War II, electoral systems have been exported to countries throughout the world under the aegis of geopolitical powers, such as Britain and the United States. Despite their superficial similarities, elections have played many different roles in these often very different political environments; in many instances, they have assumed characteristics unlike those of their countries of origin. For instance, democratic assumptions about elections—such as the belief that they allow for a greater dispersal of power—have proven rather naïve. This is most obvious in those countries where elected bodies are given virtually no power, as is the case with legislative bodies in Latin American and African dictatorships.

The Political Organization of Societies

Anthropologists commonly divide systems of political organization into two broad categories: those associated with *states* and those associated with *stateless societies*. The first category includes those structures with centralized authority and distinct administrative machinery and judicial institutions. Within this category are entities as diverse as the United States and the Kingdom of Tonga. The second category includes systems of organization commonly associated with small-scale societies, which lack the degree of specialization of state governments.

Stateless Societies
There are two types of stateless societies: **acephalous** (or headless) **societies** and **chiefdoms**. Today, both acephalous societies and chiefdoms are under the jurisdiction of encompassing state

organizations, although in some instances they are able to retain a fair degree of autonomy.

Among those societies designated acephalous are a range of small-scale polities associated with foraging, small-scale farming, and pastoral adaptations; for example, the Mardudjara Aborigines, the Cree of northern Canada, and the Nuer of northeastern Africa, respectively. The primary unit of political organization among acephalous societies consists of the people who live and work together in bands, camps, or villages. The members of these primary units commonly are organized into loose alliances, known as tribes. A **tribe** consists of a group of people who share certain cultural characteristics, have a common territory, and in general feel that they have more in common with one another than with their neighbors. It is usually an alliance without much centralized authority. Relatively little power is available to individuals in these societies, a reflection of their relative lack of surplus wealth and a manifestation of the egalitarian social organization and belief systems of acephalous societies.

Kinship often is so much a part of the political organization of acephalous societies that they sometimes are referred to as kin-based societies. Thus, political decision making in such acephalous societies as the Nuer or Tallensi is structured around clans and lineages. In these societies, political status often is based on a person's status within the web of kinship relationships, and kin groups form the primary administrative units. Alliances among kin groups are of primary political importance when intergroup disputes arise.

Chiefdoms differ from acephalous societies in that their administrative structure formally integrates a number of communities, and they are more hierarchical. The office of chief affords the incumbent a status notably above that of other members of the society. Kinship is also important, and the position of chief may be hereditary, with the chief and his kin forming an elite stratum. Chiefs accumulate goods, usually in the form of tribute, some of which is redistributed through public feasts and doles to those in need. While usually there is more specialization in chiefdoms than in acephalous societies, chiefdoms are still a good deal less specialized than societies organized into states.

Population size and growth are key factors in the transition from acephalous societies to chiefdoms—and from chiefdoms to states. Higher population densities promote a greater degree of specialization and intensification of production, and this, in turn, creates a greater potential for the accumulation of wealth and power. Acephalous organization in Africa, for example, is associated with low population densities, whereas chiefdoms and other more stratified systems are associated with progressively higher densities.

States

As defined in Chapter 11, a *state* is an autonomous integrated political unit, encompassing many communities within its territory, with a highly specialized central governing authority. This central authority claims a monopoly over those powers associated with maintaining internal order and ordering external relations. Order is maintained in states through a *bureaucracy*, the specialized administrative organization concerned with the day-to-day running of the state. States vary in degree of centralization, the extent and nature of their powers, the precise form of administration, and the extent of popular participation in running them. Over the past few thousand years, various types of states have evolved, including the city-states of ancient Greece; empire states, such as the Mongol and Roman empires; theocratic states, such as the Vatican and ancient Egypt; and more recently, nation-states, such as France and Canada. Despite many differences, these entities have enough in common to warrant being grouped within a single category, especially when contrasted with nonstate structures.

As discussed in Chapter 11, how states came into being has been the subject of research and debate for years. Careful analysis of state formation in a range of settings indicates that the process is never reducible to a single cause. A number of authors (e.g., Adams 1966; Flannery 1972; Hassan 1981) point to what seems to be the best approach, which is seeking to isolate a range of variables that interact in the process of state formation. Brumfield (1983), for example, in examining the formation of the Aztec state, focuses on several factors, including "the interplay of ecological variables and political dynamics" (p. 278).

The majority of modern states did not evolve on their own. They were the creations of various colonial powers, and their subsequent evolution often has involved the progressive realization of a nationality that was at first little more than an ideal. "Nation building" refers primarily to attempts to forge nations out of disparate peoples placed together in an artificial political creation. The modern Melanesian states of Papua New Guinea, Solomon Islands, and Vanuatu were created in the nineteenth century by European powers seeking to demarcate spheres of influence and control over peoples who recognized no common political bond beyond a few allied villages and who spoke hundreds of distinct languages. Today, the governments of these states, having achieved independence only recently, are seeking to create a sense of nationhood through language and educational policies and through a bureaucratic machinery that remains sensitive to the diversity of the people within their national borders.

CONFLICT

Interpersonal and social tensions are always present in any society. As we have seen, societies develop mechanisms for trying to deal with these tensions and the threat to order they pose. When minor problems occur, usually they can be taken care of with minimal disturbance to the social order. However, sometimes things get out of hand, and gossip or the police are not able to prevent a major disruption. Such major breakdowns of order tend to result from pressures built up in a society because of underlying conflicts in the social structure, especially conflicts concerned with the distribution of wealth and power.

Political Violence within a Society

Orderly, nonviolent transferrals of power are not common, especially when it is a matter of a transferral between different groups. Those with power want more; they are also usually unwilling to give up what they have. Likewise, those out of power often see violence as the only means of increasing their position in society.

Rebellions

Eric Wolf and Edward Hansen (1972) wrote that "the history of Latin America from independence to the present time is a history of violent struggles of 'ins' and 'outs'" (p. 235). William Stokes (1952) outlined the basic forms of rebellion common to Latin America: machetismo, cuartelazo, golpe de estado, and revolution. Machetismo (named after the long knife, the machete, carried by many Latin American peasants) is a violent seizure of power in which a leader employs a mass of armed followers. This method of obtaining power disrupts the administration and economy and may lead to substantial loss of life. In Colombia, where machetismo was common throughout much of the nineteenth and early twentieth centuries, conflicts often took a heavy toll, and affected almost every aspect of people's lives. Between 1899 and 1903 alone, more than 100,000 people were killed.

The cuartelazo involves careful planning on the part of a small group of soldiers to seize power quickly by taking over strategic locales. This transfer can be almost bloodless, and the bulk of the population may not even know about it until everything is over. The most difficult part of the cuartelazo is making it stick. Staying in power re-

quires gaining recognition from other powerful elements in the society, especially other military units. The golpe de estado (or coup d'etat) is a more widespread, violent overthrow of a government than the cuartelazo. Although the military is always involved, the golpe includes important civilian participation as well. The golpe itself is a quick attack on those in power, generally involving the assassination or immobilization of the chief executive and a large number of people.

Forceful seizures of power occur in many parts of the world besides Latin America. The South Pacific, for example, experienced its first military coup when, after 17 years of parliamentary government, the elected government of Fiji was overthrown in May 1987 (Howard 1990). This golpe, or coup, was organized by members of the former ruling oligarchy (headed by Fijian chiefs) who had lost power in a recent election, together with their civilian and military allies. The actual coup was carried out by a small group of soldiers who occupied parliament and held the prime minister and members of his party captive for two weeks, by which time the new military–civilian regime felt itself to be securely enough in power to allow their release.

These forms of political violence, and rebellions in general, do not necessarily result in any structural changes in the society, or at least may not intend to bring such changes about. The Fiji coup, for example, was intended to restore political power to the chiefs and their associates after their political party had recently lost an election. After reviewing numerous rebellions in Africa, Max Gluckman (1965) found that most involved a process of "repetitive change," since they did not result in an "alteration in the structure of authoritative offices or the character of the personnel who hold them" (p. 165). Rather than promoting change, such rebellions often served as a safety valve for pressures that had built up in the society. However, many rebellions do foster at least some important changes. Looking at the Fiji coup again, although the original intent was to restore the traditional oligarchy to power, what actually resulted was that the chiefs were forced

Fijian soldiers staged a coup in 1987 meant to restore power to the chiefs. The military, however, represented here by Lieutenant Colonel Rabuka (Fijian man in sulu, or sarong), who led the coup, in fact increased its power more than the chiefs'. Rabuka talks with the British high commissioner minutes after the coup.

to share power with the military, thereby significantly altering power relations within Fijian society.

Revolutions

Although political violence is fairly common within societies, actual revolutions are not. According to Wolf and Hansen (1972), a revolution involves "fundamental change in the nature of the state, the functions of government, the principles of economic production and distribution, the relationship of social classes, particularly as regards the control of government—in a word, a significant break with the past" (p. 235). The term *revolution* has been used inappropriately for a wide range of political violence resulting in relatively minor change for the majority of people. Fundamental breaks with the past that warrant the designation *revolution* actually are rare.

Revolutions occur infrequently for a variety of reasons. The majority's lack of power, inability to organize, or insufficient desire are relatively simple reasons. Gluckman (1965) discusses another

important factor: multiple and divided loyalties that make a drastic change difficult. People are caught up in a web of social relationships that bind their actions and thoughts and reduce their revolutionary potential. A desire for security and a fear of the unknown are common to most members of a society. Also important in constraining revolutionary tendencies are decisions by those in power to implement reforms sufficient to relieve immediate pressures and their ability to co-opt the leadership of the opposition. Even when people do rebel because of poverty or injustice, their goal often is not the revolutionary transformation of society, but merely the adjustment of the existing social order.

Revolutions are the result of very exceptional circumstances. It is not enough for people to rebel; they must also create a new social order that is drastically different from what came before. This creative process distinguishes revolution from other forms of political violence.

The complexities of the revolutionary process are best studied in an interdisciplinary manner.

Economists have contributed to our understanding through their analysis of such factors as inflation and deflation. Social psychologists have provided insights into the questions of deprivation and response to authority. Equally significant contributions have been made by historians, sociologists, political scientists, and many other specialists. Anthropologists, too, have added to our understanding of revolutions. Detailed knowledge of peasant society resulting from research based on participant observation is one of anthropology's major contributions. Despite the urban bias of most revolutionary leaders and revolutionary ideologies (and of those who study revolutions), peasants have played a decisive role in many revolutions.

For many individuals, the term *peasantry* conjures up an image of a conservative, bland mass. This is a false image. To understand the dynamics of revolution among peasants, we must look at the different segments of peasant society, for they influence the process in very different ways. In the Russian Revolution, for instance, one segment of the peasantry was of particular importance: those who were relatively affluent and more closely tied to the cities. It is this upper stratum of peasants that is most likely to find its social and economic goals frustrated by existing conditions.

To understand how a revolution comes about, we cannot simply look at general socioeconomic conditions or ideologies. We must examine the specific social context within which groups of people make their decisions and the actual exchanges that occur, with special attention to the role of intermediaries. Intellectuals may be able to provide the ideological focus of a revolution, but it is rare that such people are easily accepted by peasants or urban laborers. Comprehending how relations actually develop between segments of a population and how ideology is transmitted at an interpersonal level is prerequisite to any study of revolution. These are dynamics that anthropologists are especially well suited to explore.

Warfare between Societies

People within a society generally try to settle their differences in a peaceful and orderly manner, although they do not always succeed. While there are numerous constraints on aggression within most societies, beyond the bounds of the society there are far fewer restraints or incentives for a peaceful resolution of differences. This is particularly relevant when the outsiders are barely considered to be members of the same species. However, those who are perceived to be so different also tend to be of little social or economic relevance; hence, there is little reason to fight.

Warfare, or aggression between politically autonomous communities, most often occurs when relations break down between communities that usually interact peacefully or when societies that generally have little to do with one another find themselves in contact and competition. It is wrong to say that warfare is a natural consequence of human aggressiveness; warfare results from specific social and environmental circumstances.

Anthropologists recognize three primary categories of intergroup aggression: feuding, raiding, and large-scale warfare. The causes and patterns of each vary from one setting to another. They will also take on very different characteristics in large-scale and small-scale societies, reflecting demographic, economic, and technological differences. In all cases, the parties involved will pursue goals in a relatively ordered fashion, seeking continuously to rationalize their actions through ideology.

Feuding

A prolonged state of hostility between different families or groups of kin is known as a **feud**. It may take place within a society or between members of different societies. The feud is the most universal form of intergroup aggression, in part because of its limited requirements: all that is needed is enough people to find something to fight over.

Spencer and Gillen (1899) described a common pattern of feud among Australian Aborigines—the avenging party. Quarrels usually begin when a man steals a wife from some other group or when someone's death is blamed on sorcery by a member of a distant group. The aggrieved party then forms a group to attack those believed to be responsible. Although the members of the avenging party enter the enemy's camp fully armed with spears and spear throwers, boomerangs and shields, the quarrel is usually confined to a verbal battle, which lasts about an hour or two. Physical violence is not always avoided, however. Occasionally, the avenging party will ambush one or two of the enemy and spear them with no risk to themselves. A common feature of such feuds is that acts of violence are not necessarily carried out against specific individuals but are aimed at any individual who is a member of the kin group, reflecting a sense of shared responsibility. Feuds do not always end with the first act of revenge; there may be counterattacks, and the feud may evolve into a more general confrontation between larger groups.

Feuds also take place in large-scale societies. Gang rivalries in U.S. cities provide an example. But feuds assume particular significance when kinship and politics are closely aligned, especially when political authority is based on heredity, as with monarchies. Such feuds may easily develop into warfare. The rivalry between York and Lancaster leading to the Wars of the Roses in England provides an example.

Raiding

Among foragers and small-scale farmers, surprise predatory attacks by groups is often associated with population pressure and competition for scarce resources. **Raids** are common, for example, among agriculturalists in the more populous parts of New Guinea and in the Amazonian basin. Raiding is encouraged when neighboring peoples possess different levels of power, as with the Bushmen foragers of southern Africa and their more powerful agricultural and pastoral

neighbors. Finally, some societies come to specialize in raiding because other options are closed to them or because such an adaptation has a decisive advantage over any other available to them. The Amazonian Mura evolved from aquatic agriculturalists to almost full-time raiders during the nineteenth century in response to new opportunities created by the Portuguese invasion and occupation. The Mura raided both Europeans and other Indian groups all along the Amazon, living for long periods in isolated canoes. They raised few crops of their own, subsisting primarily on fish caught in the rivers and on what they could seize from others. Groups of Plains Indians developed a similar adaptation on the land, utilizing the horse and developing a social organization suited to their need for mobility and frequent fighting.

Large-Scale Warfare

Australian Aboriginal feuds or Mura raids involved relatively small numbers of people, as does most intergroup aggression associated with small-scale societies. Occasionally, fighting in these societies does escalate, but because of the small population and the inability of foragers and subsistence agriculturalists to afford the luxury of a prolonged period of warfare, fighting of this magnitude tends to be short-lived.

Larger agricultural populations are able to carry out more protracted forms of warfare. As population pressures become noticeable, people begin to find more to fight about. For foragers and farmers living in sparsely populated areas, warfare is rarely initiated to seize territory (although territory may be occupied as an indirect result of fighting). Rather, wars among these peoples generally begin because of interpersonal quarrels, such as disputes over women. As population pressure increases, so does the likelihood of fights for territory.

Mervyn Meggitt (1977), in his study of Mae Enga warfare in the densely populated highlands of New Guinea, noted that "in the present and in the past, the desire of local descent groups to gain and hold arable land has been the most powerful motive impelling them to make war on each other" (p. 182). Mae Enga warfare usually lasts only a few days, because longer periods of warfare place a severe strain on resources. The average number of participants in wars among the central Enga is about 360. Between 1961 and 1973, out of 46 incidents, the mean number of deaths was 1.6 per incident. This number may seem small, but in relation to the size of Enga society, it is far from insignificant.

Mortality and casualty rates from warfare in such small-scale societies can, in fact, involve a larger percentage of the total population than in the case of warfare between large-scale societies. Thus, the male mortality rates from warfare among such groups as the Yanomami and Dani appear to be significantly higher than those of the major participating countries in World War II (including Germany and the Soviet Union). Moreover, mobilization rates of adult males for warfare in such small-scale societies are much higher than in large-scale societies. Among peoples such as the Yanomami, virtually the entire adult male population may go to war, at least for a brief period. By contrast, mobilization during World War II did not exceed 15 percent in the countries involved in the fighting.

Warfare and the evolution of the state are closely interrelated. Larger and larger political units were created through conquest, and large states were supported through the collection of tribute from conquered peoples. Such warfare was never rationalized solely in terms of power or wealth; it always required some other form of justification. As Frederick Hicks (1979) noted: "Every empire has developed some high moral principle to justify its actions and for which its people would be more than willing to risk their lives than they would be just to make their rulers rich and powerful" (p. 90). Thus, for the Aztecs, support for their aggression came from their religion, which "needed" sacrificial victims.

The Aztecs of central Mexico, as did many early empires, emphasized military training. Young commoners and nobles were given formal military training and those who were most successful in battle were recruited to posts such as judge, constable, or steward. To remain in a state of readiness, the Aztecs engaged neighboring peoples in *xochiyaoyotl*, flowery wars, in which fighting was restrained and nobles refrained from killing one another (the only casualties were commoners).

Within societies such as that of the Aztec we see the emergence of the military specialist, a player generally absent in small-scale societies. Such specialization meant that a larger proportion of the male population could avoid direct participation in combat. Warfare was carried out by armies consisting of specialists and less trained soldiers recruited largely to provide bulk.

Along with specialization in personnel, another feature of warfare that varies with social scale is technological change. The most important innovation was firearms. Pettengill (1981) pointed this out in regard to the ability of professional soldiers (knights) to control the peasantry in feudal Europe: "Prior to the development of the firearm, the professional soldier did not have a preponderant advantage in weaponry over the peasant when it came to small-scale combat.... The professional's advantage lay more in his organization and discipline in the battlefield. ... This relative symmetry was destroyed once firearms were developed. Whoever possesses them has an enormous advantage over those who don't" (pp. 4–5). Firearms were invented in Europe in the 1300s, but it was not until the mid-1500s that they assumed a major role in warfare and social control. They came to play a vital part not only in warfare within Europe, but also in colonial expansion into those areas of the world that did not possess firearms.

The expansion of European empires and the spread of firearms have had important consequences for patterns of warfare among small-scale societies. In the Amazon basin, many societies that had not been particularly warlike were pushed together and forced to contend with the Hispanic invaders, as well as to compete with each other for dwindling resources. For example,

This member of Papenal (the National Liberation Army in West Papua) fights with only a bow and arrow against Indonesian troops who are armed with sophisticated modern weapons. Such resistance movements of indigenous peoples against brutal integration into modern states are fairly widespread today, as they have been in the past.

the warfare that has become endemic to the Yanomami of southern Venezuela (Chagnon 1977) is largely a consequence of their being pushed into a refuge area with relatively scarce resources. Yanomami adaptation was then influenced by the acquisition of guns by their neighbors, the Makiritare, who were able to establish dominance over them. In many parts of the world, differential access to European military technology allowed some groups to establish hegemony over their neighbors. In Africa, those states that supplied the slave trade created far-flung empires with the support of such technology. In Polynesia, petty chiefs were able to defeat their neighbors and establish island-wide kingdoms. In most of these instances, the success of the conquerors was short-lived as the Europeans who made their success possible assumed control.

Creation of the modern world system has been accompanied by warfare that is increasingly wider in scope. From the sixteenth century to the early twentieth century, various colonial wars around the world were part of a global competition among European states for colonies. This interstate rivalry culminated in the twentieth century in the so-called world wars. Such warfare witnessed the development of increasingly complex military technology, to the point that we now have the ability to initiate wars at any point on the globe within a matter of seconds, to carry out warfare in space, and to exterminate all of humanity.

Rather than end this chapter on such a pessimistic note, we emphasize that people generally have sought to live in peace. Perhaps one of the most important ideas to come out of anthropological studies of warfare is that wars are "cultural artifacts" (Mead 1967, 219); they are created by specific, nonbiological conditions. By altering these conditions, it should be possible to eliminate warfare. To do so requires that we gain a thorough understanding of the conditions that generate warfare, and it is here that such social science disciplines as anthropology can play a vital role.

The face of modern warfare: American soldiers in Saudi Arabia protect themselves against chemical warfare.

SUMMARY

Although political violence has always been with us, it is limited by norms, laws, and provisions for law enforcement and dispute mediation. Norms are conceptions of how people should behave. Often norms are elevated to the systematized status of laws—binding rules about behavior. Laws are legitimatized by reference to some general normative idea and sometimes by concepts of how a "reasonable man" would behave in a given situation. Both norms and laws change with the social environment.

Attitudes toward laws vary from society to society. Those laws based on widely accepted norms usually meet with the most compliance. In every society, however, some people will break laws, become engaged in disputes that require legal mediation, or disagree with others over some laws. Ways of handling such situations are related to the society's adaptive strategy. Foraging societies handle disputes either by informal interpersonal means or by somewhat more formal methods. Common means of dealing with disputes are through dispersal or group negotiation. In small-scale farming societies, where the potential for quarrels over distribution of surplus food, property inheritance, and land rights may be greater than in foraging societies, people may use informal interpersonal methods or more formal dispersal or decision-making methods to deal with disputes. In large-scale societies, people have so much to fight over that law enforcement and dispute mediation are highly institutionalized.

In all societies there is competition for power. Political power is based on authority, ideas, symbols, and contests. Authority is the right of an individual or group in power to make certain decisions and command obedience. When ideas about appropriate political goals and behavior are organized into a systematic program, they constitute an ideology. Organic ideologies stem from the direct experiences of members of the society; rationalistic ideologies are based on observation and introspection. Symbols support political ideas by associating them with strong emotions.

The people behind political systems can be categorized as political communities, the political elite, and political teams. Political communities are people with similar political norms, goals, and ways of operating. The political elite are those entitled to or able to compete for available power and leadership opportunities. Teams actively involved in politics include coalitions, political parties, and multipurpose organizations.

Competition for power is keenest during political contests. Societies with hereditary access to power usually have provisions to minimize rivalries for power vacuums created by the death of a leader. Elections are used in other societies to make moves into power more orderly, though they may not necessarily spread power democratically across the population at large.

Small-scale societies tend to be stateless, authority being limited to local realms of power. By contrast, in many large-scale societies power is highly centralized, with specialized administrative and judicial machinery. Stateless societies may be of the acephalous (headless) form, or they may be chiefdoms (hierarchically ordered communities integrated into a formal structure). There have been numerous types of states, with many still facing problems associated with relations among formerly distinct groups.

Tensions in society sometimes lead to violent struggles for power. There may be repeated rebellions that change the personnel in power, but leave the social structure intact. There may also be revolutions, in which the social order is radically changed, but these are rare occurrences. Warfare between politically autonomous communities may be on as small a scale as an interfamily feud or as large a scale as a world war. Each kind of warfare is linked to specific adaptations and environments.

The expansion of European empires and the modern world system have created warring patterns in some small-scale indigenous populations. An anthropological understanding could provide a basis for altering those settings, perhaps reducing the incidence of violence.

SUGGESTED READINGS

Boehm, C. 1984. *Blood Revenge: The Anthropology of Feuding in Montenegro and Other Tribal Societies*. Lawrence: University Press of Kansas.

Cohen, Robin, Peter C. Gutkind, and Phyllis Brazier, eds. 1979. *Peasants and Proletarians: The Struggles of Third World Workers*. London: Hutchinson.

Fried, Morton, Marvin Harris, and Robert Murphy,

eds. 1967. *War: The Anthropology of Armed Conflict and Aggression*. Garden City, NY: Natural History Press.

Howard, Michael C. 1981. *Aboriginal Politics in Southwestern Australia*. Nedlands: University of Western Australia Press.

Malinowski, Bronislaw. 1926. *Crime and Custom in*

Savage Society. London: Kegan Paul, Trench, Trubner.

Roberts, Simon. 1979. *Order and Dispute: An Introduction to Legal Anthropology.* Harmondsworth: Penguin.

Seaton, S. Lee, and Henri M. Claessen, eds. 1979. *Political Anthropology.* The Hague/Paris: Mouton.

Tapper, Richard. 1979. *Pasture and Politics: Economics, Conflict and Ritual among Shahsevan Nomads of Northwest Iran.* New York: Academic Press.

The Clans on Capitol Hill

Jack McIver Weatherford

J.M. Weatherford worked in the Senate as legislative assistant to Senator John Glenn (D., Ohio) in 1978–1980, after which he wrote Tribes on the Hill, *comparing the congressional organization with various tribes around the world. In addition to conducting research on politics and crime in Washington, he has worked in South America, Africa, and Europe. His most recent books,* Indian Givers *and* Native Roots, *deal with the contributions of Native Americans to the world. Dr. Weatherford teaches anthropology at Macalester College in Saint Paul, Minnesota.*

My first surprise on starting work in the United States Senate was how small and intimate a community Congress is. As I wandered through the underground maze of tunnels, cafeterias, barbershops, and small candy stores stuck in little corners, I felt very much at home, in the same way I had on the small back streets of the Bavarian village of Kahl, where I did my doctoral research. Sitting upstairs in the formal meeting rooms or dining rooms, I sensed the same kinds of political maneuvering I had seen in the barazas and religious court sessions of the Swahili community in Mombasa, Kenya. What surprised me most, however, was how important marriage and kinship are in Washington politics, just as in nearly every community or tribe I had seen anywhere in the world.

The importance of kinship and marriage first caught my attention in the case of Senator Howard Baker of Tennessee, who held the position of Senate majority leader from 1980 to 1984. He first arrived in the Senate as a political professional following in the steps of his father and his stepmother, both of whom served in Congress before him. In his early years in the Senate, Baker served with his brother-in-law, Representative William Wampler of Virginia, and with his father-in-law, Senator Everett Dirksen of Illinois, who was then Senate minority leader. After his father-in-law's death, Baker eventually succeeded him as Republican leader. In 1982, Baker's daughter, Cissy, won the Republican nomination for the House of Representatives, but she lost in the general election to the grandson of the man her grandfather had defeated two generations earlier.

In the struggle to replace Howard Baker as Republican leader in 1985, Senator Robert Dole of Kansas clobbered his opponents. It may have been mere coincidence, but at the time of his election he was married to Secretary of Transportation Elizabeth Dole, whereas none of his opponents had such kinship ties.

The importance of kinship was not confined to the Republican party; I soon found that a high proportion of the top-ranking Democrats were also connected by blood or marriage. Russell Long of Louisiana was one of the most important senators in his position as top Democrat on the Finance Committee. He first came to the Senate fresh out of law school and took the seat made vacant by the assassination of his father, Huey Long. For a while his mother, Rose Long, had also held the same seat. Other cousins and uncles of his served in

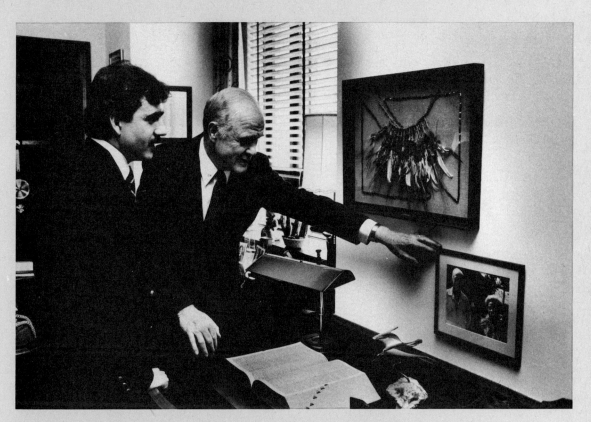

Jack Weatherford with Senator John Glenn in Glenn's office on Capitol Hill. In U.S. politics, marriage and kinship function much as they do in tribal societies.

virtually every elected office in Louisiana and in the United States Congress. A northern parallel to the Long family is the family of Rhode Island's Claiborne Pell, who was the ranking Democrat on the Foreign Affairs Committee. His father served in the House, representing New York. Other political members of Claiborne Pell's family included former Senators William Claiborne and George Dallas, and even John Pell, who served as a minister in the British court of Oliver Cromwell in the seventeenth century. More recently, Claiborne Pell served in Congress with his cousin, Congresswoman Lindy Boggs, who replaced her husband, House Majority Leader Hale Boggs, after he was killed in an Alaskan plane crash. One of her sons worked as a major Washington lobbyist after losing his own congressional race; a daughter ran for the Senate in New Jersey; and a third child, Cokie Roberts, became congressional correspondent for the government-financed public radio and public television networks.

Not only do such clans control the two parties in Congress, some of them cross party lines. Senator Jay Rockefeller (also known as John D. Rockefeller IV) arrived in the Senate in 1985 to represent West Virginia as a Democrat, the same year that his Republican father-in-law, Senator Charles Percy of Illinois, gave up his seat. Jay's uncles, Winthrop Rockefeller (former governor of Arkansas) and Nelson Rockefeller (former governor of New

York and vice president of the United States under Gerald Ford), had also won office as Republicans. Jay's wife, Sharon Percy Rockefeller, also served as chair of the board of the Corporation for Public Broadcasting as a Democrat.

In recent years, women have emerged as more important players in these political dynasties. In 1986, Elizabeth J. Patterson, daughter of the late Senator Olin D. Johnston, won election to the House of Representatives from South Carolina. Another daughter followed her father into office in 1990, when Republican Susan Molinari ran for the seat of her father, Representative Guy V. Molinari, who left Congress to become borough president of Staten Island.

Political family ties transcend state and regional boundaries. John and Edward Kennedy represented Massachusetts in the Senate and their brother, Robert, represented New York. In 1986, a new generation of the family came to office in Massachusetts when Joseph P. Kennedy II won election to the seat of retiring House Speaker Tip O'Neill, Jr. Barry Goldwater, Junior, won election in a California district while his father served as senator from Arizona. Before becoming vice president and president of the United States, George Bush served in the House of Representatives from Houston, Texas, even though his father had served in the Senate representing Connecticut. Ideology, party affiliation, and geography all are subject to manipulation for the individual with the right kinship and marriage connections.

I soon found, however, that just as in New Guinea and Amazonia, political alliances are only as durable as the marriages that bind them. Divorce in twentieth-century American politics looms as threateningly as it did in the court of Henry VIII of England or as it does today in the social order of a Big-Man in Melanesia. This appeared rather clearly in the case of Senator Gary Hart of Colorado. After he and his sister-in-law, Martha Keys, worked

together on the George McGovern presidential campaign of 1972, they won election to Congress from Colorado and Kansas, respectively. Once in Congress, Martha Keys fell in love with Andrew Jacobs, Junior, the congressman from Indiana and son of former Indiana Congressman Andrew Jacobs, Senior. Martha Keys then divorced her political scientist husband in Kansas to marry Congressman Jacobs. This started a great political clan stretching across the American heartland of Kansas, Colorado, and Indiana, a good all-American base for a presidential candidate. Representative Keys, however, failed to win reelection, and soon afterward she and second husband Jacobs divorced. The collapse of this congressional clan because of marital problems presaged the collapse of Gary Hart's presidential campaign in 1988 because of a disagreeable mixture of national and sexual politics.

Divorce might be less of a problem today if American politicians, in the manner of some tribal chiefs, were allowed to have more than one spouse at a time. As if to compensate for this lack, Congress provides itself with supernumerary aides who can inherit a position when one of the bosses dies or moves on to a higher office and does not have the right relative to take over the job. Thus, Jesse Helms of North Carolina became such a successful congressional guerilla after learning the inside workings of the system while serving on the staffs of two former senators.

Of course, the best route into office is to be related to other politicians and to be a congressional aide. Senator Nancy Kassebaum was the daughter of the 1936 presidential candidate Alf Landon, and she worked in the Senate for several years before gaining a seat. Similarly, Senator Sam Nunn worked for his great-uncle Carl Vinson, who for many years chaired the House Armed Services Committee. When Nunn was elected to the Senate, he immediately built himself a powerbase on the Senate Armed Services Committee, where he became a major force. After serving 10 years as administrative assistant to Senator Nunn, Ray B. Richard won election to Congress in 1982, whereupon he immediately got a seat on the House Armed Services Committee.

The relatives and former aides of congressional members together control approximately 20 percent of the seats in the House of Representatives and the Senate, holding most of the important leadership positions. And the power of these clans is increasing in the last decades of the twentieth century as the importance of the political parties declines. For most tribes, kinship is only one resource used by rising leaders; in Washington, however, kinship and marriage are fast becoming the defining criteria that determine who gets and who holds power. Once families and clans become as established and enduring as they now seem to be in American politics, they deviate from tribal politics and take a major step toward the familial politics of reigning aristocracies and royal dynasties.

21 Religious Belief, Behavior, and Symbolism

A Ghost Dance religious ceremony among Arapaho Indians of the Great Plains, part of a Native American millenarian movement in the nineteenth century.

In the last chapter, we considered belief systems in relation to political ideology and normative concepts of law. We stressed the importance of legitimacy and authority in discussing the bases of such systems of belief. Among the examples we used to illustrate sources of legitimacy and authority were ones derived from religion, such as the Dreamtime mythology of Australian Aborigines and, with regard to stratification, the idea of the Divine Right of Kings employed by the European monarchs. We now look more closely at religion. **Religion** may be defined as a system of beliefs involving supernatural forces or beings that provide shape and meaning to the universe.

Religious beliefs, of course, concern more than providing a justification for legal systems or the rule of kings. A system of religious beliefs, commonly referred to as "a religion," seeks to provide an all-encompassing view about how the universe works and why. It addresses the ultimate questions of our existence: Where did we come from? Why are we as we are? Why must we die? The term *supernatural*, as employed in our definition of religion, refers to a shift away from the secular order of reality into the *sacred,* the realm of symbolic meanings and actions through which people interpret the forces that ultimately control and give shape to the universe. Religion, then, involves the use of sacred symbols through belief and action. In studying religious beliefs, anthropologists are concerned with how people construct a religious view of the world—a religious **cosmology,** or philosophy concerned with the fundamental causes and processes of things in the universe.

As with human beliefs in general, religious beliefs are related to a society's adaptational strategies. They tend to reflect a society's view of the world from the perspective of its adaptational strategy and to pose questions in a way that has meaning within the context of this strategy. Thus, the Aboriginal Dreamtime mythology relates the ultimate questions of our existence to the actions of mythical creative beings, but the shape of the questions and the answers to them reflect a foraging adaptation in their focus on plants, animals, and the landscape. In examining the major religions of the world today, we see them as the products of earlier adaptive strategies. Yet, they have evolved over time so as to be meaningful in the context of modern conditions.

UNDERSTANDING RELIGIOUS BELIEF

What concerns anthropologists is not the ultimate truth of a religious assertion, but the question of why people hold a given belief. Why, for instance, have some people been drawn to the idea of reincarnation out of a range of possible ways of dealing with the question of death? Answers to such questions, to the extent that they can be found, are both complex and difficult to arrive at. In searching for answers, we must look at particular religious beliefs, their relationship to social processes, and to historical and ecological factors.

Belief Systems in Context

Religious beliefs generally are systematically centered on a core of precepts about the nature of things, presented in symbolic form. It is this core that gives direction and shape to the belief system. We can see how a belief system is shaped by looking at the Rastafarians, members of a religious cult founded in Jamaica.

The Rastafarians believe that they are eternal and shall never die. They declare, "We who are Rastafarians are the disciples who have walked with God from the time when the foundation of creation was laid, through 71 bodies, to behold the 72nd house of power which shall reign forever" (Barrett 1977, 112). According to Barrett, other core elements of their beliefs include deification of the former Ethiopian emperor Haile Selassie; the assertion that the black person is the reincarnation of ancient Israel, living in exile because of the "Whiteman"; the belief that Jamaica is the modern-day Babylon, in contrast to Ethiopia, which is heaven; and the belief that whites are inferior to blacks.

We can trace the historic origins of Rastafarian beliefs to such sources as Christianity and the early twentieth-century teachings of Marcus Garvey, an American black activist who promoted ties between New World and African blacks. The Rastafarians see the Bible as a source for many of their beliefs. They argue, however, that the Bible has been distorted by the Whiteman, and that they alone are able to interpret the meaning of its contents correctly.

The Rastafarians' interpretation of the Bible is linked to their own circumstances. For instance, they base their belief in their immortality and reincarnation on a passage from the Bible in the Book of Romans: "The wages of sin is death, but the gift of God is eternal life." This passage guaranteeing eternal life has been interpreted in many ways by different Christian sects; the Rastafarians' version is derived from the peculiarities of their life in Jamaica—their poverty, the discrimination they have faced, and their feelings of hopelessness with respect to changing things by rational means.

The Rastafarian form of Christianity is an example of what has been termed a "religion of the oppressed" (Lanternari 1963). It is an attempt by oppressed peoples to deal with their situation through the medium of religion. Such religions represent a form of rebellion, and it is from the impoverished population of Jamaica (and elsewhere in the Caribbean) that followers of the Rastafarian movement are recruited. They can be viewed as seeking to escape from their plight through faith and the promise of a reversal of the world order by supernatural forces.

Choices Available

A person's decision to become a Rastafarian often is a matter of conscious choice, but given the life of most poor Jamaicans, it represents one of only a few choices they perceive to be available. In seeking the answer to why a person chooses to become a Rastafarian, or to adhere to any other religious belief, we can look at psychological and social pressures and constraints. The Rastafarian faith offers security and hope in an otherwise insecure and often rather miserable world. The potential Rastafarian is raised in an environment of poverty and illiteracy in which individual attempts at upward mobility rarely succeed and rebellions consistently fail. That those living under such conditions will turn to such religions as the Rastafarian can be expected. To determine why a particular choice is made, we can look at what one religion offers that others do not and how each recruits its members.

The options available in choosing a religion vary from one society or situation to the next. In small-scale societies, individuals rarely have much choice in their beliefs. For example, Australian Aborigines traditionally were provided with only one basic view of the world. There was

Members of the Rastafarian cult of Jamaica attempt to adapt to their poverty and powerlessness through the belief that they are eternal and that the world order that discriminates against them will be reversed by supernatural forces. Marijuana (Ganja) is smoked as a symbol of freedom from the laws of "Babylon."

little possibility of questioning any of the fundamental tenets of this belief system. Those who lived around the various Aboriginal societies had similar beliefs, the social order and adaptational strategy were relatively stable, and their personalities were sufficiently intertwined with these beliefs to allow little room for fundamental change. The coming of Europeans to Australia altered this situation; but even today, as with many small communities in our own society, the choices of religious belief realistically available to

Aborigines living in more isolated communities remain extremely limited.

Increasing social scale presents a potential challenge to the monopolization of religious belief characteristic of traditional small-scale societies. However, when state religions are promoted, choices may still be severely limited, as they were in Spain during the Inquisition. Even in the absence of such formal constraints, there are other limiting factors. Early socialization is one such factor, when young people are conditioned to view the world from a particular perspective and to feel that their religious affiliation is a vital part of their social identity. This religious socialization may influence a person's choice of friends and potential spouses, who further encourage retention of the initial allegiance. But, as we shall see in the final section of this chapter, there are many forces at work to encourage change as well. These include culture contact, drastic changes of status, and proselytization.

Religious Beliefs and Adaptational Strategy

As a final consideration in understanding religious beliefs, certain forms tend to be associated with particular modes of economic adaptation. For example, among foragers, such as traditional Australian Aborigines, religious beliefs are closely related to those things that are of most importance in their lives: the land over which they range and the plants and animals they procure. Aboriginal religion therefore places a heavy emphasis on the procreation of important animal species.

The Gunabibi fertility ritual practiced in northern Australia contains a great deal of procreative imagery. The sacred ground on which the rite is performed includes a large crescent-shaped pit representing the uterus of the mythical rock python, which is the central image on which this ritual is based. As part of the ritual, young boys are led into the pit and symbolically swallowed by the rock python; they later emerge reborn. Many of the objects used in the ritual are phallic. In one of the final acts of the Gunabibi, the men place two large *jelmalandji* (12- to 20-foot-long poles with pads of grass and paper bark tied to them) across the pit. The rite represents a way to ensure the growth and perpetuation of the animals most important to the Aboriginal diet.

A change to agriculture results in a shift of emphasis in a people's religion. The gods, prayers, rites, and so forth now are concerned primarily with the things that influence agricultural productivity: pestilence, natural disaster, rain, time. Among the most important deities worshiped by the Maya are those associated with the weather, especially with rain. Mayan religious specialists traditionally devoted much of their effort to divining knowledge useful in planting and harvesting.

Although he is oversimplifying somewhat, Anthony Wallace (1966) has proposed four basic categories of religion that he associates with particular modes of adaptation and social formation:

1. *Shamanistic*, characterized by individualistic and shamanic cult institutions and part-time practitioners, and usually found in conjunction with relatively independent foraging bands, such as those of the Inuit and native Siberians. (Shamans are discussed later in the chapter in the section on religious specialists.)

2. *Communal*, in which communal religious institutions occur along with individualistic and shamanic practices. Communal cults are characterized by periodic gatherings of members of a society for ceremonial purposes, often in association with the seasons, harvests, or rites of passage. This type of religion is associated with relatively well-integrated foraging societies such as the Australian Aborigines, and with small-scale agricultural societies.

3. *Olympian*, which adds to the communal system a hierarchically and bureaucratically organized professional priesthood that manages rituals and beliefs. This type of religion is characterized by a hierarchy of deities that usually

includes a number of powerful high gods. It is associated with chiefdoms and nonindustrial states, such as those of the Aztecs and the Incas.

4. *Monotheistic,* which includes all the various cult forms but is unique in its emphasis on a single supreme being or concentration of supernat- ural beings or forces under the control of a single supreme being. This type of religion is closely associated with the growth and expansion of state organization and the centralization of power in the hands of the state.

SYMBOLIC EXPRESSION

The Huichol of northwestern Mexico were foragers until a few centuries ago, when they adopted agriculture as a result of Spanish influence. The Huichol have retained many social and cultural elements from their foraging past, and these continue to be reflected in their religion, which centers on what Barbara Myerhoff (1970) refers to as the Deer-Maize-Peyote complex. The influence of their foraging past is represented by deer symbolism, while agriculture is associated with maize symbolism. Through such religious practices as the ceremonial anointing of maize with deer blood, these two elements of their life are united.

Symbols, such as the deer and maize of the Huichol, draw together significant elements of a people's existence, unifying the everyday with the supernatural. Such symbols objectify experience and belief; thus, they evoke our most fundamental feelings. Because of their ability to unify and express the core elements of our lives, symbols play an important role in religion.

Culture-Specific Symbols

Certain religious symbols may be universal, but most are culturally specific, and individuals must be conditioned to understand and appreciate them. Conditioning occurs through both informal and formal instruction, as when Aboriginal youths are taught the meanings of the marks on the sacred boards that serve as physical representations of the actions of the Dreamtime beings. This learning is enhanced by creating an environment designed to stir people's emotions when they are confronted with the symbols. Such an environment may include impressive architecture or other evocative settings, a stirring ritual or ceremonial gathering, or a combination of the two. Among the Pintubi (an Aboriginal society from central Australia), through physical separation, ritual, and other means, youths are already in an otherworldly state when the elders bring forth the sacred paraphernalia, exclaiming, "Dead men held this" (Myers 1982).

The power of culture-specific religious symbolism is exemplified in the best-known Rastafarian symbol: their long and unkempt hair, the "dreadlocks." The wearing of their hair in this fashion is justified by reference to the Bible: "They shall not make baldness upon their head, neither shall they shave off the corner of their beard, nor make any cuttings in the flesh" (Leviticus 21:5). The dreadlock serves as a powerful public symbol of what the Rastafarian religion is about. It sets the Rastafarian apart as "the natural man, who typifies in his appearance the unencumbered life" (Barrett 1977, 137). But beyond this is an association with rebellion, with a refusal to accept the world as defined by the Whiteman. As Barrett (1977) has noted, hair is used by many Jamaicans as an index of social differences. By wearing long, unkempt hair, the Rastafarian is considered wild, dangerous, effeminate, and dreadful. He underscores contradictions within Jamaican society and represents a threat to the social order: "The hair symbol of the Rastas announces that they are outside Jamaican society and do not care to enter under any circumstances other than one of radical change in the society's attitude to the poor" (p. 138). The response of those concerned with maintaining the status quo has been to cut off the Rastafarians' hair.

While hair style has symbolic significance in virtually all societies, its specific symbolic significance can vary. While many Westerners would be disturbed to see the Pope or their local minister or priest with long, unkempt hair, in many other societies a man's long hair is associated with holiness; in some societies, it is a status marker. Before the arrival of the Spanish, lowland Maya, especially those of high status, commonly wore their hair long. Under Spanish influence and pressure, the Maya cut their hair, and today most Maya view long hair unfavorably. It is only among the non-Christian Lacandon that long hair continues to be worn, and this has reinforced other Mayas' aversion to long hair because of its association with paganism.

Food Symbolism

People's dietary habits are often closely associated with religious beliefs. In many religious traditions, particular animals or plants are assigned symbolic status; in religions with food taboos, people are forbidden to eat certain foods, except perhaps in specific sacred contexts. Rastafarians have relatively strict ideas about their diet, and these ideas are tied to their religion. They are for the most part vegetarians, although they may eat small fish. Pork and beef are considered pollutants. Basically, Rastafarians favor a diet that is natural and derived directly from the earth.

The cow has symbolic properties in many societies. To many North Americans it is a symbol of wealth and well-being, but has no direct religious significance. Pastoralists in the southern Sudan and western Ethiopia, such as the Nuer and Dinka, traditionally saw their lives and those of their cattle as inextricably intertwined. Dinka perceptions of color, light, and shape are connected with the color configurations of their cattle. The centrality of the cow to Dinka culture is reflected in their religion; the cow serves as the

most important element in their religious beliefs and practices. In animal sacrifice, the Dinka's central religious act, the sacrificial animal symbolizes their society as the meat is divided to represent social relations based on gender, age, and clanship (Lienhardt 1961). While most Hindus in South Asia do not depend as heavily on cattle for their survival as the Dinka, the cow has assumed an important place in their religion as well. To Hindus, the cow is "worshipped as a symbol of warmth and moisture, as earth mother, and as a producer of milk and indirectly ghi [clarified butter], so essential in sacrifices" (Heston 1971, 192). In India, this belief and the Hindu tradition of nonviolence led to a constitutional ban on the slaughter of cattle, and today the killing of cattle and eating of beef remain an emotional issue in India, contributing to communal tensions and sometimes riots.

Totems

Australian Aborigines, as do many other peoples, "conceptualize a single, unified cosmic order in which man and the natural species, ancestral beings, spirits, and other conceived entities are on equal terms. All are interrelated in a genealogical and pseudogenealogical manner" (Tonkinson 1974, 74). This view of the cosmos is referred to as *totemic*. The links between individuals and groups and particular plants, animals, and other natural phenomena are represented symbolically in the form of **totemic emblems**, and their relationship forms the basis for ceremonial and ritual activities.

Australian Aborigines recognize several varieties of totemism. Two primary types are conception totemism and ancestral totemism. *Conception totems* are associated with a person's birth; for example, plants, animals, insects, or minerals of the locale where the person was believed to have been conceived. In many Aboriginal societies, there is a strong emotional bond with this totem. Since the totem and the individual are said to be of the same flesh, individuals may refrain from eating or otherwise harming those things identi-

In India, Hindus have traditionally worshiped cows, which are allowed to wander freely through villages and cities.

fied as their totems. This caring bond is not universal. The Mardudjara of Jigalong in Western Australia feel no special attachment to their conception totem, and there are no dietary restrictions. Even within a similar environment, practices can vary. While the Aranda of central Australia place restrictions on eating their conception totems, the nearby Warramunga will eat their conception totems if they are killed by someone else, and the neighboring Walbiri assert that "men would be stupid not to eat such foods when available" (Meggitt 1962, 208).

Ancestral totems link individuals with the historical or mythical past. For the Australian Aborigines, ancestral totems are associated with activities of the Dreamtime beings. During their travels, as recorded in myth, the Dreamtime beings left objects behind; these became animated with a life force from which came spirit children waiting in plant or animal form to be born as humans. These totems place individuals within their physical environment and create a spiritual map of the terrain. It is often through these totemic beings that individuals gain access to land, in return for which the humans perform ceremonies at sites associated with their ancestral totems. Known as *increase rites*, the ceremonies usually involve activities aimed at procreating species of animals. Attitudes toward the treatment of plants and animals acknowledged as ancestral totems are similar to those involving conception totems. The Walbiri have no rules against eating their ancestral totems, although Meggitt (1962) comments that "occasionally a man would express sorrow, in a half-joking fashion, when he ate a bird or animal he called 'father.' . . . The usual comment, accompanied by winks and smiles, was: 'What a pity—I am eating my poor father! I am so sorry for him!'" (p. 209). Some anthropologists claim that restrictions on the eating of totemic animals help to preserve species in a given area, but the evidence is far from conclusive.

Myth

Since at least the nineteenth century, it has been common to use the term *myth* to refer to something considered untrue: the myth of equality, the myth of democracy, and so forth. This usage reflects the secularization of our beliefs, for in its original sense as a sacred tale, a myth did not connote falsehood. For those adhering to a particular religious tradition, their myths represented received truth. Other peoples' myths may have been false, but not their own. As used by anthropologists to describe a type of sacred narrative, a myth is more than just a tale. **Myths** express the unobservable realities of religious belief in terms of observable phenomena. As with other forms of symbolic expression, myths link the supernatural and sacred with the concrete and mundane.

Myths, in fact, serve a variety of functions. They may serve as cultural histories, alluding to past events, such as migrations; earlier forms of social organization; and natural occurrences, such as meteor showers, eclipses, or floods. The events described in myths, however, may be apocryphal. Even when the myths do have historical validity, they do not simply serve as records of the past, for myths use history for social and religious purposes.

Sacred history myths may serve as *charters* for interest groups and as justifications for particular institutions in a society. They link the present social order with a sacred past and condition behavior toward desired ends. Aboriginal youths are not instructed in their mythic traditions simply to entertain them. The myths they are told are intended to shape their view of the world and instill an attitude toward social institutions and the status quo that will ensure continuity of the existing social order. In this respect, myths often "constitute a conservative, socializing force

whose function is to sanctify existing institutions and foster the values of sociality" (Hiatt 1975, 5).

The events depicted in myths deal with fundamental questions concerning the human condition from the point of view of a particular social order. Myths represent attempts to analyze the world around us and its contradictions or paradoxes. The themes that occur over and over again are those associated with basic philosophical questions: the relationship between life and death, the origins of life and human society, and the stresses with which people in all societies must come to terms, such as tensions between parents and children or siblings.

Art

Religious symbolic expression frequently takes the form of art. We use the term **art** with reference to attempts to reflect or interpret the essential aspects of reality through images recognized as having an aesthetic quality. Artistic expression can assume a variety of forms. These may include material objects, such as paintings, carvings, weavings, and so forth. Or art may be expressed through drama, music, poetry, or literature. All art is deeply embedded in a social context. This context determines the format of expression, the nature and interpretation of reality, and the recognition of aesthetic quality. Thus, in those societies where the interpretation of the world is largely religious, artistic expression is predominantly religious. In more secular societies, such as ours, the influence of religion on art is less comprehensive.

Traditionally, in most small-scale societies, artists and their works are closely associated with religion. The artist often functions as an adjunct shaman or priest who expresses myths, sacred beings, and religious principles through art (Abramson 1976). Such art may occur solely in a religious context (for example, in the performance of rituals), or it may occur in a more mundane setting (such as in the carving of religious symbols on domestic utensils), perhaps providing a link with the sacred. Religious art in small-scale societies can serve a variety of functions; hence, it can assume a range of meanings. Phillip Lewis (1969) noted that religious art among the Melanesian people of New Ireland is connected with wealth and power in the context of displays and exchanges of wealth at ceremonies and feasts, where such art adds to the prestige of the patron (Big-Man) whose wealth has supported the occasion.

Artistic expression in small-scale societies is influenced by the environment and adaptation. Among materially poor peoples it is rare to find much elaboration of religious artistic symbolism in material terms, nor is there likely to be much opportunity for individuals to become full-time artists. For example, differences in the elaboration of artistic expression occur between Australian Aborigines living in the arid regions of central Australia and those in the tropical north, as there are differences between the art of foragers of the Great Basin and the northwest coast of North America.

Artistic expression undergoes important changes with increasing social scale. Ancient empires and city-states were able to subsidize artistic activities to an extent that allowed for greater specialization. Patronage in these societies influenced artistic creation, and more secular forms of art emerged, reflecting the particular interests of rulers and the state. For the most part, however, until fairly recently, religion and art remained closely intertwined. Thus, in the European Middle Ages, religious themes dominated artistic works in keeping with the central role of religion in European society at the time.

With the rise of capitalism and emergence of the modern world system, art has assumed an increasingly secular character. Beginning during the Renaissance and increasingly with the advent of the seventeenth- and eighteenth-century political and economic revolutions in Europe, artists allied themselves with those seeking to put an end to the old feudal order and the religious establishment associated with it: "By means of a change of artistic themes and the introduction of new ones, art helped to debunk a decrepit world

and exalt a new one" (Sánchez Vázquez 1973, 164). As modern large-scale society became more individualistic, and as artists became more independent of religious establishments and wealthy aristocratic patrons, art itself became more individualistic. To some extent, however, modern art is related to underlying social factors. Therefore, while it is possible to distinguish between secular and sacred art in contemporary societies, they are united with respect to their common social context (see Forge 1979, 280–281).

The incorporation of small-scale societies into large-scale ones has profoundly influenced the art produced by small-scale societies. In describing the art of enclave societies, Nelson Graburn (1976) distinguished that which is inwardly directed or "made for, appreciated, and used by peoples within their own part-society" and that which is made for an external, dominant world (pp. 4–5). Art that is inwardly directed has undergone changes that reflect transformations within these societies. Although the religious aspect of this art may remain important, it is likely to have been greatly influenced by the traditions and symbols of the encompassing societies. Thus, when tribal groups convert to Christianity, Christian themes often assume an important place in their art.

Outwardly directed art serves as a means of generating income (for example, in the form of so-called tourist art) and as a medium for "presenting to the outside world an ethnic image" (Graburn 1976, 5). Such art may use religious symbolism, but it is not necessarily religious in its intended purpose. Outwardly directed art can have important inward effects on a society. The work of Haida artist Bill Reid, which can be categorized as outwardly directed art, has played an important role in the cultural renaissance of the Haida people and in their claims of sovereignty over their homeland on the Queen Charlotte Islands, which they call Haida-Gwaii. As with the cedar canoe that Reid carved and painted for display in Paris in 1989 (see N. Jennings 1989), much of his work employs Haida religious symbolism that remains central to Haida culture.

In Fiji, the spread of tourism has encouraged the development of art forms catering to the tourist market. Such art is often based on an indigenous tradition, providing it with some distinctiveness.

Bill Reid's carved and painted canoe in Paris, an example of outwardly directed art playing a role in the cultural pride of a Native American people.

SUPERNATURAL FORCES AND BEINGS

All religious beliefs recognize some named force or entity. The variety of forms these entities take is extensive, and even within a single tradition there can be many different forces or supernatural beings populating the cosmos. Following the scheme of Annemarie de Waal Malefijt (1968, 146–162), we will now review briefly the major varieties.

Unseen Power

Many people believe in the existence of some *impersonal supernatural force*, a power that although unseen is believed to be everywhere. R.R. Marett (1909, 1912) referred to the belief in such a force as **animatism**. This force is conceived of as a massive reservoir of power that may infuse or possess, and perhaps be used by, individuals, gods, the forces of nature, and even natural objects. Animatism is associated with societies characterized by very different adaptational strategies. Thus, it is exemplified in the concept of *mana*, common to many religious traditions throughout the Pacific area; in the Hindu concept of *brahma*; in the ancient Greek notion of *dynamis*; and, more recently, in Western culture, as in Henri Bergson's *élan vital*. People are rarely satisfied with leaving things up to such an ambiguous entity, however. The concept of an impersonal supernatural force is almost universally accompanied by beliefs in more precisely conceived supernatural beings.

Spirits

People in many societies believe in the existence of an almost endless number of *spirits* that dwell in animals and places or simply wander about the earth. We refer to this belief as **animism**. Because of their great number, spirits usually are viewed collectively and not given individual identities.

The number and categories of spirits recognized in a society can vary a great deal. The Gururumba of Papua New Guinea recognize only two types of spirits: those who live in the highland forest and those who inhabit the lowlands along the riverbanks (Newman 1965). By contrast, the Javanese have a large number of categories, including frightening spirits, possessing spirits, familiar spirits, place spirits, and guardian spirits (Geertz 1960). A culture may assign individual names to certain spirits, but even these spirits are recognized as members of a broader category of similar beings, failing to achieve the degree of individualization reserved for gods.

Spirits sometimes are of human origin. The spirit children that form the pool from which new Aborigines are born are closely tied to the human population. And many societies recognize a category sometimes referred to as *souls of the dead*. These are supernatural beings of human origin which may for a time be remembered individually as *ghosts*; later they merge into an unnamed collectivity. The Walbiri Aborigines of central Australia believe that, upon death, a person's spirit becomes a *manbaraba*, "an ethereal, pale ghost, whose features resemble those of its previous owner" (Meggitt 1962, 192). The ghost remains near the tree platform where the corpse has been placed until the death is avenged (death is never considered to have occurred naturally). The ghost then dissipates, with its spirit joining the collective pool of matrispirits and patrispirits associated with particular kin groups.

The dead may retain their individual identity and continue to play an active role in society. These entities are called *ancestor souls* or *ancestor spirits*. In many societies, ancestor worship is important to religious beliefs and practices. Even today, for many Chinese and Japanese the ancestral shrine has a prominent place in the home, where the ancestors receive daily offerings and prayers. Swazi families of South Africa carry out rites to pacify ancestors on the occasions of births, marriages, deaths, the building of new homes, and family calamities.

Gods

Ancestors sometimes make it further up the religious hierarchy, being elevated to the status of a god. The term **god** (or deity) refers to a supernatural being with an individual identity and recognizable attributes who is worshiped as having power over nature and human fortunes. Most gods are of nonhuman origin. However, many human beings have either proclaimed themselves to be gods or been considered gods by a large number of worshipers. The Rastafarians believed that the former Ethiopian emperor Haile Selassie was a living deity, for example. Such concepts are often related to systems of social stratification, as when rulers claim divinity on the basis of their descent from gods. Until 1947, the Japanese emperor was considered divine, his divinity based on a claim of descent from the sun goddess, Amaterasu Omikami. Japan's defeat in World War II and subsequent changes in the country's system of stratification ultimately ended the emperor's official divine status.

Religious systems vary widely with respect to the number of gods worshiped. As in the Christian tradition, some religions have only one god. We refer to this as **monotheism**. In **polytheism**, as in the Hindu religion, there can be an almost limitless number of gods, or perhaps a finite number arranged in a hierarchy. Monotheism is related to the development of social stratification and the rise of large-scale societies—India providing an important exception. Thompson (1970), for example, discusses how the lowland Mayan god Itzam Na assumed an ever-greater role during the classic period; other gods were placed under or incorporated into Itzam Na. This process was closely related to the rise of the Mayan aristocracy. When the aristocrats' power apparently collapsed, so too did Itzam Na, and a more diverse and egalitarian polytheism reasserted itself.

An important role of the god or gods in most religious traditions is creation—the creation of the universe, of life, and of the prevailing order within the universe. For the Australian Aborig-ines, the creative acts of the mythical Dreamtime beings remain at the forefront of their religious practices and beliefs. Other traditions, however, take creation more for granted, emphasizing the postcreative activities of gods. Some religions also believe in an omnipotent and omniscient god. Supposedly, this god created the universe, and then more or less withdrew, leaving subsequent direction of the world in the hands of lesser deities. Such a god is called *otiose*, meaning "at rest," serving no practical purpose. Otiose deities seldom have an important place in worship or ritual. The Igbo of Nigeria believe in such a god, Chuku; but there are neither priests nor shrines dedicated to Chuku's service. Chuku is called on only in cases of great distress, but even then the Igbo feel that this will do little good.

Religions that allow for a number of gods frequently include relatively specialized gods, sometimes called *attribute gods*. Pre-Columbian lowland Maya, for example, recognized merchant gods, gods of hunting and fishing, gods of cacao growers, gods of beekeepers, a god of *balche* (a fermented ritual drink), gods of medicine and curers, gods of war, gods of poetry and music, a god of tattooing, a god of ballgame players, a god of fire, and a god of birth, to name just a few. Such supernatural departmentalization is largely a function of secular specialization in a society. Particularly important activities may have several highly specialized gods: the ancient Romans had three separate gods of the plow, since the fields were plowed three times. Activities of less importance might share a god or be lumped with some generalized deity, or do without altogether.

Minor Beings

Finally, many religions also possess a range of divine or semidivine beings of minor theological significance. In Western Europe, these include dwarfs, elves, pixies, and the like. The traditions of the Kekchi of southern Belize populate the forests with a number of semidivine denizens. These include the *chiel*, who live in caves and in pre-Columbian ruins. They are said to live much like people, and on occasion they visit human settlements. There is also Xtabai, who shakes her breasts at young men to lure them into the forest, only to cause them to go insane. She has a male counterpart. A common character in many religions is the *trickster*. This is a semidivine being who may establish cultural practices for a group accidentally, but who basically is not concerned with human welfare. Among native Americans, one of the best-known tricksters is Coyote: "He stole the sun, the moon, and the stars from the spirits who had them before, but he did not know what to do with them, so he placed them in the sky" (Malefijt 1968, 161).

RELIGIOUS BEHAVIOR AND CONSCIOUSNESS

Religious beliefs are not simply stated. They are presented in such a way as to have a strong emotional impact. Religious specialists (about whom more will be said in the next section) attempt to ensure that a complex, multidimensional message concerning the cosmos and one's place in it becomes a fundamental part of an individual's personality. While the precise aims and methods of religious practices may vary from one setting to the next, there are features that are common to most religious traditions.

Separation

One important aspect of religious behavior is separation. It involves the recognition of two relatively distinct realms, the secular and the sacred, each of which is associated with particular actions and objects. Western Desert Aborigines in Australia categorize as "secret-sacred" certain acts, beliefs, and related objects, which are reserved exclusively for fully initiated men or women because of the danger resulting from their close association with the Dreamtime. Punishment for transgressions traditionally was severe—sometimes even death. The ideological and emotional boundary between the sacred and the secular is far less extreme in most present-day Christian religions, but there is a boundary nevertheless.

Separation of the sacred often is related to an idea of exclusiveness: entry into this realm is special and not for everyone. To be able to enter, one has to meet special preconditions. Birth may be a factor, in which case only the chosen few are allowed entrance, or some sort of initiation may be required, as in the Christian practice of baptism. Special knowledge of esoteric language, rites, or symbols may also be important, and can be learned only from those already initiated.

The specialness of the sacred is emphasized further by how the transition from the realm of the secular to that of the sacred is marked. Frequently some form of purification is involved, ranging from abstaining from sexual relations to becoming thoroughly drunk to bathing and putting on one's Sunday best. There may be other transitional rites actually marking entry into the realm of the sacred, such as kneeling and praying and crossing oneself.

Ritual

Another common feature of religious behavior is its routinization and repetitiveness. Religious performances in any tradition tend to be highly routinized. While there may be variations in a Catholic Mass or an Aboriginal Gunabibi ceremony, the basic format remains much the same from one celebration to the next. Within this framework, we find even more precise routinization in the acting out of **rituals**, highly stereotyped, stylized, and repetitive behaviors that take place at a set time and place. This orderliness serves to create a sense of security and stability; participants know what is happening and they know what to expect. Religious rituals support the basic tenets of the ordered universe as perceived within a religious tradition. Repetitive chants and the use of repetitive themes in music and discourse also reinforce the primary messages of a religion.

Altered Consciousness

Practices associated with some religions attempt to place people in an extreme emotional state, sometimes taking the form of a trance. The idea is to provide experiences or visions so overwhelming as to reinforce the individual's belief in the reality of the supernatural. There are numerous means of achieving such states of consciousness, including fasting, flagellation, sensory deprivation, breathing exercises, meditation, and ritual dancing and drumming. Certain yogi practices originating in Tibet include the recitation of *mantras,* words or sounds of power, in almost hypnotic fashion. By uttering

the mantra associated with a deity, the person tries to transcend human thought and make contact with the deity. A trancelike state is achieved by voodoo practitioners in Haiti through drumming and dancing during special gatherings. Trances such as these are not random affairs. They tend to be culture-specific, following the rules or guidelines of the particular tradition and reflecting the behavioral norms of the culture.

A very ancient and widespread means of achieving trancelike states is the use of narcotics (see Furst 1972; Harner 1973; Wasson 1973). Relatively mild narcotics such as alcohol, tobacco, and marijuana are employed by many religions to assist in achieving the desired effect. Rastafarians use marijuana for symbolic purposes and because of its mind-altering properties. They make reference to the Bible to support its use: "Thou shalt eat the herb of the field" (Genesis 3:18). Other religions employ much more powerful hallucinogens to bring the individual face to face with the supernatural. The hallucinogenic mushroom *Amanita mascaria* is used by Siberian sha-

Religious gatherings among voodoo practitioners in Haiti lead to trance states induced by drumming and dancing.

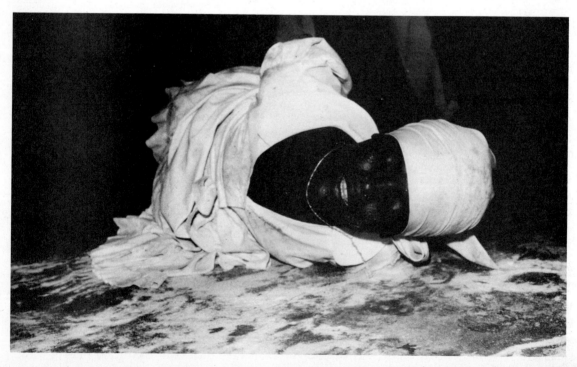

mans to communicate with the supernatural by allowing them to go into a trance in which they perceive the soul to leave the body. Some scholars maintain that narcotic-induced soul flights may have led to the initial beliefs in souls and ghosts. According to Gordon Wasson (1972), the religious complexes in Eurasia and the New World have many roots in the amanita-using shamanistic traditions of Siberia. Another hallucinogen, peyote, has become important in the religions of many indigenous peoples in northern Mexico and the southwestern United States (see Myerhoff 1974).

The use of narcotics in religion is related to a number of environmental and social factors. An obvious one is the availability of the plants. The widespread use of hallucinogenic plants in the New World is facilitated by the unusual number of narcotic plants available (Schultes 1963).

Where plants are not available locally, trade lines can be developed. The use of narcotic plants in religion can also be linked to social structure. Narcotic plants are widely used in egalitarian societies with shamanistic traditions. With increasing social stratification, their use tends to become much more restricted. In contrast to less stratified Mexican Indian societies, where the use of hallucinogens is widespread, narcotic use among the highly stratified Aztec in pre-Columbian times was restricted to a small elite. In general, the popular use of narcotics for religious purposes has survived only where there has been little or no competition from state religions. The unrestricted use of narcotics for religious purposes threatens the monopolization of sacred truth that serves as a fundamental support for these institutions.

RELIGIOUS SPECIALISTS

In most societies, there are some people who are especially skilled in the performance of certain religious tasks and who have a greater knowledge of religious traditions than most other people. In small-scale societies, where there is minimal division of labor, such individuals tend not to be full-time specialists. They are people who must perform many of the same tasks as other members of their society, but who also do a little extra. For this, they may be afforded a status somewhat above the others. As social scale increases and the division of labor becomes more complex, full-time specialists emerge—individuals who support themselves exclusively by carrying out religious tasks.

Shamans

A type of specialist common in foraging societies is the **shaman**. Michael Harner (1973) has defined a shaman as "a man or woman who is in direct contact with the spirit world through a trance state and has one or more spirits at his

command to carry out his bidding for good or evil" (p. xi). The shaman's status is highly personalistic, for it depends on perceived ability to contact and influence the spirit world rather than on knowledge of sacred lore or ritual. Furthermore, while the shaman's ritual activities adhere to a generally prescribed cultural pattern, there is a great deal of leeway in how the shaman may carry out the task of communicating with the supernatural.

The Inuit provide a good example of shamanistic practices and beliefs (Holtved 1967). The primary role of the Inuit shaman is to take charge of relations with supernatural beings who interfere with human life. This includes intervening to ensure a supply of game, driving away evil spirits, procuring good weather, divining the future, and curing the sick. For instance, if game were scarce, the Inuit would assume that Moon-man or Sea-woman, who controls the animals, was angry because someone had committed an offense, such as eating a prohibited part of an animal. To the Inuit of Greenland and Labrador these offenses become dirt in the hair of Sea-woman, and the shaman must struggle to be allowed to cleanse and comb her hair before she will promise to free the animals so that they may be hunted again. The shaman communicates with such deities by entering a trance with the assistance of a drum. The shaman is assisted by helping spirits, who take a variety of forms and who are communicated with in a special language.

An Inuit usually decides to become a shaman after a dream or some extraordinary experience. The individual may try to resist the call, giving in to his or her destiny only after great mental anguish. The next step is to consult with older shamans, providing them with a gift, and then to undergo a period of instruction that lasts anywhere from a couple of days to a few years. During the apprenticeship, the novice meets the various supernatural beings who later will serve as helpers. Another element of the shaman's preparation is experiencing the mystery of life and death through such practices as hanging, drowning, or shooting. In Greenland, while under hypnosis, the novice is attacked and eaten by a bear spirit, later awakening naked on the shore of a lake.

Keepers of the Law

Very different from the shamans are religious specialists who can be designated, in general, as *keepers of the law*—individuals whose primary roles are the performance of ritual and the interpretation and maintenance of religious tradition. In small-scale societies, keepers of the law are not usually full-time specialists. The Tzotzil-speaking Maya of southern Mexico have a large number of hierarchically ranked shamans among whose primary responsibilities is curing through communication with the ancestors (see Vogt 1970). In addition, there are religious office-holders responsible for the performance of ceremonies associated with particular Catholic saints. These offices form part of the civil–religious hierarchy or cargo system. To assume his burden (*cargo*), the cargo-holder moves from his residential hamlet to the ceremonial center of the community for one year. There, those holding religious offices engage in a series of costly ceremonies for the community, involving food, liquor, and ritual paraphernalia such as candles, incense, and fireworks. Since their role entails withdrawal from farming and other economically rewarding pursuits, cargo-holders are forced to live off sav-

The initiation of a 16-year-old Mapuche woman as a shaman in Chile after an apprenticeship of several months. The shaman's status depends on his or her ability to contact and influence the spirit world.

ings and loans for the year. Such specialists, then, are able to function on a full-time basis only periodically, at the expense of their normal economic activities. Their reward is the prestige that comes with community service.

A full-time, permanent religious functionary is a luxury that small, relatively poor communities or societies rarely can support. Occasionally, older members of a small-scale society are able to devote themselves to religious activities full-time because their age precludes normal economic pursuits as farmers or foragers and the rest of the community is willing to support them. For the most part, however, full-time religious specialists, or **priests**, are found only in large-scale societies. Only societies that can support an extensive division of labor and a large nonproductive class can accommodate religious specialists on a permanent basis. Thus, in the early 1970s, there was an estimated one full-time religious specialist per 730 persons in the United States and one per 900 persons in Europe; in the poorer countries of Latin America, the figure was one per 15,000 (Gheerbrant 1974). In southern Mexico, full-time Catholic priests visit Tzotzil communities on occasion, and one of the responsibilities of some of the cargo-holders is to collect money to pay the priest for saying mass.

Most priests can be characterized as keepers of the law because they are primarily concerned with maintaining a particular social and religious order. In fact, they can be viewed as an integral part of social order. Through their public statements, counsel, and public (as well as behind-the-scenes) maneuverings, they represent the interests of the establishment in a society. On occasion, the order they represent may come into conflict with other orders, or even with elements of their own social order, especially when secular political leaders act in ways perceived by the priesthood to be against the interests of the church (as in the case of England's Henry VIII). In such struggles, the priesthood usually acts as a conservative force. However, as we will see shortly, not all priests play such a conservative role, and they may in fact serve as catalysts for fundamental changes.

Prophets

Perhaps the most noteworthy exceptions to the conservative role of religious specialists are prophets. **Prophets** are individuals who receive divine revelation, usually through visions or dreams, concerning a restructuring or a redirecting of some aspect of society or a people's beliefs. On the basis largely of revealed truth, prophets seek to alter the existing social order through teaching or example. They do not, however, represent a complete break with the sociocultural order around them; to some extent, they are a product of their society and its religious traditions. They do, however, represent a threat to those holding religious power (and sometimes to those holding secular power as well).

Because they rely on their ability to arouse loyalty and enthusiasm and claim to communicate directly with the supernatural, prophets have much in common with shamans, although the two specialists have different aims. The goal of the prophet is the creation of a new order, whereas the shaman basically seeks to ward off disruptions to human life. Success as a prophet usually leads to the foundation of a new religious institution, transforming the seer from a renegade to a person who is at least somewhat respectable, and who may even become a deity and leader of millions.

RELIGION AND SOCIAL CHANGE

Australian Aboriginal religious dogma proclaims a perfectly ordered world in which change is unnecessary. Such a claim of permanency is common to many religious traditions, as a fundamental source of their strength. Despite this emphasis on what is unchanging in the world, however, religions and the world of which they are a part are in a constant state of flux—religions both react to the changing world and often play a role in the process of change itself.

Change through Contact or Conquest

Changes in religious belief and practices are associated with the gradual evolution of a society from one adaptational strategy or social form to another. Over the past few centuries, the process has been speeded up as a result of increasing contact between societies—in particular, contact between expansive states and small-scale societies. European expansion was not merely political and economic; it included attempts to conquer people's minds as well, largely through religion.

In establishing colonial rule throughout the world, the European conquerors profoundly influenced the religious beliefs of many peoples. Through force, or simply as a result of associating the conquerors' might with the strength of their religion, to varying degrees these peoples adopted many aspects of European religion. The result was an amalgamation of traditional and introduced elements, through a process of blending known as **syncretism**—the conscious adoption of an alien idea or practice in terms of some indigenous counterpart (Barnett 1953). Thus, in central Mexico following the Spanish conquest in the sixteenth century, Catholic and pagan beliefs were mingled to create a distinct version of Catholicism. Patron saints took on the characteristics of old pagan gods, Catholic rites were interpreted in ways quite different from those of the Spanish, and Catholic ceremony and ritual were incorporated into the political and economic fabric of the village (see Madsen 1967).

Traditional indigenous religions do not always collapse as a result of conquest; people often retain much of their traditional religion. In fact, clinging to their religious heritage can serve as a source of strength for societies. While Aboriginal religion was often destroyed or seriously undermined by the European conquest and subsequent Aboriginal integration into Australian society, in the more isolated areas, especially in the desert interior, Aboriginal religious beliefs and practices were better able to survive. Despite decades of effort by Christian missionaries, Aborigines in many settlements, such as Jigalong in Western Australia, have been successful in retaining key elements of their religion. In fact, by congregating Aborigines in more permanent settlements where there is often considerable leisure time, the whites indirectly promoted Aboriginal religious activities (Tonkinson 1974).

The activities of Christian missionaries among native peoples have been the subject of considerable controversy among anthropologists. While many missionaries actively engage in defending the rights of native peoples and in promoting socioeconomic ventures that are clearly beneficial, the work of missionaries is sometimes of questionable value to those they work among. One of the most controversial groups is the American-based Summer Institute of Linguistics/Wycliffe Bible Translators. The group's supporters point to the linguistic work that it has sponsored, including the translation of hundreds of languages into written format. The group has been attacked by Latin American anthropologists, in particular, for undermining the cultures of native peoples and for promoting conservative American cultural values in a biased manner (see Stoll 1982; Hvalkof and Aaby 1981). It has also come under attack for alleged links with the Central Intelligence Agency and American-sponsored counterinsurgency campaigns in the Philippines, Vietnam, and elsewhere. More recently, attention has focused on the conservative evangelical missionaries in Central America and the political implications of their work with governments engaged in civil wars (see Dominguez and Huntington 1984). This is a difficult area with complicated issues. A number of anthropologists have been forced to deal with such issues because of their direct bearing on the lives of the native peoples being studied.

Millenarian Movements

A weakening or disruption of the old social order, periods of social unrest, or subjugation and a loss of power frequently result in religious movements that may be categorized as **millenarian**. Millenarian movements espouse a belief in the coming of a new world, in part through supernatural action. These are religions born of frustration, despair, or bewilderment, which seek to cut through a seemingly hopeless situation with a promise of the millennium—a period of good government, great happiness, and prosperity. Millenarianists call for a complete change, although their actual visions are, of course, limited by their own sociocultural milieu. As Kenelm Burridge (1969) pointed out, their main theme is moral regeneration and the creation of a new kind of person. Such themes are often expressed or symbolized by a hero or prophet. For example, such figures as Haile Selassie, the prophet Jesus, and Buddha serve as focal points for the call for a new life.

Millenarian movements (sometimes referred to as *nativistic* or *revitalization movements*) vary somewhat according to circumstance and cultural tradition. The Rastafarian movement, with its promise of the Blackman's escape from Baby-lon, return to Africa, and black rule with the coming of the millennium, exemplifies such movements in an Afro-American context. Among native Americans, the best-known millenarian movements are those associated with the Ghost Dance (see Mooney 1965). These movements emerged among the Great Plains Indians following the failure of their armed attempts to stop American expansion; they then spread to groups in Nevada, California, and elsewhere in the American West. The central theme is a belief that the dead will return to announce the dawn of a new day. According to some versions, the earth was to open up and swallow all the whites, while leaving all their material possessions to the followers of the cult who would be spared to live in the heavenly era brought about by the Great Spirit.

In Melanesia, millenarianism took the form of **cargo cults.** In colonizing the Pacific, Europeans deprived Melanesians of power and autonomy. In addition, they failed to meet their obligations, as perceived by the native populations, to share their enormous wealth and power with the Big-Men. The resultant cults blended Christian missionary teachings concerning the eventual millenarian resurrection of Christ with the Melanesians' own myths in which ancestors would

Millenarianism in Melanesia: The Christian cross in the background, cargo cult members march with bamboo stick rifles in the belief that their "cargo" will arrive.

become transformed into powerful beings and the dead would return to life. The millennium would occur when the ancestors would return in steamships or airplanes bringing European goods (the cargo) and initiating a reversal of the social order. Those on the top would be relegated to the bottom, and those on the bottom would gain pre-eminence.

Millenarian movements commonly are associated with secular political activities. The Maasina Rule movement in the Solomon Islands began in the 1940s as a protest over wages, racism, and British colonial rule that was heavily influenced by Christian teachings. While "cargo" expectations existed from the beginning of the movement, "such ideas only became pronounced during the later years of Maasina Rule, when frustration was deepening" (Laracy 1983, 33). In fact, while earlier analyses of Maasina Rule emphasized its millenarian and religious aspects, recent scholarship has focused on its role in the movement toward the independence of the Solomon Islands, which was achieved in 1978.

Millenarian movements are not a thing of the past. Cargo cults are still important in many parts of Melanesia, as on the island of Bougainville in eastern Papua New Guinea. Bougainville has been the scene of considerable political agitation since the late 1960s, when negotiations began with local landowners to open the large Panguna copper and gold mine, which has since been a major source of revenue to the central and provincial governments. Disputes have continued to simmer over issues relating to the division of the mine's revenues, the influx of outsiders to work on the mine, and environmental problems. The tensions created by these disputes led to the founding of a cargo cult opposed to foreign business interests, to town life, to intermarriage with outsiders, to the established church, and to the central government. In mid-1989, cult members joined with political militant Francis Ona to launch attacks on the mine and mineworkers. The ensuing violence led the government to declare a state of emergency and to send in the army. Members of the cult were convinced that they could win the struggle, even against the army, because the ancestors with their "black power" would intervene on their behalf (see Albon 1989).

Religion and Revolution

The major religious traditions of large-scale societies—Christianity, Islam, and Buddhism, for example—encompass a wide range of beliefs that often are ambiguous, contradictory, and subject to differing interpretation. Such diversity allows the same religious traditions to serve both the interests of those concerned with preserving the status quo and the interests of those who desire reform or change. This situation is most apparent in the case of revolutionary movements.

Within any revolutionary setting, many religious leaders will be opposed to the threat of change. Such conservative tendencies are commonly singled out by revolutionaries and attacked, as they were, for example, by Marxists who proclaimed religion to be "the opiate of the masses." During the French Revolution in the late eighteenth century the church establishment that was associated with the aristocracy was strongly criticized by many revolutionaries, and church property was seized. Similar developments took place during the revolutions in Mexico and Russia in the early twentieth century.

Religious leaders and religious ideologies may, however, play an active and supportive role in the revolutionary process. This was true in Europe among radical clergy involved in the sixteenth-century Peasant Revolt in Germany and in the English Civil War of the seventeenth century. Radical clergy also were significant in the North American and South American wars against European colonial domination in the late eighteenth and early nineteenth centuries. As the social forces with which many of these religious ideas and movements were associated became dominant in their societies, the religions assumed a more conservative role in support of the new order.

Although revolutionary movements during this century initially exhibited considerable hos-

Influenced by the ideas of liberation theology, this priest says Mass in a warehouse occupied by striking Coca-Cola workers in Guatemala City.

tility to religion, over the past few decades religion has become important in revolutionary movements around the world. Two notable examples are liberation theology among Catholics and Islamic socialism in the Moslem world. *Islamic socialism* involves an attempt to bring about social justice based on the teachings of Islam. It has taken on various forms in particular national settings, including variants associated with the revolutionary Shiites in Iran (see Munson 1989) and Colonel Mu'ammar El Qaddafi in Libya (see First 1975). According to *liberation theology*, under conditions of widespread social and economic injustice, one must become committed to the political, even revolutionary, liberation of the oppressed (Ogden 1981). It emerged in the 1960s, under the influence of the reforms of Pope John XXIII, and has become an important and controversial force throughout the Third World (see Gheerbrant 1974; Mahan and Richesin 1981). In recent years, liberation theologists in Central America, such as Archbishop Oscar Romero (assassinated in 1980) and Ernesto Cardenal (Nicaragua's minister of culture in the Sandinista government), have received considerable attention.

In both Islamic socialism and liberation theology, religions that are major aspects of the cultural heritage of a people have come to serve as forces in revolution. Neither Islam nor Catholicism can be seen as having caused revolutions, but they have influenced the direction revolutionary movements have taken.

SUMMARY

Although religions, which assume the existence of supernatural forces or beings, are based on mystical understandings of the cosmos, their features can be analyzed on a down-to-earth anthropological level. Adherence to particular belief systems can be partially explained by local social processes, history, and environment. At the individual level, personal circumstances circumscribe the choice of a religion. For the society as a whole, the form of religion is often related to adaptational strategy; religious behaviors and beliefs are subject to change as the adaptational strategy shifts.

Symbols are often used as concrete expressions of the core elements of a religion. How people wear their hair, for instance, is often given symbolic religious significance. In many religious traditions, natural phenomena are seen as closely linked to humans within a totemic view of the cosmos.

Art, which reflects or interprets essential aspects of reality through aesthetic images, also is a common medium of religious symbolic expression. In most small-scale societies, and in many large-scale societies, artistic expression traditionally has been associated with religion. With the rise of capitalism and emergence of the modern world system, art has become increasingly secular.

Myths, which express the unobservable of religion in terms of the observable, are another way of linking the supernatural with the mundane. They may function as culture histories, as justification for the existing social order, or as attempts to deal with basic questions of the human condition from the society's point of view. In analyzing myths, we gain insight into how a social order works and how its contradictions are handled.

Religious traditions also include belief in supernatural beings. Many people believe in an all-encompassing unseen supernatural force. Often there are spirits, gods, and minor beings populating the cosmos.

Religious beliefs are presented in ways that have great emotional impact. Certain practices enhance a feeling of separation of the sacred from the secular; rituals repeat the basic messages of a belief system. Sometimes people seek experience of the supernatural by altering their state of consciousness. Hallucinogens are often employed in egalitarian societies that do not restrict access to sacred truths to a small elite.

Men and women who specialize in communications with the spirit world through trance are called shamans. Others who specialize in keeping religious laws and performing rituals usually do so part-time. Only large-scale societies with an extensive division of labor can afford full-time priests. Keepers of the law tend to be conservative upholders of a religious tradition, whereas prophets with visions of a new way are likely to encourage radical change. Even radical change, however, is shaped by the existing social order.

A religion may change as the culture itself does. Sometimes cultures slowly evolve from within; sometimes contact with or conquest by another culture brings change in religious beliefs. A conquered people may accept the conqueror's religion, assert their own, or join the two in a process known as syncretism. When conditions seem particularly bleak for an oppressed people, a millenarian movement may offer hope for a complete change. Religion may even play an important role in revolutionary movements.

SUGGESTED READINGS

Barrett, Leonard E. 1977. *The Rastafarians: The Dreadlocks of Jamaica.* Kingston: Sangster's/Heinemann.

Furst, Peter T., ed. 1972. *Flesh of the Gods: The Ritual Use of Hallucinogens.* London: Allen & Unwin.

Geertz, Clifford. 1960. *The Religion of Java.* Glencoe, IL: Free Press.

Keesing, Roger M. 1982. *Kwaio Religion.* New York: Columbia University Press. (Solomon Islands)

Lessa, William A., and Z. Evon Vogt, eds. 1979. *Reader in Comparative Religion.* 2d ed. New York: Harper & Row.

Lévi-Strauss, Claude. 1973. *Totemism.* Harmondsworth: Penguin.

Mooney, James. 1965. *The Ghost-Dance Religion and the Sioux Outbreak of 1890.* Chicago: University of Chicago Press.

Newell, William H., ed. 1976. *Ancestors.* The Hague/Paris: Mouton. (Ancestor worship)

Religious Pluralism in a Papua New Guinea Village

John Barker

John Barker is an anthropologist at the University of British Columbia in Vancouver, Canada. He lived in Papua New Guinea from late 1981 until 1983, and again in 1986, studying religious, aesthetic, and economic change among the Maisin people. Dr. Barker is the editor of Christianity in Oceania, a collection of ethnographic studies of Christianity in the Pacific Islands.

Journeying up the northeast coast of New Guinea in July 1907, the Anglican missionary Arthur Kent Chignell was delighted by the village of Uiaku. Distressed by the "semi-civilised" shabbiness of colonial towns and surrounding villages, he saw in Uiaku, by his account, "what I had hoped and expected to see—large villages and crowds of natives, dressed beautifully in native fashion." He went on to describe the setting of splendid tropical flora and towering golden mountains as one the likes of which he had never seen before "except in picture-books or dreams" (Chignell 1911, 17).

When Anne Tietjen and I stepped from a small boat to the beach at Uiaku in November 1981, we felt some of the same thrill that Chignell had experienced, despite the long passage of time. True, the Maisin people now wore European-style clothing and many were fluent in English, but Uiaku's isolation from the towns and roads of Papua New Guinea, its clean thatched houses and clear earth plazas, gave the place a pristine, "traditional" appearance. The Maisin graciously incorporated us into a daily rhythm of subsistence garden activities, punctuated by public ceremonies in which villagers exchanged exquisitely designed bark-cloth and adolescent girls had their faces elaborately tattooed. As our new friends told us of their encounters with ancestral spirits and of the need for constant vigilance against sorcerers, I was again reminded of Chignell's early impressions. Was this the same "pagan" religion he had hoped to replace with Christianity?

Even in Chignell's time, however, Uiaku had been intimately involved with a larger world. Situated at the center of Collingwood Bay, the four Maisin communities of around 1,500 people formed a hub in an extensive coastal and interior trading network in the precolonial days. Maisin initially welcomed European government officers, missionaries, and traders to their villages after 1890, but began to resist their presence as their numbers grew. In late 1900, a government patrol routed an ambush and shot dead six Maisin men. The following year, under conditions of enforced peace, the Anglican mission built a church and school in Uiaku.

Since this early defeat, the Maisin have consistently sought opportunities within the networks established by the colonial government and mission and their successors. By the 1920s, most villagers had accepted baptism and young men were routinely leaving their villages to work for 18-month stints at the distant plantation and mines. Following the Japanese invasion of 1942, most Maisin men served as laborers for the Allied forces. When the men returned, they formed councils to run the local church and to undertake economic development projects. They sent

Dancing on St. Thomas Day in Uiaku. Church holidays now provide the main occasions for dancing and community feasting in Maisin villages.

their children to new Anglican and government high schools and colleges to take advantage of the national employment opportunities opening up as the church and the government prepared for independence of Papua New Guinea from Australia. At the time of independence in 1975, the Maisin formed part of a small national elite, working as doctors, civil servants, priests, and business-people in the urban centers around the country.

The "traditional" appearance of Uiaku in 1981 was thus deceptive. While around 500 Maisin lived in the village, as many as 250 more lived and worked in distant urban centers. Family members who worked in the cities regularly sent money and desired commodities, such as clothing, fishing nets, and tinned food, back to the village. This steady flow of remittances may have actually subsidized customary activities. The steady outflow of educated Maisin from the village substantially reduced the workforce available to grow food and perform other necessary tasks. Money and commodities helped to make up for shortfalls in food from the gardens and wealth objects for exchanges.

By the same token, an exclusive focus on "traditional" religious ideas and such activities as mortuary ceremonies and shamanism would have resulted in a misleading impression of Maisin religion in the 1980s. When we lived with them, virtually all Maisin regarded themselves as Christians, and all villagers supported their church by donating money to pay the priest (a Papua New Guinean), by building and maintaining church buildings, by attending services, and by participating in church festivals—the major celebrations of the year. While the church services, which were performed largely in English, owed much more to the Church of England than to indigenous traditions, the Maisin did not regard them as foreign; they had all grown up in the church and most were second- and third-generation Christians. This was their church, a church they happened to share (as villagers told us) with millions of other members of the world-wide Anglican Communion. It was also a church they had successfully integrated with many of their own unique traditions.

For the Maisin, as for most of us, religion is a natural outgrowth of socialization. They also turn to religion in search of answers for what Max Weber called problems of meaning: Why do we die? Why does evil happen to good people? Also, just as the rest of us, the Maisin live in an increasingly pluralistic world; they are simultaneously members of clans, villages, Papua New Guinea, and world Christendom. People experience conundrums and crises at different levels of their social experience, and they typically respond to these problems of

meaning with corresponding types of religious action. Thus, when a young person suddenly died in the village, the Maisin understood the death and sought redress in terms of local beliefs concerning sorcery and spirit attacks. When a person became seriously ill, villagers approached both indigenous healers and Western specialists for help. They understood illness not only in terms of local beliefs, but in terms of Western beliefs as well. And in attempting to make sense of their community's situation in the wider world of nation-states, capitalism, and diverse ethnic groups, the villagers referred to their church and the Christian God. "Now that Europeans and Maisin are Christians," said one woman, the wife of a church teacher and herself a traditional healer, "we are brothers and sisters and our children can now marry one another." Christianity for Maisin involves the recognition that they are members of a wider world community—a community in which the differences and inequalities that separate cultures and races can be transcended through the sharing of a common morality and faith in a single deity. At the same time, the Maisin are aware and proud of their cultural distinctiveness, which they have successfully maintained since missionaries first landed on their shores a century ago.

22 Illness and Curing

A hospital serving a commune in Canton, in the People's Republic of China. Although this health-care setting provides a specialized locale for treatment and trained practitioners, it is backward by Western standards.

Illness is common to all human societies. However, the types of diseases that occur, how these diseases are treated, and how people regard illness vary considerably from society to society. In Western Europe and in North America, cancers are of major concern. In many tropical and subtropical regions, people worry more about such diseases as malaria, cholera, and dysentery. Treatment of illness in Western societies focuses on curing specific diseased organs or controlling a specific virus. In many non-Western societies, greater emphasis is placed on the social and psychological dimensions of illness.

Anthropologists emphasize that patterns of disease and methods of curing exist within particular physical and sociocultural settings. The medical systems of the United States and Nicaragua are as much a product of their respective environments as are the systems of Australian Aborigines and Amazonian Indians. By *medical system* we mean "the culturally based behavior and belief forms that arise in response to the threats posed by disease" (Foster and Anderson 1978, 33). Anthropologists study the medical systems of both small- and large-scale societies.

In studying medical systems, it is important to distinguish between disease and illness. **Disease** refers to a pathological condition of some part of the body in which functioning is disturbed or deranged. **Illness** is a cultural concept: a society's idea of pronounced deviation from what is considered a normal healthy state. Even though beliefs about disease and patterns of incidence may be viewed as sociocultural phenomena, diseases themselves are physiological conditions. Illness, on the other hand, is a broad concept referring to how people conceive of deviant mental and physical states.

EPIDEMIOLOGY

Epidemiology is a branch of medical science concerned with the factors that determine the frequency, distribution, and control of diseases in societies. On a worldwide basis, the leading categories of disease that people die from are cardiovascular, respiratory, infectious and parasitic, and cancerous types. However, if we compare more developed Western societies with poorer Third-World societies, we find significant differences in the relative frequencies of these types of disease. In developed Western countries, cardiovascular diseases remain the number-one killers; the number two spot is held by cancers, with communicable diseases being relatively insignificant. By contrast, communicable diseases are of considerable significance in Third-World countries. But even among developed societies, there are marked differences. While Scotland and Finland have the highest mortality rates from heart disease—over 700 and 600 deaths, respectively, per 100,000 population a year—the figure for France is just over 150, and for Japan only around 50.

Epidemiological patterns are also related to gender and age. Looking at mortality from heart disease again, in the United States and Canada, while the rate for men is in excess of 300 deaths per 100,000 population a year, for women it is only around 100 (a ratio that is relatively constant in other countries). In terms of age, heart disease is primarily a killer of adults. The epidemiological picture for children is different. Diarrhea is the leading cause of death among children worldwide (some 5 million a year), while it is responsible for relatively few adult deaths.

Whereas many of the disease-related deaths in the Third World can be linked to poverty and poor sanitary conditions, understanding patterns in developed countries is more complex. Why do more Scots die from heart disease than French people? Smoking, high blood pressure, and high cholesterol levels are often cited as major causes of heart disease. Thus, epidemiologists compare smoking and dietary habits of populations and measure the extent to which they are related to differing levels of heart disease. Recent studies, however, have pointed to personality type as an extremely important factor (Eysenck and Grossarth-Maticek 1989). Thus, the epidemiologist must study a complex set of cultural, social, and psychological variables to be able to interpret the different rates of death from heart disease.

One of the best-known examples of the contribution of anthropology to epidemiological research is the case of *kuru*, a disease of the central nervous system that was discovered in the 1950s among the South Fore of the eastern highlands of Papua New Guinea. No known treatment will cure or arrest kuru, which usually leads to death within 6 to 12 months. The disease was found to be unique to the South Fore, and among them it was limited to women, children, and occasionally young men.

Initial investigation revealed that kuru tended to follow family lines, but the cause of the disease remained elusive (Hunt 1978). The first break came when "slow virus infections" were identified as the result of studies with sheep and chimpanzees. Such diseases appear only after a long

A kuru victim is treated by "bleeding" by a medicine man (Papua New Guinea, 1962).

period of incubation. Kuru proved to be the first-known human disease caused by a slow-acting virus.

The discovery of the slow-acting virus failed to explain the epidemiological characteristics of kuru, however. Why was the disease limited to the South Fore, and why to only a limited segment of the population? Also, why had its incidence changed over time? The disease had first appeared during the early part of the twentieth century, becoming more frequent up to the late 1950s and declining thereafter. Anthropologists Robert and Shirley Glasse provided a clue to the mystery (see Lindenbaum 1979). They noted that cannibalism among South Fore women had

been introduced around 1910, roughly the same time that the disease first appeared. In particular, eating the brains of deceased kinswomen became part of the society's mourning ceremonies. The brains were prepared and eaten primarily by women, with small portions occasionally being given to children of both sexes. It was found that the virus was transmitted in the preparation; the women who touched the mucous membrane of the brains contracted the disease either through ingestion (see Gajdusek 1977) or through handling the corpses and then "rubbing the eyes and the eyes of children with contaminated hands" (Steadman and Merbs 1982, 619). The decline of kuru was linked to the cessation in the 1960s of this ritual cannibalism. In 1986, there were only six reported cases.

Endemic Diseases

A society's characteristic diseases are closely related to its physical environment as well as to its cultural practices. Part of a population's adaptation to a particular environment entails biocultural adjustment to the local disease-causing features. When the population and its adaptation are rather stable, relatively constant epidemiological patterns will emerge. One result is the development of **endemic diseases**. These diseases have a relatively low incidence but are constantly present in a given community. In our own society, they include the common cold, flu, and chicken pox.

Evidence indicates that during the thousands of years of our existence as foragers, disease patterns were fairly constant (Dunn 1968). The original immigrants to the New World carried few diseases with them, and in their isolation they developed tolerances for the limited selection of disease-causing agents in the New World. One of the endemic diseases to develop in the New World was syphilis. A syndrome of the worldwide disease treponematosis, syphilis evolved as a disease that was unique to the New World. Among New World inhabitants, it was not a particularly serious problem. Only after 1492, once it had spread to Europe and Asia (the first epidemic in Europe occurred in Italy in 1494 or 1495), did syphilis take on the more severe characteristics for which it has been known subsequently (Crosby 1972).

Epidemic Diseases

Migration and contact between previously isolated human populations are the prime causes of epidemics. An **epidemic disease** is not commonly present in a community; it is characterized by high incidence and rapid and extensive diffusion. Perhaps the most devastating series of epidemics in world history were those brought about by the opening of regular contact between the New World and Europe after 1492. The long isolation of the New World population made it especially vulnerable to diseases from outside. Smallpox was one of the leading killers. Endemic to the Old World, it was a steady, predictable killer, responsible for less than 10 percent of the yearly deaths in Europe. But among people with no previous contact, smallpox will infect nearly every individual. Within 10 years of its initial contact with Europeans, the population of central Mexico declined from 25 million to 16.8 million, primarily because of the direct and indirect effects of epidemic diseases such as smallpox.

Epidemics are not merely something of the past; nor are they something to which those in developed countries are immune. One disease that has been spreading at an epidemic rate in recent years, especially in developed countries, is skin cancer (malignant melanoma and squamous-cell skin cancer). There were an estimated 500,000 new cases of skin cancer in the United States in 1987, and the number could soon be in the millions. The epidemic has been linked to both environmental and cultural factors. In 1922, fashion figure Coco Chanel returned to Paris from a holiday "beautifully tanned." Before long, the lily-white look was out and tanned skin, which until then had been frowned upon and linked with manual outdoor labor, was in. Since then, the popularity of tanning in the West has increased dramatically and even came to be associated with good health, although it is now known to be a cause of skin cancer. In addition to fashion trends, environmental changes also have contributed to the rise of skin cancer—primarily a thinning of the ozone layer, due mainly to chemical pollution.

Easily the most highly publicized modern epidemic is associated with AIDS (Acquired Immune Deficiency Syndrome), largely a sexually transmitted disease and fatal. The earliest known AIDS virus was found in Zaire in 1959. The disease spread as a "silent epidemic" in the 1970s, gaining public awareness only in the 1980s. Of the more than 150,000 officially reported cases of

AIDS in some 120 countries in 1989, about 90,000 were in the United States (with just over 2,000 in Canada). By the mid-1990s, AIDS will probably cause more deaths in the United States than any other disease.

Because of the stigma attached to the disease and technical problems in testing for it, official figures indicating the incidence of AIDS must be viewed cautiously. Unofficial estimates are nearly twice the official figures. Taking Zambia as an example, sensitive to the country's international image, the government refused to recognize the

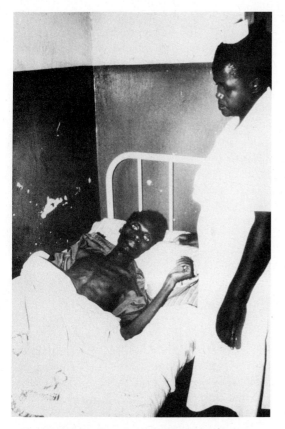

The worldwide epidemic associated with AIDS has hit the people of sub-Saharan Africa particularly hard, placing a strain on already inadequate health-care facilities and threatening to cause economic havoc.

disease until 1986. A major change in government policy occurred the following year, when one of President Kenneth Kuanda's sons died of AIDS. But official figures for Zambia still do not reflect the true picture. In 1989 there were still only 1,300 reported AIDS cases, while semiofficial estimates ran as high as 70,000. Moreover, as many as 350,000 people are believed to be carriers of the virus—out of a total national population of 7 million.

Anthropologists and other social scientists are not interested solely in the relationship of sociocultural factors and disease; they are also concerned with the social consequences of diseases. Severe epidemics affect societies profoundly. For example, a popular theory argues that the sixteenth-century collapse of the various indigenous empires in the New World, such as those of the Aztec and Inca, was caused primarily by the ravages of newly introduced epidemic diseases. The more subtle effects of diseases are also significant. Endemic malaria in a region may kill only a small percentage of the population, but it debilitates a much larger proportion, contributing to a general malaise that adversely affects all aspects of life.

Diseases of Development

Charles Hughes and John Hunter (1972) coined the term "diseases of development" to refer to "those pathological conditions which are based on the usually unanticipated consequences of the implementation of development schemes" (p. 93). Such diseases can be divided into three general categories. First, there are those diseases that result from integration into large-scale industrial societies: diabetes, obesity, hypertension, and so on. For example, the people of Nauru experienced a dramatic increase in disposable wealth in the 1960s and even more of an increase in the 1970s as a result of increased earnings from phosphate mining on their isolated South Pacific island (Howard 1987). With this new-found wealth came a rise in food consumption (virtually all food being imported and much of it high in sugar and salt content and low in nutritious value), reaching an estimated daily average of around 6,000 calories per person. By 1983, out of a total population of some 5,000 Nauruans, about 400 were known to be suffering from diabetes, and the actual figure was probably much higher. Obesity appears to be a precipitating factor in adults with a tendency toward diabetes. If neglected, diabetes can result in such complications as respiratory diseases, heart ailments, kidney diseases, blindness, gangrene, stillbirths, and congenital abnormalities. When the government of Nauru launched a program of medical check-ups for those suffering from diabetes in 1983, some individuals had already become too ill to travel to the hospital on their own.

In the second category are bacterial and parasitic diseases, introduced or augmented by changes in the physical environment. For example, onchocerciasis (African river blindness) is a disease that traditionally has affected the population living in the Volta River basin in West Africa. Carried by a tiny blackfly, it results in reduced vision or blindness. In 1974 and 1975, the disease, which had been present in Mexico since the 1940s, was reported to be spreading throughout the northwestern part of the Amazonian Basin in South America (Davis 1977). The indigenous population of the region proved particularly susceptible. Among some groups of Yanomami, up to 100 percent of the population became infected. Two American scientists, Robert Goodland and Howard Irwin (1975), found that the blackfly population was thriving in the cleared areas along the newly constructed Northern Perimeter Highway, which penetrated the territories of these indigenous groups.

The third category includes diseases that result from poverty, undernourishment, and poor sanitation, reflecting a failure of development programs to integrate people into large-scale societies in a satisfactory manner.

Diseases of development present difficult problems. Understanding the causes of the diseases helps to solve some of these problems, and anthropology plays an important role in analyzing the complex social, cultural, and natural factors that influence diseases. However, diseases such as diabetes or onchocerciasis will not be eliminated simply through the development of wonder drugs or spraying with pesticides. Finding cures can result only from a willingness to see the disease in its total context.

MALNUTRITION

Hundreds of millions of people are undernourished; thus, understanding the causes of malnutrition and finding solutions to this problem are among the most important challenges facing scientists today. Minor cases of malnutrition can impair people's ability to perform normal daily tasks. Malnutrition also reduces resistance to disease. More severe cases of malnutrition can lead to permanent brain damage or to death. The causes of malnutrition are both cultural and social. They are related to people's ideas about what they eat (what they consider desirable food) and to social factors (such as economic impoverishment), influencing what people can eat and how much.

Malnutrition and Subsistence Patterns

In his research on hunter-gatherers, Frederick Dunn (1968) cited numerous studies indicating the relatively good nutritional status of more traditional foraging societies. Hunger was rare among these societies, and their diets usually met their nutritional needs. The same was true for small-scale farming societies where adequate land was available. In both cases, periodic hunger might have occurred as a result of natural disasters, but hunger resulting from the pressures of overpopulation usually was avoided by migration or innovation.

The extent to which malnutrition exists today among foraging societies is mainly a result of their competition for resources with nonforagers and their disadvantageous integration into modern states. In a study of nutrition among Australian Aborigines living at the Edward River settlement of the Cape York Peninsula, John Taylor (1977) noted that since giving up their traditional nomadic existence in the 1950s, the Aborigines' diet has been characterized by shortcomings in most important nutrients. The postsettlement diet of most rural-dwelling Aborigines consists of damper (flour and water), sweet black tea, and occasionally meat. Such a diet is particularly lacking in protein, calcium, vitamin A, and vitamin C. It provides poor nourishment, especially during pregnancy, resulting in newborns of less than optimal weight and impaired resistance to disease. Health problems continue through the life cycle, and Aborigines today have higher disease and death rates than do other Australians.

Perhaps the most significant finding of Taylor's study, however, is that improvement in economic conditions for the Edward River Aborigines has not resulted in dietary improvements. In fact, just the opposite. Increased earnings have been diverted toward satisfying demands for nonfood consumer items rather than being used for food. One problem is that Aborigines think their diet is adequate: the flour and tea are, after all, filling. As a result of their dietary outlook and these economic changes, the nutrition of the people has deteriorated to the point where some people are unconsciously starving themselves, even though their material well-being seems to have improved.

For many small-scale farming societies, nutritional problems begin to emerge as they are integrated into large-scale market economies. As peasant agriculturalists, they find a large percentage of what they produce usurped by nonagriculturalists, and what they retain plus the payment they receive for their product is rarely sufficient to meet their nutritional requirements. Their diet begins to suffer in both quantity and quality. Protein intake, in particular, tends to be

greatly reduced. The protein intake of most rural peasants in Ecuador, for example, is less than half of that of the Achuara Jivaro, who maintain something of their traditional subsistence adaptation in the eastern jungles of the country.

Modern agricultural techniques of large-scale societies are able to produce a tremendous amount of food, but there are also a lot of people to feed. In many Third-World countries, it is difficult simply to keep up with population growth, despite innovations that increase productivity. Often, however, the problem is not just a matter of producing enough food. Third-World countries also face infrastructural problems in storing, preserving, and distributing food. In addition, problems are exacerbated by relative socioeconomic inequality. And this is not a problem faced by poorer countries alone. In the United States, a nation with an abundant supply of food and an overfed and overweight middle and upper class, there are also millions of undernourished people occupying the lower economic rungs of society.

Cultural Perceptions of Food

Malnutrition also can develop in the midst of plenty because what people are willing to eat is largely a matter of cultural definition. Not only do relatively poor and uneducated people, such as the Aboriginal inhabitants of Edward River, remain unaware that their diet is lacking in vital nutrients; the same can be said of many educated and affluent North Americans.

In every society, people designate certain items as "food" from a range of edible plant and animal matter. People of other cultures include in their diet things that most Westerners would never consider eating; for example, dogs, commonly eaten in parts of East Asia and the Pacific. (Ishige {1977} provides a Ponapean recipe for roasting dogs in an earth oven.) Less obvious are numerous nutritious insects and "weeds." They are plentiful enough, but because they are not considered food, people will go hungry or even starve while living in what members of many tra-

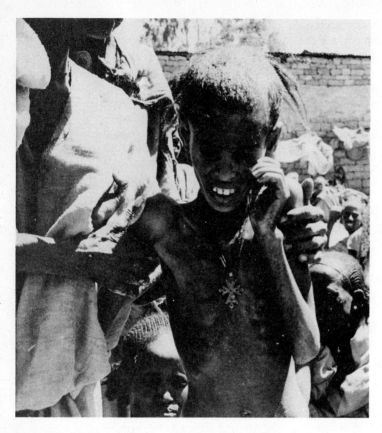

Human and environmental factors have combined to produce a famine in Ethiopia that has threatened millions of lives.

ditional foraging societies would consider a veritable supermarket.

Trying to change people's notions about food is a very difficult task; improving their dietary habits is rarely as simple as providing alternative types of food. We all know how little good it does to tell a child (or adult, for that matter), "Here, eat this, it's good for you." Cross-cultural innovations may be even more difficult, especially when there are existing prejudices against foods ("We feed that to pigs!"). Furthermore, schemes to boost nutrition through food innovations may in fact result in a lowering of nutritional standards because of the context within which the innovation is attempted. For example, Third-World programs to promote the use of dietary formulas for infants by transnational corporations such as Nestlé often have resulted in health problems because of the lack of education, the poverty, and the unhygienic surroundings of many mothers.

MENTAL ILLNESS

All peoples recognize illnesses that take the form of mental states perceived as abnormal. **Mental illness** includes disorders caused by physiological conditions as well as those caused by unsatisfactory adaptations to sociocultural conditions at the individual level. In the latter case, mental illness is associated with stress in coping with the environment.

Stress is a feature of life in all societies. It may result from such natural events as earthquakes or volcanic eruptions, or it may be induced intentionally, as in torture. It may also be a "normal" part of the life cycle, such as the stresses caused by births, deaths, marriages, and the like. Beyond this are the stresses that arise from the nature of our society—those caused by commuting, unemployment, and overwork.

Patterns of Stress Disorders

After decades of research on mental illness in different cultures, it now appears that the major patterns of mental illness known to Western psychiatrists are universal (J.G. Kennedy 1973). However, since patterns of stress-producing situ-

ations will vary from one setting to another and because cultural methods of dealing with stress differ, the distribution of forms of mental illness varies among societies. Physical surroundings, economic conditions, childrearing practices, religious traditions, and so forth, all combine to produce particular patterns of stress. It is thus possible (although difficult) to study mental illness from an epidemiological perspective: to note distributional patterns and search for variables in the environment that appear to influence such patterns.

In addition to universal forms of mental illness, there are unique configurations that result

---

Life in slums such as this one in Port-au-Prince, Haiti, is difficult, often leading to both physical and mental health problems.

from particular environments and cultural traditions. These are commonly referred to as *culture-bound syndromes*. Among these disorders are "Arctic hysteria," found among a number of circumpolar peoples; "running amok," a frenzied violent behavior of males in certain Asian societies (see Spores 1988); and "koro," a fear among Chinese that the penis or breasts and vulva will withdraw into the body. While most of these disorders are based on universal forms of mental illness, they have taken on certain unique characteristics as well.

Arctic hysteria is marked by periods of silence followed by seizures, in which the individual typically tears off his or her clothing, takes flight, and runs about in the snow. Arctic hysteria is a variant of the universal condition known as agoraphobia (a morbid fear of being in an open space), but with characteristics unique to the arctic environment and Inuit culture. Thus, Edward Foulks (1985) writes: "While Arctic hysteria can be partially understood in universal psychological terms, a more complete understanding is offered by consideration of the unique framework of Eskimo culture" (p. 307). Anthony Wallace (1972) noted the important role of calcium deficiency in bringing on Arctic hysteria. Climatic factors also are important because winter conditions serve to intensify insecurity.

Studies of Arctic hysteria conducted by Foulks (1985) have provided insights into how such syndromes are influenced by culture change. Behavioral stress among Inuit today is associated with the consumption of alcohol. Foulks identified a traditional segment of Inuit society that exhibited a transformed version of Arctic hysteria involving the use of alcohol; others exhibited behavior patterns characteristic of the urban United States.

Social Change and Stress

Rapid social change is a primary source of stress for many people. Often such stress is temporary, but it may be sufficient to cause severe mental disorders. Migration commonly results in considerable stress. In an early study, Margaret Mead (1947) pointed out that migrants are frequently culturally disoriented and subject to special strains; at the same time, they are without the accustomed means of reducing tensions. The problem may be even worse if the migrant must make difficult physiological adjustments. Peruvian Indians moving to the coastal city of Lima from the Andes are not only faced with social and cultural problems of adjustment, but also have difficulty adjusting to the higher oxygen content at the lower elevation. The combination of factors results in a syndrome characterized by anxiety and depression, as well as by a number of circulatory, respiratory, neurological, and gastrointestinal symptoms during the initial period of their stay in Lima (Fried 1959).

Migration and other forms of rapid social change can result in a state of **anomie**: disorganization of personality and a feeling of alienation. In his famous study of suicide, Emile Durkheim (1951) described anomie as resulting from the abandonment of community goals and of the social rules for reaching them. In small, closely knit rural communities, people's lives tend to be highly organized and closely regulated. There are constraints, but there is also a sense of security. Movement to the city may liberate a person from many of the constraints of rural life, but suddenly the individual is faced with living in a very unfamiliar environment, with no sure way of finding happiness in this new setting.

For many indigenous peoples around the world, rapid social change has meant the destruction of the existing social order, and, all too often, its replacement with a social order based on impoverishment and exploitation. The psychological consequences often are great, sometimes resulting in suicide or loss of a will to live. For those who persist, the stress of life under new conditions still may lead to mental illnesses that blend characteristics of disorders associated with the old and the new cultural patterns.

CONCEPTS OF ILLNESS CAUSALITY

The ways in which people attempt to cure a perceived illness are based on their notions of what caused it. Such ideas vary widely. Within large-scale societies there are many beliefs, reflecting the complexity of the societies (see Worsley 1982, 339–346).

Mind–Body Dualism

Western medical traditions make a distinction between illnesses originating in the mind and those originating in the body; that is, between psychological and physiological illnesses. Other traditions take a more holistic approach, viewing health and illness as manifestations of the totality of a person's life. For instance, most non-Western medical systems do not have a separate category for "mental illness." Mental illness and physiological illness in such systems are placed in the same general category. To the Azande of the southern Sudan, mental illnesses are viewed in much the same way as malaria and smallpox, and all kinds of illness are believed to be ultimately caused by sorcery. Categorical distinctions between mental and physiological illness by Western medical traditions are in part a reflection of greater specialization (occupational and otherwise).

The traditional mind–body division of Western medicine increasingly has been called into question by Western medical practitioners themselves, who now recognize the close relationship between psychological and physiological disorders. Thus, on the one hand, it is now apparent that many physiological illnesses (such as cancer) are related to psychological problems influenced by the environment. On the other hand, research has shown that many psychological disorders are influenced by biochemical factors. These psychological disorders include some forms of depression, "possession," and perhaps schizophrenia.

Personalistic versus Naturalistic Explanations

Not until after the sixteenth century did modern scientific concepts of disease causality begin to develop. In many parts of the world people still adhere to alternative beliefs. Although these beliefs differ markedly from one another, there appear to be basic principles common to many of them. In very broad terms, Foster and Anderson (1978) have identified two major belief systems of disease causality: personalistic and naturalistic.

In a **personalistic system**, illness is thought to be purposefully caused by a supernatural being (such as a ghost or evil spirit) or a human being (such as a witch or sorcerer). Personalistic belief systems are found in small-scale societies throughout much of sub-Saharan Africa, throughout the Pacific Islands, and among tribal peoples in eastern Asia. According to this system, the sick person is a victim—the object of personally directed aggression or punishment. Such a belief system lacks a concept of accident. If a person falls from a tree and dies, it is assumed that some person or some being caused the death. This is not to say that people subscribing to such beliefs do not recognize more immediate causes of illness or injury, but they believe that there are other forces at work beyond the more apparent ones. The Azande exemplify this type of thinking:

> Azande attribute sickness, whatever its nature, to witchcraft or sorcery. This does not mean that they entirely disregard secondary causes but, insofar as they recognize these, they generally think of them as associated with witchcraft and magic. Nor does their reference of sickness to supernatural causes lead them to neglect treatment of symptoms any more than their reference of death on the horns of a buffalo to witchcraft causes them to await its onslaught. On the contrary, they

possess an enormous pharmacopoeia . . . and in ordinary circumstances they trust drugs to cure their ailments and only take steps to remove the primary and supernatural causes when the disease is of a serious nature or takes an alarming turn. Nevertheless, we must remember in describing the Azande classification of diseases and their treatment that the notion of witchcraft as a participant in their origin may always be expressed, and that if Azande do not always and immediately consult their oracles to find out the witch that is responsible it is because they consider the sickness to be of a minor character and not worth the trouble and expense of oracle consultation. (Evans-Pritchard 1937, 479)

By contrast, **naturalistic systems** explain illness in impersonal terms, attributing good health to the maintenance of equilibrium within the body. Illness results when the balance is upset by such natural external forces as heat or cold or internal forces, such as strong emotions. Most contemporary naturalistic systems are derived largely from the medical traditions of ancient classical civilizations, particularly those of Greece, India, and China. Thus, some systems are based on the concept of *bodily humors,* a belief that originated in ancient Greece. The Greeks believed that there were four humors, or fluids, in the body: blood, phlegm, black bile (or melancholy), and yellow bile (or choler). Each humor was associated with certain qualities: blood with heat and moisture, phlegm with cold and moisture, black bile with cold and dryness, and yellow bile with heat and dryness. Illness or suffering resulted when one of these humors was either deficient or excessive, or if the humors failed to mix properly. Curing was largely a matter of restoring the balance.

In a contemporary Latin American variant of humoral pathology, illness is ascribed to an imbalance of heat and cold. This may be related to the actual temperatures of substances with which one comes into contact (such as water, air, and food), but more often actual temperature is not important, "hot" and "cold" being cultural categories. Foods are especially important in maintaining a balance between hot and cold, and the system classifies foods according to their "temperature." According to Margaret Clark (1970), in one Mexican-American community, white beans, garlic, and chili peppers are considered to be "very hot"; salt, pork, and onions to be "hot"; corn tortillas, lamb, and radishes to be "cold"; and cucumbers and tomatoes to be "very cold." Illness is often attributed to eating an excess of hot or cold foods, and curing commonly entails eating things that will restore the balance.

Beliefs in disease causality are rarely so rigid as to ascribe all illness or misfortune to a single cause. Even the Azande do not ascribe certain diseases that afflict infants exclusively to witchcraft or magic. In fact, their ideas about the causes of these diseases are fairly vague. In part, this reflects the status of infants in Azande society. There is a very high infant mortality rate, and small children are barely considered social beings, their life at this time being very tenuous.

CURING

How people attempt to cure illness primarily reflects social and cultural factors rather than any inherent properties of the illness itself. It is not surprising that cultural beliefs about causality influence how people set about to treat illnesses. If an imbalance of humors is seen as the cause, then the cure will rest in trying to effect a balance. The Aztec believed that headaches were caused by excessive blood in the head. Curing therefore involved the use of medicines that produced violent sneezing and nosebleeds to remove the excess blood. If this approach failed, they would remove more blood by making an incision with an obsidian point (Ortiz de Montellano 1977). If the cause of an illness is believed to be bacteria or other microorganisms, the cure will probably include use of antibiotics. If sorcery is to blame, something may have to be done about the sorcerer.

The Effectiveness of Cures

Assessing the effectiveness of different curing systems is not as simple as it might seem. All healing systems seem to work at least part of the time, and all have rationales to explain their failures. Moreover, because of the psychological and cultural dimension of illness and curing, just because a cure does not work in one culture does not mean that it might not be effective in another. When an Aboriginal inhabitant of Welles-

ley Island in northern Australia comes down with *malgri*, an illness characterized by drowsiness and abdominal pain, said to be brought on by concern over violation of food taboos, the Aboriginal curer kneels and begins massaging sweat from his armpit into the victim's body. A belt of grass or hair then is unraveled and tied to the person's foot. The cord is run down to the water to point the way home for the intruding spirit. The curer begins to sing, continuing into the night until a shooting star (the incarnation of the malgri's eye) is seen, indicating the disposition and banishment of the spirit. The cord is then snapped and the victim recovers (Cawte 1974). It is doubtful that this cure would work on someone in our own culture suffering from simi-

Two curers attend an old man who is complaining of a headache (Jigalong, Western Australia).

lar symptoms, nor would it necessarily be effective if the patient were suffering from some disease with similar symptoms, but it does work for this specific illness.

All curing systems are able to treat at least some illnesses, but this does not imply that all systems are equally effective. Clearly, some cures work better than others, and some cures in fact do not work. But assessing cures from one system to the next is not an easy matter, and experience has taught many Western medical practitioners not to dismiss the curative capabilities of other systems out of hand. It was not so long ago that Western doctors scoffed at the claims of acupuncture, which is now widely judged in the West to be an effective treatment for many diseases. Likewise, Western scientists are giving more attention to the medicines employed by many so-called primitive medical systems. Many of the plants and potents used in these systems may be of little value, but some of them are effective; in fact, many have provided Western researchers with valuable information in developing modern drugs.

The ambiguity that exists in all curing systems and the number of systems available create both difficulties and opportunities for healer and patient. For someone trying to cure a patient, diagnosis and an appropriate cure are rarely automatic, and there is always the possibility of error. Failure to arrive at a successful cure may be attributed to the nature of the affliction or to a lack of skill on the part of the curer. More rarely, the effectiveness of the curing system may be questioned. If more than one curing system is available, the patient can resort to an alternative system if the first one fails. In fact, there are many instances of individuals who have been cured only after turning to another system. However, searching for cures across systems also leaves the sufferer vulnerable to "quacks." Most medical systems recognize the possibility of charlatanism, although it is more commonly acknowledged in large-scale societies. These societies have the means to set scientific standards, but such standards do not necessarily apply across systems.

Health-Care Delivery Systems

The social components of curing include aspects of the overall social structure that influence the curing process and, more specifically, what may be referred to as the *health-care delivery system* (Colson and Selby 1974). A health-care delivery system mobilizes resources to care for those who are ill. Patient, curer, and auxiliary personnel all have role expectations. The system also includes available or appropriate technology and the physical setting within which the curing process takes place.

Health-care systems may prescribe different settings for treatment of the ill, and within the same system settings may vary. There are two dimensions to the question of setting: privacy and specialization. Among the Azande, diagnosis takes place in public. Heralded and accompanied by drums, diagnoses of patients are considered "local events of some importance," drawing spectators from throughout the neighborhood (Evans-Pritchard 1937, 154). Hausa barber-surgeons in Ibadan, Nigeria, place their operating tables under a tree in public view (Maclean 1971). By contrast, in Western medical systems a premium is placed on privacy for both diagnosis and treatment.

In many non-Western settings, curing takes place in a nonspecialized locale, such as the village center or the patient's or curer's own home. Among the Maya of southern Belize, patients traditionally often moved into the home of the curer for the duration of their treatment, sometimes bringing their entire family with them. Curing in a Western medical system often takes place in a specialized setting, such as a hospital. Hospitals have evolved into very complex institutions, functioning as small societies with many of their own cultural attributes. Thus, hospitals can be studied in much the same way as we would study a Mayan village or a South Sea island, with attention to the interplay between the external environment and the local hospital community (see Freidson 1970).

In addition to prescribing the appropriate setting for curing, every society recognizes only a limited number of people who are able to treat illnesses. Contrary to popular belief, the practice of medicine is probably the oldest profession, as well as the most universal. The role of the curer, however, varies from one society to the next. In societies with personalistic views of disease causality, there is a need for someone who is able to determine who caused an affliction and why—usually someone with ties to the supernatural. In such societies the curer usually is a shaman, sorcerer, or "witch doctor." On the other hand, societies with naturalistic beliefs require "doctors" who have learned curing skills through practice and observation of illnesses and the properties of medicines.

In most small-scale societies, curing is not a full-time vocation. There is simply not enough work, and the curer generally will engage in the same primary economic activities as other members of the society—hunting or farming—much of the time. In large-scale societies, curing is more often a full-time occupation.

Most societies also recognize specialization within the medical profession. Although by far the greatest degree of specialization occurs in Western medical systems, even very small non-Western societies may have different types of curers (see Worsley 1982). Peasants in the Philippines recognize midwives, bonesetters, and general practitioners (Lieban 1962). The Maya of southern Belize divide medical roles according to level of skill and specialty. At the lower level of skill are midwives and snakebite doctors. At higher levels there are several grades of general practitioner.

Analysis of curers requires attention not only to their roles, but also to other career-related factors, such as recruitment, training, and reputation. In personalistic systems, recruitment may be by personal dream or by physical affliction, such as epilepsy. Recruitment in other instances may be linked to the would-be curer's personal inclination, ability, or social status. In some cases, only the children of curers can become curers, or recruitment may be limited to members of cer-

tain socioeconomic classes. Often a combination of these factors is necessary.

For shamans or sorcerers who engage in curing, training may be transmitted via dreams induced by supernatural beings. In many systems, a period of apprenticeship is involved, sometimes lasting for a number of years. At the end of the training period, there is commonly a rite of passage. From Eric Thompson (1930), we have the following account of the training and initiation of a Mayan curer in southern Belize:

> The instructor and the initiate retire to a hut in the bush for a month so that there may be no eavesdropping. During this period the initiate is taught by his master all the different prayers and practices used in causing and curing sickness. At the end of that period the initiate is sent to meet Kisin {a deity}. Kisin takes the form of a large snake called Ochcan (otskan), which is described as being very big, not poisonous and having a large shiny eye. When the initiate and the ochcan meet face to face, the latter rears up on his tail, and approaching the initiate till their faces are almost touching, puts his tongue in the initiate's mouth. In this manner he communicates the final mysteries of sorcery. (pp. 68–69)

Although this initiation may be somewhat more dramatic than graduation from a Western medical school, the result is much the same: the legitimacy of the curer is sanctioned by those who set professional standards.

The ability of a curer to continue working is in large part a matter of reputation. Curers generally must have a good record, although within any system a good public relations effort can compensate for a lack of success in curing patients. All systems have norms regarding appropriate "bedside manner" which play an important part in assessment of the curer. Success as a physician can have its pitfalls, however. Inuit shamans and Western surgeons alike run the risk of negative sanctions resulting from the envy of others or feelings that they have too much wealth or power.

In addition to the chief curers, health-care systems often include auxiliary personnel, who assist in the treatment process. In Western systems, these include nurses, orderlies, and assorted administrators. In non-Western systems, assistance may be provided by an apprentice or by readily available nonspecialists. Assistants among the Azande may include musicians or chanters, who provide an accompaniment to the curer's activities.

The other essential participant in any health-care system is the patient; patients, too, are expected to conform to behavioral norms. One of the most important parts of any health-care system is the interaction between the patient and those responsible for his or her treatment—an interaction based on the patient's belief in the healers' power to diagnose and cure and on the mutual understanding of what should take place. The significance of such interaction becomes especially clear when patient and curer come from different sociocultural backgrounds and communication is impaired. Among the Bomvana Xhosa of southern Africa, the diviner starts the consultation by intuitively guessing what the illness is:

> He is not supposed to take "the medical history" by interviewing the patient and/or his relatives. On the contrary, he is the one who has to give answers to all the questions about the patient and the causes of his disease. (Jansen 1973, 43)

Thus, when a Xhosa patient is confronted with a Western-trained doctor's "What seems to be the matter?" the patient usually is puzzled. It is the doctor, not the patient, who is supposed to answer that question.

An important part of disease treatment in contemporary societies involves promoting public awareness of the nature of diseases and their cures. Screening clinics, educational programs,

and advertising campaigns are used in this regard. To be effective, such programs must be sensitive to the cultures of those to whom they are addressed. Thus, in campaigning against the spread of AIDS, public-health workers have had to take into account how people of different cultures view sex and what they consider appropriate ways of discussing sexual matters. One Swedish campaign against AIDS features a bikini-clad woman in a "love bus" going about dispensing brochures, T-shirts with slogans, and condoms. Such an approach clearly would not be appropriate in many cultures. In the case of Uganda, priests and even the president have sought to fight the epidemic by exhorting people to limit their sexual partners. An anti-AIDS advertisement in Australia aimed at Aborigines contained the following dialogue: "What's this AIDS? This a white man's disease?" Response: "Hah! AIDS is a killer, like the pox, VD. Once yah got it, you're dead."

The Costs of Health Care

Whereas the discovery of miraculous cures used to be the primary focus of attention in Western medicine, in the past 20 or 30 years the cost of medical care increasingly has been in the limelight. Medical care costs something in all societies; what it costs, how costs are determined, who pays, and how the payment is distributed vary. Whether Western-trained physicians or African witch-doctors, curers expect some compensation for their services. Even in societies relatively poor in material goods, treatments can be expensive. Among the Inuit of North America, payment traditionally ranged from the offering of a wife or daughter as a sexual partner, when the shaman was a man, to the gift of an *umiak* (a boat), a substantial fee (Spencer 1959).

Curers are not always wealthy, however. Part-time curers in the Mayan community of Zinacantan in southern Mexico receive only a bottle or two of rum, a few tortillas or a loaf of bread, and a chicken or two for their work. Fabrega and Silver (1973) found that the incomes of Zinacantan curers were roughly the same as those of other villagers, the primary difference being that the payments received by the curers were not in a form that could be used readily for commercial purposes. As a result, many of the curers were among the poorest people in the village; generally, only poor people became full-time curers because of the lack of economic rewards.

In small-scale societies and many non-Western health-care systems, most of the cost of being cured involves the curer's fee. But in Western health-care systems, the curer's fee may, in fact, be only a small part of the overall cost. Greater specialization has meant that a wider range of auxiliary personnel must be paid for. There is also the cost of maintaining the more elaborate settings for curing—hospitals, doctors' offices, clinics, and so on. Then there is the costly research and technology that is the cornerstone of modern Western medicine. Finally, there is the cost of the medicine itself. Rather than the curer using locally available herbs and other medicines on the basis of knowledge and traditions built up over generations at minimal cost to society or the patient, Western medical practitioners rely on medicines produced by other specialists. Western medicine devotes great effort and expense to research in developing new medicines (sometimes derived from traditional non-Western medicines) and to marketing these medicines. All these factors have combined to make Western medicine an extremely costly undertaking. The ability and willingness to devote so many resources to curing are a part of the adaptational strategy of a modern society.

The costliness of Western medicine is of great concern to poorer, underdeveloped countries. The high cost of training medical personnel is a particularly thorny issue because such expensively trained people often seek employment in developed countries, where they hope to earn more money. There is also the cost of building and maintaining hospitals and clinics. While it may be possible to find donors willing to finance the construction of such buildings, the cost of maintaining them usually falls on the recipient country, which may have great difficulty obtaining the necessary capital.

The price of medicine, most of which is produced and sold by a few large multinational firms, is another issue. A number of Third-World countries and researchers have accused these firms of pushing drugs that are overly expensive, useless, and in some cases known to be harmful. There are numerous instances where, in order to boost sales, even potentially beneficial drugs are wrongly promoted by pharmaceutical companies in the Third World, with serious consequences. Silverman, Lee, and Lydecker (1982) refer to "the bribery, the mislabeling, and the medically unjustified overpromotion" of drugs by such companies in the Third World (p. xi). They cite, for example, the antibiotic chloramphenicol. Chloramphenicol has proven to be very successful in treating many serious diseases that plague poorer countries (such as typhoid fever). In the United States, Canada, and other developed countries, physicians are warned not to use the drug in the treatment of trivial infections because of its potentially harmful side effects. By contrast, in many Third-World countries, recommendations for its use are extremely broad, and few or no warnings are provided concerning its potential dangers. This has served to boost sales of the drug but has also led to its overuse, if not abuse, in treating many minor diseases.

Muller (1982) has pointed to the need for Third-World countries to use drugs that are both more effective and "efficient"; that is, drugs that people can afford. Governments and organizations in countries such as Bangladesh, India, Mexico, and Mozambique have dealt with this situation by attempting to reduce dependency on drugs produced by foreign firms by developing their own pharmaceutical industries, tightening controls on the marketing of drugs, and exploring uses of existing traditional medicines (see Melrose 1982). Success in these efforts remains limited, however.

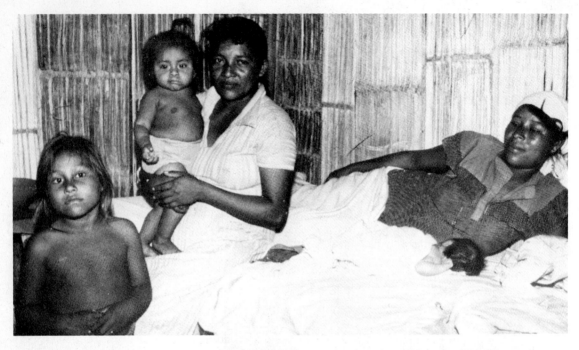

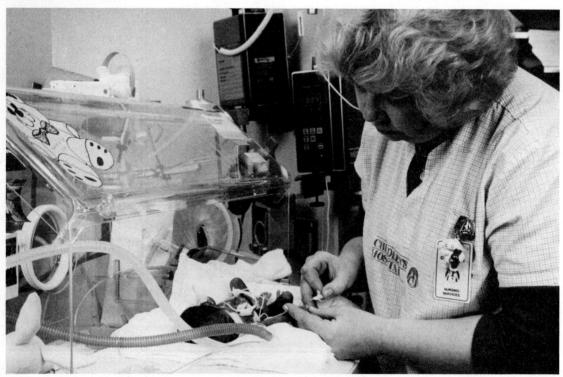

(opposite) The quality of a country's medical facilities depends largely on its wealth, just as the quality of personal health care often depends on one's ability to pay. These two childbirth sites—a health-care center in Nicaragua (top) and a high-tech center in the United States (bottom)—contrast drastically in the quality of service they are able to provide.

Western medical technology poses a problem in terms of cost, appropriateness, and dependency. Poorer tropical countries often have difficulty maintaining expensive equipment that has little tolerance for the added strains of heat, humidity, and an undependable supply of electricity. These things can be dealt with, but often only at a great deal of added expense. The question of dependency has both an economic and a political dimension. For example, Nicaragua found itself in a desperate situation when the Reagan administration imposed an economic embargo in the early 1980s because virtually all its medical technology came from the United States (H. Williams 1984). While Third-World elites can go to developed countries for treatment requiring expensive technology, this is not an option for the majority of people. Thus, such countries as India are seeking ways of overcoming this problem by developing their own technologies and exploring alternatives.

SUMMARY

Illness and disease cannot be understood outside their cultural context. Epidemiologists working from an anthropological perspective have helped to explain the occurrence of mysterious diseases, such as kuru. They have shown how environmental factors are linked to the incidence of both endemic and epidemic diseases. The environmental context is also critical to an understanding of "diseases of development."

Malnutrition, although not a disease itself, may have debilitating or fatal effects. Its occurrence is linked to subsistence patterns: it is more common in large-scale agricultural and industrial societies than in small-scale societies. Foragers and small-scale farmers are usually malnourished only when their traditional subsistence pattern has been severely disrupted. Even in societies such as ours, in which more than enough food is produced to feed the entire population, inequalities in distribution reflect socioeconomic inequalities and leave many people hungry. Hunger is also linked to people's perceptions of food: potentially nutritious resources may be defined as "nonfood," and nutrition is not clearly understood, even by so-called experts.

In addition to physiological diseases and malnutrition, mental illness is recognized in all cultures. Often it is caused by the stress of trying to deal with a particular environment. Certain patterns of mental illness are universal; others are culture-specific, linked to particular physical environments and cultural traditions. Sometimes rapid social change can be so stressful that individuals become seriously disoriented or lose the will to live.

Notions of the origins of illness vary considerably. Western medical specialists have traditionally viewed mind and body as two separate systems, each accounting for its own type of illness. Other traditions take a more holistic approach. Another distinction can be made between personalistic systems, in which illness is thought to be intentionally caused by some malicious being, and naturalistic systems, in which impersonal factors are recognized as the cause of illness.

Attempts to cure illness take many different

forms, but all traditions can claim some degree of success. Precisely how and why some cures work is hard to prove, however. In social terms, the health-care delivery system consists of a culturally defined setting for curing, curing specialists and their helpers, and the patient. Treatment always costs something, and in Western medical systems, in particular, a wide range of factors contributes to such costs.

SUGGESTED READINGS

Bloom, A.L., and J. Reid, eds. 1984. *Anthropology and Primary Health Care in Developing Countries*. Special issue, *Social Science and Medicine* 19(3).

Colombo, J.R., ed. 1983. *Windigo: An Anthology of Fact and Fantastic Fiction*. Lincoln: University of Nebraska Press.

Henderson, George E., and M.S. Cohen. 1984. *The Chinese Hospital*. New Haven: Yale University Press.

Kunitz, Stephen J. 1983. *Disease, Change, and the Role of Medicine: The Navajo Experience*. Berkeley: University of California Press.

Logan, Michael H., and Edward E. Hunt, Jr., eds. 1980. *Health and the Human Condition: Perspective on Medical Anthropology*. North Scituate, MA: Duxbury.

Ohnuki-Tierney, Emiko. 1981. *Illness and Healing among the Sakhalin Ainu*. Cambridge: Cambridge University Press.

Reid, Janice. 1983. *Sorcerers and Healing Spirits: Continuity and Change in the Aboriginal Medical System*. Canberra: Australian National University Press.

Rubel, Arthur S., C.W. O'Nell, and R. Collado-Ardón. 1984. *Busto, a Folk Illness*. Berkeley: University of California Press.

Simons, Ronald C., and C.C. Hughs, eds. 1985. *The Culture-Bound Syndromes*. Boston: D. Reidel.

A View of Health and Sickness from Aboriginal Australia

Janice Reid

Janice Reid is a medical anthropologist at the University of Sydney, Australia. In 1974 and 1975, she lived for 12 months with the Yolngu people of Yirrkala. On subsequent visits in 1978, 1979, and 1981, Dr. Reid studied the effect of social change on the indigenous medical system.

The Yolngu of Australia live in the far northeast of the Northern Territory, one of the remotest parts of the continent. Until just before World War II, most of the Yolngu had never seen any of the white Australians whose ancestors had settled their land 150 years before. Arnhem Land, the rectangular peninsula that is home to the Yolngu and other Aboriginal groups, was an afterthought in colonial exploration. When it finally attracted the attention of governments and missions, it was declared an Aboriginal reserve. To this day, there are no all-weather roads into Arnhem Land from either the north or the south. The annual tropical monsoons regularly isolate its scattered communities, which have come to depend on sea-going barges for food and goods and air services for travel.

Although this impressive region is geographically remote from the urban centers of Australia, it is no longer socially or politically isolated. In the late 1960s, one of the largest bauxite mining operations in Australia was established in Nhulunbuy, and with it was built a town to house 4,000 white workers and their families. Aboriginal resistance to this development and an increasing concern all over Australia with the rights of Aborigines led to the declaration of the Aboriginal Land Rights Act in the Northern Territory in 1976 and the transfer of reserves to Aboriginal hands. Thus, a few societies now legally own the land they have occupied for 40,000 years. Family and clan groups who had been living in crowded mission settlements decided to "go home" and reestablish small communities on their own lands.

The "outstation movement," as this development was called, was motivated by the Aborigines' complex set of needs and fears—the specter of further allocation of land for mining and development; the social conflicts, inflamed by alcoholism, in the mission settlements; the desire for autonomy; and love of the land and the livelihood, religious inspiration, and identity it gives. Another factor that motivated the movement was the severe breakdown in physical and emotional health on settlements. Because of the high incidence of infectious and degenerative diseases, low life expectancy, and high infant mortality rates in contemporary Aboriginal society, it has been described as "a developing country within a developed country."

Yolngu clearly perceive the postcolonial breakdown in health. Much of it they attribute to the lack of public amenities, poor living conditions, and the processed store food most settlement-dwellers eat. Critical illnesses and deaths, however, are often attributed to sorcery.

Medical anthropologist Janice Reid with the Yolngu people of Northern Territory, Australia.

Sorcerers in Yolngu society are either people from hostile clans to the west and south or other Yolngu seeking revenge for past wrongs and conflicts (murder, adultery, theft, trespassing, jealousy, and gossip, for example). Many Yolngu claim that frictions and fights among them are on the increase because of the poor conditions of settlement living, alcohol, the waning of Yolngu social controls, and the imposition of Australian laws and values. Accordingly, they fear that serious illness and premature deaths will continue to increase; changes for the better will come only when the Australian government permits them the resources and freedom to reassert their own authority, laws, and values.

When Yolngu speak about health and illness, two themes emerge: first, the contrast in the quality of life on the settlement and on outstations and, second, the risks to health and peace of mind posed by sorcery. They think about health in both "naturalistic" and "personalistic" terms. The naturalistic model accords in some aspects with Western ideas of illness causation. The personalistic model is essentially a social model that attributes health or illness to the quality of relationships between groups and individuals (Foster 1976). Conflict causes sickness. Harmony brings health. In Yolngu thinking, naturalistic and personalistic ideas coexist and are invoked according to the circumstances and severity of an illness.

One clan leader spoke to me of the value of outstation living in the following terms:

When the old men living at the outstations come to {the settlement} they get sickness every time. When they go back to their homeland and taste many different foods they die at the right time {that is, not prematurely}. The young people always change when they go to the outstations and become strong. But even when people go to the outstations, tobacco, sugar, and tea will follow the people and make them sick in their land. But we get hunted food, bush honey, wild meat and many other foods. When I go there I have oysters, crabs, fish, turtle eggs, and stingray and it makes me happy and strong and opens my life.

Describing the establishment of his clan's outstation, another senior member affirmed the health benefits of the move:

We've had no diarrhea or other illnesses since being here—no flu or bad colds. I think the fresh spring water may contribute to this. Our food consists of fish, waterlily, wild honey, wild yams, kangaroo, emu, goanna, blue-tongued lizard, blanket lizard, freshwater turtles, flour, Uncle Toby's Oats, Cornflakes, Weetabix, rice, sugar, tea, syrup, jam, and tobacco.

But when life-threatening illness or death occurs among the Yolngu, according to one of the most respected and prominent community leaders, "people talk and worry." This man undertook to teach me about the various modes of sorcery and its causes because he believed such knowledge could benefit both Europeans and Aboriginal people:

Nobody, no doctors and nurses, have been taught this way before. This is something in our lives we fear—that sorcerers will come and destroy our people. This is for people who are interested in these things. Now that Europeans are living in Arnhem Land, Yolngu are afraid to fight with spears

because they'll go to jail. So they now fight secretly {with sorcery}. So many people have died suddenly from this over the years.

Of the numerous modes of sorcery believed to be used, the most feared and often mentioned is *galka*:

Galka hunt for people at night. They are real people. First the galka spears his victim or cuts him open {after hypnotizing him magically} and damages his liver, or pierces his heart so the blood flows out. Then he'll heat his spear in the fire and put it on the wound to seal it so no one can see it. After this there are several things he might say to the victim. For instance, "When you go back to camp you'll only be alive for two days and a crocodile {or snake, or shark} will kill you." Or, "When you go back to camp you'll get in a fight with your wife or relatives, someone will hit you with a spear and you'll die straight away." Or the victim might just go home, forgetting what has happened to him, and drop dead. Even if the person goes to the hospital he'll still die, because the galka has spoiled his lungs, his liver, or his heart.

For the Yolngu, most of the short-term, readily treated sicknesses of daily life either are not given much thought or are attributed to natural causes. But, as in many societies in other parts of the world, Yolngu explanations of tragedy and suffering reflect the Yolngu experience of the order of things, emphasizing human relations and the control of threats to life that are found in all societies.

23 Anthropology and Human Problems

Brazilian Indians, assisted by government agents, build a new village. The old village was destroyed by the building of a road through the rain forest.

Over the past century we have created an increasingly more integrated world system with the help of technological innovations that have given us a productive capacity far in excess of anything previously imagined. The benefits we have derived from this system are considerable. We know much more about the universe, and we are better able to solve many of the problems that confront us.

Such advances have not been without their price, however. The creation of the modern world system has left great destruction in its wake and has given us the potential to do even more damage. Millions of people have been killed and millions more left impoverished and on the verge of starvation. The environment has suffered destruction on an unprecedented scale. Furthermore, despite the advances that we have made over the past century, the majority of people today have benefited little or not at all from them. Most of the products of our modern technology are available to a minority of the world's population. The modern world system has, in fact, seen a deterioration of the quality of life for hundreds of millions of people. Their previous ways of life have been destroyed, forcing them to adjust to new circumstances that often leave them in despair.

Anthropologists have responded to these problems on a number of levels. Generally, they try to make people more aware of the social and environmental forces surrounding them. Frequently, however, anthropologists are not content to merely describe problems and point to their causes; they often take an active role in finding and implementing solutions. Their work as applied anthropologists may be within their own society or in other societies with which they are familiar.

CONTEMPORARY ADAPTATION PROBLEMS

Many of the problems in the modern world system center on adaptation. As we continue to evolve as a human society, our adaptation changes, and so do the adaptational problems we face. Among the most crucial problems of our age are those associated with economic inequality and poverty; ethnic and national conflict and, often accompanying it, violence; the denial of fundamental human rights; and the threats posed by environmental pollution. These problems are massive and highly complex; however, past experience has shown how resourceful and adaptable we are at meeting the challenges before us. With its holistic perspective and its understanding of adaptation and the world system, anthropology offers a unique vantage point for confronting the crucial problems of our day.

Development and Underdevelopment

In its most general sense, **development** means improvement in the quality of human lives. In material terms, this entails ensuring an adequate level of nutrition and suitable physical surroundings. Development means more than just meeting material goals, however. It is important that social, political, and economic systems help realize the human potential more broadly. All societies in the world today fall short of achieving such goals. Those countries that come closest to achieving them (such as Canada, Sweden, Japan, and the United States) are referred to as **developed** countries. Those countries that are further from achieving these goals, especially the material ones, are called **underdeveloped**.

As noted in Chapter 15, there are major differences between countries that have achieved a high level of development and those that are the most underdeveloped. While the vast majority of people in the United States and Canada live relatively comfortable, if not affluent, lives, in the most underdeveloped countries even the barest necessities are out of the reach of most people.

This is as true in the case of the so-called LDCs (Least Developed Countries), such as Laos or Bhutan, with per capita annual Gross Domestic Products (GDPs) of around $160 and $140, respectively (as of 1988), as it is of wealthier underdeveloped countries, such as the Philippines, with per capita annual GDP of about $670. The United Nations categorizes 41 countries as LDCs. These countries have a total population of 402.4 million people, with an average per capita GDP of $227, compared with an average of $877 for all developing countries. Average adult literacy in these countries is 32 percent, compared with 58 percent for all developing countries. And the average life expectancy is 49 years, compared with 59 years for all developing countries.

The United Nations Human Development Index (HDI), which includes factors relating to health, nutrition, and education (see Westlake 1990), is a much broader index than the GDP. Ranking countries from 130 to 1, the top-ranked country on the HDI is Japan (Canada is given a ranking of 126 and the United States 112). By contrast, there are some two dozen countries that are ranked below 30 (Niger is assigned a rank of 1), while the Philippines is near the middle with 65.

Averages such as per capita GDP and the HDI serve to highlight disparities between poor and rich countries in general terms. However, the situation for many of the people in underdeveloped countries is even worse than reflected in the figures because of the extremely unequal distribution of resources. Such inequality is one of the fundamental problems facing many underdeveloped countries. In the Philippines, for example, which suffered for years from dictatorship and has long been dominated by a small wealthy and powerful elite, 1988 figures indicate that the bottom half of the population earned only 20 percent of the national income, while the top 20 percent earned 35 percent. One study (see Cohen 1990) of the "intensity of poverty" in the Phil-

Peasant children in Guatemala. In the 1980s, 82 percent of Guatemalan children under the age of five had nutritional problems.

ippines indicated that 30 percent of the population was surviving on an average of $50 a month for a family of six (the "poverty level" in Manila for such a family being $175).

Moreover, despite the ending of the Marcos dictatorship in 1986 and subsequent growth in the GDP, poverty in the Philippines has not been reduced. In most parts of the country, poor families received an even smaller share of the income in 1988 than they did in 1985; thus, a greater proportion of preschool children were severely malnourished in 1988 than in 1985. The country has long suffered from widespread underemployment (the underemployed work less than 40 hours a week but desire to work more). In 1989, an estimated 21 percent of the workforce was underemployed. This is the same percentage as in 1985, which is bad enough, but to make matters worse, it represents an additional 700,000 people in real numbers because of rapid population growth. In the rural areas of the Philippines, where land ownership is highly concentrated in the hands of a few, the vast majority have access to little or no land and minimal employment. An estimated 67 percent of families in rural areas appear to live in poverty.

While living standards generally have risen for many developing countries over the past decade,

poverty remains widespread. Real growth in GDP for the developing world for the 1980–89 period was 4.3 percent. However, at the end of the 1980s over 1 billion people still were surviving on incomes of less than $370 per year. Moreover, such growth has done little to alleviate the poverty of the poorest of the poor, many of whom, especially in sub-Saharan Africa, are worse off than they were a decade ago. Many poor countries find themselves weighed down with debt and have little to invest in alleviating poverty. Also, by the end of the 1980s, developing countries were transferring record amounts of their financial resources to the developed world. That is, the amount they were paying to service their debts to the developed world exceeded the inflow of funds from the developed world in record amounts— a deficit of $42.9 billion for 1989, up $5 billion from the year before.

The Evolution of Underdevelopment

Underdevelopment is a relatively new phenomenon that differs considerably from the lack of material wealth traditionally associated with many small-scale societies. People living in traditional Aboriginal societies had far less than many people living in modern societies, and many of their descendants living in modern Australia also are poor. But the nature and causes of the poverty of the traditional and contemporary groups are very different. Small-scale foraging societies were materially poor because they had not developed technological complexity. They were **undeveloped**. By contrast, most of the poor people in the world today are poor largely because they have been unable to benefit from the wealth available in the modern world, largely by being denied access. They are poor as a result of the progressive *underdevelopment* that has accompanied the spread of the present world system.

Underdevelopment is a reflection of how people are integrated into the modern world system. Thus, underdeveloped parts of the world occupy disadvantageous positions within the international division of labor. Their resources are drained to support the wealthier portions of the world, and their people are the most poorly rewarded for their labor in extracting the resources and producing the goods consumed by the world economic order.

The historical aspect of underdevelopment is nicely illustrated by the example of Guatemala. When the Spanish conquered Guatemala in the sixteenth century, they transformed it from a relatively self-sufficient region into one that produced primarily in the interests of the Spanish conquerors. To support Spanish demands, the indigenous population was deprived of its land and forced to work on farms and in mines under adverse conditions. By providing the Indians with few rewards for their work, the Spaniards were able to export goods at a favorable rate and at the same time extract a large profit. After meeting the demands of the export market and the local Spanish elite, little was left for the Indian population, which was barely able to meet subsistence needs.

Little changed for the majority of Guatemalans with independence in the early nineteenth century. By mid-century, however, the condition of most Guatemalans took a definite turn for the worse as the Guatemalan elite, with foreign interests, sought to increase the production of export crops, particularly coffee. Coffee provided wealth for a few but pushed most people even further into poverty. More land was seized from the Indians and given to wealthy coffee-growers, and laws were passed to force Indians to work on the coffee plantations for what was very little pay even by the standards of the day. Not only did the local elite become still wealthier, but foreigners benefited as well. United Fruit, W.R. Grace, and other companies purchased large plots of land to grow export crops such as bananas. These companies extracted large profits from Guatemala, while spending relatively little within the country.

Guatemala today remains a source of inexpensive labor and goods; output is now diversified to include textiles, beef, cotton, and other agricultural products. The country is also a source of nonrenewable natural resources, such as oil and nickel, the profits from which are divided between foreign corporations and the local elite. This situation has evolved at the expense of the majority of the people, as food crops have been taken out of production to make way for export crops and cow pastures, and as people are pressured to work on plantations and in factories at low wages and under unsafe conditions. Guatemala also serves as a market, though small, for foreign companies. Luxury goods produced in the United States and elsewhere are sold to the Guatemalan elite. Pharmaceutical, chemical, and other companies are able to sell a range of goods, often under more favorable conditions than at home. In addition, countries such as Guatemala serve as dumping grounds for toxic wastes that may be banned or restricted in more developed countries.

Attempts to overcome Guatemala's underdevelopment have met with little success in the face of opposition from the national elite and foreign corporations. Social upheaval, widespread violence, and denial of human rights have persisted for decades, with no solution in sight.

The Plight of Indigenous Peoples

Those who probably suffered the most from the spread of Western industrial society and the re-

Only foreign tourists and the wealthy elite can afford the comfort of this luxury hotel in Antigua, Guatemala.

sultant underdevelopment were the indigenous peoples of newly colonized or incorporated lands: native peoples of the United States and Canada, Australian Aborigines, Amazonian Indians, and the like. As these peoples were conquered and incorporated into the world system, they lost their land, their autonomy, and often their lives. Many fought back, and sometimes were successful in postponing their fate. Ultimately, however, those who survived were rounded up on reservations to become wards of the state or left to roam, broken and impoverished, on the margins of society in a land that had once been theirs.

The progressive destruction of such peoples is exemplified by the history of the Kaingang, an indigenous group in Brazil. At the turn of the century, the Kaingang lived a seminomadic ex-

istence inland from the growing city of São Paulo. As railroad construction began through Kaingang territory, and as settlers started moving onto their land, clearing the forests and planting coffee trees, the Kaingang found themselves forced into a war for survival. They had tried to make peace with the settlers, but to no avail. Their subsequent attacks on railway workers and settlers led to preparations in São Paulo to launch a campaign to destroy the Kaingang, who were seen as impeding the march of civilization. Although their destruction was avoided by the Indian Protection Service, the Kaingang population declined from 700 to 200 between 1912 and 1916, primarily because of deaths from newly introduced diseases such as influenza and measles (Ribeiro 1970).

The remaining pacified Kaingang were placed on a small reserve, as the man who gained control of the lands they had occupied previously became wealthy. In 1949, the state governor took away half of their reserve, handing over the land to three business enterprises, he himself profiting greatly in the process. Over the next couple of decades, much of the remaining reserve land was logged by private companies and even by the government Indian agency. Most of the profits from logging went to the companies and to employees of the Indian agency, with only a small amount being turned over to the Kaingang.

The Kaingang and other local Indians began to organize a resistance movement in the 1970s, managing to expel 2,200 non-Indian families from their lands in 1977. The government response was to establish schools to train Indian leaders who would be more receptive to government control. One of the Kaingang leaders of the resistance movement was killed in 1980, and other leaders were subjected to attacks. Having weakened Indian resistance, the government initiated construction of hydroelectric dams that would flood a large portion of the Kaingang reserve; squatters encroached further on the remaining territory.

By late 1984, the Kaingang once again were on the offensive, as were other native groups around Brazil (see Howard 1987). Members of the Kaingang community took part in a hunger strike that led authorities to agree to recognize their rights to a portion of the land threatened by squatters. However, delays in implementation of the agreement resulted in a group of Kaingang marching on the national capital, Brasilia, in October 1984, and to their staging a nationwide march on the capital in March 1985. Finally, in January 1986, the government announced creation of the Kaingang Indian Reserve.

The problems faced by the Kaingang are common to many indigenous peoples around the world. Decimated by outright attacks and diseases introduced by their conquerors, they have seen what little they have left gradually taken away by those seeking to profit at their expense. Their attempts at resistance are met with subtle maneuvers to overpower them, and if these are not successful, with a return to violence.

Genocide

Many indigenous peoples have been the target of **genocide**, the deliberate and systematic destruction of a cultural or political group. From the seventeenth to the early nineteenth centuries, the settlers of Newfoundland hunted and killed the local indigenous people, the Beothucks, "first because they were considered a nuisance, and later for the sport of pursuing such elusive game" (Harwood 1969, 72). The Beothucks' peaceful overtures were constantly met with violence, and settlers frequently would organize parties to hunt them, much as they hunted game. Genocide did not end with the early colonial era. Australian Aborigines continued to be attacked into the 1920s, with organized gangs of whites attacking the Aborigines' camps and ranches, going so far as to leave out poisoned flour for them to eat. Raids on peaceful groups of Indians by organized groups of non-Indians continue to occur in parts of South America today.

When, out of desperation, indigenous minorities try to fight back because peaceful means have been denied them, their "belligerence" is used as an excuse to slaughter them. When the Embera Indians of Colombia sought to retain control of a gold mine that one of their people had discovered in the late 1970s, they were subjected to constant attacks by local landowners and prospectors. As a result of pressures from the landowners, fueled by rumors that the Embera were subversives, in early 1981 the government sent in the police. In the ensuing battle, several Embera were killed and others captured (International Work-Group on Indigenous Affairs 1981). Similarly, dozens of Indian leaders have been killed in other parts of Colombia by gunmen hired by wealthy landowners without a single case of murder ever having been brought to trial.

Ethnocide

Even when ethnic minorities are not wiped out, their cultural traditions may be. Maintenance of a distinct cultural identity by indigenous peoples is difficult in the face of expanding industrial society. As their resources are seized and as they are overwhelmed by the new technology, such peoples find the very bases of their societies undermined. The destruction of a people's culture carried out on a systematic basis is referred to as **ethnocide**. Ethnocide is the result of extreme policies aimed at incorporating minorities into the dominant culture through coercion or incentive. It is based on the belief that the indigenous culture is inferior, and that it should be superseded by the dominant culture, believed to be superior. Ethnocide is ethnocentrism acted on in the extreme. A common means of promoting ethnocide is to force parents to send their children to distant schools, where they will learn to accept the values of the new culture. Another tactic is to provide the first converts to the new ways with material rewards in the hope that others will be encouraged to follow. Traditional customs also may be banned. Such actions almost always are defended on the grounds that they benefit indigenous peoples—"bringing them from the stone age into the space age." More significant, however, are the benefits accruing to the "civilized" in terms of access to land and other resources. The gains of the dominant culture usually far outweigh those of the native peoples.

Some indigenous peoples readily accept their cultural loss, hoping for greater rewards in the new order; others accept the change fatalistically. However, there are those who choose to resist. To the chagrin of people convinced of the superiority of Western industrial culture, not everyone embraces it with open arms. One of the major struggles confronting the world today concerns the right of indigenous peoples to retain their own identities and to use the resources they feel belong to them in ways they consider appropriate. In the United States, Canada, Brazil, and Australia, this struggle centers on **land rights**—the right of native peoples to control what happens on the lands they occupy and to be compensated for the lands they have lost.

While today the struggle for land rights in the United States and Canada takes place mainly in the courts, frustration over perceived injustice sometimes still leads to violent confrontations. Protests by Sioux at Wounded Knee, South Dakota, over the loss of treaty rights in 1973 erupted into a violent confrontation with federal authorities involving gunfire and the taking of hostages. More recently, a July 1990 protest by Mohawks from Oka, Quebec, escalated into a prolonged armed confrontation in which a police officer was killed during an assault on Mohawk barricades. Such violence is much more common in countries where native peoples have little recourse to the courts. The Karens, Kachin, and other indigenous peoples have been fighting the government of Mayanmar (formerly Burma) since that country became independent in 1948. Likewise, the Melanesian people of Irian Jaya (also known as West Papua) have been fighting for independence since their territory was occupied by the Indonesians in the early 1960s. Such resistance is based on cultural as well as economic grounds. For many of these people, giving in does not simply mean being unable to dance in a certain way or dress after a certain fashion; it means being pushed to the bottom of the heap in the world system, following the path of the Kaingang into ever deeper poverty.

Environmental Destruction

As our world becomes increasingly urbanized and industrialized, we are producing pollutants at an unprecedented rate. Disasters such as occurred at the Chernobyl nuclear power plant in the Soviet Union and at the Bhopal chemical plant in India have no historical parallel. The range of pollutants discharged into the air, soil, and water is far greater today than at any time in the past. The air quality in Mexico City with its vast number of industries and 3 million vehicles would have been unthinkable in cities of the past. Many of the deserts and treeless landscapes throughout the world are testimony to past destruction of the environments by an expanding human population, but now we are destroying our environment at a far more rapid pace. In the past, we were comforted by the thought that

In 1990, the Mohawk Indians of Oka, Quebec, protested injustices concerning land rights.

there were always more resources to be had and that the atmosphere, oceans, and soil could always absorb the pollutants we produced. But today, in the face of unparalleled environmental disaster, we are quickly coming to realize that such assumptions were naive. The environment is under major stress from air and water pollution, and we are being exposed to increasing levels of dangerous solar radiation as by-products of human technology destroy the atmosphere's protective ozone layer.

One of the most serious ecological problems is the large-scale destruction of tropical rain forests (see the Rain Forest Portfolio earlier in Part Three). If the current rate of deforestation continues, tropical rain forests may virtually disappear within the next couple of decades as a result of logging, burning, acid rain, and other factors. This possibility is of immediate importance to those living in the forests. Also threatened are many archaeological sites within the rain forests. Acid rain in southern Mexico, partly resulting from oil refineries and tourist buses, is now threatening millions of acres of tropical rain forest as well as pre-Columbian ruins and forest-dwellers such as the Lacandones. Moreover, since the world consists of a single large ecologi-

cal system, the loss of such a major natural component as the tropical forests has serious global implications.

Clearly, the destruction of rain forests is an extremely complex and important issue. The lives of indigenous peoples are being ruined, and local lands are being eroded into uselessness by excessive logging; improper forest farming; wasteful ranching practices; migration leading to overpopulation; road construction; and commercial pursuits such as mining, industrial agriculture, and hydroelectric dams. As the delicate ecological balance of vast regions is being thrown into disarray, many species of plants and animals are becoming extinct. In recent years, erosion in areas that have been subject to severe deforestation has resulted in flooding, with considerable loss of life and damage to property.

Research also has shown that deforestation disturbs both local and global climatic patterns, including rainfall and temperatures. One reason is that the forests return significant amounts of moisture to the atmosphere and play a major role in converting carbon dioxide to oxygen. Many scientists believe that a reduction in this conversion, as well as an increased level of carbon dioxide from burning of the forests, contributes in a major way to the **greenhouse effect**—a warming of the atmosphere caused by air pollutants that trap heated air near the earth's surface. The greenhouse effect could result in drier and warmer weather in extensive portions of the northern temperate zones, including the American and Canadian grain-growing belts.

Concern with environmental problems poses special questions for the poorer countries of the world. As they strive to improve their standard of living, such countries are faced with difficult contradictions. How are they to reconcile the imperative of development with their reliance on exports of timber from their forests, food from their fragile soils, and nonrenewable mineral and oil resources? Likewise, if they seek to limit the development of such energy sources as hydroelectric dams, they risk creating even greater pressure on their forest resources as sources of firewood. Even more than developed countries, the poorer countries also face difficulties in trying to bring about environmental improvements. Cleaning up the waste that already exists and reducing the amount of pollutants from vehicles and factories is expensive. Moreover, stricter enforcement of regulations puts an even greater strain on the already limited resources of governments.

TOWARD SOLVING THE PROBLEMS

Given the immensity of the problems facing people around the world today, it is little wonder that many people seek to ignore them, give up in despair, or retreat into cynicism. Yet thousands of organizations, agencies, and individuals are working toward solutions. That so many problems persist attests not so much to the failures of those seeking solutions as to the scale and complexity of the difficulties we face in searching for an adaptational strategy that provides a more equitable standard of living on a worldwide basis.

The Role of Sociocultural Anthropology

From its very inception, sociocultural anthropology has been intimately caught up in the problems associated with underdevelopment and with efforts to find solutions. In particular, this subfield of anthropology has played an important role in improving dialogue and understanding between cultures. For example, the work of developmental planners and administrators has become more attuned to the needs of communities they are seeking to help as sociocultural anthropologists provide them with relevant information concerning the beliefs and feelings of the local people.

Applied Anthropology

While the role of many anthropologists in seeking solutions to human problems is indirect through their teaching and writing, some anthropologists have determined to take a more active role in effecting change. Those who engage in such activities are called applied anthropologists. The term **applied anthropology** refers to research and activities intended to produce a desired sociocultural condition that optimally will produce a marked improvement in the lives of the people concerned. This may be simply a matter of keeping them from being exterminated or being reduced to even lower levels of poverty.

Applied anthropology originated under the sponsorship of European and American colonial authorities as "a kind of social work and community development effort for non-white peoples" (James 1973, 41). British anthropologists, for example, helped to train colonial officers and also conducted research on behalf of colonial governments on such topics as indigenous legal systems, land tenure, religious movements, diet and nutrition, and migration. Anthropologists were sometimes commissioned to do ethnographic research in crisis-ridden areas to facilitate the establishment of colonial authority.

In the 1930s, U.S. anthropologists were hired by the Bureau of Indian Affairs and the Soil Conservation Service to work on problems concerning reserve-dwelling Native Americans. During World War II, anthropologists were hired to study problems associated with the forced displacement from the West Coast of Japanese Americans and Japanese immigrants who had not become citizens. After the war, anthropologists worked with the American administration in its new Micronesian colonies.

The destruction of the colonial order following World War II left anthropologists, particularly applied anthropologists, open to attack. In many parts of the world, nationalist leaders who had replaced colonial administrators identified anthropologists with the former colonial regimes, viewing them as agents of colonial repression. Although this attitude in some instances was justifiable, overall it represented a distorted oversimplification. Some anthropologists were active proponents of colonialism, but most sought in limited ways to improve conditions for those living under colonial rule.

With applied anthropology in ill repute in the immediate postcolonial period, many cultural anthropologists opted to retreat to colleges and universities. Some continued to work for international development agencies, for government departments, and for industry, but their work was far from the mainstream of anthropological research. Applied anthropology survived the demise of colonialism best in the United States, partly because of the relatively large indigenous population and partly because of U.S. global geopolitical activities. The kind of work done by applied anthropologists during this period and their tendency to avoid larger issues in favor of solving smaller problems was much the same as in the colonial era.

The late 1960s and early 1970s were a critical period for applied anthropology in the United States. Of particular concern was the employment of anthropologists by business and government, at the risk of serving the interests of the rich and powerful instead of those supposedly being helped. Debate was especially intense over the role of anthropologists in relation to America's military involvement in Southeast Asia.

While anthropologists continue to debate the ethics of applied work, the number of full-time applied anthropologists and academics doing part-time applied work has expanded markedly in recent years. Their activities are wide-ranging, including helping to implement culturally sensitive educational programs, studying the social impact of highways and oil pipelines, and helping indigenous peoples with land claims. For the most part, such activities fall into two categories: development planning and advocacy on behalf of cultural groups.

Development Planning

Anthropologists help in both formulating and implementing development plans. Most often, they serve as part of a multidisciplinary team including other experts such as agronomists, engineers, physicians, economists, and geographers. The anthropologist brings to such a team detailed knowledge of the people in the area and the holistic, integrated perspective essential to successful planning.

One of the most valuable roles played by anthropologists in development projects is to promote discussion between the planners and the local population. Typically, the local population distrusts the planners. Such distrust may be warranted, as planners often lack knowledge of the local culture and the specific needs and goals of the people they are to serve. Peter Weil (1980) argued that to bridge the gap between the residents and the planners, the anthropologist must (1) identify and explain local decision-making processes and (2) help both residents and planners adapt local structures to better meet developmental needs as expressed by the residents. These steps clarify which residents the planners should interview; they also help to ensure that local customs will be preserved to the extent possible and that plans truly reflect the needs of the people.

In addition to their work on specific projects, anthropologists also contribute to the development process through studies on the culture of development, in which the planning process is examined in the same way other sociocultural phenomena are examined. This includes a consideration of the culture and social organization of the planners themselves. Thus, planners are seen as social beings with their own goals, whose actions are influenced by their own environments. For example, to understand the developmental work of an international agency such as the World Bank, it is important to understand the world of those working for the agency (e.g., the political context of their work, their career goals, how information is received and translated into practice).

Advocacy

Anyone engaged in planning or implementing change is, in a sense, advocating particular goals and a particular way of life. In most applied work, this advocacy role is not made explicit. The applied anthropologist is viewed more or less as a technician utilizing his or her particular skill in pursuit of some neutral goal. But applied anthropologists do not always claim to be neutral, or even try. Many feel compelled by the poverty and exploitation of people with whom they work to serve as lobbyists on their behalf, as suggested by Thomas Melville's (1981) plea for the embattled Mayan Indians of Guatemala:

> Anthropologists have sat at the tables of Guatemalan Indians, eaten their meager food, laughed, smoked, and drunk with them, and made livings writing about their culture. It will be a shame if we leave the stage in silence. (p. 1)

This advocacy approach by no means implies that local populations are incapable of speaking for themselves. Instead, it recognizes the social responsibility of the anthropologist to lobby on behalf of people in need and to promote values associated with fundamental human rights.

Advocacy on the part of anthropologists has been particularly evident with respect to the rights of native peoples. Anthropologists have been involved with a number of groups promoting indigenous rights, including Cultural Survival, Survival International, and the International Work-Group for Indigenous Affairs. Such groups publicize the problems faced by indigenous peoples and act as lobbyists on their behalf; they also attempt to provide indigenous peoples with opportunities to make their own voices heard. The groups have been especially active in petitioning governments on behalf of indigenous peoples threatened as a result of the exploitation of natural resources. Thus, in 1990 Survival International took part in a campaign to have the government of the Philippines cancel the logging concession given to a company in the southern part of the country after it was discovered that the company had tortured and murdered local native peoples opposed to its activities.

Anthropologists also have become involved in major political issues concerning domestic and foreign policies in their own countries. They have worked as advocates for those with drug-related problems, for the homeless, for retired people, and for the terminally ill. They have sought both to educate people about the cultures of these groups and to promote policies designed to assist them. In terms of foreign policy, perhaps the most controversial activities of anthropologists have been associated with recent wars. In the United States, anthropologists were prominent among those who organized teach-ins during the Vietnam War in the 1960s and early 1970s. In the 1970s and early 1980s, anthropologists were active in trying to stop U.S. assistance to military regimes in Central America. Such activities still generate debate among anthropologists themselves over their roles as scholars and citizens. Such debate illustrates the extent to which anthropologists are active participants in the modern world system.

Survival International, a group concerned with the rights of indigenous peoples, has conducted a campaign against logging in the Philippines.

Applied Medical Anthropology

Medical anthropology makes use of the methods and theory of all branches of anthropology in the study of human health. This rapidly growing field often views human health from an evolutionary and ecological perspective, addressing such questions as What is the evolutionary basis of the differences in how various populations contend with diseases? What are the essential factors influencing the growth and development of children? and What effect does modernization have on local populations? As with other applied work, applied medical anthropology also is strongly interdisciplinary. Medical anthropolo-

gists commonly work with people in the fields of medicine, psychology, sociology, and demography. In this context, they broaden the point of view of other scientists. McElroy and Townsend (1979) noted that "anthropology's comparative framework helps medically trained people avoid a limited one-culture perspective, to see how social and environmental factors affect health, and to be aware of alternative ways of understanding and treating disease" (p. xvii). This perspective leads to a deeper understanding of the biological basis of disease, defines the role environment plays in illness (including social factors, such as poverty, stress, and pollution), and provides insights into new ways of treating disease.

Medical anthropology contributes in many ways toward developing more effective policies and programs that address health problems caused by rapid culture change and modernization. For example, had planners known about the culture and ecology of the people living in the Sahel region of Africa, a terrible famine might have been avoided. The Sahel is a dry region occupied by farmers and pastoralists. During the 1960s, government planners encouraged pastoralists in the Sahel to increase the size of their herds. While the number of wells in the area was increased, the amount of vegetation needed for grazing was decreasing, largely because of destruction of the forest cover by farmers and others. Competition for use of the Sahel's limited resources reached crisis proportions when the area experienced a period of abnormally low rainfall. The result was a famine of major proportions.

As the Sahel crisis worsened, an international relief program was launched. Unfortunately, the food-distribution program proved to be inadequate, especially for the pastoralists living in more remote regions. In addition, because the policymakers had a poor understanding of the people's adaptation, in some instances the wrong kind of provisions were sent. This included grain for the nomads, who were accustomed to a diet composed largely of dairy products. The grain gave them stomach cramps and diarrhea. Again, a problem could have been avoided with better

Provisions have gone to the famine area of Sahel, Africa. The food-distribution program, however, was inefficient, largely because of policymakers' poor understanding of the people's adaptation.

understanding of the people's ecology and culture.

Medical anthropology not only benefits people in poorer countries, it also can help those in more developed countries. For example, it can be of considerable help in providing medical care sensitive to the wide cultural variety we find in most large cities. A background in anthropology can make clinicians more aware of the biophysical differences that exist within and between populations. According to Tripp-Reimer (1983), "nurses and other health professionals are coming to recognize that standardized growth and development charts have been based on Caucasian norms" (p. 249). Recently, medical anthropology has played a role in formulating policies concerning AIDS in the United States. Michael Gorman's (1986) study of AIDS in San Francisco was conducted to help government policymakers prevent the spread of the disease. As a medical anthropologist, Gorman contends that "effective prevention policy must incorporate a thorough understanding of the individual behavior that places people at risk for the disease, and social and cultural factors that influence this behavior" (p. 157).

Applications of Biological Anthropology and Archaeology

As is true of cultural anthropology, biological anthropology and archaeology have moved toward directly serving the needs of contemporary humans. This trend includes both a focus on practical applications and a growing sense of social responsibility. Some of the service occurs on a "small" scale—helping individuals to be proud of their heritage, identifying war dead, or assisting law-enforcement officials gather evidence. Other work serves humankind on a "large" scale, pointing to the global implications of environmental degradation.

Practical applications of biological anthropology and archaeology address many of the problems discussed earlier in the chapter, including those related to nutrition and health, the destruction of the natural environment, and eth-

nocide and loss of cultural pride. Biological anthropology has additional applied fields and areas of social responsibility, including legal applications of forensic anthropology and sociopolitical ramifications of advances in biology, such as those resulting from recombinant DNA research. One of the applied fields of archaeology is research-oriented contract archaeology.

Forensic Anthropology

In the process of studying human paleontology and biology, anthropologists gain an intimate understanding of the human form and structure. An important application of this knowledge is **forensic anthropology**, which deals with legal questions relating to human physical remains or traces. Most forensic anthropologists are human osteologists, **osteology** being the scientific study of bones. From human remains, forensic anthropologists may be able to determine the sex, age at death, ancestral background, and stature of the individual. The cause of death may also be ascertained. This knowledge can assist in identifying crash victims, war casualties, homicide victims, and skeletal remains in unmarked graves (see the Focus section at the end of Chapter 6).

Forensic anthropologists are sometimes enlisted to assist legal authorities in solving crimes. For example, Angel and Caldwell (1984) described a case in which an unidentified skull was found on a golf course. The police first suspected that it came from a nearby cemetery, but the medical examiner, because of soil stains and sun bleaching on the bone, was able to determine that it had not been buried. Details of the skull indicated that it was that of a young white female. Using dental records of local young women reported missing, the medical examiner matched the teeth to those of an individual referred to as "S.S." A more thorough search turned up more of the skeleton and evidence that a crime had been committed, including a broken handgun butt and a noose of insulated wire, attached to a piece of wood.

The evidence was examined by a forensic anthropologist to help determine the cause of death and to firmly establish the individual's identity.

Dr. Clyde Snow, forensic anthropologist, testifying at the 1985 trial of Argentinian junta leaders who were accused of the mass murder of civilians. Dr. Snow helped convict the leaders by presenting physical evidence, such as this skull, of their crimes.

The anthropologist established that the remains were those of a young white adult female, from 62 to 65 inches tall, who had been active in athletics—all of which helped to confirm the remains as being those of S.S. Further, some of the skeletal damage, including fracture lines and other patterns of stress, indicated that extreme pressure had been applied to her chin and neck while she was alive. The wire attached to the wood proved to be the best way to explain the pattern of damage and was the most likely instrument of death, through strangulation. The forensic anthropologist later was enlisted as an expert witness for the prosecution of a man accused of S.S.'s murder.

Because of the need for credibility and caution in such legal matters, the American Academy of Forensic Sciences has established strict guidelines for certification of forensic anthropologists. This reflects the fact that they work closely with other forensic scientists, including dental experts, pathologists, toxicologists, psychiatrists, and criminologists.

Archaeology and Cultural Heritage

In many nations, the management of historical and archaeological sites is a major political and governmental concern. The issues that must be dealt with are complex and often emotionally charged, as noted in the Focus section at the end of Chapter 8. While the preservation of cultural resources may appear to be in direct conflict with economic development, its importance is hard to deny: "Archaeological heritage management has an ideological basis in establishing cultural identity, linked with its educational function, it has an economic basis in tourism, and it has an academic function in safeguarding the database" (Cleere 1989, 10).

The means of managing archaeological resources varies with country, culture, and site. At Stonehenge, England, the government seeks to preserve an important monument while accommodating the economically important tourist trade. In countries such as Egypt and Mexico, the situation is similar. Preservation is desired, but the demands of tourism must be met. These countries must also contend with problems of theft because collectors are often willing to pay high prices for items from archaeological sites. Theft is not the only problem with respect to the disposition of artifacts. There is also the more difficult ethical and legal question of who owns the past. In Egypt and Mexico, most artifacts are considered national property; hence, the work of foreign archaeologists is carefully monitored.

Questions also arise when archaeologists excavate sites held sacred by native peoples. For example, considerable controversy surrounds the issue of the preservation versus the reburial of Native American human remains and artifacts (Ubelaker and Grant 1989). Such materials are used by paleoanthropologists to study the culture and physical diversity of prehistoric populations. However, a strong Native American political movement contends that the excavation of native sites is racist and disrespectful. Leaders in this movement argue that if an excavation has taken place, then the materials must be reburied. Others defend the preservation of these materials and contend, for example, that scholarly study of the human remains is not racist, but entails the "exploration of the proud heritage of a great people" (p. 249). In some instances, tribal councils and government authorities have arrived at compromises; for example, some remains have been placed in vaults, with access to them by the scientific community controlled by tribal authorities.

The expansion and growth of human society in modern times has changed the face of the land to an unprecedented extent. In the course of building highways, factories, and new homes; clearing land for agriculture and settlement; and flooding lands under dams, prehistoric and historic sites often are destroyed and valuable scientific information lost forever. Because of increased sensitivity to the issue of cultural heritage, however, many countries have established policies regarding the rescue of such information before a project can proceed.

In the United States, both federal and state governments have enacted laws and provided for funding to mitigate adverse effects of projects on archaeological sites. The National Historic Preservation Act of 1966 and the National Environmental Policy Act (NEPA) of 1969 de-emphasized "salvage archaeology" with a new focus on planned, research-oriented archaeology. Prior to enactment of such laws, archaeologists often had to carry out excavation just ahead of construction crews, and usually without the benefit of an integrated research design and sufficient funding. What the new laws did was to ensure that the effects of construction or development on cultural resources would be considered *before* a project began. The laws also provided for funding to mitigate the effects of construction through research-oriented excavation projects (McGuire and Schiffer 1982; see also McGimsey and Davis 1977; Schiffer and Gummerman 1977).

A result of this legislation has been an increasing number of **contract archaeologists**—professional archaeologists contracted by govern-

Contract archaeologists in Arizona are concerned with conserving the artifacts of the local Native American way of life.

ment or industry to perform surveys and excavation projects to comply with the laws. For example, Czaplicki (1989) directed a contract archaeology team hired in response to the federal Central Arizona Project (CAP), which was designed to provide water from the Colorado River to central Arizona. In compliance with federal laws, the Bureau of Reclamation had to identify the archaeological sites that could be damaged or destroyed by construction of the final segment of the CAP. The Arizona State Museum (ASM) was awarded a contract to survey the final segment that consisted of two sections (Phases A and B) totaling about 115 miles of aqueduct corridor. The intensive survey resulted in the recording of 133 sites from a variety of periods spanning a few thousand years and including camps, villages, field houses, farmsteads, a reservoir, and agricultural features. Because avoidance was not possible, in 1985 the ASM was awarded another contract to conduct excavations in the Phase B section. (Another contract firm was awarded a contract to conduct excavations in Phase A.) Of the 47 sites located in Phase B, 13 sites with the best research potential were excavated. Because of its research orientation, this contract project provided new information about Hohokam archaeology (Czaplicki and Ravesloot 1989).

As a result of the federal laws enacted over the past two decades, most contract archaeology today is research oriented, carefully planned, and usually adequately funded—a far cry from the salvage archaeology of the 1950s and 1960s.

ANTHROPOLOGY IN THE CONTEMPORARY WORLD

Anthropology and all its subdisciplines have changed a great deal since the nineteenth century. Anthropology has grown in its professionalism, in its understanding of human evolution and cultural and biological diversity, and in its methodology. It has not grown in a vacuum, however. Anthropologists are influenced by their environment as we all are. The state of the discipline today is very much a reflection of the nature of the contemporary world system. Greater world integration and improved communication, for example, have broadened the discipline to include professionals from every part of the globe—it is no longer the exclusive domain of a few Europeans and North Americans.

The small-scale societies that were the focus of sociocultural anthropologists for decades remain an important part of anthropological study. Because ways of life associated with these societies are disappearing more rapidly every year, contemporary anthropologists share the concern of their predecessors in recording these vanishing life-styles. There remain many important lessons to be learned from studying people who live in smaller, nonindustrial societies. These people can tell us much about ourselves, about our past, and about how human beings relate to the physical environment. Perhaps most important, knowledge about small-scale societies reinforces the notion that humans are highly adaptive. Furthermore, small-scale societies illustrate that many of the characteristics we often assume to be instinctive, or biologically based, such as aggression, are not—they are largely based on cultural shaping within an environmental context.

Anthropologists' continuing interest in small-scale societies involves a different theoretical approach than that of the past. There has been a shift from looking at smaller societies as isolated entities to examining how they fit into the broader environmental context. And no longer do anthropologists merely study these societies. As noted earlier, many work as planners and advocates to help overcome the poverty, genocide, and ethnocide that have often characterized integration of small-scale societies into the modern world system.

Anthropologists, of course, do not study only past and present small-scale societies. Many anthropologists today study people who are fully integrated into large-scale industrial societies. Urbanism is one of the major features of modern life; within a few years over half of the world's population will be living in urban areas. Anthropologists have come to devote considerable effort to understanding all aspects of life in these rapidly growing cities.

The recording of human cultural diversity continues to be one of anthropology's main concerns. It has become commonplace to talk about how everything and everyone is becoming homogenized—we wear the same clothes, eat the same foods, watch the same television programs. But while many aspects of Western industrial society have spread across the globe, considerable diversity remains. The resurgence of pride in ethnic identity attests to the tenacity of many cultural traditions. Moreover, while many of the distinctive "tribes" of the past are gone, they have been replaced by many new forms of tribalism relating to such things as occupation, residence, and religion.

It has always been anthropology's role not only to look at human diversity, but also to analyze it holistically. In an age subject to specialization and simplistic glosses passing for generalized understanding, the holistic perspective remains important, for it is a view that is vital to an informed understanding of both the diversity and the integration of the totality of human experience in the context of the modern world.

SUMMARY

The modern world system, integrated and technologically advanced, is nevertheless a source of major human problems, including environmental destruction and widespread poverty, hunger, and disease. With its holistic perspective and focus on adaptation, anthropology deepens our understanding of the problems and helps us find solutions.

Economic inequality in the modern world system is reflected in the difference between developed and underdeveloped countries. The indigenous peoples of colonized or incorporated lands have suffered the most from underdevelopment. Some groups have been the targets of genocide, while other ethnic minorities have suffered ethnocide.

Among the causes of environmental destruction are pollution, technological disasters, and the large-scale destruction of tropical rain forests. Deforestation has profound consequences. Local and global climates are disrupted, plant and animal species become extinct, and the quality of life of local peoples is severely undermined.

Sociocultural anthropology plays an important role in solving human problems. Applied anthropologists actively promote beneficial changes by providing information, making policy recommendations, and working directly with local populations. Such activities fall largely within two categories: development planning and advocacy.

Medical anthropology is a rapidly growing interdisciplinary field in which human health is viewed from an evolutionary and ecological perspective. A major function of medical anthropology is broadening the point of view of health-care providers and scientists. Medical anthropology contributes to the development of policies and programs that address health problems caused by modernization in underdeveloped countries; it also helps provide better medical care within developed nations.

Biological anthropology and archaeology also demonstrate a growing trend toward directly serving contemporary human needs by emphasizing practical applications and promoting a sense of social responsibility. Forensic anthropologists investigate legal questions relating to human physical remains or traces. Archaeologists assist in the management and preservation of historic and prehistoric sites. Contract archaeologists excavate sites that are in immediate danger of being destroyed by construction or technological projects.

SUGGESTED READINGS

Frank, André Gunder. 1980. *Crisis: In the Third World.* New York: Holmes and Meier.

Franke, Richard W., and Barbara H. Chusin. 1980. *Seeds of Famine: Ecological Destruction and the Development Dilemma in the West African Sahel.* Montclair, NJ: Allenheld, Osmun.

Hong, Evelyne. 1987. *Natives of Sarawak: Survival in Borneo's Vanishing Forests.* Pulau Pinang, Malaysia: Institut Masyarakat.

Howard, Michael C. 1987. *The Impact of the International Mining Industry on Indigenous Peoples.* Sydney, Australia: University of Sydney, Transnational Corporation Research Project.

Janes, Craig R., Ron Stall, and Sandra M. Gifford, eds. 1986. *Anthropology and Epidemiology.* Dordrecht, Holland: D. Reidel.

Jorgensen, Joseph G. 1984. *Native Americans and Energy Development II.* Washington, DC: Anthropology Resource Center.

Rathbun, Ted A., and Jane E. Buikstra, eds. 1984. *Human Identification: Case Studies in Forensic Anthropology.* Springfield, IL: Charles C Thomas.

Shennan, S.J., ed. 1989. *Archaeological Approaches to Cultural Identity.* London: Unwin Hyman, Ltd.

von Furer-Haimendorf, C. 1982. *Tribes of India: The Struggle for Survival.* Berkeley: University of California Press.

From Filmmaking to Advocacy

Scott S. Robinson

Scott Robinson did his doctoral dissertation research for Cornell University in Ecuador (1968–69), where he became infatuated with documentary film production. After making three films in that country (with Michael Scott), he decided to devote his career to anthropological film. An opportunity to show his first films took him to Mexico, where he had lived as a child and where he lives now. Beginning in 1972, he and his wife began to apply their self-taught skills, producing documentaries throughout Mexico and Latin America.

In 1981, a contract documentary obliged me to film the construction of a large hydropower dam south of Mexico City. Federal Power Commission (CFE) executives wanted a documentary about the technical aspects of dam construction, illustrating the geophysical preliminaries, including the preparation of the bedrock on which the dam's curtain (in this case, layers of impermeable clay) would be slowly deposited and packed and the construction of an underground powerhouse. During helicopter flyovers of the dam site and the upstream basin to be flooded, I noticed a series of small villages and a good-sized town, Balsas, in the state of Guerrero. When I repeatedly asked my engineer clients what would become of all the small farmers (*campesinos*) once the reservoir inundated their homes and fertile lands, I always got the same response: "Not to worry, they'll be given new homes in the new towns we're constructing for them." The completed film made no mention of the involuntary resettlement provoked by the dam.

The following year I began teaching social anthropology at the Universidad Autonoma Metropolitana-Iztapalapa campus in Mexico City. The undergraduate degree at the UAM-I requires all students to engage in two field-research trips prior to presenting their theses. It was evident that groups of students, distributed through the dam region's mestizo, Spanish-speaking villages, could effectively gather ethnographic data as well as monitor the changes about to occur in the lives of the 5,500 inhabitants of the reservoir basin. From 1983 to 1986, at the end of each year's rainy season (October to December) students settled in the modest homes of local residents and began taking notes, making maps, and conducting interviews. During the final field trip, the students and I became caught up in the frantic moving of household goods, pigs, poultry, scarce corral posts, and roof beams above the waterline, once the flooding began. The experience of witnessing others—informants who had become friends—lose their homes, chapels, schools, and cemeteries, not to speak of valuable farmland, made a profound impression on us all.

Each field trip generated a set of student papers describing kinship patterns; maize, bean, squash, and cash-crop farming; diet; fiestas; and village outmigration (primarily to Chicago, U.S.A.). Also detailed in these reports was the factionalism born of the ongoing, improvised negotiations with the CFE engineers and

This village is empty after resettlement resulting from the construction of a dam.

representatives of the Guerrero state government, apparently more concerned about the project's smooth management than the well-being of its constituents. Each field report was distributed to the project engineers and members of the state governor's office, as well as to the leadership of the six communities scheduled to be resettled. Our field reports were providing information not to be found elsewhere, given the absence of any comprehensive resettlement plan within the CFE. The legality of other such large-scale resettlements in Mexico; the vociferous

international campaign to make multilateral lending institutions accountable for the social impact of their loans; the local information gap; the growing campesino distrust of the CFE, state, and federal authorities; and the haphazardness and nonparticipatory nature of the resettlement process inadvertently placed us in the role of advocates for the disenfranchised villagers. What began as a simple student field-research project became a controversial call for respect for human rights and due process, a novelty in the history of involuntary resettlement in Mexico and elsewhere.

As our research generated discussion and resentment among the CFE project engineers, it also became apparent that some research about resettlement precedents and policy inside the CFE was in order. I approached my wife's brother, then director of construction for the CFE, and offered to prepare a review paper of the "state of the resettlement art," an issue of growing visibility in what has come to be called development anthropology. He accepted my offer, and my team's consultancy report was circulated among CFE top management. We received almost no feedback, however, and no discussions about policy changes took place. The traditional pattern of resettlement occurring as a function of the personal concerns and whims of the responsible project engineer was not to be modified so easily. Subsequent events proved that policy changes would be made only when the professional careers of top-level project engineers were jeopardized by the news of campesino resistance to arbitrary resettlement schemes under their jurisdiction. (Caracol dam project engineers, to whom, by the end of field trip 3, 1985, we were persona non grata, never could discount the possibility that I was an informant to their administrative superior. Thus, the lines between research and action were blurred.)

At the beginning of this endeavor, I had not realized how the social organization of a government or private agency responsible for an infrastructure project with a resettlement component (such as dams, airports, tourist resorts, railways, ports, and urban-renewal projects) could be a priority research objective similar to the culture and economy of the affected communities. Because resettlement was a basic policy issue, and planning was largely nil, its reformulation became a political process as community resistance obliged the CFE bureaucracy to adapt and improvise.

In 1986, the fourth group of student researchers discovered in the archives of the Ministry of Agrarian Reform that all but 33 hectares of the 1,447 hectares of the lands to be flooded had never been legally expropriated before the dam's reservoir was filled. This information was shared with a group of dissident villagers who were unwilling to pick up and move across a then imaginary body of water, far from their fields and with insufficient space on their assigned urban lots to build small corrals for their livestock. A community of resisters to the planned resettlement evolved and, persuaded by a charismatic leader and able negotiator, decided to literally "move up the hill," refusing to accept their paltry cash indemnification for their soon-to-be flooded homes—a decision that chagrined the CFE engineers. Thus, although in hindsight this resettlement can be considered a case study of how not to do it, it taught planners and administrators some valuable lessons. In the final analysis, without some form of local participation, consensus, and accountability, any resettlement process is bound to generate resistance, raising the political costs for all responsible parties.

The outcome of the 1988 Mexican federal elections redefined the way in which many federal programs were planned and administered at the local level. Accountability became a major issue, and the negotiation of the two new loans for a hydropower project financed by the World Bank led to a dramatic turnaround of CFE resettlement planning and policy implementation. The policy of the World Bank went like this: "If you don't comply with our resettlement guidelines, you don't receive the loan disbursements on schedule." Although it is still too soon to evaluate the impact of these recent changes in resettlement planning, it is clear that independent researchers are vital to the monitoring process.

From my experience with involuntary resettlement, several crucial aspects of the process became clear to me. First of all, all participants must be made aware of the larger political arena in which the terms and costs are negotiated and the corollary political strategies are defined. Fax machines, laptop computers, and portable video camcorders allow feedback to occur swiftly between village-level leaders, the responsible government agency, and monitoring personnel. Secondly, it is essential that independent researchers define their ethical and analytical criteria regarding when and how to monitor a project. By providing reliable information about what a government agency may or may not be doing, such researchers *can make a difference*. They can create a common ground or neutral negotiating space for the resettlers and those being resettled. Finally, the local and regional context in which guidelines are implemented must be understood. Those responsible for implementation have families and kin obligations and are continually engaged in adjusting their political relations with neighbors and others beyond the community. Resettlement studies, then, must focus on the political process obtaining at *all* levels of society—a complex task and theoretical challenge, to say the least.

Glossary

absolute dating A category of dating techniques that determines an object's age in actual years. Also known as *chronometric dating*. (Compare *relative dating*.)

acclimatization Reaction to an immediate environmental stress consisting of reversible physiological responses that occur over relatively short spans of time.

acculturation A cultural process in which a society acquires new traits as a result of contact with another culture. In contrast to diffusion, acculturation always entails the large-scale influence of one society on another and direct contact between the societies.

acephalous society A "headless" society; i.e., one with a highly decentralized and relatively egalitarian form of political organization.

Acheulean A tool-making tradition of the later part of the Lower Paleolithic, characterized by symmetrical hand axes.

adaptation As a *process,* the means by which individuals or populations react to environmental conditions in order to maintain themselves and survive. As an *object,* the product of adaptation-the-process: a particular behavior, social system, or physical structure.

adaptive radiation Repeated speciation from a single ancestral stock due to adaptation to different environmental conditions. When a generalized and adaptable parent population confronts an area having a wide range of empty econiches, groups move into the open econiches and adapt to each particular set of conditions, leading to a rapid diversification of life.

adaptive strategy The set of solutions consciously or unconsciously applied by members of a population to contend with basic environmental or biological problems.

affinity Social relationships brought about by marriage.

age grades A series of recognized age-based categories.

age set A group of individuals of similar age and of the same sex who share a common identity, maintain close ties throughout their lives, and together pass through a series of age-related statuses.

agriculture The cultivation of plants based on the continuous intensive use of labor and land resources.

allele An alternative form of a gene at a particular locus.

allomorph A variant of a single morpheme.

allophone A variant of a single phoneme that does not affect meaning.

ambilineal descent A means of tracing descent in which both male and female lines are recognized; it is up to the individual to choose between them.

ambilocal residence Residence after marriage with or near the parents or kin of either the bride or groom.

amino acids Small organic molecules that form the molecular subunits that make up proteins.

analogy (biological) An independently evolved similarity that usually arises as the result of adaptive responses to similar conditions. An analogy is not based on common evolutionary descent.

animatism Belief in an impersonal supernatural force or power; although unseen, it is believed to be present everywhere.

animism Belief in the existence of innumerable spirits that dwell in animals and places or simply wander about the earth.

anomie Disorganization of personality and a feeling of alienation.

anthropoids The so-called higher primates, including all monkeys, apes, and humans, that are the most changed in form from the earliest primate.

anthropology   The scientific study of humanity.

applied anthropology   Goal-oriented research and activities which, by providing information, making policy recommendations, or initiating direct action, are intended to produce a desired sociocultural condition.

arboreal theory   The theory that primate characteristics evolved in response to life within the complex world of treetops.

archaeology   The study of the cultural past through the material remains left by people.

art   Attempts to reflect or interpret the essential aspects of reality through images recognized as having an aesthetic quality.

artifacts   The products of human behavior. Archaeological artifacts are the durable remains of a society's material culture.

ascribed group   A group in which membership is acquired at birth.

assemblage (archaeological)   All the artifacts contained within one component of an archaeological site.

assimilation   The process by which distinctions between ethnic groups are eliminated. (Compare *boundary maintenance.*)

Aurignacian   A tool-making tradition associated with the Upper Paleolithic, in which raw materials such as bone, antler, and stone were used, as well as a variety of tools.

australopithecine   A member of the hominid genus *Australopithecus.*

authority   The right to make a particular decision and to command obedience.

avunculocal residence   Residence after marriage near the husband's mother's brother or father's brother.

band   The primary group for social interaction and economic production and exchange among foragers. Each band uses a specific territory for foraging purposes.

bases   A pair of biochemical substances bonded so as to form the rungs of the ladderlike structure characteristic of DNA molecules.

bilineal descent   A means of tracing descent along patrilineal lines for some purposes and matrilineal for others.

bilocal residence   Residence with or near the bride's parents for a period and, for another period, with or near the groom's.

biological anthropology   The branch of anthropology that deals with the biological aspects of humankind, particularly from the standpoint of evolution and biological diversity of human populations.

biological clines   The graphic representation of the gradual variation of a particular biological trait over geographic space.

biological evolution   The change in a population's genetic or physical makeup, or both, through time.

bipedalism   Walking on two feet and habitually standing upright.

blending inheritance   The principle that the traits of the parents are blended in the offspring.

boundary maintenance   The process by which ethnic distinctiveness is maintained. (Compare *assimilation.*)

brain endocasts   Impressions made of the inside of craniums.

bride service   Service performed by a future husband for his bride-to-be's parents.

bridewealth (brideprice)   The passage of wealth of some sort from the husband's group to the wife's as a result of the marriage.

Bronze Age   The period of human culture that began between 3000 and 4000 B.C. characterized by the use of bronze.

bureaucracy   The specialized administrative organization concerned with the day-to-day running of the state.

capitalists   In a modern, class-based, industrial society, those who own the means of production, appropriate what is produced, and control the circulation of what is appropriated. (Compare *proletariat.*)

cargo cult   A millenarian movement found in the southwest Pacific, characterized by the expectation that Western material goods will be received through supernatural means.

carrying capacity   The maximum population of a species that a particular ecosystem can support under a specific set of conditions.

caste   A system of occupationally specific, hierarchically ordered statuses to which members of society are assigned at birth. The Indian caste system is perhaps the most comprehensive and striking.

catastrophism   The doctrine according to which supernatural causes, rather than natural and commonplace forces, are responsible for earth-bound events. Based on the Biblical account of creation, catastrophism was popular during the late eighteenth century and the nineteenth century.

cerebral cortex The outermost layers of the brain, containing the nerve cells most directly responsible for higher mental functions.

Chain of Being A scheme for classifying life in which each form was placed on a graduated scale of "perfection."

chiefdom A stateless political structure integrating a number of communities and composed of several parallel units, each headed by a chief, subchief, or council.

chromosomes The threadlike structures in the nuclei of living cells; they carry a cell's genetic information.

city The residence pattern characterized by a large and densely concentrated population.

civilization An adaptive cultural mechanism for organizing very complex societies through the control and concentration of power, as expressed by the social structure of the state and the residence pattern of the city.

civilized world view An impersonal view of the universe that stresses human separation from and dominance over nature. (Compare *tribal world view*.)

cladistic approach An approach to taxonomy in which closely related organisms are grouped on a branch, or "clade," homologous traits serving to indicate descent from a common ancestor. This approach eliminates the need to distinguish among closely related species.

clan A group of kin who believe themselves to be descended from a common ancestor, but who cannot specify the actual links back to that ancestor.

class See *social class*.

coalition A temporary alliance for a limited political purpose.

cognates Words that have evolved from a common ancestral word.

cognatic descent A means of tracing descent through all ancestors, male and female.

cognitive archaeology An approach to anthropological archaeology focusing on understanding the thought processes of people who lived in ancient societies.

commerce The exchange of goods among different countries or regions.

common descent The principle that new species are descended from earlier forms, and that organisms with similar characteristics are likely to have descended from the same ancestor.

communication The exchange of information between senders and receivers.

compadrazgo A term used in many hispanic cultures in reference to social links created by sponsorship of children in rites of passage, such as baptism or confirmation.

comparative method A method established by Aristotle in which different life-forms are compared to decipher which traits are shared and which are unique.

complex morphological traits The most noticeable characteristics of humans, such as height, weight, body shape, and so forth.

complex trait (genetic) A phenotypic trait, the nature of which is determined by the interaction of a number of gene pairs. (Compare *simple trait*.)

component (archaeological) A distinctive occupation of an archaeological site by one specific group of people.

composite tools Implements made from several components.

consanguinity Social relationships based on presumed biological links.

context (archaeological) How material remains are placed in space and time and the environmental conditions under which they were found.

contract archaeologists Archaeologists contracted by government or industry to perform surveys and excavations in compliance with federal laws.

convergence (evolutionary) A microevolutionary pattern in which different species evolve similar traits as the result of functional adaptations to similar environmental conditions.

core values The fundamental values that serve as the basis for social behavior and the goals pursued by the members of a society.

corporate group A theoretically permanent group, the members of which have common interests or property. Their rights and obligations as group members are specified by recognized rules or norms.

cosmology Study of the general structure and evolution of the universe.

cranial capacity A measurement of brain size, usually expressed in cubic centimeters.

Creationists Those who believe that the story of creation as told in the Book of Genesis should be taken literally.

creole A *pidgin* that has become the mother tongue of a people.

cross-cousins The children of a parent's sibling of

the opposite sex; e.g., children of the father's sister. (Compare *parallel cousins*.)

cross-dating An absolute-dating technique in which objects of known age are used to determine the age of associated materials.

crossing over An occurrence during the production of gametes, leading to the exchange of genetic material between the members of a chromosomal pair.

cultural ecology The scientific study of the ways in which human groups interact with and adjust to their environments, especially through the process of adaptation.

cultural evolution The patterns of culture change through time.

cultural relativism A manner of judging and interpreting the behavior and beliefs of others in terms of their traditions and experiences.

culture The customary manner in which human groups learn to organize their behavior in relation to their environment.

culture and personality A school of thought in which people are believed to assume certain personality traits in keeping with dominant themes in their culture.

culture shock The psychic distress caused by the strains of adjusting to a different culture.

debris (archaeological) Artifacts that are the discarded by-products of human activity; the "garbage" of human behavior.

demography The statistical study of population composition, distribution, and trends.

dendrochronology An absolute-dating technique based on growth rings added by trees each year.

descent Socially recognized links between a person and his or her ancestors.

development Improvement in the quality of human life by ensuring an adequate level of nutrition and suitable physical surroundings, as well as by forging social, political, and economic systems that recognize individual potential and promote self-esteem.

deviants Individuals in a society identified by the majority or by influential and powerful members as thinking or acting in ways too different from what is considered normal or acceptable.

dialect A patterned language variant associated with a geographically or socially distinct speech community or speech context.

diffusion "Cultural borrowing," in which a society adopts traits from other societies.

diffusionism The view that the main process by which cultures grow, change, and develop is by diffusion, or cultural borrowing.

diglossia A situation in which two varieties of one language ("standard" forms, *dialects*, *pidgins*, or *creoles*) are spoken by people in a speech community under different conditions.

directional selection The type of natural selection in which a population adapts genetically to different pressures resulting from shifts in the environment. (Compare *stabilizing selection*.)

disease A pathological condition of the body, or some part of it, in which its functioning is impaired or deranged.

dispersion and fission The stage of family evolution that begins with the first marriage of one of the children and continues until all the children are married.

divergence (evolutionary) The genetic separation of groups descended from a common ancestral population.

division of labor The technical and social manner in which work is organized in a society.

DNA (deoxyribonucleic acid) A large molecule present in living cells that contains the genetic code and transmits the hereditary pattern. The long strands that make up DNA act as the blueprints for the synthesis of proteins.

domestication The adaptation of wild plants and animals for human use.

dominant (genetic) A form of a gene that, if present in the genotype, will be expressed in the phenotype and will suppress the expression of a recessive form of the same gene.

dowry The woman's share of her inheritance from the group of her birth, which is taken with her upon marriage.

durable remains Objects associated with ancient cultures, either preserved or not completely destroyed by natural deterioration processes; a major form of archaeological evidence.

ecofacts A major category of durable remains consisting of objects reflecting an ancient group's natural environment.

ecological niche (econiche) The environment within which members of a species live and how they live within it. A species' econiche encompasses both its habitat and its life-style within its habitat.

ecology The study of the relationship between organisms and their physical, biotic, and social environments.

ecosystem An interacting community consisting of

all living organisms and their physical environments within a specific area.

education   Systematic instruction or training.

egalitarian society   A society characterized by few individual or group differences in wealth and power.

ego   In kinship studies, the individual from whose point of view relationships are being traced.

enculturation   The process by which rules and values of a specific culture are learned through social interaction.

endemic disease   A disease that is constantly present in a given community, but with a relatively low incidence.

endogamy   A pattern, preference, or requirement that marriage be within a social group, class, or category. (Compare *exogamy*.)

environment   Physical, biological, and social surroundings.

epidemic disease   A disease not typically present in a community, characterized by high incidence and rapid and extensive diffusion.

epidemiology   The study of the interrelated factors that determine the frequency and distribution of diseases in societies.

ethnicity   Selected perceived cultural or physical differences by which people are grouped in categories considered to be significantly distinct.

ethnoarchaeology   An approach to ethnographic analogy in which archaeologists make their own observations of contemporary cultures, rather than relying on information provided by cultural anthropologists.

ethnocentrism   Evaluation of the behavior of others in terms of one's own cultural values and traditions.

ethnocide   The destruction of a people's culture carried out on a systematic basis.

ethnographic analogy   The use of existing cultures for generating hypotheses to test in the archaeological record and for testing hypotheses derived from the record.

ethnography   The process of describing cultures, largely through fieldwork.

ethnology   The systematic comparative study of patterns and processes in living and recent cultures.

ethnoscience   An approach to the study of culture involving detailed analysis of ethnographic data in the attempt to discover structural principles of specific societies.

ethogram   A careful and complete catalogue of a species' behavior, including how it moves, communicates, and breeds.

ethology   The scientific approach to animal behavior based on long-term, nonintervening, naturalistic fieldwork, focusing on the total organism within its environment.

exchange   The pattern of trade in resources, goods, ideas, and services.

exogamy   A pattern, preference, or requirement that marriage be outside a social group, class, or category. (Compare *endogamy*.)

expansion   The stage of family evolution that begins with marriage and lasts until all the children of the family are born and raised to reproductive age.

experimental archaeology   An "active" type of ethnographic analogy in which prehistoric material culture is replicated in controlled experiments.

experimental psychology   The study of animals under laboratory conditions so as to manipulate variables that influence behavior.

extended family group   A residential group consisting of two or more families of at least two generations.

faction   A political group that acts together within and in opposition to some element of a larger unit.

family   An intimate kin-based group consisting of at least a parent–child nucleus; the minimal social unit that cooperates economically and assumes responsibility for the rearing of children.

features (archaeological)   The nonportable artifacts of human activity; they cannot be removed intact from a site.

feud   Prolonged violence between different families or groups of kin.

feudalism   A social and economic system whereby land is held by conferred right by members of a privileged class who command the labor of a lower class to work the land. In medieval Europe, the privileged were referred to as lords, and the lower class as serfs.

First World   Western industrial capitalist nations.

fission-track dating   An absolute-dating technique using uranium-238, contained within tiny crystals of zircon found in volcanic rock.

fluorine analysis   A relative-dating technique used to date fossilized bones and teeth.

foraging   Collecting wild plants and animals for subsistence.

forensic anthropology   A subfield of anthropology concerned with legal questions relating to human physical remains or traces.

fossils   The remains of ancient plants and animals preserved through mineralization.

founder effect   A random event (rather than natural

selection) that causes a new population's gene pool to differ from that of the parental population; by chance, the founding group's gene pool is not identical to the original.

fraternal polyandry A marriage pattern in which a woman is married to a group of brothers.

function The purpose and effects, the intended and actual consequences, of particular beliefs and actions.

functionalism The theoretical perspective from which culture is seen to consist of complex interrelationships of elements in a total cultural system; each element is assumed to serve a function in that system.

gamete A sex cell. It contains half the complement of an individual's chromosomes and combines with another gamete during sexual reproduction.

gene The basic unit of heredity. It consists of DNA code that specifies the structure of a particular protein or section of a protein.

gene flow An evolutionary process in which a subpopulation of a species mates with individuals from another subpopulation, thus counteracting the effects of isolation and preventing genetic differentiation of subpopulations.

gene frequency The proportion of an allele of a gene in relation to other alleles of the gene within a given population.

gene pool All the genes within a particular population of a species; a compilation of the population's gene frequencies.

general cultural evolution The pattern of large-scale changes in culture with emphasis on major shifts in sociocultural development that occur over long periods of time. (Compare *specific cultural evolution*.)

general-purpose money A medium of exchange that can be used to pay for a wide range of material goods and services. (Compare *special-purpose money*.)

genetic fitness The relative measure of differences in reproductive success among individuals of a population.

genetics The scientific study of biological inheritance.

genocide The deliberate and systematic destruction of a political or cultural group.

genotype All or part of the genetic constitution of an individual.

geologic time scale The general climatic and temporal framework on which the study of evolutionary history is based.

ghost marriage The custom in which a woman is considered married to, or may simply bear children in the name of, a man who is deceased.

glottochronology The technique of estimating the dates at which two languages diverged from one another through comparison of core vocabularies.

god A supernatural being with an individual identity and recognizable attributes who is worshiped as having power over nature and human fortunes.

greenhouse effect A warming of the atmosphere caused by air pollutants that trap heated air near the surface of the earth.

habitat The specific physical space a species occupies within the larger environment.

hacienda A large estate, especially in a Spanish-speaking country, characterized by a feudal system of social stratification.

Hardy-Weinberg law A key concept in population genetics providing a mathematical formula used to predict what the next generation of a population will be like if it is not evolving. A real population can then be compared with its mathematical ideal.

heritability A complex statistical measure of the variability of a particular trait within a population in terms of how much variability is attributable to genetic factors.

heterozygote A pairing of two different forms (alleles) of a gene. (Compare *homozygote*.)

historical archaeology The branch of anthropological archaeology devoted to the study of the material remains of societies possessing written records.

historical linguistics The study of how languages change.

historical particularism An approach to anthropology in which the unique histories of individual cultures are investigated so as to reconstruct historical and psychological processes of cultural change.

holism The anthropological concept that all aspects of the human condition are to be comprehended in relation to the whole.

hominid A species on the human branch of the primate phylogenetic tree after it diverged from the rest of the order.

hominoid A member of the taxonomic group that includes all apes and human species, both living and extinct.

homology (biological) A characteristic shared by organisms as the result of common evolutionary descent.

homozygote A pair of genes of the same form (allele). (Compare *heterozygote*.)

horizon (archaeological) A pattern characterized by cultural traits dating from the same time and distributed over a broad geographic area. These traits serve to link the sites together culturally over large distances and over relatively short spans of time. (Compare *tradition*.)

horticulture   Garden cultivation.

human universalism   The anthropological principle that all peoples are fully and equally human.

hypothesis   A general scientific statement based on observable facts.

ideology   Values and beliefs about how the world is or should be ordered that are consciously and systematically organized into some form of program.

idiolect   The speech system of each person within a linguistic community.

illness   Pronounced deviation from what is considered to be a normal healthy state.

incest taboo   A rule prohibiting sexual intercourse between specific categories of kin.

inclusive fitness   The *total* likelihood that an individual's set of genes will be passed on to the next generation, both directly, through the individual's own children, and indirectly, through the offspring of close relatives.

indirect rule   The practice whereby ranking individuals in native populations assisted foreign colonial authorities in administering those in their charge.

inheritance   The process by which status and property are transmitted from one generation to the next.

innovation   The invention of new ideas or practices within a culture, either by accident or as the result of purposeful action.

instincts   Inheritable and unalterable behavioral tendencies to make complex and specific responses to environmental stimuli.

institutionalization   The standardization of modes of joint activity.

institutions   Practices based on similar principles that display some degree of regularity.

integration (anthropological)   A concept that emphasizes how the various aspects of life function together.

interference (linguistic)   The process by which deviation from speech norms occurs as a result of familiarity with multiple languages or dialects.

Iron Age   The period of human culture characterized by the smelting of iron and its use in industry beginning somewhat before 1000 B.C.

jajmani relationships   Patron–client relationships between families of different castes.

joint family group   A residential group consisting of two or more relatives and their spouses and children.

judgment sampling   Collecting data from a limited number of key informants who have been selected on the basis of criteria deemed critical to research.

kin selection   A concept used to explain seemingly maladaptive social behaviors. Such behaviors adaptively occur among closely related individuals to ensure that a greater proportion of one's genes will be passed on to the next generation.

kindred   The network of individuals linked to ego through ego-focused cognatic principles.

kinesics   The study of gestural communication.

kinship   Social relations based on culturally recognized ties by descent and marriage.

land rights   The right of native peoples to control what happens on the lands they occupy and to be compensated for the lands they have lost.

language   A highly flexible and complex system of communication that allows for the exchange of detailed information about both interior and exterior conditions. As a creative and open system, new signals may be added and new ideas transmitted.

large-scale societies   Societies characterized by a high degree of social complexity and dependence on extensive and highly specialized interchange of goods, ideas, and people. (Compare *small-scale societies*.)

latent functions   Effects that are not overly apparent, often emerging only after careful study. (Compare *manifest functions*.)

law   A binding rule, created through enactment or custom, that defines right and reasonable behavior.

leader (political)   An individual who has the power to make decisions within and for a group.

learning   Modifying behavior in response to experience within an environment.

legitimacy   A term used with reference to general normative concepts based ultimately on the traditional moral system of a society.

levirate   The custom of a brother of a man who has died, or some other member of his kin group, marrying his widow. (See also *sororate*.)

liberation theology   A belief that under conditions of social and economic injustice, one must become committed to the political—even revolutionary—liberation of the oppressed.

life cycle   The life process through birth, maturation, old age, death, and, in some traditions, beyond.

lineage   Descent in a line from common ancestors through known links.

linguistic anthropology   The branch of anthropology that concentrates on the study of language.

linguistic community   Any group within which

communication occurs having a recognizable communicational boundary.

linguistic density   The number of languages spoken within a population.

linguistic expansion   The spread of a language throughout a new population.

linguistic multiplication   The process of differentiation within a language; the development of variant forms.

linkage   The association between genes for different traits, located on the same chromosome.

Linnaean hierarchy   A scientific system of classifying living things based on traits common to different organisms; used as the basis of the binomial method of labeling life-forms.

literacy   The ability to read and write in a given language.

locus   The location of a gene on a chromosome.

macroevolution   A form of biological evolution over long periods, resulting in major changes in form. (Compare *microevolution*.)

manifest functions   The most obvious purposes or results of beliefs or actions; those that are explicitly stated. (Compare *latent functions*.)

marriage   A socially sanctioned sexual and economic union between members of the opposite sex (occasionally between members of the same sex).

Marxist anthropology   An approach to the process of social evolution focusing on the transformation of social orders and the relationships between conflict and cultural change.

matrilineage   A lineage formed on the basis of *matrilineal descent*.

matrilineal descent   A means of tracing descent through female lines.

matrilocal residence   Residence after marriage with the wife's kin.

medical anthropology   A field in which theory and methodology from all branches of anthropology are used in the study of human health.

mental illness   An illness associated with a mental state perceived as abnormal.

Mesolithic   A major stage of Old World prehistory, also known as the Middle Stone Age, representing an increased diversification of the subsistence strategies that characterized the Paleolithic.

microevolution   A form of biological evolution consisting of short-term changes within a population between generations. (Contrast *macroevolution*.)

microliths   Very small, geometrically shaped flint blades, particularly abundant during the Mesolithic.

middle-range archaeological theory   An approach to archaeology that seeks to bridge the past and present worlds by focusing on how the dynamic processes of culture and behavior are reflected by the static remains of extinct cultures.

millenarian movement   A social movement espousing a belief in the coming of a new world (a millennium), in part through supernatural action.

mineralization   A lengthy process by which the molecules of organic tissues are either chemically changed or replaced by molecules of minerals, such as lime or lime oxide.

mitochondrial DNA   DNA contained in the mitochondria, rather than in the nuclei, of the cells of multicellular life-forms.

modal personality   The central tendencies of the personality characteristics of a given population.

moiety   A division of a society into two social categories or groups.

molecular clock studies   A research area in which biochemical and genetic differences among species are taken as a measure of the time elapsed since the forms last shared an ancestor.

money   A medium of exchange characterized by durability, transferability, and acceptability over a wide range of functions.

monogamy   Marriage of one man to one woman at a time. (See also *serial monogamy*.)

monotheism   Belief that there is only one god.

morpheme   The smallest combination of sounds that conveys meaning.

morphology (linguistic)   The study of how simple sounds are organized to form units of meaning.

Mousterian   A tradition that includes diverse sets of tools associated with the Middle Paleolithic; consists mostly of flake tools.

multivariate studies   A technique for analyzing human diversity which examines the distribution of several polymorphic genetic traits at the same time.

mutagen   An environmental agent that raises the frequency of mutation above the spontaneous rate.

mutation   A mistake in the self-replication of a DNA molecule that can lead to genetic variability by introducing new alternative genes (alleles) into a population's gene pool.

myth   A sacred tale expressing the unobservable realities of religious belief in terms of observable phenomena.

natural selection   The evolutionary principle that when differences in form exist within a population, individuals with traits best suited to the environment will live the longest and produce the most offspring. Over time, beneficial traits become increasingly common within the population, while less desirable ones decrease in frequency.

naturalistic belief system A way of thinking in which impersonal factors are recognized as the cause of illness. (Compare *personalistic belief system*.)

neoevolutionism The belief in technological advancement as the key factor in social evolution.

neofunctionalism An attempt to reform the functionalist perspective by recognizing conflict as a normal part of human culture.

Neolithic A major stage of Old World prehistory, also known as the *New Stone Age*, associated with a transition from foraging to agricultural societies.

neolocal residence Residence of a couple after marriage in a new household, not linked to the households of either of their families.

neutral mutation A mutation that has neither positive nor negative effects on the genetic fitness of an organism. Substitution of one base for another does not affect the functioning of the protein or the fitness of the individual.

norms Conceptions of appropriate or expected behavior.

nuclear family A group composed of a man, a woman, and their children.

Oldowan The earliest recognized tool-making tradition, consisting of primitive stone tools of limited variety; named after materials discovered at Olduvai Gorge in Tanzania.

omnivore An animal that feeds on both plants and animals.

osteology The scientific study of bones.

ownership Acknowledged supremacy, authority, or power over a physical object or process.

paleoanthropology The multidisciplinary study of human biocultural evolution.

paleoecology The scientific study of ancient environments.

Paleolithic The earliest major stage of Old World prehistory, also known as the *Old Stone Age*.

paleontology The scientific study of extinct life.

palynology The scientific analysis of pollen; used by archaeologists to reconstruct the plant life that characterized an area in ancient times.

paradigm A fundamental intellectual framework that governs the nature of scientific theory and method.

parallel cousins The children of a parent's siblings

of the same sex; e.g., children of the father's brother. (Compare *cross-cousins*.)

parallel descent A means of tracing descent through female lines only, in the case of women, and through male lines only, in the case of men.

participant observation A research method that entails living among a group of people, observing their daily activities, learning how they view the world, and witnessing firsthand how they behave.

pastoral nomadism An economic adaptation and life-style characterized by a lack of permanent habitat and primary dependence on the herding of animals for subsistence.

patrilineage A lineage formed on the basis of *patrilineal descent*.

patrilineal descent A means of tracing descent through male lines.

patrilocal residence Residence after marriage with the husband's kin.

personalistic belief system A way of thinking in which illness is ascribed to the actions of a malicious supernatural being. (Compare *naturalistic belief system*.)

personality The totality of an individual's behavioral and emotional characteristics derived from the interaction of physiological and environmental influences.

phenotype An individual's observable characteristics.

phoneme The smallest linguistically significant unit of sound. Phonemes cannot be substituted for one another without changing meaning.

phonology The study of a language's sounds.

phratry A descent group composed of a number of supposedly related clans, the actual links usually being unrecognized.

phyletic evolution A form of macroevolution in which a whole species gradually changes through time until it can be called a new species. Phyletic evolution does not increase the number of coexisting species at any given time.

phylogeny The evolutionary history of a group of organisms.

physiological responses Functional means of contending with environmental stress based on the body's capacity to adjust to its surroundings.

pidgin A simplified hybrid language developed to fulfill communication needs in the absence of a common language.

plasticity The ability of an organism to respond and adjust to a wide range of conditions, especially as it is growing and developing.

plate tectonics The geologic theory that the earth's outer shell consists of individual plates in relative motion with respect to one another.

plural marriage Marriage to more than one person at the same time.

political leader See *leader.*

political norms Standards concerning appropriate political goals and behavior arrived at through the process of political socialization.

politics Competition for power.

polyandrous family group A group resulting from a polyandrous marriage, consisting of a wife and her husbands and children. The men live under a single roof with their wife or jointly occupy a separate men's hut.

polyandry Marriage of a woman to two or more men at the same time.

polygamy Marriage to more than one person at the same time.

polygynous family group A group resulting from a polygynous marriage, consisting of a husband, his wives, and his or their children, all living in a single household or, occasionally, the wives living in separate dwellings.

polygyny Marriage between one man and two or more women at the same time.

polymorphism (genetic) The presence in a population of two or more forms of a gene (alleles) at a particular gene site.

polytheism The belief that there can be an almost limitless number of gods, or a finite number arranged in some sort of hierarchy.

population An interbreeding group of individuals living within defined boundaries; also, a group of individuals from whom data is obtained as part of a research study.

population genetics The complex statistical study of the generational changes in a population's genetic constitution.

potassium–argon dating An absolute-dating technique using inorganic materials, usually rock formed by volcanic activity; based on the rate at which radioactive isotopes in ancient environments naturally decay into nonradioactive chemicals.

potlatch An elaborate, and at times quite dramatic, feast and gift-giving ceremony performed among Northwest Coast Indians; a form of redistribution of wealth.

power The ability to act effectively over people or things.

prehistoric archaeology The archaeology of societies that did not leave written records.

priest A person authorized to perform religious functions.

Primates The order of mammals that includes prosimians, tarsiers, monkeys, apes, and humans.

primatology The scientific study of the morphology (form and structure) and behavior of the nonhuman primates.

primitive A term sometimes used in reference to small-scale, nonindustrial societies, often derogatorily; also used in reference to simple forms of technology.

primogeniture The practice whereby the eldest child inherits most or all of the parents' property. (Compare *ultimogeniture.*)

probability sampling A research technique in which the responses of a selected segment of the population are taken as a miniature, relatively unbiased replica of the larger population.

processual archaeology An approach to archaeology that focuses on cultural processes—understanding social behavior and *why* cultural patterns exist as they do.

production Significant transformation of an object for cultural purposes.

proletariat In a class-based, industrial society, those who are engaged in the production of agricultural and industrial goods and who sell their labor for a wage. (Compare *capitalists.*)

prophet An individual who receives divine revelation, usually by visions or dreams, concerning a restructuring of some aspect of society or of a people's beliefs.

prosimians The so-called lower primates—those most similar in form to the earliest primate.

proteins Complex molecules, composed of amino acids, that make up living cells.

proxemics The study of the cultural use of space.

psychic unity The principle that all people have essentially the same mental capacities and potentials.

punctuated equilibrium A macroevolutionary theory stating that evolutionary change is not a gradual, ongoing process, but that species are stable for long periods; change, when it does occur, is characterized by rapid bursts.

race As a biological concept, a means of grouping individuals into categories on the basis of shared physical traits.

racial typology The division of human groups into discrete categories on the basis of "ideal types."

racism The use of perceived racial differences to determine people's position relative to one another.

radiocarbon dating An absolute-dating technique in which isotopes of carbon-based (organic) materials are measured; based on the rate at which radioactive isotopes in ancient environments naturally decay into nonradioactive chemicals.

raids Surprise predatory attacks generally by small groups of people on their neighbors.

random genetic drift An evolutionary process by which chance, instead of natural selection, causes a population's gene pool to change through time. Since each generation's gene pool represents a sampling of the previous generation's gene pool, the alleles of a particular gene may or may not be passed on in proportions equal to those of the parental generation.

random sample A significant number of people selected from a population on a random basis to serve as subjects in a research project.

rank society A society in which people differ in prestige according to a series of recognized graded ranks; associated historically with relatively productive foraging and farming societies organized on a multicommunity basis.

recessive (genetic) A genetic trait, the expression of which will be suppressed if paired in an individual's genotype with a dominant form of the same gene.

reciprocity The mutual exchange of goods and services.

recombination (genetic) The reshuffling of genetic material in each generation as the result of sexual reproduction, through the random assortment of chromosomes and through crossing over.

redundancy (linguistic) The repetition or reinforcement of a signal or message.

relative dating A category of dating techniques that sequentially orders a set of objects in time. (Compare *absolute dating*.)

religion The worship of supernatural forces or beings that provide shape and meaning to the universe.

replacement The stage of a family's evolution that includes the death of the parents and their replacement in the social structure by families of their children.

rite of passage A ritual associated with a transition period in a person's life cycle.

ritual Highly stereotyped, stylized, and repetitive behavior that takes place at a set time and place.

role A socially expected behavior pattern for an individual in a given situation.

role models Fictional or actual people whose activities provide an ideal for role performances.

salvage archaeology The attempt to rescue as much archaeological data as possible from a condemned area, no specific scientific questions as yet having been formulated.

sampling See *probability sampling*.

Sapir-Whorf hypothesis The hypothesis that language imposes restrictions on people's perceptions of the world and influences how they interpret their experiences.

science A branch of study concerned with systematically observing and classifying facts and establishing verifiable laws.

scientific method A precise way of designing and conducting research that involves establishing and testing hypotheses.

Second World Industrialized socialist countries.

sedentism A residence pattern characterized by permanent, year-round settlements, such as villages or towns.

seed-crop cultivation A relatively simple horticultural system involving the reproduction of a few domesticated plants through the annual introduction of seeds derived from the fruit of the plant. (Compare *vegeculture*.)

self-concept The mental image one has of oneself.

serial monogamy The marriage pattern in which an individual enters into a series of marriages, but still has only one spouse at a time.

seriation A type of relative-dating technique in which the attributes of artifacts are used to arrange assemblages that reflect temporal patterns of popularity in style and design.

sexual dimorphism Morphological or behavioral difference between the sexes of a species.

shaman A person believed to be in direct contact with the spirit world through trance and who may command spirits to do his or her bidding.

sign Anything that can convey information, including physical objects, colors, sounds, movements, and even silence.

simple trait (genetic) A phenotypic trait, the nature of which is determined by only one gene pair (at one locus). (Compare *complex trait*.)

site (archaeological) A spatial concentration of durable remains, the usual unit of an archaeological excavation. The composition of a site reflects the human activity that occurred within its boundaries.

slash-and-burn agriculture A form of shifting cultivation in which trees are cut down and brush set afire to prepare land for the planting of crops. As new sections are cleared, the older, less rich fields are left to return to a more natural state, until they are again used by the farmers.

small-scale societies Societies characterized by highly localized social interaction and the exploitation of local resources. (Compare *large-scale societies.*)

social class A division of society, defined in terms of its relationship to the means of production, with a collective identity and interests.

social networks The social bonds and links that form the social web within which members of a society act.

social relationship A regularized pattern of interaction between individuals within a particular social context.

social stratification The division of members of a society into strata (or levels) with unequal wealth, prestige, and power.

social structure The interrelations of individuals in the whole of society.

socialization The process of learning social roles through social interaction.

society An abstraction of the ways in which interaction among individuals is patterned.

sociobiology The scientific study of the evolution of animal social behavior (including human), emphasizing natural selection acting on individuals as the underlying evolutionary mechanism.

sociocultural anthropology The study of the social, symbolic, and material lives of humans.

sociolinguistics The study of the relationship between language and social factors, such as class, ethnicity, age, and gender.

sororal polygyny The custom that, upon marriage to a woman, a man acquires the right to claim her younger sister in marriage.

sororate The custom of a man marrying the sister of his deceased wife. (See also *levirate.*)

special-purpose money A medium of exchange only in limited contexts and only for a particular range of goods and services. (Compare *general-purpose money.*)

speciation The macroevolutionary process by which a lineage splits, resulting in the formation of new species. Life becomes more diversified with the increase of coexisting distinct species.

species The largest breeding unit within which a group of organisms, under natural conditions, are mat-

ing or can mate to produce healthy and fertile offspring.

species selection An evolutionary process in which natural selection occurs between competing species rather than between individual organisms from the same population.

specific cultural evolution The pattern of change in particular societies over relatively short spans of time. (Compare *general cultural evolution.*)

speech Patterned verbal behavior.

speech community A subunit of the *linguistic community* characterized by shared rules regarding speech and the interpretation of at least one linguistic variety.

speech network Links between speech communities formed on the basis of interaction and social ties among people across community boundaries.

stabilizing selection A type of natural selection in which a population's status quo is maintained within a stable environment by the weeding out of disadvantageous extreme forms from the most successful forms. (Compare *directional selection.*)

state An autonomous integrated political unit, encompassing many communities within its territory, with a highly specialized central governing authority.

status Relative social position assigned on the basis of birth or attained through individual efforts.

stratified sample A significant number of people selected from distinct subgroups within a population to serve as subjects in a research project.

stratigraphy The most common relative-dating technique, based on the premise that objects found buried in the deepest area of a site are the oldest, while the youngest objects are those found closest to the surface.

structural functionalism A theory that emphasizes how various elements of social structure are integrated and how they function to maintain social order and equilibrium.

structuralism An approach to the study of culture in which the human mind is viewed as the origin for the universal principles that order our behavior.

subpopulation A small and relatively isolated breeding segment of a species.

symbol A sign, the meaning of which is arbitrary, being determined by social convention and learning.

symbolic anthropology An approach to the study of culture that focuses on shared symbols and meanings in the context of social life.

syncretism The conscious adaptation of an alien

idea or practice in terms of some indigenous counterpart.

syntax Standardized conventions for combining words to form statements that make sense to other speakers of the same language.

synthesis In formulating scientific theory, a major explanatory step in which diverse ideas are combined into a unified whole. A synthesis is more than the sum of its parts because it explains how the pieces fit together.

taxation A form of redistribution of wealth in which individuals of a society surrender part of their wealth to the government in exchange for services provided them.

taxonomy The science of classifying living things.

technology The skills and knowledge by which people make things and extract resources.

Third World A loose category of about 120 countries characterized by low standards of living, high rates of population growth, and general economic and technological dependence on wealthier industrial nations.

tool tradition Artifacts grouped according to similarity of form, taking into account how they are associated in the archaeological record.

totem See *totemic emblem.*

totemic emblem A symbolic representation linking individuals or groups with human ancestors, plants, animals, or other natural phenomena.

tradition (archaeological) A pattern characterized by artifacts with similar attributes of widely varying ages and confined to a small geographic area. Traditions reflect ideas passed on from one generation to another, without necessarily having been spread over a large geographic area. (Compare *horizon*).

transhumance An economic adaptation and lifestyle characterized by residence in a permanent village and subsistence based on limited crop production and migratory herding of animals.

tribal world view A personal view of the universe in which humans are seen as united with nature, rather than separate from it. (Compare *civilized world view.*)

tribe A group of people who share patterns of speech, some cultural characteristics, and a common territory; in general, they feel that they have more in common with one another than with those around them.

ultimogeniture The practice whereby the youngest child remains in the parents' household and eventually inherits their property. (Compare *primogeniture.*)

underdeveloped society or country A society or country with persistent low standards of living that can be linked historically and structurally with the manner of its integration into the world system.

undeveloped society A society that is materially poor because it has not developed a complex technology.

uniformitarianism The geologic principle that the earth is tremendously old and subject to continuous and gradual change due to such everyday forces as wind, heat, pressure, and water.

unilineal descent A means of tracing descent through a single line—male or female.

unilineal evolutionism The belief that all cultures pass through essentially the same stages along a single line of development, moving from the "savage" to the "civilized."

values Emotionally charged beliefs about what is desirable or offensive, right or wrong, appropriate or inappropriate.

varna The four primary caste divisions in India, ranked according to their relative ritual purity: Brahmin, Kshatriya, Vaisha, and Shudra.

vegeculture A relatively complex horticultural system in which plants are propagated by direct cloning, such as cutting stems and dividing roots.

visual predation hypothesis The hypothesis that primate characteristics reflect an adaptation to a life of foraging in the shrub layer of forests.

voluntary association A special-purpose group the members of which are recruited on a nonascriptive basis.

warfare Formalized armed combat by groups representing rival political communities.

wealth Objects or resources that are useful or that have exchange value.

wife inheritance The custom of an heir of a deceased man marrying his widow.

world system A social system encompassing the entire world and entailing a single division of labor.

world systems theory An approach to cultural anthropology in which human societies are viewed as part of a worldwide interactive social system.

world view The basic cultural orientation of the members of a society.

ziggurat An ancient Mesopotamian temple tower consisting of a lofty pyramidal structure with outside staircases and a shrine on top.

Bibliography

Aberle, David F. 1966. *The Peyote Religion among the Navaho.* Chicago: Aldine.

Abramson, J.A. 1976. Style change in an Upper Sepik contact situation. In *Ethnic and Tourist Arts,* ed. N. Gradburn, 249–265. Berkeley: University of California Press.

Achebe, Chinua. 1961. *No Longer at Ease.* New York: Fawcett Books.

Adams, Robert M. 1966. *The Evolution of Urban Society.* Chicago: Aldine.

————. 1981. *Heartland of Cities.* Chicago: University of Chicago Press.

Adovasio, J.M., J.D. Gunn, J.L. Donahue, and R. Stuckenrath. 1978. Meadowcroft Rockshelter, 1977: An overview. *American Antiquity* 43:632–651.

Albon, Carrie. 1989. Church intervention fails: Could secession succeed? *Islands Business* 15(6):24–30.

Alexeev, V.P. 1979. The differential geography of races. In *Physiological and Morphological Adaptation and Evolution,* ed. William A. Stini, 97–109. The Hague: Mouton.

Allan, Mea. 1977. *Darwin and His Flowers.* New York: Taplinger Publishing Co.

Alper, Joseph, Jon Beckwith, and Lawrence G. Miller. 1978. Sociobiology is a political issue. In *The Sociobiology Debate,* ed. Arthur L. Caplan, 476–488. New York: Harper & Row.

Amadi, Adolphe O. 1981. *African Libraries: Western Tradition and Colonial Brainwashing.* Metuchen, NJ: The Scarecrow Press.

Angel, J. Lawrence, and Peggy C. Caldwell. 1984. Death by strangulation: A forensic anthropological case from Wilmington, Delaware. In *Human Identification: Case Studies in Forensic Anthropology,* ed. Ted A. Rathbun and Jane E. Buikstra, 168–175. Springfield, IL: Charles C Thomas.

Ardrey, Robert. 1976. *The Hunting Hypothesis.* New York: Atheneum.

Armstrong, Este. 1979. A quantitative comparison of the hominoid thalamus. I. Specific sensory relay nuclei. *American Journal of Physical Anthropology* 51:365–382.

Arnove, Robert F. 1981. The Nicaraguan national literacy crusade of 1980. *Comparative Educational Review* 25 (June):244–260.

Asad, Talal. 1970. *The Kababish Arabs: Power, Authority and Consent in a Nomadic Tribe.* London: Hurst.

Ayala, Francisco J. 1978. The mechanisms of evolution. *Scientific American* 239(3):56–69.

Ayunga, Hazel. 1986. Polygamy in the '80s. *Connexions* 20 (Spring):8–10.

Bailey, Fredrick G. 1969. *Stratagems and Spoils: A Social Anthropology of Politics.* Oxford: Blackwell.

Baker, Paul T. 1976. Work performance of highland natives. In *Man in the Andes,* ed. Paul T. Baker and Michael A. Little, 330–344. Stroudsburg, PA: Dowden, Hutchinson and Ross.

Baker, Paul T., Gabriel Escobar, Gordon De Jong, Charles J. Hoff, Richard B. Mazess, Joel M. Hanna, Michael A. Little, and Emilio Picon-Reategui. 1968. *High Altitude Adaptation in a Peruvian Community.* Occasional Papers in Anthropology, No. 1. University Park: Pennsylvania State University.

Baker, Paul T., and Joel M. Hanna. 1986. Perspectives on health and behavior of Samoans. In *The Changing Samoans,* ed. Paul T. Baker, Joel M. Hanna, and Thelma S. Baker, 419–434. New York: Oxford University Press.

Baker, Paul T., and Michael A. Little, eds. 1976. *Man in the Andes.* Stroudsburg, PA: Dowden, Hutchinson and Ross.

Baldwin, J.D., and J.I. Baldwin. 1976. Vocalizations of howler monkeys (*Alouatta palleata*) in Southwestern Panama. *Folia primatol.* 26:81–108.

Barash, David P. 1977. *Sociobiology and Behavior.* New York: Elsevier.

Barker, John. 1985. Missionaries and mourning: Continuity and change in the death ceremonies of a Melanesian people. In *Anthropologists, Missionaries, and Cultural Change,* ed. Darrel L. Whiteman, 263–294. Williamsburg, VA: College of William and Mary.

———. 1989. Western medicine and the continuity of belief: The Maisin of Collingwood Bay, Oro Province. In *A Continuing Trial of Treatment: Medical Pluralism in Papua New Guinea,* ed. Stephen Frankel and Gilbert Lewis, 69–94. Dordrecht: Kluwer.

———. 1990. Mission station and village: Cultural practice and representations in Maisin society. In *Christianity in Oceania: Ethnographic Perspectives,* ed. John Barker, 173–196. ASAO monograph no. 12. Lanham, MD: University Press of America.

Barker, John, and Anne Marie Tietjen. 1990. Female facial tattooing among the Maisin of Oro Province, Papua New Guinea: Changing significance of an ancient custom. *Oceania* 60(3):217–234.

Barnett, Homer G. 1953. *Innovation: The Basis of Cultural Change.* New York: McGraw-Hill.

Barrett, Leonard E. 1977. *The Rastafarians: The Dreadlocks of Jamaica.* Kingston: Sangster's/Heinemann.

Barth, Frederick. 1969. Introduction. In *Ethnic Groups and Boundaries,* ed. F. Barth, 9–38. Bergen/Oslo: Universtetsforlaget.

Baumel, Howard B. 1978. *Biology: Its Historical Development.* New York: Philosophical Library.

Beattie, John. 1964. *Other Cultures: Aims, Methods and Achievements in Social Anthropology.* New York: Free Press.

Belshaw, Cyril S. 1965. *Traditional Exchange and Modern Markets.* Englewood Cliffs, NJ: Prentice-Hall.

Belsky, J., and E. Pensky. 1988. Developmental history, personality and family relationships: Toward an emergent family system. In *Relationships within Families: Mutual Influences,* ed. R.A. Hinde and J. Stevenson-Hinde, 193–217. Oxford: Clarendon Press.

Benedict, Ruth. 1934. *Patterns of Culture.* Boston: Houghton Mifflin.

———. 1946. *The Chrysanthemum and the Sword.* Boston: Houghton Mifflin.

Berlin, Brent, and Paul Kay. 1969. *Basic Color Terms: Their Universality and Evolution.* Berkeley: University of California Press.

Berman, C.M. 1990. Intergenerational transmission of maternal rejection rates among free-ranging rhesus monkeys on Cayo Santiago. *Animal Behaviour* 39:329–337.

Berndt, Ronald M. 1965. Law and order in Aboriginal Australia. In *Aboriginal Man in Australia,* ed. R.M. Berndt and C.H. Berndt, 167–206. Sydney: Angus and Robertson.

Berreman, Gerald. 1962. Pahari polyandry: A comparison. *American Anthropologist* 64:60–75.

———. 1972. *Hindus of the Himalayas: Ethnography and Change.* 2d ed. Berkeley: University of California Press.

Bhola, Harbans S. 1981. Why literacy can't wait: Issues for the 1980's. *Convergence* 14(1):6–22.

Binford, Lewis R. 1962. Archeology as anthropology. *American Antiquity* 28:217–225.

———. 1967. Smudge pits and hide smoking: The use of analogy in archeological reasoning. *American Antiquity* 32:1–12.

———. 1968. Post-Pleistocene adaptations. In *New Perspectives in Archeology,* ed. Sally R. Binford and Lewis R. Binford, 313–341. Chicago: Aldine.

———. 1972. *An Archaeological Perspective.* New York: Seminar Press.

———. 1977. *For Theory Building in Archaeology.* New York: Academic Press.

———. 1978. *Nunamiut Ethnoarchaeology.* New York: Academic Press.

———. 1983. *Working at Archaeology.* New York: Academic Press.

———. 1989. *Debating Archaeology.* San Diego: Academic Press.

Binford, Sally R., and Lewis R. Binford. 1968. *New Perspectives in Archeology.* Chicago: Aldine.

Birdsell, J.B. 1975. *Human Evolution.* 2d ed. Chicago: Rand McNally.

Birdwhistell, Ray L. 1960. Kinesics and communication. In *Explorations and Communications,* ed. E. Carpenter and M. McLuhan, 54–64. Boston: Beacon Press.

Bishop, J.A., and Lawrence M. Cook. 1975. Moths, melanism and clean air. *Scientific American* 232(1):90–99.

Blaug, M. 1966. Literacy and economic development. *The School Review* 74 (4):393–415.

Bloch, M. 1983. *Marxism and Anthropology.* Oxford: The Clarendon Press.

Block, N.J., and Gerald Dworkin. 1976. IQ, heritability, and inequality. In *The IQ Controversy,* ed. N.J. Block and Gerald Dworkin, 410–440. New York: Pantheon Books.

Bodley, John H. 1985. *Anthropology and Contemporary Human Problems.* 2d ed. Palo Alto, CA: Mayfield Publishing Co.

Bodmer, W.F. 1972. Evolutionary significance of the HL-A system. *Nature* 237:139–145.

———. 1980. The HLA system and disease. *Journal of the Royal College of Physicians of London* 14(1):43–50.

Bogin, Barry. 1990. The extinction of *Homo sapiens.* In *Anthropology: Contemporary Perspectives,* 6th ed., ed. Phillip Whitten and David E.K. Hunter, 289–295. Glenview, IL: Scott, Foresman/Little, Brown.

Boissevain, Jeremy. 1974. *Friends of Friends: Networks, Manipulators and Coalitions.* Oxford: Blackwell.

Bolinger, Dwight. 1968. *Aspects of Language.* New York: Harcourt, Brace & World.

Bonner, John Tyler. 1980. *The Evolution of Culture in Animals.* Princeton, NJ: Princeton University Press.

Bordes, François. 1968. *The Old Stone Age.* New York: McGraw-Hill.

Bordes, François, and D. de Sonneville-Bordes. 1970. The significance of variability in Palaeolithic assemblages. *World Archaeology* 2:61–73.

Boserup, Ester. 1965. *The Conditions of Agricultural Growth.* Chicago: Aldine.

———. 1981. *Population and Technological Change.* Chicago: University of Chicago Press.

Bower, Bruce. 1987. Family feud: Enter the "black skull." *Science News* 131(4):58–59.

Bowler, Peter J. 1984. *Evolution: The History of an Idea.* Berkeley: University of California Press.

Brace, C.L., Harry Nelson, and Noel Korn. 1979. *Atlas of Human Evolution.* New York: Holt, Rinehart & Winston.

Braidwood, Robert J. 1958. Near Eastern prehistory. *Science* 127:1419–1430.

———. 1971. The earliest village communities of Southwestern Asia reconsidered. In *Prehistoric Agriculture,* ed. Stuart Struever, 236–251. Garden City, NY: The Natural History Press.

———. 1975. *Prehistoric Men.* 5th ed. Glenview, IL: Scott, Foresman.

Braverman, Harry. 1974. *Labor and Monopoly Capital.* New York: Monthly Review Press.

Briggs, Jean L. 1970. *Never in Anger: Portrait of an Eskimo Family.* Cambridge, MA: Harvard University Press.

Brockelman, W.Y., and S. Srikosamatara. 1984. Maintenance and evolution of social structure in gibbons. In *The Lesser Apes,* ed. Holger Preuschoft, David J. Chivers, Warren Y. Brockelman, and Norman Creel, 298–323. Edinburgh: Edinburgh University Press.

Brown, James A., and Robert K. Vierra. 1983. What happened in the Middle Archaic? Introduction to an ecological approach to Koster site archaeology. In *Archaic Hunters and Gatherers in the American Midwest,* ed. J.P. Phillips and J.A. Brown, 165–195. New York: Academic Press.

Brumfiel, E.M. 1983. Aztec state making: Ecology, structure, and the origin of the state. *American Anthropologist* 85(2):261–284.

Bryne, Malcolm. 1987. *The Documented Day-by-Day Account of the Secret Military Assistance to Iran and the Contras.* New York: Warner Books.

Budnitz, N., and K. Dainis. 1975. *Lemur catta:* Ecology and behavior. In *Lemur Biology,* ed. I. Tattersall and R.W. Sussman, 219–235. New York: Plenum Press.

Buettner-Janusch, John. 1973. *Physical Anthropology: A Perspective.* New York: John Wiley.

Buikstra, Jane. 1976. *Hopewell in the Lower Illinois Valley.* Evanston, IL: Northwestern University Archeological Program.

Bunker, Stephen G. 1985. *Underdeveloping the Amazon: Extraction, Unequal Exchange, and the Failure of the Modern State.* Urbana: University of Illinois Press.

Burridge, Kenelm. 1969. *New Heaven New Earth: A Study of Millenarian Activities.* Oxford: Blackwell.

Buskirk, Elsworth. 1976. Work performance of newcomers to the Peruvian highlands. In *Man in the Andes,* ed. Paul T. Baker and Michael A. Little, 283–299. Stroudsburg, PA: Dowden, Hutchinson and Ross.

Butzer, Karl W. 1971. *Environment and Archeology.* 2d ed. Chicago: Aldine/Atherton.

Cachel, Susan. 1981. Plate tectonics and the problem of anthropoid origins. *Yearbook of Physical Anthropology* 24:139–172.

Campbell, Bernard G. 1985. *Humankind Emerging.* 4th ed. Boston: Little, Brown.

Campbell, J.K. 1974. *Honour, Family, and Patronage: A Study of Institutions and Moral Values in a Greek Mountain Community.* Oxford: Oxford University Press.

Cancian, Francesca. 1975. *What Are Norms? A Study of Beliefs and Action in a Maya Community.* New York: Cambridge University Press.

Cann, Rebecca L. 1987. In search of Eve. *The Sciences* 27(5):30–37.

Caplan, Arthur L. 1978. *The Sociobiology Debate.* New York: Harper & Row.

Carneiro, Robert. 1970. A theory of the origin of the state. *Science* 169:733–738.

———. 1981. The chiefdom: Precursor of the state. In *The Transition to Statehood in the New World,* ed. Grant D. Jones and Robert R. Kautz, 37–39. Cambridge: Cambridge University Press.

Carrier, James G., and Achsah H. Carrier. 1989. *Wage, Trade, and Exchange in Melanesia: A Manus Society in the Modern State.* Berkeley: University of California Press.

Cartmill, Matt. 1972. Arboreal adaptations and the origin of the order Primates. In *The Functional and Evolutionary Biology of the Primates,* ed. Russell Tuttle, 97–122. Chicago: Aldine.

Caspi, A., and G.H. Elder. 1988. Emergent family patterns: The intergenerational construction of problem behavior and relationships. In *Relationships within Families: Mutual Influences,* ed. R.A. Hinde and J. Stevenson-Hinde, 218–240. Oxford: Clarendon Press.

Cavalli-Sforza, L.L. 1977. *Elements of Human Genetics.* Menlo Park, CA: W.A. Benjamin.

Cavalli-Sforza, L.L., and W.F. Bodmer. 1971. *The Genetics of Human Populations.* San Francisco: W.H. Freeman.

Cawte, John. 1974. *Medicine Is the Law: Studies in Psychiatric Anthropology of Australian Tribal Societies.* Honolulu: University Press of Hawaii.

Chagnon, Napoleon A. 1977. *Yanomamo: The Fierce People.* 2d ed. New York: Holt, Rinehart & Winston.

Champion, Timothy, Clive Gamble, Stephen Shennan, and Alasdair Whittle. 1984. *Prehistoric Europe.* London: Academic Press.

Chance, N.A. 1966. *The Eskimo of North Alaska.* New York: Holt, Rinehart & Winston.

Chandler, Michele. 1986. Widows ripped off. *Connexions* 20 (Spring):14.

Chang, K.C. 1983. Sandai archaeology and the formation of states in ancient China: Processual aspects of the origins of Chinese civilization. In *The Origins of Chinese Civilization,* ed. David N. Keightley, 495–521. Berkeley: University of California Press.

Chignell, A.K. 1911. *An Outpost in Papua.* London: Murray.

Childe, V. Gordon. 1936. *Man Makes Himself.* London: C.A. Watts & Co.

———. 1952. *New Light on the Most Ancient East.* London: Routledge & Kegan Paul.

———. 1957. *What Happened in History.* Baltimore: Pelican Books.

Ciochon, Russell L., and A.B. Chiarelli, eds. 1980. *Evolutionary Biology of the New World Monkeys and Continental Drift.* New York: Plenum Press.

Ciochon, Russell L., and R.S. Coviuccini, eds. 1983. *New Interpretations of Ape and Human Ancestry.* New York: Plenum Press.

Ciochon, Russell L., and John G. Fleagle, eds. 1985. *Primate Evolution and Human Origins.* Menlo Park, CA: Benjamin-Cummings.

Clammer, John R. 1976. *Literacy and Social Change.* Leiden: E.J. Brill.

Clark, J.G.D. 1954. *Excavations at Starr Carr.* Cambridge: Cambridge University Press.

———. 1972. *Starr Carr: A Case Study in Bioarchaeology.* Reading, MA: Addison-Wesley.

Clark, Margaret. 1970. *Health in the Mexican-American Culture: A Community Study.* Berkeley: University of California Press.

Clark, W.E. Le Gros. 1971 [1959]. *The Antecedents of Man.* New York: Quadrangle/The New York Times Book Co.

Cleere, Henry F. 1989. Introduction: The rationale of archaeological heritage management. In *Archaeological Heritage Management in the Modern World,* ed. H.F. Cleere, 1–19. London: Unwin Hyman, Ltd.

Codere, Helen. 1950. *Fighting with Property.* Seattle: University of Washington Press.

Cohen, Abner. 1969. *Custom and Politics in Urban Africa.* Berkeley: University of California Press.

———. 1974. *Two-Dimensional Man.* Berkeley: University of California Press.

Cohen, Margot. 1990. A menu for malnutrition. *Far Eastern Economic Review.* 149(28):38–39.

Cohen, Mark. 1977. *The Food Crisis in Prehistory.* New Haven, CT: Yale University Press.

Coles, John. 1979. *Experimental Archaeology.* London: Academic Press.

Colson, Anthony C., and Karen F. Selby. 1974. Survey article on medical anthropology. *Annual Review of Anthropology* 3:245–262.

Conkey, Margaret W. 1981. A century of Palaeolithic cave art. *Archaeology* 34(4):20–28.

Conklin, H.C. 1955. Hanunoo color categories. *Southwestern Journal of Anthropology* 11:339–344.

Conway, William. 1985. Saving the lion-tailed macaque. In *The Lion-Tailed Macaque: Status and Conservation,* ed. Paul G. Heltne, 1–12. New York: Alan R. Liss.

Coon, Carlton S. 1962. *The Origin of Races.* New York: Alfred A. Knopf.

Crane, Julia, and Michael Angrosino. 1974. *Field Projects in Anthropology: A Student Handbook.* Glenview, IL: Scott, Foresman.

Crawford, M.H. 1983. The anthropological genetics of the Black Caribs (Garifuna) of Central America and the Caribbean. *Yearbook of Physical Anthropology* 26:161–192.

Creel, N., and H. Preuschoft. 1984. Pathways of speciation: An introduction. In *The Lesser Apes,* ed. Holger Preuschoft, David J. Chivers, Warren Y. Brockelman, and Norman Creel, 427–430. Edinburgh: Edinburgh University Press.

Crosby, Alfred W., Jr. 1972. *The Columbian Exchange: Biological and Cultural Consequences of 1492.* Westport, CT: Greenwood Press.

Culbert, Sidney S., ed. 1990. *The World Almanac and Book of Facts.* New York: Newspaper Enterprise Association.

Curr, E.M. 1886–87. *The Australian Race.* 4 vols. Melbourne: Government Printer.

Czaplicki, Jon S., and John C. Ravesloot. 1989. Hohokam archaeology along Phase D of the Tucson Aqueduct, Central Arizona Project. 5 vols. *Arizona State Museum Archaeological Series* 178. Tucson: University of Arizona Press.

Daggett, Richard. 1987. Toward the development of the state on the north central coast of Peru. In *The Origins and Development of the Andean State,* ed. Jonathan H. .as, Shelia Pozorski, and Thomas Pozorski, 70–82. Cambridge: Cambridge University Press.

Dagmar, Hans. 1978. *Aborigines and Poverty: A Study of Interethnic Relations and Culture Conflict in a Western Australian Town.* Nijmegen, The Netherlands: Katholieke Universiteit.

Damas, David. 1972. The Copper Eskimo. In *Hunters and Gatherers Today,* ed. M.G. Bicchieri, 3–50. New York: Holt, Rinehart & Winston.

Darwin, Charles. 1972. *The Voyage of the Beagle.* Reprint. New York: Bantam Books.

Datta, V.N. 1988. *Sati: A Historical, Social and Philosophical Enquiry into the Hindu Rite of Widow Burning.* New Delhi: Manohar.

Davis, Shelton H. 1977. *Victims of the Miracle: Development and the Indians of Brazil.* Cambridge: Cambridge University Press.

Day, Michael H. 1986. *Guide to Fossil Man.* 4th ed. Chicago: University of Chicago Press.

DeCamp, David. 1971. Introduction: The study of pidgin and creole languages. In *Pidginization and Creolization of Languages,* ed. D. Hymes, 13–39. Cambridge: Cambridge University Press.

Deetz, James. 1967. *Invitation to Archaeology.* Garden City, NY: The Natural History Press.

Dentan, Robert. 1968. *The Semai: A Nonviolent People of Malaya.* New York: Holt, Rinehart & Winston.

Dethlefsen, E.S., and James Deetz. 1966. Death's heads, cherubs and willow trees: Experimental archaeology in colonial cemeteries. *American Antiquities* 31:502–510.

Devevan, William M. 1970. Aboriginal drained-field cultivation in the Americas. *Science* 169:647–654.

Diamond, Jared. 1988. Founding mothers and fathers. *Natural History* 97(6):10–15.

Dienske, H., W. van Vreeswijk, and H. Koning. 1980. Adequate mothering by partially isolated rhesus monkeys after observation of maternal care. *Journal of Abnormal Psychology* 89:489–492.

Divale, William, and Marvin Harris. 1976. Population, warfare and the male supremist complex. *American Anthropologist* 78:521–538.

Dobbs, Michael. 1987. In Iraq, one of the world's earliest civilizations is pushed to the brink of extinction. *International Herald Tribune,* December 12:5.

Dobzhansky, Theodosius. 1962. *Mankind Evolving.* Toronto: Bantam Books.

———. 1972. Genetics and the races of man. In *Sexual Selection and the Descent of Man,* ed. Bernard Campbell, 59–86. Chicago: Aldine.

———. 1974. Chance and creativity in evolution. In *Studies in the Philosophy of Biology,* ed. F.J. Ayala and T. Dobzhansky, 309–339. Berkeley: University of California Press.

Domhoff, G. William. 1974. *The Bohemian Grove and Other Retreats: A Study of Ruling Class Cohesiveness.* New York: Harper & Row.

Dominguez, Enrique, and Deborah Huntington. 1984. The salvation brokers: Conservative evangelicals in Central America. *NACLA Report on the Americas* 18(1):2–36.

Douglas, Mary. 1958. Raffia distribution in Lele economy. *Africa* 21:1–12.

DuBois, Cora. 1960. *The People of Alor: A Social-Psychological Study of an East Indian Island.* 2 vols. New York: Harper & Row.

Dumont, Louis. 1970. Homo hierarchicus: *The Caste System and Its Implications.* London: Weidenfield and Nicolson.

Dunaif-Hattis, Janet. 1984. *Doubling the Brain.* New York: Peter Lang.

Dunn, Frederick L. 1968. Epidemiological factors: Health and disease in hunter-gatherers. In *Man the Hunter,* ed. R.B. Lee and I. deVore, 221–228. Chicago: Aldine-Atherton.

Durkheim, Emile. 1951. *Suicide: A Study in Society.* Glencoe, IL: Free Press.

Durutalo, Simione. 1985. Internal colonialism and unequal development: The case of Western Viti Levu. Unpublished master's thesis. Suva: University of the South Pacific.

———. 1986. *The Paramountcy of Fijian Interests and the Politicization of Ethnicity.* Working paper 6. Suva: USP Sociological Society, South Pacific Forum.

Duvignaud, Jean. 1970. *Change at Shebika: Report from a North African Village.* New York: Random House.

Eibl-Eibesfeldt, Irenaus. 1975. *Ethology.* 2d ed. New York: Holt, Rinehart & Winston.

Eidheim, Harald. 1971. *Aspects of the Lappish Minority Situation.* Bergen/Oslo: Universtetsforlaget.

Eiseley, Loren. 1961. *Darwin's Century.* Garden City, NY: Anchor Books/Doubleday.

Eisenstadt, Shmuel N. 1969. *The Political Systems of Empires: The Rise and Fall of Historical Bureaucratic Societies.* New York: Free Press.

Eldredge, Niles. 1982. *The Monkey Business.* New York: Pocket Books.

———. 1985. *Time Frames.* New York: Simon & Schuster.

Eldredge, Niles, and Stephen Jay Gould. 1972. Punctuated equilibria: An alternative approach to phyletic gradualism. In *Models in Paleobiology,* ed. T.J.M. Schopf, 82–115. San Francisco: Freeman, Cooper and Co.

Eluyemi, Omotoso. 1989. The archaeology of Yoruba: Problems and possibilities. In *Archaeological Approaches to Cultural Identity,* ed. S.J. Shennan, 207–209. London: Unwin Hyman, Ltd.

Evans-Pritchard, E.E. 1937. *Witchcraft, Oracles and Magic among the Azande.* Oxford: The Clarendon Press.

———. 1940. *The Nuer: A Description of the Modes of Livelihood and Political Institutions of a Nilotic People.* Oxford: The Clarendon Press.

Every, R.G. 1975. Significance of tooth sharpness for mammalian, especially primate, evolution. In *Approaches to Primate Paleobiology.* Vol. 5, *Contrib. Primat.,* ed. F.S. Szalay, 293–325. Basel: S. Karger.

Eysenck, Hans J., and R. Grossarth-Maticek. 1989. Prevention of cancer and coronary heart disease and the reduction of the cost of the National Health Service. *Journal of Social, Political and Economic Studies* 14(Spring): 25–47.

Fabrega, Horacio, Jr., and Daniel B. Silver. 1973. *Illness and Shamanistic Curing in Zinacantan: An Ethnomedical Analysis.* Stanford, CA: Stanford University Press.

Fagan, Brian M. 1986. *People of the Earth.* 5th ed. Boston: Little, Brown.

———. 1988. *In the Beginning.* 6th ed. Glenview, IL: Scott, Foresman/Little, Brown.

Falk, Dean. 1980. Hominid brain evolution: The approach from paleoneurology. *Yearbook of Physical Anthropology* 23:93–107.

Fedigan, Linda Marie. 1986. The changing role of women in models of human evolution. *Annual Review of Anthropology* 15:25–66.

Ferguson, Charles. 1959. Diglossia. *Word* 15:325–340.

Fiedel, Stuart J. 1987. *Prehistory of the Americas.* Cambridge: Cambridge University Press.

Flannery, Kent V. 1972. The cultural evolution of civilizations. *Annual Review of Ecology and Systematics* 3:399–426.

———. 1973. The origins of agriculture. *Annual Review of Anthropology* 2:271–310.

Flannery, Kent V., ed. 1976. *The Early Mesoamerican Village.* New York: Academic Press.

Flannery, Kent V., and Marcus C. Winter. 1976. Analyzing household activities. In *The Early Mesoamerican Village,* ed. Kent V. Flannery, 34–47. New York: Academic Press.

Fleagle, John G. 1988. *Primate Adaptation and Evolution.* San Diego: Academic Press.

Fleagle, John G., Richard F. Kay, and Elwyn L. Simons. 1980. Sexual dimorphism in early anthropoids. *Nature* 287:328–330.

Folsom, Franklin, and Mary Folsom. 1982. Sinodonty and Sundadonty: An argument with teeth in it for man's arrival in the New World. *Early Man* 4(2):16–21.

Forde, C. Daryll. 1964. *Yako Studies.* London: Oxford University Press.

Forge, Anthony. 1979. The problem of meaning in art. In *Exploring the Visual Art of Oceania,* ed. S. Mead, 278–286. Honolulu: University Press of Hawaii.

Fortes, Meyer. 1958. Introduction. In *The Developmental Cycle in Domestic Groups,* ed. J. Goody, 1–14. Cambridge: Cambridge University Press.

Foster, George M. 1965. Peasant society and the image in limited good. *American Anthropologist* 67:293–315.

Foster, George M., and Barbara G. Anderson. 1978. *Medical Anthropology.* New York: John Wiley.

Foulks, Edward F. 1985. The transformation of Arctic hysteria. In *The Culture-Bound Syndromes,* ed. R. Simons and C. Hughes, 307–324. Boston: D. Reidel.

Fouts, Roger, and Richard L. Budd. 1979. Artificial and human language acquisition in the chimpanzees. In *The Great Apes,* ed. David A. Hamburg and E.R. McCown, 375–392. Menlo Park, CA: Benjamin-Cummings.

Fraenkel, M. 1964. *Tribe and Caste in Monrovia.* London: Oxford University Press.

Frank, André Gunder. 1972. The development of underdevelopment. In *Dependence and Underdevelopment,* ed. J.C. Cockcroft, A.G. Frank, and D.L. Johnson, 3–18. Garden City, NY: Anchor Books.

Freeman, J.D. 1958. The family system of the Iban of Borneo. In *The Development Cycle in Domestic Groups,* ed. J. Goody, 15–52. Cambridge: Cambridge University Press.

Freidson, Eliot. 1970. *Professional Dominance: The Social Structure of Medical Care.* New York: Atherton Press.

Fried, Jacob. 1959. Acculturation and mental health among Indian migrants in Peru. In *Culture and Mental Health,* ed. M.K. Opler, 119–137. New York: Macmillan.

Frison, George C. 1978. *Prehistoric Hunters of the High Plains.* New York: Academic Press.

Furst, Peter T., ed. 1972. *Flesh of the Gods: The Ritual Use of Hallucinogens.* London: George Allen & Unwin.

Futuyama, Douglas J. 1983. *Science on Trial.* New York: Pantheon Books.

Gajdusek, D.C. 1977. Unconventional viruses and the origin and disappearance of Kuru. *Science* 197:943–960.

Galbraith, John K. 1977. *The Age of Uncertainty.* Boston: Houghton Mifflin.

Galdikas, B.M.F. 1979. Orangutan adaptation at Tanjung Puting Reserve: Mating and ecology. In *The Great Apes,* ed. D.A. Hamburg and E.R. McCown, 195–233. Menlo Park, CA: Benjamin-Cummings.

———. 1984. Adult female sociality among wild orangutans at Tanjung Puting Reserve. In *Female Primates: Studies by Women Primatologists,* ed. Meredith F. Small, 217–235. New York: Alan R. Liss.

Galdikas, B.M.F., and G. Teleki. 1981. Variations in subsistence activities of female and male pongids: New perspectives on the origin of hominid labor division. *Current Anthropology* 22:241–256.

Garn, Stanley M. 1965. *Human Races.* Springfield, IL: Charles C Thomas.

———. 1981. The growth of growth. *American Journal of Physical Anthropology* 56:521–530.

Geertz, Clifford. 1960. *The Religion of Java.* Glencoe, IL: Free Press.

———. 1973. *The Interpretation of Cultures: Selected Essays.* New York: Basic Books.

Gheerbrant, Alain. 1974. *The Rebel Church in Latin America.* New York: Penguin.

Gingerich, Philip D. 1984. Primate evolution: Evidence from the fossil record, comparative morphology, and molecular biology. *Yearbook of Physical Anthropology* 27:57–72.

———. 1985. Eocene Adapidae, paleobiogeography, and the origin of South American Platyrrhini. In *Primate Evolution and Human Origins,* ed. Russell L. Ciochon and John G. Fleagle, 94–100. Menlo Park, CA: Benjamin-Cummings.

Glasse, R.M. 1969. Marriage in South Fore. In *Pigs, Pearlshells, and Women,* ed. R.M. Glasse and M.J. Meggitt, 16–37. Englewood Cliffs, NJ: Prentice-Hall.

Gluckman, Max. 1949. *Malinowski's Sociological Theories.* The Rhodes-Livingstone Papers, no. 16. Oxford.

———. 1950. Kinship and marriage among the Lozi of Northern Rhodesia and the Zulu of Natal. In *African Systems of Kinship and Marriage,* ed. A.R. Radcliffe-Brown and C.D. Forde, 166–206. London: Oxford University Press.

———. 1956. *Customs and Conflict in Africa.* Oxford: Blackwell.

———. 1965. *Politics, Law and Ritual in Tribal Society.* Chicago: Aldine.

———. 1973. *The Judicial Process among the Barotse of Northern Rhodesia (Zambia).* 2d ed. Manchester: Manchester University Press.

Godelier, Maurice. 1977. *Perspectives in Marxist Anthropology.* Cambridge: Cambridge University Press.

Godfrey, Laurie R. 1981. The flood of antievolutionism. *Natural History* 90(6):9–10.

Goodale, Jane C. 1971. *Tiwi Wives: A Study of the*

Women of Melville Island, North Australia. Seattle: University of Washington Press.

Goodall, Jane. 1964. Tool using and aimed throwing in a community of free-living chimpanzees. *Nature* 201:1264–1266.

————. 1971. *In the Shadow of Man.* New York: Dell Publishing Co.

Goodland, Robert, and Howard Irwin. 1975. *Amazon Jungle: Green Hell to Red Desert?* New York: Elsevier.

Goodman, Morris, and Richard E. Tashian. 1976. *Molecular Anthropology.* New York: Plenum Press.

Goody, Jack R. 1970. Cousin terms. *Southwestern Journal of Anthropology* 26:125–142.

Gorman, Chester. 1977. A priori models and Thai prehistory: A reconsideration of the beginnings of agriculture in Southeastern Asia. In *Origins of Agriculture,* ed. Charles A. Reed, 321–355. The Hague: Mouton.

Gorman, E. Michael. 1986. The AIDS epidemic in San Francisco: Epidemiological and anthropological perspectives. In *Anthropology and Epidemiology,* ed. Craig R. Janes, Ron Stall, and Sandra M. Gifford, 157–172. Dordrecht, Holland: D. Reidel Publishing Co.

Gould, Richard. 1978. The anthropology of human residues. *American Antiquity* 80:815–835.

————. 1980. *Living Archaeology.* Cambridge: Cambridge University Press.

Gould, Stephen Jay. 1977. *Ever Since Darwin.* New York: W.W. Norton.

————. 1980. *Panda's Thumb.* New York: W.W. Norton.

————. 1981. *The Mismeasure of Man.* New York: W.W. Norton.

Gowlett, John. 1984. *Ascent to Civilization.* New York: Alfred A. Knopf.

Graburn, Nelson. 1976. Introduction: The arts of the fourth world. In *Ethnic and Tourist Arts,* ed. N. Graburn, 1–32. Berkeley: University of California Press.

Grant, Verne. 1985. *The Evolutionary Process.* New York: Columbia University Press.

Green, Ernestene L. 1984. *Ethics and Values in Archaeology.* New York: Free Press.

Griffin, James B. 1978. The Midlands and northeastern United States. In *Ancient Native Americans,* ed. Jesse D. Jennings, 221–279. San Francisco: W.H. Freeman.

Gumperz, John. 1962. Types of linguistic communities. *Anthropological Linguistics* 4:28–40.

Haas, Jonathan. 1982. *The Evolution of the Prehistoric State.* New York: Columbia University Press.

————. 1987. The exercise of power in early Andean state development. In *The Origins and Development of the Andean State,* ed. Jonathan Haas, Shelia Pozorski, and Thomas Pozorski, 31–35. Cambridge: Cambridge University Press.

Hall, Edward T. 1966. *The Hidden Dimension.* Garden City, NY: Doubleday.

Hallam, Anthony. 1987. End-Cretaceous mass extinction event: Argument for terrestrial causation. *Science* 238:1237–1242.

Hamilton, W.D. 1964. The genetical evolution of social behavior. I,II. *Journal of Theoretical Biology* 7:1–52.

Hancock, Ian F. 1971. A survey of the pidgins and creoles of the world. In *Pidginization and Creolization of Languages,* ed. D. Hymes, 509–523. Cambridge: Cambridge University Press.

Haring, Douglas. 1949. *Personal Character and Cultural Milieu.* Syracuse, NY: Syracuse University Press.

Harlow, H.F., and M.K. Harlow. 1965. The affectional system. In *Behavior of Nonhuman Primates,* vol. 2, ed. A.M. Schrier, H.F. Harlow, and F. Stollnitz, 287–334. New York: Academic Press.

Harner, Michael J., ed. 1973. *Hallucinogens and Shamanism.* New York: Oxford University Press.

Harris, David R. 1977. Alternative pathways toward agriculture. In *Origins of Agriculture,* ed. Charles A. Reed, 179–243. The Hague: Mouton.

Harrison, G.A., J.M. Tanner, D.R. Pilbeam, and P.T. Baker. 1988. *Human Biology.* 3d ed. Oxford: Oxford University Press.

Hart, C.W.M., and A.R. Pilling. 1979. *The Tiwi of North Australia.* Fieldwork edition. New York: Holt, Rinehart & Winston.

Hartl, Daniel L. 1983. *Human Genetics.* New York: Harper & Row.

Hassan, Fekri A. 1981. *Demographic Archaeology.* New York: Academic Press.

Helms, Mary W. 1976. Competition, power and succession to office in pre-Columbian Panama. In *Frontier Adaptations in Lower Central America,* ed. M.W. Helms and F.O. Loveland, 25–36. Philadelphia: Institute for the Study of Human Issues.

Henry, Jules. 1963. *Culture against Man.* New York: Random House.

Heston, Alan. 1971. An approach to the sacred cow of India. *Current Anthropology* 12:191–209.

Hewes, Gordon. 1971. New light on the gestural origin of language. In *Language Origins: A Bibliography,* ed. Gordon W. Hewes, vii–vxi. Boulder: Department of Anthropology, University of Colorado.

Heyerdahl, Thor. 1950. *The Kon-Tiki Expedition.* London: Allen and Unwin.

Hiatt, Les R., ed. 1975. *Australian Aboriginal Mythology.* Canberra: Australian Institute of Aboriginal Studies.

Hicks, Frederick. 1979. "Flowery war" in Aztec history. *American Ethnologist* 6:87–92.

Hinde, Robert A. 1974. *Biological Bases of Human Social Behaviour.* New York: McGraw-Hill.

———. 1982. *Ethology: Its Nature and Relations with Other Sciences.* Oxford: Oxford University Press.

Hoare, Q., and G.N. Smith, eds. 1971. *Selections from the Prison Notebooks of Antonio Gramsci.* London: Lawrence and Wishart.

Hockett, Charles, and R. Ascher. 1964. The human revolution. *Current Anthropology* 5:135–168.

Hodder, Ian. 1982. *Symbolic and Structural Archaeology.* Cambridge: Cambridge University Press.

Hoebel, E. Adamson. 1940. *The Political Organization and Law-Ways of the Commanche Indians.* Memoir 54. Menasha, WI: American Anthropological Association.

Hole, Frank, Kent V. Flannery, and James A. Neely. 1969. *Prehistory and Human Ecology of the Deh Luran Plain.* Ann Arbor: University of Michigan Press.

Holtved, Erik. 1967. Eskimo shamanism. In *Studies in Shamanism,* ed. C.-M. Edsman, 23–31. Stockholm: Amquist and Wiksell.

Honigmann, John J. 1970. Sampling in ethnographic fieldwork. In *A Handbook of Method in Cultural Anthropology,* ed. R. Naroll and R. Cohen, 266–281. New York: Columbia University Press.

Hopkins, David M., John V. Matthews, Charles E. Schweger, and Steven B. Young, eds. 1982. *Paleoecology of Beringia.* New York: Academic Press.

Horwood, Harold. 1969. *Newfoundland.* Toronto: Macmillan of Canada.

Howard, Michael C. 1977. *Political Change in a Maya Village in Southern Belize.* Greeley: Katunob, University of Northern Colorado.

———. 1980. Ethnicity and economic integration in southern Belize. *Ethnicity* 7:119–136.

———. 1981. *Aboriginal Politics in Southwestern Australia.* Nedlands: University of Western Australia Press.

———. 1987. *The Impact of the International Mining Industry on Indigenous Peoples.* Sydney: Transnational Corporations Research Project, University of Sydney.

———. 1990. *Fiji: Race and Politics in an Island State.* Vancouver: University of British Columbia.

Howell, John M. 1987. Early farming in Northwestern Europe. *Scientific American* 257(5):118–126.

Howells, W.W. 1980. *Homo erectus*—Who, when, and where: A survey. *Yearbook of Physical Anthropology* 23:1–23.

Hrdy, Sarah Blaffer. 1981. *The Woman That Never Evolved.* Cambridge, MA: Harvard University Press.

Hughes, Charles C., and John M. Hunter. 1972. Diseases and "development" in Africa. *Social Science and Medicine* 3:143–193.

Hume, David. 1748. Of national characters. In *Essays Moral, Political, and Literary.* 3d ed. Essay 21. London: A. Millar.

Hunt, Edward E., Jr. 1978. Ecological frameworks and hypothesis testing in medical anthropology. In *Health and the Human Condition,* ed. M.H. Logan and E.H. Hunt, Jr., 84–99. North Scituate, MA: Duxbury Press.

Hurlbutt, Robert H., III. 1965. *Hume, Newton and the Design Argument.* Lincoln: University of Nebraska Press.

Hvalkof, Søren, and Peter Aaby, eds. 1981. *Is God an American?* Copenhagen: International Work Group for Indigenous Affairs.

Hymes, Dell. 1972. Models of the interaction of language and social life. In *Directions in Sociolinguistics,* ed. J.J. Gumperz and D. Hymes, 35–71. New York: Holt, Rinehart & Winston.

Independent Commission on International Humanitarian Issues. 1986. *The Vanishing Forest.* London: Zed Books.

International Work-Group on Indigenous Affairs. 1981. Colombia: Embera Indians killed by police. *IWGIA Newsletter* 25/26:43–44.

Irvine, William. 1955. *Apes, Angels and Victorians.* New York: McGraw-Hill.

Ishige, Naomichi. 1977. Roasting dog in earth oven (Ponape). In *The Anthropologists' Cookbook,* ed. J. Kuper, 203–205. New York: Universe Books.

Issac, Glynn. 1978. The food-sharing behavior of protohuman hominids. *Scientific American* 238(4):90–108.

James, Wendy. 1973. The anthropologist as reluctant imperialist. In *Anthropology and the Colonial Encounter,* ed. T. Asad, 41–70. London: Ithaca Press.

Janes, Craig R., Ron Stall, and Sandra M. Gifford, eds. 1986. *Anthropology and Epidemiology.* Dordrecht, Holland: D. Reidel Publishing Co.

Jansen, G. 1973. *The Doctor-Patient Relationship in an African Tribal Society.* Assen, The Netherlands: Van Gorcum.

Jelinek, Arthur J. 1982. The Tabun Cave and Paleolithic Man in the Levant. *Science* 216:1369–1375.

Jennings, Jesse D. 1973. *The Social Uses of Archaeology.* Reading, MA: Addison-Wesley.

———. 1974. *Prehistory of North America.* 2d ed. New York: McGraw-Hill.

Jennings, Nicholas. 1989. Haidas on the Seine. *Maclean's* 16 October: 67–68.

Jensen, Arthur R. 1969. How much can we boost IQ and scholastic achievement? *Harvard Educational Review* 33:1–123.

———. 1981. *Straight Talk about Mental Tests.* New York: Free Press.

Johanson, Donald C., and Maitland Edey. 1981. *Lucy: The Beginnings of Humankind.* New York: Simon & Schuster.

Johanson, Donald C., and Tim D. White. 1979. A systematic assessment of early African hominids. *Science* 203:321–330.

Jolly, Alison. 1985. *The Evolution of Primate Behavior.* 2d ed. New York: Macmillan.

Jolly, Clifford J. 1970. The seed-eaters: A new model of hominid differentiation based on a baboon analogy. *Man* 5:5–26.

Jolly, Clifford J., and Fred Plog. 1987. *Physical Anthropology and Archeology.* 4th ed. New York: Alfred A. Knopf.

Jones, Delmos. 1971. Social responsibility and the belief in basic research: An example from Thailand. *Current Anthropology* 12:347–350.

Jorde, L.B., P.L. Workman, and A.W. Ericksson. 1982. Genetic microevolution in the Aland Islands, Finland. In *Current Developments in Anthropological Genetics. Vol. 2, Ecology and Population Structure,* ed. Michael H. Crawford and James H. Mielke, 333–365. New York: Plenum Press.

Karn, M.N., and L.S. Penrose. 1951. Birth weight and gestation time in relation to maternal age, parity and infant survival. *American Eugenics* 16:147–164.

Kawai, M. 1965. Newly acquired pre-cultural behavior of the natural troops of Japanese monkeys on Koshima Islet. *Primates* 6:1–30.

Kay, Paul, and Chad K. McDaniel. 1978. The linguistic significance of the meanings of basic color terms. *Language* 54:610–646.

Kay, Richard F. 1977. Diets of early Miocene African hominoids. *Nature* 268:628–630.

———. 1981. The nut-crackers: A new theory of the adaptation of the Ramapithecinae. *American Journal of Physical Anthropology* 55:141–151.

———. 1985. Dental evidence for the diet of *Australopithecus. Annual Review of Anthropology* 14:315–341.

Kay, Richard F., John G. Fleagle, and Elwyn L. Simons. 1981. A revision of the Oligocene apes of the Fayum Province, Egypt. *American Journal of Physical Anthropology* 55:293–322.

Kay, Richard F., and Elwyn L. Simons. 1980. The ecology of Oligocene anthropoids. *International Journal of Primatology* 1:21–38.

Keightley, David N., ed. 1983. *The Origins of Chinese Civilization.* Berkeley: University of California Press.

Kennedy, G.E. 1980. *Paleoanthropology.* New York: McGraw-Hill.

Kennedy, John G. 1973. Cultural psychiatry. In *Handbook of Social and Cultural Anthropology,* ed. J.J. Honingmann, 1119–1198. Chicago: Rand McNally.

Kerr, Richard A. 1987. Searching land and sea for the dinosaur killer. *Science* 237:856–857.

Kimura, Kunihiko. 1984. Studies of growth and development in Japan. *Yearbook of Physical Anthropology* 27:179–214.

Kimura, Motoo. 1979. The neutral theory of molecular evolution. *Scientific American* 241(5):94–104.

———. 1983. *The Neutral Theory of Molecular Evolution.* Cambridge: Cambridge University Press.

King, Glenn E. 1975. Socioterritorial units among carnivores and early hominids. *Journal of Anthropological Research* 31:69–87.

———. 1976. Society and territory in human evolution. *Journal of Human Evolution* 5:323–332.

King, James. 1981. *The Biology of Race.* Berkeley: University of California Press.

King, Marie-Claire, and Allen C. Winston. 1975. Our close cousin, the chimpanzee. *New Scientist* 67(956): 16–18.

Kinzey, Warren G., ed. 1987. *The Evolution of Human Behavior: Primate Models.* Albany: State University of New York Press.

Kitahara-Frisch, Jean. 1978. Stone tools as indicators of linguistic abilities in early man. *Annals of the Japan Association for the Philosophy of Science* 5(3):101–109.

Kohl, Philip. 1987. The use and abuse of world system theory: The case of the pristine West Asian State. In *Advances in Archaeological Method and Theory,* vol. 11, ed. Michael B. Schiffer, 1–35. San Diego: Academic Press.

Kolata, Alan L. 1983. Chan Chan and Cuzco: On the nature of the ancient Andean city. In *Civilization in the Ancient Americas,* ed. Richard M. Leventhal and

Alan L. Kolata, 345–371. Albuquerque: University of New Mexico Press.

Kolosi, Tamas, and Edmund Wnuk-Lipinski, eds. 1983. *Equality and Inequality under Socialism: Poland and Hungary Comparison.* Beverly Hills, CA: Sage.

Konigsson, Lars-Konig, ed. 1980. *Current Arguments on Early Man.* Oxford: Pergamon Press.

Kortlandt, A. 1980. The Fayum primate forest: Did it exist? *Journal of Human Evolution* 9:277–297.

Kroeber, Alfred. 1944. *Configurations of Cultural Growth.* Berkeley: University of California Press.

Kuhn, Thomas S. 1970. *The Structure of Scientific Revolutions.* 2d ed. Chicago: University of Chicago Press.

Kurtén, Björn. 1972. *The Age of Mammals.* New York: Columbia University Press.

Kyburg, Henry E., Jr. 1968. *Philosophy of Science: A Formal Approach.* New York: Macmillan.

Lack, David. 1974. *Darwin's Finches.* Cambridge: Cambridge University Press.

Lamberg-Karlovsky, C.C., and Jeremy A. Sabloff. 1979. *Ancient Civilizations.* Menlo Park, CA: Benjamin-Cummings.

Lambert, Wallace E., et al. 1960. Evaluational reactions to spoken languages. *Journal of Abnormal and Social Psychology* 66:44–51.

Langness, L.L. 1969. Marriage in Bena Bena. In *Pigs, Pearlshells, and Women,* ed. R.M. Glasse and M.J. Meggitt, 38–55. Englewood Cliffs, NJ: Prentice-Hall.

Lanternari, Vittorio. 1963. *The Religions of the Oppressed: A Study of Modern Messianic Cults.* New York: Alfred A. Knopf.

Laracy, Hugh. 1983. *The Maasina Rule Movement.* Suva: Institute of Pacific Studies, University of the South Pacific.

Lasker, Gabriel, and Henry Womack. 1975. An anatomical view of demographic data: Biomass, fat mass, and lean body mass of the United States and Mexican human populations. In *Biosocial Interrelationships in Population Adaptation,* ed. Elizabeth Watts, Francis S. Johnston, and Gabriel Lasker, 43–53. The Hague: Mouton.

Lathrap, Donald W. 1968. The hunting economies of the tropical forest zone of South America: An attempt at historical perspectives. In *Man the Hunter,* ed. R.B. Lee and I. DeVore, 23–29. Chicago: Aldine.

———. 1977. Our father the cayman, our mother the gourd: Spinden revisited, or a unitary model for the emergence of agriculture in the New World. In *Origins of Agriculture,* ed. C.A. Reed, 713–731. The Hague: Mouton.

Leacock, Eleanor. 1982. Marxism and anthropology. In *The Left Academy,* ed. B. Ollman and E. Vernoff, 242–276. New York: McGraw-Hill.

Leakey, Richard E. 1981. *The Making of Mankind.* New York: Simon & Schuster.

Lee, Richard. 1969. Eating Christmas in the Kalahari. *Natural History* 78 (December):14–22, 60–63.

———. 1979. *The !Kung San.* Cambridge: Cambridge University Press.

Leone, Mark P., and Parker B. Potter, Jr. 1988. *The Recovery of Meaning.* Washington, DC: Smithsonian Institution Press.

Lévi-Strauss, Claude. 1961. *Triste Tropiques: An Anthropological Study of Primitive Societies in Brazil.* New York: Hutchinson.

———. 1969. *The Elementary Structures of Kinship.* Boston: Beacon Press.

Levine, Nancy E. 1988. *The Dynamics of Polyandry: Kinship, Domesticity, and Population on the Tibetan Border.* Chicago: University of Chicago Press.

Levinton, Jeffrey. 1986. Letter: Punctuated equilibrium. *Science* 231:1490.

Lewin, Roger. 1981. Ethiopian tools are world's oldest. *Science* 211:806–807.

———. 1982. Creationism on the defensive in Arkansas. *Science* 215:33–34.

———. 1986. Anthropologist argues that language cannot be read in stones. *Science* 233:23–24.

———. 1987. Africa: Cradle of modern humans. *Science* 237:1292–1295.

———. 1988. Modern human origins under close scrutiny. *Science* 239:1240–1241.

Lewis, Oscar. 1966. The culture of poverty. *Scientific American* 215:19–25.

Lewis, Phillip. 1969. *The Social Context of Art in Northern New Ireland.* Chicago: Field Museum of Natural History.

Lewontin, R.C. 1972. The apportionment of human diversity. *Evolutionary Biology* 6:381–398.

———. 1974. *The Genetic Basis of Evolutionary Change.* New York: Columbia University Press.

———. 1976. Race and intelligence. In *The IQ Controversy,* ed. N.J. Block and Gerald Dworkin, 78–92. New York: Pantheon Books.

Lieban, Richard W. 1962. Qualifications for folk medical practice in Sibulan, Negros Oriental, Philippines. *The Philippine Journal of Science* 91:511–521.

Lienhardt, Godfrey. 1961. *Divinity and Experience: The Religion of the Dinka.* Oxford: The Clarendon Press.

Lindenbaum, Shirley. 1979. *Kuru Sorcery: Disease and*

Danger in the New Guinea Highlands. Palo Alto, CA: Mayfield.

Linnaeus, Carolus. 1758–59. *Systema naturae per regna tria naturae, secundum classes, ordenes, genera, species, cum characteribuus differentiis, locis....* 10th ed. Holmiae, impensi: L. Salvii.

Little, Kenneth. 1965/66. The political functions of the Poro. *Africa* 35:349–365; 36:62–72.

Long, Norman. 1975. Structural dependency, modes of production and economic brokerage in rural Peru. In *Beyond the Sociology of Development,* ed. I. Oxaal, T. Barnett, and D. Booth, 253–282. London: Routledge & Kegan Paul.

Lorenz, Konrad, and Paul Leyhausen. 1973. *Motivation of Human and Animal Behavior.* New York: D. Van Nostrand.

Lovejoy, C. Owen. 1981. The origin of man. *Science* 211:341–350.

MacKinnon, J.R., and K.S. MacKinnon. 1980. The behavior of wild spectral tarsiers. *International Journal of Primatology* 1(4):361–379.

————. 1984. Territoriality, monogamy and song in gibbons and tarsiers. In *The Lesser Apes,* ed. Holger Preuschoft, David J. Chivers, Warren Y. Brockelman, and Norman Creel, 291–297. Edinburgh: Edinburgh University Press.

Maclean, Una. 1971. *Magical Medicine: A Nigerian Case-Study.* New York: Penguin.

MacNeish, Richard. 1964. Ancient Mesoamerican civilization. *Science* 143:531–537.

————. 1971. Early man in the Andes. *Scientific American* 224(4):36–46.

————. 1972. The evolution of community patterns in the Tehuacan Valley of Mexico and speculations about cultural processes. In *Man, Settlement, and Urbanism,* ed. Peter J. Ucko, Ruth Tringham, and G.W. Dimbleby, 67–93. Hertfordshire, England: Gerald Duckworth & Co.

————. 1978. *The Science of Archaeology?* North Scituate, MA: Duxbury Press.

Maddock, Kenneth. 1972. *The Australian Aborigines: A Portrait of Their Society.* London: Allen Lane.

Madsen, William. 1967. Religious syncretism. In *Handbook of Middle American Indians,* vol. 6, ed. R. Wauchope, 369–391. Austin: University of Texas Press.

Magner, Lois. 1979. *A History of the Life Sciences.* New York: Marcel Dekker.

Mahan, Brian, and L. Dale Richesin, eds. 1981. *The Challenge of Liberation Theology.* Maryknoll, NY: Orbis Books.

Malefijt, Annemarie de Waal. 1968. *Religion and Culture: An Introduction to Anthropology of Religion.* New York: Macmillan.

Malina, Robert M., Bertis B. Little, Richard F. Shoup, and Peter H. Beischang. 1987. Adaptive significance of small body size: Strength and motor performance of school children in Mexico and Papua New Guinea. *American Journal of Physical Anthropology* 73:489–499.

Marett, Robert R. 1909. *The Threshold of Religion.* London: Methuen.

————. 1912. *Anthropology.* New York: Holt, Rinehart & Winston.

Mariner, William. 1827. *An Account of the Natives of the Tonga Islands, in the Pacific Ocean.* 2 vols. London: Oxford University Press.

Marks, Jon. 1983. Hominid cytogenetics and evolution. *Yearbook of Physical Anthropology* 26:131–159.

Marshack, Alexander. 1972. *The Roots of Civilization.* New York: McGraw-Hill.

————. 1976. Some implications of the Paleolithic symbolic evidence for the origin of language. *Annals of the New York Academy of Science* 280:289–311.

Marshall, Lorna. 1961. Sharing, talking, and giving: Relief of social tensions among !Kung Bushmen. *Africa* 31:231–249.

Martin, M.K. 1974. *The Foraging Adaptation—Uniformity or Diversity?* Reading, MA: Addison-Wesley.

Martinez-Alier, Verena. 1974. *Marriage, Class and Colour in Nineteenth-Century Cuba.* Cambridge: Cambridge University Press.

Maybury-Lewis, David. 1968. *The Savage and the Innocent.* Boston: Beacon Press.

Maynard-Smith, John. 1975. *The Theory of Evolution.* New York: Penguin Books.

Mayr, Ernst. 1970. *Populations, Species, and Evolution.* Cambridge, MA: Harvard University Press.

————. 1978. Evolution. *Scientific American* 239(3):47–55.

————. 1982. *The Growth of Biological Thought.* Cambridge, MA: The Belknap Press/Harvard University Press.

Mayr, Ernst, and William B. Provine. 1980. *The Evolutionary Synthesis.* Cambridge, MA: Harvard University Press.

McBryde, Isabel, ed. 1985. *Who Owns the Past?* Oxford: Oxford University Press.

McCown, Theodore D., and Kenneth A.R. Kennedy. 1972. *Climbing Man's Family Tree.* Englewood Cliffs, NJ: Prentice-Hall.

McElroy, Ann, and Patricia K. Townsend. 1979. *Medical Anthropology*. North Scituate, MA: Duxbury Press.

McGimsey, Charles R., III, and Hester A. Davis, eds. 1977. *The Management of Archaeological Resources: The Airlie House Report*. Special Publication of the Society for American Archaeology. Washington, DC: Society for American Archaeology.

McGuire, Randall H., and Michael B. Schiffer. 1982. *Hohokam and Patavan, Prehistory of Southwestern Arizona*. New York: Academic Press.

McHenry, Henry M. 1982. The pattern of human evolution: Studies on bipedalism, mastication and encephalization. *Annual Review of Anthropology* 11:151–173.

Mead, Margaret. 1947. The concept of culture and the psychosomatic approach. *Psychiatry* 10:57–76.

—————. 1967. Alternatives to war. In *War*, ed. M. Fried, M. Harris, and R. Murphy, 215–228. Garden City, NY: Natural History Press.

Meggitt, Mervyn J. 1962. *Desert People: A Study of the Walbiri Aborigines of Central Australia*. Sydney: Angus and Robertson.

—————. 1977. *Blood Is Their Argument: Warfare among the Mae Enga Tribesmen of the New Guinea Highlands*. Palo Alto, CA: Mayfield.

Meidl, Richard S. 1987. Hypothesis: A selective advantage for cystic fibrosis heterozygotes. *American Journal of Physical Anthropology* 74:39–45.

Meillassoux, Claude. 1981. *Maidens, Meal and Money*. Cambridge: Cambridge University Press.

Meintel, Deidre. 1973. Strangers, homecomers, and ordinary men. *Anthropological Quarterly* 46:47–58.

Mellaart, James. 1975. *The Earliest Civilizations of the Near East*. London: Thames and Hudson.

Mellars, P.A. 1969. The chronology of Mousterian industries in the Perigord region of southwestern France. *Proceedings of the Prehistoric Society* 35:134–171.

Melotti, Umberto. 1977. *Marx and the Third World*. London: Macmillan.

Melrose, D. 1982. *Bitter Pills: Medicines and the Third World*. Oxford: Oxfam.

Melville, Thomas. 1981. Guatemala: The Indian awakening. *ARC Newsletter* 5(2):1.

Mielke, J.H., E.J. Devor, P.L. Kramer, P.L. Workman, and A.W. Eriksson. 1982. Historical population structure of the Aland Islands, Finland. In *Current Developments in Anthropological Genetics*. Vol. 2, *Ecology and Population Structure*, ed. Michael H. Crawford and James H. Mielke, 255–332. New York: Plenum Press.

Milisauskas, Sarunas. 1978. *European Prehistory*. New York: Academic Press.

Miller, G. Tyler, Jr. 1982. *Living in the Environment*. 3d ed. Belmont, CA: Wadsworth.

Mitchell, Andrew W. 1986. *The Enchanted Canopy*. New York: Macmillan.

Miyamoto, Michael M., Jerry L. Slightom, and Morris Goodman. 1987. Phylogenetic relationships of humans and African apes from DNA sequences in the 4n-globin region. *Science* 238:369–373.

Molnar, Stephen. 1975. *Races, Types and Ethnic Groups*. Englewood Cliffs, NJ: Prentice-Hall.

Mooney, James. 1965. *The Ghost-Dance Religion and the Sioux Outbreak of 1890*. Chicago: University of Chicago Press.

Moore, Lorna, Peter W. Van Arsdale, JoAnn E. Glittenberg, and Robert A. Aldrich. 1980. *The Biocultural Basis of Health*. St. Louis: C.V. Mosby.

Moran, Emilio F. 1982. *Human Adaptability*. Boulder, CO: Westview Press.

Morgan, Lewis H. 1877. *Ancient Society*. New York: Henry Holt.

Mörner, Magnus. 1967. *Race Mixture in the History of Latin America*. Boston: Little, Brown.

Morris, Desmond, Peter Collett, Porter Marsh, and Marie O'Shaughnessy. 1979. *Gestures, Their Origins and Distribution*. New York: Stein and Day.

Morris, Laura Newell. 1971. *Human Populations, Genetic Variation, and Evolution*. San Francisco: Chandler Publishing Co.

Mouer, Ross, and Yoshio Sugimoto. 1986. *Images of Japanese Society*. London: KPI, Ltd.

Mourant, A.E. 1983. *Blood Relations: Blood Groups and Anthropology*. Oxford: Oxford University Press.

Mourant, A.E., Ada C. Kopec, and Kazimiera Domaniewska-Sobczak. 1978. *Blood Groups and Diseases*. New York: Oxford University Press.

Moynihan, Martin. 1976. *The New World Primates*. Princeton, NJ: Princeton University Press.

Muller, M. 1982. *The Health of Nations: A North-South Investigation*. London: Faber and Faber.

Munson, Henry. 1989. *Islam and Revolution in the Middle East*. New Haven, CT: Yale University Press.

Murphy, Robert. 1981. Julian Steward. In *Totems and Teachers*, ed. Sydel Silverman, 171–208. New York: Columbia University Press.

Myerhoff, Barbara. 1970. The deer-maize-peyote symbol complex among the Huichol Indians of Mexico. *Anthropological Quarterly* 39(2):60–72.

————. 1974. *Peyote Hunt: The Sacred Journey of the Huichol Indians*. Ithaca, NY: Cornell University Press.

Myers, Fred R. 1982. Ideology and experience: The cultural basis of politics in Pintupi life. In *Aboriginal Power in Australian Society,* ed. M.C. Howard, 79–114. Honolulu: University Press of Hawaii.

Napier, J.R., and P.H. Napier. 1985. *The Natural History of the Primates*. Cambridge, MA: The MIT Press.

Nash, Dennison. 1963. The ethnologist as stranger. *Southwestern Journal of Anthropology* 19:149–167.

Newman, Philip L. 1965. *Knowing the Gururumba*. New York: Holt, Rinehart & Winston.

Nichol, John. 1990. *The Mighty Rain Forest*. London: David and Charles.

Nimuendaju, Curt. 1967. *The Apinaye*. Oosterhout: Anthropological Publications.

Nind, Scott. 1831. Description of the natives of King George's Sound (Swan River Colony) and adjoining country. *Royal Geographical Society Journal* 1:21–51.

Norman, Colin. 1987. Supreme Court strikes down "creation science" law as promotion of religion. *Science* 236:1620.

O'Brien, P.J. 1972. Urbanism, Cahokia, and Middle Mississippian. *Archaeology* 25(3):188–197.

Ogden, Schubert M. 1981. The concept of a theology of liberation: Must a Christian theology be so conceived? In *The Challenge of Liberation Theology,* ed. B. Mahan and L.D. Richesin, 127–140. Maryknoll, NY: Orbis Books.

Olson, Storrs L., and D. Tab Rasmussen. 1986. Paleoenvironment of the earliest hominoids: New evidence from the Oligocene avifauna of Egypt. *Science* 233:1202–1204.

Ortiz de Montellano, Bernard. 1977. The rational causes of illness among the Aztecs. *Katunob* 10(2):23–43.

Overton, William R. 1982. Creationism in schools: The decision in the McLean versus the Arkansas Board of Education. *Science* 215:934–943.

Patterson, F., and E. Linden. 1981. *The Education of Koko*. New York: Holt, Rinehart & Winston.

Peters, Charles. 1987. Nut-like oil seeds: Food for monkeys, chimpanzees, humans, and probably ape-men. *American Journal of Physical Anthropology* 73:333–363.

Pettengill, John S. 1981. Firearms and the distribution of income: A neoclassical model. *The Review of Radical Political Economy* 13(2):1–10.

Peyrony, Denis. 1934. La Ferrassie. *Prehistorie* 3:1–54.

Pickford, M. 1982. New higher primate fossils from middle Miocene deposits at Majiwa and Kaloma, Western Kenya. *American Journal of Physical Anthropology* 58:1–19.

Pilbeam, David. 1978. Rethinking human origins. *Discovery* 13(1):2–9.

————. 1982. New hominoid skull material from the Miocene of Pakistan. *Nature* 295:232–234.

————. 1984. The descent of hominoids and hominids. *Scientific American* 250(3):84–96.

Polanyi, Karl, Conrad M. Arensberg, and H.P. Pearson, eds. 1957. *Trade and Market in the Early Empires*. Glencoe, IL: Free Press.

Pollack, J.I. 1975. Field observations on *Indri indri*: A preliminary report. In *Lemur Biology,* ed. I. Tattersall and R.W. Sussman, 287–311. New York: Plenum Press.

Post, Peter W., Farrington Daniels, Jr., and Robert T. Binford, Jr. 1975. Cold injury and the evolution of "white" skin. *Human Biology* 47:65–80.

Potts, Richard. 1986. Temporal span of bone accumulation at Olduvai Gorge and implications for early hominid foraging behavior. *Paleobiology* 12:25–31.

————. 1987. Reconstructions of early hominid socioecology: A critique of primate models. In *The Evolution of Human Behavior: Primate Models,* ed. Warren G. Kinzey, 28–47. Albany: State University of New York Press.

Prasad, K.N. 1982. Was Ramapithecus a tool-user? *Journal of Human Evolution* 11:101–104.

Premack, D., and A.J. Premack. 1983. *The Mind of an Ape*. New York: W.W. Norton.

Preuschoft, Holger, David J. Chivers, Warren Y. Brockelman, and Norman Creel, eds. 1984. *The Lesser Apes*. Edinburgh: Edinburgh University Press.

Prieto, Abel. 1981. Cuba's national literacy campaign. *Journal of Reading* 25(3):215–221.

Radinsky, Leonard. 1977. Early primate brains: Facts and fiction. *Journal of Human Evolution* 6:79–86.

Rak, Y., and B. Arensburg. 1987. Kebara 2 Neanderthal pelvis: First look at a complete inlet. *American Journal of Physical Anthropology* 73:227–231.

Ramos, Alcida R. 1984. Frontier expansion and Indian peoples in the Brazilian Amazon. In *Frontier Expansion in Amazonia,* ed. Marianne Schmink and Charles C. Wood, 83–104. Gainesville: University of Florida Press.

Rappaport, Roy A. 1967. Ritual regulation of environmental relations among New Guinea people. *Ethnology* 6:17–30.

————. 1977. Maladaptation in social systems. In *The Evolution of Social Systems*, ed. Jonathan Friedman and Michael Rowlands, 49–73. London: Duckworth.

Rathbun, Ted A., and Jane E. Buikstra, eds. 1984. *Human Identification: Case Studies in Forensic Anthropology*. Springfield, IL: Charles C Thomas.

Redfield, Robert. 1952. The primitive world view. *Proceedings of the American Philosophical Society* 96:30–36.

Redford, Kent H. 1991. The ecologically noble savage. *Cultural Survival Quarterly* 15(1):46–48.

Redman, Charles L. 1977. Man, domestication, and culture in southwestern Asia. In *Origins of Agriculture*, ed. Charles A. Reed, 523–541. The Hague: Mouton.

————. 1978. *The Rise of Civilization*. San Francisco: W.H. Freeman.

Reed, Charles A., ed. 1977. *Origins of Agriculture*. The Hague: Mouton.

Reichs, Kathleen J., ed. 1986. *Forensic Osteology*. Springfield, IL: Charles C Thomas.

Renfrew, Colin. 1978. Trajectory discontinuity and morphogenesis: The implications of catastrophe theory for archaeology. *American Antiquity* 43:203–222.

Repetto, Robert. 1990. Deforestation in the tropics. *Scientific American* 262(4):36–42.

Ribeiro, Darcy. 1970. *Os Índios e a Civilzaçâo*. Rio de Janeiro: Editora Civilizaçâo Brasileira.

Richard, Alison F. 1985. *Primates in Nature*. New York: W.H. Freeman.

Riesman, David. 1953. *The Lonely Crowd: A Study of the American Character*. Garden City, NY: Doubleday.

Roberts, D.F. 1968. Genetic effects of population size reduction. *Nature* 220:1084–1088.

————. 1978. *Climate and Human Variability*. 2d ed. Menlo Park, CA: Benjamin-Cummings.

Rodman, Peter S., and Henry M. McHenry. 1980. Bioenergetics and the origin of hominid bipedalism. *American Journal of Physical Anthropology* 52:103–106.

Roughgarden, Jonathan. 1979. *Theory of Population Genetics and Evolutionary Ecology: An Introduction*. New York: Macmillan.

Rudé, George. 1980. *Ideology and Popular Protest*. New York: Pantheon.

Ruhlen, Merritt. 1976. *A Guide to the Languages of the World*. Stanford: Stanford University Press.

Ruse, Michael. 1979. *The Darwinian Revolution*. Chicago: University of Chicago Press.

Ryan, Alan S., and Reynaldo Martorelli. 1987. Preface: Ross Laboratories Symposium on Child Nutrition and Growth and Development. *American Journal of Physical Anthropology* 73:447.

Sade, Donald Stone. 1973. An ethogram for rhesus monkeys. I. Antithetical contrasts in posture and movement. *American Journal of Physical Anthropology* 38:537–542.

Sade, Donald Stone, B. Diane Chepko-Sade, Jonathan M. Schneider, Shauna S. Roberts, and Joan T. Richtsmeier. 1985. *Basic Demographic Observations on Free-Ranging Rhesus Monkeys*. New Haven, CT: Human Relations Area Files.

Sahlins, Marshall. 1965. On the sociology of primitive exchange. In *The Relevance of Models for Social Anthropology*, ed. M. Banton, 139–236. London: Tavistock Publications.

Sánchez Vázques, Adolfo. 1973. *Art and Society*. New York: Monthly Review Press.

Sanders, William J., and Barbara J. Price. 1968. *Mesoamerica: The Evolution of a Civilization*. New York: Random House.

Sapir, Edward. 1929. The status of linguistics as a science. *Language* 5:207–214.

Sarich, Vincent M. 1974. Just how old is the hominid line? *Yearbook of Physical Anthropology* 17:98–112.

Sauer, Carl O. 1952. *Agricultural Origins and Dispersals*. New York: American Geographic Society.

Schapera, I. 1940. *Married Life in an African Tribe*. London: Faber and Faber.

Schiffer, Michael B., and George J. Gummerman, eds. 1977. *Conservation Archaeology: A Guide for Cultural Resource Management*. New York: Academic Press.

Schmink, Marianne, and Charles C. Wood. 1984. *Forest Expansion in Amazonia*. Gainesville: University of Florida Press.

Schultes, Richard E. 1963. Botanical sources of the New World narcotics. *Psychedelic Review*. 1:145–166.

Service, Elman R., and R. Cohen, eds. 1978. *Origins of the State: The Anthropology of Political Evolution*. Philadelphia: Institute for the Study of Human Issues.

Shackleton, N., and C. Renfew. 1970. Neolithic trade routes re-aligned by oxygen isotope analyses. *Nature* 228:1062–1065.

Shackley, Myra. 1980. *Neanderthal Man*. London: Gerald Duckworth & Co.

————. 1981. *Environmental Archaeology*. London: George Allen & Unwin.

Shannon, Thomas R. 1989. *An Introduction to the World-System Perspective*. Boulder, CO: Westview Press.

Shapiro, Judith. 1968. Tapirapé kinship. *Boletim do Museu Paraense Emilio Goeldi, Antropolgia* 37.

Shea, Brian T. 1985. On aspects of skull form in African apes and orangutans, with implications for hominoid evolution. *American Journal of Physical Anthropology* 68:329–342.

Shipman, Pat. 1981. *Life History of a Fossil.* Cambridge, MA: Harvard University Press.

———. 1986. Scavenging or hunting in early hominids: Theoretical framework and tests. *American Anthropologist* 88:27–43.

Silverman, Milton, P.R. Lee, and M. Lydecker. 1982. *Prescriptions for Death: The Drugging of the Third World.* Berkeley: University of California Press.

Simons, Elwyn L. 1972. *Primate Evolution.* New York: Macmillan.

———. 1977. Ramapithecus. *Scientific American* 236(5):28–35.

Simons, Elwyn L., and H.H. Covert. 1981. Paleoprimatological research over the last 50 years: Foci and trends. *American Journal of Physical Anthropology* 56:373–382.

Simons, Elwyn L., and David R. Pilbeam. 1972. Hominoid paleoprimatology. In *The Functional and Evolutionary Biology of Primates,* ed. Russell Tuttle, 36–62. Chicago: Aldine/Atherton.

Sinha, D.P. 1972. The Birhors. In *Hunters and Gatherers Today,* ed. M.G. Bicchieri, 371–403. New York: Holt, Rinehart & Winston.

Skinner, B.F. 1966. What is the experimental analysis of behavior? *Journal of the Experimental Analysis of Behavior* 9:213–218.

Smith, Bruce D. 1989. Origins of agriculture in eastern North America. *Science* 246:1566–1571.

Smith, Fred H., and Frank Spencer, eds. 1984. *The Origins of Modern Humans.* New York: Alan R. Liss.

Smith, Jason. 1976. *Foundations of Archaeology.* Beverly Hills, CA: Glencoe Press.

Smith, M.G. 1960. *Government in Zazzau, 1881–1950.* London: Oxford University Press.

Smouse, Peter E. 1982. Genetic architecture of Swidden agricultural tribes from the lowland rain forests of South America. In *Current Developments in Anthropological Genetics.* Vol. 2, *Ecology and Population Structure,* ed. Michael H. Crawford and James H. Mielke, 139–178. New York: Plenum Press.

Solecki, Ralph. 1972. *Shanidar: The Humanity of Neanderthal Man.* Baltimore: Pelican Books.

Sootin, Harry. 1959. *Gregor Mendel: Father of the Science of Genetics.* New York: Vanguard Press.

Sorensen, Arthur P. 1973. South American Indian linguistics at the turn of the seventies. In *Peoples and Cultures of Native South America,* ed. D.R. Gross, 312–341. Garden City, NY: Doubleday/Natural History Press.

South, Stanley. 1977. *Method and Theory in Historical Archeology.* New York: Academic Press.

Spencer, Baldwin, and F.J. Gillen. 1899. *The Native Tribes of Central Australia.* London: Macmillan.

Spencer, Robert F. 1959. *The North Alaskan Eskimo: A Study in Ecology and Society.* Bull. 171. Washington, DC: Bureau of American Ethnology.

Spindler, Louise S. 1977. *Culture Change and Modernization.* Prospect Heights, IL: Waveland Press.

Stanley, Steven M. 1979. *Macroevolution.* San Francisco: W.H. Freeman.

———. 1981. *The New Evolutionary Timetable.* New York: Basic Books.

Steadman, L.B., and C.F. Merbs. 1982. Kuru and cannibalism? *American Anthropologist* 84(3):611–627.

Stebbins, G. Ledyard. 1977. *Processes of Organic Evolution.* Englewood Cliffs, NJ: Prentice-Hall.

Stebbins, G. Ledyard, and Francisco J. Ayala. 1981. Is a new evolutionary synthesis necessary? *Science* 213:967–971.

———. 1985. The evolution of Darwinism. *Scientific American* 253(1):72–82.

Steegmann, A.T., Jr. 1975. Human adaptation to cold. In *Physiological Anthropology,* ed. Albert Damon, 130–166. New York: Oxford University Press.

Steward, Julian H. 1937. Ecological aspects of southwestern society. *Anthropos* 32:87–104.

———. 1938. *Basin-Plateau Aboriginal Sociopolitical Groups.* Bull. 120. Washington, DC: Bureau of American Ethnology.

———. 1955. *Theory of Culture Change: The Methodology of Multilinear Evolution.* Urbana: University of Illinois Press.

———. 1977. *Evolution and Ecology.* Urbana: University of Illinois Press.

Steward, Julian H., et al. 1956. *The People of Puerto Rico.* Urbana: University of Illinois Press.

Stini, William A. 1979. Adaptive strategies of human populations under nutritional stress. In *Physiological and Morphological Adaptation and Evolution,* ed. William A. Stini, 387–407. The Hague: Mouton.

Stokes, William. 1952. Violence as a power factor in Latin American politics. *Western Political Quarterly* 5(3):445–468.

Stoll, David. 1982. *Fishers of Men or Founders of Empire?* London: Zed Press.

Stringer, C.B., and P. Andrews. 1988. Genetic and fossil evidence for the origin of modern humans. *Science* 239:1263–1268.

Struever, Stuart. 1968. Woodland subsistence-settlement systems in the Lower Illinois Valley. In *New Perspectives in Archeology*, ed. Sally R. Binford and Lewis R. Binford, 285–312. Chicago: Aldine.

Struever, Stuart, and Felicia A. Holton. 1979. *Koster: Americans in Search of Their Prehistoric Past*. Garden City, NY: Anchor Press/Doubleday.

Sunderland, E. 1979. Skin color variability in the Middle East. In *Physiological and Morphological Adaptation and Evolution*, ed. William A. Stini, 7–18. The Hague: Mouton.

Suomi, S.J., and C. Ripp. 1985. A history of motherless mother monkey mothering at the University of Wisconsin Primate Laboratory. In *Child Abuse: The Nonhuman Primate Data*, ed. N. Caine and M. Reite, 49–78. New York: Alan R. Liss.

Susman, Randall L. 1988. Hand of *Paranthropus robustus* from Member 1, Swarkrans: Fossil evidence for tool behavior. *Science* 240:781–784.

Svejgaard, A., M. Hauge, C. Jersild, P. Platz, L.P. Ryder, L. Staub Nielsen, and M. Thomsen. 1979. *The HLA System*. 2d ed. Basel: S. Kager.

Swadesh, Morris. 1971. *The Origin and Diversification of Language*. Chicago: Aldine/Atherton.

Szalay, Fredrick S. 1972. Hunting-scavenging protohominids: A model for hominid origins. *Man* 10:420–429.

Szalay, Fredrick S., and E. Delson. 1979. *Evolutionary History of the Primates*. New York: Academic Press.

Tainter, Joseph A. 1988. *The Collapse of Complex Societies*. Cambridge: Cambridge University Press.

Tanner, Nancy Makepeace. 1981. *On Becoming Human*. Cambridge: Cambridge University Press.

———. 1987. The chimpanzee model revisited and the gathering hypothesis. In *The Evolution of Human Behavior: Primate Models*, ed. Warren G. Kinzey, 3–27. Albany: State University of New York Press.

Tattersall, Ian. 1986. Species recognition in human paleontology. *Journal of Human Evolution* 15:165–175.

Taylor, John C. 1977. Diet, health and economy: Some consequences of planned social change in an Aboriginal community. In *Aborigines and Change*, ed. R.M. Berndt, 147–158. Canberra: Australian Institute of Aboriginal Studies.

Terborgh, John. 1983. *Five New World Primates*. Princeton, NJ: Princeton University Press.

Thesiger, Wilfred. 1985. *Arabian Sands*. New York: Penguin Books.

Thompson, J.E.S. 1930. *Ethnology of the Mayas of Southern and Central British Honduras*. Pub. 274. Chicago: Field Museum of Natural History.

———. 1970. *Maya History and Religion*. Norman: University of Oklahoma Press.

Thomson, Glenys. 1983. The human histocompatibility system: Anthropological considerations. *American Journal of Physical Anthropology* 62:81–89.

Tierney, John. 1988. The search for Adam and Eve. *Newsweek*, January 11, 46–52.

Todd, Loreto. 1974. *Pidgins and Creoles*. London: Routledge & Kegan Paul.

Tonkinson, Robert. 1974. *The Jigalong Mob: Aboriginal Victors of the Desert Crusade*. Menlo Park, CA: Benjamin-Cummings.

———. 1978. *The Mardudjara Aborigines: Living the Dream in Australia's Desert*. New York: Holt, Rinehart & Winston.

Topic, John, and Theresa Topic. 1987. The archaeological investigation of Andean militarism: Some cautionary observations. In *The Origins and Development of the Andean State*, ed. Jonathan Haas, Shelia Pozorski, and Thomas Pozorski, 47–55. Cambridge: Cambridge University Press.

Toth, Nicholas. 1985. The Oldowan reassessed: A closer look at early stone artifacts. *Journal of Archaeological Science* 12:101–120.

Tozzer, Alfred M. 1907. *A Comparative Study of the Mayas and Lacandones*. New York: Macmillan.

Trinkaus, Erik. 1983. *The Shanidar Neandertals*. New York: Academic Press.

———. 1986. The Neandertals and modern human origins. *Annual Review of Anthropology* 15:193–218.

Tripp-Reimer, Toni. 1983. Human variability and nursing: A neglected aspect of clinical anthropology. In *Clinical Anthropology*, ed. Demitri B. Shimkin and Peggy Cole, 245–257. Landam, MD: University Press of America.

Tylor, Edward B. 1891. *Primitive Culture*. 2 vols. London: John Murray.

Ubelaker, Douglas H., and Lauryn Guttenplan Grant. 1989. Human skeletal remains: Preservation or reburial? *Yearbook of Physical Anthropology* 32:249–287.

Ucko, Peter J., and A. Rosenfeld. 1967. *Palaeolithic Cave Art*. London: Weidenfeld and Nicholson.

United Nations Educational, Scientific, and Cultural Organization. 1957. *World Illiteracy at Mid-Century*. Paris: UNESCO.

Valdman, Albert. 1975. The language situation in Haiti. In *The Haitian Potential*, ed. V. Rubin and R.P. Schaedel, 61–82. New York: Teachers College Press.

Van Gennep, Arnold. 1960. *The Rites of Passage*. Chicago: University of Chicago Press.

Vincent, J. 1979. On the sexual division of labour, population, and the origin of agriculture. *Current Anthropology* 20:422–425.

Voegelin, Charles F., and F.M. Voegelin. 1977. *Classification and Index of the World's Languages*. New York: Elsevier.

Vogt, Evon Z. 1970. *The Zinacantecos of Mexico: A Modern Maya Way of Life*. New York: Holt, Rinehart & Winston.

Wagley, Charles. 1977. *Welcome of Tears: The Tapirapé Indians of Central Brazil*. New York: Oxford University Press.

Wallace, Anthony F.C. 1966. *Religion: An Anthropological View*. New York: Random House.

————. 1970. *Culture and Personality*. 2d ed. New York: Random House.

————. 1972. Mental illness, biology and culture. In *Psychological Anthropology*, ed. F.L.K. Hsu, 362–402. Cambridge, MA: Schenkman.

Wallace, Robert A. 1987. *Biology: The World of Life*. 4th ed. Glenview, IL: Scott, Foresman.

Wallace, Robert A., Jack L. King, and Gerald Sanders. 1988. *Biosphere: The Realm of Life*. 2d ed. Glenview, IL: Scott, Foresman.

Wallerstein, Immanuel. 1979. *The Capitalist World-Economy*. Cambridge: Cambridge University Press.

Wasson, R. Gordon. 1972. The divine mushroom of immortality. In *Flesh of the Gods*, ed. P.T. Furst, 185–200. London: George Allen and Unwin.

————. 1973. *Soma: Divine Mushroom of Immortality*. New York: Harcourt Brace Jovanovich.

Watanabe, K. 1981. Variations in group composition and population density of two sympatric Mentawaian leaf monkeys. *Primates* 22:145–160.

Watson, William. 1979. The city in ancient China. In *The Origins of Civilization*, ed. P.R.S. Moorey, 54–77. Oxford: The Clarendon Press.

Weil, Peter. 1980. Mandinko adaptation to colonial rule in the Gambia. *Cultures et développement* 12(2):295–318.

Weiss, Mark L. 1987. Nucleic acid evidence bearing on hominoid relationships. *Yearbook of Physical Anthropology* 30:41–43.

Weiss, Mark L., and Alan E. Mann. 1985. *Human Biology and Behavior*. 4th ed. Boston: Little, Brown.

Wessman, James W. 1981. *Anthropology and Marxism*. Cambridge, MA: Schenkman.

Westlake, Melvyn. 1990. Money can't buy you wealth. *South* 116:18–19.

White, J. Peter, and James O'Connell. 1982. *A Prehistory of Australia, New Guinea, and Sahul*. Sydney: Academic Press.

White, Leslie. 1949. *The Science of Culture*. New York: Grove Press.

————. 1959. *Evolution of Culture*. New York: McGraw-Hill.

White, Tim, and Gen Suwa. 1987. Hominid footprints at Laetoli: Facts and interpretations. *American Journal of Physical Anthropology* 72(4):485–514.

Whitehouse, Ruth, and John Wilkins. 1986. *The Making of Civilization*. New York: Alfred A. Knopf.

Willey, Gordon R., and Jeremy A. Sabloff. 1980. *A History of American Archaeology*. 2d ed. San Francisco: W.H. Freeman.

Williams, B.J. 1987. Rates of evolution: Is there a conflict between neo-Darwinian evolutionary theory and the fossil record? *American Journal of Physical Anthropology* 73:99–109.

Williams, George C. 1966. *Adaptation and Natural Selection*. Princeton, NJ: Princeton University Press.

Williams, Glyn. 1979. Welsh settlers and native Americans in Patagonia. *Journal of Latin American Studies* 11:41–66.

Williams, Harvey. 1984. An uncertain prognosis: Some factors that may limit future progress in the Nicaraguan health care system. *Medical Anthropology Quarterly* 15(3):72–73.

Williams, Thomas. 1858. *Fiji and the Fijians*. London: A. Heylin.

Wilson, Edward O. 1975. *Sociobiology: The New Synthesis*. Cambridge, MA: Belknap Press/Harvard University Press.

Wilson, Edward O., and William H. Bossert. 1971. *A Primer of Population Biology*. Stamford, CT: Sinauer Associates.

Wilson, J. Turzo, ed. 1972. *Continents Adrift: Readings from Scientific American*. San Francisco: W.H. Freeman.

Wilson, Monica. 1963. *Good Company: A Study of the Nyakyusa Age-Villages*. Boston: Beacon Press.

Wilson, Rex L., and Gloria Loyola, eds. 1982. *Rescue Archeology*. Washington, DC: The Preservation Press.

Wittenberger, James F. 1981. *Animal Social Behavior*. Boston: Duxbury Press.

Wittfogel, Karl A. 1957. *Oriental Despotism: A Comparative Study of Total Power*. New Haven, CT: Yale University Press.

Wolf, Eric R., and Edward C. Hansen. 1972. *The*

Human Condition in Latin America. New York: Oxford University Press.

Wolpoff, Milford. 1980. *Paleoanthropology.* New York: Alfred A. Knopf.

Worsley, Peter. 1982. Non-Western medical systems. *Annual Review of Anthropology* 11:315–348.

Wright, H.E., Jr. 1977. Environmental change and the origin of agriculture in the Old and New Worlds. In *Origins of Agriculture,* ed. Charles A. Reed, 281–318. The Hague: Mouton.

Yoffee, Norman, and George L. Cowgill, eds. 1988. *The Collapse of Ancient States and Civilizations.* Tucson: University of Arizona Press.

Young, M.W. 1971. *Fighting with Food: Leadership, Values and Social Control in a Massim Society.* Cambridge: Cambridge University Press.

Zihlman, Adrienne L., and Jerold M. Lowenstein. 1979. False start of the human parade. *Natural History* (Aug./Sept.):86–91.

Credits

PHOTOGRAPHS

Unless otherwise acknowledged, all photographs are the property of ScottForesman.

Color Portfolio—Primates (following p. 114): First page, Steve Kaufman/Peter Arnold, Inc. Second page (top), Gerard Lacz/Peter Arnold, Inc.; (center), D. Agee/Anthro-Photo; (bottom), Doug Wechsler/ANIMALS ANIMALS. Third page (top left and top right), Loren McIntyre; (bottom), Luiz C. Marigo/Peter Arnold, Inc. Fourth page (top), P.J. DeVries/ANIMALS ANIMALS; (bottom), S. Howe/Anthro-Photo. Fifth page (top), Irven De Vore/Anthro-Photo; (bottom), S. Howe/Anthro-Photo. Sixth page, B.G. Murray, Jr./ANIMALS ANIMALS. Seventh page (top), McGuire/Anthro-Photo; (bottom), Evelyn Gallardo/Peter Arnold, Inc. Eighth page, Wraugham/Anthro-Photo.

Color Portfolio—Rain Forest (following p. 498): First page, Loren McIntyre. Second page (top), Luiz C. Marigo/Peter Arnold, Inc.; (bottom), Loren McIntyre. Third page (top and center), Loren McIntyre; (bottom), N. Chagnon/Anthro-Photo. Fourth page (all), Loren McIntyre. Fifth page (top), Jacques Jangoux/Peter Arnold, Inc.; (bottom), Martin Wendler/Peter Arnold, Inc. Sixth, seventh, and eighth pages, Loren McIntyre.

Text photos

Abbreviations following page numbers are as follows: T (top), C (center), B (bottom), L (left), R (right).

2 George Steinmetz **6–7** Historical Pictures Service, Chicago **8** From the !Kung San by Richard Borshay Lee, © copyright Cambridge University Press, 1979 **10** Des Bartlett/Photo Researchers **11** Irven DeVore/Anthro-Photo **12** William Franklin McMahon **14** Irven DeVore/Anthro-Photo **15** Yoram Kahan/Peter Arnold, Inc. **26** From F. Peron, *Voyage de decouvertes aux terres australes*, Paris, 1807–1816 **33** John Dawson **37** Culver Pictures **40(L)** Dr. Emma Shelton **40(R)** L.B. Shettles/SS/Photo Researchers **45** Milt & Joan Mann/Cameramann International, Ltd. **50** From LIFE Nature Library/*The Primates*/Time-Life Books, Inc. **57(T)** Alon Reininger/Leo de Wys **57(B)** Peter Baker/Leo de Wys **58(L)** M.W.F. Tweedie/Photo Researchers **58(R)** M.W.F. Tweedie/Photo Researchers **64** The Granger Collection, New York **65** Ruth Silverman/Stock Boston **78** Peter Veit/DRK Photo **81(T)** Michael Dick/ANIMALS ANIMALS **81(BL)** John Chellman/ANIMALS ANIMALS **85(L)** Richard Kolar/ANIMALS ANIMALS **85(R)** Mittermeier/Anthro-Photo **87** Dr. Carol Berman **88** Doug Wechsler/ANIMALS ANIMALS **89(T)** Dr. Nigel Smith/Earth Scenes **89(B)** Earth Scenes **95** Dr. Janet Dunaif-Hattis **96** From Eible-Eibesfeldt, Irenaus (© 1975 *Ethology*, 2d ed. Holt, Rinehart & Winston copyright) **101** Dr. Janet Dunaif-Hattis **116** John G. Fleagle **130(L)** Neg. No. 324543, Courtesy Department of Library Services, American Museum of Natural History **130(R)** Neg. No. 319565, Courtesy Department of Library Services, American Museum of Natural History **135(all)** Trustees of the British Museum of Natural History **147** Irven DeVore/Anthro-Photo **156(all)** Courtesy University of California Dept. of Anthropology, Berkeley, from White, Tim, and Gen Suwa, 1987 article "Hominid Footprints at Laetoli: Facts and Interpretations," *American Journal of Physical Anthropology*, 72(4):508 **161(TL)** R.I.M. Campbell/Bruce Coleman Ltd. **161(TR)** Neg. No. 315446, Courtesy Department of Library Services/ American Museum of Natural History **161(B)** Neg. No. 318956, Courtesy Department of Library Services/American Museum of Natural History **163(TR)** From *Paleoanthropology* by M.H. Wolpoff, Published by Alfred A. Knopf, Inc. Copyright© 1980 **163(BL)** Museum of Man **163(BR)** Neg. No. 109227, Courtesy Department of Library Services/American Museum of Natural History **167** Neg. No. 16227, Courtesy Department of Library Services/American Museum of Natural History **174** Dr. Robert Pickering **180** Courtesy Joiner Associates **183(T)** Robert Frerck/Odyssey Productions, Chicago **183(B)** Milt & Joan Mann/Cameramann International, Ltd. **190** Loren McIntyre **191(L)** Smithsonian Institution **191(R)** Anthro-Photo **200** Courtesy Benetton **205** Dr. Carole Ober **208** Courtesy of the Center for American Archaeology, Kampsville Archaeology Center **216** William Franklin McMahon **217** Dr. Robert Pickering **221** The British Association for the Advancement of Science **223(L)** John Dumont **223(R)** D.R. Baston **225(T)** Alan Pooley, Yale, Peabody Museum **225(B)** Biophoto Associates/Photo Researchers **240** UPI/Bettmann **242** Hans Hinz **246** Jeff Schultz/Alaska Stock Images **255** Field Museum of Natural History, Chicago **260** Neg. No. 114399, Courtesy Department of Library Services/American Museum of Natural History **261** Museum of Man **262** Museum of Man **267(L)** Neg. No. 117004, Courtesy Department of Library Services/American Museum of Natural History **267(R)** University of Colorado Museum **274** Tom Gorman **279** AP/Wide World **282(T)** Milt & Joan Mann/Cameramann International, Ltd. **282(B)** Robert Gardner Carpenter Center/Harvard University **286(TL)** Neg. No. 39604, Courtesy Department of Library Services/American Museum of Natural History **286(TR)** Danish National Museum **286(B)** Courtesy, Museum of Fine Arts, Boston **288** Courtesy of the Trustees of the British Museum **293** Peabody Museum of Archaeology, Phillips Academy, Andover, MA **298** Milt & Joan Mann/Cameramann International, Ltd. **301** Ekdotike Athenon, Athens **307** Susan Griggs Agency **309** Robert Harding Picture Library Ltd., London **310(T)** Museum of Science & Industry, Chicago **310(BR)** The Metropolitan Museum of Art **311** Art Reference Bureau, NY **312** Royal Ontario Museum of Arts, Toronto **313** Courtesy of the Peabody Museum of Natural History, Harvard **316(all)** Loren McIntyre **317** Loren McIntyre **319(all)** Courtesy, Cahokia Mounds State Historic Site **325** Dr. K. Anne Pyburn **328** Ted Spiegel/Black Star **331** AP/Wide World **332** Anthro-Photo **334(T)** Jerry Jacka Photography **334(B)** Jean-Claude LeJeune **338** Jerry Cooke/Photo Researchers **342** Leonard McCombe **345** Christa Armstrong/Photo Researchers **352** Courtesy The United Nations **355** Dr. Joan Gross **358** William Hodges/National Maritime Museum, Greenwich, England **361** The Granger Collection, New York **365** Courtesy Helena Malinowski Wayne **367** Ken Heyman **368** Library of Congress **371** Courtesy of the Peabody Museum of Natural History, © President and Fellows of Harvard College **376** Photograph by Campbell Grant. From *Rock Art of the American Indian*, Campbell Grant. © 1967 by permission of the author **378** Nichter/Anthro-Photo **380(T)** Michael Howard **380(B)** Stacey Pick/Stock Boston **383** Irven DeVore/Anthro-Photo **387** Anthro-Photo **389** Fronick/Anthro-Photo **394** Dr. Hans Dagmar **396** Foto de Monde/The Picture Cube **401** Tremblay/Peter Arnold, Inc. **404** Milt & Joan Mann/Cameramann International, Ltd. **407** Foto de Monde/The Picture Cube **410** Smithsonian Institution **411** Library of Congress **413(T)** Stuart Franklin/Magnum Photos **413(B)** Smetzer/Tony Stone Worldwide **415** Courtesy of the Royal British Columbia Provincial Museum, Victoria, BC **417** Catherine Koehler **421** Dr. Melvyn C. Goldstein and Dr. Cynthia M. Beall **424** Brian Seed & William S. Nawrocki/Tony Stone Worldwide **426** Lee Sackett, University of Adelaide **428** Culver Pictures **437** Loren McIntyre **439** Courtesy of the Royal British Columbia Provincial Museum, Victoria, BC **442** Western History Collection/University of Oklahoma Library **446** Dr. Donna Winslow **450** The Museum of Modern Art, New York **453** BBC Hulton/The Bettmann Archive **455** Schuler/Anthro-Photo **457** Bloss/Anthro-Photo **459(L)** Thompson/Anthro-Photo **459(R)** Dr. Janet Dunaif-Hattis **463(T)** Courtesy ABC/WLS-TV, Channel 7 Chicago **463(B)** Phil Savoie/Bruce Coleman, Inc. **466** Ellis Herwig/The Picture Cube **468** Reprinted under license from Morriseau Syndications, Burlington, VT **470** Jonathan I. Hattis/Dr. Janet Dunaif-Hattis **476(T)** Pierres/Peter Arnold, Inc. **476(B)** P.Ward/Stock Boston **477** Bob Daemmrich/The Image Works **479** Robert Frerck/Odyssey Productions, Chicago **481** Courtesy SAVE THE CHILDREN FEDERATION, INC. **484** AP/Wide World **486** Dr. James Loucky **488** Rick Reinhard **491** Levison/Minneapolis–St. Paul Star/Tribune **494** Turnley/Black Star **501** UPI/Bettman **502** Arthur Tress **504** Dr. Philip Herbst **506** Bischof/Magnum Photos **507** The Bettmann Archive **510** AP/Wide World **512** Dr. Beatriz Manz **514** AP/Wide World **519** Dennis Brack/Black Star **523** Suan Meiselas/Magnum Photos **524** Talal Asad, from *The Kababish Arabs*, © 1970, London, England **525** AP/Wide World **528** Abraham Rosman **532** AP/Wide World **536** Annette Kentie **537** J. Langevin/Sygma **541** Terry

Arthur/TIME Magazine **544** National Anthropology Archives, Bureau of American Ethnology Collection/Smithsonian Institution **547** Peter Simon/Peter Arnold, Inc. **551** Van Bucher/Photo Researchers **554(T)** Dr. Michael Howard **554(B)** AP/Wide World **558** McConnell/Bruce Coleman, Inc. **560** Margarita Melville, University of Houston **563** Kal Muller/Woodfin Camp & Associates **565** P. Schnall, Real to Real Productions **568** Dr. John Barker **570** Alice Grossman/The Picture Cube **573** Robert M. Glasse **575** Mark Peters/Sygma **578** AP/Wide World **579** Helene Tremblay/Peter Arnold, Inc. **583** Robert Tonkinson, University of Western Australia **588(T)** Cordelia Dilg **588(B)** Hyman/Stock Boston **592** Dr. Janice Reid **594** Loren McIntyre **597** Eric Vandeville/Gamma-Liaison **599** Andrew Rakoczy/Photo Researchers **602** LaGazette/Sygma **606** Candy Hernandez/SIPA-Press **607** Courtesy The United Nations **609** Courtesy Dr. Clyde Snow, Photo: Daniel Muzio **610** Arizona State University **615** Dr. Scott S. Robinson

FIGURES

22–23 Figure 2.1(a) from *Grand Valley Dani: Peaceful Warriors*, 2d ed., by Karl G. Heider, copyright © 1991 by Holt, Rinehart & Winston, Inc., reprinted by permission of the publisher. Figure 2.1(b) and (c) from pp. 354 and 430 in *A Handbook of Living Religions*, edited by John R. Hinnells. Copyright © 1984 by John R. Hinnells and Penguin Books Ltd. Reproduced by permission of Penguin Books Ltd. **24, 43** Figures 2.2 and 2.7 from *Biosphere: The Realm of Life*, 2d ed., by Robert A. Wallace, Jack L. King, and Gerald P. Sanders. Copyright © 1988, 1984 HarperCollins Publishers **35** Figure 2.5 from *Biology: The World of Life*, 5th ed., by Robert A. Wallace. Copyright © 1990, 1987, 1981, HarperCollins Publishers. **53, 55, 71, 73** Figures 3.2(a), 3.3, 3.12, and 3.13 from *Human Biology and Behavior: An Anthropological Perspective*, 5th ed., by Mark L. Weiss and Alan E. Mann. Copyright © 1990 Mark L. Weiss and Alan E. Mann. Published by HarperCollins Publishers. **59** Figure 3.4 from *Biosphere: The Realm of Life*, 2d ed., by Robert A. Wallace, Jack L. King, and Gerald P. Sanders. Copyright © 1988, 1984 HarperCollins Publishers. **63** Figure 3.6 from *The Neutral Theory of Molecular Evolution* by Motoo Kimura. Reprinted by permission of Cambridge University Press. **67** Figure 3.7 from "Genetic Architecture of Swidden Agricultural Tribes from the Lowland Rain Forests of South America" by Peter E. Smouse, in *Current Developments in Anthropological Genetics*, vol. 2, edited by Michael H. Crawford and James H. Mielke, 1982. Reprinted by permission of Plenum Publishing Corporation and Peter E. Smouse. **68** Figure 3.8 from *Primate Adaptation and Evolution* by John G. Fleagle. Copyright © 1988 by Academic Press, Inc. Reprinted by permission of Academic Press, Inc., and the author. **82, 83** Figures 4.1 and 4.2 from *Biology: The Science of Life*, 2d ed., by Robert A. Wallace, Jack L. King, and Gerald P. Sanders. Copyright © 1986, 1981 HarperCollins Publishers. **91** Figure 4.3 from *Primate Adaptation and Evolution* by John G. Fleagle. Copyright © 1988 by Academic Press, Inc. Reprinted by permission of Academic Press, Inc., and the author. **95** Figure 4.5 from "An Ethogram for Rhesus Monkeys" by Donald Stone Sade in *American Journal of Physical Anthropology* 38: 537–542, 1973. Reprinted by permission of Wiley-Liss, a division of John Wiley & Sons, Inc. **116, 119** Chapter-opening photo and Figure 5.1(b) from *Primate Adaptation and Evolution* by John G. Fleagle. Copyright © 1988 by Academic Press, Inc. Reprinted by permission of Academic Press, Inc., and the author. **123** Figure 5.2 from *Biology: The World of Life*, 5th ed., by Robert A. Wallace. Copyright © 1987, 1981 HarperCollins Publishers. Reprinted by

permission. **124** Figure 5.3 from *Continents Adrift* by J. Tuzo Wilson. Copyright © 1972 Scientific American, Inc. Reprinted by permission of W.H. Freeman and Company. **125** Figure 5.4 from "False Start of the Human Parade" by Adrienne L. Zihlman and Jerold M. Lowenstein, illustrations by Douglas Cramer, *Natural History*, August–September 1979. Reprinted by permission of Douglas Cramer. **130** Figure 5.7(a) from *Human Biology and Behavior: An Anthropological Perspective*, 5th ed., by Mark L. Weiss and Alan E. Mann. Copyright © 1990 Mark L. Weiss and Alan E. Mann. Published by HarperCollins Publishers. **140** Chapter-opening photo from *Ascent to Civilization: The Archaeology of Early Man* by John Gowlett, 1984. Reprinted by permission of Roxby Press. **143** Figure 6.1 reprinted by permission of Macmillan Publishing Company from *The Ascent of Man* by David Pilbeam. Copyright © 1972 by David Pilbeam. **144** Figure 6.2 from *Human Biology and Behavior: An Anthropological Perspective*, 5th ed., by Mark L. Weiss and Alan E. Mann. Copyright © 1990 Mark L. Weiss and Alan E. Mann. Published by HarperCollins Publishers. **157** Figure 6.6(a) from *Humankind Emerging*, 5th ed., by Bernard G. Campbell. Copyright © 1988 by Bernard G. Campbell. Published by HarperCollins Publishers. **186, 188, 194** Figures 7.5, 7.6, and 7.7 from *Human Biology and Behavior: An Anthropological Perspective*, 5th ed., by Mark L. Weiss and Alan E. Mann. Copyright © 1990 Mark L. Weiss and Alan E. Mann. Published by HarperCollins Publishers. **197** Figure 7.8 from "Testing for Order and Control in the Corporate Liberal State" by Clarence Karier, *Educational Theory*, vol. 22, no. 2, pp. 154–180, Spring 1972. Reprinted by permission. **219, 226** Figures 8.2 and 8.5 redrawn from *In the Beginning*, 7th ed., by Brian Fagan. Copyright © 1991 The Lindbriar Corp. Published by HarperCollins Publishers. **223** Figure 8.4(a) from *Azania*, vol. 8, 1973. Reprinted by permission of the British Institute in Eastern Africa and John Bower. **229** Figure 8.7 from *Invitation to Archaeology* by James Deetz. Copyright © by James Deetz. Used by permission of Doubleday, a division of Bantam Doubleday Dell Publishing Group, Inc. **230** Figure 8.8 from Bryant Bannister and Terah L. Smiley, in *Geochronology*, ed. Terah L. Smiley, copyright © 1955. Courtesy of the Laboratory of Tree-Ring Research, the University of Arizona. **234–235** Figure 8.11 from *Ascent to Civilization: The Archaeology of Early Man* by John Gowlett, 1984. Reprinted by permission of Roxby Press. **249** Figure 9.1 redrawn from *The Old Stone Age* by Frances Bordes. Copyright © 1968 by Frances Bordes. Reprinted by permission of Weidenfeld & Nicolson Ltd. **257** Figure 9.2 from *The Gods of Prehistoric Man* by Johannes Maringer, edited and translated from the German by Mary Ilford. Copyright © 1960 by Benziger Verlag AG, Zürich. Reprinted by permission of Benziger Verlag AG, Zürich. **266** Figure 9.4 from *The First Americans* by G.H.S. Bushnell. Reprinted by permission of Thames & Hudson Ltd. **269** Figure 9.5 from *Prehistory of North America*, 3d ed., by Jesse D. Jennings. Copyright © 1989 by Jesse D. Jennings. Reprinted by permission of Mayfield Publishing Company. **283, 305** Figures 10.2 and 11.2 from *Demographic Archaeology* by Fekri Hassan. Copyright © 1981 by Academic Press, Inc. Reprinted by permission of Academic Press, Inc., and the author. **288** Figure 10.3(b) from *The Neolithic of the Near East* by James Mellaart. Reprinted by permission of the author. **294** Figure 10.5 from *European Prehistory* by Sarunas Milisauskas. Copyright © 1978 by Academic Press, Inc. Reprinted by permission of Academic Press, Inc., and the author. **304** Figure 11.1 from *Physical Anthropology and Archaeology* by Clifford Jolly and Fred Plog. Copyright © 1976 by McGraw-Hill, Inc. Reprinted by permission of McGraw-Hill, Inc. **341** Table 12.1 from *The World Almanac and Book of Facts*, 1991 Edition, copyright © Pharos Books 1990, New York NY 10166. Reprinted by permission. **498** Map from *In the Rainforest* by Catherine Caulfield. Copyright © 1984 by Catherine Caulfield. Reprinted by permission of Alfred A. Knopf, Inc.

Name Index

Subject Index